SELF-INFLICTED WOUNDS

SELF-INFLICTED WOUNDS

From LBJ's Guns and Butter to Reagan's Voodoo Economics

HOBART ROWEN

To Alice

*Lover, best friend, and
companion of a lifetime*

All rights reserved under International and Pan-American Copyright
Conventions. Published in the United States by Times Books, a
division of Random House, Inc., New York, and simultaneously in
Canada by Random House of Canada, Limited, Toronto.

Library of Congress Cataloging-in-Publication Data

Rowen, Hobart.
Self-inflicted wounds : from LBJ's guns and butter to Reagan's
voodoo economics / Hobart Rowen. — 1st ed.
p.   cm.
Includes index.
ISBN 0-8129-1864-9
1. United States—Economic policy—1961–1971.   2. United States—
Economic policy—1971–1981.   3. United States—Economic
policy—1981–1993.   4. International economic relations.   I. Title.
HC106.6.R69   1994
338.973—dc20   94-4081

Book design by Brooke Zimmer

Manufactured in the United States of America
9 8 7 6 5 4 3 2
FIRST EDITION

Contents

Introduction

When I began in journalism more than fifty years ago, the United States was struggling to survive the hardships of the Great Depression and soon would face the privations of the Second World War. Ironically, both experiences would leave the nation more prosperous than ever before. Because of the structural changes introduced by the New Deal, and the impetus given to technology and business by the war effort, America emerged in the late 1940s with the most powerful economy in the world. And for several decades it was able to maintain its unrivaled position.

Today, in the early 1990s, America can no longer boast that it is number one. Indeed, we are the world's largest debtor nation, and many critics insist that we have become a second-class power unable to lead the world by virtue of either our unmatched economic prowess or our political sagacity. Our decline in self-esteem puzzles both our allies and rivals. It bewilders our people most of all. Many of us search for a scapegoat to blame for our manifold ills. But the bitter truth is that we have no one to blame for our condition but ourselves.

For the wounds to our economic health and to our national pride have been largely self-inflicted. I intend in this book to trace the trajectory of our slow but steady self-strangulation. It is a story of blunder, mismanagement, stupidity, and irresponsibility by officials whose chief obligation to govern the nation was betrayed by their embrace of policies misconceived and ineptly applied.

It is a story that begins with President Lyndon B. Johnson's inheritance of a level of prosperity—with good jobs and without significant inflation—that had never been achieved in the nation's entire prior history. But Johnson's embrace of a forlorn and unwinnable war in Vietnam, his insistence that the country could have, in the phrase of the time, both "guns and butter," put America on a course from which it has yet to recover. The buildup in Vietnam, which occurred without regard to its cost, destroyed the delicate social fabric that had steadily been woven during the Eisenhower and Kennedy years and by Johnson's own Great Society. Johnson faced two unpalatable choices: either to cut other government spending to match the new costs of his escalating war, or to raise additional taxes to pay for it.

Unhappily, Johnson did neither. In his hubris, he thought he could have it all, and so let the inflation genie out of the bottle, touching off a devastating spiral that, ultimately, the Federal Reserve Board would be forced to battle by imposing higher interest rates. This decision, indulged by a spineless Congress, helped to generate a flight from the dollar. Johnson's gamble was that somehow an economy already overheated by a business boom could absorb the bloated costs of an increasingly bloody war—and still escape inflationary price increases.

America was thereby set on a course in which—over time—its fundamental economic health became debilitated. Six presidents—two Democrats and four Republicans—would fail, at critical times, to make the right decisions that would have insured the nation's health as it struggled to survive a period of extraordinary technological change and fierce competition from allies formerly prostrate but now straining and eager to quite literally give us a run for our money.

We have been the victims over the past thirty years of an almost sublime mismanagement in Washington. We have stumbled through an era of breathtaking greed and malfeasance, from LBJ's failure to finance the Vietnam War through the multiple failures of Reaganomics, which always had more to do with the arts of alchemy than with the profession of economics. In between, we have suffered the duplicity of Richard Nixon, the ineptitude of the well-meaning but bumbling Gerald Ford, the notorious malaise of Jimmy Carter, and, throughout, a futile chase for dollar stability under Ronald Reagan and George Bush after the Bretton Woods system collapsed in the 1970s and trade imbalances mounted. And at no time was any American president willing or able to combat the menace of the oil cartel, the swindlers on Wall Street, or the industrial assault on the environment.

How could the world's greatest economy have been humbled so

quickly? What were the policies that president after president devised to cope with the economic maelstrom into which each of them was plunged? And who, exactly, were the men (and sometimes women) who concocted the plans and measures and instruments of such policies? Why were those policies not challenged? And what are the chances for restoring our reputation?

As we attempt to answer such questions, we can glimpse, in the twists and turns of particular policies, the character and ability of those whose task it was to govern the nation wisely and to stand guard over its physical treasure and moral effectiveness.

EVEN AS A TEENAGER growing up in New York City in the early 1930s, I knew I wanted to be a newspaperman, and nothing else. I am one of the lucky ones who lived out a dream. In grade school, I devoured anything in print and kept an ear tuned to politics, usually baiting my father, who voted a straight Republican ticket and once was a minor (nonelected) GOP official in Manhattan. Newspapers and the New York Yankees were my twin passions, although I never wanted to be a sportswriter.

My first chance to work on a newspaper came when, at age fifteen, I entered the freshman class at the City College of New York (CCNY) in February 1934. The *City College Campus* was published three days a week, and I immediately signed on as a cub reporter—and, of course, was assigned initially to write sports. Soon, I became so heavily involved in general reporting and the *Campus* editing process that I forgot one was supposed to go to classes. Of that small requirement, a just-in-time warning from Morton Gottschall, the revered dean of men, preserved both my academic career and future service on the *Campus.*

After I was graduated in January 1938, I came face to face with economic reality: a recession was on, and few newspaper jobs were available. I was offered a post as a tutor in mathematics at Syracuse University, and my parents—naturally—wanted me to take it: better to teach math than to starve, they argued. But I wanted to be a newspaperman.

A friend of a friend tipped me off that there was an opening for a copy boy at the *New York Journal of Commerce,* then the leading business newspaper in the country, with editorial offices at the legendary old World Building, 63 Park Row, across from City Hall. I hustled down there and was interviewed by Night Managing Editor Arthur Krahmer, a prototypical cigar-smoking, shirtsleeved, gruff old newspaper pro. All I remember about the interview is that I got the job—four P.M. to midnight, six days a week. Salary, paid in cash in a tiny brown envelope, ten dollars a week. Thus my career as a business journalist was launched. I didn't think seriously, then, of business or financial reporting as a permanent occupation, or, as sportswriter Frank Deford put it recently about his equally accidental first connection with *Sports Illustrated*, "being in for life."

For me, the thrill was that I was working for an honest-to-God newspaper. I was happy with my ten bucks a week, half of which went to my mother as partial "rent" for living at home. A copy boy's life meant running errands of all sorts: down to Wall Street for financial reports (no fax machines then), to police and fire headquarters for overnight reports, across City Hall Park as soon as I came in each day to pick up the stock market "mats" from the *New York Sun*. The stock tables, like everything else in those days, were hand-set on Linotype machines; borrowing the mats from which steel plates for the presses were made saved the *JOC* a lot of money. Another of my chores was to take the subway to Times Square every night—a ten to fifteen minute ride—and to wait for the arrival of the first or "bulldog" editions of *The New York Times* and the old *New York Herald Tribune*, which hit the streets about eleven P.M. My assignment was to buy two of each, and rush them back to the *JOC* newsroom. Krahmer and his two chief aides on the news desk, Bill Russell and Shelley Pierce, would then quickly go through the financial sections of those two great newspapers, find any Washington financial stories that the *JOC*'s Washington bureau might have missed, and prepare quick rewrites for the *JOC*'s final edition.

Today, among better newspapers, the lifting is more deft—and when material is "borrowed," it is considered only proper to credit the originating publication by name. But in 1938 there was no such sensitivity. I observed the process for a while to see the kind of story that Krahmer expected his Washington bureau to report on, and one day in the early fall of 1938 I took a yellow legal-sized lined pad with me on the subway. On the way back, I rewrote a piece from the *Times* I hadn't seen in our first edition. Sure enough, when I got back to 63 Park Row that night, Krahmer tossed the *Times* over to Shelley Pierce, and told him to rewrite the story I had picked out. I waited until the final edition was "up," and when Krahmer was finished going through it, I told him what I had done, giving him my version in longhand on yellow paper. He read it slowly, then asked: "Did you have any help with this?" I assured him that the only help came involuntarily from *The New York Times*. "OK," he said, "you have a job as a reporter, eighteen dollars a week, as soon as we find another copy boy."

I spent the next three years reporting on financial markets and commodity markets under the guidance of a brilliant economics editor, a German national named Heinz Luedicke, who later was interned at the Greenbrier Hotel, in West Virginia, for the duration of the Second World War. In December 1940, the *JOC* asked me if I would be interested in joining the Washington bureau to report on the war mobilization effort, and to begin editing what they proposed to call a "compendium" of new economic regulations relating to the growing crisis. Was I interested! I had had my own love affair with Washington ever since I had taken a day trip from New York to the capital, on the Pennsylvania Railroad, ten years before when I was about twelve (for an excursion rate, as I remember it, of $8 round trip). I wandered all over town, from the White House to Capitol Hill, and vowed one day to return.

Almost nothing—except the Watergate affair, which happened while I was an assistant managing editor at *The Washington Post*—has been as exciting as those early years as a reporter in Washington. In a city getting ready for war, I discovered the nexus between politics and economics, and became convinced that the specialty I had lucked into as a copy boy would be a lifetime endeavor. On Pearl Harbor Day, December 7, 1941, at age twenty-three, with less than a full year under my belt, I was a Washington correspondent busily writing stories about the reaction to the devastating Japanese attack that compelled America's entry into the war.

A perforated eardrum frustrated my effort to beat the military draft by volunteering for the Naval Air Intelligence Command, and then the same eardrum kept me out of the Army when my draft number came up in 1942. I stayed with the *JOC* until early 1942, when I joined the public affairs staff of the War Production Board. That was a great education in how a large government bureaucracy works—a brief, and my only, venture to "the other side."

In 1944, Ernest Lindley, then bureau chief for *Newsweek* in Washington, offered me a staff job covering business news. Lindley also wrote a column syndicated by the *Des Moines Register* that appeared in *The Washington Post*, and when he would go on vacation, a few of us on his staff were invited to fill in for him. Once I saw a column of mine on the editorial pages of *The Washington Post*, I was hooked; in 1960, while still at *Newsweek*, I started the syndication, on my own, of a twice-weekly column called "Economic Impact." I continued to work for *Newsweek* in Washington through 1965, until Ben Bradlee, having moved from the magazine to the *Washington Post*, offered me a chance to get back into daily journalism as the paper's financial editor. I jumped at the chance, and joined the *Post* on January 1, 1966, where I have since served as reporter, senior economics correspondent, editor, and columnist.

It has been a great satisfaction to me to see economic and financial journalism come of age. When I started at the *Post*, business writers were second-class citizens. Only rarely did a business or economic policy story hit page one. Bradlee, whose great strength as an editor was in other areas, especially politics and national news, nonetheless sensed that the *Post*, to be a rounded and great newspaper, needed a major upgrade of its financial reporting. Around the same time, as inflation was stimulated by guns and butter under LBJ, and exacerbated by the oil cartel, editors everywhere sensed that economic news was becoming more important.

I acknowledge here my great debt to Ben Bradlee, friend and colleague now for thirty-seven years—he first came to *Newsweek* in 1957. The best thing that ever happened to me in my career as a journalist was to be rescued by Bradlee from the drudgery of weekly magazine reporting and to be plunged back into work on a daily. Bradlee and I also shared a close relationship with John F. Kennedy—he, to be sure, had one that was much more intimate and important than mine. But it was JFK, as Bradlee relates in his moving book of recollections, *Conversations with Kennedy*, who got me started on my specialty in international economics by suggesting to Bradlee in 1962 that *Newsweek* send me to Europe to explore why economic growth there was proceeding at a faster pace than here. *Newsweek* did, and I have been covering global economic news and events ever since.

Others who greatly influenced my career as a writer and editor include Kenneth G. Crawford, a heroic war correspondent on D-day in Normandy, who succeeded Lindley (and preceded Bradlee) as *Newsweek*'s Washington bureau chief. Crawford was the best writer and the most sympathetic editor I ever worked for. My colleague and office roommate at the *Post* for seventeen years, Haynes Johnson, is another fine writer and author whose judgment I cherish, and from whom I have learned much.

Outside of the world of journalism, I owe a debt to that marvelous and energetic group of New Economists, many of whom came to prominence in Washington with Kennedy in 1962—Walter Heller, James Tobin, Kermit Gordon, Joseph Pechman, Arthur Okun, Gardner Ackley, Paul Samuelson, Lester Thurow, Robert Solow, Otto Eckstein, James Duesenberry, William Capron, Gerhard Colm, Alfred Reifman, Frank Schiff, Barry Bosworth, Charles Schultze, and Stanley Surrey, among others.

I have also picked the considerable brains of economists George

Shultz, John Kenneth Galbraith, Franco Modigliani, Arthur Burns, Alan Greenspan, Paul McCracken, Nat Goldfinger, and Stanley Ruttenberg, among others.

I have kept in touch over the years with countless businessmen and business groups, but must single out for their especially consistent help Robert Hormats of Goldman Sachs & Co., formerly a State Department official; Fred Bergsten, director of the Institute of International Economics; and two of Wall Street's major forces for good, Felix Rohatyn of Lazard Frères, and Henry Kaufman, formerly of Salomon Brothers and now head of an investment company bearing his name.

In recent years, I have maintained a close association with the Brookings Institution in Washington, where then Director of Research Charles Schultze kindly allowed me to use valuable space as a Brookings Scholar in 1990; there, I began work on this book. I have benefited from my association with Brookings, especially with President Bruce MacLaury, and Senior Fellows Edward Bernstein, Walter Salant, George Perry, Thomas Mann, and Henry Aaron; and am privileged to participate in the "Friday lunch at Brookings," pioneered by Joseph Pechman.

Needless to say, none of these economists, friends, businessmen, and others named here have the slightest responsibility for any failures or errors in this book—but deserve much credit for having influenced its reasoning.

I would be remiss if I did not mention another group important in my professional life—too many colleagues for the past twenty-seven years at *The Washington Post*, to list individually, and many journalists outside the *Post* who were friendly and tough competitors. There have been many long hours of shared experiences and confidences—often abroad covering economic summits or meetings of the IMF and World Bank—with Art Pine, now with the *Los Angeles Times*; Walt Mossberg of *The Wall Street Journal*; Richard Janssen, formerly of both the *Journal* and *Business Week*; and Charles E. Egan of *The New York Times* and Sterling Green of the Associated Press, who shared with me, in 1950, the feat of breaking through the fabled secrecy of the Business Advisory Council, a group of 100 top corporate CEOs who met privately with government officials, and exposing it to public view.

Finally, this book would not have become a reality without the persistence of Robert Barnett, lawyer and book agent extraordinaire, who persuaded me at a book party for Bill Greider of *Rolling Stone* to write about my experiences as an economics journalist; or without the continuous encouragement of Peter Osnos of Times Books and

Random House, who allowed me to write it at my own pace, especially when a bout with prostate cancer slowed me down in 1991. Peter told me to forget deadlines and get better, and I did both. I am indebted also to Osnos's editorial staff, including Steve Wasserman and Sarah Flynn; and to librarian Melody Blake of *The Washington Post,* whose skill as a researcher and whose sunny disposition helped me to shape the final draft. Gregg Pentecost, Brookings's computer whiz and guru, was an invaluable adviser on how to make WordPerfect 5.0 do what it is supposed to do.

Nothing I say here can adequately express what I owe to my wonderful wife of fifty-two years, Alice S. Rowen, for her love, patience, and forbearance as this work consumed the bulk of my so-called free time for the past four years; or to my three children, and their spouses, who gave me encouragement throughout to finish "the book."

BLUNDER

I

Guns and Butter

I N 1965, Lyndon Johnson made two decisions that would have a profound effect not only upon his presidency but also upon the future of the American economy. In February, he started the systematic bombing of North Vietnam. Then, in July, he made the commitment—kept secret from the nation—to bring troop strength in South Vietnam up to 500,000, all the while maintaining the fiction that the ceiling was 200,000.

The decision to escalate the number of troops being sent to Vietnam, also kept secret from his closest economic advisers, would require a multibillion-dollar boost in the military budget, with no provision for paying the bigger bills. Johnson, of course, had a passion for secrecy that infected all of his relationships, and he went to great lengths to detect leaks and punish leakers.

Like all presidents who try to manage the news, LBJ himself was an accomplished leaker. Once, after an impromptu Oval Office press conference, the president buttonholed Marguerite Higgins, the accomplished war correspondent for the *New York Herald Tribune*. Maggie had given a small press lunch at her home for Johnson a few days before. Now, evincing displeasure, LBJ said: "Maggie, I didn't see a line in the papers about our little talk." Higgins replied with some astonishment: "Well, Mr. President, you said it was off-the-record!"

"Yes," LBJ snapped, "I said it was off-the-record. But goddamn it, I didn't say not to write about it!"[1]

Johnson bet the country on the proposition that an economy already overheated by a business boom could absorb the bloated costs of an escalating war—and still escape inflationary price increases. Critics who refused to be fooled by the evidence at hand warned him he would lose the bet. But Johnson, bent on preserving to the fullest his domestic Great Society programs, was willing to gamble, even though he felt trapped, and didn't know how to get out of the increasingly ugly war. That became painfully evident to me one warm afternoon in the spring of 1965. One of Lyndon Johnson's habits was to break the tensions of the day by walking his beagles, Him and Her. But LBJ never liked to be alone when he could use the press as a sounding board, so he would sweep up any reporters he could find, and in best Pied Piper tradition—with the dogs on leashes and the journalists crowding around—start a circuit or two of the South Lawn of the White House. It was wonderful theater, exposing us to the president in some of his most revealing moments. On this particular day, I happened to be in the White House press room, on assignment for *Newsweek*, when word came that Johnson was about to begin one of his processionals. We joined him in the Rose Garden, as he started walking briskly toward the South Gate. LBJ was a big, bulky man, but his shoulders drooped, and his eyes betrayed his fatigue. As we scrambled to keep up with him, he launched into a discourse on Vietnam. We peppered him with questions that mirrored the growing discontent in the country. Were we getting overcommitted? Did we know the true costs? When was it all going to end? What was he doing to end the nightmare?

Suddenly, he jerked the dogs to a halt, turned, and said: "I don't know what the fuck to do about Vietnam. I wish someone would tell me what to do." That ended the conversation—and the walk.

As it became clear that Johnson never would find the answer to his Vietnam dilemma, Democratic politicians began to wonder how to ease him out of the White House. Then, on Sunday evening, March 31, 1968, in a hastily arranged prime-time television address to the nation, Johnson announced his "irrevocable" decision not to run for reelection that fall and pledged to take a "turn toward peace" and restrict future air raids on North Vietnam.

Later that night, I had the rare opportunity to visit the family quarters of the White House to hear Johnson explain his decision to de-escalate the war and quit the presidency. After the speech, LBJ's press secretary, George Christian, had phoned *The Washington Post* to say that "the boss" would talk to reporters "right away." Executive Editor Ben Bradlee tore through the newsroom to see who was around in possession of permanent White House press credentials.

He found the *Post*'s national editor, Richard Harwood, and me—and told us to get moving, fast, to the White House. Joining a group of about twenty, including Lady Bird Johnson, Christian, other White House staffers, and about eight or ten reporters from other papers, Harwood and I were greeted by a relaxed Johnson in the family parlor on the second floor of the White House. Immediately, we could sense that a great weight had been lifted from the president. He had changed from the shirt and tie he had worn for his TV appearance into a blue turtleneck, and he sat on a couch, spooning chocolate pudding, while the rest of us sat crowded together on the rug in front of the couch or on chairs encircling the president.

Johnson conceded that the war had caused "dissension in the country," and that its final resolution, as well as the political leadership of the nation, now had to be put in someone else's hands. Clearly, he still didn't know what to do about the war, but he had decided at least to let someone else figure out the answer. "I don't feel very good about asking one-half million [American] men to stand out there [in Vietnam]. I want to put myself in the position to do my job as successfully as they do theirs. If I don't have the aura of political campaigning around me, my efforts might be a little more fruitful," he said. It was a symbolic admission that America faced a costly defeat, its first ever in war. Johnson realized that his presidency had also become a casualty of a war he could no longer contain or win.

Johnson's sudden decision to neither seek nor accept the nomination of his party was triggered as much by an international gold crisis as by public opposition to the war—though this was barely recognized at the time. Trouble over gold had erupted during the previous year, and had intensified with the closing of the "London gold pool" (the eight-nation consortium that helped to keep the price of gold level throughout the world) only two weeks before Johnson's announcement—a reflection of loss of confidence in the dollar and in the American economy. And, as a retreat from the commitment made at Bretton Woods in 1944 to sell an ounce of gold for $35 in U.S. paper money when presented by another government, the gold pool closing was a critical sign that a limit on America's financial resources had been reached. Johnson, however, was preoccupied with matters he considered more important—the war and his Great Society programs.

But if Johnson's pursuit of both guns and butter was a costly option for the nation, the blame should be shared by others who didn't speak up early enough. For a long time, many Democratic economists were slow to challenge Johnson's failure to propose a tax increase to pay the mounting bills. When Johnson inherited the presidency after the assassination of John F. Kennedy, he turned to key members of the Kennedy cabinet for help, first to Walter W. Heller, chairman of Kennedy's Council of Economic Advisers (CEA). Heller was one of the great economists of this period, the leading figure among a group of energetic "New Economists"—Keynesians in their thirties and early forties—who came to power with Kennedy in 1961, committed to "get the economy moving again." Also included in this group were Kermit Gordon of Williams College and James Tobin of Yale University, who constituted the Kennedy CEA. Their staff included Joseph A. Pechman, who had a distinguished career as a tax reformer and later as director of research for the Brookings Institution, and a younger clutch of economists who established reputations on their own—Arthur M. Okun, who at age thirty-two had been a member of the Kennedy CEA in 1964, and at thirty-six succeeded Gardner Ackley in 1968 to become LBJ's third Economic Council chairman; Otto Eckstein of Harvard; and Robert M. Solow of the Massachusetts Institute of Technology.

They were all brilliant, but Heller was special. His most telling contribution was his successful campaign to get Kennedy to propose a stimulative tax cut in the face of a pending deficit, until then heretical theory. His talent for blending economic with political advice, spiced with witty observations, was unique. His fellow economists admired him for his integrity and drive, and he was a positive force in educating not only Kennedy and the Congress but journalists and other members of the public on economic issues.

It was Heller who had initiated for Johnson the idea of a war on poverty. Just three days before his fateful trip to Dallas, Kennedy, who had been impressed by Michael Harrington's just-published book, *The Other America: Poverty in the United States*, and by Heller's sales pitch on the need to fight poverty, told the economist to get to work on such a program, to be sent to Congress after the election in 1964.

With Kennedy gone, Heller broached the idea to Johnson in one of their first meetings. He pointed out that Johnson could legitimately claim the program as his own because nothing was down on paper, and Kennedy had not planned to push it right away. LBJ instantly seized the opportunity to construct a "War on Poverty" as a major theme for his fledgling administration. It quickly became the core of his vision of a "Great Society."

Almost immediately, Johnson learned that the budget for the next fiscal year being prepared by Kermit Gordon's Budget Bureau was to be the first-ever to top $100 billion. Johnson was determined that he would not be the first president to cross that threshold. Daniel Patrick Moynihan, then an assistant secretary of labor, recalls that LBJ gathered about thirty subcabinet officers in the Roosevelt Room, gave them coffee, and then began "bellowing." According to Moynihan, LBJ said: "I know that this room is full of mean, scheming little SOBs who've got special plans to put their special little pet projects into this budget, so I'll be the first damn fool in history to send a $100 billion budget to the United States Congress. Let me tell you, you are not going to succeed because I'm gonna make you wish you were never born. I'm gonna make you so unhappy because I'll never let you go easy. It's going to be long, and slow, and hard. It's gonna hurt." When the budget went to Congress, the headlines in the daily papers read: "$99 billion budget."[2]

Apart from Heller, another key Kennedy operative who caught LBJ's eye was Secretary of Defense Robert S. McNamara, the former Ford Motor Company executive whom Kennedy, Johnson remembered, had described as "half genius, half SOB."[3] After meeting McNamara in 1962 at Kennedy's first cabinet session, LBJ told a friend: "That fellow with the Stay-Comb in his hair is the best of the bunch."[4] Now, as president, Johnson was attracted to McNamara not only by what he recognized as tough single-mindedness, but because of his successful track record in business. McNamara would become a de facto deputy president, a sort of economic czar, troubleshooting assignments for Johnson that normally would go to other cabinet members or economic advisers. Soon, with LBJ's blessing, McNamara was second-guessing Heller.

The tip-off came when the Detroit auto companies began to boost prices over the then-existing national price guideposts. Alert to the threat of a snowballing consumer price inflation, Heller had sent Johnson a memo suggesting that Detroit be told firmly that, under the guideposts, auto prices should be going down, not up. Instead, Johnson tossed Heller's proposal over to McNamara, who touched base with his old buddies in the auto business. In the end, Heller's idea to squeeze back rising auto prices was deep-sixed, and Detroit was allowed to boost prices.

The guidepost or guideline concept was another Kennedy legacy. It had evolved from the fertile mind of Kermit Gordon. Gordon sold Heller—who sold Kennedy—on the notion that if wage increases could be limited to an average of 3.2 percent, matching the then-prevalent rate of gain in national productivity—that is, worker output—inflation could be contained. Prices would also be geared to productivity, allowed to rise only if an industry's labor costs were rising. These would not be "controls," anathema to both conservative businessmen and labor leaders, but merely guidelines or "guide-posts" or government standards that all would be urged to follow.[5]

Thus Johnson's cave-in to Detroit was a jolt not only to Heller but to Gordon as well. Both men had been led to believe by Johnson that he would be an even stronger advocate of the wage-price guide-posts than Kennedy. After all, in his 1964 Economic Report, Johnson had specifically endorsed the guidepost principle. On November 15, 1964—just short of a year after the Kennedy assassination—Heller resigned.

Nevertheless, the economic expansion that had begun under Kennedy continued through 1964, the fourth year of unprecedented prosperity—high economic growth, full employment, yet low infla-tion. It was probably the most satisfactory economic performance in America in modern times. But the additional inflationary pressures generated even then by the growing conflict in Vietnam were begin-ning to take a toll.

In the absence of a sound fiscal policy—including a tax hike to restrict consumer buying power—Federal Reserve Board chairman William McChesney Martin Jr. wanted to use the only other broad tool available, monetary restraint, to reduce the level of credit avail-able to business and consumers. He and Federal Reserve governor J. Dewey Daane publicly announced that they supported an increase in the key discount rate, the rate charged member banks borrowing from the Fed. It was then 4 percent. A boost would be the signal for most other interest rates in the economy to go up—thus cooling down the boom.

But aware that the seven-man board of governors was split almost down the middle, with Sherman J. Maisel, just named to the board by Johnson, and others opposed, Johnson played for time. At a critical meeting at the White House early in October 1965 among Johnson, Martin, and their economic aides, Johnson, due to be hospitalized for a gall bladder operation on October 8, turned to Martin and, in the wheedling tones he reserved for such an occasion, said: "You wouldn't do that to me while I'm in the hospital, would you?"

Finally, on December 6, 1965, the Fed, in a 4–3 vote, raised the discount rate by half a point to 4.5 percent, Governors Maisel, J. L. Robertson, and George W. Mitchell vigorously dissenting. In the next four or five months, the Fed also reduced the availability of credit by lowering reserves, a step Maisel feels, in retrospect, would have been even more effective had it been taken in December at the time of the discount rate increase.

Many businesses began to raise their prices. For example, in No-vember 1965, when the aluminum industry—profiting from boosted defense orders—raised prices, Johnson chose McNamara to get a simple message across to the corporate leaders: in a twilight zone that was neither all war nor all peace, business was not totally free to make its own decisions. Gardner Ackley, who had succeeded Heller as head of the CEA, had already sternly, but unsuccessfully, lectured the aluminum companies, warning that the rise was unjustified and inflationary. To drive the point home, Johnson threatened to release 200,000 tons of aluminum from government stockpiles.

Still, the industry wouldn't move. Johnson then ordered McNamara to "Get in there and get rid of that stockpile." McNamara read the riot act to the industry, and Alcoa, which had initiated the price increase, promptly withdrew it. McNamara called a press conference at the Pentagon, announced his victory, and added boldly: "I know of no major commodity in our economy today on which a price increase is justified." In making that judgment (which was probably correct), McNamara—with LBJ's assent—was usurping not only Ackley's role, but Treasury Secretary Henry H. (Joe) Fowler's as well. When a reporter raised that question, McNamara snapped: "Well, as secretary of defense, I'm the largest buyer of aluminum in the country." Then came copper. After ten days of negotiations with copper industry officials, McNamara announced a government program to expand copper supplies while holding down prices. All elements of the program were to be under the supervision of civilian agencies outside of McNamara's jurisdiction. No matter—they marched to McNamara's orders.[6]

Speaking for Johnson, McNamara made clear that LBJ was willing to risk the cozy consensus he had built up with the business community after Kennedy's assassination to enforce a sort of government by ad hoc pressure: if Johnson wasn't willing to raise taxes to hold down Vietnam-induced inflation, he was more than willing to use the naked power of government through jawboning, suasion, and whatever economic clubs he could find in the closet. And McNamara would be his point man.

McNamara kept Johnson's regular economic advisory team in the dark on the full extent of the Vietnam buildup—and what its impact on the economy was likely to be. Paul A. Volcker, then an assistant secretary of the Treasury, for instance, feared in the fall of 1965 that he might unintentionally be "lying" in his public speeches about the economic outlook. He also suspected that reports from the Pentagon about the cost of the war were "phony."

Deep down, Johnson loyalists like Arthur Okun, a member of the CEA, were also skeptical of what they were being fed by McNamara. As Okun remarked to me at the end of 1965, "Of course, everything depends on Vietnam spending, but we can't get a goddamn word out of McNamara."[7]

Yet, by the fall of 1965, what Okun couldn't get confirmed out of the Pentagon was common knowledge in Washington. Congressmen close to the Pentagon, such as Senator John C. Stennis (D.-Miss.) were saying publicly that the following year's budget would run $10 billion to $12 billion over earlier estimates for fiscal 1967.[8] But on September 9, 1965, still working in the dark, Gardner Ackley made a speech in Philadelphia in which he said that estimates such as Stennis's "can at this point only be pure figments of someone's imagination. The estimates we at the Council have put into our tentative projections do not even approach that order of magnitude."

Ackley and Okun, of course, had been sold down the river by Johnson and McNamara, who were masters of deceit. It would get worse. A month later, Treasury Secretary Fowler told a meeting of the American Bankers Association in Chicago that "If I thought defense was going to add $10 billion to $15 billion to our fiscal 1967 budget, I'd be back in my office right now considering proposals for tax increases to pay for it."

In November, Lloyd Norman of *Newsweek* reported that the Pentagon was "pushing for—and predicting—a force of 400,000 to 500,000 men [in Vietnam] later in 1966." Norman, it turned out, had the right numbers on the president's buildup, but the administration denied it.[9] As the year moved along, Lloyd Norman's and John Stennis's assessments of the American commitment in Vietnam proved to be all too accurate. By November 19, Fowler in public speeches was not repeating his brave, uninformed words in Chicago, saying only that Vietnam had thrust "greater economic burdens" on the nation.[10]

By the end of the year, Ackley tried to alert LBJ to the dangers ahead. He told Johnson that any major increase in Vietnam appropriations, without a tax increase to pay for them, threatened the remarkable stability in wages and prices with which the country had been blessed since 1961.

This was the approximate point—as 1966 began—when Johnson should have decided on a tax increase, but he didn't begin that process for another year. It is hard to overestimate the impact of this basic blunder. Still, it isn't hard to understand Johnson's reluctance. He reasoned that if he did the fiscally responsible thing—which would have been to ask Congress to raise taxes—the treasured Great Society programs, which would assure him a place in history, would be imperiled. He believed, no doubt correctly, that if Congress had to choose between guns and butter, it would cut back on the butter. And Johnson was determined not to sacrifice the Great Society, a resolve that led him to hide the extent of the military buildup.

To Johnson's dismay, the public became preoccupied with the bloody, televised war that invaded its living rooms every night, overshadowing the social gains of the Great Society. He became the butt of an ugly chant—*Hey, hey, LBJ, how many kids did you kill today?*—that could be heard from the second-floor bedrooms at 1600 Pennsylvania Avenue.[11]

Johnson was devastated by that taunt. He saw his own, rightful place in the history books as the befriender of the poor and the Mexicans, the man from the Deep South who had signed both the Civil Rights Act of 1964 and the Voting Rights Act of 1965, besmirched, obliterated. From his own humble beginnings, he would tell friends, he had a gut feeling for disadvantaged people, and limited patience for those who, having emerged from similar backgrounds, quickly forgot their origins. But the war, he felt, had blocked all of that out.[12]

EARLY IN 1966, all of Johnson's economic advisers except Fowler urged removal of the 7 percent investment tax credit, which had been created during the Kennedy years to stimulate business expenditures for new factories and capital equipment. The tax credit was a lavish handout for business—a 7 percent cut in costs of expansion—and companies could take the credit even if the purchases or additions had been planned beforehand. Obviously, the investment credit wasn't needed by an economy already overheating. But Fowler prevailed, and the tax credit was continued, even as Fowler—belatedly sensitized to what was happening—fruitlessly begged businessmen to voluntarily trim back their expansion plans, now barreling ahead 16.5 percent over the 1965 pace.

In September, Heller, who had returned to his teaching post at the University of Minnesota, recommended a moratorium on the 7 percent investment tax credit, saying that even if the nation could afford guns and butter, "it does not follow that we can afford both guns and fat." A few weeks later, Heller, calling himself a "cautious hawk" on the economy, came out for an across-the-board surtax.

That was really late in the game, well over a year after the huge troop escalation. Johnson had succeeded in his masquerade: despite the escalation in the commitment of ground troops, he had only asked for a Vietnam supplemental appropriation of $700 million. His own Budget Bureau, concealing the real costs of the war from the

American people, was estimating the probable cost for fiscal 1967 at only $10 billion to $12 billion, rather than a realistic number about double that amount.

Finally, late in 1966, Johnson overruled Fowler and suspended the investment tax credit. The Fed was encouraged to loosen the monetary strings a bit. But the debate over whether to raise taxes raged throughout the year. Johnson and his advisers chose to ignore the work of Murray L. Weidenbaum, a mere Republican associate professor from Washington University in St. Louis, who had pointed out in his doctoral thesis that inflationary impact of the Korean War—like that of the Vietnam War now—had spread through the economy before becoming fully evident in federal statistics.[13]

Johnson, however, had to take the chairman of the Federal Reserve Board more seriously. In close touch with businessmen and bankers, Martin, the very embodiment of monetary integrity since his appointment by President Harry S. Truman in 1951 to head up America's central bank, drew the same inflation warning from the Vietnam business inventory buildup. Martin sensed quickly that Pentagon orders were overtaxing the economy, and warned Johnson that the huge expansion would soon send prices skyrocketing.

Early in March 1966, *The Washington Post* polled thirty-two top business, academic, and labor economists, asking: "Do you favor a prompt increase in federal taxes to combat inflation?" Included in the survey were Republicans and Democrats, conservatives and liberals. The result was twenty-two for, eight against, two undecided. The poll showed that liberals, including many adherents of the so-called New Economics—Keynesians closely associated with the Kennedy or Johnson administration—were in the forefront of the group urging LBJ to raise taxes to yield up to $5 billion a year in additional revenue. Opposition to raising taxes to pay the government's bills came not from the liberals but from a strange combination of labor unions and conservatives such as Milton Friedman. The labor unions feared that taxes, by slowing down the economy, would add to unemployment. Friedman, who paid no attention to unemployment as a guide to policy making, was concerned only with controlling inflation by manipulating the supply and price of money. A genius with a narrow focus, Friedman attributed inflation and the threat of further price increases to an excessively easy monetary policy, meaning that he thought the Federal Reserve was not pushing interest rates high enough. The only effective way to prevent inflation, Friedman argued, "is to restrain the rate of monetary growth. That is a task for monetary policy and not fiscal policy." But others, not so dedicated to monetarist theory, argued that reliance only on tight money, which means high interest rates, could put the economy through an unneeded crunch, resulting in high unemployment.

The issue heated up. In May 1966, at a meeting of the American Bankers Association in Madrid, Chairman Martin said that "the real problem is that we don't know where it [the cost of the war] ends." To the administration's annoyance, Martin got strong support in Madrid from an urbane Frenchman, Pierre-Paul Schweitzer, managing director of the International Monetary Fund, set up in 1944 to supervise the international monetary system. It was unusual for the head of the IMF—an international civil servant—to comment on a member nation's economic policy, but Schweitzer was willing to incur the wrath of American officials.[14]

Johnson tried to finesse the situation by urging everyone, including businessmen, to spend less money and thus help to control inflation without formal government action or tax increases. It was a campaign that one businessman called "government by inhibition." Exercising his famous jawbone. Johnson invited 150 blue-ribbon executives to a White House dinner in April. The hostility to government that is a near religion for many corporate bigwigs has never dampened the allure of an invitation to a White House dinner or reception—regardless of the president or his party affiliation. No one knew the magic of this attraction better than LBJ. Dishing out the corn pone with a generous hand, LBJ reached the peak of his personal persuasiveness with the business community on this occasion, which one moderately sensitive participant likened to a revival meeting. Johnson told them to slow down plant expansion, among other things. His audience promised to cooperate, and praised Johnson's initiative. Given the high cost of money and materials, and rising labor costs, that was not too surprising. In effect, Johnson was giving them a tool with which to hold wages down: they could plead patriotism. When LBJ assured them he would urge union leaders to hold the line on wages with the same vigor with which he demanded price restraint, the business leaders nodded approvingly.

But the era of goodwill with the business community began to erode as the Vietnam buildup raised havoc with the economy. Business had good cause for a case of jitters. In midsummer 1965, General William C. Westmoreland had put his maximum troop requirements at 200,000 men. By the start of 1966, Westmoreland had raised the ante to a staggering 459,000 men, and McNamara was in the process of meeting his demand.[15] Not until July 1966 did Johnson admit that a "substantial supplemental [appropriation] for Vietnam" would be needed "if we carry on the war at the present rate."

Steel mills were told that same month that they would have to reserve 30 percent more tonnage for the military in the final three months of 1966 than in the three preceding months. The news, combined with rising interest rates, turned the stock market bearish. Already down 150 points from a level of 1,000 early in the year, the Dow Jones industrial index dropped sixteen points in a single day toward the end of July, the biggest break since Kennedy's assassination.[16] The stock market had been going almost straight up, from the Cuban missile crisis in October 1962 until January 1966, and it may have been ready for a burst of profit taking. But now Wall Street knew that Vietnam was bad news for financial markets because normal business operations would be disrupted. The popular myth that war is good for business was rapidly collapsing. More and more people could see that war breeds higher taxes, shortages of materials, and a controlled economy.

The once-solid phalanx of liberals supporting a tax increase began to crack, as the economy was battered by the impact of high interest rates triggered by the Fed's boost in the key discount rate. Economists Paul A. Samuelson and Leon H. Keyserling, for example, who had taken a pro-tax stance in *The Washington Post* poll, waffled a bit as the summer rolled along.

But the high interest rates didn't slow the economy or curb inflation—which was the classic result to be expected. As interest rates soared to forty-year highs, they appeared merely to enhance the business appetite to borrow money to expand capacity. Only the home construction industry was hit by the traditional tight-money reaction, because funds that ordinarily would have moved into mortgages flowed instead into a whole new range of investment possibilities, such as certificates of deposit.

The money markets' growing sophistication was defeating the Fed's anti-inflation goal: yes, it cost more to borrow money, but it was available. The supply of money ballooned, and the inflation careened upward. The lesson for future textbooks seemed clear: monetary policy, unaided by fiscal policy, is useless to control an inflation that is triggered by excessive demand. More and more, Johnson's failure to act on the tax side of the equation was undermining his policies everywhere else.

Without a slowdown on the spending side of the budget, Johnson's economic team was reduced to begging the banks to say "No!" to their customers, a gambit about as effective as telling kids to watch less television. Andrew F. Brimmer, a new Johnson appointee to the Fed board, said that "the crying need today is for more effective bank restraint on loan expansion." But the only way to get such restraint was by tax increases. Failing that, businessmen would borrow, banks would gleefully lend, and interest rates would continue up.[17]

Vietnam was leaving such an indelible imprint on the economy that Budget Director Charles L. Schultze stitched a unique "excluding special Vietnam costs" line throughout key tables in the fiscal 1967 budget message that Johnson sent to Congress. Vietnam included, Johnson was forecasting budget expenditures of $113 billion, with a deficit of nearly $7 billion. Without Vietnam, a record sixth year of the Kennedy-Johnson boom would have yielded a $4 billion surplus—enough money to have tripled what LBJ could afford to spend on Great Society programs.[18]

By any accounting, the undeniable fact was that a substantial part of the nation's overall economic muscle—nearly two-thirds of the fiscal 1967 federal budget—was to be devoted to the Vietnam War. Wealth was being created in the hands of business and labor. But because there was no equivalent supply of consumer goods to soak up the buying power, a classic case of "demand inflation"—too many dollars chasing too few goods—was in the making. Johnson had opted for guns and butter—not as much butter as there had been the year before, but still a 20 percent boost. Setting an example for later presidents, Johnson said he would count on economic growth, rather than a tax increase, to pay for escalating budget deficits.

But the situation was worse than Johnson had let on: at the end of November 1966, Schultze and White House aide Joseph A. Califano brought twenty-one civilian agency heads into the Roosevelt Room to hear that the $10.2 billion figure penciled in for Vietnam had exploded to nearly $20 billion, and that the deficit estimated in January at under $2 billion now looked like $7 billion, despite revenues enlarged due to hefty corporate profits.

Meanwhile, Johnson's solicitation of the business community's support and understanding had left him on the outs with the trade union movement—which not only didn't get invited to the White House to be massaged by the president, but had been ignored when it earlier had urged Johnson to puncture the inflation bubble by withdrawing the 7 percent investment tax credit. Labor sulked. AFL-CIO president George Meany complained that there was no one in the White House entourage, such as Arthur J. Goldberg in the Kennedy administration, who could speak labor's language. After working hard for LBJ against Goldwater in the 1964 election campaign, labor felt that it had been jilted.[19] Since 1962, going back to the Kennedy administration's imposition of a 3.2 percent wage increase "guidepost," union leaders had concluded that labor was getting screwed: prices and profits were rising, but workers were being asked to be "responsible" by forgoing reasonable wage demands. Despite bitter complaints, however, organized labor had moderated its wage demands. The level of inflation, and the average level of wage boosts for five years, had remained remarkably close to the 3.2 percent figure. The unit cost of labor had moved up only fractionally in this period.

But in the early months of 1966, prices began to move up sharply, in the absence of any well-defined policy, well ahead of wage gains. Arthur Okun said in a speech to a business writers' group in Minneapolis that "if we move into 1967 with a strong head of steam in the economy, with exceedingly tight labor markets, with a record of very substantial increases in consumer prices, and with a continuing rise in profit margins, then we would have to expect a marked acceleration in wage increases."[20]

By summer, as prices soared in an overheated economy, it was no longer possible for a Democratic administration to persuade labor leaders to limit wage increases to the low 3.2 percent standard embodied in the wage guidepost. James Tobin, a member of the Kennedy CEA that had devised the guidepost, admitted in August 1966 that rising prices and business profits "have made it virtually impossible to ask labor to adhere strictly to guideposts."[21]

What ended the guideposts was the threat that an airline industry dispute would be settled with a 4.3 percent wage boost for the airlines' machinists. By itself, that would not have been unique: there had been many settlements in the 4.0 percent to 4.5 percent range, but all had been resisted by the administration. This one, however, Johnson tried to pass off as a justified, noninflationary wage hike, because the machinists' productivity was rising at a 6 percent annual level.

But that was heresy in terms of the guidepost concept: wage increases in a given industry were to be held to trend level in the overall economy. There were also subtle violations of the price guidepost, which had never been well understood by Congress or the public. On prices, the idea was that industries enjoying productivity *above* the national average should reduce their prices, because the high productivity they experienced translated into lower labor costs. Adherence to this concept, for example, called for a reduction in auto prices. Walter P. Reuther, president of the United Auto Workers, estimated that General Motors could have cut prices by an average of $100 per car while maintaining profit levels. Instead, GM boosted prices by $56 a car for 1967 models—and that was cheered by the Johnson administration because it was less than Ford and Chrysler had got away with despite a protest by Ackley.[22]

Labor's complaint that it was not sharing equally in national prosperity seemed confirmed by testimony by Gardner Ackley on Capitol Hill. From 1960 to 1965, industry's before-tax profits plus depreciation allowances had increased from 26.2 percent to 28.6 percent of national income. The "swing" in industry's share of national income implied by the extra 2.4 percent was equal to about $7 billion to $8 billion annually. That left the unions almost no option except to try to catch up by demanding wage boosts exceeding the increases in the cost of living.

With industry and labor engaged in all-out warfare, the public took it on the chin, paying higher prices while the companies accumulated greater profits and workers got above-guidepost wage increases. Another body blow to the guidepost concept came when the steel industry caught the administration by surprise with a totally unexpected $3 per ton price increase—again, over the guidepost. But after talking it over with Ackley and White House press secretary Bill Moyers, Johnson decided there was nothing he could do about it, even though he felt "the public interest had been violated."[23]

Johnson and his key advisers were still hoping for miracles, deluding themselves into believing that, somehow, Vietnam War costs would quit escalating. The Pentagon kept promising that the costs of the war would soon "peak out." The economy was booming, but Johnson had no desire to go to Congress for a tax boost so soon after the 1964 tax cuts.

"Mr. Taxes," as Representative Wilbur D. Mills (D.-Ark.), chairman of the House Ways and Means Committee, was known, and Senator Russell B. Long (D.-La.), chairman of the Senate Finance Committee, also had no taste for raising taxes after just having reduced them, knowing the sentiment on the Hill. "Let me put it to you this way," one senator told me at the time. "If I vote for a tax increase, my opponent in November is going to hang me with that record of the rollcall. Now, I recognize that without a tax increase, maybe prices will get out of hand. But no one can pin that on me."

If Johnson's "government by inhibition" policy didn't make business and labor happy, his own advisers were soured by his propensity to keep them in the dark. When he speculated out loud to a group of visitors that he might, after all, have to recommend a tax increase of "five, six, or seven percent," Ackley and Okun had to learn about it from a wire service report.[24]

At that stage, Ackley and Okun believed they had to take the risk that a price spiral could be avoided (even though they had serious private doubts). True, it was not an open and shut case: prices had not yet boomed out of control as they had in 1955, a year often cited as a parallel to 1966. As Okun told me: "We don't want to give up on a dream: for the first time in ten years, we're at the point where we can have full employment, continued growth, and reasonable price stability. Every other society that has come up to this challenge has foundered. We get a lot of advice which in effect says: 'When you get to Heaven, knock yourself to Hell again.' We believe that even though it's a tricky tightrope to walk, there must be a better way."[25] Meanwhile, Heller and Eckstein, having returned to their respective universities, were warning Ackley and Okun that it had already become too big a risk to assume that a price spiral could be avoided.

Johnson simply refused to view it in those terms. He reasoned, in mid-1966, that if he decided to ask for a boost in corporate and personal taxes to deflate a booming war economy, the obvious response of the Republicans would be to propose a cut in Great Society expenditures, so he decided to ride it out.

Private dissensions among LBJ's advisers soon began to break out. Bureau of Labor Statistics commissioner Arthur M. Ross said publicly that the gross national product for 1966 could hit $735 billion, $13 billion over the revised official forecast, helping to generate inflationary pressures. (Ross—an economist from the University of Michigan—would be the only Johnson administration official to quit because of the escalating costs of the Vietnam War.[26])

Ackley and Okun prepared their economic forecasts without knowledge of McNamara's planned jump in troop commitments; thus their first GNP estimate for 1966 was only $710 billion, based on the theoretical assumption supplied by McNamara that the war would end by July 1967. The final result, according to later official tallies, was $749.9 billion.[27] But in January 1967, when the preliminary figures had shown the 1966 GNP to have swelled to at least $740 billion, the pretense that the war would be over by midyear had to be abandoned for a budgetary assumption that "the war will continue indefinitely" at then-current levels.

Even so, Johnson and McNamara played everything close to the vest, which meant that economic projections were largely guesswork. Ackley, Okun, and CEA member James S. Duesenberry nonetheless confidently predicted a better-balanced 1967, with real growth of 4 percent, inflation held to 2.5 percent, and the GNP expanding to a record $785 billion to $790 billion.

Sidney Weinberg, the brash investment banker who was a power in the Business Advisory Council (later the Business Council), put it in a graphic way: "As long as we're not doing what we should on the fiscal side, money will stay tight—and history shows us that this pattern almost always ensures recession. If the man at the corner delicatessen can't borrow $600 at reasonable rates, he can't buy the kind of corned beef you want to eat."[28]

Finally, in January 1967 Johnson suggested a tax increase in the form of a 6 percent surcharge on top of normal tax rates. Later, the surcharge request was boosted to 10 percent, designed to yield $7.4 billion in the new fiscal year.

By that time, the damage was done. When Budget Director Schultze testified in August 1967, he had to admit that of a $44 billion increase in projected spending for fiscal 1968, $29.7 billion had gone to defense, all but $3.8 billion of which was for Vietnam.

All of Johnson's Great Society spending in that period—lumping housing, antipoverty, education, and welfare programs together—had increased by only $6.2 billion—and Schultze warned that future programs would be even less generous. Bitterly, Wilbur Mills sent a public message to Johnson: "We have been kept too much in the dark. . . . There has got to be recognition that we can't go forward and do everything else we want to, like going to the moon, and still fight this war to a successful conclusion. We need some advice on priorities, and we haven't gotten it. And the buck has been passed to us."[29]

In his memoirs, Clark M. Clifford, who succeeded McNamara as secretary of defense in February 1968, details the incredible lengths to which the Johnson White House went, in the early months of 1968, to keep from the public the true measure of the disastrous losses being inflicted on the American forces in Vietnam after the Tet offensive began in January, at the same time that McNamara, General Westmoreland, and General Earle G. Wheeler, chairman of the Joint Chiefs of Staff, were lobbying for delivery of 206,000 more troops and a huge buildup of reserves.[30] On March 4, Clifford—who opposed the buildup—writes, Fowler "followed me [in a presentation to LBJ] with a brutal description of the fiscal and monetary implication of the buildup of the Reserves. I could see that it had a strong impact on the president and on Secretary of State Dean Rusk, and even on Wheeler, who surprised me by backing away from the Wheeler-Westmoreland troop request."[31]

That final buildup never took place. Instead, Johnson made his surprise announcement on March 31. Yet it wasn't until June that he and Congress agreed on legislation authorizing a tax surcharge designed to bring in $11 billion in extra revenue and cutting spending by $6 billion. Counting the extension of excise taxes, there would be about a $20 billion swing in the fiscal balance. It was the end of the pretense that guns and butter could both be paid for forever. Yet the two-year delay in beginning to pay for the war in Vietnam came only when fears of inflation were joined by open concern that failure to act would precipitate a run on the dollar.

The British pound had been devalued in November 1967, and the dollar was under siege. In March, LBJ's own Kerner Commission, created in the wake of the 1967 urban rebellions, declared that the United States had become "two societies, separate and unequal." Despite LBJ and McNamara's grand deceit, there would not be guns and butter: it would be mostly guns. The Great Society had become a not-so-great society—and, in human terms, the worst was yet to come before we would be expelled from Vietnam.

Eventually, labor and management's greedy competition for increasing shares of the national income continued; it has never been resolved in the national interest. In the absence of a firm policy line from the White House, the companies and unions proceeded to squeeze the last nickel out of a booming, fully employed, semiwartime economy. Thus they set in motion the process of losing market shares to more competitive Asians and Europeans.

It wasn't until the publication of their final Economic Report of the President in January 1969, as Johnson turned the government over to Richard Nixon, that LBJ's economists offered a public mea culpa. With great candor, Arthur Okun, who had succeeded Gardner Ackley as CEA chairman in February 1968, and his two colleagues admitted that they had missed the boat with their forecasts in 1968. Inflationary forces gained a momentum "more than was realized," the report said.

Johnson had gambled that the pressures of war, superimposed on an economic boom, would somehow evaporate by themselves. They didn't, and today, a generation later, America is still paying for his irrational wager that the nation could have "business as usual" at home while fighting a guerrilla war abroad.

2

The Retreat from Gold

W HILE POLITICIANS, government officials, businessmen, and bankers were wrestling with the nation's economic woes that spring of 1968, the public's attention was preoccupied by the assassinations, in quick succession, of Martin Luther King Jr. and Robert F. Kennedy. The war in Vietnam raged on, opposition to it grew ever more vociferous, and 1968 would turn out to be one of the most tumultuous years in our nation's recent history. Within days of Johnson's announcement that he would not run for reelection, King was murdered and the nation's capital erupted into a weekend of devastating riots. I will never forget the sight of Washington burning, the flames devouring long lengths of Seventh and Fourteenth Streets.

Business leaders, acutely aware that the dollar was in trouble and that Vietnam was still draining the nation's resources, had expected, prior to Johnson's surprise withdrawal statement, that once the election was over, Johnson—if victorious—would impose formal wage-and-price controls. To be sure, there were disclaimers. But his—and the government's—credibility was at a low ebb. For the first time, the seriousness of the gold drain, and its impact on the dollar, began to seep into congressional awareness. Representative William S. Moorhead (D.-Pa.) warned that without a tax increase at a time the nation faced back-to-back annual budget deficits in excess of $20 billion, the international monetary system could break down, "precipitating a worldwide depression of catastrophic dimensions."

There is a mystique and glamour to gold—for those who treasure and fawn over it, but not for the miners who sweat to dig it out of the earth's crust. From time immemorial, gold—once labeled "that barbarous metal" by Fed chairman William McChesney Martin—has been used by kings and princes as money: it can be melted into bars and fashioned into coins, lovely to look at, touch, and fondle. Yet gold is not an earning asset, like stocks or bonds, which pay dividends or interest: if you put gold coins or bars in a bank, there is a cost for insurance and safekeeping. To make a profit by owning gold, the price has to keep rising more than the annual cost of storing or insuring it. And the weakness of gold as a basis for a monetary system is that its supply depends on the shifting economic or political needs of the gold-exporting countries. Still, there have been "goldbugs" in every generation, people with a passionate devotion to the metal as the single most desirable standard for money, or as the most trustworthy store of value, or as the underpinning for the most rigorous economic discipline.

In the beginning, gold had value because people would not only fight and kill for it but would barter goods for it. In modern times, gold had a value because politicians and governments arbitrarily declared that it did. In the postwar era, its price was set at $35 an ounce when the United States, as part of the bargain creating the International Monetary Fund at the famous Bretton Woods, New Hampshire, conference in 1944, agreed that it would always buy and sell an ounce of gold to and from the central banks of other governments for that many dollars. More precisely, the gold price would be kept within one-quarter of 1 percent of $35—or between $34.9125 and $35.0875.[1]

Under the management of the IMF, with the gold-dollar relationship at the core of the international monetary system, the world enjoyed an era of global prosperity, based on stable and fixed exchange rates, that lasted almost twenty-five years. The idea was simple: each country, except the United States, would adopt par values for its currency, and agree to keep the exchange rates in the market within 1 percent of those values by buying or selling dollars. The American role was to freely buy and sell gold to settle international transactions. There was a tacit understanding among the major powers of the Western world who dominated the IMF that Britain, West Germany, and all the other large holders of official dollar balances would not cash them in for gold.

Thus all the world's currencies were linked to the dollar, and the dollar was pegged to gold at $35 an ounce. By establishing that fixed relationship, the Bretton Woods conferees judged, they would end once and for all the undisciplined currency markets of the 1930s, when countries jockeyed for advantage by competitive depreciation of exchange rates—as well as trade restrictions—so as to shove their domestic problems, including unemployment, onto others.[2] But limiting the growth of the world's money supply irrevocably to a metal in short supply, dug out of the ground primarily by two pariah nations, South Africa and the Soviet Union, would also limit global economic growth and expansion. To be sure, gold exerted an economic discipline, but many critics of the gold standard believed that trade and investment relationships among nations should be governed by flexible, rather than rigid, exchange rates. The price of gold, like that of any other commodity, they argued, should be determined by the demand of industry and the jewelry trade. But bankers and many businessmen were unhappy with the unpredictability of floating exchange rates. They preferred fixed rates because such rates allowed corporations to plan exports and imports years ahead, with assurance that their costs and profits would not change merely because currency values fluctuated.

In the early 1950s, President Dwight D. Eisenhower departed from the original Bretton Woods agreement to allow the Bank of England to sell small amounts of gold to the private market in order to stabilize the official price against the onslaught of a growing black market. There always had been a thirst among the rich and powerful, especially in the Far East and Middle East, to own gold—not certificates or stock in gold mines, but the real, shiny metal one could touch and feel. Miroslav Kriz, one of the world's foremost experts on gold, has calculated that in the late 1960s private hoards of gold amounted to about $20 billion, or about double the value of the gold bars sitting in Fort Knox. Of the private hoard, at least half had probably been accumulated in the prior ten years. The culture of hoarding gold was global. For example, in India, savings were traditionally kept in gold, rather than in paper money or in stocks and bonds. Even in France, it was hard to find a prospering farm family that didn't have gold coins tucked away in the mattress. Reasonable guesses placed the French hoard at about 150 million ounces, almost $6 billion at $35 an ounce.

It was not until late in 1968 that American officials began to take seriously the likelihood that greater exchange rate flexibility would have to replace the rigidity of the Bretton Woods system. By then, it was becoming clear that if the already poor balance of payments situation was not to worsen, there would have to be some depreciation of the dollar. The reason: a cheaper dollar in effect lowers the price of American goods in foreign markets, stimulating exports. Of course, as the dollar goes down, the value of foreign currencies goes up, making imports more expensive. All else being equal, depreciation discourages the volume of imports—and, coupled with rising exports, improves the trade and current account balances. These account balances—the two chief elements in the balance of payments—are abstract concepts that can be best understood if they are thought of as determinants of jobs and economic growth. The balance of payments measures the excess or deficit in the amount of goods a country sells abroad compared to what it buys. The sale and purchase of services, such as insurance, is also included. The greater the surplus a country enjoys, the more jobs are likely to be created at home to produce the goods that others buy. But when there is a deficit, it means that a country is buying from foreigners more than it is selling. Therefore, the surplus country is probably generating more factory jobs (and profits) than the deficit country. (This description is something of an oversimplification since large imports also imply more jobs in the services and distribution sector—for example, in maintaining imported cars.)

When the earnings from the U.S. trade surplus—plus earnings on foreign investments—were not enough to cover the dollars flowing out of the country in the form of investments—or, as was true of the United States in the 1960s, large overseas military expenditures for troops and their maintenance—dollars piled up abroad. But the United States, tied under the Bretton Woods system to a fixed price for gold in dollars, could not alter its own exchange rate—unless it altered the system. Japan and West Germany were enjoying large trade surpluses that could be cut only if the deutsche mark and yen were revalued upward. But politically, it wasn't easy to do. The ideal system would be one in which exchange rates could be changed as an ordinary event, not risking the stigma attached to a major devaluation.[3]

Thus, from the onset of Bretton Woods, the world operated according to what might be called a dollar exchange standard. But it began to creak at the seams in the early 1960s, and actually to crumble in the final stages of the Johnson administration, when a worsening inflation, stimulated by the costs of the Vietnam War, and the accumulation of balance of payments deficits began to pump huge amounts of dollars abroad, and generated the biggest international money crisis since the Great Depression. So long as other countries were willing to hold dollars, there was no problem. But under the Bretton Woods system, the United States was obligated to exchange gold for dollars, at $35 an ounce, when presented by other friendly governments who were parties to the Bretton Woods system. The outflow of gold, when our reserves began to be tapped, was thus a result, not a cause, of our economic problems.[4]

The American gold hoard in Fort Knox dwindled to an estimated $12 billion in mid-1967 from more than $20 billion a decade earlier, as it dawned on foreign central banks that there could come a time when the United States would say "Sorry, no more gold for dollars." From the end of 1949 to the end of 1956, the major European countries had added only $3 billion in gold to their reserves, a 46 percent increase in their total monetary resources. But from the end of 1956 to 1966, these same countries added $11.9 billion in gold, or a 90 percent increase in their total reserves. This flow of gold had, of course, come straight out of U.S. holdings at Fort Knox. Against the remaining $12 billion in gold reserves, the "overhang" of dollars held by foreigners in 1967 amounted to an estimated $35 billion by the end of that year. And so long as the United States' balance of payments continued to be a negative number, the gap between the foreigners' dollar holdings and the American gold reserves—the linchpin of the Bretton Woods system—would grow.

During the Nixon-Kennedy campaign in 1960, a flurry of speculation in the private gold markets sent the price to around $40 an ounce, and that prompted the United States, Britain, France, Germany, Belgium, Holland, Italy, and Switzerland to make arrangements, through the Bank of England, to keep the price as close as possible to $35 an ounce. They established the "London gold pool," largely hidden from public view, to feed a supply of gold to private operators as demand for it rose. By providing steady access to gold, the London pool more or less successfully kept a lid on prices until new worries about inflation were touched off by Vietnam. In anxious times—especially when a war is going on—people abandon paper money and turn to physical investments: real estate, diamonds, other jewels, art, stamps, gun collections. Gold is considered by many the best hedge against rampant inflation.

By 1967, the gold pool had degenerated into a sort of transfer agent that allowed private holders of large amounts of paper dollars to convert them to gold, straight out of central bank monetary reserves.[5] Recognizing that gold hoarding had deep psychological roots that couldn't be ignored, the major nations had begun casting about, in 1965 and 1966, for a way to increase their monetary reserves without increasing the price of gold. With Treasury Secretary Henry Fowler's leadership at a mid-1966 meeting of the Big Ten powers[6] in London, it was agreed that the IMF would create a supply of "paper gold," to supplement gold and dollars, to be known by the awkward term special drawing rights (SDRs). The SDRs would be backed by the credit of the United States, West Germany, Britain, France, and Japan, and allocated to all member nations of the IMF. In essence, a nation needing hard currency could exchange the SDRs given it by the IMF—for dollars or deutsche marks, for example. By using SDRs, the system would be less dependent on both gold and the dollar for additional international reserves. This deal was ratified at the IMF's annual conference in Rio de Janeiro in 1967, to become effective in 1969. It was considered a great achievement at the time, marking a step toward the creation of international monetary reserves and away from a blind dependence on gold miners in South Africa and the Soviet Union.[7]

As the American economy reflected the strains of the escalating war in Vietnam, however, other governments increasingly favored gold over paper. American officials continued to argue that the dollar was as good as—even better than—gold. But few were convinced. Nevertheless, dollars were still the almost universal medium of exchange: a cab driver in London or Paris could be talked into taking dollars if a tourist didn't have the requisite amount of pounds or francs. But the London cabbie would surely reject Dutch guilders or Italian lira or French francs, and the French driver would turn down pounds or pesetas. The European cabbies were like businessmen all over the world who not only accepted, but eagerly sought, dollars as a medium of exchange not matched by any other paper currency. Those who held dollars could easily invest them, even in their own country, at good rates of return. Or they could be exchanged for other national currencies with no trouble. Yet, while the strength of the dollar as a medium of exchange was unquestioned, the anxiety building up over the gold-dollar relationship triggered talk in banking circles about the need for a change in U.S. gold policy.

The Chase Manhattan Bank published an article on April 4, 1967, by John Deaver, a vice president, arguing that in a "crisis," which he defined as a continued run on gold supplies, the United States could stop buying and selling gold at $35 an ounce, as required by the Bretton Woods agreement. Deaver said that the United States should quit being so defensive about the dollar and "employ a strategy that takes account of the dollar's strength and stability."[8] The Deaver article made the front pages when it was quoted favorably in a speech by Rudolph A. Peterson, head of the powerful Bank of America, to a New York business audience. Now, it seemed, two big American banks were joining in a demand that the United States shut off the outflow of gold, triggering a belief abroad that a new American policy was being tested for reaction. The result was an acceleration of the gold drain. That appeared to give the Chase Bank some sober second thoughts about the Deaver article and the Peterson endorsement. A week later, the bank backtracked, saying that halting the sale of gold would be risky and a confession of global policy failure.[9]

A crisis came two months later when France, a member of the London gold pool with a 9 percent share, refused to put in the $50 million in gold needed to cover its share of the recent drain. It then pulled out altogether, and the United States, which had a 50 percent share, agreed to pick up the French quota. The French were upset by the Deaver-Peterson statements, assuming that the two bankers were fronting for Fowler. They regarded talk about suspending gold convertibility as scandalous, a trick that would allow the United States to perpetuate its balance of payments deficits by pumping the world full of paper dollars that then had no gold backing. President Charles de Gaulle was further irritated that Johnson and Fowler had struck a deal with Bonn, under which the West Germans agreed to hold on to their surplus dollars. For their part, Johnson administration officials were tired of being scolded by de Gaulle for flooding the world with dollars via a large and growing balance of payments deficit. French complaints about redeeming dollars for gold were regarded as a crude threat.

René J. Larre, the economic counselor at the French embassy in Washington, liked to tell a story to illustrate how his country reacted to the American suggestion that Europe should help America solve its balance of payments problems. "Once upon a time," he said, "there was a small shopkeeper living in a narrow street in Paris. He lay awake one night because he had to pay back, the next morning, a few hundred francs to his moneylender, who happened to live across the street. And he didn't have the money at hand to do so. He was turning in his bed, unable to go to sleep, when he had an idea. He jumped to his feet, opened his window, and shouted: 'Samuel, I will not pay you back tomorrow!' Then he went back to his bed and told his wife: 'Now, Samuel is the one who will not be able to sleep!' "[10]

That was not only a French view: it summed up a European concern that America, with an inexhaustible supply of paper dollars that could be rolled off the printing presses, was not only forcing its trading partners to hold an excessive amount of greenbacks in their own reserves, but at the same time was using dollars to buy up huge investments in Europe. Of course, the countries receiving the investment flows also enjoyed substantial benefits for their own economies.

The French tantrum was a precursor to an event that American authorities had been trying to stave off for years, the devaluation of the British pound. In November, the Labour government of Harold Wilson cut the value of sterling by 14.3 percent, from the equivalent of $2.80 to $2.40, and boosted basic interest rates to 8 percent, the highest level in fifty-three years. Thus one ounce of gold was now worth fifteen British pounds, instead of twelve and a half, confirming the view among small and large speculators alike that gold was a better store of value than paper currency of any kind. The intended effect from the British perspective was a boost in exports, because a cheaper pound (so long as other countries didn't follow suit) would mean lower prices for British goods sold abroad. At the same time, however, imports would be more costly because the pound would be depressed, hitting hard at the real income of the average British wage earner, due to the island nation's heavy dependence on imported goods.

The devaluation of the pound was a shock to the international system: if the pound's value could change dramatically, it was a sign that big monetary forces were loose in the world, and that—despite routine denials—those same forces could affect the dollar. It precipitated an immediate boost by the Federal Reserve in the discount rate, from 4 to 4.5 percent, a defensive move to slow a potentially heavy flow of dollar investments into Britain to take advantage of the new high interest yields offered there.

In the two months following the British devaluation, the seven remaining gold pool members lost $1.5 billion from their gold stockpiles as they tried desperately to check the speculative flight from paper currencies. For all of 1967, the collective loss was estimated at $2 billion by Otmar Emminger, governor of the Bundesbank, who warned that if the American balance of payments deficit continued to grow, "there would be such a loss of confidence in the dollar that the whole international monetary system would be in danger."[11] Emminger, who died in 1986 at the age of seventy-five, was one of the great, innovative financial minds of Europe and a fixture on the international economic scene for more than thirty years. He worked tirelessly at two goals he saw as related—the revival of the German economy after the Second World War (he had worked on the distribution of the Marshall Plan) and the creation of a monetary system that could put an end to recurrent crises. An overstuffed briefcase always at hand, stocked with English translations of his latest speeches and papers, Emminger would carefully spell out the pros and cons of an issue, and predict—usually accurately—which governments would support which proposal, and for what quid pro quo. His ultimate ambition was to become president of the Bundesbank, a post he held for three years, from 1976 to his retirement in 1979. Emminger liked to joke that European coexistence with America "is like being in a boat—or a bed—with an elephant." That showed Emminger's sympathy with the general European view that America too often ignored the impact of its policies on friendly countries—"benign neglect," as critics less friendly than Emminger put it. But he was a strong believer that the United States should be the leader in world financial affairs, and was convinced—in contrast to the French—that the dollar, not gold, ought to be at the center of the international monetary system to maintain that leadership.

As gold began to move out of Fort Knox—both through the London pool and to central banks that were tempted to avail themselves of the Bretton Woods promise—it became clear to Washington that some specific actions would be needed: after all, the U.S. stock of gold at the end of 1967 was edging dangerously close to the $10.6 billion bare minimum required by law—a figure equal to the statutory 25 percent gold "cover" against U.S. currency, the amount of gold required by law to be held as a reserve against U.S. paper dollars.

The Johnson administration considered asking Congress to remove the gold cover, but failed to pursue the idea. It would be too plain an admission that the economy had been put under stress by the guns-and-butter approach. Instead, officials privately begged allies, such as Germany, to hold onto dollars and not cash them in for gold. The Germans reluctantly agreed. But de Gaulle urged that the price be doubled, from $35 an ounce to $70, as an incentive to flush out existing private hoards. Cooler heads noted that this would provide a windfall not only for the world's two unpopular producing nations, but would penalize those friendly countries that had held onto their dollars, refusing to unload them for gold. Fed chairman Martin labeled the idea "disruptive," Emminger said it was "terrifying," and IMF managing director Pierre-Paul Schweitzer said that his fellow Frenchman's notion was "crude."

What de Gaulle had in mind, of course, was an attack on what he had labeled the "exorbitant privilege" that allowed the United States to escape economic discipline, under a system in which the rest of the world depended on the dollar to increase its monetary reserves. De Gaulle knew that if the United States were forced to trade gold for dollars held by France and other countries, Johnson would have to modify his guns-and-butter policy, which was dumping huge amounts of dollars overseas.[12] If gold were boosted to $70 an ounce, the United States would have a gold stock worth $24 billion, and then could afford to let France and all other dollar claimants turn up at Fort Knox with paper money in hand and cart off the gold bars.

But that would likely touch off an inflationary boom: the in-

creased cash equivalents accruing to individual investors could
spark a wild spree in the stock, bond, and commodity markets.
Moreover, a doubling of the price of gold would not likely quiet the
speculative fever: having once been rewarded with a bonanza, speculators would want more. Beyond that, no one could predict the potential effects on trade: a dollar worth only one-seventieth of an
ounce of gold instead of one-thirty-fifth would, in effect, be under-
going a devaluation of 50 percent. Unless every other nation cut its
own currency values by half, American goods would gain an enormous trading advantage. There was no way to make sure that an
increase in the price of gold would not set off a series of competitive
devaluations, or a round of "beggar thy neighbor" protectionist restrictions that would lead to a global trade war. A gold price increase
would also, of course, encourage speculation in gold-mining ventures.[13]

As a sense of anxiety mounted, a variety of ideas were pro-
pounded: Yale economist and *Newsweek* columnist Henry C. Wallich advanced a plan for a 10 percent emergency tariff on all imports,
designed to cut the trade deficit by $3 billion a year. There were calls,
such as one from Donald C. Cook, president of American Electric
Power Company and a former Johnson aide, for cutting loose from
gold entirely and establishing flexible exchange rates, permitting
them to fluctuate according to supply and demand in the markets.
And Stanford University economist Emile Despres suggested a
novel, partial demonetization of gold by continuing to sell at $35 an
ounce but not promising to buy it back at that price. That, Despres
argued, would validate the favored American homily that the dollar
was not only as good as gold but better, and effectively remove the
"floor" price that stood as a guarantee against any loss for speculators.[14] But Treasury officials feared that any such move would simply convey the notion that Uncle Sam was tinkering with a
hard-and-fast commitment, and might thereby encourage, rather
than discourage, speculators.

Instead, the United States, represented by Treasury Undersecretary Frederick L. Deming, calmed things down at a meeting of the
London gold pool in Frankfurt in early December by renewing the
pledge to maintain both the $35 price as well as the buying and sell-
ing operations of the London gold pool. But in just two weeks' time,
the confidence generated at Frankfurt was dissipated by a nearly incredible American blunder, a violation of a cardinal rule of high finance: never betray anxiety. Seeking to further reassure the
international community, Deming succeeding in doing exactly the
opposite by turning up at Basel, Switzerland, as a gate-crasher.

The picturesque, small Swiss city of Basel is the site of the Bank for International Settlements (BIS), which economist Robert Triffin once described as a "jealously closed club, or mecca of central bankers." A sort of central bankers' central bank, the BIS meets behind closed doors every month to exchange views and informally coordinate the interest-rate decisions of national central banks. It jealously guards its privacy, and never invites outsiders in. The Federal Reserve system, of course, is a charter member: Chairman Martin was the board's regular representative at the Basel meetings during this period. But central bankers look down their noses at ministers of finance, such as Treasury officials, who are considered politicians first and financial experts second. None had dared show a face in Basel until Deming showed up. It was more than a personal goof: obviously, Deming was there on Fowler's orders. A European central banker who was present later told me: "Deming's sudden appearance at the BIS was a stunner, like an uninvited guest walking into somebody else's harem. Anyone taking such a risk must have something on his mind, and the way they figured it at Basel, there could be only one answer: the dollar must be in real trouble."

To top off the American indiscretion, Deming held a press conference in Basel and talked of "even closer cooperation" among the gold pool countries. But when no talks were forthcoming, rumors ran rife—the United States would stop the sale of gold; there might be two or three different "tiers" or variations in gold prices; or the gold pool would find other ways to block speculators' access to gold. The net result, a week later, was an estimated $400 million loss of gold, the amount of paper dollars cashed in by foreign governments for gold. To be sure, in a volatile market, some gold drain would have occurred anyway. But the Deming escapade showed that the Treasury wasn't yet adept in the high-stakes poker game in which markets could be panicked by the slightest miscalculation.

On New Year's Day, President Johnson made the dramatic announcement that the United States would reverse its insistence that voluntary controls were adequate to handle the balance of payments problem, and instead would enforce mandatory controls to choke off the flow of dollars abroad. It was a complete renunciation of the policy that had been reiterated just six weeks earlier, when new voluntary "guidelines" had been issued for investment and lending overseas. Clearly, Johnson had been pushed hard in the interim by his European allies to recognize that the voluntary efforts were not working well enough. An internal Treasury memorandum early in December acknowledged that a further deterioration of the balance of payments "is no longer acceptable."[15] It conceded for the first time that the balance of payments deficit could no longer be blamed exclusively on the Vietnam War. To be sure, the war was costing $1.5 billion per year, about one-third of the total deficit. But there was an additional outflow of around $3 billion that had to be accounted for elsewhere. Indications were that the red ink in that overall measure of the international accounts would swell to about $3.5 billion, triple the $1.2 billion of 1966, with the annual rate in the final quarter of 1967 over $7 billion. Fowler pressed the point to the president that maintenance of balance of payments accounts among the major partners in the system was a shared responsibility. That meant that the wealthier European countries, benefiting from the expenditures of American dollars to maintain troops on their soil in a common defense against the ever-present threat of the Soviet Union, had to chip in, especially by picking up a larger share of the burden for aid to less developed countries.

Johnson's new mandatory program to reduce the flow of dollars abroad included limits on "unessential" tourist travel outside of the Western Hemisphere and on government expenditures abroad, but the primary emphasis was to be on the reduction of investment in Western Europe, where American companies had been boosting their ownership stake and incurring the wrath of the local competition. Still, Johnson did not ask Congress to eliminate the gold cover, a step that the Europeans insisted was needed to instill lasting faith in the dollar and endorsed by Chairman Martin. (The gold-cover elimination step could have been taken earlier by Kennedy, with less traumatic effect. But Kennedy's Treasury secretary, C. Douglas Dillon, had not been keen on the idea.)

Johnson's New Year's Day program, while welcome, was an inadequate response to a basic problem. Moreover, the proposed travel ban couldn't be justified on any logical grounds. White House propagandists said the proposed limit was triggered by a jump of $100 million in the travel "gap" to about $2 billion in 1967. But that was due entirely to the popularity of Expo '67, held in Canada. Johnson's response—an effort to minimize tourist traffic to Europe— made no sense at all: tourist travel to Europe helped undergird billions in sales of jet aircraft to foreign airlines. But Johnson had concluded that corporations couldn't be asked to limit their investments in Europe while no limitations were placed on tourists. It was a cheap public relations ploy, not an economic judgment. For years, State Department officials had resisted persistent efforts by Treasury to impose a "head tax" or other measures to discourage civilian travel abroad. But now Secretary of State Dean Rusk had caved in.

Two weeks after the announcement of his highly touted program designed to ease tensions about the dollar, Johnson finally included a request to remove the gold cover in his State of the Union message, revealing that the cover left only $1.3 billion of the nation's $12 billion gold stockpile available for sale against foreign dollar holders. The squeeze was readily apparent: Fowler's tally showed that with a $500 million normal increase in the domestic paper money supply each year, and about $150 million worth of gold a year that would go into domestic industrial or artistic uses, "there is but two years grace at most, even if one assumes that no gold at all will be needed for international purposes."[16]

These events boosted the existing pressures throughout the world for an increase in the price of gold: it was abundantly clear that the price would already have broken through the $35 ceiling set by the Bretton Woods agreement and reinforced by the gold pool if the major nations had not fed $1.5 billion worth of gold into the private market toward the end of 1967, much to the delight of Arab and European speculators, business corporations hedging against a plunge in paper money, and even some smaller central banks, including those in Spain and Argentina. That meant, without a doubt, that if the price were to remain at $35, there would be further drains from "official" supplies.[17]

Behind closed doors at the Treasury, the Federal Reserve, the IMF, and in academic circles here and abroad, government officials and other experts put their heads together, seeking to devise some clever scheme that would block the flow of gold and help reduce the American balance of payments deficit—yet not give the goldbugs a psychological victory over the central bankers. For the truth of the matter was that the central bankers and the goldbugs were engaged in a nasty, no-holds-barred scramble for available gold supplies. The amount of gold flowing into monetary reserves had actually declined in 1967: production in South Africa—the world's biggest supplier— and in the rest of the noncommunist world had leveled off in the prior few years, which meant that the world was heavily dependent on increases in sales by the second-largest producer, the Soviet Union.

Edward Bernstein, one of the founders of the Bretton Woods agreement, cut to the heart of the matter at a seminar for House Republican members: "As the U.S. gold holdings go down, the good fellows who have been standing on line and saying 'We're going to hold on to those dollars forever' begin to say 'Those fellows who are pushing up to the window aren't playing fair—we better get ours before we get stuck.' Even those central bankers who criticize us the most only fear that someone else is going to get the gold, and then they will be told that they failed to protect the interests of their country. You would be astonished at the amount of ingenuity that central bankers are applying right now to devising techniques by which they will be able to tell their public, 'Look, we protected our interests, even if something happens to gold.' In my opinion, we have reached the stage where we must do something now, or the movement to a gold crisis will accelerate."[18]

A major clearinghouse for tackling the problem was a task force set up under former Treasury secretary Dillon, who had returned to Wall Street. Dillon brought together the best brains on the subject, including Guido Carli, head of the Italian central bank, who suggested that the central banks freeze the amount of gold in existing reserves, agree to buy and sell gold only to each other, and forever bar the purchase of newly mined gold. That would automatically create an "outside" or unofficial market for gold in which prices could fluctuate freely, and presumably accelerate the move toward some form of "paper gold," because the world would need some new form of reserves. The Carli plan proved to be pretty close to the final decision of the gold pool nations, and as word of the Dillon committee discussions leaked out tensions around the world increased. Bankers and businessmen wondered aloud about the strength of the dollar and Johnson's ability to continue to lead his bitterly divided nation. Even in Saudi Arabia, if Israel remained the number one concern, the dollar was a close number two.

But with the shock waves of the British devaluation still reverberating, the gold pool partners announced after the Basel meeting that they would continue to keep the system pegged to gold at $35 an ounce. That, however, was for public consumption; privately, all members put quantity limits on further contributions to the pool, validating the judgment offered by Bernstein that no big nation would be stupid enough to strip its holdings down to the last bar to satisfy private speculators. Smaller nations would be driven by self-interest to add to their gold hoards while the getting was good, an instinct that reflected declining confidence in the dollar. One of the greatest monetary theorists, Yale professor Robert Triffin, got it right when he said bluntly that "the gold-exchange system is dead or dying."

The inevitable was about to happen, a partial demonetization as had been suggested by Despres, in which newly mined gold would still have a value—but not as money within the international monetary system. On Thursday, March 14, 1968, after a wild day of speculation in gold markets, and a drop of more than eleven points in the Dow Jones index (then a big slide), the Fed raised the discount rate another notch, to 5 percent, and Johnson hurriedly placed a phone call to British prime minister Harold Wilson, asking for a temporary closing down of the London gold market. Wilson promptly complied, shutting down not only the gold pool but banks and securities exchanges. In addition, Fowler and Martin announced there would be an unprecedented emergency meeting of the gold pool's central bankers, along with the IMF's Schweitzer, at the Fed headquarters in Washington on Saturday and Sunday, the 16th and 17th.[19] Significantly, the key players decided to meet as members of the gold pool rather than as members of the Group of Ten industrial nations, which would have included the French. It was a tip-off to their determination to deflate the role of gold and to ignore de Gaulle (who had withdrawn from the pool the year before), even though that might risk the evolution of the IMF's special drawing rights, for which France's assent, as a major IMF nation, could be critical.

Meanwhile, the market action shifted to the small French gold market in Paris, the only significant gold exchange that hadn't been closed. Keeping it open was de Gaulle's response to the snub from his former gold pool partners. On Saturday, as the gold poolers began their huddle over lunch at the Fed, the price of gold skyrocketed to $44.36 an ounce, up 26.7 percent, then settled at $42, up 20 percent.

On Sunday evening, after two days of brainstorming, the gold pool partners announced that the gold pool they had operated for six and a half years would be closed and that it was no longer "necessary" to "buy gold from the market." There would be a dual-price gold system, with the United States still pledging to sell gold at $35 an ounce to official buyers, and a higher price to be countenanced for private market dealings. The Treasury said its understanding was that the cooperating governments would not cash in dollars for gold at $35 an ounce with the intention of reselling the gold on the higher private market.

The announcement was intended to sound like an ironclad commitment among the seven gold pool nations that they would never again buy newly mined gold. But the six European members viewed the ban on buying gold "from the market" as merely part of the strategy to encourage South Africans to sell gold to private buyers, which would help keep the free market price from shooting sky-high. And even more telling, the six cooperating European central banks made plain that they had not pledged in any formal way that they would quit tapping American gold reserves. That meant that the United States would have to be on its good behavior: if the large holders of paper dollars again were to lose confidence in America's stability, the process of cashing dollars for gold would start all over. The European central bankers "don't want to rock the boat," one of them told me, "but there may come a time when they have no options." So began an uneasy era of the two-tier price system for gold, in which newly mined gold would have a value, but not as money in the international system. The only gold that would count as money would be the $40 billion or so already held by central banks and the IMF. That meant that the central banks not only would not sell any of their gold, but that they would no longer buy new gold from the private market.

And why was it no longer "necessary" to buy gold from the market? Because, according to the gold pool announcement, "the existing stock of monetary gold is sufficient in view of the prospective establishment of the facility for special drawing rights." In plain language, that meant it was up to de Gaulle whether he wanted to isolate France from the mainstream. The gold pool partners hoped that a final meeting on the SDRs in Stockholm at the end of March would put the final touches on a formal agreement making paper gold a reality and allowing the London gold market to reopen April 1 without the old, official $35 floor to support it; and that France would "come to its senses" and join in freezing the existing supply of monetary gold.

De Gaulle branded the new system as inequitable, and called for a return to the "immutability" of the gold standard. "Let him rant and rave," a Johnson aide said.[20] But a social upheaval in France, which reached a crescendo of widespread riots in May, was shaking Gaullism—and the French franc—to the core. France would lose as much as an estimated $2 billion in gold and hard currency reserves. After years of running a balance of payments surplus, while heckling the United States and Britain for their pattern of red ink, France was suddenly thrown into trouble itself.[21] A 10 percent boost in overall wages, including a 35 percent increase in French minimum wages, was won by rebelling French workers. Inflation was sure to follow. Nevertheless, de Gaulle avoided devaluation. But the following year, the new French president, Georges Pompidou, with Valery Giscard d'Estaing running the Ministry of Finance, devalued the franc by 12.5 percent, conceding that the franc had been overvalued by at least that much.

For the French, it was an extraordinary reversal of government policy. Giscard gave up the fight to revalue gold, and endorsed the idea of activating a small issue of SDRs, perhaps on the order of $4 billion, which would give France a modest addition to its reserves, which had been cut in half by the speculative run that followed the events of May. It was a classic example of the "if you can't lick 'em, join 'em" philosophy. The clear lesson for the world was that posses-sion of a huge stockpile of gold (France had an estimated $6 billion worth) did not ensure political tranquillity, if at the same time the standard of living of the entire workforce, in real terms, was not al-lowed to grow.

Although the two-tier gold price system established in March 1968 had temporarily ended the drain of American gold abroad, it also had the unintended effect of providing a convenient barometer of confidence in the U.S. dollar—the unofficial price of gold. So far, it had held stable, drifting close to the $35 official price, after the brief flurry when the gold pool was closed down. But it was an uneasy situation: if the unofficial price started up again, it was clear that one alternative would be abandoning gold altogether, or yielding by the other powers to de Gaulle's demand that the official price be doubled or tripled.

At a private conference sponsored by the American Bankers Asso-ciation at Dorado Beach, Puerto Rico, in May, the world's financial elite—meeting, as Milton Friedman once remarked they had a habit of doing, in one of the garden spots of the globe— debated the pros-pect that the fixed-exchange-rate system, tied to gold, might have to be junked altogether. Word that this might be a real possibility came from an unexpected source, Karl Blessing, the short, chunky cigar-smoking president of the German central bank. In between first-ever forays at the roulette tables, Blessing confided to his colleagues that exchange rates might have to be allowed to "float"—that is, to arrive at their own value, just like wheat or any other commodity. His belief stunned other establishment stalwarts, such as Emile van Len-nep, the director-general of the Organization for Economic Coopera-tion and Development, the Paris-based research and study group organized by the twenty-four industrialized countries. But a palpable rumble went through the assemblage of the world's largest commer-cial bankers, as they sensed they were poised on the brink of a finan-cial revolution of major proportions, in which exchange rates would be set by actual supply and demand, instead of by some fixed, arbi-trary rule.

The possibility of floating rates had been formally raised at the meeting by University of Chicago professor Harry G. Johnson, a highly respected theorist who had long criticized the fixed-rate sys-tem. Glumly listening to his presentation, Maurice Parsons, deputy governor of the Bank of England, snapped that Johnson's ideas would lead to "sinking instead of floating." To which Johnson replied: "I wonder what you would call what happened in Britain last Novem-ber!" At heart, Blessing—who among Europeans was as much a symbol of irreducible monetary integrity as was Fed chairman Martin in America—was no more enthusiastic than Parsons about giving up fixed rates. "We should avoid a system of fluctuating rates as long as we can," he said. But unlike Parsons, Blessing was a pragmatist who recognized that forces were loose that might leave the world no option. Either the existing system, which was producing large balance of payments surpluses and deficits, had to be made to work better, or the pressures for floating rates would be irresistible. "Something must be flexible, either the system or the rates," Blessing observed.

LBJ's economists stuck stubbornly to the notion that the fixed-rate system could be repaired. It wasn't until its very last days in office, in the final report of the Okun Council of Economic Advisers, that the Johnson administration cautiously recommended that reforms of the international monetary system should be studied, including "wider bands" of permissible rates. But the Okun CEA also cautioned incoming president Richard Nixon not to raise the price of gold.

The following year would see an agreement to create just under $10 billion in SDRs over a three-year period, a decision that Edward Bernstein said was more important, in some ways, than Bretton Woods itself. For the first time, governments established a way of creating reserves that would allow the global economy to grow, breaking their total dependence on gold. "Paper gold" was calculated in terms of the major currencies, which, through the dollar, had a relationship to gold. But paper gold would not be convertible to gold. Meanwhile, the two-tier system was working well, with the free market price running around $6 per ounce over the official $35 price.[22]

For a change, the French had been forced to be less arrogant. In September 1969, as we sat alone in the French government's office set up at Washington's Sheraton Park Hotel for the annual meeting of the World Bank and IMF, Giscard even had kind words for Schweitzer, whom he had denounced back in 1965 as a purveyor of "inflationist claptrap." Now, Giscard acknowledged that the Gaullist dream of an increase in the price of gold was dead: "There is no longer a discussion of the revaluation of gold," he said, acknowledging that the two-tier system of pricing was "functioning smoothly." Still, he was not sold on the idea of flexible or floating exchange rates. "Nobody wants lasting, floating rates, [but] perhaps we can consider the use of broader margins, because technically, it might be a useful thing in the better management of reserves."[23]

Nevertheless, 1968 demonstrated that the Bretton Woods system had begun to come apart, and only an ad hoc, jerry-built structure was left standing. It couldn't last.

The only question was how long before the collapse would take place. And that, of course, would depend on whether the rest of the world would be content to hold dollars. If the closing of the London gold pool was merely Act 1 in the retreat from the Bretton Woods linkage of the dollar to gold. Act 2 in the saga was to be left to Richard Nixon.

MISMANAGEMENT

3

Gradualism and the Final Break with Gold

P ROBABLY NO PRESIDENT of modern times faced as complicated an economic challenge as did Richard M. Nixon when he
assumed office in January 1969. He inherited eight years of virtually
unbroken domestic prosperity in the Kennedy-Johnson years, symbolized by a fifteen-year-low monthly unemployment rate of 3.3 percent in November 1968. Nixon pledged that good times would
continue. But Johnson had also bequeathed him a raging inflationary
cycle, which Nixon had promised to break. Underneath it all, discontent festered in black America, exposing the need for reforms in
the welfare system and changes in the tax law, which clearly favored
the upper income brackets at the expense of the poor. In 1969, 12.1
percent of the population lived and suffered below the poverty line;
the percentage for whites was 9.5 while the percentage for blacks
was 32.2.[1] Meanwhile, Nixon had to confront the existence of a fragile stock market, reacting both to the growing balance of payments
crisis and the threat of a new credit shortage at home. What's more,
in the closing stages of the campaign, Nixon had announced he
would escalate the nuclear arms race with the Soviet Union, already
set in motion by Johnson. Any budget reductions to be yielded if the
Vietnam War moved toward a resolution would likely be gobbled up
by an antiballistic-missile system and an accelerated Navy ship-
building program. The key to eventual resolution of the interrelated
problems was a slackening of the pace of the Vietnam War. But the
immediate economic puzzle was how to taper off the inflationary

binge, which was pushing consumer prices up at an annual rate of almost 5 percent as Nixon took office.

Under William McChesney Martin, the nation's central bank was moving on its own to wring some of the exuberance out of the economy, having boosted the discount rate at the end 1968 to 5.5 percent, a step expected to slow civilian spending and to result in an increase in the unemployment rate. At 3.3 percent, the unemployment rate was barely over the level said to reflect "frictional unemployment"—mostly the number of workers between jobs. America had not only full employment, but "overfull" employment. Most Americans believe that low jobless rates trigger inflation, and that high jobless rates ease the pressure on prices. The acceptance of the "trade-off" argument between unemployment and inflation was almost universal among establishment economists of both parties, too, contested only by a handful of liberal Democratic economists, including Harry S Truman's chief economic adviser, Leon Keyserling, and labor specialists such as Sar A. Levitan of George Washington University. The trade-off argument has dominated classical economic theory ever since the English economist A. W. Phillips found a statistical relationship between wage and unemployment data. The Phillips curve, as his theory became known, said, in effect, that if the unemployment rate fell below a given level—say, 3 percent or 4 percent—inflation would rise. The connection, simply, was that with jobs seeking workers because the labor force was so fully employed, wage rates would rise, inevitably driving up prices. The Phillips curve, thus, was the underpinning for the conservative argument that the government should intervene as little as possible in the economy, accepting unemployment as the way to fight inflation. Levitan and others demonstrated that there had been periods in recent history when the trade-off did not seem to exist, when low unemployment had in fact coexisted with low inflation rates.[2] Phillips curve backers would say that special circumstances could adequately explain all seeming exceptions to the rule. But Levitan, supported by labor unions and—off and on—by Democratic politicians, contended that measures to deal with "structural" unemployment, that is, those made jobless by the special circumstances of their youth, race, sex, or location in depressed areas, could cut the unemployment rate without boosting inflation.

Nixon's economists weren't interested in such a theory, and were not seriously challenged by their Democratic counterparts at the time. "I almost feel sorry for Nixon," said Arthur Okun, who had moved on to the Brookings Institution as a senior fellow, "because from 3.3 percent unemployment, it can only go one way—up." The rate at the end of 1968 was 3.2 percent. For the year as a whole the unemployment rate was 3.6 percent. It would edge down to 3.5 percent in 1969, then rise to 4.9 percent in 1970.

Nixon immediately abandoned Johnson's efforts to persuade business and labor to restrain prices and wages. "I do not go along with the suggestion that inflation can be effectively controlled by exhorting labor and management and industry to follow certain guidelines," he told his first press conference six days after taking office. Pierre Rinfret, a New York business consultant and a Nixon adviser, immediately wired his business clients to raise prices. There would be no presidential interference, Rinfret assured them.

Nixon had named a group of mostly middle-of-the-road, solidly professional conservatives to his economic advisory team: Paul W. McCracken of the University of Michigan as chairman of the Council of Economic Advisers; Chicago banker David M. Kennedy (who had been considered for the job by Lyndon Johnson) as Treasury secretary, with his chief deputies being Paul A. Volcker, who had returned to the Chase Manhattan Bank in 1965, and Charls E. Walker, an economist who for eight years had been chief lobbyist for the American Bankers Association;[3] Robert P. Mayo, a Chicago banker who had worked with Kennedy, as director of the Budget Bureau; University of Chicago professor George P. Shultz as secretary of labor; and Arthur F. Burns, head of the National Bureau of Economic Research and perhaps the nation's most respected economist. McCracken's two colleagues on the CEA were Herbert Stein of the University of Chicago, who had worked for the Committee for Economic Development, a business research organization, and Hendrik S. Houthakker, a financial affairs specialist from Harvard. Stein's and Houthakker's jobs were "upgraded" by invitations to them to sit in on cabinet meetings, a privilege that had not been accorded to CEA members other than the chairman in the Kennedy-Johnson years. Conspicuously absent were the flamboyant Rinfret, Milton Friedman, and other ultraconservatives.

The bantamweight and underrated McCracken, who had been a member of the Burns CEA during the Eisenhower administration, was highly regarded by most other economists, including members of the departing Johnson team, even though he leaned somewhat to Friedman's monetarist dogma, which held that stable growth of the money supply was the single most important element in determining the nation's economic health. ("I'm Friedmanesque, if not a Friedmanite," McCracken would say.) Burns's inside-the-White House job as presidential counselor appeared on paper to deflate McCracken's authority, but Burns—who had painfully recon-

structed the Council of Economic Advisers in 1953 when Eisenhower became president, after it had undergone a credibility gap
under Leon Keyserling in the Truman administration—was a strong
believer in the CEA's institutional role and took pains not to undercut McCracken.[4]

Nixon, nonetheless, felt close to Burns, who had accurately perceived during the 1960 campaign against John Kennedy that Eisenhower's policies were exacerbating the recession. Without change,
which was not forthcoming, Burns said then, Nixon could lose the
election.

Eisenhower's refusal to heed Burns's advice may have tipped the
balance toward Kennedy in what turned out to be an extremely close
election. Unemployment was rising, and Kennedy successfully
milked the theme of "getting the economy moving again."[5]

Richard Nixon was many things, but he was not stupid. He never
forgot the lesson he took away from his loss to Kennedy that year:
you can't be elected—or stay in office—if you ignore the political
impact of high unemployment. When Nixon finally gained the presidency in 1968, Arthur Burns was the first man he tapped for his
Washington team. Until his economic game plan began to go awry in
1970, and he and Burns began to drift apart, Nixon would say: "Let's
see what Arthur thinks." In effect, Arthur Burns was assistant president for economic affairs.

The way Nixon constructed his inner economic circle, Burns at
the start was first among equals, enjoying direct access to the Oval
Office without going through White House staff, content with his
private deal with Nixon that he would be moved over to the Federal
Reserve Board as chairman when Martin's term expired in February
1970. Treasury Undersecretary Charls Walker, who resembled a
more suave version of Lyndon Johnson, also quickly became a key
figure. On a first-name basis with every important member of Congress, Walker was a glib, cigar-smoking lobbyist from Texas who
liked his double bourbons neat. In the banking business, he had been
regarded as a rough, tough competitor, smart as a whip, the kind of
guy you had better not tangle with. Lyndon Johnson himself, commenting approvingly on most Nixon appointees, said of Walker:
"Every administration has to have its own SOB, and Charlie Walker
will be Nixon's." David Kennedy, a genial, white-haired banker,
looked the part of a Treasury secretary, but he proved to be out of his
depth as the nation's chief financial officer, and would never have
much influence.

The underlying economic policy strategy crafted by McCracken
was to achieve a gradual and painless—if possible—deflation.

McCracken liked to say that Johnson had tried to get too quickly to full employment, but Nixon wouldn't make the equally grave error of trying to cool things down too quickly. Surprised and pleased, Democratic economists—although they argued it was a mistake to give up all forms of jawboning and private suasion—applauded the emergence of "gradualism," having feared that Nixon would sacrifice other national objectives in a cold-turkey effort to achieve price stability. Nixon also deflected Democratic criticism by pursuing a compassionate policy toward the poor and disadvantaged.

Indeed, Nixon was a big surprise to the Republican faithful, who expected he would be a safe and sound traditional conservative. Instead, he launched far-reaching initiatives in the areas of welfare, income-sharing, and tax equity, even if he reneged on some and agreed to water down others. Because of his ultimate disgrace over Watergate, this early Nixon phase has largely been forgotten. On the welfare front, Nixon went further to accept government responsibility for meeting minimal needs of the poor than any of his predecessors. He proposed to double the number of welfare recipients, and assure a minimum annual allowance of $1,600 for a family of four, at an annual cost of $4 billion. To help hard-pressed states and cities, Nixon turned to a version of the Heller-Pechman "revenue-sharing" plan. Heller, when he had been Johnson's CEA chairman, and his close associate, Joseph A. Pechman of the Brookings Institution, had tried mightily to sell this plan to the Democrats as a way of assuring that some states and localities would be able to maintain essential services. But Johnson would have none of it.

As to tax reform, Nixon fired the opening salvo in a long and arduous battle to amend the tax laws to force rich taxpayers with comfortable access to built-in loopholes to pay at least a minimum tax. The Nixon tax-reform plan was minimal, and achieved even less, but Nixon at least sensed the growing public interest in tax equity, in sharp contrast to Johnson, who had scuttled more meaningful tax proposals by Assistant Treasury Secretary Stanley S. Surrey and Pechman.

But as Nixon tried to break new ground, veering to the left of center on social programs, he also had to try to reassure his conservative constituency. And one way to convince the party regulars that he was the trustworthy, safe bet they had helped elect was to try to break the existing inflationary psychology by old-fashioned, traditional methods. That meant pursuing an exceptionally tight money policy (interest rates were at their highest point in 100 years),[6] and seeking to produce a balanced budget. He would neither raise taxes nor sharply cut government spending, for that could rapidly generate recession and even bring about civil disorder: an unemployment rate just over 3 percent meant jobless levels of around 6.5 percent for blacks.

Then there was the 7 percent investment tax credit. By early 1969, a revised investment tax credit was having precisely the perverse effect labor had feared: many corporate investment decisions were being made not with the goal of adding capacity or modernizing equipment for long-term economic objectives, but with an eye only to boosting the company's short-term profits-per-share scorecard.

After about two months in office, the Nixon team decided to aim at a budget surplus of about $6 billion instead of the $3.2 billion Johnson had projected for fiscal 1970 in his final budget. That would require Nixon to abandon the investment tax credit (as Democrats were demanding) and to continue the 10 percent surtax for another year. There was a nice irony in that decision: while still president-elect, Nixon hadn't agreed until the last minute to continue the surtax, even through 1969. Johnson's budget director, Charles Zwick, counseled LBJ—required by law to prepare the ensuing year's budget even though Nixon was to take over on January 20—to get the new president's acquiescence to preserving the surtax or to present an entirely different set of projections. Without the surtax, for example, a planned government pay hike would have to be postponed. Zwick advised Johnson to get Nixon to share some of the political heat for continuing the surtax or junking it. But Nixon couldn't make up his mind to go for the surtax until January 10, just five days before the Johnson budget was sent to Congress, leading a frustrated Johnson to tell Zwick that Nixon's "economic advisers must be as stupid as mine."[7]

At midyear, the Nixon administration adopted yet another new goal: to cut the real growth rate of the economy to 2 percent in the last half of calendar 1969, a sharp drop from the strong 6.5 percent real growth rate in the first half of 1968. But gradualism, which McCracken hoped would encourage businessmen to cut back on a planned 14 percent increase in plant expansion, didn't produce the desired results. The nation's gross national product boomed ahead at a $16 billion annual rate in the first quarter of the year, at least one-third more than expectations. Higher interest rates weren't deterring capital expansion: an 8 percent interest rate, after all, represented only a "real" interest rate of 4 percent, since a convenient tax deduction cut in half the actual cost of borrowing money.

Toward the end of the year, McCracken told 1,600 business leaders in the cavernous main ballroom of the Washington Sheraton Park Hotel that "a certain amount of pain" lay ahead, although "we can't use the word depression—and even recession is illegal." He went on: "The flat period ahead will only be an interlude." Look beyond, he urged his audience, "to the other side of the valley." They got the message. "What I get from him," said Joseph B. Hall, retired board chairman of the Kroger Company, "is that we can't solve our wage-price inflation without a recession, whatever you want to call it. And the only question is—what's the degree of the recession?"[8] Even Okun was endorsing the need for a crunch: "Unfortunately, we must say, 'Yes, Virginia, there is a trade-off between employment and price stability.' "[9]

INCREASINGLY, administration talk began to turn toward abandoning the game plan that relied exclusively on tight money and expenditure control. The irrepressible John Kenneth Galbraith suggested that the administration "is about to come up with something new—a combination of an intolerable level of unemployment with an intolerable level of inflation." Even the AFL-CIO's George Meany, who basically hated controls, which he saw as interference with the unions' ability to get fair wages, acknowledged that "legal controls" could stop inflation if they covered all forms of income, including business profits.[10] Gradualism was a failure; the economy was worsening. It was clear, as 1970 began, that the surplus would be paper thin, if any, in part because Congress was allowing the income tax surcharge to expire before the war in Vietnam ended. The final scorecard on Nixon's 1970 budget showed a deficit of $2.8 billion, and that would balloon to $23 billion in fiscal 1971.[11]

In February 1970, Nixon made good on his promise to Arthur Burns that he would succeed Bill Martin at the Fed. That set the stage for an easing of monetary policy; indeed, some wondered publicly whether the extremely close relationship Nixon and Burns had enjoyed over the years would undercut the highly trumpeted independence of the central bank. Although the Fed had acknowledged, over the years, that "independence" meant "within," not "from," the rest of the government, Fed chairmen traditionally had resisted pressure from the White House—usually to relax tight money policies—as a form of political interference with their mission. Now Burns, a vocal critic of the Fed's tight monetary policy, was moving from the White House to the Fed. But he would prove to be no exception to the mystique that endows almost every member, especially every chairman, with the conviction that there should be absolutely no interference from the outside with the Fed's control over monetary policy. Although he was well aware that critics could say that

Burns owed him a special obligation, Nixon made a revealing faux pas during Burns's swearing-in ceremony at the White House. When applause greeted Burns as he stepped to the podium in the East Room, crammed with Burns's family, associates, and friends, Nixon couldn't resist saying: "There's a strong vote for lower interest rates and more money." Burns made a bland, noncommittal response. But he told me just a few days later that he was deeply offended that Nixon had been that careless. Burns resented any implication that he could be influenced.

Nonetheless, in 1970 McCracken was staking out a position from which he could pressure the Fed more directly, reacting to a wider acceptance of the Friedmanite view that monetary policy ought to get more attention than Keynesians—devoted to the supremacy of fiscal policy—were willing to give it. In the 1970 Economic Report, Nixon's first after a full year in office, and coincident with Burns's move from the White House to the Fed, McCracken laid claim on behalf of the White House to a share of the responsibility for the evolution of monetary policy. Until then, the national government's responsibility under the Employment Act of 1946—calling on it to promote maximum employment, production, and purchasing power—had been exercised largely through fiscal policy. The Federal Reserve Board had traditionally expected to be left alone to determine monetary policy, in Martin's famous phrase, "leaning against the wind" to counteract inflation or deflation. But McCracken—Friedmanesque, as he had described himself—didn't want to be shut out of the picture. The Nixon administration's economic policy, according to the CEA's report, would be built on an effort to keep a modest surplus in the budget, combined with "moderate monetary restraint."[12]

So far as McCracken was concerned, that would imply monetary expansion at a rate somewhere between the 1967–68 pace and the severe credit restraint of the last half of 1969. No administration had ever offered such an explicit guide to the Fed on what monetary policy should be followed—and this one was inserted in the Economic Report over the objections of Treasury Secretary Kennedy and Budget Director Mayo. It was an overt nod in the direction of Friedman's monetarist school of thought that demanded of policy makers that in formulating monetary policy they give more attention to the aggregate measures of money, such as the stock of money and monetary reserves, rather than focus exclusively on interest rates.

The pressure brought to bear on the Fed to follow a Friedmanite money supply guide in making policy judgments would have been even more explicit if McCracken, supported by Stein and Houthakker, had been able to insert a demand in the Economic Report, as they had proposed, calling on the Fed for an immediate easing of policy. Friedman's views had split Nixon's economists down the middle. Stein was the leading advocate of pure Friedmanism, which held not only that money supply mattered most in stabilizing the economy but that fiscal policy hardly mattered at all. Stein believed that monetary policy was "the most manageable instrument" to assure stability "because the competing claims upon it are fewer than the claims on fiscal policy."[13]

Stein was joined by Houthakker, Labor Secretary Shultz, and to a lesser extent by McCracken, a middle-of-the-roader who nonetheless had come increasingly to believe that monetary policy was decidedly more important than pure Keynesians conceded. In the extreme, Keynesians believe almost the opposite of monetarists, that fiscal policy mattered most and monetary policy very little. Battling Stein, Houthakker, and Shultz were Nixon's Treasury group of Volcker, Walker, and Assistant Secretary Murray Weidenbaum; Mayo; Assistant Budget Director Maurice Mann; and Assistant Commerce Secretary Harold Passer.

But Stein, McCracken, and other Nixon administration officials could only talk about monetary policy; Burns, as the nation's new central banker, would be the one to set it. His three-hour appearance on February 18, 1970, before the Joint Economic Committee was the first of Burns's spellbinding performances as Fed chairman on Capitol Hill. His iron-gray hair severely parted down the middle, peering benignly down on his inquisitors through gold-framed glasses, pipe at hand for that extra fraction of a second needed to compose a thought or sentence, Burns delivered to the respectful senators and congressmen what would come to be his standard Sermon on the Mount—a reasoned explanation of events, with the assured tone of the well-informed professor suffering the sometimes scatterbrained queries of untutored students. If Burns had any self-doubts, they were never evident, either in private or during these vintage appearances before congressional committees. "Your appointment is probably the best that President Nixon has made," Senator William Proxmire, a Democrat from Wisconsin, cooed. Privately, and with satisfaction, Burns agreed.

But when Proxmire tried to pin Burns down to precisely how much the Fed's restrictive policy had been eased, and for other details, citing various statistics illustrating the economy's troubled state, Burns quickly forgot Proxmire's kind personal words and snapped: "I know all the facts you do, and I'm not asleep, and neither are my colleagues. The Fed hasn't been asleep in the past—at least, not in the recent past." Burns then reviewed the mistakes everyone else had made in the past year—including the Fed's staff—reporting that in his first eighteen days on the job that he had already reversed, albeit gently, the prior monetary policy, which he described as "highly restrictive." He freely ranged over the whole gamut of domestic and foreign economic issues, rejecting the notion of a wage-price freeze or credit controls. He faulted Martin for holding too long to a tight monetary policy, and said he would give "a little more" attention to the importance of money supply than his predecessor had. He also took an open poke at McCracken, belaboring the Nixon administration for sustaining inflationary expectations by talking "a little too much about gradualism."[14]

Burns's appointment to the Fed marked the transition from Nixon's first year, dedicated to fighting inflation, to the second, in which he would worry more about recession than inflation. The initial policy, relying on the broad, normally deflating tools of fiscal and monetary policy, had succeeded in depressing the economy and the stock market—which hit a six-year low. But it had failed to control inflation. Back on February 3, 1970, Daniel Patrick Moynihan, as assistant to the president for urban affairs, had warned Nixon in a brilliant private memo that he should concentrate on maintaining economic expansion. "If a serious economic recession were to come along to compound the controversies of race, Vietnam, and cultural alienation, the nation could indeed approach instability," Moynihan had written.[15]

Moynihan was ignored, despite the fact that the unemployment rate was 4.2 percent, a big jump from 3.5 percent just two months before. The jobless total was 1 million more than it had been the day Nixon had been sworn in. Less than a week after Stein, Walker, and others had all publicly warned against any sudden turnaround in policy, and after a brainstorming session with McCracken, Kennedy, and Mayo in which they urged him to hang tough, Nixon in mid-March left them all twisting in the wind, lifting a construction freeze sufficiently to permit $1.5 billion in federally assisted state construction projects (highways, hospitals, and the like) to go forward. These decisions emerged from a Nixon huddle with White House assistants H. R. (Bob) Haldeman and John D. Ehrlichman.

Into this uncertain picture, Nixon dropped a bombshell—literally. He widened the Vietnam War by bombing Cambodia in late April, foreshadowing—just as Johnson's escalation of the war in Vietnam had done five years before—huge further military expenditures and a new, bitter divisiveness in the nation, soon to be exacerbated by the killing of four Kent State University students by trigger-happy National Guardsmen. And in an uncanny replay of LBJ's blunder, Nixon kept all his economic advisers in the dark. Ehrlichman and Assistant to the President Peter M. Flanigan controlled all access to the Oval Office. Even Treasury Secretary Kennedy and Budget Director Mayo were required to report to Flanigan. Only McCracken could report directly to Nixon, and even when he did manage to see Nixon, he would find either Flanigan, Haldeman, or Ehrlichman present. Flanigan was a Wall Street entrepreneur and personal friend of Nixon's who, in the period between the launching of the strike against Cambodia and the onset of Watergate, wielded enormous power. Flanigan had the authority to summarily demand the appearance of Kennedy, Mayo, McCracken, and others in his office in the White House.

By midyear, Nixon had formalized a shift of all domestic decision-making power, including authority over the budget and the economic advisers, creating the Office of Management and Budget (OMB) and the Domestic Policy Council. By naming George Shultz OMB director and Ehrlichman to head the Domestic Council, Nixon at one stroke downgraded Kennedy and McCracken, even though McCracken was said to retain his direct line to Nixon. He virtually decapitated Mayo, who quickly was replaced by Caspar W. Weinberger. Now, increasingly, Nixon would turn to Shultz rather than to Burns for economic guidance. The old Burns role of "assistant president" was split about equally between Shultz and Ehrlichman. As director of the OMB, Shultz not only had an office in the White House itself, but took a seat on the traditional "quadriad" of top economic policy makers that included Kennedy, McCracken, and Burns. It was a special humiliation for Kennedy and the Treasury, a situation that would not be reversed until John B. Connally arrived on the scene early the following year.

Meanwhile, financial markets were stunned: the earlier announced—and highly trumpeted—budget surpluses for fiscal 1970 and 1971 had disappeared altogether, a mute symbol that federal indebtedness would have to increase. Corporate profits were down, unemployment was up—everything was going exactly in the opposite way from the future Nixon had promised.

The bombing of Cambodia and the continuing slide of the economy led to an open break between Burns and Nixon. Addressing bankers at a meeting in Hot Springs, Virginia, Burns said that by relying exclusively on fiscal and monetary policy to curb the persisting inflation, and avoiding what had come to be called "incomes policy"—direct pressure on labor and management to restrain wages and prices in a manner similar to the old Kennedy wage-price guideposts—Nixon was flirting with the possibility of "a very serious business recession."[16] As Burns summarized his words for reporters, McCracken sat by uncomfortably, and later chided the Fed chairman for holding out a hope for controlling inflation by measures that had no record of success. Secretary Kennedy, who a year earlier at the Advertising Council had himself talked of mandatory controls, stuck to the Nixon party line and said Burns was on his own.

Nonetheless, Burns triggered a national debate over the wisdom of incomes policies, and reawakened Democrats in Congress to what promised to be a key issue in the November midterm elections. Nixon, more and more influenced by Shultz, and made wary of Burns by Haldeman and Ehrlichman, adopted the line that "controls don't work," even though various studies, by think tanks, Wall Street firms, and others, showed that in some circumstances controls could be effective, or at least would be less traumatic to the economy than uncontrolled inflation. Shultz was highly emotional on the wage-price controls issue.[17] McCracken, Stein, Kennedy, and Commerce Secretary Maurice H. Stans were also opposed to controls, but without Shultz's ideological vigor. In varying degree, Burns had support from HUD Secretary George W. Romney, Transportation Secretary John A. Volpe, Interior Secretary Walter J. Hickel, and Postmaster General William Blunt. He soon gained converts among a second layer of advisers from the top: Charls Walker, Maurice Mann, and Murray Weidenbaum. Democrats like Walter Heller, Gardner Ackley, and Arthur Okun spoke out frequently in favor of different formulas that might induce government and the unions to consider the public, as well as their own, interest. "Both business and labor know by now that they are caught up in an inflationary rat race that's getting nowhere; they want and need some leadership in slowing down the treadmill they're on, and eventually getting off it," Ackley said.[18]

But with White House speechwriter William Safire wielding an effective pen, Nixon's political henchmen, including Vice President Spiro T. Agnew and Attorney General John N. Mitchell, continued to pour out a torrent of words designed to reassure the business community that despite declines in the securities markets, there would be no recession, and that no consideration was being given to controls. Nixon volunteered that if he had the money, he would be buying stocks. He then invited forty important private sector leaders to dinner at the White House for a Johnson-style massaging, after which Milton Friedman observed that "the major defect has been in the talk. The administration correctly decided that it was not going to follow a policy of 'fine tuning,' but it has tried to substitute for it a policy of 'fine talk.' " On a single day toward the end of May,

Shultz, McCracken, Walker, and Assistant Commerce Secretary Harold C. Passer gave speeches assuring that everything was just fine. Friedman, for one, was unimpressed: "What we need now is a moratorium on speeches on the economy."[19]

The escalating criticism from Nixon supporters in the business community couldn't be ignored. On June 17, Nixon reversed himself and officially resurrected "jawboning." In a formal address to the nation, he declared: "Now is the time for business . . . to take price actions more consistent with a stable cost of living, and now is the time for labor to structure its wage demands to better achieve a new stability of costs. . . . There is a new social responsibility growing in our economic system, on the part of unions and corporations. Now is the time for that social concern to take the form of specific action on the wage-price front."[20] This tactic was hammered out by Flanigan. Shultz, wanting no part of it, suggested instead a long-range study by a commission on productivity. Stein also continued to resist any change. Kennedy and Walker pushed a Republican congressional proposal for an "inflation alert"—publication of reports on wage-price actions by the McCracken CEA. Volcker and Weidenbaum went further, arguing for a voluntary wage-price freeze to last six months. Assistant Budget Director Mann wanted a congressional advisory board that would, in effect, reestablish guidelines. McCracken came up with the compromise blessed by Flanigan—a return to jawboning, along with the inflation alert, to be managed by CEA member Houthakker, plus Shultz's productivity commission. The outcome was a mild intervention program, not as tough as Volcker, Weidenbaum, and Mann had suggested, yet far beyond what Shultz and Stein had endorsed. Around the White House, the Nixon team referred to the new tactic as "soft jawboning," and openly wondered what their boss might do next.

Thus, as the economy turned sour, Nixon unhesitatingly embraced policies and financial strategies he had loathed all his political life. In Congress and as vice president, he had bitterly opposed wage and price controls, supposedly expressing an antipathy to regulation when he was a government lawyer at the Office of Price Administration during the Second World War. That, at least, was the myth built up in Washington dinner-party chitchat. The fact is that Nixon's OPA experience was exclusively with rationing affairs, and had nothing whatever to do with price controls.[21]

Nixon's entry into the incomes policy arena touched off a number of novel proposals, including one by Yale professor Henry Wallich to put "teeth" in guidelines by attaching a tax penalty or concession according to the degree of compliance. Wallich's tax incentive plan was put forward in similar form by Okun, who stressed the concession rather than the tax penalty as the better way to go. (Such plans were widely debated in academic circles for years after that, but were always rejected as not feasible by politicians of both parties.)

If there had been hope that Nixon's mild exercise of his jawbone would settle things down, disillusionment soon came. Federal spending, the budget deficit, and the balance of payments deficit all continued to mount: for fiscal 1971, the deficit ran to $23 billion. The first inflation "alerts" issued by the CEA were serious and professional efforts, detailing the record of wage and price increases that continued to spiral out of control. It came as a shock to the public to learn that the price of coal had gone up 35 percent from January to September 1970, and that interest rates were more than one-fifth higher than they had been the previous year. In the so-called free market, wages and prices were running amok. For example, tire workers were getting wage increases of 7 to 8 percent annually, even though productivity was increasing at only a 5.1 percent rate. Thus unit labor costs for the manufacturers were 2 to 3 percent higher. Since labor costs represented only about 30 percent of the final cost of tires, the wage hike translated into the need for about a 1 percent price increase for manufacturers' profits to stay level. Instead, the tire companies in mid-1970 announced a 5 percent increase. Nixon's "soft jawboning" couldn't touch that kind of greed. Senate Majority Leader Mike Mansfield put it succinctly when he said: "The things that should be going up—home building, take-home pay, and real economic growth—are coming down. At the same time, the things that should be coming down, such as interest rates, the cost of living, and unemployment, are going up."[22]

But Nixon and his advisers were not willing to listen to such warnings. The day after the consumer price index for September 1970 went up at double the rate of the August advance, Vice President Agnew was telling a political rally in Tucson, Arizona, that "we have solid evidence that your cost of living is no longer going through the roof."

The reality was otherwise: after twenty-one months in office, the Nixon administration had failed in its effort to rescue the economy from the mistakes of the Johnson era. The witty Okun told an enthusiastic audience at the Woman's National Democratic Club in Washington that "they've had seven interceptions, are forty points behind, it's the fourth quarter, and they're sticking to the same game plan."[23]

In the capitals of Europe, presidents and prime ministers were deeply concerned that Nixon was paying inadequate attention to a swollen balance of payments deficit, which had been allowing dollars to pile up abroad. IMF managing director Pierre-Paul Schweitzer—first privately, and then increasingly publicly—sharply criticized Nixon for not reducing the large American international deficit by tapping its reserves of gold, or by borrowing at the IMF—which would have subjected American policy to a degree of international discipline.

Schweitzer made his case in Copenhagen in September at the annual meeting of the IMF and World Bank, formally declaring that the United States should quit piling up dollars overseas and use its gold and other reserves to pay for what it owed. Schweitzer's sting brought an immediate retort. When I grabbed Volcker on the run at the IMF session, he said: "Schweitzer's concern over our deficit is legitimate. If someone is looking out over the future, and throws out cautionary words, I accept that. At the same time, I don't think anyone should be unduly alarmed by short-term fluctuations in our balance of payments deficit."[24] Volcker revealed that in fact the United States had been following Schweitzer's guidance, and had reduced reserves by about $2.5 billion. But Volcker and other American officials were bitter, fearing that Schweitzer's dramatic critique of U.S. dollar policy would encourage dollar-holders abroad to cash in some of their paper greenbacks for gold—while the getting was good. (Volcker was determined to punish Schweitzer, a hero of the French resistance during the Second World War and, prior to his IMF appointment, deputy governor of the Banque de France.[25] His refusal to kowtow to American policy preferences got on Volcker's nerves. When the question of a third five-year term at the IMF for Schweitzer came up, Volcker vetoed it.)

Two days after Schweitzer's declaration, Treasury Secretary Kennedy startled the financial world by telling a press conference in Copenhagen that the United States was willing to convert dollars into gold. Clearly angry at Schweitzer for bringing the subject up, Kennedy said: "Well, if the holders don't want to take dollars, let them take something else, and the reserve assets of course would be available there."[26]

Despite American unhappiness, Schweitzer's IMF had begun to encourage consideration of a degree of flexibility in exchange rates, breaking away from the rigidities of the fixed-rate Bretton Woods system, which could work with inflation contained but was strained when prices got out of hand. At the same time, there emerged for the first time the prospect of a monetary union in Europe. There was a strong linkage between the talk of more flexibility in international

exchange rates—something that had been a mere academic dream—
and more closely related European currencies. Such talk diluted the
resistance of the French, who worried that flexibility might
strengthen the German mark against the franc. But if the franc and
mark were tied together, then France would be better protected
against its chief rival-cum-partner. The remaining question for the
French would be the psychological one of the dollar as the centerpiece of whatever monetary system evolved. As I shared a taxicab in
Copenhagen with Valery Giscard d'Estaing, the French finance minister, this sentiment came through strongly. Holding my tape recorder for me—so I could also scribble notes—Giscard said: "When
the question is asked of the American delegation whether it [more
flexibility] would apply to the dollar, they always have said, 'No, no.'
There is no question about that. And certainly, we would not accept
such a solution . . . because it is impossible for the international
community to accept such a discrimination."

At Copenhagen, the IMF took a tentative, but limited, step toward introducing more flexibility into the system with a report discussing three methods by which the relative values of currencies
could be changed fairly frequently. But the United States wasn't
ready for such a change. "We're not talking about a revolution here,"
Volcker said.[27] Thus nothing much was accomplished except for
Schweitzer's critique.[28]

At home, despite efforts by Agnew, Stein, and Ehrlichman to play
down the inflation problem, it wouldn't go away. For one thing, they
couldn't silence Burns. Stein was never kind to Burns, once trying to
deflate a typically sonorous declaration by Burns by observing that
"we all don't talk with the language of an Old Testament prophet."
Burns indeed had a massive ego, and delivered his messages in apoca-
lyptic style. On the other hand, Burns brought to the government the
experience of a lifetime of study and experience with the business
cycle, and had earned respect around the globe for his wisdom and
integrity. Stein's claims to fame were more modest. The friction between the younger Stein and the older Burns became stronger as
Burns talked increasingly of the need for a form of incomes policy to
hold the income shares of business and labor fairly stable through
voluntary means.

Burns's conversion to incomes policies was a flip-flop from his
1965 attack on the wage-price guideposts under Lyndon Johnson.[29]
In December, Burns made a speech at Pepperdine College in which
he suggested the need for a voluntary wage-price board, a step
beyond "voluntary" incomes policy. He did so to challenge a
McCracken statement a month earlier that incomes policy advo-

cates were mouthing mere generalities. With McCracken and Stein among others in mind, Burns chided "the White House theologians" who, he felt, were failing to tackle a new phenomenon—persistent inflation in the face of high unemployment.[30] He confided to me that he had argued directly with Nixon that inflationary pressures would continue to mount until some sort of direct government intervention in the wage-price setting process was sanctioned.

Following the Pepperdine speech, Burns began to have an impact on Nixon, aided by outrageously inflated construction industry wages. The turning point was a 12.5 percent price increase announced by Bethlehem Steel in January 1971, even higher than the figure the company had privately forecast for McCracken. Nixon denounced the increase, and forced a partial rollback, finally recognizing that classic laissez-faire remedies couldn't cope with inflation in the midst of recession: you could deal with one or the other but not both simultaneously without some sort of intervention.[31]

On February 21, Burns had the Federal Reserve Board formally endorse the ideas contained in his Pepperdine speech with a strong statement he read to the Joint Economic Committee arguing that traditional means of solving the inflation problem would not be adequate. But McCracken, supported by Stein, stuck to his guns, calling for an expansion of the money supply and continuation of classic Republican doctrine calling for minimal government interference with "the market." In July, the White House "theologians" sanctioned a personal and bitter attack on Burns, clearly designed to force a resignation.[32] The attack backfired, with expression of outrage from domestic and foreign markets, and Nixon was forced to issue a personal statement reaffirming his support of Burns.

There were new elements in the equation. First, the United States had begun to run an unacceptably high balance of payments deficit—an annual rate of $5.1 billion, a huge number for 1970.[33] And second, John Connally strode on the scene, replacing the ineffective if likable David Kennedy. Connally, the former Democratic governor of Texas, stunned the political world by accepting Nixon's invitation to become secretary of the Treasury on February 8, 1971. Nixon not only promised Connally a free hand as the nation's chief financial officer, but designated him "chief economic spokesman" for the administration.

For the next two years, from early 1971 until 1973, Connally dominated the Washington economic scene. A wheeler-dealer trained in the Lyndon Johnson school, he twice seemed to be within reach of the vice presidency in the late 1960s (and had he made it on one of those occasions, might have become president when Nixon was forced to quit.)[34] Connally was a hawk on the war, and thus fit right in at the White House. Once, he told Volcker, in an echo of General Curtis LeMay's notorious quip, that "we ought to bomb North Vietnam back to the Stone Age." A narrow-minded chauvinist, he also didn't like foreigners. "My view is that the foreigners are out to screw us, and therefore it's our job to screw them first," he once told a group of prominent economists.[35]

Connally brought to the Nixon administration a brand-new source of energy, political smarts, and a penchant for bold speech and action—all of which a battered Nixon badly needed in early 1971. "He'd go into the Oval Office with an agenda," recalled Murray Weidenbaum, who served as assistant secretary for economic policy under both Kennedy and Connally, "and he'd come out with more assignments than he went in with. He [Nixon] would say, 'John, why don't you do this,' and 'John, why don't you do that?' "[36] A showboat with a great sense of what makes news, Connally loved the catbird seat, and soon became the dominant force in the Nixon cabinet. "He was a breath of fresh air, in contrast to Kennedy, who was a wonderful fellow, but weak," Volcker remembered.[37] The anxiety and discord in Washington in the spring and early summer of 1971 was tailor-made for Connally. Articulate, a fast learner, and not averse to getting his name in the papers, Connally was soon a favorite of the Washington press corps. There was even speculation that the three-time Democratic governor of the Lone Star State might cut his life-long ties to Lyndon and other Democrats for a chance at the vice-presidential nomination with Nixon in 1972. His only real rivals for Nixon's attention were Ehrlichman and Haldeman. Burns, as tough an autocrat who ever ruled the Fed, was ahead of the curve in his willingness to junk conservative doctrine by going for wage and price controls. But Burns had no stomach for devaluing the dollar, or for Connally's determination to strong-arm the Germans and Japanese into revaluing their currencies. Though Connally amazed Congress and his international counterparts with his forcefulness and style, he knew little about domestic economics, and even less about the complicated international financial picture—and problems in both areas soon began to pile up on his doorstep.

Increasingly, a wage-price freeze began to be seriously considered, although OMB director Shultz—who as a University of Chicago academic had strongly opposed the Kennedy-Johnson wage-price guidepost experiment—was against it. So were McCracken and Stein at the CEA. But Shultz began to waver as wages and prices barreled upward, provoking complaints from Nixon's business friends.[38] To promote the notion that the economy was in good shape, White House communications director Herbert G. Klein in April had put out a list of ten stocks up sharply in the prior year. This inexcusable flackery had no precedent.[39] But it was symptomatic of a White House effort to cover up the weakening economic fabric and make it appear the nation could get by without a major shift in direction.

At a meeting in May with the powerful Business Council at Hot Springs, Virginia, Shultz was stunned by the intensity of the private criticism from David Rockefeller and other influential Republican businessmen and bankers of the Nixon administration's failure to handle the wage spiral, symbolized by a manifestly inflationary bargain between the steel industry and the steel workers' union.[40] Arnold R. Weber, a Shultz assistant at OMB, later recalled that when Shultz came back from Hot Springs, he instructed him to "get stuff together on what controls would look like."[41]

What we didn't know then, and know now, is that Nixon and Connally cut a deal soon after "Big John" came to Washington: to talk against controls but put them into effect at the most propitious time. Many years later, Connally readily admitted—and defended— the devious strategy: say one thing and do the opposite. CEA chairman McCracken, who wasn't in on the fix, argued against the notion of a wage-price freeze as the possibility began to be debated in Congress and the press. Controls, McCracken believed, would distort economic relationships—and even if for a time they appeared to defeat the market, in the end the market would win out. In mid-1971, many liberals, while distressed with the way inflation was getting out of hand, also feared that a wage-price freeze would raise expectations among the public because many escalating service costs or seasonal food price variations would not be within its reach.

Publicly, Connally denied that any consideration was being given to wage-price controls or dollar devaluation, while privately he was telling Nixon to ignore the cautious McCracken. In fact, Connally advised Nixon that McCracken's advice was a "disaster."[42] In a widely publicized address to the American Bankers Association in Munich in May, Connally firmly asserted that the dollar would not be devalued, and that there would be no increase in the price of gold. And at a press conference in June, he assured the world that there would be no move toward wage-price controls. Burns added private assurances to other central bankers that there would be no closing of the gold window—because Burns believed that to be true.

But Connally, almost from the moment of his arrival in Washington, knew otherwise: he had his secret go-ahead from Nixon to plan on wage-price controls and to devalue the dollar. In Connally's view, there was nothing duplicitous about that: in the real world, that's what you have to do. Connally was convinced that, unless bold steps were taken, Europe and Japan "would continue to take advantage of the United States," even to the point of allowing their central banks to speculate against the dollar. Connally was not being paranoid; by the spring of 1971, there was a great deal of volatility in exchange rates accompanying inflationary pressures at home, and estimates that the widening balance of payments deficit could hit $16 billion to $17 billion in 1971. The Germans revalued the deutsche mark, and all European nations complained that they were now unwilling holders of too many dollars.

The final steps to generate a new policy were taken after Connally talked to Nixon in the Oval Office in the week of August 9, pending the arrival of a convenient trigger: convincing evidence of the threat from the foreign side—enough to counter Burns's strong opposition to closing the gold window—had to be found.[43] That trigger arrived with sudden French and British demands for gold in exchange for their paper American dollars. On Friday, August 13, the British decided to turn in $3 billion more in greenbacks for gold.[44]

Finally, Nixon decided on August 15 to adopt a system of mandatory wage-price controls as part of a "New Economic Policy" to curb inflation.[45] Nixon, on Connally's advice, seized the economic initiative from his critics by using controls-authority legislation put on the books by a Democratic Congress. The Democrats had bet that Nixon wouldn't touch controls, but they were outsmarted by Connally. The Democrats' intended political strategy was transparent: if the economy should worsen, as seemed likely, then Nixon could be flailed for rejecting the proposed authority. But when, as the Democrats expected, Connally's Treasury staff sent him a draft of a proposed Nixon message vetoing the proposed wage-price authority, Connally decided it would be smarter politics to have the power in hand. Connally would later recall telling Treasury aide James E. Smith that he had learned never to turn down a new power, "just in case you have to use it."[46]

So Nixon signed the bill granting wage-price authority, and actually used it to establish a ninety-day wage-price freeze as part of his "New Economic Policy." At the same time, he took the extraordinary step of suspending the gold convertibility of the dollar, in effect devaluing the dollar, and further imposing a 10 percent surcharge on U.S. imports as Connally had demanded, a transparently protectionist weapon to help reduce a growing balance of payments problem, in itself an additional devaluation of the dollar.

"What precipitated wage and price controls more than anything else was Arthur Burns's feeling that if we [only] closed the gold window and devalued the dollar that it would cause absolute consternation in the world monetary system," Connally later told me. "Burns had the most dire prophecies about what would happen. He argued vehemently and vociferously against closing the gold window and devaluing the dollar and [argued against] the imposition of the surcharge. He said he thought the Dow Jones index would go to 500 [from the 850 level in early August 1971] and precipitate a crisis equal to the depression of the 1930s."[47]

In his memoirs of the period, Herbert Stein, who was CEA chairman in 1972–74 following his stint as a member, suggested that Nixon reversed policy and "made the final concession" to the pro-controllers because Nixon couldn't "enter the active period of the 1972 election with an economic policy that was not working and that did not utilize all measures that might make it work."[48]

There also was an important intangible: Nixon was still basking in the afterglow of his July announcement to open negotiations with Mao's China, which even before his meeting with the Chinese Communist chief was viewed, even by Nixon-haters, as a high-water mark of presidential achievement. One of Nixon's confidants said at the time: "Peking was a blockbuster—a dramatic breakthrough was achieved on the foreign side, so why not try something like it on the domestic side? Bold transitions don't bother Richard Nixon." His oldest associates had long contended that Nixon was neither a true conservative nor a liberal, merely—as one put it—"the most pragmatic man I've ever met." John Kenneth Galbraith said when he heard Nixon's announcement on controls: "I felt like the streetwalker who had just learned from [New York] Mayor Lindsay that the profession was not only legal, but the highest form of municipal service."[49]

It was, by any measure, a dramatic reversal. Moreover, wage-and-price mandatory controls had never been tried in peacetime, and went far beyond the controversial wage-price guideposts introduced by the Kennedy administration in 1962, and the erratic efforts by Lyndon Johnson to use wage-price jawboning as a substitute for the more rigorous anti-inflation tax policy that his economic advisers were hoping for. And if, in the end, Nixon's wage-price control scheme would prove temporary, the accompanying demise of the Bretton Woods international monetary system proved to be permanent. Breaking the gold–dollar link was a shock heard around the world—to say nothing of the consternation it triggered at William P. Rogers's State Department, and Henry A. Kissinger's National Security Council office in the White House: neither Rogers nor Kissinger (who was out of the country) had been invited to Camp David when the New Economic Policy was debated and made final. On that fateful Sunday, August 15, Deputy National Security Adviser Alexander M. Haig, who had also been left out of the Camp David conclave, phoned National Security Council staff economist Robert Hormats at home and said: "Bob, they've devalued the dollar up at Camp David. How important is that?"[50]

Hormats, a career official, was stunned, realizing at once that America's partners—not consulted or forewarned—would be bitter. That afternoon, huddling in the White House with Haig and Volcker—who by then had returned from Camp David—they drafted hasty cables to Tokyo, London, Paris, and Bonn explaining what had happened, and promising a hurry-up visit by Volcker to elaborate. It was bizarre, Hormats would remember, sitting in the White House, eating hamburgers ordered from the White House mess—the television turned to the Redskins-Vikings football game—filling in not only world capitals on the stunning decision, but the State Department as well. Hormats phoned State Department economic aide Sidney Weintraub, who refused to believe the news. Had Kissinger or Haig gone to Camp David? Weintraub asked. No, Hormats said, the NSC had been left as far out of the picture as Rogers had. "It was after that," Hormats said, "that Kissinger decided he had better take an interest in economics."[51]

4

A Question of Control

P RESIDENT NIXON'S New Economic Policy was an explosive
surprise, given Nixon's well-known ideological opposition to
wage and price controls. It was, after all, the very antithesis of sound
Republican doctrine, which held that the market—not government—was the best judge of economic factors. Part of the stunning
impact of Nixon's about-face on gold was its unilateral aspect—there
was no prior discussion with other governments of the sort that typically precedes action on the international scene. Now, with the gold
"window" closed, France and other governments that had been tapping Fort Knox for gold in exchange for excess dollars could either
hang on to them or dump them in the market for what they could
bring, in effect revaluing their own currencies. Put another way, the
dollar, which had been linked to gold since 1944, could now float—
which it did, making American goods cheaper. If the allies didn't like
it, they could lump it.

Forever, it seemed, American presidents and their chief financial
officers had been saying: "The dollar is as good as gold." But in the
real world the dollar in 1971 was not worth one-thirty-fifth of an
ounce of gold, the official rate. In the unofficial gold market, the
price of gold was over $40 an ounce, which meant that the dollar was
worth only one-fortieth of an ounce of gold. In turn, that meant the
dollar was worth fewer marks, yen, or francs than the exchange rate
tables called for—based on $35 being equal to one ounce of gold.
From an American viewpoint, closing the gold window made good

sense, because it prevented a further drain on gold and other monetary reserves in a useless effort to protect an unrealistic value of the dollar. From the viewpoint of foreign holders of dollars, it meant that they were stuck with a paper currency that was a depreciating asset.

Connally didn't give a hoot what other nations might think. Following his post–Camp David meeting at the Treasury, when Connally talked of the need to screw the foreigners, C. Fred Bergsten, a consultant at the Brookings Institution, warned National Security Adviser Henry Kissinger (for whom he had worked earlier) that he had to deal "with a xenophobe at the Treasury." Kissinger listened and said, "I will bide my time."[1] But Connally had carefully briefed Nixon on the political dangers of devaluing the dollar. Cutting the value of one's own currency had always been regarded as a confession of failure: a strong currency meant a strong country, a weak currency, a weak country. That was especially true of America, for the dollar was the most widely used international transaction currency.

Sensitive to the possible political implications, Connally sounded Nixon out after a meeting of finance ministers in London in September 1971, where he had heard almost a unanimous call for cheapening the dollar's international value. In effect, America's partners were saying: "It's your problem, so you devalue the dollar." As he recalled the conversation, Connally later said he told Nixon that "there's almost a political conspiracy out there that we devalue the dollar. Whether we devalue or they revalue, or whether we do some of both, it's really immaterial to me. But does it bother you politically to devalue the dollar?" Nixon, according to Connally, replied: "Not a bit. If you want to [devalue], do whatever you want to." Connally felt that Nixon "had given me almost carte blanche authority."[2]

The dollar devaluation and import surcharge elements of the new policy brought Connally up against the redoubtable Burns, who, according to Paul Volcker, privately considered Connally a "wild man." Burns was in accord with Connally on wage-price intervention, but worried about closing the gold window and the 10 percent import surcharge. Burns's idea was to ask a friendly European central banker, Jelle Zijlstra, to be an "honest broker" between the American and European positions. At Burns's urging, Volcker carried the Burns proposal to Connally, but Connally rejected the plan.[3] Following the August 15 decision to devalue the dollar, Burns and Kissinger worked tirelessly to persuade Connally to drop the surcharge. The surcharge would remain a source of bitter contention until the end of the year.[4]

Connally acknowledged that Burns was desperately opposed to closing the gold window, devaluing the dollar, and the surcharge, which Burns feared not only would be considered underhanded by America's allies, but could trigger a depression rivaling that of the 1930s. Burns's opposition to the surcharge was widely endorsed by most economists at that time, including almost all Democrats, who regarded it as a protectionist device. That created an unusual political lineup after August 15: Democrats, because they believed in the global trading system, were supporting the conservative Burns, against Democrat-for-Nixon John Connally, who had isolationist tendencies. In turn, Burns joined forces with Kissinger, even though he regarded Kissinger as a neophyte on economic issues. There was a natural rivalry between Connally and Haldeman, who not only vied for Nixon's attention but genuinely didn't like each other.[5]

In October, Connally went back to Europe to address the monetary managers from Europe and Japan. "We had a problem," he said mischievously, "and we're sharing it with the world—just liked we shared our prosperity. That's what friends are for."[6] Connally was convinced that the United States needed a depreciation against global currencies averaging 12 to 15 percent to provide a new advantage for American exporters. Much of the international community did not think this was unreasonable, but argued that a good share of such a devaluation could be accomplished by a rise in the price of gold—say, from the official value of $35 an ounce to $38 an ounce. This was the view of Pierre-Paul Schweitzer at the IMF, of distinguished economist Edward M. Bernstein, and even of Representative Henry S. Reuss, the Wisconsin Democrat who until then had been opposed to a gold price increase.[7]

The gold issue was emotionally charged, and difficult for the public to understand. Those favoring an increase argued that if the United States raised the price of gold to, say, $38 an ounce, it would automatically be a devaluation, because one dollar would be worth only one-thirty-eighth of an ounce of gold instead of one-thirty-fifth of an ounce. That way, if there were to be a net average appreciation of other currencies against the dollar by 12 to 15 percent, the contribution from the other countries would be less, and politically easier to do. (A revaluation, of course, raises the effective price of a nation's goods in world markets—so the smaller the number, the better for those that are revaluing. In other words, it would be a two-sided affair—the United States devaluing some, the others revaluing some.)

Such a system, it was also argued, would facilitate a return to fixed-rate relationships, similar to what existed prior to Nixon's unilateral action. Perhaps there could be a bit more flexibility through

wider margins, and the $38 rate would discourage speculation, be-
cause it would remain under the unofficial gold market quotations at
$40 an ounce or more. "If the other countries have to do all of the
rectifying [of exchange rates], it makes them look like the sole sinners," Reuss said.[8] But Reuss conditioned his support for a higher
price on keeping the gold window closed, maintaining the dollar in a
nonconvertible position.

Connally's pledge earlier in 1971 that the United States would
never increase the price of gold—a commitment that brought him
into conflict with European nations and the IMF—was merely a bargaining chip: he knew all along that the price of gold would have to
go up and that the surcharge imposed at Camp David would be abandoned.[9] Shultz had convinced Connally that the American objective
ought to be to emerge from the crisis with a floating exchange rate
for the dollar, in which it would seek its own level in the markets.
Connally thought the United States might have an ally for such a
system in Canada, which was floating the Canadian dollar against
the U.S. dollar. But Connally got no support for a floating rate from
Canada's or other finance ministers. The pressure focused on a U.S.
devaluation, and, as Connally remembered it, the most ardent advocate for the United States to assume the biggest share of the burden
was Britain's chancellor of the Exchequer, Anthony Barber.[10]

The import surcharge had been fashioned by Connally as a club to
force the realignment of exchange rates that he concluded was necessary to reduce the negative trade balances between the United States
and Japan and the United States and Europe. He soon became known
as the international "bully boy."[11]

A much more subtle argument against a gold price increase was
that a long-term reform of the monetary system, away from reliance
on gold, was needed: one of the weaknesses of the original Bretton
Woods system from the beginning, but especially during the 1960s,
was its dependence on gold as the basis for economic expansion.
Inasmuch as the supply of new gold was in the hands, principally, of
South Africa and the Soviet Union, gold clearly was not a steady or
reliable asset. Former Treasury undersecretary for monetary affairs
Robert V. Roosa said it would be unfortunate if the European countries "as a sort of penance" expected the United States "to glue back
together some pieces of the broken idol through a hastily conceived
'return to gold.' "[12] But in the real world, the "float" of the dollar
triggered by Nixon's decision had produced a dollar devaluation averaging only 3 to 4 percent, because our friendly competitors found
ways of offsetting the action through capital controls and other de-

vices. And clearly, a gold price increase would make things easier for them.

The logjam in the negotiations over dollar devaluation wasn't broken until the weekend of December 17 and 18, when Connally, Burns, and Volcker worked out a realignment of the world's currencies with their counterparts in the Group of Ten industrial nations in a tense weekend at the Smithsonian Institution in Washington. It included a $3 increase in the price of gold, accounting for a 7.89 percent devaluation of the dollar. The 10 percent surcharge and the "Buy American" provision of the investment tax credit imposed by Nixon at Camp David were dropped, while West Germany agreed to revalue its currency by 13.58 percent, the British and French theirs by 8 percent, and the Japanese theirs by 16.88 percent. Other major currencies would go up by varying amounts, resulting in a net overall appreciation against the dollar of about 12 percent. With Connally at his side, Nixon announced the package at an impromptu press conference as "the most significant monetary agreement in the history of the world."[13] It wasn't: but like most of Connally's and Nixon's promises, the Smithsonian Agreement, as it came to be known, made effective headlines.

At the Smithsonian, Nixon and Connally had made devaluation, normally associated with hard times or political disaster, sound like a triumph. They had reason to feel they had pulled off a coup of sorts. They had been denounced by their allies for the New Economic Policy of August 15, especially the 10 percent import surcharge, and for the "Buy American" investment tax credit. Because America was losing out in foreign trade to its competitors, Connally was using the surtax as a weapon to force a revaluation of their currencies by an average of 11 to 12 percent. He also had on his shopping list a reduction of trade barriers against American goods, and a sharing of the burden of the global defense bill. Connally, in effect, was presenting America's allies with a "bill" of about $13 billion: that was the annual shift, in favor of America, that he was seeking in the nation's trade balance.

Naturally, America's trade partners bristled, charging that the surtax and America's own discriminations against foreign products were unfair. Yet the Smithsonian Agreement accomplished much of Connally's objective—and privately, the Europeans admitted that nothing would have changed without the bludgeon of the surcharge. But Connally had to make his own concession, raising the price of gold. In the end, Connally achieved about a 12 percent revaluation of other currencies, on a trade-weighted, average basis. That meant about a 12 percent reduction in the price of American goods in foreign markets.

Connally liked to tell a story about how the Japanese fell in line, revaluing the yen to a smidgen under 16.9 percent—16.88 percent. Connally and his Treasury team headed by Volcker had set a 17 percent Japanese revaluation as the target for a change that would benefit American exporters. During the weekend of the Smithsonian Agreement, Connally continued to press the Japanese for a 17 percent appreciation, and the Japanese continued to argue that the amount was excessive. As he was preparing to take the podium on Sunday morning, December 19, to announce that a deal had been struck with all others, a deputy to Japanese finance minister Mikio Mizuta sought one final audience with him and reiterated that 17 percent was too much for his government to swallow.

"All right," Connally said, "I'll announce that we have an agreement with everyone else, but your government won't agree."

As he prepared to go to the press conference, Connally said, the Japanese deputy tugged at his sleeve. "You don't understand," he said. "It's politically impossible—in 1930, a Japanese minister of finance approved a 17 percent revaluation, and he had to commit suicide."

Unmoved, Connally said, "I understand, but I'm going out to make the announcement."

"But we can't do 17," the Japanese pleaded. "Give me another number."

"Sixteen point nine!" Connally snapped.

"It's a deal," said the Japanese official.[14]

In fact, the Japanese official Connally remembered as the deputy finance minister was actually Toyoo Gyohten, an assistant to and translator for Mizuta. A Princeton-educated Japanese civil servant, Gyohten recalled that after Mizuta told Connally that 17 was "a very, very ominous number," Connally asked: "How much can you go?" It was then that Mizuta, through Gyohten, suggested 308 yen to the dollar, an appreciation of 16.88 per cent.[15] (But the most interesting angle to Gyohten's version—recounted in *Changing Fortunes*, written with Paul Volcker in 1992—is that the canny Mizuta had actually played a cat-and-mouse game with Connally: the Japanese had decided in Tokyo in advance of the trip to Washington that they could swallow a revaluation of as much as 20 percent. Volcker apparently didn't find that out until collaborating with Gyohten on their book: "I am chagrined to learn, twenty years too late, that another 3 percent might have been possible," Volcker said.[16])

To Japan, even though Mizuta had emerged with a smaller appre-

ciation of the yen than had seemed inevitable, the new Nixon policies represented brute force, the first display of a "Fortress America"
attitude that made America's trading partners wary. Yet Japan absorbed the revaluation without too much difficulty. What the Smithsonian Agreement and the bargaining that preceded it told the
Japanese was that they would come under persistent international
pressure, and could no longer afford to play a defensive role on the
international scene. For them, it was actually the second Nixon
"shoku," the first being Kissinger's secret visit to China, that served
to warn Japan it had to speak out for itself, and not play junior partner to Washington. Gyohten later recalled of the Smithsonian period: "There was a lot of talk here in Tokyo about how successful our
economy was. The word 'internationalization' was already popular—in the sense that we Japanese were supposed to understand and
meet international standards—American and European standards.....
If we hadn't revaluated by 17 percent—if we had held the line at say
10 percent—we just would have had to go back in a very short time
and negotiate another revaluation. It did not ruin us at all. But in
1971, there was virtually nobody in Japan who realized that. So despite the talk of internationalization, we were . . . too isolated. We
were unable to see ourselves objectively and accurately."[17]

Connally's style was consistently combative, and that made for
some tense bickering, especially between him and Burns. For example, at a meeting in Rome of the major nations' finance ministers and
central bankers just before the Smithsonian Agreement, Connally
brusquely sent his fellow finance ministers out of the conference
room and told them to come back when they could agree on a single
position, a tactic that made Burns wince. This, after all, was a meeting of the financial elite of ten countries, the dominant international
managers in an era before the creation of the superelite Group of
Seven.[18]

"Arthur kept saying to me, 'Why don't you let me talk to the
central bankers, we can work this out'," Connally would say later.

"This went on time and time again, and I got a little bit irritated
with him at the meeting in Rome—I must say, the only time I got
irritated with him—and I said, 'Arthur, goddamn it, you can't work it
out. Who are you going to work it out with?'

"And he said, 'I'm going to work it out with these central bankers.'

"And I said, 'These central bankers have no authority to work out
anything. These finance ministers here have no authority to work
out anything.' I said, 'I'm the only one at this table who has the authority to do anything, and that's because President Nixon has told

me to do whatever I thought we had to do, whatever we needed to do.' I said, 'There's not a single person in this room that can agree to one single thing without calling back to his head of government. So there's no way that you can do that.' I said, 'You're the only central banker in this room that has any authority—these other fellows all work for the finance ministers, they're not independent like you are.' And I said, 'The idea that you can work this out is ridiculous.' "

Connally was right: no one else had the extraordinary powers Nixon had conferred on him as secretary of the Treasury, and among central bankers only the chairman of the Fed had a major degree of independence from political control (to a lesser degree, the president of the West German central bank had some ability to distance himself from the Finance Ministry). Nixon didn't really much care about monetary matters. His attention to economic affairs had been distracted by the publication of the Pentagon Papers in June.[19] It was during this period that the "plumbers" unit was created, triggering the Watergate era, further distancing his mind from economic affairs.[20]

The other element of Nixon's New Economic Policy was the institution of wage-price controls. After Phase I's ninety-day freeze, Phase II was to begin. It called for average price increases of no more than 2 to 3 percent a year, and pay increases of 5.5 percent by big business and big labor. AFL-CIO president George Meany—who of course would have preferred no limits at all on labor's ability to bargain collectively—lobbied for an independent wage-price board split equally among labor, business, and public members. The board would run the show: having set the standards and issued the regulations, the board would also be responsible for enforcing them.

The business leaders, of course, did not want to share power with George Meany in such a meaningful way. They were convinced that excessive wage increases were the sole cause of America's economic problems, and wanted the program to be run from the White House, where, not surprisingly, they assumed they would be able to exert more influence than Meany. Their "inside man" on this issue was Secretary of Commerce Maurice Stans, who did his best—which was not good enough—to sell Nixon on putting labor down. But Meany, a foreign policy hawk and an old master at political maneuvering, let it be known that if labor didn't have a critical share in managing the wage-price program, its support for the Vietnam War, so crucial to Nixon, could easily wane.

As could have been predicted, the result was an organizational nightmare with overambitious goals. But if achieved, the potential political gains for Nixon in 1972 would be obvious: Nixon would have converted the economic issue, to which he set great store, from a negative to a positive.

After what Walter Heller called "a shaky start," the Nixon controls experiment, which had wide public support, began to work. But in early January 1973, the effort was junked in favor of "a semivoluntary and haphazard" Phase III, even though the economy was then responding to the overstimulation of fiscal and monetary policies put into effect in 1972. In a controversial article by Sanford Rose in *Fortune*, Burns was accused of deliberately easing Fed policy during the 1972 election. Burns denied the allegation, and other governors on the Federal Reserve Board, including Andrew Brimmer, supported him. But it is clear that the Fed eased policy during 1972. Whether Burns tipped the scales to aid Nixon is uncertain. It is doubtful that Burns would have abandoned principle to save Nixon, who had allowed "those guys in the basement" to beat up on him. When I confronted Burns with the charges, he said, "For God's sake, I'm not a rich man. Goddamn it, the only thing I have to will to my children is my reputation for integrity!"[21]

The general criticism of the Nixon wage-price controls experiment was that it proved that controls were artificial and created distortions that interfered with the operations of the free market. It is closer to the mark to say that forces inside and outside of the Nixon administration, having lost the fight to block wage-price controls from the beginning, gave it no moral support and encouraged its demise. We don't know just how well the system would have worked if it had been administered by people who believed in it.

Meany endorsed the wage-price program, although he said he thought a 4 percent inflation target would be more acceptable than 2 to 3 percent. But Meany also told reporters: "I want to make it clear that we would like to see it [inflation] come down because it would solve a lot of problems for us. After all, our members are consumers, too."[22]

But there was a great deal of bewilderment about Phase II. Over the strong objections of public members of Phase II's Pay Board, many wage settlements far in excess of the 5.5 percent standard were allowed on the excuse that they were needed to take care of "severe inequities," including a pay raise of 15 percent for coal miners in which the five management members lined up with the five labor members to outvote the public members.

This was an odd twist in the history of tripartite boards, in which business tycoons and labor bosses had typically offset each other, leaving the "swing" power to the public members. But at the start of Phase II, the public members took a stronger position against giving in to labor on key issues than did the management members, who proved to be more flexible. Thus the management group provided the swing votes in the coal case, while the public members either voted against the 15 percent boost for the miners or indicated their opposition in other ways.

But the Price Commission, chaired by economist and educator C. Jackson Grayson, displayed that it had some of the spine that the Pay Board's management team lacked. Grayson said that the 15 percent coal increase was inflationary and not compatible with the overall target of limiting price increases to a 2 to 3 percent level by 1972. So the Price Commission whittled back the coal operators' request for a 15 percent price increase by two-fifths to 9 percent.

The only hope that Phase II would stay glued together seemed to depend on whether the management members on the Pay Board would listen to other leaders in American industry, who knew that pay increases would have to be rolled back toward the announced standard in order to avoid a profits squeeze. Again, labor's response would be crucial.

With Congress bent on exempting some areas from control when it extended the legislation, it looked doubtful that the system could generate the prosperous economy promised by Nixon and Connally. From early September 1971, at the peak of Wall Street's enthusiasm over the new policy, to November 10, the Dow Jones industrial index fell by 110 points, leading to an unprecedented appearance by Burns at the New York Stock Exchange to assure assembled brokers that the Fed would provide "adequate bank reserves . . . to finance a vigorous but sustainable expansion." Said one investment man: "If the chairman of the Fed has to come to New York to tell us everything is really okay, they may be more worried than they're letting on."[23]

As often happens in Washington when things go wrong, both Connally and Stein blamed the press. Connally said that "misconceptions" about Phase II were being spread by journalists, and Stein contributed the comment that "the fog about Phase II is at least as much in the press as in the program."[24] Connally tried to instill some confidence in the program with his own ebullience, promising at a televised press conference that the nation could approach 1972 with great certainty. He predicted that controls would begin to wind inflation down, although he confessed disappointment in the Pay Board's decision in favor of the miners. And he brushed off the stock market's decline, attributing the drop in the Dow Jones index to "smart people" who had figured out that Phase II would work in a counterinflationary way.

What was the verdict on wage-price controls? The bulk of the American economics "establishment" was—and is—philosophically opposed to wage and price controls. The distaste ran across party lines. But, bit by bit, somewhat grudgingly and without total logic or consistency, the Phase II controls system took hold. When McCracken left as CEA chairman late in 1971, after three years in office, to return to the University of Michigan, he predicted that government would have to show "continuing concern about the cost level and the price level for a long time to come, even after Phase II has 'done its thing.' "[25] This view was quite a shift for McCracken, who was succeeded by Stein. The mild-mannered man from Michigan, who first had impressed academic colleagues as a member of the Eisenhower CEA in 1956–58, had been deeply opposed to controls for most of his life, but told a press conference that he had come to believe there was no way to avoid a wage-price freeze well before it had been imposed on August 15. (That, of course, was not what he was saying publicly.) McCracken confessed he had learned that it takes longer to effect changes in the economy than he had believed earlier. He also took a parting shot at the notions of Milton Friedman, who believed that economic policy should be managed mainly by manipulating the money supply through the Federal Reserve System rather than by Keynesian or fiscal policy through manipulation of taxes and the budget.

McCracken had the courage to say that he found himself increasingly "less Friedmanesque. I find myself inclined to see monetary expansion as an essential accompaniment [of other policies], with the case a little less clear that monetary expansion itself will produce the desired result." McCracken could see the need for Phase II extending through 1972, beyond the election. "We cannot take the view that we can forget about [controls] in a year or two."[26] Like Burns, McCracken had reluctantly come to the conclusion that there are times when controls have to supplement the classic fiscal and monetary tools to beat inflation, because the only alternative is unacceptable: serious recession, with accompanying high levels of unemployment. McCracken had surmounted the ideology with which he had come to Washington.

George Shultz immediately took issue with McCracken's prediction that controls would have to last a while, and Stein told *The Washington Post* in an interview that the controls process should be wound down, with a possibility they would disappear completely before the election. Stein had been assigned by Nixon the responsibility for planning a Phase III for decontrol—and that, he said, would now take a high priority. Reminded of famed New Deal economic

planner Robert Nathan's quip that putting Stein in charge of controls
planning was like putting Polly Adler, the notorious madam, in
charge of a convent, Stein retorted that he was more like a nun who
had been put in charge of a brothel.[27]

Yet it was hard, even for Stein, to ignore the facts: the shock of
the freeze had broken the inflationary psychology. From August to
November 1971, wholesale industrial prices fell slightly. The danger
looming ahead was that the conservative wing of the Republican
Party, which had been dismayed by the freeze and Phase II, would
induce Nixon to declare a victory over inflation before it was at
hand, and junk the wage-price machinery too early. Ironically, the
Democrats who knocked the New Economic Policy at the beginning
were now rallying to its support. Walter Heller stressed in 1971 that
Phase II was accomplishing a significant moderation of inflation to
about the 3 percent level.[28]

Not surprisingly, Nixon, with one eye on the November election,
gave assurance in his Economic Report to Congress in January 1972
that controls would be kept through the end of the year and possibly
beyond, and Stein, as author of the report, was forced to go along. At
the same time, Nixon abandoned the long-standing target of getting
unemployment down to 4 percent. The jobless rate, at the beginning
of the year, was 5.9 percent, a level that the administration was seeking to suggest was tolerable because some of the rise represented an
increase in the percentage of women and teenagers in the labor force.
Democratic economists, such as Okun, were sharply critical of abandoning the target, however difficult it might be to achieve, telling
Congress that the way to cut unemployment "is to try to move the
mountain."[29] But Federal Reserve Board governor Henry Wallich argued for expanded retraining programs, contending that "the 4 percent full employment level no longer had the significance that it
used to have. Today, 4 percent unemployment unfortunately is more
inflationary than in the past."[30]

The disenchantment with Phase II set in early and quickly. By
March 1972, Meany and two others of the five labor members had
walked off the Pay Board, citing rising prices and the fact that large
areas of the economy were not controlled. Meany, of course, had
been itching to get off the Pay Board the minute he had reluctantly
joined. From the very first day, he had been sniping at the public
members, especially Arnold Weber, a former Shultz aide, and Kermit
Gordon, the distinguished economist who was now president of the
Brookings Institution. A Meany aide said that Weber was "an administration flunky" and Gordon "a no good, incompetent son of a
bitch."[31] Labor's bitterness toward Gordon, one of the brightest,

most level-headed economists ever to serve the nation, went back to 1962 when Gordon, as a CEA member, was the inspiration for the famous Kennedy 3.2 percent wage-price guideposts, which Meany contended put a limit on labor's share of the national income.

While on the board, Meany displayed his contempt for the whole program, even though, with the help of the management members of the Pay Board, he was winning double-digit wage increases for a number of unions, notably a 14.9 percent boost for the dockworkers. But Meany could argue, with reason, that with so many exemptions on the price control side, especially for food, it was silly to think that anything like a 2 to 3 percent price standard could be maintained. He could point to the fact that Secretary of Agriculture Earl L. Butz was running around the country openly cheering every boost in meat prices. But Meany was willing to add fuel to the fire from the wage side; to underline his unhappiness, he rarely showed up for Pay Board meetings, instead sending AFL-CIO research director Nat Goldfinger in his place.

The way chairman George H. Boldt, a U.S. district court judge from Washington state, Gordon, Weber, and other public members looked at it, the management team on the Pay Board was also "soft," because it proceeded on the assumption that the Price Commission would automatically pass on to the consumer as price increases the excessive wage increases it approved. That, of course, would make a shambles of the whole program, especially if a precedent were set for "catch-up" increases in the steel, aerospace, rail signalmen, and dockworker cases.

The problem that remained was how to sell controls to other Nixon administration officials whose ideological bias had always been against them. George Shultz, for one, had at best accepted controls at Camp David as a necessary quick political fix, but nothing more. Kissinger had been conducting a behind-the-scenes campaign against Connally's 10 percent surcharge, and Burns, in a Montreal speech on May 12, 1972, to a bankers' group, had delivered a not-so-subtle warning to Connally: "The task of statesmanship is to tap the great reservoir of international goodwill that now exists and to make sure that it remains undiminished in the future." Shultz, who would succeed Connally in May 1973, had stayed close to Nixon, and offered the promise of smoother relations with the allies.[32]

MEANWHILE, THERE were signs that the Smithsonian Agreement on currency rates might come unglued. In her monumental history of the International Monetary Fund during this period, Margaret

Garritsen de Vries wrote that "hindsight suggests that the exchange rate realignment" agreed on at the Smithsonian "was doomed at the start. Unrest in exchange markets and disturbing flows of speculative capital persisted throughout much of 1972. Early in 1973 the Smithsonian exchange rates collapsed."[33] The American economy continued to show the effects of the deep distortions of the Vietnam War, which had drained the nation's wealth, triggered the inflation, and exacerbated the balance of payments and trade deficits. The dollar's devaluation, said former Fed chairman William McChesney Martin, while a necessity, was a confession of the failure of economic policy.[34] Not too subtly, Nixon officials began to refer to the inflation target of Phase II as "3 percent or under," rather than the old formulation of 2 to 3 percent.

Even so, the existence of Phase II, especially the 5.5 percent wage guideline, was having a moderating effect on prices, despite the fact that some big unions had won more. For smaller unions, and where labor was not organized, the 5.5 percent wage yardstick remained an inhibition against bigger increases. The typical employer was delighted to be able to turn aside individual requests for bigger pay boosts as unpatriotic. Unemployment remained high, but by mid-1972 the dollar had steadied, business began picking up, and the stock market rose. "Those of us who were skeptical about the ability of Phase II wage and price controls to moderate the rate of inflation, to say nothing of those economists who claimed that controls would not work or would make the problem worse, have been pleasantly surprised by the results in the first six months of 1972," said MIT's Paul Samuelson.[35]

But the budget was still not under control, and when I wrote several columns on the danger of renewed inflation, I touched a raw nerve in the Nixon White House, although Connally had told me at the time that my raising questions about the size of the budget deficit in prospect was "right on the button." Nevertheless, things were about to get personal.

On July 26, Stein wrote Nixon aide Alexander P. Butterfield and White House assistant press secretary Kenneth W. Clawson a memorandum saying: "I assume you both understand, despite his protestations, that he [Rowen] is an implacable and unscrupulous enemy of this Administration. . . . I could write a book, or at least a chapter, on the reporting and analysis of Hobart Rowen. I don't have the time for that now. But if you want any information on the subject, ask me." In the margin of a separate memo from Clawson to Butterfield, Nixon scrawled: "Herb is absolutely right. Rowen is just too smart to get caught in his lies—except by someone just as smart, as our Herb

Stein."[36] Stein wasn't the only Nixon aide who wanted me scalped. Charles Colson sent a memo to Fred Malek, Nixon's personnel chief, suggesting that "the Army [should] take over *The Washington Post* . . . immediately after the Army took over, we would have Hobart Rowen beheaded." Colson also wanted to try my boss, Ben Bradlee, and other *Post* colleagues as war criminals, and asked a member of the White House staff to let him know when any of the *Post*-owned TV stations came up for license renewals. Colson was upset, he told Malek, by one of my columns suggesting that the Nixon administration was trying to downplay the significance of the unemployment rate by pointing out that an increasing share of the jobless was among women.[37] The Colson memo continued: "We do not play this theme any more. Rowen loves to stick the knife in us any place he can. We are no longer saying that the fact that women are unemployed is not unhealthy to the economy. We've stopped that, but there is no way you can stop Rowen printing his nasty little jabs at us. Short of the suggestion I have proposed, of course." Such private griping, while ugly, was par for the course at the Nixon White House. It was all the more grotesque as many of Nixon's new policies had begun to work.

The consumer price index in the first year after August 15, 1971, rose by only 2.9 percent, compared to 3.8 percent from December 1970 to August 1971, and 5.9 percent for all of 1970. The gross national product "deflator," which measures inflation not just in the consumer sector but in the whole economy, was cut in half—from 4.8 percent to 2.4 percent. That was a better showing than any other industrial nation could claim. These data, assembled by Brookings economist Barry Bosworth, also showed that average pay increases had fallen to a 5.5–6.0 percent range from an average of nearly 8 percent before the freeze. Moreover, the first year bump-up for negotiated union contracts in all industries averaged 6.6 percent in the April–June quarter of 1972 compared to 10.1 percent before the freeze.[38]

These were impressive figures, even if they did not represent complete success, as Nixon claimed in extravagant terms on the first anniversary of the New Economic Policy. But the burden had been placed on disbelievers in wage-price controls to say what sort of system should be followed by Phase II to preserve its benefits while restoring more freedom to markets. Nixon's self-congratulatory statement had its petty side, of course. Secretary of Commerce Peter G. Peterson, an industrialist who could think for himself, never got along well with the White House mafia. When he showed up just seconds late for a press briefing on the success of controls, he was teased by Communications Director Herbert Klein. The irreverent Peterson responded: "Having been on the White House staff, I know the disdain with which some of my associates hold some of us lowly cabinet officials, and therefore I try to exhibit my independence in trivial but symbolic ways, like being ten seconds late. Is that all right, Herb?" Klein responded good-naturedly. "Touché!" But the exchange was expunged from the official White House transcript, and Peterson was gone from the Nixon administration the following spring.[39]

Senator George S. McGovern of South Dakota, the Democratic nominee for president, was right when he said in March that there had been a recession, and only a slow recovery that left 2 million more out of work in mid-1972 than when Nixon took office in 1969. But McGovern couldn't bring himself to credit the wage-price controls program with the achievements cited by Samuelson and Bosworth, notably the slow-down, by half, in the rate of increase in inflation.

Treasury Undersecretary Charls Walker suggested a kind of voluntary post–Phase II controls system to crunch the power of business and labor to create new cost-push inflation, a general increase in prices caused either by advancing wage rates or higher material and finished-product prices. Former CEA chairman Gardner Ackley suggested decontrolling almost all of the economy, but keeping big labor and the big companies controlled. And McGovern endorsed something like the Walker and Ackley ideas, essentially the same sort of voluntary guidelines.[40] Although it was derided by Stein and others as a surefire prescription for inflation, Nixon's Phase III turned out to be almost exactly the voluntary program McGovern had suggested.

Instead of weakening the program, Arthur Burns began to talk publicly and privately of the need to lower the 5.5 percent pay ceiling to 4.5 percent, so as to keep the rate of inflation from rising again in 1973. But Connally soon left, and Shultz, as Treasury secretary, was in the ascendancy, soon to be designated chief economic spokesman and, like others before him, a sort of assistant president for economic affairs. Shultz, whose academic expertise was in labor economics, was sensitive to the criticism, especially from the unions, that the system had been more effective in controlling wages than prices or profits. So he wanted to put off any reduction in the pay standard until the cost of living index showed further improvement. Shultz's influence on Nixon diminished Burns's role.

Meany, for his part, smarting from criticism that his walkout had destroyed the program, countered with an "all or nothing" proposal to put the whole economy, including dividends and interest, under control, with an adequate bureaucracy to run it. In that, he had been consistent throughout the years.

After Nixon overwhelmed McGovern in the 1972 presidential election—with the revival of the economy under the controls system a major plus in the Nixon landslide—the administration began a formal examination of how to unwind Phase II, assuming, as CEA member Marina von Neumann Whitman said, that the successful controls effort had "squeezed out" the cost-push pressures from the economy with a controls program that "has been more successful than anyone dared dream."[41]

At year's end, after a bitter internal fight among the factions within his administration, Nixon decided to ask for extension of authority to control wages and prices beyond the expiration date of April 30, 1973, delaying a return to a controls-free economy on pragmatist Shultz's conclusion that inflation had not yet been whittled back to manageable proportions. But Shultz overruled Burns's 4.5 percent pay guideline proposal. For the time being, Nixon and Shultz fudged the question of the exact shape and duration of Phase III—but allowed the impression that it would continue to be mandatory.

But the country couldn't be sure what to expect from Nixon. After the election, savoring his devastation of McGovern as well as an economic boom, the unpredictable Nixon bombed Hanoi and Haiphong at Christmas time, 1972, and then, on January 11, 1973, scrapped all mandatory wage-price controls, including rent controls, except in the areas of food, health, and construction, in favor of voluntary guidelines. The Pay Board and the Price Commission got the ax, while the Cost of Living Council continued under director John T. Dunlop, who succeeded Donald H. Rumsfeld. Nixon said that where business and labor didn't heed the voluntary guidelines, Dunlop could intervene to restore mandatory standards. Pointing to a closet door in the Oval Office when Dunlop was sworn in, Nixon said: "There's a stick in that closet—a very big stick—I will never hesitate to use it in our fight against higher prices and taxes."[42] And a new ten-man Labor-Management Advisory Committee to the council was established, bringing George Meany back into the picture. Phase III was a softer approach, cheered by business, by labor— and by Democratic economists such as Okun, who long had preferred a self-administered program backed by mandatory authority. But the question was: Would it work?

It didn't. The stock market, sensing that Nixon had pulled the plug too quickly on Phase II, began a retreat. Consumer food prices soared, threatening a revolution in the supermarkets, while industrial raw material prices also soared. In what was probably an early—

and missed—warning signal, funds started to move out of the savings and loans institutions into better-yielding investments.[43]

Reaction in Europe was that a toothless Phase III would do little to control inflation. There was a new and immediate burst of speculation against the dollar, and a new monetary crisis was quickly set in motion, forcing a new devaluation of the dollar by 10 percent, the price of gold moving up from $38 an ounce to $42.22. In addition, Japan decided to let the yen float, which widened the yen-dollar relationship by an additional 10 percent, the object being to cut the growing Japanese surplus by making Japanese goods more costly in this country. For the second time in fourteen months, Nixon had devalued the dollar, and the crisis didn't simmer down until an agreement among the major nations in Paris, in June, which the new French president, Georges Pompidou, labeled the third devaluation of the dollar. Economists and officials put more credence than justified in the "magic" that could be produced by changes in exchange rates.[44]

In April, with the cost of living index up 8 percent in the first two months of the year following junking of mandatory controls, and food prices in the grocery stores up 28 percent, Nixon tried a ceiling on beef, pork, and lamb. It too didn't work.

By then, Nixon's preoccupation with the growing Watergate scandal, which had begun to heat up in January and was reaching major proportions, was interfering with his ability to concentrate—and Shultz, Stein, and Budget Director Roy L. Ash were urging the president to tough it out on economic issues. To advocate anything else would be an admission of a monumental blunder, they counseled. But to do nothing was a policy fraught with disaster: the Fed was already trying to slow the inflation with tight money, and Stein began to talk of "something in the tax field."[45] Burns tried to promote a new freeze, and even Arnold Weber, the former member of the Pay Board and no devotee of controls, thought that controls might be reinstituted with clear standards imposed on the biggest companies and unions.

Eventually in June, the weakened, semivoluntary Phase III was replaced by Nixon, on urging by White House counselor Melvin R. Laird, with a new sixty-day price freeze. This action, which was taken over Shultz's objection and triggered his eventual departure from the administration, was reflective more of Nixon's desperate search for a headline that would convey the sense his government was alive and well, despite Watergate, than of his floundering. Shultz told me in a long and revealing "exit interview" when he finally quit in April 1974 that he had gone to Nixon, intending to leave on the spot, when the second freeze was announced. But Nixon was about to meet Soviet leader Leonid Brezhnev to discuss trade issues, and persuaded Shultz to delay resigning long enough to wind the controls process down. "So I did," Shultz recalled. "I mulled about that for quite a while . . . and I just didn't take any interviews [because] I didn't want to be in a position of giving a fudging answer."[46]

When Nixon told a disillusioned Stein he was considering a new freeze, Stein said it couldn't be done. "I said, quoting Heraclitus, that you cannot step into the same river twice. He replied that you could if it was frozen. . . . The decision went his way, a freeze was restored. And the outcome went my way, the new freeze was an instant flop. That experience tells us something about advising, too."[47]

The new freeze pointedly did not touch wages. In turn, it was to be supplanted by a new set of mandatory controls, known as Phase IV, in some aspects intended to be even tougher than Phase II. But Phase IV, which went into effect on August 13, also set the stage for full decontrol of the wage-price system, industry by industry. The way Nixon ran the controls program, from freeze to thaw, back to freeze again and a final dissolving, it is little wonder that the very idea of controls would come to be tarnished.

The opposition to wage-price controls—indeed, to any form of economic regulation by government—comes naturally to those who have a commitment to the wisdom of the "free" market, the strength of Adam Smith's "invisible hand" to sort out all of the pressures and to make the "right" decisions on prices and wages, successes and failures. The overzealous believe, simply, that government should get out of the way and let market forces do their job. Yet those same Adam Smithers are among the first to rush to the government for help in bailing out failing enterprises, or to look for protection against foreign competition for markets, invariably labeled "unfair." So the questions of controls can be seen to be a highly subjective one: the government should not step in to control the ability to make any degree of profit, some of the free-marketers seem to be saying. But please come in to block the competition, or save a company from going belly-up.

The trouble with following Adam Smith's commitment to the invisible hand is that pure, perfect competition doesn't exist. If it did, prices wouldn't rise at times of excessive resources.[48] In the year preceding Nixon's heretical act of freezing prices and wages, inflation had shot ahead by more than 5 percent, while unemployment was over 5.5 percent. According to classical economic theory, price increases should have begun to taper off with that much slack in the economy—allowing for some time lag in which prices reflect earlier upward pressures. Those opposed to controls argued that the only way to control inflation was for the Federal Reserve to clamp down on money supply growth, creating even higher jobless rates.

The choices were plain: put the economy through a crunch, using the Federal Reserve Board; accept inflation, which would further strain a weakening international competitive situation; or impose some restraint on prices and wages. To the distress of much of his inner circle, Nixon opted for controls—and to the dismay of noninterventionists, it worked.

In retrospect, dropping Phase II was a monumental blunder. The accepted rationale at the time was that "distortions" were beginning to creep into the economy, and would be exacerbated if mandatory controls were to continue. There were indeed some distortions, as in the lumber industry. But the administration never proved the general case. Phase II should have been left in place: it wasn't broke, and didn't need fixing. There is good reason to believe that the tough elements of Phase II were pulled in part because of Shultz's gut antipathy to the whole idea, and in part to appease Meany, who wanted to get rid of a single wage yardstick—which interfered with big individual union settlements, but which was followed almost religiously by the nonunion sector of the economy, three times as big as the organized sector.

The disastrous Phase III was followed by an ineffective Phase IV that began almost two years to the day after the original freeze had offered so much promise. And whatever glimmer of hope might have attended Phase IV soon had to be measured against a new crisis: the first OPEC oil shock. The fiscal hemorrhage that had begun with Vietnam was now about to become a torrent.

5

OPEC Shocks the World

A S THE NIXON administration continued its efforts to tame the
economy—even as the Watergate crisis deepened—along came
an unexpected shock that would shake the world. Crude oil, which
had been one of the cheapest commodities, became expensive. From
a global market price of nearly $3 a barrel at the end of 1970 (the cost
of extracting it from Middle East desert sands was only ten cents a
barrel), crude oil was marked up by the Organization of Petroleum
Exporting Countries (OPEC) on December 23, 1973, to $11.65 a bar-
rel, an increase of some 400 percent.[1] It amounted to a de facto tax
increase of some $50 billion to world consumers of oil. The OPEC
bombshell exacerbated the inflationary effects of the Vietnam-
induced American budget deficit, and when followed by a second oil
price shock in 1979, triggered massive increases in energy costs for
all importing countries that themselves did not produce oil. One result was the Third World debt crisis.

At first, the West was slow to recognize the implications of
OPEC's pricing decisions; then it overestimated OPEC's power. It
was preposterous to assume, as some did, that the oil producers
would follow any policy except one that reflected their self-interest.
Successive price hikes should have taught consuming nations the
vital urgency of developing alternative energy sources or risking vulnerability to periodic upheavals in the Persian Gulf. But it did not.

For the American automobile industry, the oil shocks brought
humiliation, and exposed the shortsightedness of some of the most

highly paid executives in the business world. Detroit had been contemptuous of small Japanese cars, but began to wake up to the fact—albeit slowly—that Japanese carmakers had a head start with "compacts," and that it would be a struggle to catch up. (Even two decades later, Detroit hadn't fully caught up with the technological production and marketing skills originating in Yokohama and Toyota City, but it could thank Japanese competition for some advances in efficiency and quality.)

In the 1970s, the view took hold in the West that the OPEC cartel, dominated by the major Arab oil-exporting states in the Persian gulf—and especially by the biggest producer, Saudi Arabia—did not really need all of the oil revenue it could extract from the consuming nations, and therefore could turn the oil spigot on or off at will. If true, OPEC would have enormous leverage over price increases. This view was supported, oil economist Eliyahu Kanovsky has observed, "by numerous forecasts projecting long-term oil shortages which would necessarily entail higher real prices; increased dependence on OPEC, and in particular on Middle East oil; and huge and growing financial surpluses accumulated primarily by the Middle East oil exporters."[2]

Conventional wisdom maintained that dependence on Middle East oil would not only continue but would expand. Never have so many been so wrong for so long. For example, Alfred L. Atherton, assistant secretary of state for Near Eastern and South Asian affairs, told a House Foreign Affairs subcommittee in 1974 that "a small group of countries in the [Persian] Gulf are well on their way to becoming financial giants, since the world must continue to depend on the oil resources of the region."[3]

The basis for this view was that oil—crucial to the operation of all modern industrial economies—was a finite resource that was fast being depleted, and therefore prices could reasonably be expected to go up. Yet, as energy expert and economist S. Fred Singer has observed, it would have been accurate to have said the same thing about oil at almost any time in the past century.[4] Most forecasts and forecasters, despite being wrong, had an enormous influence on the shaping of foreign and economic policy in the United States, Europe, and Japan.

One expert, at least, got it right: Eliyahu Kanovsky, a big bear of a man, an Orthodox Jew with unorthodox opinions. His wisdom about the oil market finally won him a following in the mid-1980s among State Department and CIA officials. Although as a Jew he had been banned from Saudi Arabia, Kanovsky so accurately analyzed the Saudis' financial condition and so intuitively anticipated their production and pricing decisions over the years that the royal family, it was said, believed that he had a covert operation in Riyadh. He also published papers on the economic situations in Syria, Jordan, Iran, and Iraq that were more revealing than any information published by the countries themselves.

Kanovsky maintained that the underlying trends in the oil and energy markets were largely determined by economic forces, not by political forces such as Arab hostility to Israel (although the Arab states were anxious to build and capitalize on that fear in the West). Rather, he contended, the Saudis and the rest of OPEC set their oil prices exclusively on the basis of what seemed the optimum course for their own economic interests. Others disagreed. James E. Akins, for example, had written in 1973 that because of American vulnerability on oil, the Arabs' threat "to use oil as a political weapon must be taken seriously."[5] The tilt to Akins's view became clear when he was named by Nixon to be the new ambassador to Saudi Arabia.

Another unheeded voice of reason after the first oil shock in 1973 was that of John B. Kelly, a leading British authority on the modern history of the Persian Gulf states. Kelly traced the origin of the oil crisis directly to the British withdrawal from the area toward the end of 1961, leaving a power vacuum that was filled by OPEC.[6] Just a week after the outbreak of the 1973 Yom Kippur War, the Arab oil-producers in the Gulf, with the help of the shah of Iran, imposed an embargo on the export of oil to the United States and to the Netherlands (which was supporting Israel), and blackmailed other countries that might have been sympathetic to Israel.

"Although the embargo caused panic and created a sense of almost hopelessness in the consuming countries," Benjamin Shwadran of Tel Aviv University later wrote, "the leaders of the embargo were themselves, apparently, more than dissatisfied with the results and were seeking means to ease the embargo and even lift it altogether."[7] It was fully canceled within five months, on March 18, 1974—but the huge price boost instituted in December 1973 stayed in effect, an achievement of the larger cartel rather than the Arab group within it.

The relationship of the Arab-Israeli dispute to the shock of higher oil prices is not well understood. The Arab nations milked the notion that it would bestow special favors on those nations that would join in ganging up on Israel. In the early years after the first oil shock, the Europeans and Japanese took the bait, stepping over one another to curry favor with OPEC. By New Year's, France, Britain, Germany, Italy, and Japan had concluded or were negotiating a total of $11 billion worth of bilateral oil deals, involving not only cash but aircraft, arms, civilian goods, loans, and services. And as a separate but related issue, Japan participated in the Arab-directed boycott of Israel. Not until 1990, when Israel sent an economic attaché to Japan, and Japan responded by dispatching its own first commercial diplomat to Tel Aviv the following year, did meaningful trade relations with Israel resume.

But the OPEC price boost, and the Arab embargo, had deeper roots than the ongoing Arab-Israeli conflict, although it provided a good cover, as it had during the Six-Day War in 1967. Until then, Saudi Arabia, Kuwait, and Iraq had resisted using the oil weapon as part of the pan-Arab campaign against Israel. But when war between Israel and Egypt broke out in June 1967, a wave of emotion that "swept the Arab world," resulted in a decision to block the flow of Arab oil to "any country that supported Israel . . . [But] the negative economic consequences of these measures were soon apparent, and the producing countries rushed to revoke them."[8]

OPEC had been formed in 1960 in the belief that the Seven Sisters—the big Western oil companies—were deliberately holding down prices. But the cartel in its early years had been ineffective: a worldwide glut continued to keep prices low. In the Gulf, the producers, notably the shah of Iran, were desperate to get higher prices for their one good "crop," so as to finance the costly development schemes they had undertaken. Nevertheless, even today the fiction that somehow the Israelis were to blame for the first oil shock is perpetuated by distinguished journalists and others. My former *Washington Post* colleague Robin Wright, for example, who won awards for her reporting from Iran, wrote in a 1989 book that the 1973 price hike was a "response to Western support for Israel during the latest Arab-Israeli war."[9] Rising revenues gave the shah new independence, financed his grandiose schemes of development, and, at least temporarily, gave him the upper hand in his long battle with the clergy, notably with Ayatollah Khomeini. No doubt the shah, along with the group of elite Iranian families supporting him, would have tried to boost Iran's oil income without regard to the enmity between Israel and the Arab nations.

OPEC touched off a new set of global inflationary trends when it decided to cut production by 25 percent and pledged further monthly cuts of 5 percent. The original 400 percent price boost simply staggered the poorer countries such as Ghana, Kenya, and Tanzania that imported small but crucial amounts of petroleum. It also shattered the development prospects and hopes of countries like Bangladesh that desperately needed special concessions on prices.[10] World Bank staffers and the International Economic Policy Association, a research group specializing in global energy problems, pointed out that for the developing countries the oil bill had gone up $11 billion in 1974, just about wiping out $11.3 billion in official development assistance.[11] But higher oil costs limited the ability of the industrialized nations to offer more help to the Third World, and OPEC itself refused to make concessions, except to a group of Arab states. The impact on the more advanced developing nations was also profound. Brazil, for example, suddenly found that, instead of a trade surplus, it had a trade deficit. The result was to widen the disparities between those developing nations that had oil resources of their own, such as Mexico, Venezula, and Indonesia, and all the others.

In early 1974, the economists Walter Heller and Charles Schultze suggested that, for America, higher oil prices in effect were like a consumer tax increase of $15 billion to $20 billion annually.[12] That, of course, was before the second oil shock, which came in 1979, after a series of lesser increases that escalated the price to $35 a barrel (and more on a spot basis when producers or shippers could get it). Despite these extortionate prices, State Department officials continued to refer to Saudi Arabia—the cartel leader—as a friendly country.[13]

These are not judgments made exclusively with the benefit of hindsight, although with hindsight one can see how poorly Nixon—preoccupied with extracting the country from Vietnam and himself from Watergate—served the nation. Kanovsky, for one, argued at the time that the importance of Middle East oil to the United States—in particular, Saudi oil—was not overwhelming. He rightly predicted that the huge bulge in OPEC prices would unleash additional oil resources in the non-OPEC world; that the major nations would reduce their need for OPEC oil by massive conservation and conversion efforts; and that ultimately the Saudi Arabia–led cartel would have to lower prices because most of the cartel members were "one-crop" nations that needed to sustain the revenue flow they had generated with higher prices.[14]

Nevertheless, oil consultant Walter J. Levy, with better Establishment credentials than Kanovsky, said that a preliminary study had convinced him by the end of 1973 that the boost in oil prices had created a "nearly disastrous" outlook for the less-developed countries, and that it would be "very difficult if not unmanageable" for many of the industrial countries of Europe and Asia.[15] Levy, who had spent a lifetime on oil, energy, and related financial affairs, had begun warning about the problem in 1972, trying to get the importing nations to understand the need to coordinate their response to OPEC. Toward the end of 1973, Levy was gloomy: "It is not a question of supply availability, but a financial problem, a balance of payments problem—it's not too much to say that it's a bankruptcy problem. No importing country except the United States can begin to handle the problem, and even we cannot survive in a world of depression which would bring political and social unrest." He tended to blame Western disunity, rather than Arab greed, for the stark predicament.[16]

The World Bank, in an internal document, said that the consequences of higher prices "present a radical turning point in the outlook for the world economy." One official predicted that "the direct consequences for the developing countries could be reduction in their rate of growth, either because of reduced energy supplies at higher prices, or because of the reduced capacity to import goods and services other than oil." What would happen next, he said, was that the Third World nations would begin to cut their purchases from the United States and other nations, depressing economic activity all around.[17]

This is precisely what happened (although it is puzzling how many of those who today worry about the trade deficit fail to connect high oil prices and Third World debt on the one hand and Third World debt and the loss of American export business to Latin America on the other). By 1984, the United States had a $39.3 billion trade deficit with Third World countries (excluding the OPEC nations themselves), or more than the $37 billion trade deficit with Japan that year.[18] From 1980 through 1984, the decline in American exports to the poor countries cost 560,000 jobs, mostly in manufacturing and trucking.

In the first half of 1974, the Nixon administration failed to confront the problem, anxious not to offend Arab sensitivities by demanding price moderation. William J. Casey, undersecretary of state for economic affairs, echoed a call by Senator Jacob K. Javits, the New York Republican, for the major Western industrial nations to coordinate their energy policies.[19] But nothing happened: prices simply kept going up. Within the administration, astonishingly, a debate broke out over whether or not there really was an energy crisis. Deputy Treasury Secretary William E. Simon, doing double duty as the nation's "energy czar," talked in ambitious terms of generating new sources of energy to replace oil, and of sharing new technology with European nations. He also warned the cartel that the big price boosts "have made oil in the ground a relatively poor investment because its value will fall over the next decade."[20] But Simon had to contend with Budget Director Roy L. Ash and CEA chairman Herbert Stein. Ash, an icy executive from Litton Industries, insisted that there was no oil crisis, and that whatever was going on was "manageable, one-time, and short-term." Simon wasn't pleased, declaring on national television that Ash "should keep his cotton-pickin' hands off energy policy. Perhaps I should call a press briefing on the budget."[21]

Stein, meanwhile, dedicated to noninterference with the private markets, was critical of Simon's Federal Energy Office, which was considering rolling back the price of certain categories of crude oil produced in the United States. That, Stein said, would lengthen the gas lines. Cut the demand, he suggested, by letting gasoline prices go up another ten cents a gallon. This would have been a mistake, because worldwide oil prices were then just turning down in response to the sharp curtailment of gasoline consumption. What was needed was a gasoline rationing system that could have ended the lines at the gasoline pumps. That never came about, but Washington did ban Sunday gas sales, which helped to curb the national addiction to driving.

At a Washington energy conference in mid-February 1974, Secretary of State Henry Kissinger persuaded other large consuming countries to try to evolve a concerted response to OPEC. Walter Levy circulated a paper to the conferees estimating that the increase in the global cost of oil from 1972 to 1974 would be a stunning $79.3 billion, of which the European share would be $39.7 billion; the American, $15.9 billion; and the Japanese, $12.8 billion. Levy pointed out that the unilateral deals some of the nations had been chasing had not met expectations, and that none could hope to avoid the disruptive effects of the price explosion or "escape the worldwide repercussions of potential international economic chaos."[22]

Finally, in March, the Arab nations announced that the embargo would be temporarily shelved, subject to a review in three months. But it was a mistake to assume that the crisis was over: so long as prices remained triple what they had been before the embargo, and so long as OPEC could control production, the oil crisis would continue. Israel alone, said the Arab statement, will bear responsibility "for more severe oil measures, in addition to the other various resources which the Arab world can muster in order to join the battle of destiny."[23]

Unhappily, the shelving of the oil embargo had the effect the politically astute Arabs intended: it vitiated the sense of urgency that Kissinger and Levy had been able to generate a month earlier at the Washington conference. Europe continued to succumb to Arab blackmail, pursuing bilateral deals to assure a steady flow of oil. With the ability, at that time, to supply 85 percent of its own needs, the United States did not have to respond in the same way. Yet, diverted by Watergate, Nixon was unable to focus on the most effective response, and by August he would be forced to resign, replaced by his new vice president, former House minority leader Gerald R. Ford of Michigan.

The World Bank also turned a deaf ear to the plight of poor countries made even poorer by the rise in the price of oil. Although under the leadership of Robert McNamara the World Bank had achieved a reputation for compassion for the needs of the poor nations of the former British and French colonial empires—McNamara himself was known to weep as he confronted these needs—it maintained that the high price of oil was a fait accompli, and that it was up to the Third World importers to pull themselves out of the hole by boosting exports. Bank officials, despite their responsibility to ease the economic burdens on the poorer developing nations, also did nothing to bring pressure on OPEC to lower its prices, but concentrated instead on efforts to encourage the rich Arab nations to recycle their monetary surpluses as loans to needy Third World countries. For example, World Bank vice president and chief economist Hollis B. Chenery said, "We have taken it as a given that the bank cannot influence the price of oil. It's none of our damned business to be concerned with the price of oil. We're a lending organization, not a trade organization."[24] At the same time, there was an eagerness at the World Bank to accord the OPEC nations, especially the Saudis, a place in the bank's power structure commensurate with its new wealth. The reason was not hard to divine. As one bank staffer told me: "The bank is remaining essentially silent on the oil-price impact on the less-developed countries in order to have access to OPEC capital."[25] Within the bank, middle- and high-level officials privately criticized McNamara's and Chenery's stand, believing that the bank should at least battle for a split-price structure for oil, with the less-developed countries getting not only lower prices for oil but grants (rather than loans) to help restore economic growth.

An internal bank study in 1973, just before OPEC boosted prices fourfold, indicated that if the price of Saudi light oil rose to merely $8 a barrel by 1980—or unchanged in real terms, after allowance for inflation—the Third World oil bill would rise from $5.2 billion in 1973 to $27 billion by 1980. But by the end of 1973 the price was already $12, and the estimates of the costs to consuming nations were wildly outdated. In 1974, an updating of the 1973 report estimated that OPEC's accumulated monetary reserves would explode from $25 billion in 1973 to over $600 billion in 1980, and to over $1 trillion in 1985. In 1975, a revised and still secret report more or less accepted high oil prices as a fact of life, despite objections within the bank staff. The poor countries, the report concluded, would have to pull themselves out of the crisis by boosting their exports.

Outside the bank, others worried not only that the jump in oil prices would drain funds out of consuming nations, rich and poor alike, but questioned the ability of the cartel members, largely undeveloped economically, to absorb the huge financial surpluses soon to be generated. These huge funds, Benjamin Shwadran pointed out, "would endow them with strong financial as well as political powers."[26] He cited "a very penetrating and gloomy" account written by IMF official Gerald A. Pollock for the April 1974 issue of *Foreign Affairs,* suggesting that ballooning oil prices might touch off "violence and anarchy" in the Third World. But such gloomy thinking did not preoccupy McNamara at that time.

A series of *Washington Post* stories I wrote in 1975, initiated by Harry Rosenfeld, the national affairs editor, raised questions about McNamara's activities; whether they reflected a pro-Arab stance and whether they conformed with the rules of conduct for an international civil servant. The stories incurred McNamara's wrath. He accused me of trying to misrepresent the bank as anti-Semitic, and was angry enough to suggest to his good friend, *Post* publisher Katharine (Kay) Graham, that I be fired, a proposal that—after some agonizing—she rejected.[27]

A question had arisen over McNamara's participation in high-level State Department discussions of Arab-Israeli problems. As president of the World Bank, after all, McNamara was no longer secretary of defense but an international civil servant whose role in the political affairs of member nations was highly restricted by rule and convention. Under bank rules, McNamara was barred from participation in political meetings called by a member nation, unless he had explicit permission from the bank's board of directors.

Yet McNamara ignored this rule when he advised Kissinger on Mideast policy in 1973, and on other foreign policy issues as part of a "wise men" group that included about a dozen former government officials, including secretaries of state Dean Rusk and William P. Rogers, McGeorge Bundy, Peter Peterson, Cyrus R. Vance, and George W. Ball. They endorsed Kissinger's demand that Israel abandon its military confrontation with Egyptian forces. The existence of the group, including McNamara, had been revealed in a book by *New York Times* columnist William Safire. I phoned Kissinger in 1975, and he confirmed Safire's account.

Safire had written that at the time of the bombing of Cambodia in 1970, "Henry told me [that McNamara] came into Kissinger's office at the peak of the furor and put on his desk a list of ten prominent Americans, saying quietly, 'You pick five and I'll call the other five, to get their support.' "[28] On the phone with me, Kissinger said: "I would say the Safire quote is 80 percent true. McNamara came into my office the day we went into Cambodia, and said: 'Henry . . . it's going to be a real problem. I have here a list of ten people who might give you trouble. I'll call five and you call five.' " Kissinger said in his conversation with me that McNamara himself was opposed to the invasion, and his offer was "an example of his desire to help keep the country from tearing itself apart. . . ."[29]

The series of stories I wrote for the *Post* was highly critical of the World Bank and of McNamara. In addition to showing that McNamara was playing a political role he was supposed to have left behind, the series reported that, in his determination to keep the oil-rich OPEC countries happy, McNamara had not only failed to induce them to follow more reasonable pricing practices but had knuckled under to Saudi Arabia's insistence that members of bank missions to Saudi Arabia produce baptismal certificates, a transparent and senseless effort to bar Jews working for the bank from entering the country. This was a limitation that the U.S. State and Treasury departments had refused to honor. In an interview, McNamara denied being aware of such a procedure, and said firmly that he would oppose any such restriction. I was happy to hear that, but when I said I would like to quote his statement, he flatly refused.[30]

McNamara's game was to stay in the good graces of OPEC leaders, so as to assure the bank's continued access to their funds. In 1974, the bank had tapped the newly wealthy cartel for $2.2 billion, and overall had borrowed about $3 billion, or 25 percent of the bank's then outstanding debt.[31] As I went about my reporting task, McNamara's many critics within the bank as well as some highly placed Ford administration officials said that McNamara was giving top priority to keeping OPEC happy, and a much lesser priority to the negative effects that OPEC price hikes were having on the poor developing countries. There was a great deal of tension within the bank during this period. Some high officials, fearing McNamara's wrath, would take phone calls from me only when I used a code name. One key source met me secretly in the stalls of Sidney Kramer's bookshop, then near the bank on H Street NW.

After the *Post* published my reports, McNamara withdrew the bank's recognition of the Saudis' demands for a baptismal certificate (which had kept his financial genius, Treasurer Eugene H. Rotberg, among others, off missions to Riyadh). McNamara also withdrew a proposal he had made earlier to reduce the bank's liquid reserves, a policy he had justified on the ground that he anticipated "continued access" to OPEC's resources. This change of heart came after I cited in my *Post* story on July 24, 1975—one of the series—views inside and outside of the bank that McNamara's open reliance on the cartel "took the heat" off OPEC to make gifts and low-interest loans to poor countries.

Then the bank held what French and American executive directors called a "history-making" session at which, for the first time, the impact of high oil prices on the economic activities of the Third World was discussed. Moreover, a policy under which the Arabic edition of a World Bank/IMF publication was allowed to drop articles by Jewish authors was reversed. The series had the kind of impact that Ben Bradlee had repeatedly demanded of reporters. But McNamara's complaints had created an uncomfortable situation for me with the publisher, Kay Graham, who was a close friend of McNamara. In time, things cooled down, and I got along passably well with McNamara. On the way home from the World Bank IMF annual meeting in Manila in 1976, the bank's public relations staff contrived to have us sit together on the plane, and we talked for long hours unemotionally and smoothly about World Bank affairs, with no further references to the confrontation we had had or to his complaint to Kay Graham.

Kay told me in an interview on July 9, 1991, which she arranged for a book she was writing, that while she recognized she might have been "frosty" to me, she never had the notion of firing me. It was the first time we had discussed the McNamara affair since 1975, and our conversation effected a rapprochement between us.[32]

The desire to play the international oil barons' game overwhelmed not only the World Bank but much of official Washington in the mid-1970s. The shah of Iran was wined and dined by President Ford, Vice President Nelson A. Rockefeller, and Secretary of State Kissinger even as the shah in May 1975 talked of the need for another $2 a barrel price increase over the prevailing $11 per barrel. The shah was playing from strength. A Ford administration official was candid: "I was teed off like nobody's business to hear the shah tell us he was going to give us a screwing, while we smiled and told him we loved him."[33] By this time, the cartel had cut production 30 to 35 percent to keep prices high, and a Democratic-controlled Congress had failed to carry through on a commitment to write even a semi-tough energy conservation program. The politically powerful automobile industry was successfully resisting proposals to pass a higher gasoline tax or regulations that would penalize gas-guzzlers.

Meanwhile, the French, British, and Japanese were stumbling over each other trying to set up bilateral deals for oil. Anthony Barber, British chancellor of the Exchequer, humbly paid a call on the shah at his Swiss chalet, and agreed to trade British products and industrial know-how for Iranian oil. The servile wooing of the shah guaranteed economic problems for the West. Instead of guts and leadership, the West displayed only fear. The shah made clear in a *Der Spiegel* interview that the Gulf nations intended to use their leverage over oil prices to move up in the world power structure. "In ten years' time, we are going to have a tremendous purchasing power. We will have the same per capita income as in Germany today. We are going to become a member of your club. It is a question of readjusting the relation between the industrial world and the oil-producing countries. We have said that the era of cheap oil is finished. We must add that the era of exploitation is finished."[34]

The boost in the power of the cartel, especially the clout of the Arab states within OPEC, was equated in the OPEC leaders' minds—and in the minds of Arabists within the U.S. government—with a weakening of the American bond with Israel. As we have seen, of course, there was no real connection between the energy crisis that had been precipitated by the first OPEC oil price shock and the Middle East conflict between Arabs and Israelis. Assistant Secretary of State Joseph J. Sisco—one of the best State Department experts on the Middle East—was an exception. He understood that the energy crisis and the Middle East troubles "constitute in fact two separate sets of problems, each of which should be viewed primarily in its own context." Nevertheless, King Faisal of Saudi Arabia responded to Sisco by making it clear that if the United States did not alter its total commitment to Israel, the Saudis would keep their oil in the ground rather than pump it to satisfy American consumption needs.[35] So the policy was clear: unless the United States changed its commitment to Israel, it wouldn't get all the oil it wanted from the Gulf states, which would, instead, divert some of their vast oil revenue to strengthening Arab armed forces for an ultimate victory over Israel.

In response, some Americans urged a massive effort to generate new energy sources—from shale, low-sulfur coal, and atomic and solar sources. Government energy expert Charles J. DiBona argued that there were "sound economic reasons" for the Saudis to keep some of their oil in the ground. "For many reasons, we have to take a closer look at what we can do to make it to their advantage [to export oil to us]. And we need a greater sense of urgency in finding different sources."[36] The "sound economic reasons" that DiBona cited for the

Saudis to keep some of their oil untapped were many. Even the Saudis' huge reserves were not unlimited, and drilling at a reckless rate could diminish the long-term value of the oil. But it was foolish to assume that the Arab nations were so caught up in their anti-Israel campaign that they would ignore their own economic interests.[37]

OPEC, in fact, was pragmatic. For example, the oil cartel countries would cough up only small amounts of money, out of their huge booty, to help Third World countries out of the mess they had helped put them in.[38] Dr. Abderrahman Khene, the organization's secretary-general, defended the policy by insisting that it was not OPEC soaking the poor countries with high oil prices but the greedy industrial nations, like the United States and Canada, that had impoverished the Third World with extortionate prices for food. OPEC, said Khene, was not truly rich like the industrialized countries, merely more "liquid" than it had been before. Moreover, he insisted oil prices were still below the level that needed to be achieved to balance Western-generated inflation in other commodities, including food.[39]

Yet we and our friends in Europe deluded ourselves into thinking that the crisis had been met because Arab moneys were being "recycled" into loans for the oil-importing countries. But recycling would be a solution only if the OPEC nations were to move into deficit by importing more goods than the value of their one export "crop." And that wasn't happening. The OPEC surpluses stayed close to their peaks, and the poor nations of the world were paying more in interest and principal to cover their debts than they were receiving in new aid. "We ought to drop the word recycling from our vocabulary," Fed chairman Arthur Burns said indignantly in late 1974. "It means piling debt on top of debt, or more accurately, bad debt on top of good debt. The talk about recycling is an escape from reality. The nations of the world are not facing the real problem, the 400 percent increase in the price of oil." It wasn't the embargo that hurt, Burns said, but the power to set prices. Oil, like money, was fungible: if the Arabs blocked the shipment of "x" barrels of oil, it would be shipped elsewhere, and another shipment of oil would take its place in the distribution system. But the price would go up.[40]

The Third World nations had to admit, reluctantly and grimly, that they were wrong when they had applauded OPEC as striking a blow for all the underprivileged nations of the world, who then could raise their commodity prices to compensate for the higher costs of oil. Instead, the oil shock recession of the early seventies had caused a general collapse of global commodity prices. Now, the poor nations looked for a break from their brothers in the cartel—a concessional price, or loans (hopefully to be canceled later) to finance the higher costs. But OPEC had no intention of making life easier for anyone.

By 1975, the outlook had turned bleak: President Ford allowed the oil and energy problem to fester throughout his first year in office, exacerbating double-digit inflation and rising unemployment. It was the beginning of a long period of uncertainty: other oil shocks were to come. More than ever, the nation needed an energy policy that at a minimum would cut about 1 million barrels out of consumption approaching 7 million barrels a day through some combination of higher gasoline prices and direct/indirect rationing. Dependence on OPEC for a major share of oil needs at the prices the cartel had set was deepening the trade deficit. What citizens deserved was a forthright decision that would enforce austerity in the use of gasoline at home and encourage joint action with Europe, Japan, and other consuming nations to bring counterpressure on OPEC. MIT's Morris A. Adelman suggested the imposition of import quotas, requiring oil sellers to submit sealed bids for a share of the American market. If total quotas were cut, say, 20 percent from normal importers, oil suppliers would begin to cut their prices. But the process would also create lines at gas stations as supplies dwindled, raising the question of how to devise a rationing system. Fed chairman Burns said that without an energy policy, "the alternative of drift, I fear, may lead to a permanent decline of our nation's economic and political power in a very troubled world."[41] But Burns clung to a tight monetary policy, which without question exacerbated the downturn in the economy. By the end of 1974, even CEA chairman Alan Greenspan, who had replaced Herbert Stein, had to acknowledge that "the economy is slipping rather perceptibly at present," arguing nonetheless that it would be "a false alternative" to shift economic policy away from the fight against inflation to a fight against recession.[42] Privately, Greenspan assured Ford in one of their many one-on-one Oval Office meetings that the problem was largely that of an "inventory correction."[43]

The situation was much worse: the nation faced a stagnating, double-digit inflationary economy, onto which was imposed the energy problem. Manipulation of oil prices and supplies by the OPEC cartel pointed to the need for curtailment of gasoline use. But any logical method—taxes, tariffs, quotas, rationing, allocation, or any combination—would further depress the hard-hit auto industry.

Around the beginning of 1975, Secretary of State Henry Kissinger began to show for the first time that he understood the depth of the energy crisis, worsened by the political malaise into which government seemed to have sunk following the Watergate scandal. He began to talk publicly about the use of military force to extract the West from OPEC's grip.[44] That was unnecessary bluster. There were many elements of a tougher economic and political policy that could have been brought to bear against OPEC before military alternatives merited consideration. OPEC was not only dependent on the West to absorb its oil exports but counted on the Free World for technical assistance, banking, markets, and transportation. If Kissinger had been truly serious about confronting OPEC, first consideration should have been given to Adelman's import quota plan and the building of a strategic oil stockpile.

Arthur Okun suggested that the cartel could be put on notice that a new embargo would be met with an immediate break in diplomatic relations. Given another oil shutoff by the cartel, "we ought to cancel all trade and revoke all visas the next day," he said. Senator William E. Brock (R.-Tenn.) called for a declaration of national economic emergency is response to an "economic Pearl Harbor."[45]

President Ford responded with nothing that bold. Worried about upsetting the auto industry, Ford, who had served thirteen terms as a congressman from Michigan, decided against a straightforward quota cutting oil imports. Moreover, he approved a deal between Federal Energy Administrator Frank G. Zarb and the Detroit auto companies that lowered emission standards. He rejected, as well, a retail gasoline tax—and, of course, gas rationing—but asked for standby power for quotas, mandatory allocations, and rationing. The energy-economic package he designed to cope with the oil crisis and threatening recession left all of Ford's advisers uncomfortable. The package included a boost in crude oil prices and decontrol of the domestic oil and natural gas industries.

In Detroit, the auto barons continued to ignore the trend. The Big Three automakers decided that the Volkswagens and other foreign "toys"—as they contemptuously referred to them—would attract only poor families, and "real American families" with "real money" would never give up the comfort and power of big American cars. In the boardroom and on the golf course, American business managers joked that you had to close the doors of a Japanese car gently or you would bend them. As for the humble, picture-taking, tape-recording Japanese visitors who came to inspect their big, modern plants— well, they must have thought, who needed to take these little yellow-skinned foreigners seriously? Yet the industry had known for some years—even before OPEC—that a shortage of refining capacity and dwindling reserves soon would threaten the availability of cheap gasoline. But that possibility was not yet visible to consumers, and men like Henry Ford II decided to tough it out and keep pumping their gas-guzzlers onto the unsuspecting market.

How could we have really known, both industry and union officials lamented, that there would be an oil embargo, a fourfold increase in prices, and the subsequent trauma? "They failed to see the handwriting on the wall," said UAW vice president Irving Bluestone. "They wouldn't give up the immediate buck on large cars with all the options. . . . Now, we all are hurt."[46]

It wasn't until mid-1975, facing the 1976 model year and beyond, that the Big Three made the reluctant decision to reduce the variety of cars, styles, and engines, and to concentrate on those that would weigh less and consume less gasoline. "Let's be honest," said Lee Iacocca, then president of Ford, "we're doing all this because our customers are forcing us to do it. . . . Since we want to stay in business, we're going to provide what they want."[47]

They were horribly wrong, of course: there *was* a market for the smaller car as well as the gas-guzzler, and as the foreign cars continued to make inroads, Detroit of necessity turned to its first "compacts"—GM's Corvair, Ford's Falcon, Chrysler's Valiant. For four or five years, these challengers to the imports did well. Then, as so often happens in America, greed took over: the compacts began to get bigger and more powerful, with more "extras" available. The bigger the car, the bigger the price, the bigger the profit—and the bigger the auto workers' hourly wages. "So imports came back stronger than ever," said former United Auto Workers president Leonard Woodcock.

In May 1975, as I sat talking to Henry Ford II in his Dearborn office, it was plain that he was living in the past, virtually out of touch with the reality of what was going on in the industry. I asked him why he had waited to hear from his customers before moving partially away from gas-guzzlers and toward smaller cars, given the growing popularity of imports, especially Japanese cars. He said: "I don't think the public wants [small cars] today. . . . They're buying small cars, but they're buying big cars in a greater percentage than they are small cars, if you want to take out the imports." Ford didn't seem to understand that overall he was losing market share to the imports. Models such as GM's Vega or Ford's Pinto (700 pounds heavier than the Toyota Corolla and Datsun B-210) certainly were not stylish. As more and more Americans switched to Japanese (and some German) imports, that meant that a "greater percentage" of those who stuck with Detroit were buying its big ones. It wasn't until Henry Ford II stepped down as chairman of the board on March 12, 1980, and relinquished his hold to a new generation of corporate managers, that the company would regain its competitive edge.

Ford seemed pathetic, an anachronistic hangover from the time that his father passed the business down. The original Henry Ford was a genius who built the Model T as cheap, utilitarian transportation. As was said at the time, you could get a Model T in any color you wanted, so long as it was black. Then General Motors came along in the 1920s with a better idea: its managers saw that there were wide variations in taste among the public, that people would pay more for style and for what they believed to be higher quality. Proceeding on this assumption, General Motors made a lot of cars and a lot of money, and the Ford Motor Company was forced to follow suit. "We were heroes in those days," a Ford man remembered in 1975, "because we created not only the profits but jobs. And the economy boomed." But by the late 1950s, as American cars grew bigger, fancier, and more expensive, European strategists sensed that there still existed in America that market Henry Ford had tapped with the Model T, then the Model A—a market for basic, reliable transportation at a low cost. Small, four-cylinder imports, led by the Volkswagen Beetle and the British Hillman and Austin, began to appear on American roads.

The average American's love affair with a big boat of a car, the kind that Henry Ford II would have liked to perpetuate, didn't die out easily. Although more efficient use of gasoline by smaller cars cut consumption and forced OPEC into some mild price cutting in early 1976, every time the price of gas at the pump dropped a few cents a gallon the demand for larger cars went up. The hottest Chrysler at the time was its top-of-the-line luxury New York Brougham, leading General Motors president Elliott M. Estes to complain at the Chicago auto show that year that "we got a little out in front of the market with small cars."[48]

Yet it wasn't exactly as Detroit wanted it to appear. Sales of American small cars were sluggish in 1976, in part because many of the imports were of better quality. Another factor was the absence of a four-door compact in the GM and Chrysler lines (the Ford Granada was an exception among the Big Three). And finally, Detroit was pushing its full-sized cars as "the last year" they would be easily available, because of the minimum fuel efficiency standards mandated by Congress: 20 miles per gallon by 1980, 27.5 by 1985. Car buyers had also become lax: they had all but forgotten the cheap oil prices prior to the 1973 shock. Consumers were getting used to the current levels. What Detroit was learning was that price and gas economy were not enough to sell cars: style and comfort still counted, and that was good news for the oil cartel.

THE SHARPLY HIGHER oil prices that began in 1973 were one of the basic underlying causes of the explosion of Third World debt and of the massive American trade deficit. In 1973, the United States had accumulated a modest trade surplus after the devaluation of the dollar. But with imported oil prices rising, and steadily declining production from our own oil fields in the Southwest, America faced a 1974 trade deficit of $10 billion. The United States would encounter an exploding balance of trade deficit in the years to come, with imported oil accounting for an increasingly significant percentage. By 1992, oil imports would constitute more than half—$43.9 billion—of a total merchandise trade deficit of $84.5 billion.[49] Few understood the grave implications of the OPEC shock—least of all President Ford.

6

Gerald Ford's Recession

RICHARD NIXON's legacy for Gerald Ford was a nation whose faith in the presidency had been shaken, economy in serious trouble, heading into recession, and universal uncertainty where the unsolved energy crisis would lead. In the last few days before August 9, 1974, when Nixon finally resigned, financial markets had exhibited a severe case of the jitters, responding initially to exchange market speculation that had caused the failure in June of Bankhaus Herstatt of Cologne, West Germany. In addition, the wholesale price index for July, announced the same day the disgraced president left office, jumped by an annual rate of 44.4 percent.[1] That was quickly followed by a run on the Franklin National Bank of New York, which for weeks had been described by the Federal Reserve Board as "solvent." On September 8, the day that Ford granted his predecessor a "full, free, and absolute pardon," the Franklin was declared insolvent.

Since Nixon had junked the wage-price controls system, inflation and declining national output had plagued the economy. Higher energy prices were helping to fuel inflation, but the public appeared to be resigned to the prospect of the OPEC cartel's ascendancy. The shah of Iran was still a power to be reckoned with: he had arranged to buy four nuclear reactors from France, bought a 25 percent share of the vast German Krupp works, and established his credits in London with a $1.2 billion loan to help bail out a sinking British economy.

Ford moved into the Oval Office cautiously with little to support him except the goodwill of the American people, who were happy to have a man with an established reputation for honesty and decency in the White House once again. Ford immediately generated rapport with businessmen and economists of both parties by demonstrating that, if he was not a brilliant and commanding presence, at least he had an open mind. There was hope that there could be respect again for the presidency.

Fortunately for Ford, in the dying days of the Nixon administration Alan Greenspan had been named to succeed Herb Stein as chairman of the Council of Economic Advisers and was confirmed by Congress shortly after Ford was sworn in. Greenspan was not an economics professor—the normal qualification for the CEA chairmanship—but a business economist, head of Townsend-Greenspan, Inc., a staid, old-line consulting firm with a long list of blue-ribbon corporate clients. Although considered by some an ultraconservative—he was an early follower of Ayn Rand—Greenspan was widely respected for his forecasting ability and professional integrity. Journalists quickly discovered that he would return their calls, although he couched his responses mostly in an intricate web of "background," "deep background," and "deep-deep background." (It was a formula he preserved in a later incarnation as chairman of the Federal Reserve Board under Presidents Reagan, Bush, and Clinton.) When he wanted to be understood clearly by financial markets, however, he had no trouble delivering a crisp sentence that told the story. But when Greenspan wanted to leave some measure of doubt about his views, or about official policy, he had a rare talent for exuding gobbledygook.

He had met Ford only a few times during Ford's brief vice presidency, but they soon developed what Greenspan considered "an ideal relationship." In fact, Ford and Greenspan enjoyed one of the great, intimate working partnerships between president and chief economist, rivaling and perhaps surpassing the strong ties John Kennedy had established with Walter Heller. Heller had never been able to move into JFK's tight social circle—a circle that included Treasury Secretary C. Douglas Dillon and journalists Ben Bradlee and Charles Bartlett. But Ford and Greenspan discovered a common passion for golf, time on the links—in the American tradition—being one of the best backdrops against which to develop business or advisory relationships. Tongue in cheek, Greenspan recalled: "If waiting on the fourteenth tee, the president would say, 'Alan, what's your view on this or that?' I obviously couldn't say, 'Well, Mr. President, let's wait until the next economic policy council meeting.' "

Greenspan was secure enough in his relationship with Ford to reject the role of chief economic spokesman—which was coveted by and assigned to Treasury Secretary William Simon, who had been held over by Ford—when Ford chief of staff Donald Rumsfeld broached the idea to him. "You've got to have a political slant to be able to support the president whether he's right or wrong. I don't know how to do that," Greenspan said.[2] Instead, Greenspan's own job description of his role as CEA chairman was as head of a research and analysis team for the president, giving the widest possible range of advice from professional economists. "I avoided giving him an editorial. In effect, I always gave him option papers, and when I had a recommendation, I also always argued the other side."[3]

Greenspan shared the economic advisory role for the brief Ford presidency with Simon; L. William Seidman, a businessman from Michigan, who was deputy chairman of the Economic Policy Board, the main advisory board on economics headed by Simon; Roy Ash, the carryover Office of Management and Budget director; and the venerable Burns—who had been virtually shut out by Nixon in the former president's final year, but now enjoyed something of a renaissance because Ford liked him and Greenspan treated him with respect.

Greenspan was content to let Simon, Ash, Seidman, and Burns make the headlines. The biggest weakness of Nixon's economic policy had been a lack of consistency of purpose. It was a case, as John Connally admitted, of doing whatever was politically urgent at a given moment.[4] When Nixon came into office in 1969, the inflation rate was running around 5 percent, and the level of unemployment was 3.3 percent, reflecting the hyperactive pace generated by the war in Vietnam. As Ford took over, the inflation rate was running between 10 and 12 percent, and unemployment was over 5 percent and rising (it would soon hit 9 percent). The most optimistic forecast for economic growth for the six months ahead was zero to 2 percent.

Such was the economic mess that faced Ford and Greenspan—a recession with prices accelerating, with labor leaders in the wings ready to try to recover the ground they had lost in wage negotiations during 1973–74, when Cost of Living Council director John Dunlop—mostly through his own energy and contacts with the union leaders—kept wages from going through the roof. But Dunlop had now gone back to Harvard. In the first eleven business days of the Ford administration, the Dow Jones index plunged 108 points, suggesting that the markets were more impressed with the hard facts pointing to continuing recession and inflation than by the new tone of civility that distinguished Ford from his predecessor. Moreover, as Chase Manhattan Bank president David Rockefeller had warned, there were sober doubts spreading about the viability of the financial system itself, fears that the problems in the United States would spill over into global recession.

Treasury notes were paying 9 percent—the highest coupon in more than a century—a clear signal to Greenspan that Ford needed a quick infusion of confidence, something dramatic, if possible. First, Ford issued a sharp rebuff to General Motors for boosting prices $500 on 1975 cars, and then announced there would be a two-day national economic summit conference on inflation at the end of September to take place "in full view of the American public."[5] Such a summit, it was hoped, would provide a vehicle for national unity—and would demonstrate the importance Ford placed on solving the hard economic questions. The plan was warmly received by the public. Even the AFL-CIO's grumpy George Meany said that "there's a great sense of relief." But it soon would be clear that it would take more than gimmickry, more than sloganeering, to turn the economy around.

Ford needed to break with the past, to get rid of incompetents in the Office of Management and Budget, in the Council of Economic Advisers, and in the housing agencies. In seeking a new team, he needed to follow a bipartisan approach that would draw on a range of talent outside the Republican Party. And for a while, judging by the broad list of people invited to his economic summit, and Ford's public declaration while still vice president that he was seeking "new ideas," the prospect for sweeping changes looked good.[6]

Burns, worried by a third-quarter inflation rate running close to 12 percent, yearned for a reinstitution of some form of wage-price controls, even though they had become badly discredited by the manner in which they had been administered by the Nixon crowd. He immediately resumed his role as a public "noodge"—the one he played in the months before Nixon reversed direction in 1971 to embrace controls—telling reporters that there was "a fair probability" that Ford's summit would reach a consensus to adopt wage-price guidelines. Treasury Secretary Simon also believed that the Council on Wage and Price Stability, which had been begun as part of Nixon's wage-price control apparatus and was given an additional lease on life by Congress in mid-August, "obviously" would have to set some guidelines for acceptable wage-price increases. But Simon, a reluctant player in wage-price controls games, believed such guidelines should be flexible, not like the 5.5 percent standard that had operated under Phases II and III of the old controls system that had lapsed in April 1974. The stock market won't stop falling, Simon said, "until it is convinced that the government is serious about [attacking] inflation. . . ."[7]

Ford had made clear on a number of occasions that a return to mandatory wage-price controls would not be considered. At his first press conference, on August 28, he had declared that "Wage and price controls are out, period." Briefed by Greenspan, Ford fingered excessive federal spending as the basic cause for inflation, pledged that in his administration belt-tightening would be the rule, and suggested that private citizens also follow an austerity plan "for an interim period." And he carefully shunted aside a $4 billion public service jobs program that had been recommended by Burns and a bipartisan group of congressmen.[8]

On September 5, President Ford convened a "presummit" exploratory session among twenty-eight prominent economists of both parties in the East Room of the White House—with the nation, at Ford's invitation, able to look on via television. "We come together as allies to draw up a battle plan against a common enemy, inflation," he said. Unfortunately, that was about as gross a misassessment of the prevailing situation as could have been made. The real enemy, as plunging auto sales and rising unemployment would demonstrate within a few weeks, was a deepening recession. At the Federal Reserve, the staff had come up with the gloomy assessment that real growth would continue to decline through 1974, with unemployment rising to more than 7 percent by mid-1975. At best, the problem was stagflation, not inflation, but Ford, before calling his summit into being, was committed to fight the wrong enemy with his fruitless WIN campaign, an acronym for "Whip Inflation Now," dreamed up by political adviser Robert T. Hartmann. It combined Madison Avenue flackery with deflationary economics that had not worked before and held no promise to do so now.

Leading off the discussion in the East Room, Greenspan conceded that the economy was "turgid" and "sluggish," but stressed that the nation was in the grip of an inflationary psychology. Then four well-known forecasters—Harvard professor Otto Eckstein, economist Beryl Sprinkel of the Harris Bank of Chicago, Walter E. Hoadley of the Bank of America, and David L. Grove of IBM—debated the issue from their differing ideological perspectives.

Eckstein, a liberal who had been a CEA member in the Johnson administration, said that the economy was "heading for a middling recession," with the only question being how bad it would be. Assuming that the Federal Reserve would continue to back off a tight monetary policy (as Burns had just begun to do), Eckstein predicted that unemployment would peak around 6.5 percent in 1975, with inflation coming down from the then-current 10 percent level to about 8 percent at the end of 1975.

Sprinkel, an adherent of the Chicago "monetarist" school of economics, said the economy was not in a conventional recession. But for the following six months, he saw slow growth of perhaps only 1 to 2 percent in the real gross national product—the measure of all of the sales of goods and services, discounted for inflation.[9] Sprinkel told Ford that "if we are to reap the benefits of less inflation, we as a nation must be prepared to accept the short-run costs of less expansive government policies." Sprinkel's advice, snorted Walter Heller in a critique from the floor, was an endorsement of the "old-time religion" that ignored the perils of unemployment.

Hoadley, from the world of big banking, like Sprinkel saw a flat economy, and volunteered the idea that the public's lack of confidence "is now a force unto itself." He went on to urge government retrenchment in the international field. "We can't police, feed, finance, or heal the world," he said. Grove, for his part, representing one of the nation's biggest industrial empires, delivered the gloomiest forecast of all. He saw "very little likelihood of strength anywhere in the economy," predicted that business would soon quit building up its inventories, and that there would be a sharp decline in corporate profits.

Although Ford and Greenspan listened carefully to the four presentations, and to all of the others who participated, the analysis they bought, in advance of the end of the September summit, was Sprinkel's "old-time religion." The chubby monetarist from Chicago, later dubbed "Beryl the Peril" by his European counterparts, was strongly supported by Milton Friedman, the father of the monetarist school; by George Shultz, who had been Nixon's Treasury secretary and director of the Office of Management and Budget; and by former price controller C. Jackson Grayson Jr.[10] With Ford hanging on every word, Friedman acknowledged that the "cure" available through the "old-time religion" would cause a "prolonged" recession, but argued that "the public is ahead of its leaders at the moment and . . . will recognize and accept that, and is willing to bite the bullet and take the cure."[11] To which MIT professor Paul Samuelson snapped: "I don't think we will get down in the next couple of years to 3 percent inflation no matter if we bite every bullet in sight."[12] (History would prove Samuelson right and Friedman wrong in this instance: in advance of what turned out in 1975 to be the worst recession since the Great Depression, Friedman had stated assuredly in 1975: "We are not, and I emphasize the *not*, in danger of a major depression or even a severe recession."[13])

Friedman was enormously influential in persuading new generations of economists—as well as many foreign governments—that monetary policy (the manipulation of the economy by regulating the supply of money) is infinitely more important than fiscal policy, which works through changing the levels of taxes and spending. Eventually, even most of the antimonetarist Keynesians, who believed firmly that fiscal policy was more important, came to agree that "money also matters." But they never bought the Friedman view that "only money matters." Shultz, himself a long-time academic devotee of Friedman's, once quipped that "I wish I could be as sure of anything as Milton is of everything."[14]

As the recession threat accelerated in 1974—even if Ford was hung up on the WIN campaign—there was another persuasive argument against applying Friedman's "old-time religion" to the situation: even if tightening the monetary screws would work against a so-called "demand-pull" inflation, in which too much money chased too few goods, it was not designed to work against an inflation caused by a wage-price spiral and by commodity shortages. Risking the ire of George Meany, Walter Heller and Arthur Okun advocated some sort of "circuit breaker" or "social compact" that would interrupt the wage-price spiral. Heller suggested beefing up the authority of the new wage-price council by giving it subpoena powers and the right to suspend proposed increases. Others, including Brookings Institution economists Charles Schultze and George L. Perry, suggested a deal whereby labor leaders would quit trying to recover "lost" wages from the prior controls era in exchange for tax cuts, carefully crafted to increase take-home income for low- and middle-level taxpayers.[15]

By and large, all ideas for a nonconventional approach were rejected by Ford and Greenspan, who decided to stick with a tight fiscal policy. Greenspan never departed from the conviction that federal borrowing for both regular and "off-budget" purposes drove interest rates up in the private market, providing the main cause of inflation.[16] Buttressed by Greenspan's and Seidman's conservative advice, Ford—for all of his talk of a fresh approach—was content to follow a stand-pat policy. The biggest overt shock to the economy came later in the fall when Detroit introduced its 1975 car models with price boosts ranging up to $1,000 per car. As usual, the Detroit moguls misjudged their market: a disgusted public refused to nibble, sales plummeted, production stalled, and news of daily layoffs dominated the financial pages for the rest of the year.

Within a few days of the presummit gathering in the East Room, the Dow Jones index dropped below 630, a twelve-year low for stocks. International financial markets were on the edge of disaster, waiting daily for new bank failures. And the oil cartel still had the

industrial world literally over a barrel, gleeful as the consuming nations stood frozen without a response to rising oil prices and mounting balance of payments deficits.

When the summit itself finally took place—with 800 in attend-
ance—speaker after speaker assailed the restrictive policies of
Burns's Federal Reserve Board. Ford—who chaired the meeting himself—gave Burns "equal time" to answer his critics. The response
was vintage Burns: "The Federal Reserve will not win a popularity
contest. . . . It's our job to help protect the jobs of American workers
and the integrity of their money. But we operate in an environment
created by others. The Fed has to make some hard decisions, only if
some hard decisions are avoided by others. . . . I received a good deal
of advice this morning, all of which suggested that the money spigot
should be opened up. If I followed that advice, inflation would be
more intense, and interest rates would go higher. It would worsen
our troubles."[17] (In just two weeks, Burns would change his mind.
Although Burns did not like to agree with Heller and Okun, whom
he considered too "liberal,"[18] the old curmudgeon himself was
forced to identify the 1974 downturn as something different. In a
colloquy October 11 with Senator Lloyd Bentsen, the Texas Democrat, Burns said the recession was unusual because it was accompanied by "galloping inflation" and "booming" capital investment at
the same time. "I have been a student of the business cycle for a long
time," Burns intoned, his corncob pipe clamped between his teeth,
"and I know of no precedent for it in history."[19])

After the first day of the two-day summit, "discordant" was the
word used by many of the participants to describe its deliberations.
Senate Majority Leader Mike Mansfield and House Speaker Carl Albert declared that Ford's honeymoon was over, signaling the onset of
a more conventional period of political conflict. The euphoria that
had surrounded Ford's entry into the White House just six weeks
before was quickly evaporating.

Ford proceeded to make an incredibly inept "major" speech on
economic issues in Kansas City two weeks later, in which he essentially blamed the public for inflation, as if the companies, the unions, and the government itself had nothing to do with it. Ford urged
the public to retrench—spend less money—oblivious to the probability that even if enough citizens took him seriously, it would
exacerbate the already clear downward trend in sales, production,
and jobs. "Bring budgeting back in style," Ford told consumers,
". . . make economizing fashionable. Shop wisely, look for bargains.
Go for the lowest-cost items and brag that you are a bargain-hunter."
Exactly a month later, Ford switched his advisory gears as the econ-

omy drifted downhill. To a business audience in Las Vegas, he said: "To you in sales, I say, sell harder. Sell more aggressively. What we need at this time in this country are more tough Yankee traders and more supersalesmen."[20]

According to government figures released at the end of the year, the country's economic decline had changed from a gradual erosion to a precipitate slide: from March through August 1974, unemployment rose by only 323,000 persons, or 0.3 percent with a jobless rate in August of 5.4 percent. But by October the jobless rate was 5.8 percent, zooming to 6.5 percent in November, and then to a shocking 7.1 percent in December. The economy had entered a tailspin triggered by a collapse in auto output and sales, a sharp falloff in housing construction, and a weakening in business investment. But nobody, including Democrats critical of Ford and Greenspan, foresaw the rapidity of the decline.

In reality, what the nation needed to restore a badly shaken faith in institutions, reflected in an exceedingly low voter turnout in the congressional and gubernatorial elections in November, was not patronizing (and bad) advice, but a genuine antirecession program, including a stimulus policy from the Fed. Ford needn't have told citizens, as he had in Kansas City, that economizing was fashionable: consumers were retrenching out of fears of a serious recession, even depression. In the face of the government's own data showing that the GNP in real terms had declined for the third quarter in a row, by 2.9 percent, following dips of 7.0 in the first quarter and 1.6 percent in the second quarter, and a Greenspan CEA projection of a fourth-quarter slide of another 4.0 to 4.5 percent, Ford stubbornly kept hawking WIN buttons. Unbelievably, Ford's WIN program included a 5 percent surtax proposal, just as recession was gathering force with palpable effects around the country. To raise revenues, Ford proposed plugging some tax loopholes that favored special interests, along with his surtax. He also suggested a 10 percent investment tax credit for business. The combination appeared to provide a business benefit financed by middle-income taxpayers. And there would no tax relief for the poor.[21] Yet the recession was shaping up as the worst in fourteen years.

In the end, the surtax proposal was quietly buried, never to be mentioned again as the recession deepened, and the Ford administration tried to forget the ill-starred WIN campaign. But the administration was floundering, and Ford's other efforts to address his manifold problems were also inept. For example, in early October, Ford presented a ten-point economic program to Congress more notable for its omissions than for its concrete proposals. Faced with a broadening energy crisis and a manifest need to cut oil consumption, Ford not only ducked the sensitive issue of gasoline taxes but refused to recommend mandatory conservation measures. Instead, he regurgitated the same tired suggestions for "voluntary" energy savings that had been around for years, including a toothless warning to Detroit that it should produce more gasoline-efficient cars.[22] He also wholly avoided the wage-price controls question, not even asking business and labor leaders to exercise discretion, although wage settlements were averaging 11.1 percent at midyear, double the 1973 rate.[23] And having rejected any action on wages and prices, Ford also was stopped from recommending any stimulative action to move the country out of recession. Essentially, Ford looked immobilized: he would offer no dramatic initiatives against either the recessionary or inflationary influences in the economy, which condemned the nation to continued stagflation.

Meanwhile, the Democrats, who had a clear opportunity to seize the economic leadership by pushing an inflation-control program, also abdicated their responsibility. They had a special problem, and its name was George Meany. Meany was adamant against a new wage-price control program. Under Nixon, wages had been rather rigidly controlled, but prices and profits had not been. Labor's drive for higher wages in 1974 was almost irresistible because of the need to catch up with rising inflation. Over a year's time, despite the advance of wage settlements into the low double digits, labor's real compensation had fallen because consumer price increases were running close to an annual rate of 15 percent. Meany was not about to endorse yet another wage-control experiment, and without labor's support the Democrats felt they couldn't tackle Ford on the issue.

So wages and prices continued to chase each other up the scale, with no relief in sight, posing a major test for the capitalist system. If prices failed to come down in the face of a degenerating economic outlook, observed Otto Eckstein, "it will look as if the market isn't working well, and [it will seem as if] all of those accusations about administered prices are largely true."[24] A group of economists recommended to the Democratic Advisory Council of Elected Officials, an adjunct of the Democratic National Committee, late in the year an eleven-point program calling for across-the-board controls on prices, wages, executive compensation, profits and rents—a formulation meant to appease Meany. It also suggested a new Reconstruction Finance Corporation to make loans to ailing businesses; and mandatory conservation steps to save energy. Additional proposals called for a more generous jobs-creation program, for tax cuts, and for an easier monetary policy at the Fed.

With the jobless rate already past the mark that the pessimists had foreseen for mid-1975, all bets on the outlook were off. The talk began to focus on whether the economy could avoid a dreaded double-digit unemployment rate, not experienced since the Great Depression. Every increase of 1 percent in the unemployment rate represented slightly more than 1 million Americans out of work. Arthur Okun had devised a clever "Discomfort Index"—a simple addition of the unemployment and inflation numbers—that enabled anyone to measure the relative extent of the trouble in the economy. As inflation moved into the double digits, the "Discomfort Index" approached new heights. But, it turned out, Democratic politicians were no bolder than their Republican counterparts. Among some Democratic—and Republican—economists, however, there were calls for massive tax cuts to stimulate new spending. This chorus was joined by former Nixonites Stein—who just a few months back had been holding to the "old-time religion"—and Shultz. Stein made his switch known in a private session at the White House, and Shultz went public with a speech at the annual economists' convention in San Francisco, calling for a $25 billion tax cut. The return of Shultz and Stein to the mainstream of economic thinking symbolized dramatically the rapid deterioration of the economy in a brief period of time. What now loomed ahead for the country was the first set of back-to-back years of negative economic growth since the Great Depression, except for 1945–47, a period of postwar adjustment not generally considered a recession.

Even the normally supercautious West Germans recommended a similar policy to Ford. Chancellor Helmut Schmidt, on a visit to Washington, urged Ford and Simon to follow his lead in cutting taxes to spur private investment and boosting public expenditures. Others in Europe worried that America would wind up being the most depressed among the industrial nations in the Organization for Economic Cooperation and Development, dragging most of the West into a serious recession.[25]

Yet, in the midst of the nation's economic distress, there arose the familiar charge that things were really not so bad, and that the problems would go away if journalists would just quit writing about them. Walter B. Wriston, chairman of Citicorp, told a sympathetic audience of businessmen in Boston in November that "the traditional American sense of optimism has been replaced by doubt and gloom." One reason for the "cynicism and pessimism," he said, "is the omnipresence of the media. And dispassionate assessment would have to conclude that our journalists are better than they ever have been. . . . But one indisputable fact stares us in the face: the profession as a whole lacks a sense of history, which is essential to balance, to perspective, and to optimism."

Wriston was wrong. The notion that a sick economy would look better or recover more quickly if the news media soft-pedaled the bad news made no sense. Journalists couldn't keep secret the existence of recession in 1974 even if they had wanted to. The additional 1.3 million workers who had lost jobs in the past year didn't need the newspapers to tell them that the economy was in a decline. Moreover, to the extent that the public was better informed of the details of the intertwined domestic and international pictures, and congressional responses were subject to scrutiny in a democratic way, the better would be the chances for sensible solutions. Yet there always has been, for as long as I can remember in my reporting career, a certain element at the very top in the business world that thinks the media ought deliberately to serve up more optimistic appraisals, like cheerleaders rooting for the home team. Along with Wriston, some of the biggest sinners during the Ford recession were auto executives, such as General Motors boss Thomas A. Murphy, who were staggered by the biggest percentage drops in car sales since the Great Depression. American families were not rushing into dealers' showrooms because the newspapers were recording the decline in sales but because they had lost confidence in the economy. Surveys by public opinion analysts William Watts and Lloyd A. Free showed that since 1972 the number of persons who felt that the economy had lost ground had doubled from 22 percent to 44 percent, and the number who felt that ground had been lost in the fight against inflation had zoomed from 58 percent to 88 percent.[26]

But as against Wriston and Murphy, who wanted sugarcoated "facts" fed to an unsuspecting public, most intelligent businessmen wanted the news dished up with accuracy. That's why *The Wall Street Journal* was a success, and that's why the newsletter put out by the First National City Bank, a subsidiary of Wriston's Citicorp, had a wide circulation. The November 25, 1974, edition of that newsletter, for example, reporting on the recession "mess," said that the downturn actually "began as a failure of perception" on the part of "optimistic business managers" who missed "recessionary signals." So much for Wriston and his complaint that it was journalists who lacked proper perspective.

The Ford administration itself had trouble taking off the blinders. In mid-November, Press Secretary Ronald H. Nessen admitted that "the country is moving into a recession," and White House economic coordinator L. William Seidman confided that the 1976 budget would show not a balance but a deficit.[27] But then President Ford took off for speechmaking and press conferences in Las Vegas and Phoenix, where he soothingly confided that all was well, that the economy would recover and inflation would turn down. And those reassurances came on the same day that the Bureau of Labor Statistics announced that wholesale prices had jumped 22.6 percent in the prior year, the most for any twelve-month period since 1947.

IN FEBRUARY 1975, Ford sent a budget for fiscal 1976 to Congress not only acknowledging candidly that a recession in fact was at hand but that it would be twice as deep as any other in the postwar period, with unemployment projected to rise to 8 percent in 1975 and stay that high throughout 1976.[28] Ford's budget sketched out a period of stagnation and high unemployment, with economic growth an unsatisfactory 1 percent, lasting four years.

In the Eisenhower years of 1957–58, in a brief two-quarter recession, the real gross national product had dropped 3.9 percent, the largest postwar slide. The first Eisenhower recession, four quarters in 1953–54, had resulted in a 3.4 percent GNP decline. But now things were worse: already, in the four quarters of 1974, there had been a drop of 5 percent from the peak in the final three months of 1973. The Ford budget projected a continuation of the decline at least through mid-1975, and probably into the third quarter, with an overall GNP loss of 7.3 to 7.5 percent.

The projected inflation rates were equally disturbing: from 6.2 percent in 1973, the consumer price index had shot up 11.0 percent in 1974, and was expected to go to 11.3 percent in 1975 before falling back to a still unsatisfactory 7.8 percent in 1976. Without exception, Democratic economists were stunned by the willingness of Ford and Greenspan to publish such bearish projections—and no plan to cope. Okun, in a private conversation, told me: "No president I ever worked for would ever have put these numbers into print. If we believed [such projections], we'd be proposing something else [in terms of policy changes]." But Greenspan, commenting on the Economic Report that followed the budget, said the function of presidential advisers is "not to think up a report to restore confidence—our job is to tell it as it is."[29]

Ford and Greenspan were telling the nation that for the next six years it would have to suffer two solid years of unemployment in the 8 percent range, and four years of hard times after that before nudging the jobless rate under 7 percent. George Meany predicted the jobless rate would hit 10 percent by mid-July, but even an 8 percent national unemployment rate would, of course, mean black unemployment around 15 percent and teenage unemployment of 23 to 25 percent. Acceptance of such results betrayed a sense of political unreality, and foretold with almost infallible certainty that Ford would lose the election in 1976, no matter who was on the Democratic ticket. Ford was not saying that the economic outlook was horrible, and that he proposed to do something about it. Stubbornly, he was saying that the outlook was horrible—and the only antirecession medicine would be a one-shot tax cut that Greenspan conceded would not halt the decline in output but merely shave it a little. Ford and Greenspan were willing to drag the nation through a long period of recession and stagnation, in which layoffs would mount, profits shrink, and business expansion be postponed—all in the hope that austerity would cure the inflationary menace.

Greenspan's argument was that pumping up the economy offered no guarantee that the unsatisfactory rate of unemployment would be cut much—and whatever further reduction of the jobless rate might be produced by that method would be at the expense of a new, long-term burst of inflation. But the recession had gained so much momentum that in the two weeks between Ford's 1975 State of the Union address and the printers' final lockup of the pages of the budget document, the projected deficit for fiscal 1976 had jumped $5 billion, from $47 billion to $52 billion. "Suffer, it will be good for you in the long run," was one way of translating Ford and Greenspan's decision. Ford and Greenspan, honest if misguided men, had concluded that pumping up the economy offered no guarantee of reducing unemployment—and that if pump priming did manage to cut the jobless rate, the price might be inflation later on.

For all the noise Democratic politicians made about the inadequacy of Ford's economic programs, however, they pretty much bought his line. There was little to distinguish the unemployment and budget deficit targets set by the Democratic-controlled Congress from Ford's. Both parties more or less accepted Greenspan's analysis that excessive stimulus would merely regenerate inflation. And that left only diehard liberal economists such as Heller and Okun calling for more expansionist policies, making them uncomfortable bedfellows with Meany, who angrily denounced Republicans and Democrats alike for opting for high unemployment "in the sacred name of holding down the size of the budget deficit."[30]

The course that Ford, Greenspan, and Burns had chosen assured high unemployment. The president and Greenspan never considered going back to wage-price controls or to some form of "social contract" as insurance against the inflationary impact of a more stimulative program. After Ford and Greenspan came front and center with their bleak projections, a national debate ensued over how to rescue the economy from the disaster, which was compounded by Ford's inability to cope with it.

A year later, Ford reversed gears. In January 1975, he proposed a moderate tax cut that was boosted by Democrats on the Hill to a total of $23.1 billion—and Ford reluctantly signed the bill on March 29. In a brief radio and TV speech to the nation that day, Ford also raised his estimate of the fiscal 1976 deficit to $60 billion, well below congressional estimates of the real red-ink flow. Burns and Simon had recommended a veto, but Ford overruled them and was guided instead by Greenspan, Seidman, and John Dunlop, whom he had appointed labor secretary in February.

Dunlop, square-jawed and bow-tied, was one of the bright spots in a below-par cabinet. In twenty-five years of prior service, including the chairmanship, under Nixon, of the now-defunct Cost of Living Council, Dunlop was one of a rare breed of bureaucrats who had a record of pragmatic dealings with union leaders and a reputation for being sympathetic to their cause. But it was less a pro-labor bias that enabled Dunlop to carve out an unusual role than his belief that the federal government must create a series of "structural changes" in the way business and labor conduct their affairs. As a microeconomist, Dunlop thought that macroeconomists, by concentrating on the big picture, tended to miss critical deficiencies in specific sectors of the economy. Dunlop wanted more attention focused, for example, on how to bring teenagers into the labor market. The high jobless rates among young people, he thought, represented a failure of the labor market as well as of the educational system. Liberal economists, most of whom were macrospecialists, didn't care much for Dunlop, arguing that he had an ideological bias against wage-price controls. But Dunlop was committed to getting people back to work, and he brought to the Ford administration a sympathetic channel to a disenchanted labor movement.

The tax cut bill Ford signed was a hybrid of the good and the bad, something for everybody. On the positive side, while it averaged a not-insignificant 14.3 percent reduction from 1974 tax liabilities (including rebates of up to $200 per taxpayer), the biggest cuts were in the lower brackets—as much as a 47 percent reduction for those earning less than $10,000, with the use of the first "earned income credit," a form of negative income tax, at the lowest end of the scale. On the bad side, there was an inexcusable giveaway, estimated at $600 million, in the form of a credit up to $2,000 for the purchase of a new house or mobile home if it were under construction by March 26, 1975. This was a bonanza designed for the benefit of home builders, financed by Uncle Sam, one of many illustrations of the political clout of the housing lobby.[31] There were other deficiencies in the tax legislation, including and especially an increase in the investment tax credit to 10 percent, in effect price cuts for equipment that companies in most instances would have bought without the tax credit. That credit alone was worth about $3.3 billion to business.

But on the whole, the tax-cutting effort was praised by Democrats as the magic potion that would pump some life into a dormant economy, provided consumers had the courage to dig into their fatter purses and spend some of the money. The critical question, however, was directed to the Fed. Now that fiscal policy was eased, what would Arthur Burns do? And as he tenaciously clung to a restrictive policy, the criticism of Burns reached a crescendo, triggering a congressional resolution that for the first time required the Fed to present to both banking committees quarterly estimates of the Fed's targets for the growth of the money supply.[32]

Burns, at seventy-one, was outwardly unperturbed by the controversy swirling about him. His workaholic pace, seven full days a week, wore out younger subordinates. Burns had a sense of mission, an overwhelming ego, and the belief that, while others might waver, he would stick to his convictions. Yes, he told me, "recession is the number-one problem in the short run. But inflation is the number one in the longer run. It is because of the past inflation that we now have a recession. If we are to have prosperity in the long run, we must guard very carefully against inflation in the future."

Others disagreed. Former CEA member James Tobin said bluntly that "the Fed's tight-money policy caused the recession." Arthur Brimmer, who had bucked Burns's iron rule when he was a member of the Fed board, also argued that monetary policy under Burns was "stuck," and instead should be shifted into a generous creation of monetary reserves that—along with the tax cut—would lubricate economic recovery.

But Burns regarded the new requirement to publish monetary growth targets at a public hearing as a challenge to his and the Fed's authority. He had never accepted the new and popular emphasis on monetary targets and the monetary supply as advocated by Friedman. The Fed, he would say, can do only so much to increase the money supply, and the rest depends on "velocity," that is, the willingness of businessmen and consumers to hold, use, and borrow money. He feared that if the Fed was forced to pick a precise target for money growth for political reasons, there would be pressure brought on the central bank to achieve the target, whether or not the number fitted the needs of a shifting economy. What Burns ignored was the fact that the target could be changed if the economic needs changed.

When he appeared on May 1, 1975, before the Senate Banking Committee, he made the first-ever announcement of a 5 to 7.5 percent target for the growth of the basic money supply—currency and checking accounts—known as M-1. That would be larger than 1974's 4.7 percent growth, but implied a steadier pattern, long demanded by monetarists, contrasting with the wild swings that had thus far prevailed—from a minus 9 percent in January to plus 12.7 percent in March, for an average of plus 3.5 percent. Burns thought that too much attention was being paid to M-1, and that M-2, which included savings deposits other than large certificates of deposit, was a better indicator. That measure of the money supply had grown by 8.5 percent.[33]

He turned aside suggestions from senators that the Fed should follow a more stimulative policy, accepting risks in view of the high unemployment rate. "I'm not going to say other economists are wrong," Burns said slowly, "but"—his voice rose—"I have found that most economists these days move from one platform to another, and they pay too little attention to the business cycle. They've never really studied it thoroughly, or if they have, they've forgotten what they once knew."[34]

Burns was unmoved by suggestions that he ease up his severely restraining money policy, foiling the expectations of those economists who had predicted economic recovery once the tax cut took hold. Milton Friedman and John Kenneth Galbraith, the strangest of bedfellows, contended still that inflation, not recession, was the problem; and they were joined by Andrew Brimmer (who changed his mind later), Beryl Sprinkel, and Walter Hoadley, among others. They were terribly wrong. "Most of the [Ford] summit forecasts turned sour because they didn't predict Arthur Burns properly," Brookings economist George Perry shrewdly observed.[35]

Burns had only one vote of seven on the Fed board, and one of twelve on the Federal Open Market Committee that established policy for the overall Federal Reserve System. By force of prestige, knowledge, personality, and respect, Burns dominated the process. On Capitol Hill, he was equally in command. But there was trouble inside the institution. Independent-minded governors like Brimmer chafed under Burns's sometimes schoolmasterish methods, including rules on speechmaking and restraints on interviews with reporters that they considered tantamount to censorship. "We have an extremely powerful central bank," Brimmer confided after he left the board, "and it is not being run by a board, as was intended by

Congress, but by the chairman."[36] The high-level staff members, traditionally anonymous and unseen, were mostly younger and more liberal than Burns, and anguished that monetary policy was not being used effectively to tackle high unemployment, on the certain edge of double digits. Some staff members told me privately that they were ashamed, in such circumstances, to admit that they were economists.

Burns was challenged also by a growing expertise in monetary affairs in Congress. Where Representative Wright Patman, a Texas Democrat, could rail at Burns in the old days out of his populist convictions, a new sophistication was being developed on the Hill, especially on the Banking Committees and at the Joint Economic Committee, enabling Congress members to grapple with Burns in his own language and, if necessary, with the same arcane skills. Thus a private memorandum from his staff to House Banking Committee member Henry Reuss of Wisconsin (who came from a banking family) questioned Burns's claim that he had attempted to expand the money supply in the final two quarters of 1974, only to be frustrated by inadequate loan demand: "The Federal Reserve could have expanded the money supply adequately if they had pursued a more aggressive policy of reserve expansion."

The central bank's principal way of affecting the supply of money in the hands of the public is through buying and selling federal government bonds and other securities in the open, or private, market. When it buys securities, the cash it hands over adds to deposits in the banking system, expanding total bank reserves. Thus when the Fed chooses to expand the money supply, it announces that it is a buyer of federal securities. Conversely, when the Fed wants to tighten the money supply, it sells government securities, thus draining cash out of bank reserves. Since bank reserves are the base on which banks make loans to business, the fatter the reserves, the more lending power the banks acquire; and when reserves are skimpy, then the banks have fewer dollars to lend. And when reserves are plentiful, then the banks are willing to lend money at lower interest rates; when reserves are drained by Fed action, the banks can and do charge more. So there is a direct relationship between the level of bank reserves and interest rates: the larger the reserves, the easier it is for business to borrow money—to expand operations, or perhaps to build up supplies and inventories. When they do, that adds to the money supply: as a business borrows money, it opens up a line of credit at the bank, actually creating money as it writes checks and passes them on to suppliers and others in the system. Each dollar of reserves held by the bank can support about six dollars of money created through loans.

That was the theory, in any event. Burns's contention was that the money supply hadn't increased as expected because business wasn't anxious to borrow. His critics were saying that he didn't move rapidly enough to supply reserves to the banks. Burns was afraid of creating too much money because his number-one target was inflation, Brimmer said.

In retrospect, it seems clear that Burns's overweening focus on the evils of inflation over a four-year period, starting from his first day as Nixon's chairman of the Fed in 1970, had helped precipitate the debacle of the 1974–75 recession. New York investment banker Henry Kaufman theorized that Burns's basic mistake was in being "duped" by the private banking system during that period, in which he failed to check their speculative excesses. By the time Burns caught on, in 1974, to the bankers' greed, "he had created an environment in which there was an explosion of debt creation," Kaufman said. Then, to prevent the possibility of another collapse like that of the Franklin National Bank of New York, he had to apply the screws. Thus the economy was condemned to suffer a painful period of stagnation to satisfy Ford's and Burns's fears of inflation.

IN MID-1975, as President Ford struggled with recession and high unemployment at home, he had no coherent foreign economic policy. One problem was the absence of any administrative vehicle for consideration and development of such a policy—a situation that America's friends in Europe found astounding. The Nixon administration had created a Council on International Economic Priorities (CIEP) in 1971 to deal with overlapping foreign economic responsibilities. But Ford chose not to name an executive director for the council, and its function, in a practical sense, vanished. Thus there was no one available to referee differences cropping up daily among the State, Treasury, Commerce, and Agriculture departments—and sometimes between members of the cabinet and Arthur Burns.37

Our friends abroad had firsthand evidence of this policy failure. In mid-June 1975, at a bankers' conference in Amsterdam, Burns told a group of American and European journalists that after years of refusing to discuss the "overhang" of American currency abroad—a surplus of some $100 billion to $150 billion in U.S. greenbacks held by foreign central banks that they could no longer turn in for gold—Washington was willing to discuss how to whittle that overhang down as part of the process of reshaping the international monetary system.

At the precise moment that Burns was talking, Treasury Secretary Simon's public relations assistant was distributing the text of a luncheon speech to the bankers in which Simon downplayed the seriousness of the overhang problem. But when Simon learned what Burns had said, he scrapped that part of his speech and, after the lunch, hastily called a press conference of his own to try to paper over the difference.

Back in Washington a few days later, however, Treasury Undersecretary Jack F. Bennett debunked the urgency of the problem as outlined by Burns, adding that in his view the dollar overhang didn't even exist "in the old-fashioned sense." For foreigners, it was confusing. In the end, nothing came of Burns's idea, which was to let the foreigners trade in some of their dollars to the International Monetary Fund for special drawing rights (SDRs), the IMF's bookkeeping unit of account that could be used as a way of getting convertible currencies of real value. Over the years, Burns had proposed, the United States would gradually pay off the debt to the IMF.

The split between Simon and Secretary of State Henry Kissinger on energy issues was even more basic. In mid-1975, Kissinger overrode Simon's objections, and rammed down Ford's throat an inflationary energy policy conjured up by Assistant Secretary of State Thomas O. Enders, consisting of a proposed "floor" price on imported oil for all consuming countries, as well as a $2 per barrel added tariff that Ford had decided to impose. It was, in effect, an open invitation to OPEC to raise its prices, but it did very little for America's economic security.

Kissinger and Simon also locked horns on the question of how to give poor world producers of such basic commodities as cocoa, copper, and tin greater stability for the price of what they sold in world markets, which was critical to sustaining their levels of income. In a series of speeches—the first in Kansas City, followed by two in Europe—Kissinger recognized that the United States and other rich nations had to meet some of the demands of the poor nations for price stability for a whole range of raw materials. He didn't propose anything very radical, merely that new arrangements be considered on a case-by-case basis. It hardly met the extreme demands for a "new world economic order," including insistence that the "have" nations transfer some of their wealth to the "have-nots," then being mounted by many of the producer countries.

All such radical, interventionist ideas, as well as Kissinger's more modest tokenism, didn't sit well at the Treasury, where Simon and

Assistant Treasury Secretary Gerald L. Parsky were devoted to preservation of the old economic order, based on unregulated free markets. Simon, a successful and wealthy Wall Street investor, had succeeded George Shultz as Nixon's Treasury secretary, and stayed on for Ford. Simon was Adam Smith reincarnated. In a speech to business journalists in 1975, Simon had said that "we must begin to place more reliance on ourselves and the free enterprise system and less upon government. The government has become so huge and domineering—and we have turned to it so often for solutions that have fallen short of our dreams—that the time has come to rediscover how much can be accomplished by price enterprise and by men and women who are free to determine their own destinies."[38]

Simon was especially irked by Kissinger's penchant for secrecy. Already vexed by Kissinger's proposal for a "floor price" for oil, Simon was stunned when Kissinger's Kansas City speech came to the Treasury for clearance. Kissinger had quietly worked out the details with Undersecretary of State Charles Robinson, and with Enders, and hadn't tipped off Simon, head of Ford's Economic Policy Board, the senior policy group within the White House. Simon sent Parsky over to State to get the language toned down: for example, Kissinger's earlier draft proposal for "indexing" the prices of key raw commodities—so that they would automatically move up with inflation—was abandoned. And Simon got a promise that his council would be cut in on any future Kissinger adventures into foreign economic policy making. He was backed, in this instance, by Burns, who had similar free-market commitments. Nonetheless, it was clear to Simon that he would have to fight a rearguard action to prevent Kissinger from going too far.

Simon became a leading and articulate spokesman for the far right. With a straight face, he said to congressional Republicans: "We're talking about the difference between freedom and socialism." In his view, he and Ford were the apostles of freedom, and the Democrats were socialist big spenders who wouldn't let the private sector manage its own money. What bothered Simon was what he regarded as an explosion of government. Simon was Ronald Reagan in disguise, six years ahead of time. In August, he made a speech to the Junior Achievers Conference in Bloomington, Illinois, in which he declared: "We are trying to lift the dead hand of governmental regulation so that the spirit of free enterprise can flourish again."[39] Simon couldn't acknowledge—or understand—that Adam Smith's invisible hand was not perfectly discriminating in a modern, complex society, that government had to act to protect the public in the many instances when the so-called free market failed. Instead of looking to achieve government efficiencies with sound cost-benefit ratios, Simon talked wistfully of "deregulation" and abandonment of what he considered the "welfare state."

There was a good contemporaneous rebuttal to Simon's fear that every dollar of expanding government services represented a new achievement for socialism: Arthur Okun published a fine book, *Equality and Efficiency: The Big Tradeoff*, arguing that the nation had an efficient mixed system, for all its warts, and certainly one not drifting into socialism. "The rights and powers that money should not buy must be protected with detailed regulations and sanctions, and with countervailing aids to those with low incomes," Okun wrote. The nation should be happy, he added, that "the Government got in the business of pensions and unemployment insurance, of financing basic research, and of electric power."[40]

ON THE HOME FRONT, given a boost by rising domestic oil prices, inflation rates jumped into double digits. The consumer price index rose a stunning 15.4 percent in July 1975. At annualized and compounded rates, the price of fuel was up 32 percent, and food was up 22 percent—and no part could be blamed on a worldwide commodities boom, on shortages, or on excessive demand. Rather, a whole raft of American industries experiencing falling demand, including autos, steel, aluminum, and paper, were able to raise their prices in defiance of normal free market rules. In addition, as of September 1, all domestic oil prices were decontrolled. Enormous new sales of grain to the Soviet Union helped drive up the price of wheat and corn. Yet the Ford administration was seemingly incapable of action. The president and his aides prayed for good weather that would boost grain harvests, and for restraint by the oil industry after decontrol.

Ford's excuse for vetoing legislation that would have extended control over oil prices was that extension of regulation would have delayed indefinitely "America's start on the road to energy independence." But decontrol actually had little to do with "independence" from imported oil, and everything to do with assurance that there would be further oil price increases, from American producers as well as from OPEC. This additional upward thrust to energy prices came at a time when economic recovery from a serious recession was fragile at best in the United States, and hadn't got started anywhere else in the world, still suffering from the OPEC sting of 1973. Energy independence was then, and is now, a faulty concept because there was little prospect that America could do without substantial oil imports; and given the fact that half of the world's known oil reserves were in the Middle East, it was certain that we would always need to import much of those requirements from the OPEC producers.

Decontrol also assured that the profits of the multinational oil companies would skyrocket, as they marked their prices up to the world level, or to whatever price OPEC would set. "Decontrol," said Milton Friedman, "will not produce a sharp immediate rise on the price of petroleum." Instead, "ultimately it will lower prices as the free market works its magic."[41] The Ford administration was in accord with this blind devotion to free-market principles, even though the oil market was in effect being run by a foreign cartel that had set a monopoly price—and by a powerful, concentrated oil industry at home.

But the blame had to be shared by a Democratic-controlled Congress that did not reduce reliance on OPEC crude oil. The United States continued to waste enormous amounts of energy, and was ill prepared for the second oil shock in 1979, which made a shambles out of the predictions of Friedman and others who sold Ford on decontrol. By that time, of course, Jimmy Carter was in office, and the economic consequences of the failure to generate a meaningful energy policy would help make Carter a one-term president, setting the stage for Ronald Reagan.

No one can be sure that the October 30, 1975, New York *Daily News* headline—"Ford to New York: Drop Dead!"—actually cost Ford reelection in the race against Carter in 1976: Ford was carrying a lot of other negative baggage. But when Treasury Secretary Simon, speaking for Ford, rejected Mayor Abraham Beame's plea for financial help to keep the city afloat, New Yorkers were stunned, and that reaction was accurately summarized by the *Daily News* headline. Carter went on to win New York State's thirty-six electoral votes by a skinny 300,000 vote margin, Ford getting 724,000 fewer votes than Nixon had received in 1972. Carter thereupon squeaked by with 297 electoral votes to Ford's 240. Had Ford held New York, the electoral college vote would have been 276 for him to 261 for Carter.

At stake in the New York City crisis was $10.3 billion in city bonds, and $12.5 billion in New York State obligations that were in potential jeopardy. A recently created New York Municipal Assistance Corporation (MAC), chaired by New York banker Felix Rohatyn, had refinanced another $2 billion of city bonds. That still left almost $23 billion in combined city-state obligations that might be defaulted, a bankruptcy six times the largest corporate bankruptcy in American history—the default on $3.7 billion worth of bonds by the Penn Central Railroad. Nonetheless, Simon blandly told New York municipal leaders that they could avoid default by cutting spending. And if they did have to tell their bondholders New York couldn't make good, the city "would continue to exist and operate." New York governor Hugh L. Carey, echoing concerns expressed by almost every major banker in New York, warned that a New York City default would "start an exodus of business firms from New York from which it will never recover." Calmly, Simon counseled the city to declare a voluntary bankruptcy, saying that would assure it a sufficient cash flow from taxes to maintain essential services and to pay off long-term bondholders. In any event, Simon said, the default wouldn't affect the economic health of the rest of the country. Simon, about as compassionate as was Jonah for the wicked biblical city of Nineveh, had concluded that New York had been profligate and now deserved to suffer. He believed that the "costs and risks" of help to New York "would outweigh the benefits." In terms of the impact on the rest of the country, he told me, "default would be tolerable and temporary."

Ford and Simon were comforted by the knowledge that there was little love lost for New York City in the rest of the country. Indeed, as Bank of America president A. W. (Tom) Clausen told the Senate Banking Committee, there existed in the rest of the country a sort of "perverse glee" at New York's plight. Yet, he noted, "the financial markets are floundering" as a result of New York's inability to raise money. Clausen told me that he had started out philosophically opposed to aiding New York, and then altered his views "the hard way."[42] As president of what was then America's largest bank, Clausen said that "you start with the premise that the survival of the fittest is the law of the land, or ought to be, and that's okay up to a point. But when we started to think really seriously about the problem and discussed all of the ramifications—what might happen and what the ramifications were—it just started to become clearer and clearer that federal assistance was the least onerous of the alternatives." Yet other senior figures in the business world were disposed to feel that a New York going "belly-up" would have only temporary effects that would be quickly absorbed by the economy.[43]

It was undeniable that every time interest rates went up a half point taxpayers in cities and states across the country, excluding New York, found the bill for their own municipal bond issues rising by an aggregate of $1 billion a year. Yet the distaste for New York in some parts of the South and Midwest was there, part of middle America's provincialism and ethnic prejudice.

A background report by the Congressional Budget Office—a bipartisan body established in 1974 to provide expert analysis of budgetary issues for use by members of Congress—said that unless the rest of the country decided to take some of New York's poor blacks and Puerto Ricans, and parcel them out among "suburban and rural jurisdictions," there was no alternative but to relieve the city of "some major portions of its current fiscal responsibility." New York City had indeed been a big spender, even profligate, as Simon had said. But the political stupidity of ignoring the problem was evident on all sides. Some fourteen mayors of other American cities, representing the entire membership of the U.S. Conference of Mayors, showed up in Washington to announce their angst: if New York City were allowed to go belly-up because it couldn't pay off bondholders, the same fate could befall others. "We all look on New York as symptomatic of a national urban crisis overlooked in Washington," said Detroit's Coleman A. Young.

If New York could go broke, the mayors asked Ford in a two-hour meeting at the White House, why not any city in the nation? Mayor Henry W. Maier of Milwaukee, a city with a fabled triple-A credit rating, warned that a New York default would have a "chilling effect" in his town and elsewhere. In mid-October 1975, the city of Rochester, New York, like Milwaukee triple-A rated, had to pay an interest penalty of $540,000 on a twelve-month $27 million borrowing at 6 percent. Were it not for the "investment stigma" arising from New York City's woes, according to the Dow Jones News Service, Rochester could have borrowed the money at about 4 percent. But all such evidence, and warnings that there would be more such bad news, didn't move Ford and Simon.

Temporarily, at the risk of its own credit standing, New York State came to the city's aid. But clearly, federal help was urgent. The first hint that the administration's Calvinist reaction would be amended came in an interview I had with Simon, in which he said that if New York State were threatened with default, "that would add a dimension to the problem that would require close scrutiny."[44] Belatedly, Simon—schooled by Arthur Burns—began to understand that the crisis was generating not only great uncertainty in global financial markets, but a feeling among key allies that common sense had taken a holiday.

Michael Getler, *The Washington Post*'s Bonn correspondent, reported that West German chancellor Helmut Schmidt had concluded that Ford was playing with fire by not coming to New York's assistance, and was preparing to tell him so face to face in a Washington visit. Ford's arm was also twisted in an Oval Office meeting attended by three leading New York bankers—David Rockefeller of Chase Manhattan, Ellmore C. Patterson of the Morgan Guaranty

Trust Company, and Walter Wriston of the First National City Bank.

The extreme narrowness of Ford's view of the problem was revealed by none other than Vice President Nelson Rockefeller—who of course had been lobbied by his brother David—but who was being bypassed by Ford and other White House officials on the New York issue. In an interview in the *U.S. News & World Report*, Rockefeller revealed that in April, when Abraham Beame first appealed for financial help, Ford complained to the diminutive mayor of the nation's biggest city that New York provided free tuition at the City University.

"Mr. Mayor," Rockefeller quoted Ford as saying to Mayor Beame, "I understand you have free tuition in your city university, and you're asking us to provide money for the city. We don't have free tuition in Lansing, Michigan. Why should the federal government provide free tuition for the students in New York City and not in other cities of the nation?"[45]

In his less than satisfactory defense of a great democratic principle, Beame responded, according to Rockefeller: "If we hadn't had free tuition, I wouldn't be here." Ford's willingness to belittle New York's far-sighted approach to a free education for talented but poor New York City high-school graduates was evidence that he essentially was a small-time politician propelled into a job far beyond his talent and capacity.[46] Ford should have been able to understand that if New York went bust, so could Lansing, Michigan—whether or not the City University of New York provided free tuition.

Rockefeller, however, was increasingly isolated in the Ford White House. Riding with him in his limousine from the Capitol to the White House in October, I found he could barely conceal his disgust with the way in which the president and Simon were dealing with the critical situation in New York City. He felt that a default would be a "catastrophe," with unpredictable consequences for the nation as a whole. He didn't even want to think of the dilemma that would be posed if the New York police or sanitation workers didn't get their regular paychecks. "Nobody can tell how far it can go, or what form it will take," Rockefeller said. Reminded that Simon had calmly assured anyone who would listen that a New York failure to meet its payments due on bonds would be "tolerable and temporary," Rockefeller shook his head. "It would be wonderful if he's right," he said. "But it's a pretty big gamble for the country. I'm the kind of guy who is not crazy about an uncertain situation. I like to take action in advance and have contingency plans ready."[47] Congress had a unique opportunity, Rockefeller felt, to help a Democratic mayor and a Democratic governor, even though he had been

critical of Carey for failing to call a special session of the state legis-
lature to advance funds to the city—essentially, a prepayment of
state funds scheduled to go to the city anyway.

To Europeans, it had always been incomprehensible that anyone
would even think of allowing New York City to go down the drain.
In Paris, an American businessman who had lived in Europe for
twenty years told me: "What you don't understand is that to Europeans, New York is America, and America is New York."

In the end, after flailing New York in stump speeches across the
country, Ford relented and came to New York City's aid in a limited
way after forcing some concessions from city and state politicians. In
the process, Ford earned the anger and distrust of some of the more
important men of the banking and business community who
thought he had played a dangerous game, risking damage to the national economy at a time when it seemed likely that unemployment
would continue to rise. With federal assistance, Rohatyn's MAC
pulled New York City back from the brink of bankruptcy. It would
again enjoy what Rohatyn would call "a remarkable renaissance, accompanied by a burst of civic enthusiasm."[48]

AT THE SAME time he was ignoring New York's plight, Ford was
trying to get Congress to agree to $28 billion worth of tax cuts, in
exchange for $28 billion in reductions in the ensuing year's budget,
to be made effective nine months later. It was a clever ploy, never
intended to do anything but knock out a Democratic proposal for
extending the 1975 tax cut, estimated to cost about $17 billion.

For months, Simon and Greenspan had been warning about the
dangers of mounting federal deficits. Budget Director James T. Lynn
had estimated fiscal 1976 red ink at anywhere from $50 billion to an
extreme of $90 billion. Simon topped the scare stories with a guess of
around $100 billion, signifying the strong opposition of this band of
fiscal conservatives to extension of the expiring 1975 tax cuts. When
pressured by finance ministers abroad to "reflate" the economy,
Simon responded that he was concerned that American fiscal policy
was already too expansionary.

Yet, suddenly, Ford raised the tax cut ante by a neat $11 billion—
from $17 billion represented by a simple extension of the 1975 rates
to $28 billion, but tied to a $28 billion in unspecified budget reductions that would take force nine months after the tax cut.

The explanation for the nonsensical $28 billion tax cut/$28 billion expenditure cut proposal, its two parts separated by nine
months, was that Ford had heard the noises being made in the back-

ground by an ambitious Ronald Reagan, who talked about "getting the government off our backs." Ford decided that by playing louder tax-cut music, he could drown out the Democrats who merely wanted to extend the 1975 tax cuts. Then by sounding elaborate cut-spending, "knock out big government" themes, he could please the Republican right wing and undercut Reagan, who looked like a serious threat for the 1976 Republican nomination. The tax cuts would come on January 1, 1976, but the budget-cutting ax wouldn't be swung until October 1, 1976, too late to have an impact by Election Day.

On October 18, 1975, in the White House's Roosevelt Room, along with a handful of columnists and reporters invited by Ford, I listened to the president try with a straight face to suggest he wasn't playing election year politics. How come a $28 billion tax cut wouldn't be inflationary, when his chief advisers had been saying that $17 billion would run the country into the ground, Ford was asked. "I have to rely on what my economic advisers tell me on that, and they say it will have a minimal effect," Ford said lamely.

He turned first to Simon for support. Simon admitted that, with a larger deficit, the Treasury would have to borrow more money. But now Simon magically discovered "slack" in the economy, whereas until then his persistent argument was that Treasury borrowing would "crowd out" private borrowers, skyrocketing interest rates.[49]

When it came Greenspan's turn, he rationalized the prospective increase in the 1976 deficit that would be triggered by Ford's new proposal by saying that one has to "distinguish between short-term deficits and long-term deficits." In effect, Greenspan argued, it was better to accept a bigger deficit in fiscal 1976 in exchange for a reduced deficit in fiscal 1977—always assuming that Congress would agree to cut $28 billion from a budget it had not yet laid eyes on.

There were few outside the Ford White House who didn't think that $28 billion in tax cuts would provide an excessive stimulus to the economy—and that it would be difficult to get Congress later on to provide a $28 billion yank in the other direction. Liberals Walter Heller and George Perry argued only for extension of the lesser amount of expiring individual and business tax cuts.[50] Even Greenspan's old consulting firm, Townsend-Greenspan, Inc., suggested that its former owner's new idea "could introduce an undesirable element of volatility into the path of economic growth from 1976 to 1977."

In November 1975, at the request of Representative Al Ullman (D.-Ore.), chairman of the House Ways and Means Committee, CBO director Alice M. Rivlin polled seven well-known Democratic economists, and five equally famous Republican ones, on the question whether Ford's prospective failure to extend at least $12 billion of the expiring tax cuts in favor of his $28 billion offsetting scheme would thwart the recovery from recession then under way. All of the Democrats and some of the Republicans criticized Ford, warning that failure to extend the $12 billion in tax cuts would cause a sudden jump in tax withholding, thus causing consumers to retrench. He got a single unqualified endorsement, from former CEA member Marina von Neumann Whitman. There was also restrained approval from former CEA chairman Paul McCracken. But McCracken's successor, Herbert Stein, opposed Ford's program because he saw "the danger of inflationary overstimulation." Stein said that the impact of the tax cut, combined with the "monetary and psychological effects," would overwhelm any later expenditure cut—"if that would indeed materialize."[51]

Of course, all presidents play politics—especially in advance of an election—and Congress plays the game right back. What made the Ford ploy more serious was that a new congressional budget process had just been set in motion, under which a Budget Committee in each chamber had been established to work out overall spending, revenue, and deficit/surplus targets with the help of the CBO staff. The key to the exercise was a pair of concurrent resolutions, one to be passed by May 15 and the other by September 15 of each year, to set binding targets. On a dry run in 1975, Congress had started to take the process seriously, so much so that individual senators sponsoring spending legislation hesitated to challenge Edmund S. Muskie (D.-Me.), scheduled to be chairman of the new Budget Committee. Muskie was so successful on the floor of the Senate invoking the authority of the new process that George Meany began to refer to him—sarcastically—as "Mr. Fiscal Integrity." For example, Muskie successfully battled Senator John Stennis (D.-Miss.) on a defense budget authorization, and Senator George McGovern (D.-S.D.) voluntarily withdrew part of his proposal for child nutrition expenditures.

But with the new process scheduled to move from dry run to a first real effort with the new budget year beginning October 1, 1976 (a change from the then-existing fiscal year basis, which began on July 1), Ford was proposing that Congress junk the carefully blueprinted plans, in which it was taking some pride, by demanding that Congress adopt, in advance of the two newly scheduled resolutions, a budget ceiling of $395 billion, a cut of $28 billion from his projection that it would hit $423 billion.

"We don't know what goes into the $423 billion," Rivlin told the

National Economists Club. "Presumably, there is a real increase in some programs, including defense. That's the whole point. We better see what's in [the budget] before we start cutting it." Too casually, Ford seemed ready to abandon a genuine budget reform-in-the-making for his own short-term political gain. In doing so, he was willing to risk a confrontation with his old colleagues on Capitol Hill. "Apart from party," said Rivlin, "he's created a feeling that it's us against them."

Although battered and baffled by events at home, Ford was equally puzzled by economic events abroad. The vexing problems of oil costs, balance of payments, and trade protectionism remained to be solved. Ford's failure to do so had made the task of his successor all the more difficult.

7

The Birth of
Economic Summitry

IN THE MIDST of his battles with Congress and in face of the perceived need to build his political strength against the expected assault from the pro-Reagan forces in advance of the 1976 Republican convention, President Ford began to look more favorably on a proposal by French president Valery Giscard d'Estaing and West German chancellor Helmut Schmidt to participate in an economic summit at the Château de Rambouillet near Paris in December 1975.

The chain of events that began with the first economic summit, now an annual ritual, goes back to Nixon and his momentous decision in August 1971 to cut the link between the dollar and gold and to the establishment of a new set of "central" exchange rates, announced at the Smithsonian Institution. Expected to stabilize world currency relationships, the agreement had been followed by a steady slide that had brought the dollar down 40 percent from pre-Smithsonian levels. Since September 1972, a group of officials assembled by the International Monetary Fund—known as the Committee of twenty, or C-20 for short—had been studying ways in which the major nations could cooperate on trade and investment issues by a new system of exchange rates, avoiding the pitfalls of the old Bretton Woods system, whose rigid exchange rates had produced a rapid-fire series of monetary crises in the prior six or seven years. The twenty members, half from the rich nations, half from the Third World, were seeking a magical formula to provide "stable but adjust-

able" rates[1]—a nice-sounding but essentially meaningless phrase—
that they could put on the table at the September 1973 annual meeting of the IMF and World Bank in Nairobi.

Jobs, investment, and trade—these were the issues that brought
the industrial nations together at such international meetings. In the
early 1970s, the cost of producing goods in Europe and Japan for sale
in the United States (and in other markets) had been rising rapidly, as
wages moved up in Japan and Europe toward the high American standard. That process of moving toward equalization was dramatically
advanced by two dollar devaluations over a fourteen-month period
beginning in August 1971 that boosted the values of the German
deutsche mark and Japanese yen. Thus Japan and Germany—and
other European nations in a similar situation—faced an intriguing
dilemma: since they still had a comparative, although declining,
edge in terms of their labor costs, they could afford to see the dollar
move down modestly, even if that allowed America to generate a
trade surplus, hoping that such a surplus would encourage Washington to allow foreigners to cash in for gold (or something else of real
value) some of the $90 billion in excess paper dollars they then held.

But Europe and Japan could not tolerate a further sizable decline,
because that would price their goods out of the American market,
causing a serious loss of jobs in their home economies. Since the end
of 1968, for example, the deutsche mark had increased by 64 percent
in value, making German car makers (notably Volkswagen) uneasy
about their ability to export to the United States. And putting aside
questions of symbolism—does a weak currency suggest a weak nation, a strong currency a strong nation?—a dollar decline, if excessive compared to the currencies of its major competitors, could also
be unhealthy from the American perspective. Too cheap a dollar can
have two unfavorable results. First, it boosts the cost of goods imported into the United States, giving a thrust to inflation—in terms
of both higher imports and the shield given domestic manufacturers
who otherwise might find reasons to lower prices. And second, a
cheap dollar enables foreigners—using their stronger currencies—to
make sizable investments here.

There had been two tests for the economic brainpower assembled
for the annual IMF/World Bank meeting at Nairobi on September 23,
1973. For the IMF, the challenge was to evolve a halfway point somewhere between the fixed-rate relationships of the Bretton Woods system and a completely undisciplined float. For the World Bank, the
key assignment was to use the first IMF/Bank meeting ever held in
Africa—or, for that matter, in a Third World country—to highlight

the growing need of the poor countries for greater financial assistance from the rich First World.

Just two weeks before the meetings got under way, the IMF's annual report bemoaned the fact that currency values had fluctuated widely since the Bretton Woods system had disintegrated. In fact, since early in 1973, only the major European nations were maintaining close currency ties, while as a group floating their currencies against the dollar. The smaller developing nations tied, or pegged, their rates to either the dollar, the French franc, or the British pound.[2] With most currency relationships in a state of flux, the IMF report pointed out, the developing countries had to face a whole new set of uncertainties.

The Nairobi meeting was intended to provide an important test of whether the major nations could work cooperatively together—or whether they would split into competitive trade blocs to protect their export markets and jobs. They also would be tested on whether they could share their wealth with the poorer nations and—some far-thinking souls wondered—whether the West was willing to let the central economics of the East get their noses under the tent. The French were convinced that, as the world was brought closer together by technology, it made little sense to have one monetary system for the noncommunist world and another for those with other ideologies.

Such advanced thinking would have to wait for another score of years: the Nairobi meeting wasn't even up to the lesser tasks on its agenda. Instead of generating a cooperative spirit, Nairobi underscored the deep differences between the United States and its economic competitors. On the very first day, as the delegates gathered, H. J. Witteveen, the new IMF managing director, said that the target date for a monetary agreement had slipped to the fall of 1974.[3] What Witteveen and the C-20 planners could not have foreseen was that ten days after the Nairobi conference concluded, the 1973 Arab-Israeli war would break out, to be following by an Arab oil embargo and a 400 percent increase in the price of oil by December 1973. Although the embargo was dropped within five months, the first oil price shock set off serious global economic consequences, including a stunning impact on the oil-consuming nations' balance of payments deficits.

The first oil shock made moot the C-20 effort to find some kind of agreement leading to greater stability of exchange rates: the regime of floating rates would have to go on for some time.[4] (Indeed, it still prevails today.) It also wrote finis to the French drive for what their

finance minister at the Nairobi meeting called "mandatory and multilateral" convertibility, requiring those countries holding excess
dollars to turn them in, through the IMF, for other assets, presumably gold or the new special drawing rights. The Nairobi meeting
adjourned with an agreement that all unsolved questions should be
settled by July 31, 1974. It was, in retrospect, a kind of meaningless
adagio, serious men on all sides unaware of events soon to overtake
them.[5]

After the dismal Nairobi result, French president Georges Pompidou kept up the pressure to restore stability to exchange rates by
returning to at least a degree of dependence on gold. The United
States countered with a complicated proposal to create a certain degree of discipline by installing a "reserve indicator" system: if a nation's monetary reserves swelled beyond a certain level, it would
have to revalue its exchange rate, or change its domestic economic
policies in ways that would make it less attractive for foreign investment money. And the converse would be true: if reserves fell, that
would be the signal for devaluation. But the Europeans, led by
France, didn't like the idea, arguing that speculators could read the
signs in advance.

A Nixon-Pompidou summit at Reykjavik, Iceland, in December
1973, designed to bridge the differences, failed totally, despite a full
complement of the highest financial advisers on each side.[6] Then
further efforts to narrow U.S.-European differences collapsed when
OPEC boosted oil prices, which led all the countries, including those
that favored fixed currency rates, to concede they would have to
learn to live with some measure of floating.

There was one more abortive effort to patch up the differences
between France and the United States prior to the 1975 economic
summit in Rambouillet. Giscard had succeeded Pompidou as president of France, and met with Ford in a one-on-one summit in Martinique in December 1974. There Ford yielded to the Frenchman's
views on gold, whereas just the year before at Reykjavik, Nixon had
faced down Pompidou's pitch to restore gold's tarnished status. The
Martinique communiqué said that Ford and Giscard agreed "it
would be appropriate for any government which wished to do so to
adopt current market prices as the basis for valuation of its gold holdings."[7]

France for a long time had been pressing for the right to revalue
its gold reserves at the then-prevalent $190 per ounce free-market
price, almost five times the official $42.22 price. Giscard, since his
days as finance minister in 1973, had been a leading critic of the
American commitment to "export inflation." He and Banque de

France governor Olivier Wormser set in motion a campaign to give gold, revalued to about $125 an ounce, a more important role in any new international monetary system.[8] The U.S. position had been to try to demonetize gold to avoid the risk of inflating the world's monetary base (and incidentally providing a huge bonanza to the Soviet Union and South Africa); but the Martinique decision seemed to reinforce the status of gold within the monetary system.

It was against this background of the French-led European struggle to dilute the impact of floating rates generated by Nixon in the tumultuous year 1971 that talk began to generate in mid-1975 about a summit at which the heads of state would focus only on economic issues, especially the elements that the French considered to represent a monetary crisis. According to Paul Volcker, the summit process got its start when Secretary of the Treasury George Shultz invited the British, French, and German finance ministers to meet with him on March 25, 1973, in the White House library to talk about the future of the world monetary system.[9] Soon the Japanese finance minister was added, and the emerging committee became known as the Group of Five finance ministers, which met regularly, and mostly in secret, to try to keep balance in the global monetary system. Sometimes, when financial markets rumored that they had got together, the G-5 would stonewall and deny there had been a meeting. The existence of the G-5 was considered an affront by many other major nations, especially the industrial countries that were grouped with the G-5 as the Group of Ten, all of whom were called on to make extra contributions, when needed, to the resources of the IMF.[10] But it was more than two years before the Group of Five could take the next logical step—an annual summit of the heads of government in a private and intimate setting. In essence, it had to wait until Schmidt and Giscard had each graduated from finance minister to head of government and head of state respectively before the first one could take place.

Giscard's goal was to overcome American resistance on international monetary reform, as well as to create a convenient diversion from France's domestic economic problems by introducing additional world leaders into global discussions. Ford's inner cabinet was wary about the prospect that the president, no giant on economic theory, would have to face three old economic pros—Giscard, Schmidt, and British prime minister Harold Wilson—with no one at his elbow to prompt him when necessary. Ford looked to be out of his depth in such an encounter, especially after Martinique.

Helmut Schmidt's aim at Rambouillet was bold and blunt: in company with Giscard, Schmidt looked to the summit as a means of

boosting the potential of Franco-German leadership of a stronger
Europe that would in turn play a more dominant global role. A secondary objective—even as he resisted juicing up the German economy—was to get Ford to lead the world out of recession via a major
American expansionary program.

Secretary of State Henry Kissinger, meanwhile, was anxious to
establish better relations with France, and events and changed personnel in early 1975 led to new flexibility on both sides.[11] Among
other things, Edwin H. Yeo succeeded Jack Bennett as undersecretary for monetary affairs at the Treasury in the spring, and struck up
a close working relationship with Jacques de Larosière, his opposite
number in the French Treasury. Bennett, a Simon disciple, was a
conservative, strict constructionist with a dour personality. The ro-
tund, jolly Ed Yeo was more adaptable and a better negotiator. His
accord with Larosière—produced in a series of eight meetings in the
elegant Ministry of Finance office at 93 rue de Rivoli in October and
November 1975[12]—proved invaluable not only in the run-up to the
Rambouillet summit, but also in its follow-through at the summit
and immediately afterward at a January IMF meeting in Jamaica that
set up the framework of the international monetary system as it exists today. Yeo and Larosière, as they began their marathon negotiations, hoped that they might work something out in time for the
Jamaica meeting; then, as the prospect of a summit became a greater
reality, an understanding on monetary issues by the time of the
Rambouillet meeting became their top priority.

Yeo and Larosière agreed that exchange rates were less a determining factor in the economic system than a reflection of what was
going on—and that a certain amount of stability (the French goal)
was a good, rather than a bad, attribute. A final theme of the Yeo-
Larosière accord was that rather than impose a par value system,
with no "asset settlement" to give punch to the system, it would be
better to strive for improvement of basic underlying economic policies. That led to the proposal, subsequently adopted at Rambouillet
and then at the Jamaica IMF meeting, of an authorization for the IMF
to undertake a formal "surveillance" of each country's policies. That
was a far-sighted, even daring concept, because it implied a degree of
subordination of national sovereignty to an international authority.

Meanwhile, during the late summer and early fall of 1975, Representative Henry Reuss kept up a persistent campaign from his van-
tage point on Capitol Hill to argue that IMF members ought to have
the option of following flexible rates if they chose to do so. Reuss's
steady drumfire reinforced Yeo's hand. The Germans and the Japa-

nese began to shift toward the American view, and even Giscard began to talk guardedly of "limited flexibility" of exchange rates.[13]

The more Ford's strategists thought about it, the more attractive the Giscard-Schmidt summit proposal began to look: the American economy was recovering, and the appearance of the United States taking the lead on global economic issues would enhance Ford's prestige. Moreover, foreign trade—exports and imports together—began in the early 1970s to run close to 7 percent of the annual gross national product, a spectacular increase from the 4 percent that had been the experience of the past few decades, signifying that the American stake in international trade and financial matters was growing. An international economic summit, if properly launched, could be a timely vehicle through which the United States could cut back its traditional isolationism and become an activist on global economic issues. Moreover, the oil shock had introduced a new note of urgency: the sharp increase in oil prices had led to the expectation that inflation would spread to other commodities and force the advocates of monetary "reforms," such as Giscard, who wanted to return to fixed rates and the discipline of gold, to accept, even if reluctantly, the notion that currencies should be allowed to fluctuate.

"There was a sense that our conflict with the French had gone on to the point where it was destabilizing," Yeo later recalled. "The world functions best if it has a framework within which to function. If there are no rules of the game, even if not as precise as some want, or as imprecise as others want, you've got to have a structure. The French wanted a par value system, and they wanted to retain the monetary role of gold in an official sense. There were signs that French public opinion had begun to change on gold."[14] Yeo was able to report to Simon that Giscard, his close adviser and *chef de cabinet* Claude-Pierre Brossollet, and Larosière were reflecting this shift in public sentiment, and might be responsive to a compromise.

The setting for the ultimate bargain struck by Yeo and Larosière was the presidential yacht *Sequoia* on a sunny summer afternoon in 1975, as the Group of Five finance ministers and their key aides enjoyed food and drink on a cruise down the Potomac River. The principals that day included Simon, French finance minister Jean-Pierre Fourcade, British chancellor of the Exchequer Denis W. Healey, German finance minister Hans Appel, and Japanese finance minister Masayoshi Ohira. A tense argument ensued involving all five over the question of removing gold "from the center of the monetary system." The debate grew so heated that Simon quietly slipped away from the stern where the ministers were gathered and told the

Sequoia captain to delay returning to the dock, hoping that extra time cruising the Potomac might produce some consensus. Finally, Healey, tired of the wrangling over a sticky and increasingly technical issue, blurted: "Why don't we let the French and the Americans settle it—anything they agree to, I agree to!" Immediately, Appel and Ohira nodded their assent.[15] It was a big breakthrough, and it was seized by both the French and American sides as the vehicle to make a success of Rambouillet, even though, according to IMF historian Margaret Garritsen de Vries, those who gave carte blanche to Simon and Fourcade "probably did not really expect the U.S. and French authorities to settle their differences."[16]

Negotiations proceeded on two tracks: the first was through a group of senior private citizens, including George Shultz representing Ford. Quietly, Ford brought Shultz—who had left the Nixon cabinet to preside over the Bechtel Corporation—back into the picture as a member of the Carlton Group, named for the Carlton House Hotel on Madison Avenue in New York. There, in a suite belonging to the Morgan Bank, Shultz met with Raymond Barre, representing Giscard, and other private citizens nominated by heads of government, to negotiate an agenda for Rambouillet. Shultz, aided by his long-time relationships with fellow finance ministers Giscard and Schmidt, succeeded in getting Giscard—who would be the host at Rambouillet—to broaden the agenda to topics beyond just monetary matters to include recession, inflation, the oil embargo, and trade protectionism.

The other track was the nitty-gritty bargaining on the details between Yeo and Larosière, who as deputy to Brossollet had direct access to Giscard. Ford excluded his best-known expert on international financial affairs, Fed chairman Arthur Burns, from the discussions. Burns had got under Ford's skin by warning publicly about "the massive federal deficit" that the administration was piling up. Out of the loop, Burns "was beside himself," as Yeo found out when he was given the unpleasant task of filling in the Fed chairman.[17] Burns had been agitated earlier in 1975 when Yeo had set up a small committee of departmental undersecretaries, which Yeo named "Thurber's Dogs," that met regularly with their opposite numbers in other countries to make effective whatever had been decided by the G-5 finance ministers. The name "Thurber's Dogs" evolved, Yeo recalled, simply because he was a fan of James Thurber, the gifted *New Yorker* writer, whose cartoon dogs may have been his best-known signature. Burns was offended by the thought that a group of what he regarded as low-level officials would be poaching on the Fed's special domain of foreign exchange market intervention.

Yet, even after Rambouillet, "Thurber's Dogs" continued to meet every other week, sometimes in Washington, sometimes abroad, its consultations well shielded from inquiring journalists.

The news that Ford would join other world leaders at an economic summit near Paris was officially announced in a speech by Kissinger to the Pittsburgh World Affairs Council on November 11, 1975. Ford, said Kissinger, would meet in France for three days beginning November 15 with Giscard, Schmidt, Wilson, Prime Minister Takeo Miki of Japan, and Italian premier Aldo Moro—a summit involving leaders of six nations.[18] "This worldwide crisis to the democratic process is the deepest challenge before the leaders at the economic summit," Kissinger declared. "They meet to give their peoples the sense that they are masters of their destiny—that they are not subject to blind forces beyond their control."[19]

It had been Schmidt's dream that heads of the major industrial nations would be able, at such a summit, to hammer out their differences, unimpeded by finance ministers or foreign secretaries—until they called them in for advice, or as notetakers to record their agreements. The picture Schmidt had in mind was a group of gentlemen sitting in a library, over cigars and coffee or liqueurs, not distracted by functionaries—and especially not by the press. The Château de Rambouillet, thirty-three miles outside Paris, offered exactly the kind of isolation and security Schmidt had in mind. The fourteenth-century castle, set in an eighty-square-mile forest replete with canals and water gardens, was a history-soaked edifice where big men could make big decisions, far removed from the bureaucratic riffraff and the media despised by Schmidt. In 1815, Napoleon had spent his last night in the château before being banished to St. Helena. In modern times, Rambouillet had become the French president's country residence, an elegant Camp David, a setting that would encourage frequent and easy conversation among the six leaders, each of whom had his own private suite.

Kissinger, Simon, and Greenspan, Ford's principal aides, were not quartered at the castle, but were taken by helicopter in and out to hotels in Paris or at the airport. (Kissinger, of course, wanted a room at Rambouillet; but the only one left, after the needs of the presidents and prime ministers were filled, did not have a private toilet. Unhappy, Kissinger had to commute like the other foreign secretaries.) I was one of only a handful of American reporters covering Rambouillet—years later economic summits would become all-inclusive circuses with thousands of journalists stumbling over each other— and we were held at bay in the George V Hotel in Paris, far from the actual site of the meeting.

The mechanical arrangements for the summit were primitive. Kissinger had insisted that each country be allowed a "notetaker" to monitor and record the conversations of the heads of government. But when Robert Hormats of the National Security Council staff—who served as a "sherpa," or preparer, for Rambouillet and was the designated American notetaker—and British cabinet secretary John Hunt, named by Prime Minister Wilson, showed up, they found that Giscard had provided them no tables at which to work or earphones to pick up the simultaneous translation of the interpreters. Hormats and Hunt crowded behind the interpreters' booth so they could hear the translations directly. By the time of the afternoon session on the first day, Giscard relented, and arranged table space with earphones for the notetakers, and Hormats and Hunt were joined by representatives of the four other countries.

On the eve of the summit, Giscard gave an interview to *Le Figaro* in which he said that the international monetary system needed "a certain flexibility of the apparatus to enable it to absorb the shocks it is subjected to"—a tip-off that French and American differences were going to be narrowed. In fact, following from the implicit understanding carved out on the *Sequoia*, Ford and Giscard had made a deal, and trotted it out to the surprise of their four colleagues, who had no choice but to ratify it.

The work on the precise language of the compromise agreement was painstaking and tedious: participants recall Yeo and Larosière editing the final phrasing on top of a piano in one of the mirrored vestibules of the château, outside the huge old chamber in which the heads of government were meeting.

The final communiqué, issued after three days of talks, officially recognized the inevitability of floating exchange rates. It also said that the six nations' "monetary authorities will act to counter disorderly market conditions, or erratic fluctuations in exchange rates," thus placing a limit on the market freedom that some academic enthusiasts for exchange rates had desired. The key element in the deal sanctioned a controlled "float" of exchange rates to prevent wide swings. The United States, which benefited from freely floating exchange rates—the downward drift of the dollar had made American goods cheaper abroad—naturally wanted to preserve its advantage. The French, initially, had demanded a quick return to fixed rates. The compromise, involving more formal management of the rates, paved the way for a final agreement—which proved to be truly historic—at a January 1976 meeting in Jamaica of the International Monetary Fund's so-called Interim Committee.

(The Interim Committee was, as the phrase suggests, intended to be a temporary structure bridging the gap between the old system of fixed parities that was discarded with the 1971 Smithsonian Agreement and a reformed system that was supposed to be worked out later under the aegis of the C-20 group of "wise" technical experts. But the oil shock of 1973 interrupted the reform process, and the system never underwent the basic changes envisioned by the C-20 that would undo the inconvertibility of the dollar, dating back to Nixon's 1971 decision breaking the link between the dollar and gold. Therefore, the Interim Committee simply carried on as the top policy-making board of the IMF.)

Robert Hormats would say later that the artful language of the communiqué could not mask a major difference in philosophy between the United States and France: "The United States, at the time, was becoming more and more enchanted with the notion of a long period of floating rates to release it from what its officials, particularly Secretary of the Treasury William Simon, Shultz's successor, regarded as the shackles and rigidities of fixed rates. The French sought a return to the discipline of fixed rates and convertibility of the dollar."[20]

But the deal hammered out at Rambouillet, reflecting the hard initial bargaining between Yeo and Larosière, gave Giscard and Ford something they could sell to their home constituencies. For Giscard, there was the ability to say he hadn't given up the French fixation with fixed rates: even the United States was committed to try for more stability. Ford, on the other hand, had won agreement that there would be no premature return to fixed rates, and the United States could count on the considerable flexibility it felt was necessary for it to remain competitive.

Since 1973, when the move toward floating rates had begun, there had been widespread approval in American academic circles for adoption of greater flexibility on a permanent basis, on the theory that the system would allow each nation to follow its own domestic policies. Businessmen, too, were won to the idea, although many would later yearn for a return to stability. "Proponents of a system of floating rates argued that this would enable countries to pursue independent domestic policies because balance-of-payments surpluses or deficits, which resulted from differences in domestic policies, would be reflected in movements in exchange rates," Hormats said. "They in turn would reduce the payments imbalances that might result. A country with a current account deficit would expect to see its currency depreciate; one with a surplus would expect to see its currency appreciate. As a result, both types of imbalances would ultimately be eliminated."[21]

(Of course, as we know with the benefit of hindsight, the theory that flexible rates would moderate trade and balance of payments deficits didn't survive the impact of huge flows of capital in the 1980s and early '90s; specifically, changes in exchange rates did not prevent the buildup of huge American deficits accompanied by Japanese and European surpluses. The drift in the Reagan presidency under his second secretary of the Treasury, James A. Baker, was back toward elements of fixed currency relationships. But Rambouillet initiated a period of almost a decade in which flexibility was the main theme, and for a time the floating system played a positive role in softening the economic blows that otherwise would have multiplied because of the cumulative effect of the two oil shocks of 1973 and 1979.)

Essentially, the Rambouillet agreement between France and the United States was incorporated in two secret, formal memoranda initialed by Simon and French finance minister Jean-Pierre Fourcade. The first made clear that France would abandon its insistence that every country return to a single system of fixed "par values" for currencies, with minimum allowable fluctuations. Instead, floating, along with fixed rates, would be considered a perfectly acceptable system—each to come under the surveillance of the IMF through a new IMF second amendment of the basic Articles of Agreement, details of which were to be worked out in Jamaica.

Second, the United States, which until then had followed a policy of intervening in markets only to prevent so-called disorderly conditions, agreed along with other governments that it would intervene "to counter disorderly market conditions, or erratic fluctuations in exchange rates." By adding the "erratic fluctuations" criterion, the United States in effect agreed to be more active in trying to keep the dollar from rising or dropping excessively. As recently as September 2, Simon had told the IMF annual meeting that "sizable movements in exchange rates over a period of several months are not necessarily indicators of disorderly markets."[22]

Thus a new era in Franco-American understanding was at hand. A few weeks later in Jamaica, a British official told me: "Everything is sweetness and light between the French and the Americans. Every time Simon says something, Fourcade jumps up to agree with his friend Bill. And it's the same thing the other way around." France did not succeed in restoring gold as the basis for the international monetary system, but would be able to count its gold holdings, at higher prices, in its reserves. At the same time, the Americans got their way on the exchange rate system they wanted, even if monetary reform purists felt that true reform had been abandoned for the sake of political compromise.[23]

Yeo pointed out in an interview that "We [and the French] will now have a much better communication of policies and attitudes than in the past. But it is not a supranational decision-making machine. Each country will continue to manage its own economy." Gingerly, Yeo and Larosière had avoided any talk of economic policy coordination.

Interestingly enough, the Franco-American accord on the exchange rate question was the single substantive element produced by the Rambouillet summit—and it was in the area originally proposed by Giscard as the rationale for the heads of government meeting, and rejected by Ford as too narrow. The other topics included to make the meeting acceptable to Ford—energy and global recovery among them—produced a lot of talk but no significant conclusions. Regrettably, not a word that might be taken as offensive by OPEC was uttered. There was not even a promise of another summit: instead, the leaders called on existing international agencies, starting with the already scheduled IMF meeting in Jamaica, to follow up their talks. It was only when Ford later decided that a summit in 1976 would provide a convenient backdrop for his reelection campaign that he convened the second summit (including Canada), at Dorado Beach, Puerto Rico. (That set the cycle in motion; through Tokyo in 1993, there have been nineteen consecutive annual summits rotated among the seven participating countries.)

THE SHIFT IN monetary negotiations from the placid, wealthy French countryside to the turbulent, poverty-stricken Caribbean island of Jamaica six weeks later provided what my former boss, *Newsweek* editor Osborn Elliott, might have called a "neck-snapping transition" between elements of a story. In Kingston from January 7 to 10, 1976, against a background of local political violence, gang warfare, arson, and looting that escalated out of control of the civil authorities, the International Monetary Fund adopted the new Article IV that not only legalized floating rates but put into effect ironclad provisions assuring that the United States or any other nation that preferred floating rates need never go back to par values.

International economic gatherings have occasionally been interspersed with tense moments. Student demonstrations and other elements of civil disorder have been present at meetings I've covered in Copenhagen, Manila, Tokyo, London, and Seoul. But the IMF meeting in Jamaica was the only time that my colleagues and I, as economic journalists, ever had to cover gang warfare. The press corps numbered about 150, and news of riots, rather than exchange rates, soon began to pour out to the rest of the world. It was not quite civil war—although it was represented as such in one purple dispatch to *The New York Times*. Nonetheless, it was an ugly scene that forced an embarrassed Prime Minister Michael N. Manley to impose martial law in certain areas of Kingston. The trouble—long brewing in a nation whose unemployment rates ranged from 20 to 30 percent, with no unemployment insurance as a social buffer—broke out on a Tuesday night, just as Simon, Fourcade, and finance ministers from 128 nations began to arrive in Kingston. Young members of Manley's People's National Party (PNP), the dominant political group in Jamaica, demonstrated in front of the conference site, the Pegasus Hotel, against the presence of a delegate from South Africa. The antiapartheid rally had been encouraged by Manley, on the understanding that the demonstrators would limit their protest to chanting. But it got out of hand when a small group proceeded to the American embassy and began to stone the building. In the resultant melee, one Jamaican policeman guarding the embassy was killed, one of four Jamaican officers who died as the clashes spread.[24]

Meanwhile, about four miles from the Pegasus in a slum area known as Trenchtown, more than twenty homes were firebombed. There had been skirmishes before in Trenchtown, often armed, between Manley's left-of-center PNP and the rival centrists, the Jamaican Labour Party. The symbols of the struggle were public housing units, rewards for party loyalty. Trenchtown—an area of perhaps one-half mile square—had been established by the Labour Party when it held power in 1962–72, immediately after Jamaica won its independence from Britain. (Manley's party had set up a rival housing project at Arnett Gardens, whose apartments were reportedly superior to the older units in Trenchtown.) As the finance ministers tried to concentrate on their assignment, Trenchtown was reported to be burning out of control. Firemen first on the scene were driven back by armed gangs; hundreds were made homeless. The Jamaican army eventually restored order, but the damage was done.

Manley hoped that the highly publicized meeting of the IMF in Jamaica—the first of any international organization of such prominence—would serve to advertise the tourist industry, third largest after bauxite and sugar. Instead, he had to take to radio and television after the riots, stopping just short of calling the situation a civil insurrection, but imposing martial law in Trenchtown and elsewhere. The roots of the revolt went deep into the island's troubled political structure and the abject poverty that contrasted so stunningly with the beautiful beaches, rich vegetation, and rolling mountain range. But the hard reality was that the riches and beauties of the island were enjoyed largely by white foreign tourists and a wealthy white ruling class entrenched since the days of British colonial power. The black population—save for a thin upper crust of managers associated with the white elite—was in desperate straits.

Meanwhile, discussion of monetary affairs went on, as the delegates hammered out the details of a new second amendment to the IMF Articles of Agreement that permitted each nation to choose its own exchange rate regime. Among the major currencies, the American, Canadian, and Australian dollars, the British pound, and the Japanese yen were allowed to float freely. Most nations, however, decided to link their own paper money to the U.S. dollar, or to an average of a "basket" of the major currencies. Most of the European countries continued to link their currencies to the "snake," set up in 1972 as an informal range of acceptable fluctuation against each other. (The "snake" was the forerunner of the more precise European Monetary System, another product of the Schmidt-Giscard relationship.)

A beaming Ed Yeo explained how the French focus on fixed rates had been blended with the American urge for flexibility. Article IV of the second amendment promised that the IMF would collaborate with its member nations to promote "a stable system of exchange rates"—but such stability in rates was to be fostered by creating stability in underlying economic conditions. "It used to be assumed that an exchange rate system could impose or create stability," Yeo said. "The theory here works the other way." The United States, France, and the others would try to get their economies working in better harmony, hoping that "convergence"—a new buzzword—would lead to calm in the currency markets. It was a new principle, and would prove to be the basic underpinning of international efforts for the next decade and more.[25]

If the IMF should ever decide to move back to a par value system, the new agreement specified, it would have to be by an 85 percent vote—a provision that Simon and Yeo insisted upon because it gave the United States, with about a 20 percent share of the IMF votes, the ability to veto such a decision.[26] (Maintaining such a veto remains today a basic American objective in its relations with the multilateral lending institutions.) In a widely quoted article, Tom de Vries, alternate executive director for the Netherlands at the IMF, wrote that the Jamaica agreement was less a significant "reform" of the international monetary system than a patchwork response to a collapse of the system.[27] De Vries would prove to be right. The floating rate system would not yield all the benefits expected from it. To be sure, flexibility would help the international monetary system cope with major unsettling events, such as the oil price shocks. But the floating rate system would at times be overwhelmed by huge flows of capital among large trading nations. Thus floating exchange rates would by themselves fail to adjust trade surpluses and deficits, as advocates of the floating system had predicted they would.

BEFORE FORD COULD return to the relative comfort of dealing with international problems, he had to face the reality of the troubled domestic scene. Liberal critics wanted him to spend more money on reconstruction of the cities and other social problems, while his own conservative advisers, headed by William Simon, counseled retrenchment.

For a time, early in 1976, events seemed to suggest that Ford could have both. Unemployment had come down from a 1975 peak of 8.9 percent and 8.3 percent in December to 7.8 percent in January. Other indicators began to suggest recovery from the 1974–75 recession: business sales and profits were up, and the rate of inflation as well as interest rates began to turn down. That brought real wages up, and gave consumer confidence a boost. Ford began to claim that, by following Alan Greenspan's conservative advice, he had masterminded a "sound recovery" without radical measures.[28] The dollar and merchandise exports also were doing well: the trade surplus in 1975, according to the Department of Commerce, had swelled three-fold over 1974 to $21.5 billion, far above a preliminary estimate of $12.5 billion. Taking all this in, investors pushed up prices on Wall Street, not unmindful of the fact that the jobless rate, even though lower than in 1975, was staying high enough to block significant pay raises during labor negotiations in 1976.

Washington nonetheless was preoccupied with debating the durability of the apparent recovery and its potential impact on the upcoming presidential election. Senator Jacob Javits, the shrewd New York Republican, had his doubts that the economy would remain sufficiently strong to assure a Republican victory. "I'm a politician, so I know that a president can be elected with 7 million unemployed, because there are 87 million that are employed. But that's unacceptable, it's un-American, it's just not our way," Javits told a Washington conference on full employment issues.

Early in 1976, Ford decided to seek a tax cut of $15 billion or $16 billion, less than the Democrats thought necessary to stimulate the economy. Eventually, a $23.1 billion package was agreed upon, boosting the estimated deficit to as much as $80 billion, a result that Simon had warned would cause him to resign. Simon went public with his reservations (which didn't please Ford), but soon the differences were papered over. Ford was a pragmatic compromiser, willing to put aside his free-market ideology in the stress of events. Simon was not: he rebelled at the notion of additional tax cuts in the face of an already sizable deficit.

The story of Simon's years in the Ford administration would not be complete without an account of his propensity for keeping valuable gifts from foreign dignitaries, in clear violation of federal regulations, and of how he was foiled by an anonymous letter to *The Washington Post*, and by former child movie star Shirley Temple Black, chief of protocol at the State Department, who threw the book at him, resulting in a sensational series of stories in the *Post*. The tipster's letter appeared to be prompted by a November 1976 story of mine revealing that Simon, the hard-nosed advocate of reduced government expenditures, had taken a farewell junket to London and Moscow that month that cost the taxpayers $131,500 for a party of forty-two, including Mrs. Simon and two of their children.[29] The letter—apparently from a Treasury employee blowing the whistle on his boss—said that Simon, on his many trips abroad in his official capacity, and as part of his association with other finance ministers, had received scores of gifts—in exchange for Treasury mementos such as bronze medallions—but had failed to transfer all of them to the State Department. Government officials such as Simon were required by law to turn over any gift worth $50 or more to the government (the threshold is now $200).

Although as a columnist I was a persistent critic, I had a good working relationship with Simon, who was always willing to see me on short notice. He readily acknowledged, when I confronted him with the letter, that he had kept six gifts as mementos, but said he had urged the State Department to allow him to keep the gifts if he paid their appraised value. They included a Russian shotgun he had received from Soviet trade minister Nikolai Patolichev; a cigarette box from Saudi Arabia; a set of matched pistols from Argentina; a wristwatch given him by Soviet leader Leonid Brezhnev; a porcelain sculpture from Spain; and two silver-colored necklaces from Israel.

Simon's explanation for the pistols was that he was a gun collector, having purchased fifty or sixty on his trips abroad. "Whenever I have an hour or so, I go shopping," Simon said. "I've bought guns everywhere I've gone, because as everybody knows, I'm an avid collector." But there was no explanation for guns acquired as gifts—or for the other "souvenirs"—except that he wanted to keep them. Simon explained he had proposed to Henry E. Catto, Mrs. Black's predecessor at the State Department, a system whereby the government would obtain a fair market appraisal of gifts he had received and wanted to keep, and he would then pay the established price. Simon said that it was his impression that Catto thought the purchase plan a good idea, but nothing came of it.

When the story broke in *The Washington Post*, Simon appealed to Mrs. Black to arrange a way in which he could keep at least some of the gifts, but she would have none of that. She rejected a revived proposal to set things right by writing a check for the appraised value, concluding that making such a deal with Simon would be unfair to countless other government officials who had turned in gifts. "I told him I couldn't issue regulations to comply with his suggestion", she said.[30] Angrily, Simon turned the six gifts over to the State Department. Simon later acknowledged that he had kept, and then turned over to Mrs. Black's office, four other gifts. These were a ten-inch silver rose from Mexico, a nine-and-a-half-inch stone sailboat and a fourteen-by-fourteen-inch metal casting of two deer from Russia, and three clusters of decorated stone grapes.

Mrs. Black was unimpressed with Simon's apparent effort to pressure her by citing what appeared to be Catto's less-strict attitude. In fact, if Simon had reported the gifts in timely fashion—which he had not done—the rule in force then would have permitted him to make a bid for the gifts only after they had been offered for use by any federal government agency or by the states.[31] Shirley Temple Black was tough and gutsy in her decision to make Simon comply with the law. She had carefully studied the applicable 1966 statute, Public Law 89-673, and concluded there was no way in which Simon could gain title to the gifts that would not violate the spirit of the legislation. The comptroller general of the United States, Elmer B. Staats, backed her up: his General Accounting Office had issued a detailed report on the exact procedures only a year before, and Simon could not have been unaware of the regulations.[32]

"I'll never forget it," Mrs. Black told me years later. "He said, 'Them as has gits.' "[33]

In January 1977, Simon left office, claiming disillusionment. "The government doesn't run the way Washington and Jefferson thought it would," Simon said. "No president knows the sacrifices [to ideology] that he has to make until he sits there under the gun at the White House."[34]

* * *

WHILE WILLING TO give in some on taxes, Ford resisted Democratic pressures to boost government spending, endorsing Greenspan's belief that the private sector would generate its own boom in 1977, and therefore it would be a mistake to crank further stimulus into the economy through the federal budget. "Besides, if we're wrong—and we don't think we are—it's easier to cut taxes and increase spending than to do it the other way around," Greenspan said.[35] He argued that to push for a deficit bigger than the $43 billion for fiscal 1977 projected by Ford would not create new jobs but would raise inflationary expectations. Alice Rivlin, director of the new Congressional Budget Office in its influential formative years, challenged Greenspan's view, saying in the first CBO report to Congress that lower taxes or higher spending would indeed boost employment fairly quickly, although there would be an intensification of inflation later on.[36]

Also that spring, Minnesota Democratic senator Hubert H. Humphrey, the ebullient embodiment of the liberal spirit, together with California Democratic representative Augustus F. Hawkins, pushed through Congress a bill that would put the government into the economic planning business, requiring it to set and achieve specific numerical goals for unemployment and interest rates. The Humphrey-Hawkins Bill would also require the Federal Reserve Board to shed some of its secrecy by developing precise targets for monetary growth and making them public at regular congressional hearings.

Few economic issues stir up as much heat as the notion of "planning," which—to those who despise it—is a dangerous, even socialist concept. Ronald Reagan, in an interview with me in April 1976 as he sought to wrest the Republican nomination from Ford, said that "planning scares the hell out of me. It's the same thing that under Mussolini they called fascism, or at least it turns into fascism. When the government plans—the more they have to plan, the more they have to regulate. The pity is that the magic of the marketplace is so little understood."[37]

But as applied to the United States, planning involves merely a prudent way of budgeting the use of limited physical and human resources in a mixed economy, already committed to all manner of government intervention on behalf of business, labor, and consumers. Planning had enabled European governments to exceed the American rate of economic growth in the early 1960s, an achievement that had rankled John Kennedy. Jean Monnet, the brilliant French philosopher, told me in a 1962 interview in his Paris apartment that just as General Motors or General Electric plans, so should the United States. "Everyone here has knowledge of the total needs of the economy, not just his own sector. 'Le Plan' doesn't impose anything on anybody, but it gets all sectors of the economy to participate in a collective action," Monnet said.[38]

Many Democratic officeholders and economists fretted in that campaign year of 1976 that, despite Ford's blunders in 1975, things could look rosy for the Republicans, thanks to Democratic congressional initiatives that Ford, being a pragmatist, had accepted, and that had helped turn the economy around. For example, although Ford initially vetoed extension of the 1975 tax cut, the Democratic majority forced him to accept it. That generated a robust real growth rate of 7.5 percent in the first quarter. Ford was able to brag about the zip in the economy—and, of course, take credit for it.

Again, it was the federal bailout of New York City—which Ford had fought tooth and nail for months, but to which he finally acquiesced—that averted a potential cascade of municipal defaults. And finally Congress passed an energy bill that temporarily kept a lid on exploding petroleum prices. Ford had agonized over signing that bill, since he was philosophically opposed to controls. But in the end he signed it, offering the rationale that the legislation provided a fixed and assured timetable for full decontrol after forty months, and also authorized emergency powers to deal with another oil embargo.

The combination of controls on energy prices (some prices were actually rolled back) and good luck on food prices resulted in a low and politically pleasing inflation rate of 3.7 percent. Arthur Okun grumbled: "The Democrats put the fuel in the tank, and the Republicans are enjoying the ride."[39] But Ford counted on the public's notoriously short memory, and campaigned around the nation claiming that his "steady hand" on the economy had resulted in recovery.

Given the Democrats' evident intention to avoid the "big spenders" tag, Ford, guided by Greenspan, could assume that his own restraining hand on government expenditures would get little meaningful challenge from his political opponents. He also took a strong stand against the Humphrey-Hawkins Bill. And although he signed legislation extending the Council on Wage and Price Stability—a leftover from the Nixon controls era that had the power of subpoena but only limited authority to monitor wage and price decisions—he remained firmly opposed to the use of wage and price controls. Ford even passed up opportunities to "jawbone" against price increases in steel and other raw materials.

*   *   *

AS IT BECAME clear that the state of the economy could tip the balance in the upcoming presidential election, Ford decided he could enhance his image by calling a new economic summit—this time including Canada as the seventh participant—in Dorado Beach, Puerto Rico, on June 27 and 28. Rambouillet had been rated a success for his administration's diplomacy with France, certified by calmness in the international money markets. It had also carved out a significant new role for the International Monetary Fund as the top cop on the international money beat, with new tools for surveillance of individual national economies. A second summit, with Ford the host this time, could show the president off as leader of the Free World, enhancing his election chances at a time when economic uncertainty prevailed at home.

To be sure, there were denials by Kissinger and Simon that the decision to have a midyear 1976 economic summit led by Ford had anything to do with election year politics.[40] Simon, as a matter of fact, was trying to sell the idea that a "Rambouillet II" was justified because the economic recovery had accelerated so far beyond expectations that global managers had to worry about latent inflationary consequences. But no one paid attention to those denials, because the recovery, in truth, was only average, and the inflation indexes were the envy of the rest of the world.

But a summit could be a welcome showcase for Ford: as Giscard had demonstrated at Rambouillet, the host-chairman controls the agenda and the limelight. Ford, although a welcome relief from the disgraced Nixon, was not charismatic and was sure to face a serious challenge from whomever the Democratic candidate turned out to be. Moreover, with Ronald Reagan actively campaigning, Ford wasn't even guaranteed the Republican nomination. In the fall of 1974, according to Reagan biographer Lou Cannon, Ford had offered Reagan a position in his cabinet. But Reagan declined, kept his options open for 1976, and for a brief period early that year considered the possibility of running against Ford as head of a third party.[41] In the end, Reagan went all-out to block Ford from getting the Republican nomination, strongly supported by the GOP right wing.

When he talked to me in April, Reagan groused that Ford, as "a member of the Washington establishment for two-thirds of his life, believes in the ability of Washington to solve problems. I don't share that view: I believe that the government is the problem, not the answer." The central theme of Reagan's philosophy was that government had grown too big and should be cut back. "Balancing the budget is like protecting your virtue—you have to learn how to say no," he said.[42] Reagan had a draconian plan: he would cut $90 billion from federal programs, much of it in welfare and income-distribution programs, and transfer the responsibilities for those programs—and the tax revenues for them—to the states. He also promised a sweeping overhaul of the welfare system, including the "scandal-ridden food stamp program," and the highly popular Aid for Families with Dependent Children. "I still think there are a half-dozen areas where the federal government is incompetent to run things, and these should be administered at the state and local levels. It all would have to be phased in over time," Reagan said. The six areas were welfare, food stamps, housing, Medicaid, community development, and education.[43]

The difference between Reagan and Ford was that Ford, as president, had learned to make compromises with political realities—just as Reagan had made pragmatic decisions as governor of California that didn't quite match his fundamentalist line. The state of the economy around election time was sure to be a significant factor in whether the Democrats, who had lost the White House in the midst of the Vietnam War in 1968, could scramble back—and Ford had to take that into account.

It was a propitious time, politically, for a second economic summit for the other leaders as well: there wasn't one among them who couldn't benefit from a productive international conference that made headlines, if nothing else. There were other potential benefits. A United Nations Conference on Trade and Development (UNCTAD) meeting of rich and poor nations had turned into a dismal failure when the rich nations rejected a proposal from the poor that a $3 billion "common fund" be created to ease the shock of erratic commodity price fluctuations by building "buffer" stocks that would be held off the market.

Kissinger planned to use the Dorado Beach summit as a testing ground to bridge the gap between the hard-line German-American opposition and the more accommodating views of the others, especially of France and Canada. It was time, as well, to step back from the Rambouillet and Jamaica agreements, and to determine whether recent dramatic foreign exchange rate drops in the British pound and Italian lira meant that the new floating rate system was in trouble or whether, as some suspected, both countries were manipulating their exchange rates to achieve a trade advantage.[44] Britain, which had already borrowed $5.3 billion from its major partners, and Italy had indicated that they might need further help, possibly from the IMF.

At the same time, there was a growing belief that economic summits, and other meetings such as those held by the International

Monetary Fund, should be viewed with some skepticism. The influential Fritz Leutwiler, president of the Swiss central bank, argued that it was "an illusion" to think that international conferences could solve major financial issues. "For the international monetary system, the same holds true for the economy as a whole: stability begins at home," Leutwiler said. Leutwiler, representative of traditional central banking philosophy, opposed the effort to push gold out of the monetary system, and also fretted that the end result of the Jamaica accord would be to expand unnecessarily the lending role of the IMF.[45]

Ford's Dorado Beach summit did not deal effectively with any of these issues—although it did facilitate international assistance to the Italians. Once again, the leaders also failed, as they had at Rambouillet, to take any meaningful action to dilute OPEC's power by reducing their dependence on oil imports from the cartel producers.[46] The main conclusion of the summit, following the guidance of conservative Ford advisers Greenspan and Simon, was that the fight against inflation should get priority over economic growth, even though jobless rates had risen with the contraction triggered by the oil shock. The "main lesson" that the United States had learned, said Greenspan, was that "inflation creates recession, and itself is a major cause of unemployment."

Placed alongside a similar commitment made a week earlier in Paris by the foreign and finance ministers of the Organization for Economic Cooperation and Development's twenty-four member countries, the Dorado Beach policy represented a flat reversal of the postwar emphasis on the highest possible rates of growth, and an acceptance of higher rates of unemployment. The OECD's communiqué even had been explicit, saying its go-slow policy would mean that "restoration of full employment [would] take a number of years."

The tighten-your-belt pitch at Dorado Beach was a hard sell to the Europeans, battered by the oil-induced recession. On the plane returning to Washington from Dorado Beach, Simon complained that "preaching moderate growth is like trying to sell leprosy."[47] Prime Minister Takeo Miki of Japan and Prime Minister James Callaghan of Great Britain (who had recently succeeded Harold Wilson), among others, resisted an all-out war against inflation as unwise from an economic as well as a political standpoint. Helmut Schmidt, who faced an October election, pledged in a separate statement "to create new employment opportunities and thereby decrease still-existing unemployment and to achieve full employment again." Denis Healey, frustrated by the cautions against excessive economic growth, snapped that it is "oversimplistic" to think that unemployment cures inflation.

Despite their political concerns, the other six leaders accepted the Ford pitch because, in fact, the OECD rate of inflation in April was nearly 13 percent, double the level of the two preceding months, and far above the rate in the United States. Moreover, European budgets increasingly were being drained by welfare and social programs, leaving less for capital investment programs that nurtured profits and created jobs. Another factor persuading Great Britain and Italy that they had to adhere to a tough anti-inflationary line was their status as borrowers: Simon, for Treasury, and Burns, for the Federal Reserve, had already made clear when they agreed to participate in the $5.3 billion line of credit to Britain that the actual loans would go forward only when "tough conditions" were applied. "It makes no sense," Simon had said, "to throw money down the drain."

On monetary issues, the Dorado Beach summit results were almost nil. American officials were irritated by what they were convinced was a successful effort by Japan to hold down the exchange value of the yen by buying dollars in the foreign exchange markets. The cheaper yen then gave Japanese goods an edge in world markets. But although Japan felt the American pressure, there was no agreement, merely a Japanese anxiety to put Dorado Beach behind them. Japanese foreign minister Kiichi Miyazawa recognized the pressure. "The sooner this conference is over, the better," he told reporters.

THE REPUBLICAN slow-growth political message from Dorado Beach gave the Democrats solid ammunition for the 1976 election campaign. A small handful of Democratic candidates had been probing that spring for a strategy to upset Ford. The Democratic hopefuls included Georgia governor Jimmy Carter; California governor Jerry Brown; Senator Henry (Scoop) Jackson of Washington; and Representative Morris K. Udall of Arizona—all of whom could subscribe to what might be called standard Democratic expansionist theory, loosely defined.

But Carter was different from the others: a distinct degree more conservative, he sounded more like a Republican than a Democrat when he professed a devotion to the private sector. Carter struck the business community as "safer" than the other Democratic candidates. Brown and Udall, by contrast, favored a much more active role for the federal government to boost the rate of economic growth. Brown wondered openly whether the capitalist market system could generate full employment. He indicated that if the government policies he advocated to stimulate economic growth caused inflation rates to get out of hand, he wouldn't hesitate to reinstall wage and price controls. "I'm very dubious about economic planning," Brown said, "but I see that we've got to embark upon a commitment to get these kids to work, to give [everyone] a chance. That may require work-sharing." Work-sharing was a concept that the United Auto Workers had threatened to introduce into the bargaining process later in 1976, as a way of reducing unemployment.[48] It was, to be sure, an old idea. When it cropped up in the 1960s, Arthur J. Goldberg, then general counsel of the AFL-CIO, thought very little of the notion. "It shares unemployment, not employment," Goldberg would say.

Carter didn't buy many of these concepts, and as a result the Georgia governor was a disappointment to liberal Democrats. Like Udall and Jackson, Carter faulted the Federal Reserve Board for following too tight a monetary policy, but Carter told me as we sat side by side in his campaign plane flying out of Philadelphia one day that he would not try to make a scapegoat out of Arthur Burns, or challenge the independence of the Federal Reserve. But Brown, Udall, and Jackson were disposed to make the central bank bend to the needs of a full-employment economy.

Union leaders, such as Leonard Woodcock of the United Auto Workers and Jerry Wurf of the powerful American Federation of State, County and Municipal Employees (AFSCME), weren't totally happy with Carter, but decided he probably could beat Ford, whereas Udall, Brown, and Jackson couldn't. "We're comfortable with Carter, we think his answers are straight," Wurf told me before making a pro-Carter announcement.[49]

As a group, the 1976 Democratic hopefuls shied away from being tagged "big spenders." Representative Brock Adams (D.-Wash.), chairman of the House Budget Committee, neatly laid out the theme in a presentation to the Democratic Platform Committee, warning that "fiscal responsibility" was likely to be a critical campaign issue: "The first order of business for the Congress must be to demonstrate it can control federal spending. . . . I realize this has not been the usual cheery presentation, full of promise and new initiatives. I have tried to show how we can avoid these induced recessions that have been plaguing us in recent years, and stop inflation. But we can do this only if we are willing to make real-world decisions between what we want and what we can afford, what we have and what we need, and what we promise and what we can deliver."[50]

In essence, then, the Democratic strategy in mid-1976 was to portray as conservative a stance as possible without upsetting Meany, whose support at the polls and in financing the campaign would be crucial. An underlying theme was the charge that, to the extent economic recovery from the 1975 recession had occurred, it had taken place because of congressional initiatives and in spite of Ford's foot-dragging. Beyond that, the Democrats would say, recovery was far from complete: unemployment seemed to be stuck at an uncomfortable 7.5 percent rate. Ford's counterpunch tactic was to concede that while his initial approach, notably the silly Whip Inflation Now program, had been wrong, he had shifted gears in timely fashion and now should get credit for the economic surge.

"When I became president," said Ford while hunting for votes in Florida, "we had over 12 percent inflation, we were on the brink of a serious recession with unemployment going up, and employment going down. . . . Since March of last year, we have had a steady increase in jobs, and a downward trend in the unemployment rate."[51] Ford's actual strategy, although he approved a large antirecession tax cut under pressure from the Democrats, was to use his veto power to stall Democratic proposals for job expansion, and to block beefed-up funding for housing and public works the Democrats sought as an antidote to rising unemployment and urban tension. Adams, in his presentation to the Democratic Platform Committee, had condemned Ford's "government by veto." At the same time, Adams warned his fellow Democrats that if they wanted to pump more money into social programs, they could not at the same time finance upgrading of the military services, or stimulate private investment in plant and equipment.

Carter—largely unknown before 1976—won the nomination at the July Democratic National Convention in New York. In his acceptance speech, he snapped that Ford had evinced an insensitivity to the needs of the country by vetoing a $4 billion Democratic public works bill, even though the June unemployment rate stood at 7.5 percent. Carter pledged to push for "full employment," meaning a reduction of the jobless level to 4.5 percent, which he said could be achieved while keeping "the inflation rate down to 4 or 5 percent, with proper government management."[52] The latter phrase meant reliance on an "incomes policy" formulated mostly by Carter aide Jerry J. Jasinowski, who had worked on the Humphrey-Hawkins legislation. Jasinowski saw "incomes policy" not only as a government effort to hold down wages and prices, but as a way to modernize ingrained union, government, and industry practices that block competition or that in other ways add to inflationary pressures.[53]

During the primary campaign, Lawrence R. Klein, a University of

Pennsylvania pioneer in the creation of econometric "models" to forecast the economy and president-elect of the prestigious American Economic Association, was brought in to supervise an economic policy task force cobbled together by long-time Carter confidant Stuart E. Eizenstat, a young Atlanta lawyer, and John Bowles, a New York stockbroker.[54] Klein's assignment was to educate Carter, an engineer by training, who knew little about economics. Just before his nomination, Carter had voiced his innocent belief on *Meet the Press* that the nation could simultaneously enjoy low rates of unemployment, inflation, and interest, citing the happy situation at the end of the Truman administration, when the unemployment rate was below 3 percent, the inflation rate less than 1 percent, and the average budget surplus over seven years had been $2.4 billion. "And at the same time interest rates were low too. I think the FHA loan interest rate then was 4 percent. So I don't think there is any incompatibility between low unemployment and low inflation. In general, I think they go together," Carter said.[55]

Klein set out to demonstrate to Carter that the Truman record, at the end of the Korean War, was the exception that proved the rule: Klein's plan was to build a strategy for Carter that would establish "full employment" as Carter's top priority. But what represented full employment? Klein ducked pinpointing a number. He wasn't happy with the Humphrey-Hawkins Bill, which originally called for the immediate institution of a 3 percent unemployment target, with a commitment that the federal government would become "employer of last resort," at "prevailing wages." But after the target was redefined to mean "adult" unemployment of 3 percent after four years—which translated into an easier-to-achieve 4.5 percent unemployment target for the labor force as a whole—Carter endorsed the bill, and its general goals were incorporated into the Democratic platform.[56]

Faced with the commitment by the Democratic candidate to give top priority to a new economic stimulus designed to cut unemployment, the Republican convention in Kansas City nominated Ford and pledged, in its platform, a steady-as-you-go economy with "less government, less spending, less inflation," in contrast to what it said was the Democratic platform commitment to "more government, more spending, more inflation."[57] Simon, who feared that GOP politicians might be tempted to churn out a "watered-down version" of the Democratic platform, succeeded in producing a Republican campaign document that almost exactly represented the "get the government off our backs" philosophy trumpeted by Reagan. When Ford, on the eve of the Kansas City convention in August, met with a group of *Washington Post* editors and reporters, I quoted Simon's laissez-faire philosophy to the president, noting how closely it matched Reagan's thinking. I then asked Ford to what extent he endorsed the Reagan-Simon charge that bigger government, as advocated by Democrats, had become a threat to economic liberty. "I won't comment about Mr. Reagan's approach, but I will say with emphasis that my whole approach as president has been to put a greater reliance on the private sector and in the area of taxation," Ford responded. "Not only in my period of two years in the White House, but my whole philosophy in Congress was predicated on greater reliance on the private sector and a lessening of the responsibility of the federal government."[58] Ford prevailed over Reagan at the convention: the power of the incumbent carried him through despite the minimal nature of his achievements in the White House.

THE ECONOMIC CAMPAIGN strategy that would prove successful in November was devised at Carter's home in Plains, Georgia, and at his national campaign headquarters in Atlanta, by a small group of Carter aides and longtime friends headed by lawyer Stuart Eizenstat. Their underlying goal was to pin the responsibility for recession on Ford, and then defeat him by following a standard Keynesian approach to revive the economy—higher spending and lower taxes—without reigniting inflation. Eizenstat and Jerry Jasinowski planned a campaign stressing four economic goals, each within a different time frame: full employment, reduction of inflation, steady economic growth, and a balanced budget. Jobs and growth would have the top priority, but realistically no one anticipated that the July 1976 jobless rate, standing at 7.8 percent, could be brought down to the Humphrey-Hawkins target of 4.5 in the first year of a new administration. They would settle for a 5.0 to 5.5 percent range in 1977. And the balanced budget target would have to wait until 1980. Even so, some liberal Democrats such as Senator George McGovern complained that the balanced budget target had been established without regard for poor and middle-class America.[59]

Moreover, after meeting with a dozen leading Democratic economists in Plains on July 28, 1976, immediately following his nomination, Carter had agreed that government spending should not be boosted beyond the current level of about 22 percent of the gross national product. That was a relatively conservative yardstick, designed to add to Carter's appeal to moderate Republicans: by establishing a broad limit to expansion of the public sector, Eizenstat pointed out, the Georgia governor could respond to Ford administration charges "that we are reckless spenders."[60]

But in early September, with the election close at hand, Carter waffled on an earlier pledge to give top priority to battling unemployment: he promised to approve no new spending programs unless their cost "is compatible with my goal of having a balanced budget before the end of my first term." That was an effort to reinforce relations with key business leaders who were disappointed by Carter's choice of liberal Senator Walter F. Mondale of Minnesota as a running mate. Businessmen unhappily took note of endorsements of Mondale by Meany and consumer advocate Ralph Nader.[61]

As the Carter campaign against President Ford swung into high gear, the economy began to slip—even Alan Greenspan publicly acknowledged the existence of a "pause," the favorite euphemism of economists who can't bring themselves to utter the word "recession." The unemployment rate for August increased for the third month in a row, to 7.9 percent, dashing Greenspan's hope for a turnaround. As usual, the black unemployment rate was almost double that for whites—13.6 percent, compared to 7.1 percent. And black teenage unemployment shot up within the month from 34.1 percent to 40.2 percent. The overall jobless rate, as a snapshot of the whole economy, doesn't portray what may be going on in various industries or regions of the country, and never gives a full picture of economic discrimination against women and minority groups. Nevertheless, the unemployment number was the most closely watched sign of the nation's economic health. Under Ford, it had hit as high as 8.9 percent in May 1975. But after that there had been steady improvement, down to 7.3 percent a year later. Inasmuch as the rate of inflation had been cut in half from an unacceptable 11 percent in 1974, there was a degree of optimism within the Ford administration and in business circles that the worst was over. But conditions deteriorated in the campaign summer of 1976, and although confronted by an August jobless rate of 7.9 percent, Greenspan clung to a forecast that the unemployment rate by the end of the year would be less than 7 percent.[62] In the end, an uncomfortable 8.1 percent jobless rate in December proved him wrong.

Labor Day found the union movement's political machinery fully geared up to help Carter, a dramatic change from 1972 when Meany had sulked, refusing to let the AFL-CIO's political action arm, the Committee on Political Education (COPE), work for George McGovern, whom he detested. Meany never had forgiven McGovern for a Senate speech in which the South Dakotan accused the labor leader of trying to interfere with American foreign policy. Meany made clear in private conversations that as between Nixon and McGovern, he thought McGovern—who opposed the Vietnam War that Meany fully backed—the greater evil. In 1976, Meany was eighty-two, ailing, and grumpy. He had hoped his old friend Hubert Humphrey would make a comeback and get the Democratic nomination, and therefore had rejected entreaties by Jerry Wurf and Leonard Woodcock that he join them in an early endorsement of Carter. But once Carter agreed to Mondale, a labor union favorite, as his running mate, Meany decided he would actively support the Democratic ticket. In a boisterous speech to 110 AFL-CIO union presidents meeting in Washington, Meany charged that Ford had wrecked the economy. "The seven and one-half years of Nixon-Ford rule have been ruinous," Meany intoned. Thus the Meany venom that Nixon escaped was now turned loose against Ford. Meany even gave leave to COPE director Mary Zon to join Carter's Atlanta staff as labor's liaison with the campaign.[63]

Late in October, with the election only two weeks away, the Commerce Department reported that the economy had grown at a rate of just under 4 percent in the third quarter, down from 4.5 percent in the second and 9.2 percent in the first quarter of 1976, or not enough to allow for improvement in the politically significant unemployment rate. Although that was a respectable rate of growth—and the rate of inflation had moderated slightly—Carter was able to tout the result as "proof that the economy is in a downward slide." Ford was on the defensive, although there was as yet no conclusive proof in the numbers that the economy was stagnating. Yet there were signs of real economic distress: abroad, the British pound had sunk to an all-time low, and the Italian lira and French franc (to a lesser degree) were in trouble, too, telltale symbols of a global economic malaise triggered in part by the stagflation effect of the first oil shock.

As the election campaign in the United States moved toward its climax, the International Monetary Fund was debating aid packages to Britain and France, which meant, in practical terms, that the United States, West Germany, and Japan—as the biggest supporters of the IMF—would help Britain and France with an infusion of about $5 billion in new funds. At the same time, OPEC was about to administer another "tax" on its Western customers, threatening a 10 percent boost on crude oil to $13 a barrel. The U.S. federal energy administrator, Frank Zarb, one of OPEC's few outspoken American critics, asserted: "I don't think they're entitled to [another] dime, and they ought to be told that."[64]

That November, Carter squeezed by Ford with less than a 2 million vote margin in a total of 80 million. As he took office in January 1977, he would face an awesome set of problems at home and abroad—problems that none of his predecessors had managed to overcome but that were growing daily in intensity and consequence.

DRIFT

8

Jimmy Carter's Ineptitude

J IMMY CARTER would prove as inept as Gerald Ford at managing the nation's affairs, failing to recognize and to deal with the massive inflation that finally caught up with the country after the interlocking mistakes of the Johnson, Nixon, and Ford years. Carter's incompetence was symbolized by shifts of policy so frequent that they left supporters as well as critics befuddled. "Carter has not given us an *idea* to follow," said James Fallows, who worked as a speechwriter, then left the administration to write critically of his former boss: "He holds explicit, thorough positions on every issue under the sun, but he has no large view of the relations between them, no line indicating which goals (reducing unemployment? human rights?) will take precedence over which (inflation control? a SALT treaty?) when the goals conflict. Spelling out these choices makes the difference between a position and a philosophy, but it is an act foreign to Carter's mind."[1] Mark Siegel, who was executive director of the Democratic National Committee, recalled that the morning after Carter's election, Hamilton Jordan, Carter's campaign manager, phoned to ask Siegel to prepare a memo on Patricia Harris, former dean of Howard University law school, because Carter was considering her for a cabinet post. Siegel agreed, but asked: "Which cabinet position and what kind of background information do you want?" According to Siegel, Jordan's response was: "We don't know which position, we just think we may want to take a look at her. Go ahead and put together any information you think might be useful to us." (Carter later named Harris secretary of housing and urban development and to other cabinet posts.) Siegel cites Jordan's request as an example of "the lack of structure, lack of direction, and above all, lack of programmatic and ideological parameters" that dominated the Carter presidency over the four years that followed.[2]

Jimmy Carter appeared bored by inflation, trade deficits, and other problems of the domestic economy. But aware that Wall Street and the business community intuitively distrust a Democratic president, Carter worked overtime to gain that elusive commodity known as business "confidence." Instead, he should have sought only its respect. As a self-proclaimed Washington outsider, Carter was never smooth in dealing with Congress, even though his own party was in control. Indeed, he often alienated the very Democrats whose support he needed.

On the Hill, the Democrats' old-line constituencies—the liberals and the unions that had held the Great Society together for Lyndon Johnson—were in control. And indeed, those were the same Democratic constituencies that, somewhat reluctantly, had helped elect Carter. But the former Georgia governor was a fiscal conservative. "In the early stages, the need, the perceived need, both politically and economically, for economic stimulus ran against the grain of his fiscal conservatism," observed his CEA chairman, Charles Schultze. Early on, Carter aides had floated some ideas on wage-price incomes policies, but it was clear that neither business nor labor, remembering unpleasant experiences in the Nixon controls era, wanted to risk them again.[3] The public, of course, was caught in the middle: labor leaders justified the rise in wages by citing the recent history of price increases, and businessmen justified the boost in prices by the pay increases to which they already had committed themselves, and additional rises that lay inevitably on the horizon.[4] Carter, in turn, briefly blamed the inflation rate on the persistent federal deficit—a linkage that Democratic economists had shunned and Republican economists had promoted. Standard Democratic dogma was that budget deficits were the product of economic malaise, not the cause as Carter said at a press conference in May 1977.

Carter turned out to be the most conservative Democratic president in years, a deep disappointment to old-style, FDR liberals like the attorney and activist Joseph L. Rauh. Arthur M. Schlesinger Jr., for one, believed only President Grover Cleveland, among Democrats, was more to the right of center than Carter. Vernon E. Jordan of the National Urban League and Benjamin L. Hooks of the NAACP, who also had vigorously supported Carter, made the same assessment. They contended that the economic stimulus packages

Carter's aides devised in 1977 and 1978 to redeem his 1976 campaign pledge did nothing to create jobs in the ghettoes.

Alan Greenspan, who as Ford's chief economic adviser during the 1976 campaign had accused Carter of courting inflation, took a long look at the Carter White House four months after the inaugural and liked what he saw. "In my view," Greenspan said, "Carter has moved in a direction that is quite sensible."[5] Greenspan understood that Carter was intuitively more conservative than many of his chief aides.[6]

In retrospect, Carter may have condemned the nation to double-digit inflation and double-digit interest rates when he met with his economic advisory team in Plains in December 1976 to settle on the details of his economic program for the first year. At that session, Carter, strongly influenced by his friend and adviser, Georgia banker Thomas B. (Bert) Lance, rejected the reinstitution of anything as mild as voluntary wage-price guideposts, recommended by former CEA chairman Arthur Okun. Lance—originator of the "if it ain't broke, don't fix it" philosophy—sold Carter on the notion that dabbling in the controls business would shatter "business confidence." Even Schultze, a liberal economist and LBJ's former budget director, chimed in with the view that the economy could be stimulated for a year or so without seriously rekindling inflation. There was no pressure from Treasury Secretary-designate W. Michael Blumenthal to move Carter into a tougher anti-inflation posture.

Carter's first anti-inflation program, when unveiled in mid-April 1977, was ineffective. It relied almost exclusively on a plea to business and labor to show restraint, the goal being to drop the cost of living index by two percentage points from an "underlying" rate defined as 6 percent to 4 percent by the end of 1979. There were no mandatory controls. Nor were there voluntary targets against which the public could match the success of business and union efforts, as Blumenthal had suggested as a possibility. Yet the consumer price index in the first quarter had risen at an annual rate of 9.1 percent—not the 6 percent "underlying" calculation devised by Schultze's Council of Economic Advisers. By sweeping aside all controversial proposals, Carter's excessively timid program invited immediate comparison with President Ford's ill-fated WIN program in 1974.

Timidity and confusion also guided Carter's hand in a "comprehensive" energy conservation program. Carter set out to break up the average American's love affair with the family car, especially the big, expensive gas-guzzler, by proposing to make gasoline more expensive and to place a penalty tax on cars that yielded less than twenty miles to the gallon by 1980, as required by then-existing law.

Price ceilings on "new oil"—even if drilled close to existing wells—would be lifted, giving the domestic industry the bonanza it had long demanded for additional exploration. Gradually, the price of all oil, old and new, would work its way up to the OPEC levels. And once there, oil producers would be entitled to an allowance for domestic inflation, a sort of self-perpetuating price indexation system. Meanwhile, as an incentive to businessmen to convert to other energy sources, Carter sought to provide a half-dozen different kinds of investment tax credits. Yet nowhere did Carter or his aides provide an estimate of the inflationary impact of the program. Instead, Carter proceeded to sell the notion that his goals could be accomplished painlessly—that is, by boosting the consumer price index no more than one-fourth to one-half a percentage point.

Energy was not the only international economic issue to demand Carter's attention early in his term. There was the strong possibility of global recession, and the appearance of vigorous forms of trade restrictions in response to the amazing surge of the Japanese economy and the ability of Japanese companies to penetrate world markets dominated by American and European countries from the end of the Second World War through the entire decade of the 1960s.

Within days after his inauguration in January 1977, Carter sent Vice President Mondale, with help from Assistant Treasury Secretary for International Affairs C. Fred Bergsten, on a round-the-world mission to acquaint America's trading partners with a new idea: the "locomotive theory," also known as "engines for growth." The basic idea was that the Big Three nations—the United States, Germany, and Japan—could lead a global boom. The locomotive theory had been developed by three economists brought into top positions at the State and Treasury departments: Undersecretary of State for Economic Affairs Richard N. Cooper; Undersecretary of the Treasury Anthony Solomon; and Bergsten. They persuaded Carter that the Big Three nations, by expanding their economic activity, would generate a demand for greater imports from less affluent nations, spreading prosperity around the globe. Specifically, Mondale was commissioned to urge the Germans, enjoying an inflation rate of less than 4 percent, a trade surplus of $14 billion, and a 14 percent national savings rate, to boost their economic growth targets above a projected 5 percent. Unemployment was high by German historical standards, at 1 million, or 4.5 percent of the labor force.[7]

But in Chancellor Helmut Schmidt, Mondale met firm resistance to anything more than cosmetic changes in the German economic program. Schmidt was bitterly resentful of outsiders telling him how to run the Germany economy. He reflected traditional German fear of inflation; for Schmidt, any inflation rate above zero was considered dangerous. In addition, Schmidt had taken an intense dislike to Carter. "Schmidt never thought Carter was a leader," Robert S. Strauss, Carter's trade representative and former chairman of the Democratic National Committee during the 1976 campaign, said later. "He didn't think Carter knew what was going on, but Schmidt was overly critical of everybody. Ford was the only president Schmidt had any use for. . . . It wasn't anything specific: he just thought they didn't know their jobs."[8]

ON TRADE ISSUES, union leaders felt betrayed by Carter, when he seemed to part company with labor by opposing protectionism. The message was clear when Carter overturned a recommendation by the International Trade Commission for a sharp boost in tariffs on imported shoes, a ruling that had been sought by the AFL-CIO in a misguided effort to protect jobs in the declining American shoe industry. The debate on protection for the shoe industry brought the first hint of a deepening split in the Democratic Party on trade issues: eventually, the once-dominant free-trade wing of the party would capitulate to the influence of labor's economic nationalism. "Though it is early in the game," said AFL-CIO secretary-treasurer Lane Kirkland, "the recent signs and portents lead us to wonder if our support [in the campaign] was not just another triumph of hope over experience."[9] Carter's free-trade stance on the shoe issue was merely one item in Kirkland's growing list of complaints, including big business dominance of the cabinet, Carter's refusal to back a $3 an hour minimum wage, and his reluctance to push direct job-creating legislation.

Tutored by Bert Lance, Carter set out to create and then enhance "business confidence" in his administration. First, he promised a balanced budget by the end of his term. Then he foreswore any backsliding into wage and price controls, or even anything as disturbing as voluntary wage-price guidelines. He opposed a proposal for a $3 minimum wage, regardless of the impact such opposition would have on Meany: so much the better would be his reception in the boardrooms of America, he must have figured.

Meanwhile, Carter's economic team began to search for an infusion of economic strength that would help ward off labor's growing disenchantment. The Carter transition team evolved a two-year $31.2 billion stimulus package. In the first year, there would be a $15.5 billion program featuring a $50-per-person rebate of 1976 taxes, followed in the second year by a $15.7 billion spending program weighted heavily to jobs and public works. The $50 rebate idea was conceived as a quick infusion of cash for consumers by Schultze, leader of the liberal bloc of economic advisers. The Carter "left wing" also included Vice President Mondale and Secretary of Labor Ray Marshall. Schultze was highly regarded in the profession. But the union leaders in the Carter camp worried that Schultze was too much a free-trader. An even bigger sin Schultze had committed, in Meany's view, was his advocacy of "incomes policies"—the buzzword for experimentation in controlling wages and prices, sometimes voluntary, sometimes not. Schultze's rebate gimmick came under attack immediately from Democratic politicians on Capitol Hill, who questioned its effectiveness. They argued that the economy would respond better to old-fashioned pump priming. But liberal Democratic economists, such as Arthur Okun, agreed with Schultze that the rebate was worth 200,000 jobs and a half-point jump in the gross national product, at a cost of a mere one-tenth of a percentage point on the inflation index.[10]

But Schultze also had to contend with Carter's "right-wing" cronies from Georgia. There was, first of all, Carter's confidant, Charles Kirbo, a prominent Atlanta lawyer who didn't accompany Carter to Washington but who remained Carter's most frequently consulted friend when Carter had to resolve close debates among advisers. Then there was Lance, the new budget director, who had been Carter's highway administrator in Georgia. Lance acted as a counterweight to liberal labor influences within the administration until September 1977, when Carter was forced to fire him after he was caught by Comptroller of the Currency John G. Heimann in unethical banking practices.[11] Michael Blumenthal was also supposed to be something of a balance to the liberals in the Carter administration. He appeared to own the ideal résumé for a secretary of the Treasury in a Democratic administration: not only was he a Democrat and chief executive officer of the Bendix Corporation, but he had an economics degree and had played a key role in the Kennedy administration as a trade negotiator. Moreover, Blumenthal was tough. After his family had escaped the Nazis, he spent his young teenage years in the predominantly Jewish ghetto in Japanese-controlled Shanghai. Blumenthal stayed in China two years after the end of the war, scrounging for work. In 1979, thirty-two years after he left China, I accompanied Blumenthal, now a distinguished cabinet officer, on a tour of his old neighborhoods in Shanghai. He told me: "You needed a sense of survival to make it. So you lose your awe of some big shot sitting behind a desk."[12] But important elements of the business community never trusted Blumenthal. Incredibly, one negative, so far as the blue bloods were concerned, was that Blumenthal had made his mark as CEO at Bendix in Detroit, not in prestigious New York. And in the small minds of some businessmen, to possess a Ph.D. in economics, as Blumenthal did, indicated a thinker, not a doer.

The carping was unfair to Blumenthal, who was intellectually light-years ahead of the typical CEO. But Blumenthal was not a natural politician. He just didn't know how to shoot the bull with the Georgia mafia on Carter's personal staff, or with senators and congressmen on the Hill, although Robert Strauss had offered to give him pointers. Strauss thought he was doing Blumenthal a favor; to Blumenthal, it sounded patronizing.

Blumenthal was aware that he wasn't accepted by his peers in the business world, and it bothered him. At a dinner meeting in 1978 at Washington's tony F Street Club hosted for him by Time Inc., the mutual hostility was palpable. That night, Blumenthal told his fellow CEOs a story that betrayed his frustration. The job that had best prepared him for Washington, he said, was as a stagehand for the famous stripper Lily St. Cyr, a position he landed in Las Vegas soon after leaving Shanghai in 1947. Offstage, he explained, his duties were to flash colored lights on Lily, then gradually dim them as she did her striptease. "But while the customers out front were cheering what they thought they saw, I would see her as she finished her act, au naturel. That's how I learned the difference between appearance and reality. In Washington, it's the same thing."[13]

Carter aides Hamilton Jordan and Jody Powell didn't accord Blumenthal the normal deference due the nation's chief financial officer, and arguably the most important cabinet officer next to the secretary of state. Press Secretary Powell, for example, didn't hesitate to second-guess Blumenthal's public statements on tax policy. Blumenthal's regular harassment by the Georgia mafia couldn't have taken place without Carter's knowledge and participation. This would lead, later, to Blumenthal's summary dismissal by Carter in the midst of the 1979 energy crisis.

There is only one word for economic policy under Carter: disorganized. Eizenstat recalled that the intention had been to build an economic policy group modeled after President Ford's, in which William Seidman, as an assistant to the president and someone who understood the nexus between politics and economics, acted as a bridge between the economic advisers and the president and, even more important, as a bridge between the Treasury secretary, who normally acted as chief spokesman, and the president. Blumenthal needed such an intermediary because he never had quite the access to Carter that he needed. Said Eizenstat: "Mike Blumenthal was never vested with the kind of authority he should have had. There was always the question whether Mike was the chief spokesman, or was it Charlie [Schultze], chairman of the Council of Economic Advisers? There was never the laying of the president's hands on Mike [as chief spokesman], which was necessary to have him do his job. There was constant bickering about who belonged to the Economic Policy Group, and should the Commerce and Labor departments participate. But most important, we didn't have a Bill Seidman in the White House. I wanted one. De facto, it fell to me. So I said to Charlie, 'Look, why don't you come over to the West Wing and fulfill the Bill Seidman function? Be my equivalent as domestic coordinator.' My job was to coordinate development of policy for domestic agencies. I said to Charlie, 'Why don't you do that in the economic area, because we don't have that, we don't have the nexus between the EPG and the president, that link is missing.' And he said, and I think in retrospect, rightly so, 'That's not my job. My job is to give him [Carter] completely objective economic advice. My job is to be a sort of economic think tank for the president, to give objective economic advice to the president, and not to get involved in the nitty-gritty of policy development compromises and so forth.' "[14]

In the absence of a Bill Seidman to coordinate economic policy, Carter invariably was left to choose among many options. "If there were five economists," said the Brookings Institution's Barry Bosworth, who served for a period on the Cost of Living Council, "Carter usually had six options, because invariably one adviser would put in two options." Inevitably, Bosworth said, Carter accepted the middle ground."[15]

That sort of free-for-all among the economic advisers left a lot of room for a powerful influence like Bert Lance. Until his disgrace, Lance was in effect deputy president of the United States. Lance was Carter's tennis buddy and principal confidant, except for Kirbo. "I think I understand [Carter] as well as anybody in this country, with the exception of Rosalynn," Lance said. It was not an overstatement: a man of huge bulk and homespun wit, Lance became Carter's trusted emissary to the business community, a jack-of-all-trades for the president. He assured top executives they could trust Carter—confiding that his boss was essentially a Southern conservative who would spring no surprises, especially on wage-price control issues, and who was sympathetic to assigning top priority to control of inflation. It was in that context that Lance could promise them that "Jimmy may campaign liberal, but he governs conservative." Shrewd, earthy, and gregarious, Lance was the living embodiment of the aggressive, but charming, Southern politico not seen in Washington since John Connally had displayed similar snake-oil refinements for Richard Nixon. Lance became an instant celebrity. "When I walk across the hotel lobby," he told the Washington Press Club, "I just put out my hand and say, 'Hello, my name is Bert Lance.' And I see some of 'em look over their shoulder as if to say: 'When did he get loose?' "[16]

It didn't take long for Lance's antennae to pick up the bitter opposition to Schultze's $50 rebate idea among congressional leaders, who wanted the money spent on manpower and public works programs, not on what they regarded as a frivolous gesture that would do little to help the economy. Quietly, Lance, with Blumenthal now joining in, persuaded Carter on April 14, 1977, to drop the idea— even though it had just narrowly passed in the House. Carter strode into the White House press briefing room, and stunned reporters with the announcement that he was withdrawing the controversial rebate proposal because the economy had turned up. Inflation, Carter said, was now the main threat to the economy.

Carter's flip-flop on the $50 tax rebate not only generated an image of presidential indecisiveness, but was a telltale sign that on an economic issue into which Lance and Blumenthal could feed the input of the business community, they could dominate Schultze and Eizenstat. "You might as well throw $50 bills out of an airplane window," Lance remembered some businessmen saying—a judgment he passed on to Carter. "To go all out, if you didn't need it, and moreover, when it became a symbol to business of something that would destroy confidence, why persist?" Blumenthal explained.[17]

Whatever his private feelings, loyalist Schultze publicly endorsed the Blumenthal explanation, arguing that the consumer had jump-started the economic recovery, and really didn't need the inducement of a tax rebate. So did Eizenstat, excusing Carter's decision as that of a "sui generis president." But with the benefit of hindsight, and a drift toward conservatism in his own philosophy, Eizenstat years later would come to believe that Carter's major blunder in 1977 "was not focusing sufficiently on inflation early enough," a mistake he blamed on pressure from left-liberal forces in the Democratic Party.

"You have to remember that Carter was still considered fiscally conservative by the basic elements of the Democratic Party," Eizenstat said. "I think that Carter was a neoliberal, someone who fell between the cracks—too conservative for the liberals and too liberal for the conservatives. [Speaker of the House Thomas P.] 'Tip' O'Neill and [Majority Leader] Jim Wright felt the stimulus package was not ample enough, not enough [devoted to] public works spending. . . . So we did have our eye too much on unemployment. We did probably a mild amount of overstimulus on the fiscal side. I'm told that conservative economists, people like Milton Friedman and Steve Axilrod [a Federal Reserve staffer] think the problem was not fiscal policy at all, it was monetary policy, it was much too easy. But the main point is that there was a blind eye to inflation. Once there was a recognition that inflation was rising, the steps taken were too temperate, too moderate. I was very much a part of that temperance—because there was a mortal fear among mainstream Keynesians of throwing the economy into a recession and of hurting poor people, hurting our constituents. We were ill equipped to deal with inflation. Carter was more inflation-sensitive, budget-deficit-sensitive than a lot of people in his administration. He was constantly whipsawed between the Democratic groups on Capitol Hill and the interest groups there on the one hand and his own [conservative] instincts on the other. Nor, would I say, was he getting contrary economic advice from his economists. Wage and price controls were a possibility. I pushed very hard to get those in our '77 package, and although they were in our [campaign] White Paper, Charlie [Schultze] and the others were very much against it."[18]

As preparations began for Carter's first trip to Europe for the London Economic Summit, Robert Strauss saw an opportunity to get a political impetus from global leaders for the Tokyo round of trade negotiations that he was trying to bring to a conclusion. To his surprise, Henry Owen, the president's chief "sherpa," or preparer, for the discussions, told him: "We haven't received your paper yet for the summit." That's when Owen learned what made Bob Strauss tick: a simple operating credo, which held that the key to success was the projection of "the image of power."[19] Strauss told Owen not to worry about the trade paper, he'd deliver it himself to Carter in London.

"You don't seem to understand," Owen responded. "You won't be going, only the secretary of state and the secretary of the Treasury will be going, so just send me your paper."

Strauss retorted: "Mr. Owen, if you get any paper from me, it will be my resignation." He went on to say: "Mr. Owen, this is contrary to the deal I cut with the president. And I may not be going, but if I don't speak for trade at this summit, I'll have no power, and no image of power, and the only way you get anything done, you have to have the image of power. And I am close enough to this president through the campaign that he would expect me to have it. And if I show up with it I will be accepted. If I don't go to the summit, it's perfectly all right with me, I didn't want this job anyway, he'll just have to get himself another boy.' "

Owen looked stunned, and threatened to tell the president of Strauss's remarks. Strauss was unmoved, and said, "By all means be my guest, because if you don't I will."

Owen left. Ten minutes later he was back in Strauss's office, looking chastened. He said, "I've had a very interesting experience. I told the president what you said. He just smiled, and we went on to other things. As the meeting broke up, I said, 'Mr. President, what should I say to Bob Strauss?' And he said, 'Why don't you let me talk to Bob, and you make reservations on the plane [for him].' I said, 'There are only two seats in the room [one each for Secretary of State Cyrus Vance and Treasury Secretary Blumenthal].' The president told me: 'You explain to Cy that he will leave when Strauss has to talk about trade, and I'll talk to Bob.' "

Strauss thus had established the principle that he had direct access to Carter, and that ability stood him well. "I could go in to see the president with a half hour's notice, and say, 'Mr. President, you have to call Helmut Schmidt before the close of business today, and tell him so and so. Or call [Prime Minister James] Callaghan, or Giscard, and I could tell Carter these things in two minutes, it didn't take a ten-page position paper. And he'd pick up the goddamn phone right there, and get 'em."[20]

What had preceded Carter to Europe—which had rooted for "safe" Gerald Ford to win the election—was Carter's rather unflattering image on television, that of a toothy, grinning figure who "looked something like Howdy Doody," according to one senior European official. Schmidt, for one, hadn't hesitated to tell Mondale that he was unhappy that Bill Simon would no longer be Treasury secretary. "You know," Schmidt told Mondale, "we owe a lot to Bill Simon." To which Mondale grinned: "We owe Bill Simon everything—without him, we wouldn't have won the election."

Schmidt had the erroneous impression that Carter was a knee-jerk liberal, uninformed about global or serious international economic matters. It was true that Carter's only prior contact with foreign issues had been through his membership on the Trilateral Commission, a David Rockefeller–managed private group in which selected businessmen and labor leaders were brought together once a year to rub shoulders with academics and officials and ex-officials of major governments.

When Jimmy Carter burst on the scene, America's trade partners preferred Gerald Ford. Schmidt had developed a rapport with Ford, when he and former French president Valery Giscard d'Estaing first established the economic summit process in Rambouillet in December 1975.

But at least some of the negative view of Carter prevalent in Europe was dissipated at the 1977 London summit, where the American president in his first appearance on the international economic scene demonstrated an inquiring and sharp mind. He came across as much more conservative on economic issues than the Europeans had expected—but liberal on human rights issues. In part because of Chancellor Schmidt's reservations, and in part because of Carter's own caution, Carter's earlier intent to press for global economic expansion was shelved at that London meeting. Instead, the summit declaration not only reflected the more conservative German economic philosophy focusing on stabilization and control of inflation, but on a much more restricted agenda relating to human rights and control of nuclear energy. Carter accepted the much softer promise by Japan and Germany to take whatever steps were necessary to achieve previously announced growth targets. German officials could scarcely conceal their glee at having won a substantial victory over Carter.[21] They were especially elated that the summit communiqué declared that "inflation does not reduce unemployment," classic conservative doctrine they hadn't even been able to get past the two Ford summits, where Alan Greenspan had been a key influence.[22]

And any pretense that the richer nations—the "North"—would undertake more than token transfers of wealth to the poorer countries—the "South"—were put aside. "For us," said Bundesbank vice president Otmar Emminger, the go-slow approach "means there will be no more exhortation to inflate a little more to make life easier for other countries. That conforms to our thinking and experience."[23] Japan, which had been publicly battered by Trade Representative Robert Strauss and British Secretary of State for Trade Edmund Dell for accumulating huge trade surpluses, promised to cut its positive international balance of payments from $11.1 billion in 1976 to $7.3 billion in 1977 by expanding public works programs at home and cutting domestic taxes to generate consumer buying to soak up goods that otherwise would be exported.[24]

The London summit also grappled—unsuccessfully—with the question of the suppression of free trade and, despite inclusion of cosmetically acceptable antiprotectionist language, failed to reproduce the specific commitment of the Rambouillet and Dorado Beach summits "to avoid the imposition of new trade barriers." Thus neither Carter nor Strauss got what they hoped to get out of the summit, a stimulus to both economic growth and world trade. As for Strauss's charter to negotiate trade agreements that would open global markets, the summit was little short of disaster.

French president Valery Giscard d'Estaing, troubled by high unemployment, a 13 percent inflation rate, and the possibility of a Socialist-Communist victory in parliamentary elections scheduled for March 1978, surrendered to the increasingly protectionist demands of French industry and labor. Giscard filibustered his summit partners with long soliloquies on the benefits of *"dirigisme organizé"*—organized regulation of trade—with the result that the antiprotectionist language of the first two summits was dropped. French prime minister Raymond Barre was able to needle Carter by referring to the "orderly marketing agreements" that the United States—under Strauss's management—had imposed on Japan to limit its imports of color television sets and other products.

Strauss had defended such agreements as a "second best" approach. Without import quota limits, he contended, Congress was ready to apply even stronger sanctions because the United States' trade deficit for 1977 was expected to zoom to as much as $25 billion from $9 billion in 1976.[25] But Giscard and Barre could and did cite the agreements as a precedent for applying similar "antimonopoly" restraints on a wider international front.[26] The Germans were distressed by the French approach on trade—but having scored so many points on the macroeconomic issues, Schmidt didn't come to Carter's support on the trade issue. Thus the drift toward mercantilism continued. Later, Barre would refine Giscard's concept of *"dirigisme organizé"* more deftly as "organized free trade," which would allow for "orderly" growth of trade while limiting the ability of some nations, especially Japan, to succeed in any "massive penetration" of others' markets.[27]

Back in Washington from the summit with little to brag about, Carter had to confront the reality that the consumer cost of living had been growing since April at an annual rate of 10 percent, while economic adviser Schultze was trying to sugarcoat the pill by reminding the public that the "underlying" rate was only 6 percent. The "underlying" rate was economic jargon for taking the prevailing annual wage rise pattern of about 8 percent and subtracting a productivity gain of about 2 percent. The net amount of 6 percent, not matched by productivity improvement, would be reflected in an "underlying" rate of inflation.

But consumers also were paying an additional 4 percent in prices because the cost of food and fuel, largely uncontrolled by the government, was sharply higher. "Underlying" rates of inflation to the contrary notwithstanding, the public had to pay the whole bill. In the real world, double-digit inflation had come back with a vengeance, and Wall Street correctly foresaw that tight money and higher interest rates were bound to follow. Moreover, America's main trading partners/rivals, Japan and Germany, had succeeded in going the other way, Japan from a basic inflation rate of 7.5 percent down to 5 percent, while the Germans had squeezed a 4 percent rate down to a low 3 percent.

In two detailed speeches in the fall of 1977, Schultze cautiously voiced his concern that, by holding back on monetary expansion, Arthur Burns's Federal Reserve could choke off the very modest recovery that seemed to be under way.[28] The stock market ratified Schultze's analysis with a nosedive, representing traders' fears that the tenacious Burns had allowed short-term rates to climb too quickly.

In mid-October, in response to a reporter's question on where Carter stood on monetary policy, Jody Powell posted a statement (drawn from earlier Schultze speeches) in the White House press room criticizing Fed policy. Was it a signal to Burns, up for reappointment as Fed chairman in February 1978, that Carter would dump him? Schultze hastily phoned Burns that no such message had been intended. Burns also got a reassuring call from Blumenthal, with whom he had more rapport. But these signals from 1600 Pennsylvania Avenue elicited a stinging rebuke in a speech by Burns— and Carter and Schultze, who were wary of open warfare with Burns, especially because the business community was increasingly uneasy with the president, retreated under fire.

The tension between the White House and the Fed intensified a shift away from what was referred to as "the golden era of Keynesian economics" in the 1960s, when fiscal and monetary policy combined to yank the economy out of the Eisenhower recession and into a stable period of economic growth with low inflation, especially during the brief Kennedy presidency.[29] Carter, like other presidents before and after, would blame his troubles not on his own failings but on poor advice. "There's a mystic down in Smithville who's got as good a batting average as my economic advisers," Carter once said in a cabinet meeting.[30]

As Jimmy Carter headed into his second year, Lawrence Klein, a campaign adviser, said: "I grade him a 70. The main thing is that economic policy should be steady. He proposed a stimulus program, then dropped the $50 tax rebate. Tax reform was in, then out. Now, there's a big tax cut to be proposed for 1978. People feel that policy is in too much of a flux."[31] Indeed, the only certainty about Carter was his twin addictions to uncertainty and inconsistency.

9

The Failure to Control Inflation

T HE CENTRAL FAILURE of the Carter administration was its
utter inability over four years to control inflation—a failure that
would ultimately lead to the election of Ronald Reagan in 1980.
Runaway inflation in the United States, at a time when authorities
in Japan and Germany were able to keep prices under control,
smashed global confidence in the dollar and encouraged speculators
to seek a safer haven in gold. On July 18, 1978, gold broke through
the $200-an-ounce psychological price barrier that had held since the
1930s. Even in December 1974, when American citizens were allowed to buy and sell gold for the first time since Franklin Roosevelt
took that privilege away, gold did not rise over $200 an ounce, reach-
ing a peak of only $197.50 per ounce. Gold at $200 an ounce in the
hot summer of 1978 (it would rocket to $800 less than two years
later) was proof positive to America's trading partners in Europe and
Asia that Jimmy Carter didn't know how to manage the American
economy: the way Europeans and Asians viewed it, Carter was pushing the price of the dollar down and the price of gold up. What could
be more stupid?

Earlier in the year, frustrated by rising prices, Carter on April 11
announced new steps to fight inflation, including the appointment
of Robert Strauss as coordinator of the effort. Strauss again began to
explore the possibility of a new stab at wage-price guidelines, although George Meany could be counted on to object, and so would
businessmen and mainstream academics, who by and large had al-

ways been skeptical of controls and who warned Carter against trying controls again except in true emergency (or wartime) conditions.[1] Strauss begged Lane Kirkland, who would soon succeed Meany as president of the AFL-CIO, to go along with voluntary guidelines. But Kirkland, a tough-talking ex-sailor, reminded Strauss that, in a voluntary system, unions would not even have recourse to "due process," which they might get with full-fledged controls—which, of course, labor also rejected.[2] Meany later made the suggestion explicit—that if Carter was willing to embrace guidelines, he might as well "go all the way" to full controls that would give labor a voice in designing the system.[3]

Carter and the Federal Reserve Board at first tried to stem the dollar decline by a boost in the discount rate from 7.25 percent to 7.75 percent—the fourth boost in a row—on the theory that higher interest rates, by discouraging business borrowing, would reduce inflation and give those who held dollars reason to keep the greenbacks instead of dumping them on international exchange markets.

A much stronger anti-inflation program was needed, of course, but Carter dallied and temporized. Secretary of the Treasury Michael Blumenthal continued to offer a rosy outlook for the future, predicting that the inflation rate in the first half of 1978 of 10.4 percent would drop to 6.0–6.5 percent in the second half and that for 1979 as a whole the inflation rate would be below that of 1978. "But that double-digit rate [in the first half] has been planted in the minds of some people," Blumenthal lamented.[4]

Barry Bosworth put his finger on the problem in a memo to Carter: because neither business nor labor was willing for the government to intervene in the private decision-making process, "prices are headed no place but up, and the rate of inflation will accelerate over the next couple of years. The real problem is that fiscal and monetary policies don't work, and nobody is willing to accept alternative methods for decelerating inflation." Bosworth's courageous memorandum, which caused Carter great embarrassment when it was leaked, also raised the question whether the Carter administration itself was not a major source of the inflation facing the country.[5]

It was a painful period for Charles Schultze, one of the brightest of the Democratic economists, who had to sublimate some of his own liberal instincts to Carter's innate conservatism. As Carter waffled, unsure how to deal with rising prices, other Democratic economists, including Schultze's close friend, Arthur Okun, concluded that Carter was following policies hardly different from Ford's. Okun had tried to persuade Carter and Schultze to scuttle a conventional tax relief proposal amounting to $15 billion to $20 billion for businesses and individuals, and to use the money in an innovative way to support a program to break the nation away from the "8 and 6" combination, wages rising at 8 percent and prices by 6 percent.[6]

The centerpiece of the Okun plan was to be a voluntary "social contract" to limit wage increases to less than 6 percent and prices to less than 4 percent, with $15 billion offered as tax rebates for employers and employees who would go along. Another $5 billion to $6 billion in tax benefits would flow to state and local governments that cut sales taxes—another factor pushing up the cost of living indexes. Half of the $5 billion to $6 billion would be direct payments by the federal government to those local authorities who reduced or repealed sales taxes in 1978. The other half would come from higher local personal income taxes. Okun argued that unless some such conscious effort were made to break the "8 and 6" cycle, it would become self-perpetuating: "New wage decisions are made against the background of 8 percent advances in other wages and 6 percent in prices. And so they tend to center on 8 percent. Then, with hourly labor costs rising by 8 percent, businesses find their labor costs per unit of output up about 6 percent, and so their prices continue to rise by 6 percent." He believed that both businesses and workers would come out ahead under his program, and that in the aggregate the higher corporate profits and greater individual purchasing power generated by the rebates would stimulate both capital investment and the overall economy.

Okun broke with Schultze, arguing that Carter's timidity would fail to pull the nation out of its inflationary cycle. Okun, an adviser to Carter in the 1976 campaign, worried that Carter's reliance on traditional fiscal and monetary measures wouldn't work to break the pattern. "The time has come to face the likelihood that we have a losing hand, and to deal a new one," Okun said.[7]

Vice President Mondale, who liked the Okun concept, explained it to Carter. It was assigned for study to a task force on inflation control headed by Eizenstat, who, along with Schultze and Cost of Living Council chairman Alfred E. Kahn, approved it, and drafted legislation to put it into effect. But House Ways and Means Committee chairman Al Ullman (D.-Ore.) and other Democratic members rejected Okun's idea as a political nonstarter and "potential budget-buster."[8]

Ultimately, Carter would decide that it was Arthur Burns who was holding up economic recovery. On December 28, 1977, Carter said that he would appoint Textron, Inc., chairman G. William Miller—a Blumenthal find—as chairman of the Fed, despite Miller's lack of financial experience. Burns, seventy-three years old at the time of Carter's election, desperately wanted to be reappointed for another term, and had considerable support in the business community as well as in international financial circles. But Carter, Schultze, Eizenstat, and Blumenthal had grown increasingly disenchanted with him.[9] They concluded that, with Burns at the helm of the Fed, there could be no effective coordination of fiscal and monetary policy. Burns was a brilliant theorist and scholar, but for all his intelligence he had to share the blame with Alan Greenspan for the Ford recession of 1974–75, when Fed policies put the nation through an interest-rate crunch. That doomed his campaign for reappointment. Carter and Blumenthal were determined to have a Democrat running the central bank and had settled on Miller, who had a good reputation as an efficient chief operating officer for a large conglomerate.

To "save" the dollar, Burns, on March 31, 1978—his last day as Fed chairman—called on Carter to establish a credible anti-inflation policy, including a symbolic 10 percent cut in pay for Congress and all federal employees, including the president. Burns also counseled Carter to put up all $50 billion in the nation's gold stock in defense of the dollar, selling the gold for other foreign currencies, which would then be used to buy up dollars when the greenback price dropped in international markets.[10] Following his advice would have been a total break with the more timid "disorderly conditions only" foreign exchange intervention policy Carter and Blumenthal had opted for, under which government intervened in the foreign exchange markets only to combat extremely wide swings attributed to sheer speculative activity. Burns also urged the sale of $10 billion or more of Treasury bonds denominated in foreign currencies to help restore confidence among foreigners that America was determined to stop the slide of the dollar.

Blumenthal and Miller advised Carter to reject the Burns program for defense of the dollar as too radical and possibly counterproductive. They insisted that the proper course was to turn around the fundamental conditions in the economy that were weakening the dollar, including a huge drain on the nation's resources for oil imports. But they had no anti-inflation plan to reach that objective. There were lots of ideas—including academic proposals to use the tax system to help break the inflationary cycle—but no action.[11]

By early 1978, Blumenthal—who had done precious little in the first Carter year to stem the ballooning of prices—began to understand (and say publicly) that inflation, rather than unemployment, was the nation's key economic problem.[12] The consumer price index for January hit an annual rate of 9.9 percent. Because some of the jump represented an increase in food costs, Schultze persisted in talking about an "underlying" inflation rate of about 6 percent. But that ignored the reality of what was going on. Consumers were still paying the full price of inflation. Moreover, Gar Alperovitz, a liberal economist, published in April 1979 an even more disturbing analysis breaking down the overall consumer inflation statistics from December 1978 through February 1979 into three components identified as "consumer necessities."[13] The breakdown showed food rising at a 17.3 percent annual rate, gasoline at 25 percent, and all forms of energy at 17.1 percent. Alperovitz's average of the "necessities" group stood at 13.9 percent—a far cry from Schultze's theoretical "underlying" rate of 6 percent.

Toward the end of 1978, the administration would confess that Schultze's "underlying" rate of 6 percent was really closer to 7 percent.[14] And things would get worse before getting better: in April, the wholesale price index soared at the stunning compounded annual rate of 16.8 percent. Moreover, there was the prospect of even higher energy prices once a long coal strike (which began on December 6, 1977, and lasted over three months) was settled, and Carter had accepted as inevitable the deregulation of natural gas prices. Even worse, the nation was heading into an active year of collective bargaining in 1979. As Bosworth had suggested in his memo, Carter now faced a credibility gap: having acquiesced in the coal wage boost, estimated at 37 percent to 40 percent over three years, the president was hardly in a position to argue when U.S. Steel announced a $10.50 per ton boost in the price of coal.

Other government actions contributing to inflation, as listed by Bosworth, were: higher Social Security taxes, higher minimum wages, restrictions on imports, new environmental and other regulations, and larger farm subsidies. The social justification for some of these actions wasn't challenged, but the cumulative inflationary impact couldn't be ignored. And like a yellow warning signal of dangers yet to come, the dollar registered a spectacular drop in its foreign exchange value early in 1978. Off by 5 percent, just that much of a decline would add one-half point to the inflation rate by raising the prices of imports, according to economist Otto Eckstein.[15] But a weaker dollar also made American exports cheaper in foreign markets, and the trend therefore touched off angst among America's trading partners, who could translate the result into greater American exports into their markets.

Since the end of December 1977, Blumenthal had followed a hands-off policy on dollar intervention, agreeing to prop up the dollar only when there were clear "disorderly conditions" in the exchange markets. Foreigners wondered how far the dollar could sink. So did the average American. On *Meet the Press*, moderator Bill Monroe opined that citizens might worry that "the Statue of Liberty is sinking into the muck."[16]

Within three weeks of rejecting the proposal Burns had made on his last day in office, the Treasury Department was forced to announce it would auction gold on a regular basis, beginning May 23, 1978, to shore up the declining dollar and reduce the trade deficit, while maintaining the limited policy on intervention.[17] Two days later, Blumenthal pledged an all-out defense of the integrity of the dollar to an audience of top-level Arab businessmen, displaying at the same time the naïveté of the Carter administration in its evaluation of the OPEC. He and the president, Blumenthal said, were "counting" on the Arabs to "do their part" to stabilize the global economy by keeping an oil price freeze in place, at least through 1978.[18]

Meanwhile, Miller relentlessly pursued a rigid tight money policy and persuaded Carter to trim back the size of a proposed tax cut. And as the Carter administration veered toward austerity in both fiscal and monetary affairs, fear of recession returned once more. By early July, Blumenthal and Carter were on the verge of a confrontation with their own central bank chairman.

Miller had stubbornly stuck to his tight money policy. Five months after taking over from Burns, he expressed the "hope," in an interview in August 1978 that "we'll see a peaking of interest rates [high-quality bonds then yielded 8 percent to 9 percent] between now and the end of the year."[19] That was one of the all-time bad guesses in American economic history. By the end of the year, rates had neared 12 percent, on their way to a record 21 percent—a transition that would bounce Miller out of the Federal Reserve to make way for Paul Volcker.[20]

It proved to be a tumultuous year, and although it marked Carter's one great success—the Camp David Middle East accords—1978 no doubt sowed the seeds of Carter's ultimate undoing. The Camp David accords added to Carter's prestige, and his aides thought his new image might even enhance his ability to deal with the sagging dollar and rising inflation.[21] But Carter proved unable to manage the economy, or even his own economic team. There was no single person in charge, as first John Connally and then George Shultz had been for Richard Nixon.[22]

In the summer of 1978, Blumenthal's problems with Press Secretary Jody Powell and Chief of Staff Hamilton Jordan broke into the open when Powell told reporters that Carter had not authorized "the secretary of the Treasury or anyone to enter into agreements" on tax policy to be followed by the president.[23]

This dispute arose out of Blumenthal's belief that, despite Carter's opposition, Congress would pass some form of capital gains tax relief that year. Blumenthal told me before going to the Bonn economic summit in mid-July 1978 that he personally felt that some capital gains tax change made sense, and that he was working as a mediator to try to bring about a compromise between Carter's view and extremely generous proposals such as one made by Representative William A. Steiger (R.-Wis.).[24]

Blumenthal explained all of this to Carter on *Air Force One* en route to Bonn. And Carter, according to Blumenthal, told him to see what he could achieve—without making a promise to change his original opposition to a tax cut.

But Powell's public humiliation of Blumenthal was devastating. Blumenthal hadn't committed Carter to any new policy, and Powell's attack could only be interpreted—and was—as an effort by those in the White House who opposed any compromise on the capital gains issue to undercut Blumenthal's effort to make a deal.

HELMUT SCHMIDT'S ABILITY to withstand American pressure for Germany to become a global "locomotive" lasted only one year: at the Bonn economic summit, national aspirations and international needs coincided, which made it a success, even though Carter and Schmidt cordially disliked each other. Schmidt, confident and cocky, agreed that Germany should aim for an extra percentage point of economic growth in exchange for Carter's commitment to decontrol domestic oil prices, allowing them to rise to world levels by the end of 1980. This deal, carefully crafted with the guidance of Carter aide Henry Owen and help from Robert Hormats, still a National Security Council staff member (and again American notetaker at the summit), for many years stood as the most significant achievement of economic summitry. Indeed, the Bonn economic summit of 1978 is generally held to be the model of a summit that provided something for all major participants.[25]

In Bonn, Schmidt and Japanese prime minister Takeo Fukuda, who had attended his first summit in London the year before, together asserted their growing economic/political power, and boldly laid the blame for most of the world's economic problems at the door of the Americans. (Until the Bonn summit, the Japanese had been reluctant to criticize their American mentors. But Fukuda was the first Japanese prime minister to try to play a leadership role at the summits, initiating the discussion of how to fight back against terrorists interrupting global air traffic.[26]) And together with Giscard d'Estaing, Schmidt pressed for a scheme stressing European monetary unity through a new European Monetary System, firmly believing that one day a European currency unit could rival the dollar.

Later, Schmidt and succeeding governments would wonder who got the best of the bargain at the Bonn summit. Carter's promises to reduce oil imports and work harder on inflation policies were only partially kept, and Fukuda also fell short on his commitment to stimulate the Japanese economy. The Germans came to believe that the 1 percent stimulus they had agreed to was a mistake, responsible for inflation in 1979, never to be repeated. In truth, however, the inflationary period that followed was triggered by another oil shock, not the extra fiscal thrust. But the wide publicity accorded the "locomotive" theory has given German politicians ever since a rationale to resist pressure from succeeding American administrations to accept more of the burden of international economic leadership. Many feel that when Schmidt lost his chancellorship soon after the Bonn summit, the idealized notion of international coordination collapsed with him because no national leader could again assume his colleagues would or could keep their bargains.[27]

Within two weeks of the conclusion of the Bonn summit, American tax policy was thrown into reverse, typical of the jerky nature of the Carter administration. On August 4, Blumenthal and Stuart Eizenstat—who had taken a hard-line position opposing a capital gains tax cut—stood together at a press conference to announce support for a new capital gains tax cut proposal by liberal Democrats.

Carter was forced to choose between these opposing forces within his own administration. Even the business community, whose spokesmen sounded the usual free-market commitment to free and open trade, was sharply divided. "Businessmen are a bunch of frauds," said Henry Owen. "They say they are believers in the free market, but when it comes down to it, they're just as protectionist as anybody. The business community, *en principe,* had one view. But in practice, there was another."[28]

Strauss, strongly supported by Eizenstat, wanted Carter to respond to the political pressures and back away from pure free trade principles. At a minimum, Strauss and Eizenstat told the president, he would have to "do something" to protect the domestic shoe and television industries by signing new "orderly marketing agreements" (OMAs) with Taiwan and Korea, and perhaps with Japan on cars. In plain language, the agreements amounted to a restrictive quota: the exporting countries would agree to put a ceiling on their exports, dividing up the sales among their own companies. This neat, and effective, cartelization nipped any competition in the bud, and made certain that consumers, at the other end, would pay high prices. The drift into OMAs had begun in 1977 when the United States forced Japan to accept a "voluntary" agreement reducing its television exports by 1 million units, from 2.6 million to 1.6 million. Alert to a new opportunity, Taiwan and Korea together boosted their TV sales in the United States by 550,000 units, effectively cutting the protection afforded American manufacturers in half. So Strauss now was attempting to recoup with an OMA imposed on Taiwanese and Korean TV exports.

Strauss was aware of the cost to consumers, but argued with Carter that OMAs were a lesser evil, a concession to avert even more drastic legislation favored by both Democrats and Republicans on Capitol Hill and by the labor unions. Blumenthal and Schultze, fearing more OMAs tipped too far in the protectionist direction, lobbied for less restrictive understandings with the Asian exporters under which they would curtail exports. But as protectionist sentiment snowballed in Congress, Strauss won out, and proceeded to negotiate OMAs with Taiwan and Korea on TV sets and shoes. Later Strauss negotiated with Nobuhiko Ushiba what became known as the Strauss-Ushiba agreement, under which Japan agreed to increase its imports of manufactured goods and loosen its restrictive quotas on farm products. Japan agreed, as well, to stimulate its domestic economy by 7 percent. Strauss argued that the need for punitive legislation was over—and Congress dropped the idea for the time being.[29]

Having won access to the summits the year before, an increasingly confident Strauss graded his performance as a trade negotiator with an A by the time of the 1978 Bonn summit. Along with his counterparts from Japan and the European Community, he reported to the heads of government in glowing, self-congratulatory terms on the imminent successful conclusion of the Tokyo round, which was signed the next year. French president Valery Giscard d'Estaing, who had tried to deflate Strauss the year before in London, was still fighting a rearguard action to slow progress in tariff cutting. "When Giscard objected to this, that, and the other, I said to him, 'Mr. President, this is a first-rate package,'" Strauss recalled.[30] "And he said, 'How can you be so sure?' And I said, 'I'm sure because I wrote it.' And then he said, in English, 'Is it in good taste for one to speak so well of one's own accomplishment?'"

Strauss then told Giscard the Dizzy Dean story.[31] "Mr. President," said Strauss, addressing Giscard in his best folksy manner, "we once had a great baseball player in our country, and his name was Dizzy Dean. He was very colorful, he was a character, and once he pitched a no-hit game, which you may or may not understand. But that means he pitched a perfect game, and when talking to the press corps about how wonderfully he had performed, one of the reporters asked, 'Is it in good taste, Dizzy, for one to brag about his own accomplishments?' To which Dizzy Dean answered: 'It ain't bragging if ya done it.' And with that the room erupted in laughter, and I remember that when Giscard—he didn't understand that story at all—said to [Canadian prime minister Pierre] Trudeau, 'Qui est-ce Dizzy Dean?' Trudeau said back to him in English, 'If you don't understand it in English, you won't understand it in French.' "[32]

Nevertheless, when Strauss finally concluded the Tokyo round in mid-1979, after four long years of negotiation, the consensus was that it would hold back protectionism only modestly. The treaty did little to reduce growing reliance on "nontariff barriers," other ways of restricting imports. Textile imports, for example, would still be subject to the Multi-Fiber Agreement, a fancy name for a strict quota. And for the first time, those quotas were extended unilaterally to the People's Republic of China. Strauss naturally argued that he got the best possible deal, considering the compromises that had to be made. "The way you get the canoe to shore is you feed the sharks a little of this and a little of that until you get to the shore," he told *The New Yorker* magazine. But the Consumers for World Trade, a Washington lobbying group, commented: "Some observers feel the administration has fed too many goodies to the sharks."[33]

After explaining Dizzy Dean to Giscard, Strauss was persona non grata to the French president. On trade issues for the balance of the Carter years, Henry Owen had to substitute for Strauss in Paris. Owen was convinced that the French drift toward protectionism was designed to keep their agricultural prices high. Giscard apparently feared that if the European Community became the main negotiator on trade issues, France would be unable to protect the politically powerful French farm bloc.

As global financial leaders of the International Monetary Fund and World Bank prepared to descend on Washington for their annual meeting late in September 1978, Blumenthal's close friend and Treasury undersecretary for monetary affairs, Anthony Solomon, predicted that the dollar would strengthen "if markets behave rationally."[34] The annual IMF/Bank meetings, like the economic summits, had a way of concentrating the attention of national leaders on international problems. The very fact that key politicians were gathered in one place, and were forced by an agenda to consider their joint and interrelated financial or economic problems, brought coordinated action in some cases that otherwise would not have been achieved. The annual meetings were also the one venue in which the poor nations—collectively—could bring their problems to the richer ones. The poor rarely got their way, but they had a forum, through the press, that served to illuminate their problems.

As the days ticked off toward the 1978 sessions, the busiest man in Washington may have been Jacques de Larosière, forty-eight years old, the new managing director of the IMF, who had succeeded H. J. Witteveen of Holland, head of the international agency for the six prior years, which covered the period of the first oil shock—an event that eroded the IMF's resources. Larosière, who had been director of the French Treasury—the top civil service post—had the unenviable task of attempting to get the IMF's lendable resources—technically called "quotas"—replenished by 50 percent over the existing capital base of $49 billion. But Larosière would experience some foot-dragging by Carter, who hesitated to ask Congress for additional moneys—however small the actual budgetary impact might be—for international purposes.[35] Still, Carter, his international prestige enhanced by his successful sponsorship of the Camp David accords, went along with pressure from Larosière, Blumenthal, and Solomon and approved a major increase in funding for both the IMF and the Bank. Further, he pledged to fight inflation and reduce oil imports, and he articulated his belief in a sound dollar. "We recognize the international role of the dollar, and accept the responsibilities [that] involves," Carter told a plenary session.[36]

Carter's assurances were well received by a mostly polite—if worried—audience. There was a basic distrust of the dollar that had been set in motion ever since Richard Nixon had broken the link between the dollar and gold, and was now exacerbated by high U.S. inflation and a trade deficit worsened by huge oil imports. René Larre, director of the Bank for International Settlements, told me during the meetings that "the market still sees bad [balance of payments] figures. . . . People who hold large balances of dollars want to move into some other currencies or [into] gold because they are scared."[37]

It was no accident that a proposal for a European Monetary System, evolved at an earlier meeting in Hamburg by Schmidt and Giscard, was widely discussed at the Washington IMF/Bank meeting. Schmidt, especially, was skeptical about the prospects for the dollar in the years ahead. He and Giscard put before other European governments the nucleus of the EMS system that would eventually come into being—a multibillion dollar fund that would stabilize currencies of the European region within agreed limits. Schmidt and Giscard didn't view the EMS as providing a currency to compete with the dollar, but as a way of reaching greater stability—at least within Europe.

No sooner did the IMF/Bank meeting conclude than the dollar started to slide anew, and gold hit another all-time high. The public's concern about inflation was reflected in many ways. The so-called tax revolt, symbolized by Proposition 13 in California, was not so much a complaint about high taxes as a protest from citizens who knew they were not getting good value for their tax dollars. In Massachusetts, Governor Michael S. Dukakis, who four years earlier had made a campaign promise not to raise taxes, got trounced in the Democratic primary in September 1978 because he failed to live up to that commitment. When he conceded to Edward J. King, who leaned hard on the Proposition 13 concept, Dukakis pulled no punches: "The voters in this primary wanted something else."[38]

On the national front, voter dissatisfaction was translated into tax legislation far different from the tax reform ideas Carter's campaign advisers had dreamed about two years before. Instead, Carter had to accept in principle the idea that taxes on capital gains had to be eased—a mostly Republican article of faith with which only Blumenthal among Carter's advisers had any sympathy. A Senate-House conference committee was busy at work on pro-business tax legislation that would provide new depreciation deductions, as well as capital-gains changes. Lobbyist Charls Walker, Treasury undersecretary in the Nixon years, gloated: "The middle class will finally get its due."[39]

But it wasn't until November 1978 that Carter decided that beating inflation back had to become his top priority, even if it meant duplicating Richard Nixon's "old-time religion" by risking a recession in an election year. For months, while the dollar was sinking, Europeans wondered whether Carter would "take" a recession to halt the inflation that was causing the dollar's decline.

Toward the end of October, it had seemed that Carter would not: he announced a toothless program of anti-inflation guidelines that was greeted by a new speculative attack on the dollar in foreign exchange markets. And on Tuesday, October 31, the dollar plunged a shocking 5 percent—a movement of panic proportions for a single day's trading.

The next day, Carter was forced to step forward with a tough set of measures crafted by Anthony Solomon: a $30 billion rescue program for the dollar, coupled with a full point increase in the Federal

Reserve's discount rate, to 9.5 percent. The dollar package included a commitment to intervene, along with German, Japanese, Swiss, and other central banks, to buy dollars when the price moved down—up to $30 billion in U.S. funds, and unspecified amounts from the others. It went far beyond what had been traditional American intervention policy, which was to step in only to counter "disorderly markets." In practice, this had meant only token intervention by the United States to protect the value of its currency, which left the burden of the responsibility on European central banks, who naturally did not want to see the value of their huge holdings of dollars decline. This was the basis for the familiar European charge that Washington pursued a policy of "benign neglect" of the dollar. The new Carter policy called for intervening not merely when conditions in the market were "disorderly" but to stop the decline of the dollar by throwing government resources into the market in "whatever" amounts were needed.[40] And for the first time, the United States pledged to sell up to $10 billion worth of securities denominated in foreign currencies and promised to sell gold from the Fort Knox stockpile to foreign central banks unwilling to hold dollars.

This was a dramatic reversal of policy, and an open confession that the dollar could be defended only by a hands-on, rather than hands-off, intervention policy and by paying off some of the accumulated international deficit with gold and hard cash—that is, in marks and yen instead of unwanted dollars. The proposed sale of up to $10 billion in government notes or bonds carrying a payoff in marks or yen was an acknowledgment that some investors wouldn't invest in U.S. government obligations if they were to be paid back in dollars whose value might have dwindled. After all, they figured, what good was an 8 percent interest rate return if the value of the bond—in American currency—had dropped 8 or 10 percent by the time the bond matured?

For months, Blumenthal had argued that yen- or mark-denominated bonds would be counterproductive, because investors who had concerns about the dollar would sell their regular bonds—further weakening the dollar in exchange markets—so as to exchange them for the foreign-denominated issues. But in the face of the slide on October 31, there was no choice—although some White House aides wanted to delay action one week, until after congressional elections on November 7. Blumenthal and Solomon knew that any delay could be perilous. The weekend before, Blumenthal had told Carter that he had to act boldly unless he wanted to be known "as the president who had presided over an international money panic."[41]

The rescue package was applauded by European and Asian bankers. In the first three weeks, the dollar moved up as much as 15 percent against some currencies, while gold—which tended to skyrocket when the dollar was in trouble—backed off by 18 percent.

But what lay ahead was a new uncertainty: the OPEC oil cartel had scheduled a meeting in Abu Dhabi for mid-December, and rumors in the Middle East suggested that, despite private assurances by the Saudis to Blumenthal that the price rise would be no more than 8 percent, the cartel managers were thinking of a new 10 percent to 15 percent price increase—which, as Blumenthal knew, would threaten double-digit inflation rates. A new OPEC price increase in that range would artificially increase the American trade and current account deficits, and again diminish the dollar, Blumenthal figured.

On December 16, 1978, OPEC delivered the second oil shock to consuming nations, rich and poor, boosting prices by 14.5 percent. The Western world, as the 1970s moved to an end, was still struggling with the economic consequences of the first oil shock. In 1977, as Carter entered the White House, the United States was importing oil at a stunning $45 billion annual rate.

Three years later, the United States and the world faced sharply higher oil prices—10 percent immediately, with an additional 4.5 percent to become effective by the end of 1979. Revolt against the shah of Iran by Muslim fundamentalists had shut down Iranian production, emphasizing once again how exposed oil production in the area around the Persian Gulf was to upheaval or sabotage.

Yet the Carter policy on energy was essentially do-nothing. The emergency stockpile of oil that had been authorized at the time of the first oil shock had not been built. Saudi Arabia, America's "friend" in OPEC, cheerfully offered to make up an expected loss of 1 million barrels a day of Iranian oil, although it would charge a full 14.5 percent extra as a premium.[42]

In reality, the revolution in Iran cost about half of its normal 5 million to 6 million barrels a day, and soon the Saudis stopped "replacing" the Iranian oil. While publicly playing down the inflationary impact of a made-in-Riyadh American energy policy, Carter's people were saying privately that it was "a terrible blow." Clearly, the Saudis could have burst the price bubble by increasing production. But as Senator Henry M. (Scoop) Jackson, Carter's former rival for the Democratic presidential nomination, said: "They are going to make more money by producing less. I think it's bad news for Western financial institutions." Oil expert Walter J. Levy said: "The Western nations are acting like frightened children" in failing to stand up to OPEC.[43]

OPEC's new tax on oil-consuming countries further exacerbated the inflation problem for Carter. In January 1978, under Chairman Schultze's direction, the Council of Economic Advisers had recommended a further stimulus package in anticipation of an economic slowdown. But 1978 turned out to be a boom year, and the stimulus package added to it. Schultze would later admit that it was "a fatal mistake," based on "bad" forecasts on inflation.

Early in 1979, Schultze and Blumenthal knew they were on the wrong track, and desperately began a campaign through the press to try to get Miller, the new Fed chairman, to slow the economy down by raising interest rates, only to get "a very nasty note" from Carter "in effect saying lay off."[44] This was an extraordinary thing for Blumenthal and Schultze to have done: normally, economic growth-oriented Democrats in the White House push the Fed to lower, not raise, interest rates. And normally, inflation-fearing Fed chairmen resist such pressures, and tend to make monetary policy tighter. But even though the inflation rate was 13 percent in the first quarter of 1979, and the money supply was growing at a phenomenal rate, Schultze and Blumenthal couldn't move Miller, who felt their recommended half-point boost in the federal funds rate would be overkill. Ironically, Carter had unloaded Burns because he was considered a monetary "hawk." Now, Carter's aides were reduced to hoping that Miller would act as a typical Fed chairman should— which is to say, more like Arthur Burns! It was not to be. "I have to laugh at what I read in the newspapers," Miller told me that April in his office at the Fed. "There must be some lower-echelon people who are leaking their bankrupt ideas to the papers. . . . The president is committed to an independent Fed—he's told me so repeatedly."[45]

As gasoline prices soared at the pump, and frustrated drivers lined up at their local service stations hoping that there would be something left for their empty gas tanks, the Carter team tried to evolve a strategy that would deflate OPEC's power to present to the economic summit in Tokyo—the first ever in Japan—due to begin June 28, 1979. A proposal by Treasury Undersecretary Solomon, endorsed by the Department of Energy, to commit $10 billion to an international development corporation, perhaps with ties to the World Bank, for developing alternative sources of energy was shot down by an Office of Management and Budget mindful of Carter's budget-cutting proclivities.

A related plan, floated by three prominent Washingtonians, to set up a $100 billion Petroleum Reserve Corporation to create a synthetic oil industry also was a nonstarter.[46] America and other oil-consuming nations needed, as Arthur Okun put it, to shake the premise created by OPEC "that oil in the ground is worth more than the oil they pump," but struggled vainly to find a way to convince themselves or OPEC that the theory was true.

Just days before the Tokyo summit was to convene, the leaders of the Group of Seven powers received word that the June weighted average price for OPEC oil of $17.22 per barrel, including surcharges—already 57 percent higher than the official OPEC benchmark price of $13.84 at the end of 1978—and would probably be boosted another 20 percent, at a Geneva OPEC session on June 26, to $20 or $21 per barrel.

Carter was scheduled to be in Tokyo for a bilateral meeting with Japanese prime minister Masayoshi Ohira—who had succeeded Takeo Fukada the previous November—just ahead of the seven-nation summit. The symbolism was clear: if OPEC went through with its plan, it would be a classic case of the newly empowered oil producers thumbing their nose at the United States and the rest of the West, pushing the consuming nations into recession, and daring them to do something about it.

Secretly, Carter had humbly begged Crown Prince Fahd to hold the Saudi crude oil price to $18 a barrel, and to produce an extra 1 million barrels of oil a day.[47] That cast some doubt on Carter's repeated commitment to put some kind of lid on imported oil. Fahd acquiesced in a smirking note on July 4, telling Carter: "This is your gift on Independence Day."[48] On Capitol Hill, Democratic leaders talked incessantly of the need for gasoline rationing—but Carter was immobilized, unable to demand sacrifices of average citizens, irate over the ability of foreign oil suppliers to exert control over their lives. "It's dynamite," said Scoop Jackson, after a June trip back home to Seattle, where gasoline stations were closed on a weekend. "When you have this confluence of shortages and runaway prices—well, people are mad at everyone."[49] Carter should have known that the gas lines and his inability to cope with the problem they identified marked the beginning of the end of his presidency.

Carter's popularity plummeted to a new low, just above the worst of Nixon's ratings, according to a June Louis Harris poll. Ted Kennedy emerged as the preferred choice of Democrats for the 1980 nomination. "I'm afraid there is an anybody-but-Carter mood growing. And we just don't seem to be doing anything about it," lamented a midlevel White House aide.[50] Clearly, the worry was that if Carter managed to control the renomination process, as any incumbent should be able to do, he would fall easily to a Republican candidate like Ronald Reagan, growing in popularity among Republican voters.

En route to Tokyo, the gloom was palpable. Carter said in a departure statement on the South Lawn of the White House that the en-

ergy problem had to be brought under control without "panic or des-
peration," but warned that no matter what might be conjured up in
Tokyo, "gas lines and fuel shortages will not disappear overnight."[51]
Carter had no viable scheme with which to deflate OPEC's power, no
prospective deal with his European opposite numbers, who wanted
to limit Middle East imports or to enforce serious, global conservation measures. James Schlesinger, Carter's secretary of energy—the
Department of Energy was created by Carter in 1977—was ineffective, and had already been subordinated to Eizenstat in the real line
of authority.[52] In their bilateral summit in Tokyo, Carter and Ohira
rejected as too drastic a proposal by the European Community that
all major nations put a five-year freeze on oil imports at the then-
current levels. The Carter-Ohira refusal triggered an angry and public charge by Valery Giscard d'Estaing that the United States was
profligate in its use of oil.[53]

But when OPEC announced what amounted to an overall 25 percent price increase on June 26—to $18 for Saudi oil and to $23 or
more for other producers—the cartel was roundly denounced by all
summit participants, including Carter, who finally adopted a variation of the European proposal: a pledge to place a ceiling on imports
at a level slightly higher than the then-current totals, and to maintain those limits through 1985.

Japan, because of its total dependence on foreign oil, was allowed
to let its 5.5 million-barrel-a-day import level creep up to a maximum of 6.9 million barrels a day in 1985. Significantly, the Tokyo
summit did not attempt to deal with the impact that the latest round
of oil price increases would have on the Third World—but soon
would find out the cost of that neglect when the debt crisis broke out
in 1982.

For the United States, Carter said the cap would be 8.5 million
barrels a day through 1985, or about the same level it was in 1977.
OPEC's price boost meant that the world faced slower economic
growth for the next several years—and an additional diversion of
wealth straight out of Western pocketbooks into those of the oil
sheikhs. Aboard *Air Force One* on the way home from Tokyo, a
Carter administration official estimated that U.S. oil import costs
would zoom to $70 billion in 1980, up $12 billion from $58 billion in
1979, and $25 billion from oil import costs of $45 billion in 1978.

The message to the oil cartel, said British prime minister Margaret Thatcher (who had taken office six weeks earlier) "is that we are
determined to cut demand and not be so reliant on [the Middle East]
source of energy."[54] In reality, there was a deeper message that
emerged from the Tokyo summit, although it took the world a num-

ber of years to understand it: it was a delusion to continue belief in the myth perpetuated by earlier summit leaders, as a convenient way of covering up their mistakes, that the Western world's economic pie could continue to grow, despite the shift of huge resources to OPEC. With the second oil shock, the new reality was that car producers, especially in Detroit, needed to cut back on gas-guzzlers, and that conservation by both industry and individuals, along with a search for substitutes for oil, had to become the world's top economic priority.

For the immediate future, however, the killer political issue so far as Carter was concerned was the persistence of the gasoline lines. But Carter as president never was able to understand the depth of public anger and frustration over the indignity of sitting in a car for an hour for the privilege of buying gasoline at prices extortionate by American standards. On the first day of the Tokyo summit, Stuart Eizenstat had tried to explain it to Carter in a memo cabled from Washington in which Eizenstat called OPEC "a real enemy" and warned his boss that he needed to mobilize the nation to confront the cartel: "Every day you need to be dealing with and publicly seen to be dealing with the major energy problems now facing us."[55] The memo was drafted by Eizenstat assistant David Rubinstein and designed, Eizenstat later said, "to shock Carter, across several thousand miles of ocean," into understanding just how serious the situation was. "I remember stopping off at the Amoco station at Connecticut Avenue and Manor Road, and waiting forty-five minutes for enough gas to get to the White House so I could deal with the energy situation," Eizenstat recalled.[56]

Eizenstat and Rubinstein were right, but the warning was late. Like Nixon and Ford before him, Carter had waffled on the need to conserve oil and develop alternative sources ever since the first oil shock. In retrospect, the biggest mistake was the failure to ration gasoline, which would have caused an immediate, but probably temporary, spike in the retail price, after which it would have settled back to what economists call a "market-clearing" price. Carter was unwilling to take that risk because it would have exacerbated an already dangerous inflationary situation. But it would have been less risky—certainly less risky to Carter politically—than to let the gasoline shortage situation fester. Equally, Carter's economic policy overall had been indecisive. First there was to be a stimulus, then a contraction. Dollar policy began with benign neglect and wound up with the $30 billion Blumenthal-Solomon rescue package. In Eizenstat's view, this was another mistake that could be chalked up to dogmatic liberal Democratic ideology.[57]

For Carter, high oil prices and the Arab threat to American sovereignty now loomed as the biggest challenge of all. Yet he seemed unwilling to lash out, except with words. In a carefully orchestrated barrage on *Air Force One* returning from Tokyo, Carter "dropped in" on a background briefing held by his national security adviser, Zbigniew Brzezinski, to tell reporters that the United States and its allies had until then been too "timid" in dealing with OPEC: "I don't see how the rest of the world can sit back in a quiescent state and accept unrestrained and unwarranted increases in OPEC's oil prices."[58]

Initially, Carter—who had followed the stressful Tokyo summit with a state visit to South Korea—had planned a three-day rest and recreation stopover in Hawaii. But just before the president's plane touched down at Hickam Air Force Base, reporters were told Carter would skip his holiday and push right back to Washington to deal with the energy shortage—and the gas lines. The Eizenstat-Rubinstein memo had warned Carter that a holiday in the warm breezes of Honolulu would not go down well with angry Americans who expected Carter to do something about the gas lines.

That much advice Carter took, but he couldn't bring himself to translate his tough talk into action. The result was the "malaise" speech of July 15, which emerged from a solemn retreat at Camp David where he meditated on his failures. In one of the most bizarre decisions ever made by a president, Carter almost disassembled his administration, firing Treasury Secretary Michael Blumenthal and Secretary of Health and Human Services Joseph Califano Jr., and allowing three other cabinet officers to leave more or less voluntarily. It was a stunning shake-up of the cabinet that left the nation and its overseas partners bewildered.

Carter never actually used the word "malaise" in the Camp David speech that Sunday, but it was a fair characterization of the essence of his message:

> I want to speak to you first tonight about a subject even more serious than energy or inflation. I want to talk to you right now about a fundamental threat to American democracy.
>
> I do not mean our political and civil liberties. They will endure. And I do not refer to the outward strength of America, a nation that is at peace tonight everywhere in the world, with unmatched economic power and military might.
>
> The threat is nearly invisible in ordinary ways. It is a crisis of confidence that strikes at the very heart and soul and spirit of our national will. We can see this crisis in the growing doubt about the meaning of our own lives and in the loss of a unity of purpose for our Nation.

The erosion of our confidence in the future is threatening to destroy the social and political fabric of America. . . . Our people are losing faith, not only in government itself but in the ability as citizens to serve as the ultimate rulers and shapers of our democracy. . . . In a nation that was proud of hard work, strong families, close-knit communities, and our faith in God, too many of us now tend to worship self-indulgence and consumption. . . . But we've discovered that owning things and consuming things does not satisfy our longing for meaning. We've learned that piling up material goods cannot fill the emptiness of lives which have no confidence or purpose.

The symptoms of this crisis of the American spirit are all around us. For the first time in history a majority of our people believe that the next five years will be worse than the past five years. Two-thirds of our people do not even vote. The productivity of American workers is actually dropping, and the willingness of Americans to save for the future has fallen below that of all other people in the Western world. . . .

What you see too often in Washington and elsewhere around the country is a system of government that seems incapable of action. You see a Congress twisted and pulled in every direction by hundreds of well-financed and powerful special interests. You see every extreme position defended to the last vote, almost to the last breath by one unyielding group or another. You often see a balanced and a fair approach that demands sacrifice, a little sacrifice from everyone, abandoned like an orphan without support and without friends.

Often you see paralysis and stagnation and drift. You don't like it, and neither do I. What can we do?

But to this extraordinary self-indictment—who was running the government in Washington that Carter condemned?—the troubled president offered just a few palliatives for the energy crisis: a plan to make 2.5 million barrels a day of synthetic oil by 1990; a cut in imports below the levels agreed upon in Tokyo; and further conservation steps. And for the more general loss of confidence and feeling of malaise, Carter's only solution was the bizarre request to the entire cabinet to resign. It was Treasury Secretary Blumenthal who would take the fall.

In an extraordinary and extemporaneous public analysis shortly after he was fired, Blumenthal told the Washington Forum, a private business group, where Carter had "gone wrong." Blumenthal said that Carter had never developed "a clear, simple, single economic philosophy" devoted to fighting inflation. He blamed this basic flaw on a split among Carter's advisers. "The liberals believe that high interest rates are bad, that fighting inflation hurts poor people, and that we have to be very careful how we fight inflation in order not to hit 'the natural constituency of the Democratic Party.' So there has been an effort to fight inflation, but not too hard. It was 'tighten the belt,' but 'don't cut out any important programs.' 'Cut down on government regulation, but don't offend any public interest groups.' It made it difficult for the president to stand up and say, 'My economic philosophy is that inflation is the number one problem, and that's what I am going to stick to.' " Blumenthal traced Carter's economic decision-making problems to the "very first meetings" at Carter's mothers' Pond House in Plains after the election. "In Plains, all of the talk was about the necessity to stimulate the American economy. All of the concerns had to do with making sure that unemployment would not rise again." That was a basic mistake, common not only to private economists but to the outgoing Ford administration. But having misjudged the strength of the American economy, Carter could not admit that he and his aides had done so.

Blumenthal also admitted his failure to assess the potential for problems in the foreign exchange market. Blumenthal persisted in trying to "talk the dollar down" in 1978. He should have known that the administration's wrongheaded inflationary bent would create a weaker dollar, which in turn would exacerbate inflation. When Blumenthal would say, casually, that the dollar had gone down only 2 or 3 percent, he was inviting the foreign exchange markets to conclude that the key financial officer of the American government was willing to see the dollar depreciate even more.

"The [Carter] administration doesn't understand how deeply ingrained is the inflationary psychology among American consumers and businessmen. We looked at our computer runs, which are based on earlier and past relationships with inflation much lower than it is today, and said: 'If we have so much stimulus, we will have so much unemployment, and so much growth, and so much economic activity, and if we raise or lower taxes by such and such an amount, it will have such and such effect.' But it never really worked out that way, because Americans began to believe in inflation, and expect inflation, and act so that they developed a stake in inflation, and that unfortunately happened—and is happening today."[59]

Ironically, Blumenthal, at the time of his firing by Carter, had just about learned how to be a useful secretary of the Treasury. He had stopped trying to talk the dollar down, and with the help of Anthony Solomon had engineered a successful "dollar rescue" program. He fully understood that Miller, at the Fed, was letting monetary policy get out of control. But by the summer of 1979, after the Tokyo summit, the gas lines, and the malaise speech, it was too late: Carter moved Miller from the Fed to Treasury, and then tried to buy the confidence of Wall Street and world markets by installing Paul Volcker as the new Fed chairman to replace Miller.

When Juanita M. Kreps left her post as commerce secretary in November 1979 to return to her teaching post at Duke University, she echoed the feeling that the president's economic advisers "have not served him as well as we might have." But Kreps's complaint—as all of Washington knew—was that she had been excluded from a major role in economic policy-making by—as she put it—"the boys at the breakfast table," meaning the Economic Policy Group that had been chaired by Blumenthal. Kreps said that Carter had "difficulty" in understanding why his economists couldn't find answers to the nation's problems: "There've been times when I sensed that he was perplexed and maybe exasperated with the failure of the group to solve the problem."[60]

Jimmy Carter was doomed to failure from the very start when he listened to Schultze and Blumenthal instead of taking Eizenstat's advice, which was to couple his initial stimulus program with standby authority to impose wage and price controls. Schultze and Blumenthal convinced Carter, even before he took office, that seeking controls authority would lead to an anticipatory run-up in wages and prices. When OPEC skyrocketed oil prices in 1979, Schultze and Miller combined to argue that controls don't work—and that having passed up a chance to get them in 1976, to ask for controls in 1979 would ensure a bloody battle. That was probably true, but not very helpful in dealing with inflationary pressures.

More than anything else, it was Jimmy Carter's failures on economic policy that brought him down after a single term. Carter's worst mistake was his inability to control or at least contain inflation, and that happened because, from the very beginning, Carter and his aides badly underestimated the power of inflationary forces at work in the economy. They knew even less how to go about rooting those forces out.

Over a glass of fine wine in an elegant restaurant in Cologne, just before the Bonn summit, Blumenthal had moodily confessed to a small group of reporters that if he had learned anything in the past year, it was about how little power he and other officials had to alter the course of events. As they left office, Carter's people put the blame on events they said were beyond their control: OPEC; the Iran hostage crisis; the Soviet invasion of Afghanistan; crop failures that drove food prices up. But as Arthur Okun used to say, the excuses were right in line with the argument that the battleship was fine, except for the holes where the torpedo had hit.[61]

GREED

10

Voodoo Economics and the Triumph of Greed

R ONALD REAGAN'S ascension to the White House was accompanied, in many quarters, by a sense of widespread optimism. If
inflation and interest rates had got out of hand under Carter, the
handsome Ronald Reagan was riding to the rescue, as if living the
lead role in one of his B movies. Reagan took Washington by storm.
He was sure-footed, amiable, great on television, ready to restore
America's macho feeling of invincibility. He had class and charisma.
The public didn't care that he needed three-by-five cards as props for
the most simple events: to them, he quickly became the "Great
Communicator."

Reagan also had, in the person of Office of Management and Budget director David Stockman, an instrument for making his dream of
"getting the government off our backs" into a reality. Reagan promised to cut spending, reduce inflation, lower unemployment, promote economic growth, and balance the budget by fiscal 1983—later
amended to fiscal 1984. What the nation got, instead, was a series of
budget deficits that nearly tripled the national debt. The actor-
turned-president and his key aides were also allowed to indulge their
ideological passion for deregulation, which played a decisive role in
subsequent crises in the savings and loan and airlines industries. The
S&L debacle was also likely to be followed by expensive taxpayer
bailouts in less-publicized risky commitments in "government-
sponsored enterprises" that would feed huge sums into housing,
mortgage insurance, and farm credit programs.[1]

Reagan's original economics program, the "national recovery plan" he unveiled in 1981, promised to reverse the distress of the Carter years; it would simultaneously cut taxes, reduce unemployment, trim all wasteful social programs, boost defense spending, lower interest rates, expand real economic growth in calendar 1982 by 4.2 percent—and balance the budget within three years (later amended to four years). This was a commitment to accomplish what never had been done before, through the magic of supply-side economics along with monetary stringency: a rapid economic expansion—5 percent in 1983 over 1982—with a quickly declining inflation—from double digits down to 5.7 percent in 1983, induced by a stringent monetary policy.

Despite George Bush's branding of the Reagan program during the 1980 campaign as "voodoo economics," Reagan adopted supply-side economics that pledged, by cutting tax rates, enough economic growth would be triggered in the private sector to boost total government tax receipts despite lower tax rates. Its main proponent was Professor Robert Mundell of Columbia University, but supply-side thinking was popularized by economist Arthur Laffer, who had studied under Mundell; by *Wall Street Journal* editorialist Jude Wanniski; by economist Paul Craig Roberts (who would briefly serve in the Reagan Treasury); and by Senator William Roth (R.-Del.), who, along with Representative Jack Kemp (R.-N.Y.), had legislation ready (the Kemp-Roth Bill) that became the vehicle for supply-side tax cuts.[2] The Kemp-Roth Bill called for a 30 percent tax cut over three years—a proposal that became even more generous with the help of a Democratic Congress.

The magic of supply-side economics was symbolized by the famous "Laffer curve" that the economist—who once had worked for George Shultz—was said to have drawn on a paper napkin. The Laffer curve put the theory into a simplified diagram that purported to show revenues rising as taxes declined. Alas for the theorists and the country, Reagan's lower tax rates did not generate extra revenue—only sharp increases in retained wealth in the upper income brackets. Supply-side economics proved to be a bonanza for the rich. But for the nation, the outcome was a series of huge annual budget deficits. While misplaced reliance on supply-side theorists caused huge losses in government revenues, Reagan went on a spending binge.

Ironically, the unrestrained military budget touched off by Reagan in his first term was the product of a misassessment of the need, as confessed by Stockman in his tell-all book, *The Triumph of Politics*, published in 1986. But since no one was about to admit that when Reagan's military budgets were being prepared, they were defended, approved, and funded by Congress. Stockman, a thirty-four-year-old whiz kid, was pretty much in control of economic policy and programs early in the Reagan administration. In a celebrated article written by William Greider of *The Washington Post* for *The Atlantic Monthly*, former divinity student Stockman confessed that he had intentionally deceived the American people.[3]

He was a very bright man; yet he did not fully understand the potency of the bombshell he and Greider were crafting; nor did Greider, nor did a top *Post* editor who had vetted the Greider piece to make sure that Greider was not giving away something to the *Atlantic* that had not first appeared in the *Post*. The Stockman-Greider revelations confirmed what I had been arguing in my columns (along with others): it was delusionary to believe that the huge Kemp-Roth supply-side tax cut, side by side with an enormous jump in military spending, could result in a balanced budget in 1983 or 1984. New York financial expert Henry Kaufman delivered an especially effective critique of Reaganomics at the National Press Club as early as June 1981. But Greider got an admission/confession from Stockman in his own words, for all to read. Stockman said that he had cooked the books to fool Congress and the American people. Supply-side, he smirked to Greider, was really "trickle-down economics."

Stockman had his wrist slapped by Reagan, to whom he apologized. But he was forced to sit in the back of the bus for the balance of Reagan's first term, after which he joined Salomon Brothers, the big New York financial house. Then, in 1986, he wrote a book in which he revealed bitter feelings about his former colleagues, all of whom he considered stupid or venal. The Stockman book was even more a self-indictment than was the Greider article: "I soon became a veritable incubator of shortcuts, schemes and devices to overcome the truth now upon us—that the budget gap could not be closed except by a dictator. The more I flopped and staggered around, however, the more they [his colleagues in the Reagan administration] went along. I could have been wearing a sandwich board sign saying: Stop me! I'm dangerous! Even then they might not have done so. . . .

"Only later would I appreciate the vast web of confusion and self-delusion I was creating. I instilled so much confidence by appearing to know all the answers, but I was just beginning to understand the true complexities of the federal budget."[4]

Stockman would also admit that the "Reagan Revolution, as I had defined it, required a frontal assault on the American welfare state. That was the only way to pay for the massive . . . tax cut." In other words, the only way of assuring that the welfare programs carefully built up from the New Deal under Roosevelt through the Great Society under Lyndon Johnson could be torn down was to take the money away from them and pass it out to rich taxpayers through supply-side tax cuts. "To this day," said Senator Daniel P. Moynihan in 1982, "I don't think we understand that a conspiracy had seized the White House."[5]

Stockman, billed by the press as a wunderkind, dazzled Washington and the president. To an envious Donald Regan at Treasury, twice his age, Stockman was a young whippersnapper, not to be trusted. Yet Regan privately ordered his Treasury staff to make thorough studies of Stockman's Budget Bureau presentations and other papers generated by the OMB. "If these were the things the President wanted, I was ready to help get them," a pragmatic Regan later wrote.[6]

FOR A GOOD LONG WHILE, it appeared that President Reagan could do no wrong. Even his political opponents had to admire his courage and panache after the March 30, 1981, attempt on his life by a crazed gunman as he was leaving the Washington Hilton Hotel. John Wayne couldn't have handled it better. As Reagan's gurney was being rolled into the operating room at George Washington University Hospital, the president was able to joke with the surgeons: "I hope one of you is a Republican." The manner in which he confronted that personal crisis helped make him an authentic hero in his own time. His bout later on with colon cancer reinforced the impression that, even if he was probably too old to be running the country, Reagan was tough, affable, and, above all, presidential in the face of adversity. Few could have guessed in 1981 that he would serve two full terms, the first president to do so since Dwight Eisenhower.

Reagan has to be credited for the revival of the American spirit, which had sunk to a new low point under Carter. Reagan played the role of the smiling, confident president to perfection. One couldn't imagine him carrying his own garment bag slung over a shoulder, Carter-style. Everyone knew that the Carter garment bag routine was faked for "photo ops" to show that Carter was a "regular guy." But there was no pretense among the Reagan handlers that their president was ordinary. He was, instead, The President. If anything, the Reagan team tried to foster an image of Ron and Nancy that tipped more to the notion of royalty.

Nonetheless, Reagan was greeted with some coolness by his counterparts in Europe early in his presidency, although traditionally most European politicians, taking a clue from their businessmen and bankers, favored Republicans over Democrats. Although Europe had been contemptuous of Carter, Reagan was "underrated in Europe, and underrated by me as well," said Fritz Leutwiler.[7]

Europeans had been offended by a number of developments in the new Reagan administration. Treasury Secretary Regan had abruptly canceled an appearance at the International Monetary Fund's policy-making Interim Committee meeting in Gabon, and shortly after that decided not to go to a private conference in Lausanne, Switzerland, sponsored by the American Bankers Association in conjunction with foreign bankers. Ten years earlier, Nixon's Treasury secretary, John Connally, made points and won friends for America by arriving early and staying late at the same conference in Munich.[8] Regan's snub of these sessions carried a message: the new Reagan administration not only didn't care much for the international financial institutions on which the rest of the world so much depended, and which, moreover, had been created through important American initiatives at the end of the Second World War, but was downright suspicious of foreigners.[9]

Regan's undersecretary for monetary affairs, Beryl Sprinkel, a short, roly-poly economist of single-minded, conservative convictions, commissioned a study of the international lending institutions based on a concern that they were "socialistic." But the study that Sprinkel commissioned had to confess that, for the most part, his suspicions were not valid, and that there was no case to reduce American support for the Bank or the IMF. Sprinkel was also a harsh and persistent critic of the Federal Reserve Board's policies under Paul Volcker, and became known as the administration's chief "Fed-basher." Volcker, irritated by Sprinkel, asked President Reagan to rein him in.[10]

Throughout the first Reagan term, the White House and the Treasury kept up a running battle with the Federal Reserve Board. Regan and Sprinkel didn't think much of Volcker, the six-foot-seven cigar-smoking central banker with an ego to match, who enjoyed the utmost respect of the financial community, especially fellow central bankers and finance ministers throughout the world.

From the beginning, Volcker, who had assumed his post in August 1979, almost two years before the Reagan revolution hit Washington, was viewed with suspicion by the clutch of monetarists and supply-siders who dominated the Reagan administration, as well as by Keynesian economists who felt that the Volcker brake on economic growth was assuring continued recession.

But the White House took no action. Eventually, Donald Regan decided that the public squabbling had got out of hand and silenced his undersecretary.[11] Sprinkel had also upset Europeans by enunciating a hands-off policy relating to gyrations in foreign exchange markets. The United States would intervene, Sprinkel said, only in the case of "disorderly markets." What he meant by "disorderly," Sprinkel explained, was the kind of chaotic financial market that developed only rarely in very special situations—for example, in the uncertainty following President Kennedy's assassination.[12] Europeans correctly interpreted that to mean that the United States would sit by in most situations and not take action to soften the rise of the dollar in world markets, leaving the intervention job to the Europeans if they found a rising dollar onerous. Volcker tried to placate the Europeans, suggesting—at the Lausanne meeting Regan had ducked—that American policy was not all that rigid. But Sprinkel's unrelenting laissez-faire policy was not modified until White House chief of staff Jim Baker succeeded Regan in a dramatic job switch at the beginning of the second Reagan term in 1985.[13]

The Regan-Sprinkel pursuit of a highly restrictive monetary policy in the first Reagan term helped trigger an excessively strong dollar that undercut efforts of American manufacturers to sell their goods abroad. They succeeded despite the opposing views of Martin Feldstein, an economist from Harvard who in 1982 had followed Murray Weidenbaum, Reagan's first CEA chairman. Neither Weidenbaum nor Feldstein had a close rapport with Reagan, who liked few economists apart from monetarist guru Milton Friedman.

The White House regarded Weidenbaum as suspiciously liberal, which he was not, and groused that Feldstein, authentically conservative, was nonetheless not a team player. Indeed, Feldstein had principles, and argued—first privately and then publicly—that the high dollar was not the happy symbol of a strong economy that offered a "safe haven" for foreign investment, as Regan and Sprinkel contended. Rather, Feldstein insisted, agreeing with most Europeans, the high dollar was triggered by high interest rates, which in turn had been caused by the growingly oppressive federal budget deficit. When Feldstein publicly called for a tax increase so as to reduce the budget deficit, it was too much for Chief of Staff Jim Baker. Feldstein quit the CEA post in May 1984, convinced that Reagan's huge budget deficits assured a legacy of debt and economic weakness.

THE DECADE OF THE 1980s, widely heralded by those Reaganites who helped shape it as a huge success, was, in retrospect, a disaster for the nation as a whole, except for the rich who enjoyed tax cuts and tax breaks. Blame should properly be shared by Democratic

politicians who yielded to the seductive appeal of supply-side economics. Congressional Democrats, reading the polls, refused to buck
Reagan's popularity. "Support the president, that's the concern
[among the public] out there," said Tip O'Neill, the Speaker of the
House, "and Congress can read that. I've been in politics for a long
time, and I know when to fight and not to fight." But O'Neill, a master politician, knew nothing about economics. So the Democrats
went along with Reagan's cuts in everything that wasn't related to
defense, his boosts in military spending, and his tax cuts for the
rich.[14] Reagan also enjoyed a mostly friendly and uncritical press.

Reagan was motivated to push for lower taxes not only, as adver-
tised, to reduce the role of government, but because he remembered
with bitterness that, early in his movie career, he had had to pay a 90
percent marginal tax rate on "unearned income" (defined as income
from interest or dividends, as distinct from salaries or wages).[15]
When Reagan became President, the top marginal rate was still
high—70 percent. Ironically, it was the Democrats, not the Republicans, who proposed abandoning the distinction between regular and
marginal income, making the top rate 50 percent, a change warmly
welcomed by the business community.

Reagan's legislative proposals were adopted with the aid of some
subtle political pressure, including the generous use of jelly beans he
handed out at the White House. Jelly beans may sound like an in-
consequential item, and indeed they are. But they were symbolic of a
new hospitality at the Reagan White House. For all of the Kennedy-
Johnson and Carter years, there were some congressional Democrats
who had never been invited to a White House dinner—and many
Republicans who never made it, either. No matter how much time a
congressman or senator spends in Washington, he or she never gets
over the allure of an invitation to be in the presence of the president
and first lady—regardless of party affiliation. New York State Republican congressman Barber Conable Jr. was a seventeen-year veteran
of the House, and ranking minority member of the influential, tax-
writing House Ways and Means Committee. When a happy and obviously impressed Conable stepped out of a helicopter on the White
House lawn after a visit to Camp David, where Reagan did a little
arm-twisting on one of the tax bills, he told reporters: "This is the
first time I've ever been [to Camp David]."

Yet, for all of the massaging of Washington egos, doubts began to
surface, even in his own party, that Reagan could bring off his economic miracle. Peter G. Peterson, secretary of commerce in the
Nixon administration, said in a speech in the summer of 1981 that
Reagan's program, when fed into computers, "does not compute."[16]

In July 1981, economists at the International Monetary Fund judged that the "economic situation envisaged [in the United States] for 1982 is weaker . . . in real and nominal terms than the forecast published by the [Reagan] Administration."[17]

Recession, in fact, took over: For calendar years 1982 and 1983, the unemployment totals topped 10 million persons each year, for an average rate of 9.5 percent, with a high close to 11 percent, while factories operated at only 60 percent of capacity. There had been no parallels in recent history for those distressing numbers. In the 1974–75 Gerald Ford recession, the jobless rate for the year was 8.3 percent, with 7.9 million persons out of work. Under Reagan, unemployment remained at or above 7 percent through calendar 1986, when it finally began to recede.[18]

OF THE MANY self-inflicted wounds suffered by America in the last thirty years, none was as deep, corrosive, and enduring as the series of huge, chronic federal budget deficits created by the policies of Ronald Reagan in his eight years in office. During that period, the average budget deficit was $211 billion, with the result that the federal debt (which had been less than $1 trillion over the entire course of the nation's history until then, including two world wars) nearly tripled to a total of $2.7 trillion, while the size of the nation's economy increased barely by half.[19]

Bush went Reagan one better: in his four years, the deficit averaged $355 billion, adding another $1.4 trillion to the debt, for a total of more than $4 trillion. The interest cost of servicing the national debt would run $200 billion a year by the early 1990s. Worse, the real annual deficit totals should include up to another $100 billion annually that is taken directly out of Social Security and other government trust funds, and used to pay normal operating costs of government.

Over the sixteen-year period covering Johnson, Nixon, Ford, and Carter, the federal debt had risen only an average of $35 billion a year, for a total of $579 billion. Thus, in any three years of the Reagan-Bush twelve, the budget deficit expanded more than it had in the sixteen years of the four prior administrations.

Reagan presided over an economy in which investment and savings stagnated and real wages declined, transforming America from the world's number one creditor nation to the number one debtor. Incredibly, America's foreign debt began to exceed that of Mexico or Brazil, one of the "poor" nations that we, presumably, were trying to help by canceling loans made to them by international banks. If Reagan was right to suggest in 1980 that Americans were "worse off" than they were in 1976, at the beginning of the Carter years, Bill Clinton could rightly argue during the 1992 presidential campaign that they had made no gains in the entire decade of the 1980s.

"BILL SEIDMAN has fuck-you money," former Treasury secretary Donald T. Regan would say, by way of explaining the independence of the crusty and competent "Mr. Clean," who turned out to be the only government official to come out of the savings and loan mess with his reputation for integrity intact.[20] William Seidman, who had served President Ford as an economic adviser on the White House staff, was left with the unenviable job, in the Bush years, of picking up the pieces of the shattered S&L industry. Appointed chairman of the Federal Deposit Insurance Corporation (FDIC)—the regulator of the nation's 13,000 commercial banks—by Ronald Reagan early in his first term, Seidman was also named head of the Resolution Trust Corporation in 1989, created to take on the thankless task of unloading the pitiful "assets" of the failed savings and loan institutions for whatever they would bring.

Seidman, as FDIC chairman, had battled an early and misguided effort by James Miller, who had succeeded David Stockman as Reagan's director of the Office of Management and Budget, to force Seidman's FDIC to reduce its staff of supervisors, just as Miller had forced Edwin L. Gray, chairman of the Federal Home Loan Bank Board (FHLBB), into a disastrous penny-pinching effort that kept it from monitoring the S&Ls.

Years later, Seidman revealed how intent both the Reagan and Bush administrations had been on abandoning adequate supervisory controls, despite protests from the embattled Gray. While Gray made many questionable decisions during his term of office he did warn Congress of the potential for disaster, and of the fact that the OMB under Miller had forced him to reduce the number of supervisors he could keep on the payroll.

Seidman discovered this immediately after his appointment at FDIC as chairman. "I had just about settled in my chair when the OMB showed up and said that they would like to administer our budget," Seidman told me. "It was Jim Miller carrying on the thrust of his predecessor, David Stockman. Of course, they had obtained control of the Federal Home Loan Bank Board budget.

"They had a series of wonderful letters in which they exchanged insults, really, because Ed Gray was asking for more people. OMB was telling him that this was a deregulated industry and that, therefore, you didn't need any supervision anymore. When they came to see me, I went over to see Miller and I said, 'I don't see anything in your record that commends our going forward with your jurisdiction. Look at the Bank Board and what's gone on.'

"We had a series of exchanges in which he [Miller] finally ended up saying, as I left over there in the OMB, 'Bill, we've gotcha.' I said, 'Well, we'll see.' Then when he sent his people over next time, we wouldn't let 'em in. Anyway, he ultimately wrote a letter to me saying that he could not believe the way we were behaving and that I had become a disloyal Reaganite and a reregulator, which were the two biggest insults they could think of.

"I put the letter away. I never answered it. As a matter of fact, they never got control of our budget, as a result of which we have today doubled the number of supervisors that we have in the FDIC.

"Ever since then we have been fighting a little running skirmish because [Richard] Darman—who was with [James A.] Baker over at Treasury at that time—Darman's view was that we were wrong and that we should be under OMB. So when he came into OMB [as President Bush's budget director] he explored that again. But since we'd had a statute passed at that point that said that we were not under OMB, he decided not to fight that battle directly. So we have had a lot of indirect skirmishes. As a matter of fact, the bill that was passed [in 1989 to bail out the S&Ls] says that FDIC is to send [Darman] our numbers, but this no way implies control of our budget."[21]

Thus Seidman was able to resist falling into the same trap set for Gray, and banks, under Seidman, escaped the fate of the savings and loans. As Donald Regan's unsubtle remark indicated, with his own budget authorization Seidman could and did ignore Miller's penny-pinching directive. But Gray, at the Federal Home Loan Bank Board, was dependent on the Office of Management and Budget for his agency's funds. (The FHLBB was the agency responsible for controlling the S&Ls, while the Federal Savings and Loan Insurance Corporation—FSLIC—insured S&L deposits.)

Governmental financial irresponsibility came to a head with the crash of the S&Ls in the 1980s, an event that will saddle taxpayers with the cost of a huge bailout for decades to come. It gathered momentum in the Carter years, when the S&Ls began paying double-digit interest rates so as to accumulate deposits, while earning only half to two-thirds as much from their mortgage portfolios. Some mortgages, written fifteen to twenty years earlier, were earning only 6 or 7 percent or less interest for the S&Ls. As 1981 began, the average mortgages paid the S&Ls only 9 percent, while they had to offer half again as much for some of the funds flowing in. As a result, insolvent institutions had to keep increasing the interest they were paying depositors to dissuade them from withdrawing their funds. And then relatively more healthy S&Ls, to remain competitive, were forced into a bidding war, jacking up the rates they offered to pay for deposits.

Even a beginner's course in finance establishes the sound principle: "Never borrow short and lend long." That's a high-risk operation: if you make long-term loans at a fixed rate—which is the essential definition of a home mortgage—and accumulate the funds you lend out from deposits on which interest rates can fluctuate over a wide range—especially higher—you can get into trouble. The S&Ls were able to carry off this unsound operation for many years because their huge and powerful lobby had persuaded the federal government to put a ceiling on the interest rates they were required to pay on savings deposits. Under the Federal Reserve's Regulation Q, made applicable to the S&Ls in 1966, they paid no more than 5.25 percent to savers, which made it possible for them to write mortgages running twenty years or more at low interest rates. In effect, government policy required savers to subsidize the home-building industry—and home owners. (Home owners were and are further subsidized by the tax laws, which allow the deduction of interest payments from federal taxes.)

In January 1981, just a few days after Ronald Reagan took office, Alan Greenspan, former chairman of Gerald Ford's Council of Economic Advisers and once again a private business consultant, told the Joint Economic Committee of Congress that "a time bomb is ticking away in the financial system" because high interest rates inherited from the Carter administration were devastating the S&Ls. "It will eventually blow up if we do not defuse the inflationary pressures in our economy, and thereby rid ourselves of the huge inflation premiums embodied in nominal interest rates. But obviously, this cannot go on for very long under the existing rate structure. At some point, when interest income will no longer consistently meet interest cost requirements, the whole thrift institution system will undergo a massive crisis," Greenspan said.[22] His diagnosis was right on the money, but his prescription was faulty.

The cure that Greenspan and the Reagan administration devised in 1980 and 1982 was deregulation to permit the S&L industry to earn more money. Without adequate supervision, the S&Ls were encouraged by Congress and the regulators to compete with the banks and the new money-market funds—and that put them under fierce pressure to find high-yield, speculative investments. And the regulators, the Federal Savings and Loan Insurance Corporation and the

Federal Home Loan Bank Board—aware that the insurance funds they managed would be unable to cope with massive failures— looked the other way as the S&Ls in mid-1981 paid as much as 14.5 percent interest to attract deposits.

In 1980, 119 weak S&Ls had been merged into stronger thrift institutions. And as many as 600 insolvent S&Ls were kept open in 1981 and 1982 because the FSLIC didn't have enough money to shut them down. Instead, the FSLIC used accounting gimmicks to redefine what solvency meant, thereby concealing from the public the fact that many of them were in fact bankrupt. Congress, including its chief banking committees, was an active participant in this deception every year from 1982 on.[23] Ronald Reagan, for his part, was so emotionally committed to the idea that government was wicked and private industry pure that the notion that the public interest was sometimes dependent on government rules and regulation never received consideration.

At a banking conference sponsored by the Federal Reserve Bank of Boston at Harwichport, Massachusetts, on October 29, 1981, the bank's chief economist, Richard W. Kopcke, revealed that two out of every three S&Ls were actually insolvent, and—with great prescience—put the ultimate bailout cost at $30 billion to $200 billion.[24] Kopcke's calculation of insolvency was based on pricing assets and liabilities at realistic, current market levels—not the phony, overvalued asset levels that S&Ls put forward (and federal regulators accepted) as a way to keep their doors open.

But Kopcke's warning, and similar red flags raised by Professor Edward J. Kane of Ohio State University, went generally unheeded, and the press must accept a share of responsibility for inadequate coverage. Following Kopcke's and Kane's sober warnings, I wrote numerous columns on the subject. But it was difficult, in the early 1980s, to get editors to concentrate on the S&L issue. Most of my stories, including the original warning by Kopcke at the Boston Fed meeting, appeared in *The Washington Post*'s financial pages, not on page one—although the *Post* and other papers had done a good job in uncovering shoddy practices that plagued state-chartered S&Ls as far back as the 1960s.

Representative Jim Leach (R.-Iowa) has rightfully argued that the media should have focused the same spotlight on the S&L scandal it shined on national political scandals. "We're looking at an eleven-figure bailout—we're looking at an eleven-figure fraud story that's bigger than Teapot Dome or Abscam," Leach said at a National Press Club forum in April 1989. There is little doubt that in reporting financial news the press had been supercautious, unwilling at times to be the bearer of bad news. As journalists, the major criticism leveled against us is that we are more attentive to protecting the establishment than to protecting consumers and taxpayers. The critics are too often right.

The sharply higher interest rates that S&Ls began to pay in mid-1981 not only raised dramatically the costs to obtain deposits, but lowered the real market value of many of their mortgages, written years before at sharply lower rates. Higher interest rates deflate the real market value of a mortgage in exactly the same way they do a fixed-interest bond. If you own a $100,000 bond paying 6 percent interest, and try to sell it when other bonds are paying 12 percent, you will find the market value of the $100,000 bond is only $50,000. But under conventional accounting practices, an S&L was allowed to count its mortgages at face value regardless of changes in interest rates. That is precisely what was happening as the 1980s began: an old $100,000 mortgage at 6 percent was being counted as an asset worth $100,000. In reality it was worth only $50,000. That charade was the beginning of the end for the S&Ls.

Richard Kopcke proposed a commonsense standard—the current value of mortgages—as a better barometer of the real net worth of thrift institutions.[25] But obviously, an institution with a declining net worth based on actual market conditions would face the need to raise new capital. Using his current-value yardstick, Kopcke found that the average net worth of all thrift institutions worked out to a shocking minus 7 percent. By Kopcke's test, only one of three S&Ls could be said to be solvent, and the reported net worth of most of them "will drop very close to zero during the 1980s."[26]

Had the federal regulators put a true value on the S&Ls' deteriorating assets in 1981, as Kopcke suggested, they probably would have averted the severity of the crisis as it developed, and the cost would have been a moderate $30 billion to $50 billion to bring the net worth of the industry back to zero from minus 7 percent. But neither the Republicans managing the White House nor the Democrats controlling Congress had the courage to tell the American people the truth. Instead of paying what we now know would have been a cheap price to set the system straight, they perpetuated the sham, and turned a blind eye toward the phony bookkeeping. Thus brain-dead S&Ls were kept alive artificially by accounting shenanigans, enabling them to lose even more money.

The very act of deregulation, followed by inadequate auditing and inspection, produced the explosion that Greenspan hoped to avoid. With deregulation at both the federal and state levels between 1980 and 1983, the S&Ls were able to compete with the money-market funds and the banks—but that put them under fierce pressure to find even higher yield investments. And squaring the circle of mistakes, the federal government removed any need for S&L managers to act in a prudent way by guaranteeing their depositors, through the FSLIC, the safety of accounts up to $100,000. The S&L managers had every reason to throw caution to the winds—and they did, with a vengeance. What difference did it make if an S&L offered a high interest rate it could not really afford?

Until the inflation that began with the Vietnam War and deepened under Nixon and Carter, the home-building industry had been one of the more stable pillars of the long postwar boom. The thrift institutions, established to support the housing industry, made money on low, long-term loans to builders, acquiring the cash from passbook savings on deposit at even lower short-term rates. It didn't take a financial genius to figure out that money could be made by offering mortgages at 6 percent when the money came across the teller's windows at 4 percent. But the subsidy system for insuring S&Ls, of which managers could cleverly take advantage, was even worse, as Edward Kane brought out in his writings. Through 1984, the annual "explicit premium" for FSLIC insurance was one-twelfth of 1 percent of an S&L's deposits. After 1985, an additional one-eighth of 1 percent was tacked onto the costs of insuring an S&L. "Because this explicit premium does not increase with the riskiness of an insured firm's operations, FSLIC insurance can simultaneously be unreasonably expensive for a conservatively run firm and unreasonably cheap for an aggressively run enterprise that has little of its own capital at risk," Kane argued. "In effect, federal authorities offer incentive payments to undercapitalized thrifts and to any thrifts whose managers are willing and able to skew their investments toward aggressive, high-risk deals. . . . Managers' and officials' cleverness took advantage of naive and underinformed taxpayers, whose too-trusting passiveness marks them as the truly inept and unaware players in zombie enterprises."[27]

It didn't occur to many people that this cozy system, which involved a subsidy that home owners were getting at the expense of savers, could last only until such time as savers woke up to find they could earn more money with minimum effort. Gradually, savers learned they could do better (although a combination of inertia and the desire for an insured deposit kept—and still keeps—a lot of money in passbook accounts at low interest). In 1981, Greenspan estimated that the S&Ls held about $100 billion, or 21 percent of their total borrowings, in 5.25 percent passbook accounts, without which the S&L situation would have been even worse.

But other options for savers were multiplying: there were commercial bank certificates of deposit, Treasury bills, and mutual funds—all offering greater returns on their money than that available from the S&Ls. And into this menu of more attractive investments there was dumped a brand-new one, an All-Saver Certificate, concocted by the well-heeled S&L lobby in 1981. The infamous All-Saver Certificate was, in plain terms, a legalized steal.[28] Donald Regan, a Wall Streeter who accomplished little in his four years as the nation's chief financial officer—and then, as White House chief of staff, met his match in Nancy Reagan and her astrologer—bought this outrageous plan, and a spineless Congress went along with it.

The All-Saver Certificate—which went into effect on October 1, 1981—enabled the S&Ls to attract funds for a year by paying only 70 percent of the Treasury bill rate—but with a portion of the interest designated as tax-free. Since Treasury bills were paying 14 percent, the S&Ls could sell All-Savers at 9.8 percent, which would be tax-free up to $1,000 in interest to an individual and $2,000 per family. That meant an upper bracket family—around the 40 percent marginal tax rate—could shelter about $20,000 worth of investments in its All-Saver tax-exempts. But families in lower income brackets, paying a lower tax rate, would not benefit enough from the tax-exempt privilege to make it worthwhile.

The ill-advised All-Saver Certificate amounted to a quick infusion of funds, or a bailout for the S&L industry, via a new multibillion-dollar tax loophole for the wealthy. In essence, Regan, who should have known better, sanctioned not a system of real benefit to the S&Ls, or an incentive for new savings, but merely a shift by interest-sensitive investors in the upper brackets. In a way, it was a precursor of the individual retirement accounts (IRAs), which were intended to boost savings but for the most part only encouraged wealthy families to move savings from one pot of money to another, with attractive tax-postponement features.

The All-Saver Certificate was not the only bad idea floated to help the S&Ls. Worried that the number of S&Ls that had been merged out of existence in 1980—119—might be doubled in 1981, Federal Reserve chairman Paul Volcker asked Congress to impose reserve requirements on money-market funds that provided checking services. Theoretically, a cash reserve or set-aside would provide additional safety features for mutual funds, which are not insured like banks or thrift deposits. But the "reserve"—because it couldn't be invested—would reduce the competitive interest rate advantage that the money-market funds were enjoying over banks and S&Ls. One of Volcker's critics was Greenspan, who attacked the idea as arbitrary: "There is no economic rationale for it [in terms of safety for the depositor]. The idea of a reserve is to facilitate the conversion of assets. But what the money-market funds hold is all rather liquid."[29] On NBC-TV's *Meet the Press*, Citicorp chairman Walter Wriston also zapped Volcker, suggesting that the Fed was trying to "shackle" the money-market funds, whereas "all the commercial banks, under the Fed's rules, really rip off the consumer by paying him too low an interest rate." Volcker's plan died quietly.[30]

The All-Saver Certificate, as it turned out, did not put a dent into the money-market funds, which continued to grow. But it did trigger a flow of money out of passbook accounts into the higher-return, tax-free instrument, in effect forcing the S&Ls to pay about double the passbook rate of 5.25 percent. A befuddled Regan told reporters soon after the All-Savers became available: "We actually don't know what is going on. The industry is in a ferment. . . ."[31] Some economists attributed a further weakening of car sales and retail business in general to the attractiveness of the All-Saver Certificate.

Conceptually, there were other things terribly wrong with the All-Savers: tax-free S&L certificates forced state and local authorities to pay more on their tax-free bonds, in order to meet the competition, at precisely the time they had to boost regressive sales and property taxes to fill some of the gaps in social programs left by President Reagan's budget cuts in 1981 and 1982.

In the wake of the S&L fiasco, the public is entitled to wonder why more people didn't go to jail, and why more politicians weren't forced to walk the plank. But fraud and high living by ex-managers of S&Ls, while complicating the problem (and making for some of the juicier headlines), account for only a small share of the huge losses for which American citizens will still be paying ten or twenty from now. "In effect, the government assumed all the risks for hundreds of insolvent institutions," former Federal Reserve Board governor Sherman J. Maisel told a congressional committee investigating the fiasco. "It was like staking poker players [to] piles of chips while allowing them to keep any winnings, even as the government agreed to pay all the losses."[32]

The tax giveaways of the first Reagan term also contributed to the S&L disaster. As William Greider wrote in 1992, the 1981 tax legislation provided breaks for commercial real estate so generous "that it launched the nation's gaudy boom in new office buildings—the boom that collapsed in bankruptcies at the end of the decade. The new tax rules for depreciation were such that developers and investors found they could put up a new building and make money on it, even if it was half empty. They built lots of them. When the real estate lending regulations were loosened for commercial banks in the 1982 financial legislation, the stage was fully prepared for the great financial collapse that engulfed both builders and their bankers later—and led to another taxpayer bailout."[33]

But to get a total picture of the origins of the S&L mess, one has to go back to basics, to such elementary matters as lending long and borrowing short. William Seidman observed sardonically that this "was really quite a clever idea until, of course, inflation came along and they invented money-market funds."[34] Money-market funds, which got their start during the Carter inflation and expanded vigorously in the early Reagan years, offered depositors the benefit of higher rates than were actually prevalent in the market. And while money-market funds were uninsured, they offered savers many of the benefits of an account in an S&L, such as easy access to funds. Many offered checking services, much like a bank.

By the time Ronald Reagan took office, the yield on long-term government bonds had jumped to 13 percent, which meant that the markets were betting on a long-term inflation rate of around 10 percent. That posed a difficult problem for the thrifts: when the expectation was for a long-term inflation rate of no worse than 6 percent, the S&Ls could underwrite new home construction with low-interest home mortgages, pulling in the cash by paying even lower rates for passbook deposits. Lenders could make money so long as their return on mortgages exceeded the passbook payout rate of 5.25 percent. Soon the government was forced to allow the S&Ls to offer interest rates above the old ceilings. Then the new and more generous S&L interest offerings began to creep higher, on the average, than the returns they were getting on long-term mortgages written years before. As the S&Ls began to lose money, the least well managed of them began to look for better revenue producers than home mortgages—such as risky real estate ventures and junk bonds. The rest is history.

The problem can probably be traced back to 1973, when Congress authorized mutual savings banks in Massachusetts and New Hampshire to begin offering accounts known as negotiable orders of withdrawal—NOW for short. The NOW accounts allowed depositors to use their interest-bearing savings accounts to write the equivalent of checks to pay bills. Despite vigorous objection by commercial banks that this service amounted to an infringement of their special role, NOW accounts proved highly popular, and the system spread to S&Ls.[35] In some states, energetic S&Ls and credit unions worked out a system that allowed their depositors to pay for groceries at supermarkets with credit cards—also usable to get cash, or for payment of utility bills. Thus the thrift institutions made themselves over in the image of banks, vying for consumers' deposits by promising many of the same services and offering—at the start—a marginally better interest rate, as allowed by Congress. The U.S. Treasury cooperated nicely by introducing the direct deposit of Social Security checks in S&Ls already available at banks—a convenience to many Social Security recipients who then didn't have to worry about mail delays of their checks or, worse, theft.

For the thrifts, their new and expanded role meant a basic readjustment: loan operations had been dominated by the mortgages written for individual homes against a supply of funds generated by savers who were satisfied with the low, regulated interest rates set by Regulation Q. But to allow the S&Ls to compete for deposits that used to be placed in banks or in other forms of investment, those ceilings would have to be scrapped.

It was immediately apparent to experts that one price to be paid for abandoning the system whereby the small depositor subsidized the home-mortgage borrower would be to boost mortgage rates into double digits. Yet few could visualize that the transformation of the role and character of the S&Ls and savings banks, in a deregulated atmosphere, would be an invitation to disaster. And only a few, like economist Henry Kaufman, then with Salomon Brothers, were farsighted enough more than a decade ago to see that greed and speculation—accompanied by investment decisions as questionable as those made by S&Ls—would eventually trap some commercial banks into a similar mess.[36]

Incompetent Reagan administration officials decided that the answer to the problem was to let the thrift industry "grow out of it" by allowing it to go into new businesses. Losses already on the books were covered up by adopting new accounting standards that denied the fact that hundreds of institutions had become insolvent by the old standards. "What they said," Seidman recalled, "was that if we do anything now [to bail them out], these guys are all insolvent and that's very costly. We're not going to pay for it now, we're going to let them grow out of it. So they started out to encourage them to go into all these businesses and to grow out of it."[37]

This brought disaster, a classic illustration being the events surrounding the now-notorious Lincoln Savings and Loan Association of Irvine, California, acquired by an Arizona land speculator, Charles H. Keating Jr., who eventually persuaded five senators to go to bat for him. When Keating bought Lincoln at the end of 1984 for about $1 billion, the federal government was urging the S&Ls to expand with no attention to capital standards. Grow, grow, grow—that was the message. By the time Seidman took charge of the Resolution Trust Corporation in 1989, Lincoln had inflated itself into a $6 billion institution, having solicited insured deposits on which it was paying higher than average rates. Keating needed to generate higher than average returns, which he got by putting the money into speculative land ventures, junk bonds, and other questionable "investments" that didn't pay off. The institution was forced to close, after temporizing by M. Danny Wall, the chief savings and loan regulator. Under pressure from Congress to explain and defend the fiasco at Lincoln, Wall resigned in late 1989.

Lincoln came to symbolize the entire S&L mess not only because of the great loss associated with its demise—$2.5 billion—but because of the charge that U.S. senators Dennis DeConcini and John McCain of Arizona, Alan Cranston of California, Don Riegle of Michigan, and John Glenn of Ohio interceded with federal regulators to take it easy on Keating, who had contributed $1.3 million to their political campaigns or political action committees.

The mistake the "Keating Five" senators made was to plead Keating's case in private meetings with FHLBB chairman Edwin Gray and other regulators, suggesting that Gray was too tough on Lincoln. It smacked of blatant pressure to get favored treatment for a constituent who just happened to be a major contributor to some of their political campaigns.[38] The first meeting (without Riegle) took place in DeConcini's office on April 2, 1987. The second, held a week later with Gray's subordinates, included Riegle.

When the story broke in 1989, the senators protested that they were interceding only because two documents—an analysis by the accounting firm of Arthur Young, and a four-year-old letter from Alan Greenspan[39]—convinced them that Gray was being unfair to Keating. Arthur Young had given an extraordinary clean bill of health to Lincoln, which, considering its status as one of the "Big Eight" accounting firms, understandably provided the Keating Five with a good deal of ammunition. The author of the Young document later went to work for Keating.

Senator Glenn complained to *The Washington Post* about a column dated November 19, 1989, I had written calling for the resignation of the five senators. On December 4, I visited him in his office, where he reiterated his belief that he had done nothing wrong, but implied that he thought two of the other senators had a greater involvement. Spokesmen for Senator McCain also tried to put distance between himself and the others. The thrust of Glenn's argument was that he and the other senators were only doing what they would do for any constituent, and that as soon as the FHLBB revealed that a criminal proceeding was about to be instituted against Keating and his S&L they had dropped their advocacy of his cause like a hot potato.[40]

I told Glenn that the extent to which he and the others had stuck their necks out for Keating went well beyond routine "service" for an ordinary constituent. In my meeting with Glenn, in which he was polite but frosty, I suggested that he say that he had made an honest mistake and that he was sorry. He rejected my advice, repeating that he didn't believe he had done anything wrong.

As experienced as were Glenn and the other members of the Keating Five in the political game, they failed to see they had given the impression of bringing extraordinary political heat on a regulator to drop charges against a constituent who was a major contributor. At a minimum, it was unwise; at worst, it was unethical behavior, and triggered a special investigation by the Senate. In the end, the Keating Five accomplished nothing for Keating, and the political reputations of the five senators, despite an official whitewash, were tarnished. In 1991, Keating was convicted of securities fraud in California, and began serving a ten-year sentence. In January 1993, he was convicted in federal court on racketeering, conspiracy, and fraud charges, then sentenced to twelve and a half years in prison and fined $122.4 million on July 8 by U.S. district judge Mariana R. Pfaelzer in Los Angeles. Since the notoriety of the Keating Five became public, Cranston has retired, and Riegle and DeConcini have announced that they too would leave the Senate at the end of their terms.[41]

Predictably, as the Lincoln S&L debacle demonstrates, the "growth strategy" as a rescue formula for failing S&Ls was counterproductive, attracting crooks and swindlers into management. Worse, the Reagan administration was bent on accelerating the deregulation process. At the very time it was giving S&Ls a green light to grow and expand, it also decided it was time to reduce supervision. This decision represented a confluence of ideology and penny-pinching: it suited the fanatical "get government off our backs" credo of the Reaganites, and a perverse penny-pinching syndrome that coupled cutting critical budgetary expenditures with going hog-wild on defense expenditures. "In effect they gave people a credit card on the United States with no limits and said 'Enjoy yourself'," Seidman observed.

THE SAME HIGH interest rates that brought problems to the S&Ls also affected another group of savings institutions, mainly in the Northeast. These were mutual savings banks under the jurisdiction of the Federal Deposit Insurance Corporation (FDIC) rather than the Federal Savings and Loan Insurance Corporation (FSLIC) that regulated the S&Ls. The FDIC, chaired by William M. Isaac, met the mutual savings bank crisis with the opposite strategy in the late 1970s. As interest rates climbed, the FDIC told the savings banks to shrink, not expand. According to Seidman, "They told these banks: You are going to stay out of risk-type things and when the yield curve comes back, you'll be solvent again and, in the meantime, you're gonna learn how to run without rate risk by securitizing, by variable rate mortgages and other things." Today, by and large, the troubled mutual savings banks, such as the Seamen's Bank and the Bowery Bank of New York, have been returned to solvency. The total cost to the FDIC for the mutual savings banks problems is estimated at no more than $2 billion.

But instead of facing up to the S&L troubles, the federal government—which includes the regulators, the Congress, and the White House—covered up the damage with accounting gimmickry, and kept postponing the day when the bills would have to be paid. Almost all agree that delaying the cleanup from the time in 1983 when the problem was crying for a solution has added many tens of billions to a cost that had been placed at $500 billion over the next thirty years by the government's General Accounting Office. But a huge drop in interest rates in the early 1990s, as well as fewer S&L failures than projected, have cut the estimate of the ultimate cost to less than $200 billion.[42] By the same token, a rise in interest rates could once again boost the costs of the federal bailout. There is substantial evidence that if Ronald Reagan and the Congress had had the courage to bite the bullet in 1984, when all the essential facts were known, the entire bill could have been settled for just over $40 billion. But $40 billion in the mid-1980s would have added yet more to the extraordinary deficits being accumulated as a consequence of Reaganomics, and made the strategy of cover-up and deferral politically irresistible.

Sherman Maisel takes special note of the S&Ls' ability to get all the funds they wanted through Wall Street brokerage houses—paying, of course, high fees for the privilege: "S&Ls expanded too fast. Neither they nor the regulators had adequate staffs. Neither realized how many risks were being taken. All the new credit, together with larger tax benefits, greatly inflated land and building prices. When inflation subsided and interest rates rose, the inflated values were squeezed out."[43]

Only minimal attention has been given to the special role of the Wall Street "money brokers" in the buildup and downfall of the

S&Ls. One key source of funds enabling the S&Ls to carry out the hasty expansion to which Maisel referred consisted of deposits placed by big Wall Street houses, such as Merrill Lynch and Dean Witter. In the case of Keating's Lincoln Savings and Loan Association, the risky investments in real estate and junk bonds that eventually brought it down were largely financed by such brokered deposits, some of them representing foreign speculators. For example, in the first six months after Keating took over Lincoln in 1984, Merrill Lynch put almost $200 million into the institution. Later, Dean Witter became the main source, providing Keating with another $671 million to play with. Dean Witter earned a fee of 2.86 percent—in addition to interest.[44]

When Lincoln went broke, many Californians, including the elderly and widows, lost their entire life's savings because they had bought unsecured bonds from Keating, dramatizing for the public at large that the S&L mess was not merely high-risk finance among rich wheeler-dealers but a tragedy affecting ordinary people. Yet there are indications that even as Lincoln was seized by federal regulators in 1988, some of the best remaining among Lincoln's assets were sold off to liquidate investments by foreign financial institutions that had been guided by the money brokers. (An especially egregious error—made repeatedly through the 1980s for both S&Ls and commercial banks—was the regulators' decision, with congressional acquiescence, to keep alive failing institutions with little or no capital.)

The general problem of the S&Ls was exacerbated by a special situation in Texas and other states in the Southwest, where the S&L excesses had been combined with the greedy effort by banks as well as S&Ls to push oil prices sky high. No S&L owners or managers operated faster and looser than some of the disreputable ones in Texas, according to Ronnie E. Dugger, a distinguished Texas author: "Although California, Arizona, and Florida are large sumps in the U.S. savings and loan scandal, the Lone Star State is the swamp," he wrote in 1989.[45] Among the more notorious crooks was Don R. Dixon of Vernon Savings of Dallas, who, Dugger says, "wined and waxed top national politicians aboard the $2.6 million, 112-foot yacht *High Spirits* on the Potomac, spent freely on European vacations and lived in a two-million-dollar beach house at 'thrift' expense, and maintained fleets of airplanes, and [whose company] flew prostitutes halfway across the country for the entertainment of its directors."[46]

Still, these excesses were not uncovered until later. What really concentrated the public's mind was a series of big bank failures.

Thus the July 6, 1982, bankruptcy of the Penn Square National Bank of Oklahoma, the fourth biggest bank bust in American history, epitomized all the elements of avarice and abuse that had driven the financial institutions to disaster's edge.[47] In that summer of 1982, as the nation was sinking deeper into recession—despite the promises of Reagan's supply-siders—the American banking system faced a crisis caused by the dubious judgment of some of the biggest bankers in the country. John Heimann, who had been comptroller of the currency in the Carter administration, observed that most bankers, especially the biggest of the big wheels, don't like to concede that any of their colleagues behave badly.

But no one could ignore what was happening when Chase Manhattan Bank, then the nation's second largest, and Continental Illinois, the sixth, were caught making the kind of risky loans that banks of that size are not supposed to make. Chase had not only bought $212 million worth of what FDIC chairman Isaac called "shoddy, speculative" energy loans from Penn Square but had to confess to two large losses in earlier failures of two Wall Street securities dealers, Drysdale Securities and Lombard-Wall.

The sudden collapse of Drysdale and Lombard-Wall was a shocker on Wall Street; more important, it was one of the first signs of the fragility of the whole financial system that later ensnared the S&Ls, the banks, and the off-budget federal agencies such as the Federal National Mortgage Association, known as "Fannie Mae," and Federal Home Loan Mortgage Corporation, known as "Freddie Mac," which had implied guarantees from Uncle Sam. Continental Illinois Corporation, in a move that foreshadowed its own later crisis, bought $1 billion worth of Penn Square participation—advances to small energy companies that, without adequate collateral, were gambling on sharply higher prices for oil. In addition, Continental had loaned about another $1 billion to a clutch of troubled corporations, such as Dome Petroleum, themselves struggling to avoid bankruptcy. Chase Manhattan Bank, the Seattle National Bank, and the Northern Trust Company together bought another $1 billion worth of participations from Penn Square.[48]

Why did the huge banks mess up so badly? Americans like to think that bankers, like doctors, are the best, most trusted, most secure members of their community. Bankers, the symbol of money in a capitalist nation, naturally wield great power. But they have proved to be as frail as anyone else, as much subject to the temptations of greed, and as likely to fall into speculative and bad management practices, as anyone else.

John Heimann, now an investment banker, observes that in

many large banks, a loan manager operates under a quota system, something like a cop handing out tickets. "He may have $100 million that he's supposed to lend out for energy," Heimann said, "and if he comes back in and says he's only been able to place $60 million or $80 million, they'll say, 'Hey, if you can't do it, we'll get someone who can.' "[49]

So the classic, old-fashioned image of the tightfisted banker did not apply in the go-go atmosphere of the early 1980s. Performance had gradually become the criterion against which banks and bankers were measured, leading to a sacrifice in the quality of restraints on lending. Security was abandoned in the search for growth—in quickly changing "fashions." First, it had been real estate in the 1970s, then international lending in the 1980s. After all, had not Walter Wriston, the Citicorp boss, assured his peers and all others that sovereign nations did not go bankrupt? And finally, after OPEC's second oil shock drove up prices, what could be better than energy loans?

Karin Lissakers of the Carnegie Endowment for International Peace, a longtime keen student of the banking industry, said: "The banking industry is badly run, and big bankers have been making the same mistakes domestically that they have been making for years internationally."[50] But bankers tend to believe their own press releases. Bankers trust bankers, and often plunge into an incestuous business relationship, *keiretsu* style, with another bank—without the sort of cautious study that would precede an investment of another kind. It's not that banks make this mistake exclusively when dealing with other banks—witness the imprudent bank loans made almost a decade later to high-flying, high-living real estate developer Donald Trump.

But bank-on-bank is how Penn Square became such an entangling mess for larger banks such as Chase and Continental Illinois, sucking along a huge number of imprudent S&Ls. Ultimately, the size of the Continental Illinois rescue package became a shocking $7.5 billion when the FDIC, which is supposed to insure individual accounts only, up to a $100,000 maximum, stepped in and guaranteed all deposits at the nation's eighth-largest bank.

This was a highly politicized decision, triggered by White House fears that, if Continental went belly-up, it would affect President Reagan's reelection prospects in the fall of 1984. Treasury Secretary Regan and Federal Reserve Chairman Volcker cooked up the idea, which was sharply criticized by Alan Greenspan.

Contemptuous of Regan's understanding of the intricacies of the economy, Greenspan told me that the bailout would "lower the quality of the American banking system, which had been very good." He added: "You'll find some bankers more concerned about where they stand in those published lists of relative bank size than in the quality of their assets on their balance sheets."[51] The Reagan administration's formal explanation for this extraordinary change in FDIC policy that allowed the Continental bailout was that it would avert a bankruptcy that in turn would have staggered the entire global financial structure. A Regan statement read: "We want to make sure that in these perilous times, there is no doubt that we will support our banks. That doesn't mean that every bank will remain afloat, it doesn't mean that every bank will remain independent. But nevertheless, we will make certain that there will be no calamities in the banking system."[52] Thus the word went forth that some American banks would be considered too big to be allowed to fail, creating in effect a two-tier system. In smaller failures, for example with Penn Square, depositors holding more than $100,000 in a single account were allowed to take a beating. The Continental decision relegated most of the nation's commercial banks, then numbering about 14,000, to second-class status.

The idea that any bank can be "too big to fail," known in the trade as the TBTF philosophy, is nothing less than a cover-up, at taxpayer expense, for faulty loan or business judgments made by the nation's biggest bankers.[53] Banking consultant Carter Golembe, in a 1991 analysis for his clients, contended that TBTF has turned the federal deposit insurance system into a monster. Instead of limited insurance coverage as visualized at its inception during the New Deal in 1934, the FDIC has been used to cover all deposits—not just insured deposits—at most small banks and at all large banks. Instead of covering "rent and grocery money," the FDIC covers upward of $1 million (if the depositor follows simple rules that divide his money into multiple accounts.)[54] This can't be justified by the banking industry's defense that without TBTF the risk is "systemic risk." Instead, we should go back to basics, and end the practice of paying off depositors whose accounts are above the $100,000 insured level: no insurance, no payoff—NINP.

Why are there so many American banks to begin with? According to Golembe, the American banking explosion got started with the populist notion in the early 1800s that to open up a bank was a "right" that would serve the public interest.[55] The 1838 New York State Free Banking Act said, in effect, that any group of five persons "of good character" could open a bank. The spirit of the 1838 act permeated banking in America for all time. President Andrew Jackson vetoed legislation providing a national bank, concerned that it would lead to a concentration of financial power. The Federal Reserve System didn't arrive until 1914. According to the General Accounting Office, at the onset of the Great Depression there were about 25,000 banks, of which about one-fourth eventually failed during that record economic slump. In 1934, in order to allow small banks to continue to attract depositors, the Federal Deposit Insurance Corporation was established, another commitment to a decentralized system. Large banks were prohibited from branching across state lines; and even state banking administrations took pains to prevent their large city banks from dominating rural areas.

It can be argued that the populist approach to banking was in keeping with the entrepreneurial spirit that helped make America great. Moreover, experience indicates that the small banks in America are often more efficient than the large ones. It's the big banks that have made big mistakes. Consider Penn Square, which was the nation's twenty-second-largest bank. Its collapse triggered losses among 177 credit unions and S&Ls that had put gluttony ahead of good judgment by depositing money in Penn Square. Over its head in loans for oil exploration and agricultural purposes, and desperate for cash, Penn Square was paying up to two full percentage points over the going rate for funds put in uninsured certificates of deposit. Contrary to all the prudential caution that should typify thrift institution managers, the 177 credit unions and S&Ls responded to Penn Square's "bait" of those two extra points.

Penn Square was a flashing red light: the entire financial system was in trouble, but nobody was braking the slide. The federal regulators had known for some time that banks and S&Ls in Texas and other parts of the Southwest were getting overextended. As far back as February 1980, John Heimann had flagged Penn Square as a troubled institution. But there was no follow-up in the Reagan administration.

There were three predominant elements working to generate the flood of red ink. First, the capital behind most of the S&Ls—especially the capital put up by the owners of the ventures—proved pitifully inadequate when interest rates skyrocketed in the late 1970s and early 1980s. Second, the Reagan administration's ideological dedication to deregulation turned the S&Ls loose to make loans about which they had no expertise. And third, the lack of supervision after deregulation aborted any control over the rate of growth of the S&Ls and permitted extraordinary risk-taking by frequently unscrupulous operators.

Even as the crisis was growing throughout the early 1980s, the FSLIC was not doing its supervisory job well, and Congress was an accomplice in supervision-by-omission by failing to increase the FSLIC's manpower or capital resources.[56] The rapid progression of failures had been publicly documented: on average during the 1970s, eight banks and four S&Ls had failed each year, and the regulatory agencies designated fewer than 2 percent of the commercial banks as "problem" institutions. In the first half of the 1980s, there was a surge, especially in the eighteen months ending midyear 1986, when the failure rate was one and a half S&Ls and two banks every week.[57]

Congress didn't show a sense of urgency in dealing with the S&L crisis until the spring of 1989, when the anger of their constituents over the loss of $10 million to $20 million a day caught up with them. That was the estimated cost of keeping open 600 to 800 S&Ls insolvent since 1984 because the regulators didn't have enough money to close them.

Volcker argued that the failure of a bank as large as Penn Square would be a huge shock to the financial system in general, especially to the major banks that had bought the Penn Square participation. He would have preferred to merge Penn Square into another institution. But C. Todd Conover, comptroller of the currency since December 1981, supported by the FDIC and Treasury Secretary Regan, favored closing the bank and paying off the insured depositors. After several long days of heated meetings, Conover decided to close the bank on July 5, 1984, and the FDIC ended up as the receiver. Volcker's proposal would have protected the uninsured depositors of Penn Square—the big banks. Later, of course, Seattle First was sold to avoid another failure, and in May 1984 Continental Illinois, the sixth-largest bank in the country, failed and was bailed out, setting what William A. Niskanen properly calls "a very bad precedent": the federal government will not let any bank fail.[58]

The federal deposit insurance system was set up not to protect individual banks but to protect the banking system by extending protection to individual, insured depositors who otherwise would be tempted to withdraw their money at the first sign of trouble. As the 1980s ended, and the nation tried to assess the true costs of the S&L tragedy, it seemed clear that Congress would have to bite a bullet it had been trying to duck for years: the need to reform the deposit insurance system that had worked from 1934 through the 1960s but had failed in the volatile 1970s and 1980s. That will mean, ultimately, that what Ohio University's Edward Kane—the expert who predicted the emergence of the S&L crisis at a time when politicians preferred to look the other way—calls the "black magic" of federal insurance will have to be cut back, in stages, from that $100,000 level to a lower, basic figure that will cover the average person's savings or checking account. For insurance beyond that, there will have to be additional premiums that will give the insuring institutions enough funds and credibility to police the whole system.

Kane offered a parable to put the problem in perspective: A few prominent members of Congress order the most expensive meal and wine available at a fine restaurant, hoping that a lobbyist at a nearby table will recognize them and pick up the check. The manager doesn't ask to see their credit cards or bank balances, assuming that one way or another the bill will be paid. The congressmen stay long, and eat heartily, figuring that the longer they stay, the greater the opportunity for someone else to pay the escalating bill. "A parallel exists between this growing dinner bill and the unallocated deposit-insurance losses. Congress has repeatedly let the serious financial shortages at the Federal Savings and Loan Insurance Corp. (FSLIC) and many individual deposit institutions ride. Rather than submitting the bill that FSLIC has run up to taxpayers for immediate payment, Congress has been hoping for insured institutions' imbedded losses to be cured by various lucky movements in real estate, farm, energy, and bond prices and in the economies of less developed countries. The Federal Home Loan Bank Board (FHLBB), the General Accounting Office (GAO) and private experts all agree that since 1983, FSLIC and FDIC have lost billions of dollars while waiting for their luck in high-risk financial enterprises to change."[59]

Meanwhile, under the famous "new operating procedures" installed by Paul Volcker in October 1979, the Federal Reserve was under the spell of monetarist doctrine, which called for focusing entirely on controlling the money supply, with no attention to the level of interest rates.[60] With the Fed no longer caring how high interest rates would go, "real" interest rates—long-term yields minus inflation—began to creep up to an unprecedented 5 to 6 percent range, about twice the 3 percent level considered to be the balancing point of a modern economy. Referring to this disturbing phenomenon, Federal Reserve governor Lyle Gramley said in 1981: "This is a very different world from the one I grew up in. I used to think I was really a hotshot forecaster, but I have become very humble about my forecasting abilities. In part, that's because real interest rates are serving a different role than they once did. I add up the pieces— but I can't add them up anymore. I just don't know what's gonna happen . . ."[61]

THE RESULT WAS A level of interest rates so high as to be punitive not only for the S&Ls but for the whole domestic economy and for the global economy as well. High interest rates had a devastating impact on Third World nations that had taken out heavy loans, at floating rates tied to international standards, in order to finance the exploding costs of oil. It wasn't until the spring of 1982, when Mexico signaled that it couldn't pay back its loans on time, that Volcker's Fed began to back off the monetarist policy it had adopted in September 1979.

But in midsummer 1981 interest rates hovered around peak levels, and S&Ls started to go broke. Congress, the Fed, and the Reagan administration, instead of paying attention to the underlying causes of the thrift industry crisis, began to apply Band-Aids. The cover-up, redefining solvency by distorting accepted accounting standards, moved merrily along. And nothing was quite so outrageous as the way the Reagan administration—the White House and the Treasury—and Congress allowed themselves to be hustled by the well-heeled S&L lobby, which concocted the infamous All-Saver tax-exempt saving certificate.

Donald Regan fingers the White House—his old boss, President Reagan—as the main villain. Reporter Michael Binstein quoted Regan as saying: "I don't think, in the first Reagan administration, that the White House had a real knowledge of economics and finance and the financial system, and they didn't believe what they were hearing from the Treasury because they were more politically attuned. And therefore, when the politicians were saying 'Do it this way,' and the purists at the Treasury were saying 'No, no, no, that's the wrong way to go,' they went with the politics of it, with [the elections of] 1982 and 1984 in mind."[62]

Regan had a point: in the first Reagan term, with James Baker as chief of staff, politics ruled supreme. The chairman of the Council of Economic Advisers, the middle-of-the roader Murray Weidenbaum, couldn't cope with David Stockman at the Office of Management and Budget, or Reagan's corps of outside advisers led by Milton Friedman, and soon departed.

But there were no purists at the Treasury either, certainly not Don Regan, who came out of the brokerage industry that helped to fuel the insane growth of the S&Ls. Although Regan recused himself from issues that related to Merrill Lynch—Regan's old Wall Street firm—FHLBB chairman Edwin Gray later argued that Deputy Secretary Tim McNamar's close involvement in questions relating to the money brokers made Regan's recusal meaningless.[63]

But Regan wasn't content with that much disruption of savings patterns in an effort to solve the S&L crisis. He announced that he would propose legislation giving both banks and S&Ls the right to "take an equity position," that is, to own real estate and other assets. In addition, bank holding companies would be enabled to deal in securities and mutual funds.[64] These new powers for banks and S&Ls, Regan said, were in line with the Reagan administration's commitment to deregulation, and he predicted that "the ultimate beneficiary" would be the consumer. But as consumers learned painfully, deregulation opened the floodgates to disaster—buildings without tenants, projects in various unfinished stages, inventories of worthless art, antiques, and baubles on which S&L managers had loaned hundreds of millions of dollars.

Congress, the Fed, and the administration should have tried to shrink and compress the S&Ls, forcing them to follow more conservative investment practices. But managers had little if any incentive to curtail their risk-taking, because the government stood by with insurance up to $100,000 for each account, even in institutions completely insolvent. Finally, eight years after the crisis had begun, President Bush faced the facts, and sent Congress a bailout program designed by Nicholas Brady's Treasury Department that put at least $50 billion in budget money on the line to bail out the industry, anticipating that the ultimate cost would be about $100 billion. But everyone knew that the final bill would be higher. Bush and Brady deserve credit for reassessing the S&L problem at the beginning of 1989, even if the extent of the damage was underestimated and partially covered up by budgetary trickery.

THE SAME SLEAZE that generated the S&L debacle spread into the insurance industry; threatened to engulf the "government-sponsored enterprises" (GSEs), such as the Federal National Mortgage Association (Fannie Mae) and the Federal Home Loan Mortgage Corporation (Freddie Mac); spread into mergers and takeovers; helped trigger the stock market crash of 1987; and finally is being reflected in a slow-moving but inevitable weakening of some of the giants in the American banking system.

Even now, in 1994, little publicity has attended insurance company failures, which were running at the rate of more than fifty a year from 1985 to 1990, double the prior insolvency rate. Incredibly, insurance is a state-regulated industry, but even the troubles of top companies, such as Aetna, Travelers, and Primerica, did not stir Congress into a federal regulatory mode.

The sickness of the insurance industry was best illustrated by the infamous "GICs," guaranteed investment contracts, offered by major companies, which assured investors a fixed, double-digit interest rate for as much as ten years. For example, the Washington Post Company gave employees participating in a profit-sharing program the opportunity to put funds in an insurance company GIC that paid 14.9 percent a year for up to five years. When interest rates plunged in the mid-1980s, the insurance companies were forced to pay out, through their GICs, vast sums that exceeded their earnings.[65] In effect, insurance companies had made the same mistake as banks that expected crude oil prices to go up, never down.

Several columns I wrote in 1990 and 1991 brought attention to the potential for another $1 trillion bailout, this time involving Fannie Mae and the other GSEs, a hybrid public/private animal that few citizens know about and even fewer understand. The GSE story was largely unearthed by a persistent and dedicated Washington lawyer and former government employee, Thomas H. Stanton, who stirred my interest in writing about GSEs.

Besides Fannie Mae and Freddie Mac, the GSEs include the Federal Home Loan Bank (FHLB); the Student Loan Marketing Association (Sallie Mae); and the Farm Credit System. The distinguishing characteristic of all five—set up to facilitate the flow of credit to agriculture, housing, and higher education—is that they borrow funds in the private market on the strength of an implicit government guarantee. With Uncle Sam behind them, they can borrow at lower rates. In effect, the GSEs receive a valuable subsidy from the federal government, which bears a risk if things go bad. And although the federal guarantee is implicit—and not explicit as is the case with S&Ls and banks—it nonetheless is real.

At the end of 1990, the five GSEs had outstanding obligations exceeding $980 billion.[66] Stanton calculates that the federal government's exposure increases by about $100 billion a year. Yet federal regulation of Fannie Mae and Freddie Mac was limited to approval of their new mortgage programs by the Department of Housing and Urban Development, the federal department that promotes low-cost public housing. When a department in charge of promoting an activity is also in charge of ensuring that the financing is done in a safe and prudent manner, there always is the potential for a conflict of interest. Moreover, in addition to their multibillion-dollar lines of credit with the Treasury, the GSEs enjoy exemptions from most state and local taxes, and from Securities and Exchange Commission regulations that normally apply to private corporations.

Stanton, who was assistant general counsel, then associate general counsel of Fannie Mae from 1982 to 1985, first wrote about his concerns in a 1986 article for *Legal Times*, then explored the situation in 1987 for the General Accounting Office. As the S&L debacle gathered force, Stanton's one-man campaign to reduce the contingency risk in the GSEs came to the attention of Representatives J. J. (Jake) Pickle (D.-Tex.) and William Gradison (R.-Ohio), both members of the House Ways and Means Committee. They proposed to insert a clause in the Financial Institutions Reform, Recovery and Enforcement Act of 1989 (FIRREA) requiring the Treasury to study the financial risks inherent in the GSEs and to make an annual report to Congress.[67]

Immediately, Fannie Mae and Freddie Mac fought the idea and, supported by Senator Alan Cranston, who was a senior member of the House-Senate conference committee on FIRREA, succeeded in limiting the Treasury study to two years, 1990 and 1991. The good news is that those reports, pushed by a conscientious Treasury undersecretary, Robert R. Glauber, publicly demonstrated the enormous risk in the government's implicit guarantee of the GSEs. The bad news is that, in the end, Congress chickened out and took little significant action.

In February 1991, Fannie Mae's chief operating officer, David Maxwell, retired with a $27.5 million compensation package, representing his 1990 salary of $7.5 million and a lump-sum bonus of $20 million, compelling evidence that Fannie Mae, Washington's biggest unadvertised powerhouse, needs better oversight on behalf of the taxpayers.[68] Oakley Hunter, Maxwell's predecessor at Fannie Mae, blew the whistle on Maxwell in a letter to Senator Don Riegle, chairman of the Senate Banking Committee, and member Jake Garn (R.–Utah). Maxwell and the Fannie Mae board contended that Maxwell was receiving a justifiable reward for Fannie Mae's enormously profitable record.

But Oakley argued that whereas Fannie Mae had been set up to provide funding to assure adequate low- and moderate-income housing, under Maxwell the agency had been focusing on making extraordinary profits, "subsidizing the shareholders" who bought Fannie Mae stock on the New York Stock Exchange. Maxwell's $27.5 million compensation package, Hunter said, "was not justified by any rational applicable standard." He pointed out to Riegle and Garn that since Fannie Mae, like all GSEs, is insulated by the federal government from normal market risks, CEOs such as Maxwell "are not entrepreneurs." Fannie Mae's profit on equity in 1990 was 33.9 percent, Oakley calculated, more than double that of private blue-chip stocks traded on the NYSE. Stanton summed up the Maxwell story: "It's a classic example of how you can privatize the profits and socialize the risks."[69]

In April 1991, a Congressional Budget Office study said that Fannie Mae and Freddie Mac, the two largest GSEs, posed a low level of risk to the government, that the FHLB and Sallie Mae represented a "minimal risk," but that the Farm Credit System "remains quite vulnerable and continues to expose the government to more risk than any other enterprise." And although it recommended no changes, the CBO admitted that it "has not assessed the exposure to management and operations risks of any of the GSEs."[70] Yet the $900 billion to $1 trillion federal government exposure because of the GSEs is only the tip of the iceberg. In 1990, OMB director Richard Darman put Uncle Sam's potential liability for all federal credit programs—loans, loan guarantees, and deposit and other insurance—at an astonishing $6 trillion. The balance of the $6 trillion cited by Darman covers liabilities for the rest of Uncle Sam's huge credit programs, including insurance for S&Ls, banks, and credit unions. The early warning signals have been there: the government's insurance losses in 1989 were $67.2 billion. Seven years before, in 1982, they were only $4.6 billion.

Darman first cited the $6 trillion liability on David Brinkley's Sunday morning TV talk show, but Brinkley and his panel didn't follow up, nor did the general press, which was preoccupied with the possibility of a tax increase as part of the budget "summit" discussions taking place between President Bush and congressional leaders.[71] "If you look at what is a serious long-term problem," Darman told the Brinkley panel, "we're accumulating hidden liabilities, contingent liabilities, up to almost $6 trillion now. It's a staggering amount to imagine, that's totally outside of budgetary discipline at the moment, and somehow, it needs to be brought under control. There ought to be some cap overall on the government's loan, loan guarantee, and government insurance programs."

ANOTHER SYMBOL OF moral decay in the 1980s, fed by Ronald Reagan's political commitment to financial market deregulation, was the $200 billion junk bond market launched by Michael Milken. Junk bonds helped finance not only some of the biggest S&L scams, including the notorious Lincoln Savings and Loan Association, but a wave of corporate takeovers that froze American industry in its tracks, shuffling paper to avoid hostile buyouts while West Germany and Japan were attending to the mundane business of making quality goods and marketing them to eager customers around the world— and in the United States.

Before Milken was indicted for fraud in 1988, he had drawn $1 billion in salary from Drexel Burnham Lambert over four years, including an incredible $500 million in a single year. In a speech to the American Society of Newspaper Editors in May 1984, Lazard Frères' Felix Rohatyn, who made his living arranging mergers and acquisitions, said that junk bonds were helping turn "the financial markets into a huge casino. Leveraged buyouts, financed by junk bonds, bet the company on a combination of continued growth and lower interest rates, with no margin for error."

Junk bonds, securities offering high yields but considered to be of less than "investment grade," have their defenders, who argue that those high-risk pieces of paper have performed an essential function, financing economic growth, especially for emerging companies that otherwise would have had no source of capital. But as one expert, Columbia University's Louis Lowenstein, pointed out, if junk bonds began innocently enough as "reasonably good junk" at the start of the decade, by mid-1985 they were used increasingly to finance takeovers, and the quality deteriorated rapidly. The main point, as Lowenstein put it perfectly, was that the junk bond market became "comatose" after Milken's forced exit, not because Milken was no longer around, but "because the marketplace recognized that junk bonds are, well, junk."[72]

The 1980s were the decade of white-collar crime. The prosecution of a clutch of Wall Street slicksters, starting with Dennis Levine and Ivan Boesky, and culminating in the November 1990 sentencing of Michael Milken to ten years in prison, "disclosed a pattern of illegal activities that was much larger in scope and at a much higher level than anyone realized," according to Rudolph Giuliani, then U.S. attorney for the Southern District of New York, who prosecuted Boesky and Milken. "In the '30s, '40s, '50s, into the '60s, there was a whole different attitude about white-collar crime. It really wasn't until the '70s, with Watergate and the political-corruption cases and the business-corruption cases that emerged, that there was a real emphasis put on white-collar crime. . . . [Insider] information was not being treated as if it was sensitive. People weren't being trained in their obligations. The integrity of the marketplace was in jeopardy."[73]

But most American editors are interested in other kinds of stories—especially politics, sports, sex, and crime—that sell newspapers, and only barely tolerate what they consider to be arcane financial matters. So they paid no heed when alarm bells were sounded by Rohatyn. Nor did the public and Congress do much beyond yawning when Henry Kaufman testified before a House Energy Subcommittee on June 5, 1985, that "we are drifting toward a financial system in which credit has no guardian."

With President
Lyndon B. Johnson and
Walter W. Heller,
chairman of the
Council of Economic
Advisers, in the Oval
Office, December
1963. (*Photo by
Okamoto/author's
collection*)

President Lyndon B. Johnson at the Naval Medical Hospital in Bethesda, Maryland, meeting on November 17, 1966, with his economic advisers (*left to right*) William McChesney Martin, Jr., chairman of the Federal Reserve Board; Arthur Okun, member of the Council of Economic Advisers; Charles Schultze, director of the Bureau of the Budget; Henry H. (Joe) Fowler, secretary of the Treasury; unidentified notetaker. (*Photo by Okamoto/Courtesy of Suzanne Okun*)

Arthur Okun, newly appointed chairman of the Council of Economic Advisers, in his first briefing of the Cabinet, May 27, 1968. (*Photo by Okamoto/Courtesy of Suzanne Okun*)

President Richard M. Nixon announcing the appointment of Arthur F. Burns as chairman of the Federal Reserve Board, February 8, 1970. (*Photo by Harry Naltchayan/*The Washington Post)

At Camp David, three of President Nixon's top economic advisers meet (*left to right*): Paul McCracken, chairman of the Council of Economic Advisers; Herbert Stein, a member of the Council of Economic Advisers; and Arthur F. Burns, chairman of the Federal Reserve Board, August 14, 1971. (*Photo courtesy of UPI/Bettmann*)

John Connally, secretary of the Treasury, and Paul A. Volcker, under secretary for monetary affairs, meeting at the Smithsonian Institution to discuss a new exchange-rate system, December 18, 1971. (*Photo by Gerald Martineau*/The Washington Post)

With Giscard d'Estaing, France's minister of finance, in the courtyard of the Organization of American States, Washington, D.C., March 27, 1973.
(*Photo by Harry Naltchayan*/The Washington Post)

International Monetary Fund meeting in Rio de Janeiro, 1973. U.S. Secretary of the Treasury Henry H. (Joe) Fowler is seated at the center. It was at this meeting that "Special Drawing Rights" (also known as "paper gold") was created. (*Courtesy of the International Monetary Fund*)

President Gerald R. Ford convenes an economic summit in the East Room of the White House, September 11, 1974. (*Photo by Frank Johnston*/The Washington Post)

In 1977, with President Jimmy Carter attending, Arthur F. Burns speaks at the ceremony announcing that G. William Miller, right, would be the new chairman of the Federal Reserve Board. (*Photo by Larry Morris*/The Washington Post)

With Treasury Secretary Michael Blumenthal in Shanghai, 1979. Blumenthal had come to China to open the American Embassy in Bejing following normalization of relations. Blumenthal then visited Shanghai, where he had spent his childhood as a German-Jewish refugee. (*Photo courtesy of the U.S. Treasury Department*)

Donald Regan, secretary of the Treasury (*left*), and Paul A. Volcker, chairman of the Federal Reserve Board, have a breakfast meeting in the secretary's private dining room at the Treasury Department, April 28, 1982. (*Photo by Frank Johnston*/The Washington Post)

Donald Regan (*right*) chats with James Baker III, his replacement as secretary of the Treasury, moments before President Ronald Reagan announces the appointment in the East Room of the White House, February 4, 1985. David Stockman, director of the Office of Management and Budget, is engrossed with the president's budget. (*Photo by Frank Johnston*/The Washington Post)

Announcing the agreement known as the Plaza Accord, U.S. Treasury Secretary James Baker III (*left*) introduces West German Finance Minister Gerhard Stoltenberg (*far right*), September 22, 1985. Federal Reserve Board Chairman Paul A. Volcker sits at second from right. Standing at right is Assistant Treasury Secretary David Mulford. (*Courtesy of UPI/Bettmann*)

President Ronald Reagan briefing members of the press on the state of the economy, January 28, 1988. (*Courtesy of The White House*)

Kaufman felt that Congress, during the 1980s, tricked by the surface signs of well-being in the Reagan years, refused to focus on the threat to financial institutions, including serious conflicts of interest, primarily because no one could prove that danger was right around the corner. "In Congress, they would ask: 'How imminent is this?' And since there was no way you could say it was coming within a month or two or three, but it would cumulate, somewhere down the road, they would relax."[74]

The responsibility, nonetheless, falls mostly on Ronald Reagan and his determination to deregulate the economy. That allowed markets to control their own destiny. Even after 1988, when Drexel Burnham Lambert pleaded guilty to six criminal charges and paid a $650 million fine, many in Washington and Wall Street resisted tighter controls. But there is no good substitute for full surveillance and intelligent supervision of financial markets, including banks and S&Ls. Kaufman long has insisted that too much is at stake to leave the performance and conduct of financial institutions to the markets alone. In his 1985 appearance on the Hill, he urged Congress to establish a national board—comprising the Federal Reserve Board, other federal agencies, and private sector members—to oversee and set standards for financial institutions.

HAVE WE LEARNED ANY lessons from the deregulation experience? I think not: on September 20, 1990, the Federal Reserve Board approved an application by J. P. Morgan & Company to trade and sell corporate stocks, reversing a regulation dating back to the Depression era that ordained a "church-state" separation of the banking and securities businesses, the 1933 Glass-Steagall Act.[75] J. P. Morgan & Company has a solid reputation as a conservative institution, but by blurring the Glass-Steagall Act's line of safety, the federal government is once more asking for trouble.

The investigative commission appointed by Ronald Reagan to explore the October 1987 stock market crash, headed by investment banker Nicholas F. Brady, recommended that the Federal Reserve Board be made the ultimate regulator of the securities system. That idea—and the rest of the Brady Commission report—was shoved under the rug by Reagan, and ignored by Brady himself when he became secretary of the Treasury in the Bush administration.

In microcosm, the story of how greed contaminated the American financial system is encapsulated in the saga of the GRH Companies—a small Louisiana oil and gas refinery virtually unknown outside the energy business. GRH, as first reported by *The Wall*

Street Journal, managed to persuade fourteen American and foreign banks to lend it $750 million for oil exploration only two years after its predecessor company emerged from bankruptcy. In early 1982, GRH had to confess to its bankers that it had no money with which to pay back the loans. Like the Third World debtors of that era, GRH threw itself on the mercy of the lender banks, begging for "restructuring" or "rescheduling" of the debt.

And who were the banks on the hook for $750 million? They included some of the biggest names in the business, including three that had been stung in the debacles involving Penn Square Bank, Drysdale Securities, and Lombard-Wall: Continental Illinois, Chase Manhattan, and the Seattle First National Bank. The biggest loser was the giant French Banque du Paris et Pays Bas, which loaned GRH $245 million.

If some of the biggest bankers had been stung by a virtually unknown company in Louisiana, the financial community asked itself, what other goodies did they have in their portfolios? These bankers, and those who managed the savings and loan institutions, had been so anxious to roll up big bucks that they began to ignore their fiduciary responsibility to their depositors. Their risks might have been contained if inflation had continued to mask their mistakes. But now they were exposed as horribly bad managers.

"This shows that we're walking through a field of land mines," said Rohatyn of Lazard Frères at the time. "Who knows what's next?"[76] Clearly, Rohatyn couldn't have dreamed that, down the road, the next disaster would engulf a prestigious investment firm, Wall Street's own Salomon Brothers. Shock waves went around the world in 1990 when it was discovered that hanky-panky at Salomon had humbled and dishonored a famous firm with an unsullied reputation and a fine old name. The huge company was brought to its knees because chairman John Gutfreund and president Thomas W. Strauss forgot basic business ethics and tried a cover-up when it was discovered the firm had tried to corner the market in government securities.

They were caught not because government regulators were on top of the situation, but only because the fake-bidding excesses of one of them were "almost like a self-destruct mechanism." That was the phrase used by Warren Buffett, the legendary investment genius brought in as interim chairman of Salomon.[77] Gutfreund had paid almost no attention to how senior aides conducted the trading desk. Record-keeping was primitive—only oral reports were required in some cases. But Gutfreund, who did learn of the illegal activities of trading desk manager Paul Mozer by April 1991, nonetheless allowed Mozer to continue to make faked bids in May. Mozer had the audacity to rig bids for 105 percent of Treasury notes available for competitive bidding. Result: although the legal limit for any dealer was 35 percent, Salomon wound up controlling $10.6 billion out of $11.3 billion, an incredible 93.8 percent.

Incredibly, Gutfreund failed to disclose the situation to authorities in Washington until August. Then Gutfreund and his team resigned to make way for Buffett. Buffett was a breath of fresh air during his temporary leadership of Salomon Brothers. But for the beleaguered firm, Buffett's administration of CPR came too late: Salomon can never fully regain its pristine reputation.

Gutfreund decided to turn away from Salomon's highest-quality business to stress the more profitable deals, including bridge loans and junk bonds—even though he was cautioned against doing so by Henry Kaufman, who quit Salomon Brothers as a vice president and chief economist, warning that the venerable firm was getting overly involved in the junk bond market. But that's what top managements did in the 1980s—focus on short-term profits. Partners and employees who produced the biggest profits would reap rewards in huge salaries and bonuses. In doing so, Salomon's traders "became imbued with the drive for personal compensation, and began to enter a world of their own, with enormous power and accomplishment, but the inability to put them into context."[78] Tom Wolfe's best-selling novel *Bonfire of the Vanities* captured the gold rush atmosphere brilliantly.[79] In Wolfe's phrase, these traders were the self-appointed "masters of the universe," whose conspicuous consumption set the standard for a certain slice of New York society. The Salomon saga uncovered, as well, something beyond the Gutfreund/Strauss/Mozer misdeeds—a clubby, dangerous relationship between Treasury and Federal Reserve regulators on the one hand and a handful of Wall Street insiders who were in a position to corner a market and thereby extract illegal profits on the other. The "honor" system that had been worked out for Salomon and other "primary dealers" in government bonds was nothing more nor less than the equivalent of a cozy cartel.

As he attempted to salvage the company's reputation, Buffett delivered this clear directive to the Salomon staff: "Lose money for the firm and I will be understanding; lose a shred of reputation for the firm and I will be ruthless." In a meeting with *Washington Post* editors, Buffett said he told them he expected every Salomon player to hit the ball "down the middle" of an imaginary tennis court, and not play too close to the sidelines—the boundary between legal and illegal acts. To drive the point home, Buffett killed one high-profit deal that was in the works—legal, but too close to the "sidelines" for his comfort.

Buffett acknowledged in congressional testimony that "we need tough rules, tough cops, and tough prosecutors."[80] A brilliant stock market analyst who added to his fortune with incredibly timely and large investments in the common stock of the Geico Insurance Company and of the Washington Post Company, Buffett argued that it would be wrong to punish Salomon's new management for the mistakes of the old one. But even Buffett could not save Salomon from paying a price for Gutfreund's mistakes.

"There should not be a dime spent by the firm to defend the wrongdoers. These men should be in striped suits, sweeping up Wall Street," Representative James C. Slattery (D.-Kan.) told Buffett.[81] Buffett got the message: he decreed that Gutfreund and his team, already gone, would get no compensation, severance pay, or reimbursement for legal expenses, breaking Wall Street tradition for the tender care of downfallen executives.

But cracking down on Salomon Brothers, and on those regulators whose heads were in the sand, is only part of the necessary remedy. Congress is rightfully determined that no one will ever again twist the Treasury securities market around a little finger the way Mozer did. The Salomon saga was but one chapter in the financial market corruption that destroyed public confidence in banks, S&Ls, and other institutions. The blame falls squarely on greed and arrogance among top managers, who failed in their supervision of a younger generation of traders who arrived in Wall Street armed with the knowledge of how to manipulate the new computerized technologies in a way that could lead to making unheard of amounts of money.

"The biggest threat to the financial industry is a twenty-six-year-old MBA with a computer," Felix Rohatyn bitterly observed. Rohatyn has an explanation—not an excuse—for the behavior of younger money traders who stare at a computer screen, "buying and selling things that don't exist except as digital symbols. The only value they have at the end of the day is whether they made or lost money. It's a dehumanizing experience."[82] He compares their detachment to that of a soldier deep in a bunker who pushes a button launching a nuclear weapon that could devastate a far-away continent.

The backdrop for the big scam at Salomon Brothers was the huge expansion of global securities markets; instantaneous communications; and a volume of activity that went up exponentially as the U.S. government piled up record deficits in the Reagan-Bush years. Trading in the Treasury securities market averages about $125 billion *a day,* or about twenty times the value of the daily $6 billion in trades on the New York Stock Exchange. The bottom line is that with so much money sloshing around, it was essential that top management be alert to potential illegal practices. But close supervision wasn't there at Salomon Brothers.

Why do presumably bright and experienced men like Gutfreund and Thomas Strauss, each with an annual income in the millions of dollars, push for that extra buck? Why do they think they can get away with a cover-up? Recent history is replete with examples of senior managers of seemingly impeccable reputation who were accused of bad judgment or worse.[83] The chairmen of the boards of several thousand failed S&Ls and banks could call a standing-room-only financial conference of their own.

The lesson is that financial markets can no longer be allowed to police themselves. Self-regulation belongs to an old-fashioned, bygone era. It was at least partially abandoned, in respect to the stock markets, with the creation of the Securities and Exchange Commission in the 1930s. But amazingly, only the most genteel regulation is in place for the vast government securities and mutual funds markets. Powerful private market forces frustrated attorney Tom Stanton and congressmen Pickle and Gradison when they tried to force Fannie Mae and Freddie Mac to minimize the risks that taxpayers face for any bad decisions those institutions make. David Maxwell thinks that when I mentioned his $27.5 million golden handshake in a column, I did him a disservice. But the only disservice was to the taxpayers, whose subsidization of Fannie Mae helped generate the kind of profits that allowed such an excessive payment to be made.

The public is entitled to a greater degree of regulation and of oversight of financial institutions, especially where activities are guaranteed or underwritten by the government. The Reagan ideological bent that construes most government activity as bad or unnecessary was enormously costly in the 1980s. For too many who were tempted, the lack of a controlling hand was almost a license to steal. It was also a huge and draining distraction from the real crises besetting the country.

I I

Oil and Its Discontents

A MERICA'S RESPONSE to the economic and energy crises precipitated by OPEC was shaped primarily by the fear—carefully
nurtured by the oil industry—that the major producers, especially
Saudi Arabia, would consider their oil to be more valuable un-
touched in the desert sands than any princely sums they would get
for selling it. But in fact, by the end of Ronald Reagan's first year in
office, reliance on OPEC was dwindling fast. World production of oil,
which had hit 47.8 million barrels a day in January 1980, plunged to
39.4 million barrels a day by September 1981—and the 9 million barrel a day drop was entirely in the cartel's output, from 29.6 million
barrels a day to 20.6 million barrels a day.[1] Western consumption,
meanwhile, responding to conservation and use of other forms of
energy, had also dropped 9 million barrels a day—from 49 million
barrels to 40 million.

In other words, despite OPEC propaganda, the Middle East's control of the crude oil market was diminishing, not increasing: OPEC
was supplying barely 50 percent of the world's oil needs in 1981,
against 62 percent in 1980—and the trend was downward. Nonetheless, as the 1980s began, strenuous efforts were launched to identify
Saudi Arabia as America's friend at the OPEC court, and to bribe the
Saudis with military aid that would help build not only the royal
family's military security but also feed its ego. Naively, it was assumed by establishment Washington that this strategy was the best
way to ensure a steady flow of Persian Gulf oil. Sheik Ahmed Zaki

Yamani, the highly visible Saudi oil minister, had let it be known that the Saudis were actually pumping more oil than it was wise for them to do as a matter of self-interest—but America was a friend in need of oil, and his nation's extra production would keep prices down, he promised.

A proposal to sell $8 billion worth of sophisticated radar-detecting aircraft called AWACS (for airborne warning and control system) and other military hardware to Saudi Arabia toward the end of 1981 symbolized the pattern of cementing the relationship. The Reagan administration—over the objections of the Israel lobby—pushed the deal through, and in the course of the debate anti-Semitic sentiment was whipped to a high pitch by those who professed to worry about the "divided loyalty" of Americans of Jewish origin. Senator William Cohen—the Maine Republican and a Unitarian who had one Jewish parent—decided to vote for the AWACS sale against his better judgment for fear that disapproval would work against both Israel and American Jews.[2]

But those who raised the question of divided loyalty among Jewish Americans showed little concern about the well-heeled oil industry lobby, which had decided to put its financial stake in the Persian Gulf above anything else. According to the Federal Election Commission, the industry lobbyists put more than $4.5 million into congressional campaigns between 1978 and 1980, outmaneuvering the Jewish lobby.

Harold Scroggins, a lobbyist for the Independent Petroleum Producers Association, said: "We came to a decision some time ago that the only way we could change the political fortunes of the petroleum industry was to change Congress." The oil industry opened up its pocketbooks in an effort to defeat Senate liberals, and was at least partially successful. A campaign to overthrow Democratic control of the House was less productive.

The whirlwind offensive to get AWACS for the Saudis was led by the publicity-conscious Mobil Corporation, the innovator of paid corporate messages that appeared on the page opposite the editorial page of some of the nation's leading newspapers.[3] Mobil was flush with profits from high-priced oil in 1981. OPEC was a nuisance, to be sure. But Mobil, like the other oil companies, simply passed the higher costs on to the consumer. Now, it was trying to buy Marathon Oil, after being thwarted in an attempt to gobble up Conoco in a hungry grab that embarrassed even the Reagan administration. (In the end, U.S. Steel succeeded in swallowing Marathon.) Mobil ads contended that "the economic partnership" between the United States and Saudi Arabia could grow to a neat $35 billion affair—if only the Saudis were permitted to buy the AWACS. It listed some of the 700 corporations that would benefit, the implicit suggestion being that the same 700 companies would be punished by the Saudis if the AWACS sale were blocked.

The same scenario was packaged in a mailgram to scores of companies from Harry J. Gray, chief executive officer of United Technologies Corporation, and George David, president of Otis Elevator Company, who asked their fellow CEOs to wire their senators, urging them to back Reagan's request for AWACS for the Saudis. Gray and David cited Saudi "restraint" on oil prices, and calculated that Saudi expenditures of $5.7 billion for U.S. goods in 1980 had supported 250,000 American jobs.

Part of the slick Saudi-oil interest campaign was a "My Turn" column in *Newsweek* by Whittaker Corporation president Joseph F. Alibrandi, which regurgitated the Gray/David material. It was photocopied and circulated to all members of the Senate just before the vote.

Another element was a deluge of letters from American businessmen in Saudi Arabia raising the specter of a Saudi blacklist of American companies. For example, a number of congressmen received an alarm, dated July 18, 1981, from Dr. Jerrold L. Wheaton, a consultant to the international division of National Medical Enterprises based in Dhahran:

> Americans have only a bare 20 percent of the business available in Saudi Arabia. Those of us who work here have no doubt that the percentage would rapidly decrease to 5 percent or less if the sale of the AWACS and F-15 augmentation packages are refused. . . .
>
> What . . . motivate[s] me is the frustration of watching American businessmen, restricted by U.S. law, try to compete in this marketplace, and the concern that a negative decision concerning the AWACS sale will completely eliminate American private enterprise from competing for the Arab dollar. Our companies and our country need these dollars, and it takes all our ingenuity to compete favorably using the ground rules of the corrupt practices or unfair practices act, which are ultimately unfair only to us.

Wheaton's letter was transparent: the motivation for the sale of AWACS to Saudi Arabia was not, as had been argued, to promote "peace" in the Middle East, or to guarantee an uninterrupted supply of oil, but to underwrite a grab "for the Arab dollar," seemingly just out of reach because Americans, unfortunately, had to be careful about bribery ever since the passage in 1977 of the Corrupt Practices

Act. There also was another factor at work: the Department of Defense was anxious to lower the unit costs of its own AWACS, a goal that could be reached by beefing up the size of the production run to take care of the Saudis. That's what it was all about: the oil business-Pentagon lobby at its most efficient peak, a textbook example of the power and innovation of the military-industrial complex that President Eisenhower had warned about in his farewell address.

One final lesson of the pro-AWACS vote was that Gray, David, and Alibrandi, speaking for the oil lobby, were able to divert attention from the fact that the motive for Saudi oil price and supply policy was self-interest, not "restraint" or self-sacrifice for its American ally. The very day following approval of the AWACS sale, the Saudi government boosted oil prices by $2 a barrel, and announced a new production cut of 1 million barrels a day.

IN 1978, JAMSHID AMOUZEGAR, Iran's representative at the IMF, predicted that within a few years the scarcity of oil would be so acute that OPEC would no longer be needed to assure high prices.[4] Already geologists in America and Europe were busily at work trying to figure out ways of squeezing new supplies out of the ground.

As the Reagan administration completed its first year in office, the oil boom that had begun in Texas and other Southwestern states in the wake of the first oil shock gathered steam from the second wave of price increases in 1979. Forecast after forecast of supply shortages, accompanied by rising prices, poured forth from Wall Street, stoking a search for oil in a manner reminiscent of the California gold rush in the mid-nineteenth century. Such pessimism about oil supply did not serve the United States well, tending to confirm the notion carefully cultivated by the oil producers that they could dominate the oil market for the rest of the century, if not beyond. This point was well made by Washington businessman and consultant Lawrence Goldmuntz, who told a seminar in Israel that the Reagan administration instead should have been formulating an energy policy for the next decade that took into account the sea change in the world supply-demand picture.

Meanwhile, Europe's major powers were allowing the second oil shock to have a stunning impact. OPEC flexed its muscles, raised prices—and Europe generated no effective response. Robert Hormats, assistant secretary of state for economic and business affairs, returned from a visit to Brussels, and said: "Europe appears to be losing confidence in itself and in its future." The grand results of the 1960s, when Europe recorded years of 5 percent real growth, or even of the 1970s, when in some years there had been a growth rate of 3.5 percent, were a dim memory. Across the continent, economic activity was stagnant. The Organization for Economic Cooperation and Development predicted only minimal recovery in 1982, with unemployment rising to about 10 million, of which 40 percent would be young men and women under the age of twenty-five. The spells of unemployment in Europe were getting longer and longer. In 1981, two out of every five without a job in England had been on the dole for six months or longer. According to some estimates, many British teenagers would never hold down a full-time job as long as they lived. In Holland, the number of long-term unemployed was half the jobless total. In the United States, only about one out of six jobless persons had been out of work that long—and that was well above the typical experience of the 1970s. It was a period of deep despair in Europe, an onset some called "Eurosclerosis," dominated by political uncertainty and weakened governments.

Moreover, prospects were that both the United States and Japan would adjust more swiftly. In 1981, Japan enjoyed a real growth rate of 3.7 percent, and the United States had a positive growth of 1.9 percent. But the United Kingdom had a negative rate of 0.4 percent (following on a 2.3 percent downturn in 1980); France had only a plus 1.2 percent; and West Germany had a flat zero, followed by a negative 1 percent in 1982.[5]

Most countries in Western Europe were plodding along with inefficient, labor-intensive industries, protected by equally inefficient government bureaucracies. These countries, doing things the time-honored, traditional way, were hit by the baby boom about a decade after it rolled over North America, boosting the youth component of the labor force at the precise time that the two OPEC oil shocks were having their cumulative effect. As OPEC raised prices, most governments responded by adopting restrictive fiscal and monetary policies in an effort to counter the inflationary effect of higher energy prices. The overall result: European economic growth ground to a halt or even declined.

In the United States, with Paul Volcker in charge of the Federal Reserve Board, there was a fixation on monetary policy as the only anti-inflation weapon, a single-track response that had begun in 1979 when Volcker shifted the focus of monetary policy to control of the money supply and away from interest-rate targets. The double-digit interest rates that resulted in 1980 were what West German chancellor Helmut Schmidt referred to at the Ottawa economic summit in 1981 as the "highest interest rates since Jesus Christ."

Jacques Delors, the French minister of finance, referred to American interest rates as "the third oil shock" because they had an effect on the structure of interest rates in Europe. In a sense, Europe was being whipsawed by OPEC and the United States.

As if that were not enough to induce "sclerosis," superimposed on the fragile economic fabric of Europe was the ever-present fear that the continent might get caught in a giant superpower nut-cracker, and once again become a battlefield of death and destruc-tion—this time with nuclear weapons. Canada's Sylvia Ostry, chief economist for the OECD, was limited in what she could say publicly as an international civil servant; nonetheless she said soberly at the end of an OECD meeting in Paris early in May 1982: "We can't hon-estly say we have any easy answers anymore." Oxford University professor Peter Oppenheimer told me a few days later in London: "We're in a state of intellectual bankruptcy. All we know is that there isn't any single economic formula that will do the trick."[6]

But the Saudis thought they had one. Yamani began to sing a new tune. Having argued during the AWACS debate that the Saudis were doing their friends the Americans a great service by pumping extra oil, Yamani in February 1982 told a reporter: "We might do the world a greater service by producing less oil."[7]

Yamani was skirting the truth on both occasions. In 1981, the Saudis had pumped an extraordinary amount of oil—a record 10.3 million barrels a day—because there was a demand for it, and be-cause it was in the Saudi national interest to keep prices from es-calating to the point that would further accelerate the global search for alternatives to the Persian Gulf's crude oil. By early 1982, how-ever, Saudi production had slipped by at least 2.5 million barrels a day because the world was entering a period of oil glut, and prices had already sagged more than $3 a barrel. For all of the warnings of scarcity that had led the banks and the savings and loans in the Southwest of the United States to finance extravagant explorations for new oil supplies, the world was drowning in an excess of oil. Even at the more modest price that the cartel was now willing to take for oil, there was less demand. In 1982, the Saudis' production dropped to 6.5 million barrels a day, a decline of 33 percent, followed by a further 23 percent drop in 1983 to 5.0 million barrels a day. Pundits and experts alike were confounded. After all, the CIA had predicted in December 1979 that by 1982 there would be "an average excess of demand over supply of 2 million to 5 million barrels a day." Yet, between 1981 and 1983, Saudi production had been cut in half, and prices were sinking fast.

The lesson was clear, less than two years into the first Reagan administration, that there was plenty of oil in the world, with more waiting to be discovered. Moreover, the United States could set its own energy agenda if it encouraged conservation, switched away from oil, and continued to explore for oil, especially in the Third World. It needed to expand the Strategic Petroleum Reserve, the government-run safety supply created after the first oil shock, and consider other ways of reducing its exposure to the OPEC cartel.

OIL-CONSUMING NATIONS all over the world were happy with the dramatic slide in oil prices. But not the Soviet Union, the biggest oil producer outside OPEC, which had to meet the price cuts offered by the cartel in order to maintain the flow of hard currencies desperately needed to lubricate its creaking economy. Lower global oil prices also presented a problem to those who had placed their bets on synthetic fuels and tar sands, no longer an attractive investment with oil under $30 a barrel in mid-1982. Meanwhile, it was almost painfully clear that Du Pont's $7.8 billion takeover of the Conoco Oil Company, and U.S. Steel's $6 billion buyout of Marathon Oil, turned out to be excruciatingly bad deals. When consummated, the takeovers were supposed to have bought up, cheaply, Conoco's and Marathon's highly valued oil reserves. But Harry Neustein, the flamboyant oil broker and friend of Yamani who commuted regularly between New York and the Middle East, said: "It was a bad deal for both of them. A few years from now, it will be a millstone around their necks."[8]

An example of the wrongheaded consensus that dominated America's thinking about energy immediately after OPEC boosted prices in December 1979 was a gloomy article written for *The Washington Post* on March 16, 1980, by Peter G. Peterson, a prominent investment banker and a former secretary of commerce in the Nixon administration. Peterson's recommendations were an outgrowth of a commission on Third World problems headed by West German political leader Willy Brandt, which had concluded that OPEC held all the cards and that the industrial nations had to give in or risk the probability that the Third World countries would suffer an economic disaster.

Abdul-Latif al-Hamad, a Kuwaiti member of the Brandt Commission, had played what was labeled "a trump card" during the deliberations of that private but influential group of internationally minded citizens—a demand not only that the rich industrial nations increase the existing flow of resources to the Third World, but that they pay OPEC a tax of $1 per barrel of oil that OPEC sold to the poor countries—a recommendation endorsed by Peterson. In other words,

OPEC would not reduce the price of oil to help the poor countries, but would allow the West to subsidize its shipments to poor countries. It would amount to a tax, levied on the West, designed to yield $12 billion a year to assure a flow of oil to the Third World. "That's a lot of money," al-Hamad conceded in an interview with an Arab publication. "If the rich countries feel this is too much of a burden, they should consume a little less."[9]

Peterson, in his article, argued that the only way to avert financial chaos was to bow to OPEC's power and accept more predictable and gradual oil price increases in real terms, in return for security of supplies. "I was taught at the University of Chicago," he wrote, "that if one has no alternative, one has no problem. The blunt fact is that over the next five years, we do not have any other alternative for significant, increased supply. Nor, for that matter, have we any other prospect for significant increases in supply from other energy alternatives. Even with vigorous domestic oil exploration, we will be lucky to keep U.S. oil production even at its current level."

Subsequent history would prove Peterson right only on his last point: despite the exaggerated promises of those who advocated deregulation of U.S. prices and production, American oil output was stagnant. But Peterson was dead wrong on alternatives to OPEC, and failed entirely to envision the extraordinary progress in conservation. Together, other sources of supply and reduced consumption would create a tremendous glut of oil, and would eventually break OPEC's power to set prices.

By 1982, the change was so dramatic that the Chicken Littles were no longer worried that OPEC's prices were too high—but that OPEC's prices were too low, which would be devastating to the banks, S&Ls, and corporations that had taken prognostications like Peterson's as gospel. The truth was that lower oil prices would be a boon to all consumers, including those Third World nations on whose behalf Peterson had wanted to strike a deal in 1980 assuring high returns to OPEC. The Morgan Guaranty Bank estimated that the $26 per barrel oil price in 1982 (compared with spot market prices over $40 in late 1980) would save twelve Third World oil importers $7 billion in 1982 and another $5 billion in 1983.

After 1985, as the signs of speculative excesses in the S&L industry in the Southwest could no longer be ignored, conventional forecasters became more cautious. At first, as Eliyahu Kanovsky pointed out, they were "steadily postponing the arrival of doomsday." Many of the forecasters changed their predictions for rising real oil prices from the early to the late 1990s. "Some of these forecasts suggest that a mini-cartel of Persian Gulf producers, led by Saudi Arabia, will assume effective and far more powerful control of the market in the 1990s and raise prices far beyond the rate of dollar inflation."[10]

Ever since the onset of the first oil shock in 1973, there has been a steady and significant increase in energy efficiency—even after the major drop in oil prices following 1981. In the decades prior to 1973, growth in energy consumption just about matched increases in GNP. This highly significant new burst of efficient energy use meant that the economy was getting a bigger productive bang out of each barrel of oil. Steel producers turned out more steel per ton of energy, consumers got more heating or refrigeration out of a single unit of energy, and so on. Overall, a given amount of energy produced 41 percent more GNP in 1987 than in 1973.[11]

Yet the cottage industry built up around forecasting OPEC's resurgence survived in spite of its flawed record. As late as December 21, 1987, *The Wall Street Journal* reported that oil analysts generally agreed that, by not later than the mid-1990s, "OPEC's excess capacity will have been drained . . . [and] OPEC will be able to manipulate world oil markets at will." Such oil "analysts" were just guessing, not even pausing to wipe the egg off their faces. In point of fact, they didn't know how future economic growth would shape up; or what future changes there might be between GNP and energy consumption; or what future discoveries of oil would be made, especially in the Third World.[12]

Kanovsky, whose track record entitles him to maximum credibility, continued to insist that technological changes would restrain energy demand generally, and oil demand in particular, as they had since the first oil shock. Moreover, he pointed out, OPEC is a cartel, but doesn't have monopoly power. "A monopolist," he wrote, "involves one decision-maker who controls total supplies of a commodity, and can, within limits, reduce supplies, raise prices above the competitive level, and thereby increase the revenues of the monopoly."[13] There are thirteen nations in OPEC, each responding to its own internal pressures to get bigger shares of the quota limits agreed to—and every country in it is determined to cheat on the others. The annual spectacle of OPEC summits, at which the oil producers solemnly pledged to curtail production in order to raise prices, after which they departed Geneva or Vienna and promptly proceeded to flood the markets with oil, should have taught the Western analysts and the news media a lesson. But it didn't: each of the OPEC high command's secret confabs was soberly considered by markets and covered in detail by journalists who spawned learned articles on how, this time, things would be different. For the most part, the meetings and the coverage were a farce. Each member of the cartel was determined to pump oil, not keep it in the ground. Moreover, the producing nations were no longer mere exporters: each was now in the refinery business, with their own retail outlets abroad. That gave them an added incentive to maintain high production levels.

Kanovsky scoffed at oil experts like Daniel Yergin who believed that OPEC could preserve monopoly power over oil simply because the cartel possessed huge natural resurces. Yergin wrote in *Foreign Affairs* in 1979: "Saudi Arabia is favored by a unique conjunction of huge reserves, extraordinary ease of exploitation, and a population so tiny that domestic revenue needs have no practical effect on the level of oil production."[14] The following year, a similar evaluation came from the Senate Committee on Energy and Natural Resources: "Dependence on Persian Gulf oil means that for at least the next ten to fifteen years, the industrialized countries can expect to live in a world of steady increases in oil prices, lower economic growth, inflation, and stagnant or at least sluggish growth in GNP."[15]

Kanovsky spent a great deal of time debunking these pessimistic views. Summing up detailed studies made in 1980 and 1982, he wrote a definitive analysis in 1986: "It is, by now, abundantly clear that these forecasters committed gross errors not only in terms of magnitude of change, but, far more important, in terms of direction of change. Instead of increased dependence on OPEC and especially Middle East oil, there has been a very sharp diminution. . . . Oil prices have been weakening almost steadily since 1981 and there has been a collapse since the end of 1985. Instead of rising 'petrodollar' surpluses, most OPEC countries, and Saudi Arabia in particular, are incurring large current account deficits in their balances of payments, and are rapidly drawing down their financial reserves."[16]

Even Exxon, prone to exaggerate the growth in oil consumption (and therefore the need to be nice to OPEC) lowered its forecast for the annual increase in oil use until the end of the century to a scant 1 percent, a level that could easily be met from non-OPEC sources. Already, by 1981, non-OPEC output had risen to 21 million barrels a day from a mere 5 million barrels a day in 1976—and that was the result of the response to just the first oil shock.

Meanwhile, a tally by the IMF showed that Western dependence on Middle East oil had fallen dramatically. American oil imports from the Middle East were barely over 1 million barrels a day in early 1982, or 7 percent of consumption, against a 1977 peak of 3.7 million barrels, or 20.2 percent.[17] OPEC member nations, faced with huge budget increases predicated on the erroneous assumption of an ever-increasing stream of oil revenues, had to adjust to more austere times. It wasn't easy, given the conspicuous consumption by thou-

sands of Saudi princes and other privileged members of the Arab ruling classes—a consumption that stirred rising expectations among
poor Arabs.[18]

If the projections made by the World Bank in 1985 had panned
out, a barrel of oil in 1993 would have sold for $85. You could throw
a blanket over the standard forecasts of the CIA, the Department of
Energy, oil experts in the universities, the World Bank, and the Congressional Budget Office. They thought exclusively in terms of
OPEC controlling the oil tap in the Middle East, and therefore exert-
ing enough economic leverage to dominate the world.[19] No one
imagined that a single man, Saddam Hussein, would not only upset
the global balance but might destroy OPEC itself with his invasion
of Kuwait in August 1990.

WITH THE IRAQI INVASION of Kuwait there was a sharp but temporary bulge in crude oil prices, based on the fear that Saddam Hussein's military adventure would be successful and that he would be
in a position to dominate the distribution of all Persian Gulf oil, even
including that of the Saudis. Saddam also had in view Kuwait's huge
accumulation of financial reserves in gold and hard currencies, much
of it on deposit in the West, estimated at anywhere from $70 billion
to $100 billion.

At the beginning of its 1980–88 war with Iran, Eliyahu Kanovsky
had calculated, Iraq possessed about $35 billion in reserves. But by
the end of that war, Saddam had spent every dime, and had borrowed
an additional $40 billion to $50 billion from other Arab nations, plus
another $30 billion to $40 billion from the West. The internal economic pressures on Iraq were so severe that Saddam began to force
small creditors, such as Jordan, to accept payment for loans with
oil—at list, rather than real, prices. Thus the opportunity to plunder
what seemed to Saddam an undefended Kuwait was too good to turn
down, especially after the Bush administration, through April Glas-
pie, its ambassador to Baghdad, seemed to signal that it would not
interfere with Saddam's ambition.

The oil market action following the dramatic invasion of Kuwait
closely duplicated what happened after the 1980 Iraq invasion of
Iran. Although, as a consequence of the war, both Iraqi and Iranian
oil sales fell off sharply, there was a steady decline from oil price
peaks that were touched in 1981. Again, Kanovsky was right, while
less astute analysts stubbornly and inexplicably predicted rising
prices. This time the key factor was that oil demand, as Saddam
loosed his forces on Kuwait, was sluggish, while non-OPEC sup-

plies—from Mexico, the North Sea, and West Africa, among other places—were rising. Oil consumption in the United States was down 0.5 percent, even with a real gross national product gain of 3 percent in 1989. For the first six months of 1990, consumption was down 2 percent from the comparable period of 1989.

In some Western European countries, the oil consumption/ growth ratio reduction was even more dramatic. In West Germany, for example, oil use dropped 6 to 7 percent in 1989, while real GNP rose about 4 percent. Clearly, OPEC could not sustain the higher prices it desperately sought to cover its own rising budgetary outlays. In this circumstance, Saddam Hussein first bludgeoned the cartel into raising its then "reference price" of $18 a barrel to $21 a barrel (his original demand was $25 a barrel), asserting that Iraq had lost $14 billion in revenue because oil prices had been deliberately set too low by Kuwait and the United Arab Emirates. Until Saddam began to threaten his fellow OPEC producers at the end of June 1990, oil had been selling around $14 a barrel.[20]

Incredibly, prior to President Bush's decision to block Saddam's naked attempt to take over Kuwait and possibly dominate Saudi Arabia as well, some Americans gave a degree of credibility to the notion that Saddam's invasion of Kuwait might somehow have been justified because Kuwait was producing "too much oil." For example, on the Public Broadcasting System's popular *McNeil/Lehrer Newshour* one evening in July 1990, Charles Maxwell, an energy consultant for the investment firm of Morgan Grenfell, said: "Several members of OPEC were producing too much oil, and the markets couldn't absorb it and [they] adjusted by bringing the price down. [The] two perpetrators of cheating were really Kuwait and Abu Dhabi [the largest of the United Arab Emirates]. And everyone continued to warn them, 'Don't do this. You are taking the bread out of the mouths of our children. . . .' Last week he [Saddam Hussein] became the enforcer. He said, 'Stop cheating, live up to your quotas and we will all benefit.' "

Jim Lehrer responded: "So no matter what anybody thinks of Hussein, the fact is that he is right on this issue. Is he right?"

Maxwell answered: "Well, he is right on his merits. If you were paying for oil at the pump, you might have a different view. But I think that on his own system, and OPEC's system, he is correct." He added later that some increase in oil prices would be healthy for the West, because in the long run it would dampen the West's dependence on oil generally, and on the Middle East specifically.[21]

Maxwell was articulating the precise defense of oil prices by every special pleader for Middle East oil producers, many of whom were employed by Wall Street investing firms and had access to the financial press. The underlying assumptions in Maxwell's defense of Saddam were simply unacceptable to anyone believing in democracy and opposing brute force. Who has the right to decide how much is "too much oil"? Clearly, producers benefit from restrictive practices and from cartel arrangements. A sale below cartel-fixed prices was labeled "cheating" by Maxwell—not a necessity forced by market conditions that would not support the cartel's self-serving and artificial prices. Maxwell's notion that a higher price for oil would eventually benefit the West was the assertion floated by those with an investment interest—especially by explorers for oil and the banks that backed them. But consumers benefited from low oil prices that enabled them to spend their income on other needs. Maxwell was willing to say, publicly, that Saddam Hussein, who had conducted a terrible war against Iran and thus had piled up huge debts, had a good reason to impose artificially high prices for oil on other nations.

The ultimate blow to the theory that oil prices would or should zoom came when President Bush, leading the United Nations, pledged to throw Saddam Hussein out of Kuwait. The global response—no doubt the greatest achievement of the Bush presidency—isolated Iraq. Bush's defense secretary, Richard B. Cheney, later publicly acknowledged that Israel may have saved the world from an Iraqi nuclear attack by bombing, ten years earlier, Saddam's nuclear reactor at Osirak. "There were many times during the course of the buildup in the [Persian] Gulf and the subsequent conflict that I gave thanks for the bold and dramatic action taken ten years before," Cheney said.[22]

There were those who condemned Bush's decision to dispatch American troops to the Persian Gulf as an effort to protect America's supply of cheap oil. Thus James Gustave Speth of the World Resources Institute wrote in the *Los Angeles Times:* "At the root of the problem is America's addiction to cheap energy. . . . It would be a sad commentary if our leaders found it easier to send Americans to fight in the desert than to impose gasoline and other energy taxes."[23]

But there was something more at stake in the Persian Gulf than just the supply or price of oil. The world had to decide whether it would sit idly by and allow Saddam Hussein, who had just gobbled up an independent country, Kuwait, to position himself to swallow another, Saudi Arabia, and thereby control 40 percent or more of global oil reserves. Was the world ready to let a new naked aggression by a dictator succeed—a dictator who had already used chemical weapons against Iran, and against his own Kurdish population? Who would be next? Syria? Israel, in retaliation for the raid at Osirak?

Speth was right, as an environmentalist, to chastise Bush for weakening new car-efficiency rules. But with Saddam in control of Kuwait and poised to take over Saudi Arabia, it was nonsense to think that any action except the one Bush took would have deterred the Iraqi dictator.[24]

At the precise moment that Saddam invaded Kuwait, Kanovsky, still defying the conventional wisdom, was putting the finishing touches on a new study predicting that "stable or decreasing prices will be the dominant feature of the oil market of the 1990s." Saddam's invasion of Kuwait, Kanovsky said, hadn't changed his mind. "When oil prices go above $20 a barrel, it triggers all sorts of reactions—more explorations, greater efficiency, and so on. Sure, there will be a swift and powerful short term reaction, maybe even panic. But as was the case in 1980, within six months it will be over."[25]

HOW DO WE ASSESS OPEC today? The simple truth is that OPEC, the once-powerful oil cartel, has become a toothless tiger, unable to keep its members from producing and charging what they please—what Charles Maxwell called "cheating." Perhaps the emasculation of OPEC's power was symbolized by the decision of Ecuador—one of the smaller producers within OPEC—to quit the cartel altogether after Saddam's failed adventure in Kuwait. The old OPEC game of keeping its "black gold" in the ground, where it might be more valuable, no longer panics the consuming world. The old State Department instinct to "clear it first with Riyadh" is no longer how American Middle East policy operates. The sensible economic game plan today is: find oil, extract it, and sell it for whatever the market brings. And everybody is playing the new game, with the help of Western oil companies, from Russia and the smaller Muslim republics of the former Soviet Union to Vietnam. Ecuador's pragmatic decision—why pay dues to a purposeless bureaucracy?—underscores in a formal way what other and more important OPEC members, such as Iran, have been doing since the end of the Gulf War: pumping all the oil that can be pumped in order to restore their shattered domestic finances.

The Saudis, still the most important producer in the Persian Gulf, have been forced into unprecedented borrowing from commercial banks to cover a huge balance of payments deficit stemming from the war against Saddam. According to IMF data, the Saudi deficit soared to $25.7 billion in 1991, from $4.3 billion in 1990.[26] Kanovsky noted that the Saudi plans to expand its armed forces' size and quality "can only aggravate its financial situation." Moreover, the devastating war in the Persian Gulf, however brief, reversed the pattern of the 1970s and the first half of the 1980s, when massive oil revenues with little new expenses provided jobs for millions of Arabs in the poorer countries, as well as imported Asians. Now the prospects for Egypt, Syria, and Jordan to fob off their growing number of jobless persons on the richer Arab countries have all but disappeared. Kuwait alone expelled 400,000 Palestinians after the war was won against Saddam. Kanovsky concluded, examining all of these complicated threads, that the extremist Islamic movements in Arab countries will be immeasurably strengthened by rising unemployment, especially among Arab youth.[27]

The only way for the Persian Gulf nations who have oil to raise their income is to boost sales of oil, not the price. In turn, that means that there will be an abundant supply of oil, and that OPEC cannot control the price. Once the United Nations allows Saddam to resume sales—only a trickle has been moving surreptitiously and illegally through Turkey and Jordan—"Iraq will pump like mad," Kanovsky is convinced. Intelligence reports indicate that the Iraqis have been able to restore capacity to more than 2 million barrels a day, about 40 percent of the pre-Gulf War peak. Meanwhile, Iran, which had turned its back on foreign professionals and technicians when Ayatollah Khomeini overthrew the shah in 1979, once again is willing to accept outside expertise under the regime of the present ayatollahs in order to expand its oil output and revenue.

All of these developments work against the effectiveness of OPEC, which now also faces a challenge from environmentalists in the United States and Europe. In 1993, President Bill Clinton and a Democratic Congress boosted gasoline taxes by a tiny four cents a gallon, not enough to discourage consumption, especially in the wake of falling OPEC prices. But inevitably, energy taxes will rise in the United States to meet the challenge of persistent deficits in the federal budget. The United States must not shirk the responsibility that it has ducked for the past twenty years—the formulation of an overall energy policy to cope with excessive dependence on foreign oil, from any overseas source. It must, at the same time, pursue more vigorously all methods of conserving and substituting other energy sources for oil.

We should not allow the automobile industry to dictate softer terms for auto mileage standards. Once oil prices drifted down in the late 1980s, Detroit successfully lobbied the Bush administration for an erosion of strict minimum-mileage standards to help it get back in the business of selling hugely profitable gas-guzzlers. Clinton, seeking a stronger alliance with business, has appeared even more vulnerable to entreaties from the Big Three car companies. The European Community, to its credit, is considering a carbon emissions tax, which reportedly caused a Saudi diplomat to warn that such a tax would be considered a hostile act leading to a trade war. Such oil-producer threats should be ignored. A decade ago, the West quaked when OPEC spoke. Today, it can be serene: OPEC was yesterday's nightmare.

I 2

The Folly of Deregulation

IN THEIR FINE ACCOUNT of the risks of laissez-faire rule, *Dismantling America: The Rush to Deregulate*, Susan and Martin Tolchin observed that the underlying phony principle of deregulation is that regulation is incompatible with efficiency, that whatever happens in the free market is not only efficient but right. "The real problem with economic deregulation is that the transportation system, the airwaves, and the banks are national resources, [adversely] affecting many segments of the population with no immediate connection to the affected industries."[1] Thus the concept of the public interest is one that entirely escaped the ideologues in both the Carter and Reagan administrations, who were focused narrowly on the supposed efficiency of the free market. It was, in its own way, of a piece with the misguided American officer during the Vietnam War who claimed he had to destroy a village in order to save it. The deregulation of the airlines is a good case in point.

Although there was a brief period in the first days of deregulation of the nation's airlines when innovative small carriers provided cheap, basic air service, airline deregulation is—and has been, almost from the start in 1978—a failure. I have been saying so for years, much to the discomfort of some in the industry, and to the annoyance of Alfred Kahn—originator, patron saint, and chief defender of deregulation—who once complained to *The Washington Post* that I was writing an "annual" attack on deregulation. My critiques of deregulation actually appeared in print much more frequently than that.

As chairman of the Civil Aeronautics Board under Jimmy Carter, Kahn had a grand vision, but it came out of academia, not the real world. Kahn, an intense, witty, and bright economist from Cornell University, who prior to his appointment as CAB chairman had been Carter's "inflation czar," believed that "a realistic threat of entry by new and existing carriers on the initiation of management alone is the essential element of competition. It is only this threat that makes it possible to leave to managements a wider measure of discretion in pricing. It is this threat of entry that will hold excessive price increases in check."[2] The translation of that bit of bureaucratese was that airlines that couldn't meet the test of competition deserved to be thrown out of business. "It's destructive and cruel, but that's the way the market functions," Kahn once said. Or, as James C. Miller, Ronald Reagan's Office of Management and Budget director, later put it in 1982, just before both Braniff Airlines and the operation managed by Freddy Laker of Great Britain went bankrupt: "What the airlines need is a good bankruptcy."[3]

Kahn has modified his views somewhat in recent years. In congressional testimony ten years after deregulation took effect, he continued to defend it as successful, but said: "Whatever has happened in airline markets on average, and however great the benefits of price competition to the preponderant majority of travelers, concentration of the industry has increased at the national level; it has probably increased also on a significant number of routes—particularly for traffic originating and terminating at hubs dominated by one or two carriers—and deregulation has deprived those travelers of the protection of regulatorily imposed price ceilings."[4]

Kahn also criticized travel agent commissions as "bribes" offered by the airlines "to steer travelers their way," the result of which is "to insulate [hub-dominating carriers] from competitive challenges." He went on to attack the computerized reservations systems owned by the big airlines; the frequent flyer programs, which "tend also to distort competition"; and especially "deep discriminatory fare reductions in response to competition." The main argument of pro-deregulators is that the average American traveler enjoys cheaper travel through access to bargain and promotional rates. The cheaper fares, however, have major limitations: they must be bought well in advance, always require a stay over a Saturday night, and involve penalties for cancellation or changes of itinerary. A major unpublicized restriction is that the lowest fares are usually available for just a small number of seats—and not on all flights. Most of such discount fares "are unquestionably discriminatory," Kahn declared.[5]

In a fuller explanation of why the deeply discounted fares are discriminatory, Kahn expressed a view not much different from the analysis offered by University of Denver law professor Paul Stephen Dempsey, a former lawyer for the CAB and one of the most effective critics of airline deregulation, and others (Kahn himself referred to his description of the effects of price discrimination as "ambivalent"): "[T]here is no difference between the costs of carrying a business traveler who is unwilling or unable to meet the condition of staying away over a weekend, but may be equally willing to purchase his or her ticket in advance, and the discretionary traveler, who may travel on the same plane, at the same times, on the same weekdays, but is willing or able to stay over a weekend. The only difference between those two customers is on the demand side—that is, in what the respective traffics will bear—not on the cost side; and that is the meaning of discrimination."[6]

Kahn's candid observations on the trend toward hub operations is underscored by Dempsey. For example, in 1977, before deregulation, Delta had only 35 percent of the traffic at the Cincinnati airport. In 1987, after creating a hub at Cincinnati, Delta had a 67.6 percent share. In Nashville, American Airlines' share over the same period soared from 28.2 percent to 60.2 percent. "Freedom to enter and exit markets is the heart of deregulation," Dempsey explained, "and it is [more] responsible for concentration at more hub airports than is the Department of Transportation's 'abysmal dereliction' [in preventing mergers, as charged by Kahn], abysmal though it clearly is."[7]

What Delta accomplished in Cincinnati and American in Nashville, other carriers did in Houston, Memphis, Pittsburgh, and Salt Lake City, among other hubs. They all increased their flights in and out of the hubs and leased more gates. Meanwhile, their former competitors left quietly to establish dominance in their own hubs. Thus key markets were divided up by tacit agreement; in Detroit, Minneapolis-St. Paul, and St. Louis, the effective monopoly appeared traceable to the mergers allowed during the Reagan years.[8]

In the three years 1990, 1991, and 1992, the airline industry lost as much money as it made in the previous sixty years, and its debt (except for one company's) was downgraded to "junk" status—a precarious situation that left American aircraft manufacturers such as Boeing and McDonnell Douglas hanging on the ropes. In that three-year period, the airlines also suffered from the effects of the post–

Persian Gulf War recession, as well as from the added costs attributed to improving security procedures in the wake of terrorist attacks.

Fifteen years after deregulation took effect, after Pan American, Eastern, National, and other companies had disappeared from the scene—while still others operated only courtesy of the bankruptcy courts—President Clinton and the Congress found it necessary to appoint an emergency blue-ribbon bipartisan commission, headed by former Virginia governor Gerald L. Baliles. Upon appointing the National Commission to Ensure a Strong Competitive Airline Industry on May 24, 1993, Clinton directed it to report in ninety days on what "needs to be done" to preserve the industry and help it be competitive. Had deregulation been a success, why would a commission be needed fifteen years later to try to preserve the industry?

THE BASIC PROBLEMS of the airlines trace back, in the words of Sir Colin Marshall, chairman of British Airways, to "the unbridled competition which allowed carriers to enter any and every market on their own terms." That meant, Sir Colin added, that the airlines that survived deregulation had to cut costs to the bone, "leading to the search for that commercial holy grail, economy of scale."[9]

For all the mythology about "free markets" and the magical workings of the "invisible hand" inherited from economist Adam Smith, a groundswell of economic regulation had been triggered in America in the late 1880s and 1890s when evidence piled up that, in the real world, market action was far from perfect. Congress in 1887 established the nation's first independent regulatory agency, the Interstate Commerce Commission, to shield the public from discrimination and destructive competition that had developed in the surface transportation industry.[10] In 1938, the fledgling air transport industry was brought under control by the Civil Aeronautics Act, which was intended not only to generate an honest and logical method for letting air mail contracts to the lowest legitimate bidder, but to establish economic regulation of the whole industry that would avert disastrous rate wars.

But beginning in the 1970s, led by politicians skeptical of government interference with the private sector, America shifted gears and went on a deregulation binge as the controls process began to fail in some instances. President Nixon, as we have seen, too quickly abandoned a wage-price control system that had become unwieldy and inefficient under regulators who didn't believe in controls. And under President Reagan, as we have also seen, there was a mindless wave of deregulation that helped to weaken financial markets, the S&Ls, and the banks.

But nowhere has the regulate-deregulate-reregulate battle been fought with more intensity than in the air transport industry. For a third of a century, from roughly 1940 to 1975, a few airlines had been allowed to dominate the industry under the protective, benign management of the Civil Aeronautics Board. Paul Dempsey observed that the CAB in the period preceding deregulation in 1978 "proceeded on a course of wild abandonment, awarding operating authority in an indiscriminate manner to virtually all who sought it."[11] Airline routes, which belong to all the people, became a "valued right" under the CAB, assigned to individual airline companies. That was an indefensible bonanza, and Kahn was entirely right to cite this as the key flaw in the controlled regime.

The CAB was the final product of a long legislative debate on how to nurture an infant air transport industry and at the same time avoid the cutthroat competition that earlier had plagued the rail and motor carrier industries. Before carrying passengers, civilian commercial aircraft had been limited to the speedy delivery of mail. Back in 1918, air mail service had been inaugurated by the U.S. Army, and it wasn't until seven years later that the Kelly Act, also known as the Air Mail Act of 1925, allowed private airlines to share the business under contract with the postmaster general of the United States. The collusion that then developed between private air carriers and the Post Office Department led to one of the famous Senate investigations of that period, conducted by Alabama senator and later Supreme Court justice Hugo L. Black. Ultimately, President Franklin Roosevelt terminated all air mail contracts with private airlines.

The Civil Aeronautics Act of 1938 originally established the Civil Aeronautics Authority, which was reorganized in 1940 as the Civil Aeronautics Board. It "grandfathered" existing carriers, and the CAB gave them further protection by disallowing anyone to fly a route already covered by one of the others. Until shortly before deregulation, the CAB never allowed a carrier to enter a route that already had at least two carriers.[12] The CAB set the fares to be charged, and the routes to be flown, by the major airlines—first limited to sixteen, then reduced to ten. In return for their privileged status, the airlines were required by the CAB to serve many small cities, even if the business was not profitable. Other service to small communities was carried on by small feeder or commuter lines. The airlines could compete only on the basis of quality of service, notably on the frequency of flights. Meanwhile, safety rules, such as determining airworthiness of the planes, came under the domain of a separate federal bureaucracy, the Federal Aviation Administration.

Dempsey admitted that the system, as it operated under the CAB, amounted to a "regulated oligopoly"—a term used to describe a situation in which the supply is controlled by a few large companies and the demand is spread over hundreds or thousands of consumers.[13] Although Congress intended to encourage the formation of new airline companies, the record shows that the CAB effectively blocked new entrants for almost a quarter century, from 1950 to 1974. The regulated era was also the heyday of unionized airline employees and of economic inefficiencies. In the 1950–74 period, the CAB received seventy-nine applications from newcomers who wanted to establish domestic airline service, but it granted none. And between 1969 and 1974, the CAB was even more autocratic, imposing its notorious "route moratorium" policy: it refused even to consider applications for new routes. The effect was to create a Big Four—United, Eastern, American, and Trans World airlines—that dominated the market.

TODAY, FEW PROPOSE repeating all the mistakes of the CAB era by fully reregulating the airlines. But complete deregulation has proved to be an unacceptable alternative, and in some respects, worse. It plunged the nation into a laissez-faire regime that allowed the airlines to establish the routes they wanted to fly and set the fares they would charge. They could, and did, do almost anything they wanted to—including self-destruct. Fifteen years after deregulation, half of the big-name carriers were gone; almost 20 percent of the remaining companies were flying only by the grace of bankruptcy courts; and all of the airline industry's crushing multibillion-dollar debt had been downgraded to "junk" status.[14]

In the early 1980s after deregulation was set in motion, the times were ripe for change. The deregulators promised a heavenly blend of Darwinian competition: newcomers would enter the field, and the fittest airlines would survive, because they would offer lower prices, better service, and a myriad of benefits to consumers. It was an academic pipe dream: deregulation's product, after a brief spurt of excitement generated by a few new, small airlines that offered cheap, no-frills service, was an unregulated oligopoly instead of a regulated one. One such airline, People Express, developed grandiose ideas, gobbling up another small company, Frontier Airlines, which it found indigestible. Soon, People Express itself was gone, proof that real-life experience doesn't necessarily match academic theory.

The Airline Deregulation Act of 1978, which killed the CAB and phased out the system of total government control over routes and fares in a period of five years, had wide bipartisan support. It is frequently forgotten that the impetus for airline deregulation got its real thrust in 1975 under President Ford, who appointed John Robson chairman of the CAB. Robson terminated the "route moratorium" and other anticompetitive regulations, but was inhibited by the language of the Federal Aviation Act from going further toward deregulation. Key roles in the deregulation process were played by senators Edward Kennedy (D.-Mass.) and Howard Cannon (D.-Nev.), who, prior to passage of the act, held a set of hearings that effectively attacked the regulatory system as operated by the CAB and paved the way for Kahn to begin dismantling the agency.

The hearings, chaired by Kennedy, made clear that the CAB had pursued an arbitrary rate-making procedure that kept air fares too high. The CAB followed a formula ordinarily used to set the rates for a public utility, allowing costs plus a reasonable return on investment, which the agency set at 12 percent. But in determining costs, the CAB allowed the airlines to base their fares on the assumption their seats would be no more than 55 percent filled. Although efficient airlines could expect to experience a 60 percent or even 70 percent load factor, which would permit lower fares, the CAB would not change its rate-making procedure and banned any fare reductions.

Kahn was less inhibited when he replaced Robson at the CAB. With the fervor of a true zealot, Kahn took his guidance from the recommendations of the Kennedy subcommittee and began to grant certificates to new operators "by the bushel basket."[15] Kahn insisted, publicly and privately, that deregulation would result in more competition, better service, and a healthier airline industry that would not diminish service to small communities. As Kahn expected, innovators came in after deregulation to challenge the entrenched airline operators. Within the first half year in 1978, more than 3,000 new routes were established, and 7,000 more were pending. But the pressure on the existing companies that Kahn anticipated was not permanent. People Express is gone, and so are World, Capitol, Freddy Laker, and other upstart operators—swallowed up by the big carriers, which cut their fares for a long enough period to drive the newcomers out of business. And ten years after deregulation was instituted, in ten major American cities two-thirds of the traffic was controlled by a single airline. In two or three others, such as Atlanta and Chicago, two lines now divide 75 percent of the business.

When I asked Khan in 1983 if it were not true that large airlines with great economic power were driving smaller lines into oblivion, Kahn shrugged and said, with a bow to Adam Smith: "That's the way the enterprise system works."[16] Kahn did not visualize the deregulation scenario as it actually developed, in which the big airlines, left to their own devices, turned to predatory pricing in an effort to drive all others out of business. He didn't foresee that many of the smaller commuter lines would be forced to merge, or to sell out to the big carriers. These were developments that Kahn would later have to acknowledge.

Even those fervently for deregulation had to concede that the Reagan and Bush secretaries of transportation (against the opposition of their cabinet colleagues in the Justice Department) had to be faulted for allowing anticompetitive airline mergers. According to Donald I. Baker, a lawyer who was assistant attorney general for antitrust in 1976–77 and a strong defender of deregulation, the merger of Northwest Airlines and Republic Airlines gave Northwest a "virtual monopoly at the Minneapolis-St. Paul hub and the TWA-Ozark merger would do almost the same in the smaller St. Louis hub."[17] Altogether, about a dozen mergers were proposed during the Reagan years, and only one was blocked. Eventually, TWA entered bankruptcy, and Northwest at times has been on the verge of seeking Chapter 11 protection.

The hub or home-base system, under deregulation, is the modus operandi that allowed individual airlines to attain virtual monopoly control over traffic, even without the benefit of mergers. A given airline, establishing a hub or hubs, increased its flights in and out of the hubs, leasing more gates, while their competitors left to shore up their dominance in their own hubs. Neatly, they divided up the markets, and it was all legal. With fewer nonstop flights available, the typical passenger was forced to change flights at one of the hubs, usually losing an hour or more in making a connection. What used to be a routine two-and-a-half-hour flight from New York to Miami is now likely to turn into a two-hour flight, New York to Atlanta, a layover of up to an hour there, then another ninety minutes from Atlanta to Miami—over all, a minimum of about four hours. At that, the New York–Miami passenger is lucky: at least there are available connections. Some cities and areas have been deregulated out of any service. The options are to fly an uneconomic roundabout route that may take the traveler close enough to rent a car to the final destination—or to drive all the way.

Though Kahn is still a believer in deregulation, he tends to argue that the difficulties of the airline industry fifteen years after the onset of deregulation are due more to the Reagan and Bush administrations' refusal to block airline mergers than to deregulation itself. In an op-ed piece for *The Washington Post* in 1986, following the

bankruptcy of Frontier Airlines and the demise of People Express—
so much the symbols of the kind of success story he had hoped
deregulation would generate—Kahn admitted that there were questions whether giants such as Eastern, TWA, and Delta could survive
the merger wave. Careful to say "there is no basis . . . for declaring
the game lost, or deregulation a failure," Kahn—who had returned to
his post at Cornell University—nonetheless admitted: "All these
things make it impossible to say with confidence that the industry is
not already evolving into an uncomfortably tight oligopoly."[18]

The earlier, comforting assurances that deregulation would be a
bonanza for the consumer did not fool everybody. Senator Barry M.
Goldwater, who was speaking out against big government while
Ronald Reagan was still paying Screen Actors Guild dues, saw
through the deregulation sham very early. In 1983, Goldwater told
the *Airport Press* he had become disenchanted with deregulation,
although reregulation "won't help a damn bit. I thought the deregulated airline industry would revert to the virtues of private enterprise
and arrive at sensible ticket prices. Instead, you can fly to the same
place for ten or twelve different prices. The airlines are their own
worst enemy."[19]

Goldwater, a former general in the Air Force Reserve and a lifetime aviation enthusiast, also said he was outraged by the "woefully
inadequate medical kits" carried as emergency supplies on most
civil aviation flights. He complained that the airlines did not stock
drugs and other equipment useful in handling heart attacks, chok-
ing, severe allergic reactions, and bleeding, as did Air Canada and
some other foreign carriers. Some improvements in first-aid kits
stowed by the airlines have been made in the past decade, but it remains good advice for passengers not to get seriously ill flying at
35,000 feet above sea level.

In citing the air fare jungle that became the pattern under deregulation, Goldwater put his finger on one of the most frustrating results of giving the airlines complete freedom. With all fare-setting
controls abandoned, any airline could—and did—boost the price
when it had a monopoly, or a dominant presence, on a given route.
Thus a crazy-quilt pattern developed: on the same airline, the fare for
a short haul could be substantially higher than one for a longer distance. In 1983, when Goldwater sounded off, the airlines were offering a below-cost $99 fare from New York to Los Angeles, while
flights from New York to Chicago or Detroit were $300 to $400. In
1987, the fare structure remained illogical. Example: the one-way
fare for the short flight from St. Louis, Missouri, to Madison, Wisconsin, was $225. But a passenger could fly from New York to St.

Louis and connect there for a flight to Los Angeles, a distance of 2,200 miles, for $199.[20]

In mid-1993, Delta was charging $540 for a direct flight from Dallas to New York. But Delta also had a Dallas–Montreal flight for $346.50, with an intermediate stop in New York. What does a savvy Dallas–New York traveler do? He or she books the flight to Montreal, carries on any luggage, gets off in New York, tears up the New York–Montreal coupon, and saves $193.50. Newsletters and computer "electronic billboards" have helped travelers seek out the best deals, at a cost to the airlines estimated to be in the tens of millions of dollars.[21]

A *U.S. News & World Report* article on travel in 1992 outlined a scheme whereby fliers, to avoid high-priced unrestricted fares, could buy two heavily discounted tickets and use one coupon from each bargain package to complete the trip—even if the unused coupon from each excursion rate was discarded. Thus, instead of paying $724—the regular rate for a round-trip ticket between Boston and Orlando if there was no stay over a Saturday night—the traveler could buy two $218 round-trip discount tickets, one made out for beginning the trip in Boston and ending in Orlando, the other beginning in Orlando and ending in Boston, for a total cost of $436. The traveler could use the first part of the discount ticket on the flight to Orlando, discarding the return coupon to Boston. Then he or she could use the first coupon in the second ticket, allowing passage from Orlando to Boston. This so-called "back to back" ticketing provided a saving of $388.[22]

Examples of increased air fares since deregulation abound. On the heavily trafficked shuttle between Washington and New York, the regular round-trip fare offered by Delta and USAir (which operated the service for the Donald Trump interests) was $145 one way in 1993. In 1978, before deregulation, the fare was $35, rising successively to $59, $69, $75, $79, and to $99 by the tenth anniversary of deregulation, even though the original Eastern shuttle (later Trump, now USAir) had nominal competition from Pan American (now Delta). It is difficult to convince those who travel the shuttle that airline fares are really lower. The claim of *lower average* fares by deregulation defenders of course includes excursion rates and special discounts, all of which impose strict conditions. But averages can be tricky. As economist Walter Heller once observed, "there once was a six-foot-four-inch economist who drowned wading a stream he was told averaged only four feet deep."[23]

In their Pulitzer Prize-winning book, *America: What Went Wrong?*, Donald R. Bartlett and James B. Steele of *The Philadelphia*

Inquirer showed what other services and consumer products would cost if their prices had jumped the way regular coach air fares had risen under deregulation. Citing the cost of a round-trip ticket from Philadelphia to Pittsburgh, which was $86 in 1978 before deregulation, and $460 in 1992 after deregulation, the reporters noted that a similar rise would result in the following:[24]

Color TV, 19-inch	$2,022.00
Ticket to the circus	$72.22
Pot roast, 1 lb.	$9.04
One dozen doughnuts	$7.44
One pound of coffee	$14.93
One gallon low-fat milk	$7.97

Bartlett and Steele were careful to note that the $460 Philadelphia–Pittsburgh rate in 1992 was for a ticket purchased the same day of the flight. But other options, although substantially cheaper than the $460 fare, were still far above the $86 pre-deregulation cost. Thus a Philadelphia–Pittsburgh round-trip ticket purchased seven days in advance, with a penalty for cancellation, cost between $263 and $284; and a nonrefundable ticket bought fourteen days in advance cost $233 to $253.

According to an index kept by a well-known travel agency, fares at the end of 1989 were 50 percent higher for the business traveler than they were in 1980. Unrestricted coach fares, on the average, were up 77 percent. According to the Department of Transportation, however, nine out of ten airline customers could use cheaper, discounted fares, which in some cases were 40 percent lower in 1989 than in 1980.[25]

In 1983, Thomas G. Plaskett, then marketing vice president for American Airlines, tried to establish a system that would have based rates on actual mileage. "The explosion in the number and complexity of fares has produced tremendous confusion. . . . At the same time, fares have reached a point where the price paid by the customer bears no logical relationship to the distance traveled," he said.[26] Not surprisingly, Plaskett's sensible initiative was soon withdrawn.

Baliles Commission member Felix Rohatyn, who believes that the deregulated airline system has taken on some of the aspects "of legalized gambling" through highly questionable leveraged buyouts (LBOs), put in perspective the deregulators' claim that consumers have won huge benefits in terms of lower fares. On balance, he said, the fare reductions didn't necessarily benefit the country, once bankrupt carriers, losses incurred by the aircraft manufacturers, and "the lousy service on the airlines" are considered.[27]

Dempsey, in a statement to the Baliles Commission, sounded a similar note: "Not to be confused by the facts, laissez-faire theologians tenaciously point to consumer savings and declare victory. Never mind the tremendous loss of investors, creditors and workers, or the opportunity costs squandered by imprisoning business travelers in canisters of aluminum and steel and flying them circuitously through constipated hubs, or that we Americans now fly the oldest fleet of aircraft of any G-7 nation, or that bankruptcies and concentration are growing. Many market economists suffer from a severe methodological handicap by insisting that competition is perfect, and a unidimensional assessment of consumer prices is the only salient measure of sound public policy."[28]

Dempsey, in the same presentation, pointed out that two Brookings Institution economists, Steven A. Morrison and Clifford Winston, who initially calculated consumer fare savings at $6 billion since deregulation, later revised the figure down to $3 billion—"a significant confession of methodological error"—and that such studies did not take into account a long-term downward trend in fares that had set in before deregulation.[29] A study by Morten Beyer of Avmark, Inc., an airlines consulting firm, calculated that consumer savings would have been $10 billion greater if there had been no deregulation.[30]

Since the onset of deregulation, according to Dempsey's tallies, nearly 200 airlines have gone bankrupt. Prior to deregulation in 1978, 99 percent of the traffic was carried by nineteen domestic trunk lines and local service carriers. And of the nineteen, the eight biggest had eighty percent of the business. Under deregulation, the eight biggest lines had an unprecedented 90-plus percent of the market by the end of the 1980s. By January 1992, the concentration showed that the Big Four—United, American, Delta, and Northwest—had 70 percent of the business. The stranglehold of the big carriers on the airline business—despite the promises of a wonderfully competitive era under deregulation—has been reinforced by their ownership of computer reservations systems used by 95 percent of travel agents to book tickets for their customers.[31]

Perhaps no single calamity better illustrates the dubious benefits of deregulation than the demise of Eastern Airlines, which began to break apart in early 1989 after a long strike and a forced bankruptcy. Defenders of deregulation blamed the Eastern tragedy on tycoon Frank Lorenzo's determination to bust the unions and on unreasonable demands by the machinists' union for boosts in the pay of baggage handlers. But to view Eastern's problems as an old-fashioned labor-management dispute ignored the reality that it was deregulation that set the stage for it. It was the bitter competitive pressures arising out of deregulation that gave rise to the penny-pinching Frank Lorenzo, who may have been the worst of the cost-conscious operators out to make a buck.

The newer airlines that emerged in the deregulated era had much lower labor costs than the older airlines, which then had to squeeze concessions out of the entrenched unions. To meet the competition, many an airline deferred necessary maintenance. While the average age of the aircraft grew sharply under deregulation, the average age of the cockpit crew—and the quality of their training—was lower than before.[32]

Senate Budget Committee chairman James R. Sasser (D.-Tenn.), who as a new senator in 1978 voted for deregulation, later told me that he recognized his mistake. "It was the worst vote I ever cast," Sasser said regretfully.[33] Deregulation in effect has brought isolation to many rural communities. A 1988 tally showed that 140 small towns had been deprived of all air service, and in 190 others, large airlines had left, leaving only commuter lines to handle the traffic.[34] Senator Larry Pressler, South Dakota Republican, noted that after deregulation it cost more to fly 150 miles between two cities within his state than it does to fly across the continent.[35] "There have been some benefits from deregulation," said Senator Byron L. Dorgan, a North Dakota Democrat, "but they have gone largely to the population centers, while the costs have gone largely to rural areas. It's the same old economic cow—it feeds in the rural areas but is milked in the cities."[36]

Deregulation also opened a debate on whether the absence of a governmental presence resulted in a softening of air safety regulations. Investigative reporters James E. Rowen of *The Milwaukee Journal* and Larry Eichel of *The Philadelphia Inquirer*, among others, produced detailed reports indicating that deregulation was at least indirectly responsible for a series of fatal air crashes.[37]

Consider the facts surrounding the crash of Air Florida's Flight 90 into a bridge crossing the Potomac River on a wintry day in Washington, January 13, 1982, which killed seventy-three, including four in their cars on the bridge. James Rowen reported that it was deregulation that allowed Air Florida—with little experience in flying through rough, snowy weather—to enter the Washington corridor. Remember, the key change from the regulated era was that any carrier that could demonstrate that it is "fit, willing, and able" to meet Federal Aviation Agency standards for aircraft and personnel "can enter practically any U.S. market and can charge any price it wishes."[38]

The two pilots on the ill-fated Air Florida Flight 90 had done virtually all their flying in the friendlier, warmer skies of the South: "They had only ten landings or takeoffs between them in snow and ice conditions like those they confronted on that fateful day." In the CAB era, inefficient as it was, Air Florida would not have been allowed to move into the Northeast air corridor. The National Transportation Safety Board, in its report on the Air Florida tragedy, could not have been more clear in linking the accident to the deregulated era: "The Board believes that the captain of Flight 90 missed the seasoning experience normally gained as a first officer [co-pilot] as a result of the rapid expansion of Air Florida, Inc."[39]

Nothing was more bitterly contested by deregulation supporters than the notion that deregulation had caused safety as well as economic problems. The standard excuse was that only airline fares and routes had been deregulated, not air safety. Hence, said one article, by economics professor Richard B. McKenzie, "if air-travel safety was affected by 'deregulation,' it must have been affected through the impact that the airlines' greater freedom to adjust fares and routes had on the volume of travel, and on their willingness and ability to maintain the safe operations of their planes."[40] This analogy to the famous doctors' cop-out—"the operation was successful, but the patient died"—is obviously unsatisfactory.

My observation in a *Washington Post* column in 1987 that "As the grim record of near collision on the nation's airways proliferates, you and I are taking a bigger chance flying than ever before,"[41] brought a torrent of angry rebuttals. I recounted in that column comments made by Cathy Kartow of Anaheim, California, a passenger on an American Airlines flight from San Francisco to Los Angeles. Her flight had been forced to take evasive action to avoid a collision with a helicopter. Kartow said: "I was petrified. I don't know if I will fly again." There was good reason for passengers to be jittery. A week after the American Airlines incident, a helicopter carrying President Reagan had a similar near miss. Such close calls happened—and are happening—every day, in part because in 1981 Reagan banned the air traffic controllers' union (PATCO), diminishing the quality of air traffic control. But more near misses happen than are reported, because pilots and other personnel do not want to get "involved" if they can avoid it.

My 1987 and earlier pieces questioning deregulation may have triggered the McKenzie article. Its introduction starts with a quote from my column suggesting that flying was riskier than ever before, and cites Kahn's response to similar claims: "[He] bristled that any argument that deregulation has made airline travel more hazardous—despite the fact that there has been no dilution in the Federal Government's responsibility for safety—represents a triumph of preconceptions over fact."[42] But critics of deregulation who saw a connection with safety maintained their ground. Some concluded that it was only pilot awareness that airline managements were shortcutting maintenance under the economic strains of deregulation that prevented a sharp rise in airline fatal accidents. For example, it was known throughout the industry that when United Airlines absorbed Pan Am's Pacific operations in 1986, it was forced to spend huge sums of money to bring the old Pan Am fleet up to a standard that United insisted on but that a cash-starved Pan Am could not afford.[43] Concern that poor maintenance, as an outgrowth of deregulation, was becoming an increasing safety hazard was publicly expressed in 1988 by John O'Brien of the Airline Pilots Association: "With deregulation and mergers, the airlines' willingness to live up to the highest standards of safety is seriously jeopardized by the competition going on today."[44]

The operative question is less the precise link between deregulation and tragic air accidents than whether air travel is as safe as it might have been if conscientious efforts had been to give top priority to passenger safety instead of to profits. Minnesota Democrat James L. Oberstar, chairman of a House aviation subcommittee, told *The Philadelphia Inquirer*'s Larry Eichel: "I think it's fair to say that the airlines, in the rush to merge, acquire, or expand, did not put safety at the top of their ladder of considerations. Safety wasn't neglected, but it wasn't the highest priority."[45]

Brookings's Morrison and Winston, laudatory of the deregulation process, attempted to dispel any connection between airline accidents and deregulation. They said that the number of fatal accidents had fallen in the first ten years of deregulation, despite significant increases in the number of miles flown. Yet they acknowledged that pilot error and weather-related crashes had increased, and that the air safety support system—traffic controllers, safety inspectors, and airport facilities—was not growing at the same pace as air traffic volume.[46]

Some others, acknowledging a greater degree of "congestion" in the airways, put the blame on greater traffic arising from less sophisticated private planes flown by less experienced pilots rather than on commercial airlines.[47] Consolidation of routes under deregulation, and the abandonment of regular service by established airlines, has led to a proliferation of commuter lines, for which lesser standards are set, and whose pilots tend to be younger and less experienced than those working for the big carriers. Yet, because the smaller commuter planes must fly lower, in greater turbulence, into airports with less sophisticated guidance equipment, greater rather than less skill for pilots should be demanded on the commuter lines.[48]

Even Kahn has admitted that "the powerful pressures . . . on the [airline] companies to cut their costs . . . may also induce them to cut corners on safety."[49] Not only is it clear that deregulation, by unleashing a wave of competition, inspired cost-cutting and risk-taking that had the practical effect of reducing airline safety, the danger was foreseen in advance.

James Rowen dug out an internal FAA memo titled "Regulatory Reform—Potential Issues," dated August 2, 1977, or a year before the Airline Deregulation Act passed, warning about the safety hazards that might accompany deregulation. "In order to be competitive with other carriers in ticket prices, the carriers could be expected to cut economic corners wherever possible," wrote Paul L. Clark, chief of evaluation in the FAA's Flight Standards Office.[50] Where once the goal had been to exceed minimum safety standards, the pressures in the deregulated world were to do no better than meet them. The airlines, anxious to break the power of unions, began to hire less experienced pilots—and saved on their salaries.

Improper use of deicing equipment may also have been a factor not only in the Air Florida crash but in a 1985 tragedy involving an Arrow Air (charter) DC-8 that went down after takeoff in Newfoundland, killing 256 American soldiers. In discussing the Air Florida and Arrow air tragedies, Frederick C. Thayer of the University of Pittsburgh said: "The effects of deregulation can be quite literally murderous everywhere. . . ."[51] Earlier, Thayer told the Tolchins: "On larger airlines, pilots are assigned to fixed routes, where they get trained. They know about weather and about airports. By the time a pilot becomes a captain, he's been in that kind of [icy, cold] weather hundreds of times."[52]

And although Kahn insists that air travel is "unequivocally safer now than it was before deregulation," he admitted for the first time in 1988, ten years after the beginning of the deregulated era, pretty much what critics of deregulation have been saying all along: "It is possible, of course, that the margin of safety has narrowed. The number of near hits may have increased, for example, although there are no consistent statistics going back before 1979 to support this hypothesis. It is possible that the carriers, under the pressure of competition, have been cutting corners on safety. It is also possible,

however, that the increased availability to travelers of competitive
alternatives since deregulation has made airlines more averse to accidents than before: a carrier that experiences a series of crashes is
likely to be out of business."[53]

On airline safety, Thayer, who has made a general case for economic regulation—in the banking and financial industry as well as
in transportation—had this to say: "When the deregulators point to
fare-cutting wars and low accident rates as indicators that all is well,
they ignore important evidence. When airlines are losing money and
cannot raise fares because of excessive competition, they must keep
cutting costs, and perhaps by too much. When a major airline announces that it carries as many passengers as before but with 22 percent fewer employees, that is flirting with danger. Deregulation led
major airlines to abandon smaller cities to commuter lines that do
not have to meet the same standards and whose safety records are
much worse."[54]

The NTSB reported that in 1992 there were seven commuter accidents with twenty-one fatalities (a big drop from seventy-seven in
1991), while large commercial scheduled carriers had four fatal accidents and thirty-three fatalities (compared to forty-nine the year
before). The recent record for the commercial lines is substantially
improved over 1985, when seven fatal accidents cost 526 lives; in
1987, when five fatal accidents took 232 lives; in 1988, when three
cost 285 lives; and in 1989, when eleven fatal accidents took 278
lives.[55]

Kevin P. Phillips, the astute Republican political analyst, observed that if many low-income and rural residents were the losers in
airline deregulation, the winners tended to be "upscale—people and
companies well-heeled enough to profit from new business, investment, travel and communications opportunities." Phillips saw this
result—obviously not one intended by Kahn or other deregulators,
who tend to have tunnel vision—"of a piece with other Reagan-era
economic policies and beginning to stir reform demands"—even, he
thought, to the point where extremes of deregulation "would be followed by a regulatory wave." I don't believe the reaction will go that
far. But as the high costs of deregulation in the airlines, in trucking,
in environmental safeguards, and in financial institutions become
more evident, the government will be forced to reclaim a presence in
these areas. Once again, belatedly, government will have to remember that it has a commitment to the public interest.[56]

13

Third World Agonistes

On a bright Thursday morning in the spring of 1988, a
faxed copy of my *Washington Post* column of that day was
slipped under my door at Paris's Intercontinental Hotel, bearing a
scrawled note in handwriting I recognized as belonging to Treasury
secretary James Baker.[1] (Along with half a dozen other journalists, I
had come to Paris to cover Baker, who was attending a series of high-
level financial meetings on debt and related matters. All of us—including Baker and Treasury staffers—were booked at the luxurious
Intercontinental, Baker's favorite Paris hotel.) A paragraph in the column was circled, and the note read simply: "Your menu is chicken
shit." Clipped to my column was an editorial from the *Economist*
magazine, praising the so-called Baker Plan. Baker's reference to a
"menu" was shorthand for the then-current debate on a "menu of
options" that commercial banks might utilize to ease the debt burden of the Third World nations without going all the way to actual
debt forgiveness, fast becoming the consensus recommendation of
students of the debt crisis.

Baker, one of the few innovative members of a deadly dull Ronald
Reagan cabinet, had proposed a scheme to alleviate the burdens of
Third World debt in a speech to the annual meeting of the World
Bank and International Monetary Fund in Seoul, South Korea, in October 1985. His plan represented a courageous step in that the chief
fiscal officer of the U.S. government recognized that only the revival
of economic growth held out any hope for unwinding debt load in

seventeen key countries, whereas the rich nations' prior focus—on austerity—held out no hope at all.[2]

But while Baker was able to make the leap from advocacy of enforced austerity to sponsorship of economic growth in the poor countries, his hang-up was a stubborn belief that growth could be financed by a continuing buildup of debt. That was the Achilles' heel of the Baker Plan—an erroneous assumption that there would be adequate private financing to reduce debt in the seventeen countries Baker singled out for priority attention.

When his plan did not prove to be an immediate success because the banks shied away from making additional loans, Baker began to discuss a "menu of options" to broaden the scope of the plan. At a meeting of the IMF on April 9, 1987, he outlined a number of modest alternatives, such as debt-equity "swaps," an arrangement that allowed the debtor countries to pay off their debts by offering an equity stake in local enterprises or physical resources.

But many of the debtors logically regarded debt-equity swaps as yet another way in which foreigners could take over valuable slices of their national heritage.[3] Representative Charles E. Schumer (D.-N.Y.) proposed his own menu, including outright cancellation of debt as one obvious approach for the banks. In what Baker called my "chicken shit" column, I wrote approvingly of Schumer's initiative and said that Baker needed to come up with bolder ideas. When Baker and I met at lunch later that day, he grinned and asked if I had received his note and the *Economist* editorial. "Now *that*," he declared, "is what I call chicken salad." I told him I had received his message, but that I didn't care much for his salad.

Baker had become increasingly sensitive to criticism that his plan was a failure. He feared that if borrowers obtained an easy out—outright cancellation of their loans, in part or in whole—there would be little incentive for them to reform their creaky financial structures, or to adopt anything resembling a free-market approach. One way or another, however, the debt crisis would have to be faced.

THE DEBT STORY began on August 20, 1982, when Jesús Silva Herzog, Mexico's finance minister, reported to a private, sober-faced audience of big bankers who had loaned huge sums to his country—generally viewed as the most advanced nation in Latin America—that Mexico couldn't meet scheduled repayments on its debt, variously estimated at $70 billion to $80 billion, for at least three months. That session, arranged by Fed chairman Paul Volcker, took place at the offices of the New York Federal Reserve Bank on

Liberty Street. It came a week before word of the crisis exploded publicly at the annual meeting of the IMF and World Bank in Toronto. The Mexican revelation marked the beginning of what would come to be called the Third World debt crisis, which affected developing nations in Latin America, Asia, and Africa.

In modern times, there have been few cosmic financial events to compare to the Third World debt crisis of the 1980s. The bad news, coming as it did after a quasi default by Poland on its $23 billion hard currency debt and the Falklands/Malvinas Islands War, which expanded Argentina's debt to $37 billion, sent a 1930s-like chill through world financial markets. "Something must be done about the debt. . . . It is like we are on a sinking ship running around patching holes one after the other. We go from one crisis to another. It is not only very annoying, it is also very costly," said President Fernando Belaúnde of Peru.[4]

Henry Kaufman, chief economist and forecaster for Salomon Brothers, warned: "It's a crisis of confidence in the system. How did we get to this point? I strongly believe what is happening . . . is reflective of a buildup of a massive debt structure both in the United States and internationally. And [the debt] has financed not a large amount of economic efficiency, but for a long while, a large amount of inflation. But now we have it, it's there, it's got a maturity schedule and it's got an interest payment."[5]

Baker never did broaden his vista on debt relief. Along with many other officials, he continued to underestimate the scope of the debt crisis and what had to be done to grapple with it. And although the world financial structure did not totally collapse—as some initially feared it would—officials and bankers continued to show flawed judgment in lending policies, and seemed not to understand what the crisis meant to the poor populations among the debtor countries. International interest rates, which pushed as high as 17 percent in 1980 and 1981, proved to be too burdensome for Third World borrowers. Some of these loans had been written at around 7 percent, and were easy to pay off when world inflation rates were running at 7 to 10 percent. That boosted the dollar value of exports over the interest rate costs.

The interest rates charged Third World borrowers were not fixed, but were variable—that is, they rose as market interest rates rose, the benchmark being known as LIBOR, for London interbank borrowing rate. As international interest rates rose into the double digits, the loans that banks had made at relatively cheap single digits suddenly became monstrously expensive. Mexico and other borrowers suddenly found that as much as 50 percent of their earnings from exports had to be devoted to paying interest—to say nothing of the principal. And precisely at the time that interest rates soared out of sight in 1982, commodity prices began to fall, which meant that Third World exporting nations were caught in an impossible squeeze.[6] At one stroke, the bizarre outpouring of funds from Latin America to pay off their bankers in the rich countries triggered a social crisis and potential revolution among the debtors, as well as a jobs crisis in the United States—the chief source of loans—because money that used to go to purchase American goods was siphoned away to repay the banks.

There were few good guesses, at the time, of the dimensions of the Third World debt, although Jacques de Larosière, the energetic managing director of the IMF, added it up to $540 billion as of the end of 1981 among the major debtor nations, mostly Latin American countries, including Mexico's $80 billion and Brazil's $87 billion.[7] At the New York meeting, Volcker suggested to Silva Herzog that he ask the bankers for a "standstill"—a term the Fed chairman described as "a less frightening and aggressive term than a 'moratorium' or 'default,' which would have technically triggered legal action forcing banks to foreclose."[8]

News of the crisis stunned the annual IMF/World Bank meeting in Toronto. Establishment bankers, like medical patients denying symptoms of disease, refused to acknowledge the seriousness of the crisis. They chose to believe they could muddle through. Willard C. Butcher, chairman of the Chase Manhattan Bank, seriously overloaded with Third World loans, said that fears about the stability of the banking system had been exaggerated. "Reneging on debt has serious consequences . . . the loss of interest [by the banks] over the long term is highly improbable," he said.[9]

Initially, Reagan administration officials also tried to play down the seriousness of the crisis, arguing that the troubles were "manageable."[10] But Larosière and Volcker acknowledged that the problem was severe, got together to address the challenge, and in doing so probably preserved the basic structure of the world's financial system. With the concern over the banks as much in mind as the distress of the borrowers, Larosière and Volcker hatched a strategy to save the financial system. A crucial, and less well known, role was also played by Fritz Leutwiler, chairman of the Swiss National Bank and of the Bank for International Settlements, aided by Gordon Richardson, governor of the Bank of England.

Leutwiler turned his suite at the Toronto Four Seasons Hotel, headquarters for the IMF/Bank session, into a command post. Working with Richardson and other European central bank chairmen,

Leutwiler's BIS collected between $1.2 and $1.5 billion as "bridge loans" from ten members of the BIS and from Switzerland to keep the defaulting countries alive until the IMF could bludgeon the commercial banks to lend more money.[11] "It was very close to blackmail," Leutwiler admitted. "The IMF said to the banks: 'We are prepared to put up a [lending] program for these countries, if you throw in some good money after the bad.' The banks didn't like that, but what could they do? What was the alternative? This was the lesser evil. I'm still convinced that the international payments system was really on the brink.

"It all started before Mexico defaulted. The first difficulty came from Eastern Europe in 1981, when Poland became virtually bankrupt, and it spread to Hungary. The Western banks were reluctant to allow Hungary to extend its short-term loans, and the Soviet Union was also unwilling to help.[12]

"I remember a high-level Soviet delegation [that] came to see me in my office in Zurich to tell me not only that they wouldn't give the Hungarians any money, but they thought I shouldn't give them any either. I suggested that [Hungarian prime minister János] Kádár should ask [Soviet leaders Leonid] Brezhnev and [Aleksey] Kosygin to give the Hungarians some gold for collateral, because we would have taken it [as security] for loans. But they bluntly said: 'It's better to let the Hungarians go down.' "[13]

Leutwiler, Richardson, Karl Otto Poehl, president of the German Bundesbank, and other European central bankers feared that if all of Eastern Europe went down the tubes, the spillover effects on the Western European banking system would be calamitous. So they pursued the painful business of getting pledges—but found the United States uninterested until Mexico got into the same kind of difficulty. "Then," said Leutwiler, "they wanted us to get interested in their problems."

When the Mexican crisis broke, Volcker, Larosière, and Richardson met every day to monitor the calls that the New York Clearing House—the major international institution for settling indebtedness among commercial banks—would get, anywhere from $50 million to $75 million daily, to meet the bills that the Mexicans and other Latin countries couldn't pay. Leutwiler elaborated: "These needs were covered out of the BIS bridge loan to keep the New York Clearing House operation afloat. We were frankly afraid that what was happening in New York would spread to London, and we concluded that if you don't stop the domino at the beginning, you have disaster in the end."[14]

Mexico's troubles came as a shock to those who had believed that the discovery of massive oil reserves in 1976 would further strengthen Mexico's industrial and economic progress. For a long period between 1945 and 1970, Mexico had enjoyed high per capita growth rates and relatively low inflation—a benign condition flawed by great inequality of wealth and economic opportunity. The government engaged in a spending spree, counting—mistakenly, as did American savings and loan institutions—on the proposition that there was no place for the price of oil to go but up.[15]

But Mexico was only the tip of the Latin American debt iceberg. Argentina couldn't pay off its loans, and offered to put up gold. "Then we found out the gold was already pledged," Leutwiler said. But eventually Argentina got a BIS bridge loan, and every dollar was paid back, as the IMF stepped into the breach and took over. "I don't want to glorify our actions of those days. We had no parliaments, we [central bankers] could make our own decisions. We did it and we didn't lose anything."

What Leutwiler now calls "blackmail" was officially described by Larosière as a process of "rescheduling," according to which the banks would postpone required debt repayments and throw in some new money as well. Volcker's main contribution, apart from his intellectual support for the rescue scheme, was, in the fall of 1982, to back off the high-interest-rate, monetarist-oriented policy he had introduced in 1979 to check the collapse of the dollar, which had triggered double-digit American interest rates that translated at once into double-digit international interest rates.

At the time, the abrupt change in course at the Fed was explained primarily as an effort to bring an end to the severe economic recession that had caught up with President Ronald Reagan. The unemployment rate had edged into double digits—10.1 percent—the highest mark in forty-two years, and the newspapers recorded a daily flow of corporate bankruptcies. And indeed, a reversal of tight money was urgently needed to salvage the domestic economy. But the private worry at the Fed, as Volcker would admit much later, was that the rich nations found their "banking system suddenly threatened with collapse."[16] Moreover, the dollar, whose plunge in 1979 had been responsible for Volcker's dramatic, even reckless decision to let interest rates soar, had reached such record highs that American companies were threatened with a loss of overseas markets.

In his and Toyoo Gyohten's *Changing Fortunes*, published in 1992, Volcker neither apologizes for the wrenching move in 1979 into high interest rates nor explains the Fed's 1982 reversal in specific terms relating to Third World debt. But Volcker does say: "No doubt the emergency efforts in 1982, and the tortuous process that ensued to coordinate the efforts of a dozen countries, hundreds of banks, and several international institutions was energized by that most important of all instincts—that of self-preservation."[17]

It would prove difficult to get the banking community to understand the hit it would have to take. During the IMF/Bank session in Toronto, one of the most powerful private citizens in the world, Chase Manhattan Bank chairman David Rockefeller, expressed his frustration at having to deny, once again, that his bank was overexposed in Mexico. At a garden reception at the private estate of a wealthy Canadian manufacturer, just outside Toronto, Rockefeller insisted: "No, I don't think [Chase] is overexposed. You ought to remember that just a few years ago everybody was talking about Zaire, Peru, and Turkey. And what happened? Nobody lost hardly any money."[18] In fact, the banks did lose lots of money in all three countries. But they had "deep pockets," overflowing with the money on deposit from the rich OPEC cartel. Lending for Third World development had become a fashionable practice (as had lending in the Florida land boom in an earlier generation). Initial loans may have been good loans, while many subsequent loans, for less desirable projects, were bad loans.

But when it becomes fashionable to lend, borrowers in such a favored sector naturally take advantage of the availability of money. Senior partner of Brown Brothers Harriman Robert Roosa, who had been a Treasury undersecretary for monetary affairs in the Kennedy administration—one of the most innovative thinkers to serve the Treasury in modern times—faulted his fellow bankers for failing to apply a "hair shirt" standard. "They should only be lending for valid projects, and where there is a workable use for borrowed money," he said.[19] Mexico was a good example of where bankers should have applied the Roosa hair shirt but didn't. Instead, they stumbled over each other, begging the government and private borrowers to be included in their plans, especially after new—and substantial—oil discoveries were made in Mexico. Major international banks had boosted their overall lending to less-developed countries by an annual rate of 25 percent.

Karin Lissakers, who was on the staff of the Senate Foreign Relations Subcommittee on Multinational Corporations when the first oil-price shock hit the global economy in 1973, and later an adjunct professor of business and banking at Columbia University, revealed in a recent book that Mexican president José López-Portillo polled his foreign bankers late in 1980 about their future lending intentions, after his Finance Ministry officials warned him that the banks would have to pull back.[20] In a grand misassessment of the situation,

the banks interpreted López-Portillo's inquiry as a sign that Mexico
was about to put a lid on borrowing, and would use the polling results to ration the business among the lenders. So the banks inflated
their projections—one New York bank put in a fivefold projection of
its available loans in the single year 1980 to 1981. Reassured, López-
Portillo fired the Finance Ministry officials who had cautioned him
and extended Mexico's spending binge: in 1981, Mexico borrowed
$20 billion, double the figure of the year before.

"By mid-1982," Lissakers wrote, "Mexico and Brazil owed foreign banks around $70 billion each; Argentina and Venezuela owed
at least $30 billion each; Chile and the Philippines owed more than
$10 billion; and Nigeria, $7 billion. Altogether, Latin developing
countries and Eastern Europe owed foreign commercial banks nearly
$500 billion. Most of the debt was, or would soon become, sovereign
debt."[21]

The timing was exquisitely bad: an oil glut developed in the early
1980s, after the second OPEC price shock in 1979, and the price of oil
plummeted. Thus international bankers were trapped in exactly the
same situation as were large American banks after the Penn Square
fiasco: what might have been surefire, sound loans to finance oil development suddenly had to be classified as bad loans—very bad
loans.

European bankers, more exposed in Eastern Europe than in Latin
America, seemed as unconcerned as Americans. At the same
Toronto reception where David Rockefeller denied that Chase
had become overexposed, Walter Seipp, chairman of the German
Commerz-bank, rejected the notion that the crisis could be likened
to that of the 1930s. "We're all aware that we're sitting in one boat,
and if we play it cool, we have the means to avoid a crisis like the
1930s," he confided. (Interestingly enough, in view of what happened eight years later with the collapse of the Soviet empire, Seipp
explained bad loans to Poland and other Eastern European countries
this way: "The Soviet Union was never in default, so we used the
'umbrella theory.' " He meant that Moscow would protect its satel-
lites if they encountered financial stress.[22]

Even if, as Seipp guessed, the situation was not exactly analogous
to the deflationary problems of the 1930s, it was plenty bad. Banker
and former Peruvian cabinet minister Pedro Pablo Kuczynski made
the point that, despite the IMF's attempt to "blackmail" the big international banks, they "immediately and drastically cut back new
lending to most Latin American countries" the minute Mexico announced its suspension of payments in August 1982.[23] That left a gap
of as much as $50 billion in the Third World's financing needs—a gap

that the international lending agencies such as the IMF and World Bank did not have the resources to fill by themselves. "It's a situation caused by bad bankers who made bad loans to those countries," said John Heimann, then cochairman of the investment banking firm Warburg Paribas Becker, and former comptroller of currency for President Carter.[24]

Until 1973, the developing countries had not been large borrowers abroad; mostly, they had depended on foreign governments and international institutions. But when OPEC skyrocketed oil prices, the developing countries that used oil suddenly had large balance of payments deficits, and the oil exporting countries had even larger surpluses, which they placed with the large, money-center banks that specialize in international transactions. Thus there arose a huge pool of lendable "petrodollars" that the developing countries were eager to borrow. Because demand for funds was depressed in the industrialized nations (in part because of high oil prices), the banks could charge the Third World countries higher interest rates than they could get at home. "The wider interest-rate spread attracted regional banks that had not been previously engaged in international lending. To accommodate them, the money-center banks formed lending syndicates from which they earned generous fees," economist Edward Bernstein explained.[25]

Many heads of the large banks argued that the debtor nations needed to tighten their belts and make themselves creditworthy by applying austerity standards. Clearly, there had been much waste and dishonesty in the Third World countries in managing the enormous sums channeled into their countries by the commercial banks, but the solution—after the banks had been overgenerous—was hardly to be overharsh now. Even former secretary of state Henry Kissinger, who had never paid much attention to international financial problems when he was in high office, appeared well briefed on what was happening: as a highly paid private adviser to big corporate clients here and abroad, Kissinger warned that demanding austerity from poor countries as the sole solution to the debt crisis "misunderstands the nature of the developing countries." Kissinger added that when the IMF sets "conditionality" standards—the austere conditions on which it lends money—"the cure may be worse than the disease."[26]

From the standpoint of the borrowers, rescheduling of their oppressive debt would obviously be preferable to default, although many bitter politicians in Third World countries—usually in the opposition parties—were willing to go that desperate route. But rescheduling was not an ideal solution. That process, as World Bank economist Chandra S. Hardy pointed out, was crisis-oriented and un-coordinated because ninety cents out of every dollar newly borrowed by the poor countries was being used to service older loans. Re-scheduling merely postponed the day of judgment.[27] Better, some ex-perts began to think, to cancel some debt than go through with the charade of pretending that old loans were good by making new loans largely designed to pay back the old ones. That was a hocus-pocus exercise to convince bank examiners that the banks' books were in better balance than an honest accounting would show.

It was a long way, though, before debt cancellation became the accepted vogue. Debt "rescheduling" was the magic word: whereas in the 1970s there might have been one or two reschedulings a year, at least fifteen were under way by the end of 1982 at the "Paris Club" under the impact of two oil shocks and deepening debt. Not a night-spot for American tourists, the Paris Club was the meeting place at the Kleber Centre in the French capital where officials of the sixteen rich industrial nations met informally to rewrite the terms of gov-ernment-to-government loans that otherwise might fall into default. (The Paris Club's private sector counterpart was the London Club, where, on an ad hoc basis, commercial bankers got together to dis-cuss the wisdom of stretching out or easing the terms of loans they had made to developing nations.)

As the rescheduling activity at the Paris Club gained momentum, Charles Meissner, special State Department negotiator for economic matters, suggested that "what we are dealing with is a transition from a period of inflation and negative interest rates in the past fif-teen years to a period of deflation and positive interest rates." Inter-est rates are said to be "negative" when they are lower than the level of inflation. In that case, it makes sense to borrow as much as incau-tious lenders are willing to lend—which is precisely what the poor countries did.[28]

Yet it did the borrowers little good for the Paris and London clubs to work out an easier payment schedule if they couldn't sell enough of their products to the richer countries to pay back their loans, even if the payment dates were stretched out. Increasingly, while the major nations talked about the need for expanding global trade and dropping barriers, protectionism was on the rise. After years of a ris-ing volume of trade—which benefited the poor nations—the volume of global trade had begun to shrink, and each nation therefore began to try to maintain or increase its share.

The situation cried out for leadership that would devise an ac-ceptable way to transform the massive debt buildup into longer maturities at more manageable interest rates. But the mood of the moment was ad hoc, muddle through, stiff upper lip and all that. Gloomily, Horst Schulmann, a former deputy finance minister under German chancellor Helmut Schmidt, observed that "the situation may very well be that the reality of interdependence [among nations] has outpaced our intellectual power to analyze the problem, and to build appropriate models [to solve it]."[29] C. Fred Bergsten, director of the Institute for International Economics, estimated that two-thirds of the Reagan recession of 1982 could be chalked up to declining exports—a result of an overvalued dollar as well as a loss of markets among Third World debtors. He put forward what he called "the bicycle theory" of trade, according to which the system can't stand still but either becomes more open or lapses into protectionism.[30]

From think tanks, financial markets, international institutions, and other government agencies, the debt crisis generated an outpouring of plans, ideas, and schemes to solve or mitigate it. But it would take three years, as the situation degenerated, before Baker launched his initiative in 1985 in Seoul.

Actually, all the world's developing countries owed nearly twice the total of the Latin American group—or about $1 trillion—and were committed to pay back at interest rates that were variable. Triggered by the extraordinary rise in American interest rates to double digits, international interest rates had soared. Many countries that had borrowed when interest rates were 8 percent or less found themselves obligated to pay back at rates of 15 percent and 16 per cent. This became as oppressive to the commercial banks as to the borrowers, because they had inadequate capital with which to back up their loans.

According to William R. Cline of Bergsten's institute, the nine largest American banks had loaned developing countries (including some in Eastern Europe) 240 percent of their capital. Mexico had borrowed 44.3 percent and Brazil 40.8 percent of the Big Nine banks' capital.[31] Clearly, if those debts could not be paid off, or written down substantially, some of the banks would be in deep trouble. The big money-center banks—the major sources of loans to the poor countries—accumulate most of their deposits from corporations or other banks with cash to invest for short periods. The price the big banks paid when "buying" such deposits would go up as the markets observed their accumulating troubles. Worse, as the banks with heavy Third World debt had to deduct large amounts of their profits to add to their reserves against loans that might go sour, there would be less money available to lend to good customers. And the worst scenario of all would concern those banks so heavily overcommitted that the reserves were not available to cover bad loans.[32]

In 1982, the interest payments due to the nine major banks cited by economist Cline amounted to $3.66 billion, whereas the profits at those banks totaled $2.76 billion. Thus any rescheduling or postponement of interest payments necessary to tide the borrowers over would have a grim impact on the banks' bottom lines.

But whatever the problem of individual banks, the relative optimists pointed out in 1982 that the banking system itself could survive with some adjustments by lenders and borrowers. The hazard, as was only slowly appreciated in government circles, was that some debtor nations, if they could no longer finance imported food, oil, or other necessities, might face social upheaval.

"The record shows that frank and open debate does not take place in official and banking circles," World Bank chief economist Stanley Fisher observed much later. What was clear was that unless real debt "relief"—which meant cancellation—was given, most of the debtor countries could not resume economic growth. "So long as the United States was not willing to move, the international financial institutions were not free to speak—though to be sure, the repeated emphasis on debt reduction, with 'voluntary, market-based' added sotto voce by the heads of the World Bank and IMF, was signaling their conclusion that it was time to move on."[33]

The trouble with "voluntarism," as Richard E. Feinberg, vice president of the Overseas Development Council, explained, was that unorchestrated, market-oriented reductions in debt weren't likely to amount to much. To put it bluntly, if there were to be an amount of debt reduction large enough to make a difference to the debtors, it wouldn't come from noble, voluntary gestures. There had to be some oversight mechanism to organize what the banks should do.

As interest rates came down and debt payments were postponed, Mexico and other debtor countries recovered a measure of their strength. And while the structure of the banks and of the financial system—thanks to Volcker, Larosière, Leutwiler, Baker, and Nicholas Brady—has been preserved, the debtor nations lost up to a decade of economic growth, and many of them seem relegated to permanent poverty, their cities dominated by crime-ridden, polluted, overpopulated ghettos.

THERE ARE TANGLED ROOTS to the Third World debt crisis. They reside first in the famous if naive belief of influential private bankers like Walter Wriston of Citicorp that sovereign states cannot go broke. In a speech to the American Bankers Association international financial conference at Lausanne, Switzerland, in May 1981, Wriston counseled others to quit worrying about Third World debt so long as the governments pay the interest that is due. His argument was that sovereign governments are expected only to "roll over" the debt. When the U.S. Treasury sells bills every Monday morning, Wriston asked, how does that differ from debt "rescheduling" by poor countries?[34]

Only a few dared to challenge Wriston's false assurances. New York economist Henry Kaufman told all who would listen that "you don't know when you'll get blindsided" by a new crisis. Felix Rohatyn warned that, as far back as the 1960s, performance had become the test for financial institutions, leading to "an almost inevitable sacrifice in the quality of restraints vis-à-vis the desire for growth.[35] Robert Roosa also challenged the Wriston view, which he said "does a disservice two ways: it gives the public a feeling that there is no problem, and gives the borrowing countries the idea that there is no discipline in the system, that they can go on this way forever. The system may not be out of control, but a lot needs to be done to prevent it from getting out of control."[36]

But no one took on Wriston more courageously than my friend and former colleague at *The Washington Post*, the late Henry C. Wallich, who capped his illustrious career as a governor of—and leading international expert for—the Federal Reserve Board. The *Financial Times* noted that Wallich "memorably described the notion of sovereign immunity from default as being as elusive as the smile on the vanishing face of the Cheshire cat."[37]

"Over the life of a medium-term loan, lenders must recognize the possibility of major shocks," Wallich said. "That is the difference between short-term lending and medium-term lending. Evidently, the market was not well prepared to make that kind of risk assessment. Indeed, one is almost bound to conclude that the organization of international lending contained strong biases against proper risk assessment."[38]

The concept that each Third World country's creditworthiness needed to be judged carefully, as advocated by Wallich, or that "country limits" had to be set, as suggested by economist William Cline, had not yet come into vogue.

It was a lose-lose situation as the commercial banks saturated Third World borrowers. At first, of course, the poor countries had to borrow to pay the soaring costs of oil imports—the rich oil-exporting developing countries had no sympathy for the poorer, oil-importing developing countries. (Nor did the Arab members of OPEC give many, if any, concessions to Arab oil-importers.)

Later, the debtor nations needed more money from the commercial banks both because interest costs were rising—they were stuck with floating rates—and because an overvalued dollar forced them to pay higher prices for urgently needed imports. And in some countries, bad economic policies made the situation even worse.[39] The greedy banks were happy to oblige, lending at what Kuczynski refers to as "an almost dizzying pace."[40]

Cline estimated that about $400 billion of the $500 billion in increased debt among the "non-oil" debtor countries between 1973 and 1982 could be chalked up to external problems such as the higher oil prices they had to pay and a huge drop in the prices they could get for their commodities in a global recession. But there were internal causes as well, including corruption at top political levels and a flight of capital to safer havens as the big debtors plunged deeper into domestic economic debt. In some countries, like Argentina, the domestic problems were as bad as the outside pressures: of Argentina's debt of $44 billion in 1984, $20 billion was due to capital flight.[41]

Most of these heavily indebted countries could keep one step ahead of their debt repayment schedules so long as exports grew faster than the interest rate on the accumulated debt. In the 1970s, interest rates grew only about 10 percent a year, while exports were growing at 20 percent. But with the huge bulge in international interest rates after 1979, the interest costs zoomed out of sight. By 1981 and 1982, the 10 percent average interest had ballooned to 16 percent, while the recession punctured the Third World export boom. Cline reported that with the growth of exports a meager 1 percent, the debt crisis was in full bloom.

IT TOOK ALMOST THREE YEARS to evolve a coordinated approach to the debt problems of the most heavily indebted nations. Until Baker, with considerable fanfare, unveiled his debt plan at the IMF/World Bank annual meeting in Seoul in October 1985, the basic guideline since the Mexican crisis had erupted in 1982 was to deal with debt issues on a "case by case" basis—with no broad strategy in mind. Baker proposed additional lending of $29 billion over three years—$20 billion from commercial banks, $9 billion from the international institutions—to fifteen of the most heavily indebted nations, later adding Costa Rica and Jamaica, making seventeen in all. All this, in exchange for a series of economic reforms. He called it a "three-legged stool," the key elements being more commercial bank loans, more international agency loans, more economic growth among the debtor nations.

What was missing from the Baker Plan was not only any true debt relief but any central or strategic plan for government involvement. En route to Korea on Baker's plane, a National Security Council staffer confided to me that "there's not much there [in the Baker Plan], it's only an effort to buy time."

Although it fell far short of its objectives, the Baker Plan nonetheless marked a major philosophical shift in policy for the Reagan administration. Always keen on damage control—as he had demonstrated just days before on exchange rate issues at the September 22 meeting that resulted in the Plaza Accord—Baker understood that the debt crisis couldn't be solved under the Donald Regan formula, according to which governments and international institutions would treat the problem as a private one between the borrowers and their commercial bankers.

Baker accepted what Regan failed to comprehend—that the political limits of austerity in the Third World, especially in the major Latin American nations, had been reached. Some way of regenerating economic growth (especially in Mexico, with its long common border with the United States) was an imperative. In his address at Seoul, Baker recognized not only that the debt crisis was more severe than any other official had been ready to admit over the prior three years, but that a plan of action had to be set in motion—the problem couldn't be left entirely to the banks and their debtors to solve. But clearly, the specific actions blueprinted by Baker would not be enough.[42]

And despite his almost slavish dedication to free markets, Baker understood that governments, especially Washington, had to get involved in a major way. Cline credits Baker with moving from short-term "crisis management" to a broader, indeed a global, attack.[43] But at the last moment, before addressing the annual IMF/World Bank meeting in Seoul, Baker abandoned one element of the plan he had intended to put before his audience—a doubling to $5.4 billion of moneys the IMF and World Bank could use to guarantee private loans to the least-developed nations in Africa. Baker bowed to fears that such a guarantee would tarnish the World Bank's vaunted triple-A credit rating.[44]

However, the Baker Plan did abandon the "case-by-case" approach that the commercial bankers and the IMF had pursued since the beginning of the crisis in 1982, and that was a distinct step forward. Baker argued that the commercial banks had a general obligation to boost their total new lending, hoping to stimulate economic growth in the Third World and thereby help the borrowing countries to become more efficient—and in the process, better able to pay off their old loans. It was an important conceptual breakthrough that Baker had forged with help from Volcker, and Baker demanded a similar commitment from the IMF and World Bank.

The better approach would have been outright debt relief or forgiveness. But for Reagan and Baker in 1985, that was too much to swallow. Ultimately, that step would come with Bush and Treasury Secretary Brady.

The Baker-Volcker relationship during this period was interesting. Regan as Treasury secretary, influenced by his undersecretary for monetary affairs, Beryl Sprinkel, had fought with Volcker, trying to influence the management of monetary policy. Sprinkel, as a monetarist in the Friedman tradition, was an active and public critic of Fed policy. But under Baker, the Reagan administration had made a sensible adjustment to the real world and away from Regan and Sprinkel's laissez-faire policy. The famous Plaza Accord was a perfect example of Baker's pragmatism.

As part of this adjustment, Baker, as the new Treasury secretary, actively sought and received Volcker's cooperation—although Volcker was reluctant to engage in a policy of weakening the dollar. Volcker told me on Baker's Seoul-bound plane that talking the dollar down is "a tricky business," adding, "I'm just as worried about the dollar falling too far as I am about its being too high." In essence, Volcker feared that once Washington started to push the dollar down—witness Great Britain and what happened to the pound sterling—it couldn't be sure where the process would end.[45] Yet, reluctantly, Volcker went along with Baker, who was able to sum up the situation this way: "We could never have done what we did at the Plaza Hotel without the active cooperation of the Federal Reserve."[46] In similar fashion, Volcker helped in the formulation of the Baker Plan on the debt crisis, and was expected to help sell the commercial banks on the idea that they needed to boost their loans by $20 billion, as Baker requested, instead of cutting off fresh funds, as they had threatened to do. Although it was apparent around the middle of 1986 that the Baker Plan would fall short of its objectives, Baker stubbornly refused to give ground. More surprising was that Volcker also refused to budge.

One of the brilliant academic thinkers who immediately understood the good intent of the Baker Plan, as well as its basic flaws, was Percy S. Mistry, a senior financial adviser to the World Bank, who left on June 1, 1987, partly out of frustration, to return to his teaching position at Oxford. Mistry tried to convince his bosses at the Bank that, while Baker should be credited with having introduced the first major shift in conventional thinking on the debt strategy, it had to be supplanted by yet a bolder shift in strategy that would reduce the outstanding levels of debt. In a privately circulated paper, Mistry pointed out that in the five years from the revelation of the debt crisis in 1982 to mid-1987, the banks had substantially improved their position while the borrowers had not, and thus the banks "are now in a much better position to take systematically planned write-downs than they were in 1982."[47]

The concept of moving the political and banking world toward actual debt relief, as envisioned by Mistry, was finally embodied in the Brady Plan—named for Baker's successor at the Treasury, Nicholas Brady. Credit for giving debt relief the necessary political push belongs in large part to several Democrats on Capitol Hill, and especially to Senator Bill Bradley of New Jersey, who lobbied for debt relief as early as 1983 and who popularized the idea at a private conference of international experts in June 1986 in Zurich.

Bradley had struggled, along with Senator John F. Kerry (D.-Mass.) and Representatives John LaFalce (D.-R.I.) and Charles Schumer (D.-N.Y.), to find some logical answers to the debt problem that would end the practice of throwing good money after bad, actually adding to, not reducing, the huge annual interest load on the poor countries.[48] Bradley argued that wrongheaded banking and governmental policies "have stood development economics on its head. We must stop the perverse flow of resources from the poorest countries to the richest, stem capital flight, and restore the confidence in Third World countries that is necessary for growth."[49]

At the Zurich conference, Bradley proposed a daring idea: the creditor nations and commercial banks would offer to wipe out about two-thirds of Latin America's annual debt-servicing burden, then about $30 billion annually. In return for this outright debt cancellation, recipient nations would have to agree to liberalize their trade barriers, promote domestic economic growth, and help strengthen the international financial system. "The Baker Plan prolongs the policies that created the debt crisis in the first place," Bradley said.[50]

Bradley, a former pro basketball star, has been one of the truly innovative younger Democrats on Capitol Hill, perhaps better known for his contribution to tax reform, which reached a high point with passage in 1986 of legislation that traded a drop in the top marginal rates for abandonment of many tax shelters. Bradley's contribution to the coalescence of global opinion on the need to do something dramatic about debt relief for the world's poor countries is equally important. For months, he had tried to generate support for debt cancellation. It was clear that the Baker Plan had a central, crippling flaw: it attempted to solve an already burdensome debt problem by creating still more debt—new loans that would be used to pay interest on the existing loans to the banks. But Bradley's speech in Zurich, the idea of actually writing off some of the borrowed money, was daring. The Zurich conference was sponsored by two young Washington promoters who had started an international financial advisory business. David Smick, a Republican, and Richard Medley, a Democrat—both of whom had worked on Capitol Hill—sensed around the time of the Plaza Accord in 1985 that global economic affairs would be increasingly important not only to the governments involved but to private companies. They enlisted Bradley and Representative Jack Kemp (R.-New York)—who had worked together on tax reform—as congressional sponsors, and won the informal backing of Jim Baker and his deputy, Richard Darman.

For Baker and Darman, the high-profile group of public officials and interested private citizens Smick and Medley were able to corral for their private "summits"—there had been one in 1985 prior to the Zurich gathering—was a convenient marketing tool for the exchange rate intervention ideas they wanted to push in the period immediately after the Plaza Accord. The success of the early Smick and Medley meetings provided a favorable backdrop for the Zurich conference. At that three-day affair, a blue-ribbon audience of bankers, businessmen, Treasury officials, and others was rewarded by Bradley's bombshell. It was a surprise to Kemp ("I had no idea he was going to do that," Kemp later said). And it met with predictable grumbling from some of the commercial bank lenders present.

But my story from Zurich got a featured display spot in *The Washington Post* on Monday morning and good play elsewhere, and the idea began to catch on. Reagan's former ambassador to the United Nations, Jeane J. Kirkpatrick, praised Bradley's initiative in a *Washington Post* op-ed piece, and boldly concluded that the Baker Plan was flawed.[51] Invited to address the National Press Club shortly after the Zurich speech, Bradley said that the big debts and weak economies in Latin America were "an explosive combination. They create an atmosphere where democracy cannot take hold. As the debtor nations cut back on their domestic budgets, they hurt the poor. The tangible promise of a better life disappears. Discontent grows and provides a breeding ground for instability and revolution."[52] In essence, Bradley was warning that Latin America's fragile democracies could disappear unless the world listened closely to their urgent pleas for help.

Bradley did not have the field to himself: a group of Western Hemisphere leaders, including former U.S. ambassador Sol Linowitz and Galo Plaza, former head of the Organization of American States, chipped in with a stunning fact: each year from 1982 through 1985, the Latin nations had shelled out $35 billion in interest payments to the banks, out of their annual export earnings of $90 billion to $100 billion. Clearly, the huge interest payments were not only putting a severe brake on their ability to expand their home economies, and the standard of living of their citizens, but reducing their ability to import goods. In a strange way, the demands by bankers for full repayment of their loans (which had come back many times over through near-usurious interest rates) constituted a drag on the Latin nations' ability to import American goods. Third World debt, therefore, was one hidden cause of America's huge trade deficit—and debt relief, while a cost to the banks, would benefit American exporters.

World Bank figures showed that the value of U.S. exports to six major Latin American debtors had dropped from $32 billion to $22 billion from 1981 to 1985, while imports soared from $28 billion to $38 billion. In round numbers, a $4 billion surplus had turned into a $16 billion deficit, a turnaround of about $20 billion.[53]

There is little doubt that the World Bank, which should have been on top of the problem from the outset, was particularly ineffective under president A. W. (Tom) Clausen, who had been chairman of BankAmerica before beginning his five-year term in 1981. The IMF under Larosière did a much better job, even though the Monetary Fund had suffered for years with the image of being the international "Scrooge," demanding excessively austere conditions from the poor countries for its help.

Clausen, for all his thirty years as a big commercial banker, had no Washington or developing-country experience. He lacked charisma, and was a poor manager of the colossal 6,000-person bank bureaucracy. For the latter deficiency, Clausen or anyone else can probably be excused. Of all the huge, overblown agencies in Washington, the World Bank, staffed by nationals from dozens of countries, spread over two-score office buildings, changes course about as easily as a huge ocean liner on the high seas.

Clausen was and is extremely bright and good at analyzing the bank's problems—but he couldn't produce the necessary follow-through. For the first time in the bank's history, bank lending in 1984 fell behind the prior year's total by about $2 billion. Unlike

Larosière, Clausen failed to seize a leadership role for the bank as the
debt crisis developed. He acknowledged in a 1983 interview that the
bank could be "a bit more aggressive" in its lending, but flatly ruled
out any approach under which his institution would consolidate and
stretch out unpayable debts.

Clausen's bank presidency was ill-starred from the beginning.
The five-year term of the bank president does not coincide with the
four-year term of the president of the United States, who, according
to custom, nominates the bank head, who is then approved by the
multination bank board. Jimmy Carter, as he exited from the presidency, chose Clausen, a California Republican, in 1980, just before
Reagan was to be sworn in the following January. Carter cleared the
appointment with Reagan, using Washington lawyer Lloyd N. Cutler as the intermediary. But Clausen never enjoyed the full confidence of Reagan administration officials, especially Don Regan and
Beryl Sprinkel: for true Reaganites, Clausen's loyalty was somehow
flawed because Carter had had a role in his selection.

Clausen confirmed the worst evaluation of his detractors with a
weak response to the Mexican crisis as it evolved in Toronto in 1982.
The whole idea of buying up distressed loans and writing bonds
against them was anathema to Clausen. "That's not our business—
our business is development," Clausen told me in 1983. The bank's
logical role, Clausen insisted, was to let the IMF take the lead in
addressing the debt crisis, which he regarded as within its short-term
purview, while the bank continued its historic assignment of making medium- to long-term loans—fifteen to twenty years—to help
poor nations expand their export potential.

Clausen failed to see that, for some nations, there would be no
long-term survival unless the short-term problems were solved on an
urgent basis. There were strong dissenting views within the World
Bank. Vice President Munir P. Benjenk told me that the institution's
unwillingness to address the debt issue "is quite incomprehensible
and somewhat absurd." Banks that were hesitating to increase their
exposure in the Third World were now placing some excess funds in
World Bank bonds—a triple-A rated investment. "We can borrow
more, and therefore let us lend more in the present situation . . . and
let us do this so that the adjustment which is necessary in the developing countries can be gradual and not brutal."

To give Clausen his due, he lobbied hard with President Reagan
to support the proposal put forward by European leaders at the Williamsburg economic summit in the summer of 1983 to boost funds
for the Bank. And Clausen wanted the president to state forthrightly
that the Group of Seven leaders were "greatly concerned" about the

debt crisis. But Reagan and Regan weren't anxious to go to Congress for a major capital increase for the bank, and the word "greatly" was excised from the Williamsburg summit communiqué.

From about mid-1984, it was clear to me that the White House would ease Clausen out and try to replace him with a more dynamic leader—preferably one in tune with the Treasury's bias against development financing, which it regarded as somehow in conflict with pure free-market operations.[54] The dump-Clausen movement gained more force when Baker succeeded Regan at Treasury in early 1985. Baker would seek not only an ideological soul mate but someone with professional political skills or instincts. But even as Clausen readied himself in the fall of 1985 for the annual IMF/World Bank meeting in Seoul, there was no official word from the White House.

Clausen was inept, and was so judged, privately, by many career officials at the bank, who compared his weak performance to the dynamism of Robert McNamara. "Clausen held back," a high bank official told me confidentially. "He's the kind of man who wants to make sure that he's taking the right action—and he never wants it said he made the wrong decision."[55]

Indeed, it was Clausen's bad luck to be the president who succeeded Robert McNamara—an organizational dynamo who was revered among Third World clients of the lending agency. Despite my argument with him in 1975 over his complacent attitude on global oil prices, I know that McNamara was a more successful manager than any of his successors; he had a loyal following among the senior staff people at the bank, and most likely would have moved aggressively to keep the bank in the forefront of an effort to solve the debt problem had he still been president in the early 1980s.

By the time Baker readied his initiative in Seoul, the IMF was more than willing to play ball. "The international economic system has reached the point of no return," said Larosière. "There is no alternative to closer cooperation and leadership. It is now up to the international community to act, and to act together."[56]

But Clausen had his own future in mind. Bitter at being left swinging in the wind, Clausen phoned Baker on Monday, October 7, 1985, after they had both arrived separately in the Korean capital, and told him he would announce at the end of his speech the next day that he would not seek reappointment when his term expired in 1986. In an interview the day after Clausen's decision became public, Assistant Treasury Secretary David C. Mulford pointedly said that the bank had at least $2 billion available that "they are not lending." Nailing down Clausen's coffin, Mulford added: "It's been our view that the World Bank has not been using its resources effec-

tively."[57] Clausen complained to a banker friend that for four years
the Reagan administration had withheld an increase in the bank's
capital resources—which Clausen had favored and which would
have permitted the bank to expand its role in the Third World. Now,
Clausen felt, there would be a policy reversal under Baker, including
a capital increase—but Baker would have his own man running the
bank. (Clausen was right about that: the new president succeeding
Clausen was former congressman Barber Conable Jr. (R.-N.Y.), who
had no experience in commercial banking or development finance,
but who had been a fixture in Republican politics for twenty years.)

Reagan and Regan had been stingy with resources for the Clausen
bank from the beginning. There was, first of all, the Beryl Sprinkel
problem. During the first Reagan term, Sprinkel had used his Treasury post to argue that markets should be left alone, and that governments and international institutions should take on no function that
could be performed by the private sector. One of Sprinkel's first acts
in office was to commission a Treasury study of the World Bank to
determine whether, in fact, the World Bank had "socialistic" tendencies, which would be evidenced by the private sector being crowded
out by government-to-government loans. The Treasury study, in the
end, fully cleared the institution of any such evildoings, but the bank
properly resented it as a witch hunt and it touched off hard feelings
never fully erased during the Reagan-Bush era.

By way of contrast, the IMF's Larosière—who had the ability to
offer short-term bailout loans—moved quickly to put out the debt
crisis fire. Clausen, although he could not have been expected to rep-
licate the IMF emergency role, nonetheless was too slow to understand that the problems faced by Mexico would break out of the
short-term range into the area in which the World Bank could play a
massive role. Not until early in 1985 did Clausen speak of the need
for more aid from the World Bank and other international development banks, especially "in the light of the reluctance of the international marketplace [private banks] to come forward. Therefore, the
role of the [World] Bank ought to be enhanced, strengthened and encouraged."[58] That was in line with the recommendations of a special
congressional subcommittee headed by Representative Stanley N.
Lundine (D.-N.Y.), and exactly parallel to the major thrust of the
Baker Plan as outlined in Seoul. But that was too late for the problem—and for Clausen.[59]

In February 1987, one of the many fuses on the international-debt
booby trap exploded: Brazil, the largest Third World debtor—it then
owed $108 billion—announced that it would suspend indefinitely

the interest payments on about two-thirds of the total, or $67 billion. That was followed immediately by an Argentine declaration that if Buenos Aires were not accorded the same special loan terms Mexico had negotiated, it too would declare a moratorium on interest payments.

The Brazilian announcement was a deep shock to Baker because Brazil had been held up as a major example of the success of the Baker Plan and various other makeshift debt-relief schemes that had been in place since the Toronto IMF meeting in 1982. But the signs of stress had been there for anyone to see, and had been noted publicly by almost all students of the debt problem.

By the time Baker had made his scatological reference, in Paris, to my column urging a more generous approach to debt relief, he was on his way out of the Treasury, having been drafted by George Bush to take over his upcoming campaign for the presidency. He remained adamantly opposed to plans like Bradley's, arguing that debt relief was counterproductive because to lenders it was the equivalent of default.[60] "Debt forgiveness is a mirage," Baker liked to say.

Despite Baker, the movement toward outright debt relief became irresistible. At the 1987 fall meeting of the IMF and World Bank in Washington, Larosière's successor, Michel Camdessus, said that "anything that can be done without adding to the level of existing debt is welcome," provided that there are no unilateral decisions and the solutions "are rooted in the market."[61]

In September 1988, a panel of twenty-seven experts commissioned by the Economic Policy Council of the United Nations Association issued a report calling for consideration of "voluntary debt service reduction" to help relieve the crisis. This panel, chaired by former New York Federal Reserve Bank president Anthony Solomon, chairman of S. G. Warburg U.S.A., and Rodney Wagner, vice chairman of Morgan Guaranty Trust Company, began to tip the scales toward debt forgiveness, because it was the first time that big bankers had publicly endorsed debt relief as part of the menu. Bluntly, this blue-ribbon financial group faulted the rich countries, along with the IMF and the World Bank, for resisting "the trend toward flexibility and the search for innovative solutions to the debt problem."[62]

Soon thereafter, Richard Darman, of the brokerage house of Shearson Lehman Hutton, who as deputy Treasury secretary in 1985 had helped launch the Baker Plan, conceded that it had failed to increase the flow of bank money to the Third World both had envisioned in Seoul. At a press conference in December 1988,

President-elect Bush, in a straightforward way, agreed that some change had to be made. "I think we should take a whole new look at it," Bush said, without endorsing total debt write-offs.

The growing sense of dissatisfaction with the Baker Plan made it easier for Brady, prodded by David Mulford, to work on a new U.S. strategy that would lighten the burden on the Latin American debtors. When Brady took over the Treasury job from Baker in September 1988, he was surprised that so many of the Treasury staff supported the reluctance of Fed chairman Alan Greenspan, named to his post the year before, to endorse outright debt relief. But Mulford had a change of heart. There was no love lost between Mulford and Baker, who had denied Mulford a long-sought promotion to be undersecretary for international affairs. A chance to supplant the Baker Plan with a Brady Plan was not an unwelcome dividend for Mulford, who remained at the Treasury and was promoted to be undersecretary by Brady.

In the Baker Treasury, Mulford had played third fiddle behind Baker and Darman, who simply didn't like Mulford. Mulford, after all, was a Don Regan pick—both of them having arrived in Washington via the international financial markets. Mulford had been an important adviser to Saudi Arabia's central bank, and was highly regarded in banking circles; he wasn't Baker's or Darman's kind of guy who knew how to play the Washington political game. But in the Brady Treasury, Mulford was allowed to use his expertise and international financial connections. He not only became the nominal number two on international economics but, given Brady's distaste for the subject, he was considered by his foreign counterparts as the number one spokesman for the United States on debt and related issues, such as American policy vis-à-vis the World Bank and the IMF. And indeed, given Brady's laid-back attitude, Mulford acted out the number one role.

Brady and Mulford also gained a strong debt reduction ally in Brent Scowcroft, George Bush's new national security adviser, who would have gone even further on debt reduction—cutting the burden for countries friendly to the United States, whether or not those countries provided the quid pro quo of market-oriented reforms in their domestic economies. To continue to insist on full servicing of the debt would require the perpetuation of an annual transfer of $20 billion to $30 billion from the poor nations to the rich. Richard Feinberg, a former Treasury official and vice president of the Overseas Development Council, argued that this "negative" flow made no sense. He showed that in 1987, for the first time ever, the World

Bank, IMF, and Inter-American Development Bank drained more money out of Latin America than they put in.[63]

The tip-off that a major Third World debt policy change was brewing came in a Mulford speech in February 1989 to a private meeting sponsored by the World Economic Forum at Davos, Switzerland. By then undersecretary-designate, Mulford conceded that the Baker Plan had outlived its usefulness, noting that the loans commercial banks had made to some of the poor countries could be bought for anywhere from a nickel to fifty cents on the dollar in the open, secondary markets in New York or London.

The big banks—refusing for the most part to write off their loans—had been pretending that the real value of their loans was much higher. In effect, they argued that the borrowers who cried for debt relief were trying to get something for nothing. Mulford's citation of real market values of billions of dollars worth of loans was taken by his Davos business audience as evidence that debt relief made sense and was in the offing.[64]

Still, Brady temporized, anxious not to have a falling out with Alan Greenspan, who fretted that writing down the debt would discourage banks from making new loans, thus drying up a necessary cash flow to the debtor countries. But the banks were already turning away from the Third World and seeking better opportunities in Asia, Europe, and their own domestic economies. The cash flow would have to be filled out by the IMF, the World Bank, and individual national governments.

Brady was finally propelled into announcing the policy shift on March 10, 1989, by the news of sickening riots in Venezuela and the happenstance of a speaking commitment to a conference cosponsored by the Bretton Woods Committee (a private lobby that pushes Congress to be generous with support funds for the IMF and World Bank) and the Brookings Institution. The setting was the glamorous eighth-floor diplomatic reception rooms of the State Department. And while Brady is one of the world's least-inspiring public speakers, I could sense a unanimous sigh of relief in the VIP audience as he outlined the broad terms of his plan to reduce some of the huge debt among thirty-nine Third World nations.

Actual debt relief, or forgiveness, would be financed by about $30 billion put up by the World Bank, the International Monetary Fund, and Japan. But in the Brady concept, debt reduction would be voluntary, and the basic strategy would remain market-related. Brady's main focus was on Mexico, which had made enough progress immediately after sounding the warning bells for all borrowers in 1982 to attract better terms from the banks as early as 1984.[65] Brady said forthrightly that "the path toward greater creditworthiness and a return to markets for many debtor countries needs to involve debt reduction." Eugene Rotberg, the financial genius who for nineteen years, beginning in 1968 as vice president and treasurer of the World Bank, brilliantly managed the World Bank's multibillion-dollar investment portfolio, pointed out that Brady's initiative boiled down to four main points: First, it was permissible, if not desirable, for U.S. banks to confess that they had incurred some real losses on their Latin American loans. In effect, what the banks had been doing was a bit of fancy bookkeeping: in order to avoid showing losses, they "paid themselves interest by providing new loans for that purpose." Second, the banks should provide some form of real debt relief or debt reduction. Third, Uncle Sam would not provide direct, visible support for the banks. And fourth, the United States should give the green light for the IMF and World Bank to offer some form of limited guarantee that the borrowers would pay interest on the amount of debt that remained in place.

But the reality, Rotberg insisted, was that the Brady Plan would not provide a beneficial effect on the financial condition of the debtors because "they haven't been paying interest or principal anyway." At least fifteen of the twenty big Latin American debtors, including Brazil and Argentina, said unblushingly that being in arrears provided more relief than they would realize through a Brady Plan agreement. Thus, Rotberg argued, for the whole process to have meaning, the banks either had to write down or write off more of their old loans, and provide new loans that topped the value of their old loans: "Otherwise, the whole process is irrelevant."[66]

Still, as analyst Shafiqul Islam of the Council on Foreign Relations observed, the Brady Plan was a "qualitative break" from the Baker Plan.[67] Cline also credited the Brady Plan with the potential to make a key contribution to international debt management, but conceded, in effect, that it was underfunded by public money.[68]

Totally omitted from the Brady Plan strategy were the poorest among the poor countries, such as African nations and the Philippines, which had borrowed not from commercial banks but from richer governments.[69] "If debt reduction was a good idea, it was a good idea for reducing all debt, including official debt," said Sir Jeremy Morse of Lloyds Bank in commenting on that failing of the Brady Plan.[70]

Six years after the debt crisis had exploded during the IMF/World Bank meeting in Toronto, the 1988 economic summit in the same Canadian metropolis had to agree in its official communiqué that

the debt strategy had failed: "The problems of many heavily indebted developing countries are a cause for economic and political
concern and can be a threat to political stability in developing countries."[71] For the very poorest countries, the 1988 summit suggested
subsidized interest rates and partial write-offs. But no move in this
direction was ever taken, although the idea surfaced again at the
1993 Tokyo economic summit.

Events as the 1980s drew to a close demonstrated that Rotberg
was right. If the Brady Plan was an improvement on the Baker Plan,
it offered no real magic: the great majority of poor countries remained overwhelmed by massive commercial debt, their negative
per capita growth rates induced by excessive population growth.
Ironically, the biggest single act on the debt relief front was American forgiveness of $7 billion owed by Egypt (which wasn't being paid
anyway), a diplomatic gesture arising out of the Persian Gulf crisis.

Harvard economist Jeffrey D. Sachs pointed out in a *Foreign Affairs* article in mid-1989 that debt relief without economic reform
among the recipient nations could have little meaning. The IMF always (and properly) looks for fiscal discipline, he noted, and the
World Bank seeks an outward-oriented trade regime. "But both institutions have found that their message gets lost in the political fire-
storm that breaks out when excessive debt payments overwhelmed
the domestic economy."[72]

A DECADE AFTER the crisis began, although politicians and bankers liked to say that a slide in global interest rates had ended the debt
crisis, Latin America was still burdened with $435 billion in debt,
which meant that the annual interest burden would remain a dead
weight on the economies of those countries far into the future.[73] As
we head into the last years of the twentieth century, private lending
by banks is being replaced in part by World Bank and IMF loans and
guarantees. The "officialization" of the debt now runs to about 50
percent of the total, compared with less than 40 percent at the start
of the debt crisis in 1982. Now it is the turn of the World Bank and
the IMF to become overextended, just as the commercial banks were
a decade ago.

The debt crisis story suggests that bankers are among the worst
representatives of American business leadership. Almost anyone can
run a bank better than a banker. Bankers' judgments are distressingly
bad, as shown by the loans they continue to make to each other, as
well as to failing nations in Latin America. Banker competence runs
in inverse ratio to the size of the banks they are running: in good

times and bad, the most efficient banks are the small and medium-sized ones.

Not surprisingly, the banks survived the debt crisis in better shape than did the Third World, until declining interest rates in the early 1990s eased the burden on borrowers as well as lenders. Karin Lissakers, a keen observer throughout this period, argues persuasively that some banks and debtor countries haven't learned their lesson. For example, commercial banks to which Argentina still owes huge debts "have cheerfully underwritten bond issues for Argentine borrowers." And Citibank has converted the dollar loans it made to Brazil into a growing retail banking business. "Happy times are here again. Maybe," Lissakers remarked sardonically in 1993.[74]

14

End of an Era

WHEN JAMES BAKER REPLACED Donald Regan at the Treasury at the beginning of Reagan's second term in February 1985, bringing with him Richard Darman, his aide at the White House, as deputy secretary, the high-interest-rate, high-dollar era came to an end. Baker, to deflect the protectionist trend generating in Congress, sought ways of pushing the dollar down.

Baker achieved his goal with what was undoubtedly the most important event of his stewardship of the Treasury, the Plaza Accord. Signed on Sunday, September 22, 1985, among five major nations—the United States, Japan, Germany, England, and France—the Accord recognized that the dollar was overvalued against other major currencies of the world. The signatories boldly committed themselves to manage the values of their respective currencies to drive the dollar down and the other four currencies up, abandoning the policy of accepting whatever the market dictated. The communiqué did not use the word "intervention," but all understood the message: the five nations together would step into the markets to sell dollars and buy the other currencies. If successful, the operation would drive down the price of the dollar.

On Monday, September 23, the day after the meeting, just such a massive intervention took place, and the dollar fell 4.29 percent, the largest single-day's drop ever recorded.[1]

Over the course of the next two years, the value of the dollar continued to fall against the yen and major European currencies so sharply, as we will see, that by early 1987 the same powers were seeking ways of braking the fall and stabilizing the dollar's relationships to other currencies. By the end of 1993, the yen had appreciated to about 110 to the dollar, or more than double its value at the end of August 1985, when the ratio was 237 yen to the dollar. In effect, one yen at 1993's end was worth almost one cent; in 1985 one yen was worth less than half a cent. Put the other way around, the dollar had depreciated by more than half against the yen.

Baker was, of course, pleased with the immediate, post-Plaza result. But at the time it was pointed out by many observers, such as Reagan's former Economic Council chairman, Martin Feldstein, that the dollar had actually peaked against other major currencies in February 1985, and had started down before the Plaza Accord, in response to basic underlying economic conditions. Like many conservatives, Feldstein was a strong critic of the international coordination process, arguing that the benefits were minimal. Feldstein was right in asserting that the results of international cooperation could be overstated.

Baker's Plaza Accord venture, even if it misfired in its long-term objectives, nonetheless represented a huge philosophical reversal of the noninterventionist policies of Reagan, Regan, and former Treasury undersecretary for monetary affairs Beryl Sprinkel, who had been shunted aside as caretaker chairman of the Council of Economic Advisers after Feldstein was dumped by Baker in a fight over tax policy. Baker's Plaza initiative was warmly received by America's trading partners as a sign that the United States would henceforth abandon a policy, detested abroad, known as "benign neglect."

Sprinkel, as the leading administration official for monetary policy in Reagan's first term, was a vigorous opponent of intervention except in rare cases when markets were demonstrably "disorderly." But as CEA chair in 1985, Sprinkel was so far "out of the loop" of policy making that he didn't even know that Baker's famous Plaza Hotel meeting was about to take place until he read about it in the newspapers. In fact, Sprinkel's CEA office had issued the text of a speech he would make that same weekend denying rumors that any effort to manage exchange rates was afoot.

The Plaza meeting was launched with the greatest of secrecy. Assistant Treasury Secretary for International Affairs David Mulford was sent around the world to apprise officials of the G-5 countries of Baker's plan to boost the levels of their currency in relation to the dollar. It obviously had to be kept a tight secret, or speculators would make fortunes by selling dollars—which Baker and his cohorts knew would plunge after the Plaza Accord was announced. In keeping with

Baker's practice of dealing only with reporters he knew well, just three of us—Art Pine of *The Wall Street Journal,* Peter Kilborn of *The New York Times,* and myself—were called into the Treasury on Saturday, September 21, for separate briefings alerting us that the G-5 would have an important meeting the next day at New York's Plaza Hotel—with all information embargoed until Sunday morning. We were not given specific details, but enough so we could sense the drift of what would happen. Pine, working for *The Wall Street Journal,* which publishes only five days a week, would not be able to get his story into the paper until Monday morning. But Kilborn and I were able to write page one stories for *The New York Times* and *Washington Post* that fleshed out the terse, single-paragraph announcement the Treasury press office had made the day before about the Sunday meeting and a press conference to follow. Similar announcements in the other four capitals set off a mad dash by journalists and other interested observers for New York City, and the famous old hotel at Fifty-ninth Street and Fifth Avenue.

When Baker, Volcker, and their G-5 counterparts entered an incredibly crowded and hot meeting room in the Plaza after a five-hour meeting, and announced that they had agreed that "some further orderly appreciation of" the other currencies against the U.S. dollar "is desirable," there was a stampede for telephones. A Treasury press aide, about to be engulfed by a horde of reporters battling for an inadequate initial supply of the printed communiqué, took one look at the mob and tossed the batch of releases into the air, as one would scraps of food to deter an onrushing horde of wolves.

Kilborn, Pine, and I were always invited to travel with Baker. He chose us not because he had any particular fondness for us but for the pragmatic reason that we represented three of the most influential newspapers in the country. There were four or five other reporters who from time to time also joined Baker's press entourage. All in this group had countless interviews with him and his staff. The system was manifestly unfair to other reporters but typical of the way Baker worked. It was especially hard on foreign journalists, who were virtually banned from the Treasury.[2] Like other Washington journalists, I was impressed by Baker's political smarts and ability to learn the economic ropes from scratch. He was cool, calculating, and competent—an enormous improvement over Regan. At any international gathering, foreign reporters struggled to wedge their way into a Baker briefing, which was sure to be authoritative, even if slanted in favor of American policy goals. I admired Baker and his professionalism, but I also had no doubt that his decision-making process had cranked into it an assessment of how his career might be affected.

By the time the Plaza Accord rolled around in the fall of 1985, Regan, as White House chief of staff, was, like Sprinkel, safely removed from the economic decision-making process. As Baker and Darman planned the dramatic break from Reagan's laissez-faire conviction that the market should always be allowed to operate without interference, Baker had to make sure only that the Fed's Paul Volcker would go along.

Volcker had well-advertised concerns over the risks involved in depressing a national currency like the dollar. It was easy to recall the more-than-bargained-for success of Treasury Secretary Michael Blumenthal's campaign in the late 1970s, during the Carter years, to "talk the dollar down": confidence in the dollar weakened to the point that a savage deflationary effort, including double-digit interest rates, was required to restore some semblance of confidence in the U.S. currency. In the end, the adverse results of the dollar-rescue effort had a great deal to do with the collapse of the Carter presidency and the rise of Ronald Reagan in 1980. Blumenthal, nonetheless, would never acknowledge that he had set in motion a process he couldn't control; to this day, he insists that he did not talk the dollar down. But he did.

The problem with fiddling around with the value of currencies, as Volcker testified, is that depreciation does not provide a solution of fundamental problems, and is, in fact, a double-edged sword.[3] The positive aspect is that a cheaper dollar reduces the cost to foreigners of goods and services, thereby boosting exports; the downside is that a cheaper dollar, by the same token, is inflationary: it makes imports more costly, allowing domestic manufacturers, such as carmakers, a convenient umbrella for raising prices. When the United States is confronted by inflationary pressures, the Federal Reserve tends to adopt a more restrictive monetary policy; in the mid-1980s, there was also the possibility that foreign investors, who had financed much of the U.S. budget deficit by buying Treasury bills and notes, would be tempted, by a slide in the dollar, to move their cash elsewhere. That could also lead to higher interest rates.[4]

Baker placed supreme faith in the high-stakes game he was about to play at the Plaza. In many carefully documented conversations, he persuaded free-trader Volcker to go along, using as a clincher the argument that the only way to break protectionist momentum in Congress was to bring down the international price of the dollar. The logic of Baker's argument was that a cheaper dollar would boost American exports and cut the Japanese trade surplus: it had been clear in 1985 that if the U.S. trade deficit continued to rise, protectionist legislation probably couldn't be stopped.

The Plaza Accord did, in fact, delay protectionist legislation. Volcker's support of Baker was critical: he endorsed the communiqué, and the group photograph at the press conference that followed the meeting at the Plaza showed a smiling "tall Paul." Had he objected, or appeared unenthusiastic, there is no doubt that Baker could not have come away with his Accord. An influential official in Europe told me later: "Don't forget it was Volcker's credibility that made it possible for Baker's New York meeting [at the Plaza Hotel] to take place on short notice. We all have great admiration for Paul Volcker."[5]

But what Baker and Darman could not foresee in 1985 was that the stronger yen that would result from the Plaza Accord would have two unplanned consequences: the soaring yen—*endaka*—would force Japanese companies to make their operations more efficient to remain price-competitive. In order to maintain as much of their market shares as possible for autos and other products, Japanese exporters trimmed profit margins, partially offsetting the adverse effect of the higher yen. And the high yen generated such enormous financial wealth in Japan that its investors were able to buy American properties or shares in American business at bargain prices, leading to the reaction among some Americans that the Japanese were "buying up our country."

Through the late 1980s and into the early 1990s, the dollar was still cheap against the yen, but the Japanese bilateral trade surplus in 1993 was running at an annual rate of $56 billion, up a bit from $50 billion in 1985, although sharply less as a percentage of the gross domestic product. Economist C. Fred Bergsten, who had strongly influenced Baker and Darman and who is the leading exponent of exchange rate adjustment as the primary solution for curing trade imbalances, could say that, without the Plaza Accord, the Japanese trade surplus might have zoomed to $300 billion a year.[6] But that is conjecture: what we do know for sure is that the impact of exchange rate changes such as those made at the Plaza were overrated as a way to cut Japan's trade surplus.

EVEN SO, THE VAUNTED Plaza Accord marked the high-water mark of international cooperation in the Reagan-Bush era. In early 1986, Darman tried to introduce a note of realism about the limitations of the cooperation process, whether in terms of the powerful Group of Five or its slightly diluted form, the Group of Seven, which included Canada and Italy, paralleling the makeup of the economic summit partners.

At an informal conference sponsored by David Smick and Richard Medley, the two Washington consultants who had helped forge a consensus on the need for Third World debt relief, Darman warned that the world could move only slowly and incrementally toward complete integration of its international economic policy-making machinery. He and Baker knew that the big powers would have to give up a share of their national sovereignty to make a globally interdependent economy work—and that they would resist. He was right. The Plaza Accord was unprecedented. No major power had ever before agreed to deliberately increase the value of its currency, as did America's four major partners. But the major powers were not ready for much more, as Darman had divined.

With great fanfare, they formalized the Plaza Accord at the Tokyo economic summit in 1986 into an agreement among the seven powers to curb erratic fluctuations in major currencies, in effect "a managed float." At the Louvre Palace in 1987, the system was further refined by an agreement to keep currencies within specific "target zones," or allowable high-and-low ranges.

At the Venice summit in mid-1987, and again in late September, the G-7 finance ministers reaffirmed the pledges made at the Louvre. But the shallow nature of the bond among them was driven home by a running fight over interest rates between Baker and the German authorities that played a role in the stock market crash of October 1987.

The intense controversy between the United States and Germany over the proper level of interest rates first broke out in the fall of 1986. The German finance minister, Gerhard Stoltenberg, rebuffed Baker's not-so-subtle demands that Germany lower its interest rates to stimulate global economic growth. Better, said Stoltenberg after a long G-5 meeting in Washington, that the major nations, the United States included, concentrate on growth and stability, instead of squabbling over interest rates.[7] The usually unflappable Baker lost his cool, bit by bit, over the spring and summer of 1987 as Germany raised interest rates, culminating in an open threat by Baker to the Germans on *Meet the Press* on the Sunday before Black Monday, October 19, 1987.

ALONG THE WAY, the quick fragmentation of the international co-operative process led to one of the most bizarre moments in Federal Reserve Board history, when a "Gang of Four" Federal Reserve governors led a successful revolt against Chairman Volcker on February 14, 1986, forcing a reduction in interest rates that Volcker had not wanted to make. There was a face-saving patch-up of the damage, and Volcker served out the rest of his term, to mid-1987. But his influence was shattered by the Gang of Four revolt.[8]

The four rebels were Vice Chairman Preston Martin, Governor Martha R. Seger, and two freshman governors, Wayne D. Angell and Manuel Johnson. There had been bad blood between Volcker and Martin, a Reagan appointee (suspected of angling for Volcker's job as chairman), ever since June 1985, when Volcker, apprised of a Martin proposal to reduce the Third World's external debt, labeled it "incomprehensible." That's not the normal language one member of a supposedly collegial board of governors uses about another—and it was illustrative of Volcker's occasional arrogance.

The Gang of Four rebellion had its origins in the first post-Plaza meeting of the Group of Five, in London on January 18 and 19, 1986. The G-5 agreed, in a conference devoid of the attention given to the Plaza Accord, that their central banks should pursue a coordinated reduction of interest rates. But some of the central bankers, notably President Karl Otto Poehl of the German Bundesbank, already upset at the public impression that politicians—meaning finance ministers—were dictating how they, as independent central bankers, should act, resisted adoption of a specific timetable, as was desired by the finance ministers.

"The central bankers don't like the world to think that finance ministers, either within their own country or collectively among countries (e.g., the Group of Five) are telling them what to do, or even influencing them in what to do," said a Finance Ministry official who recognized the strained relations between the politicians and the central bankers.[9] Volcker joined Poehl in bucking pressure from members of his own board, including Martin, for a cut in the rates they believed necessary to stimulate the domestic economy. Martin had been urging a cut in the Fed's discount rate, then 7.5 percent, since November 1985.

There was not, and is not, any public record of the behind-closed-doors sessions of the G-5 or G-7, beyond the brief communiqués they issue, which only hint at the full range of matters discussed. But the principals, to the degree that it suits their purposes, reveal some of the events, often on a background or off-the-record basis. It soon became known that Volcker argued at the London G-5 meeting that, because economic indicators in the United States were still strong, Japan and Germany should initiate the interest rate decline without expecting the United States to follow, lockstep, with its own interest rate cut.

By the time the central bankers' regular monthly meeting rolled around in Basel on February 10, 1986, three weeks after they had met with their finance ministers at the London G-5 session, the global economic outlook had weakened, and crude oil prices had plunged dramatically. Interest rates in the market had fallen on their own, and a consensus had developed that lower interest rates the world over could be put into effect with little worry about inflation.

Normally, what transpires at the Basel central bankers' sessions is kept totally secret; there is not even the flimsiest briefing, as provided by the G-5. But I learned what had gone on in Basel on February 10 from one central banker, a tight-lipped official who usually shuns contact with reporters. As the controversy over coordinated interest rates became more intense, I phoned him, and—after he made clear that his name was not to be used—he gave me a detailed account. There had been a consensus, he said, that "present inflation prospects justify lower interest rates the world over. Obviously, Paul [Volcker] is hesitant because the dollar is in a trouble zone, and he worries about the risk of starting an avalanche down, if the element of confidence were to disappear. . . . Paul is not as convinced as we are that inflation expectations have been fully eradicated. He seems to fear there could be a flare-up of inflation in the United States, but he does believe Europeans need to expand their own economy more than they plan to do. . . . The central banks are willing to take concerted action, although there are elements of difference among us. . . ."[10]

He and his fellow central bankers thought it unwise to challenge Volcker because they judged "he is needed by the U.S. government, and he is capable of continuing to manage monetary policy in the United States. It is difficult to predict who will be president after Reagan, but it is even more difficult to replace Paul Volcker. That's a fact." But if, out of respect, his central banker colleagues would not push Volcker, the Gang of Four—whose focus happened to be on domestic rather than international affairs—would and did. Two weeks after the Basel meeting, on February 24, the four governors took the situation in their own hands and forced a vote on a motion to cut the 7.5 percent discount rate to 7 percent. Since the Federal Reserve board of governors consists of seven members—the chairman, vice chairman, and five other governors—their proposal for lower rates carried, 4–3; governors Henry Wallich and Emmett Rice voted with Volcker against the motion.

Having established their point, the Gang of Four had second thoughts about the humiliation they were about to heap on Volcker: they did not want to be responsible for his resignation, which was almost certain to follow a defeat within his own board, probably leading to turmoil in world financial markets. Led by Johnson and Angell, the four governors—before the decision was publicly announced—suggested to Volcker that the 4–3 vote would be withdrawn if he would undertake to pursue a coordinated reduction in rates with Germany and Japan. Volcker acquiesced in this face-saving solution, and a press release announcing the Gang of Four's victory was killed in the nick of time by board public relations official Joseph Coyne.[11] Volcker immediately telephoned Poehl, who told him that the Bundesbank had just agreed to lower rates and that he needed only the formal approval of the German central bank council. Volcker then pressured the Japanese central bank to go along, and finally, on March 6 and 7, the three nations voted to lower their discount rates: Germany acted first, then Japan, and finally the United States. Later Angell told me: "Johnson and I, as new members of this board, we really put our careers on the line. And let me tell you, I thought very carefully about it, and I only did it because I was so convinced I was right."[12]

Reagan did not reappoint Volcker as Fed chairman when his term expired in mid-1987, but the disappointment of global financial markets was assuaged by his selection of Alan Greenspan for the job. Greenspan, former chairman of the Council of Economic Advisers under President Ford and an informal adviser to Reagan, quickly convinced markets that Volcker's essential conservatism was matched by his own. Besides, Republican Greenspan had one great advantage: he would have the kind of immediate access to the White House that Volcker never enjoyed.

THE COORDINATED INTEREST RATE reduction that the Gang of Four helped engineer did not initiate others. In April, the United States and Japan lowered interest rates one more notch—but Germany didn't join in. At a June meeting in Boston, sponsored by the American Bankers Association and attended by his central bank friend Karl Otto Poehl of the Bundesbank, Volcker suggested that Germany take the lead in another round of interest rate reductions. But that idea was sharply rebuffed by Poehl, who said: "We already have the lowest interest rates."[13]

In one forum after another, the controversy between Baker and the Germans over interest rates percolated for the entire year. By mid-1986, nine months after the Plaza Accord, the dollar had declined 30 percent against the yen, 22 percent against the German mark, and 15 percent against the average of ten major industrial nations' currencies. Measured against the peak touched by the dollar in

February 1985, the decline was 35 percent against the yen and mark, and 24 percent against the industrial nations' average.[14]

But while Baker's G-5 partners at the Plaza—and Volcker—began to think that the dollar had gone down enough, Baker followed a policy of trying to keep markets guessing. In June, a senior Treasury official said: "You may wake up tomorrow morning and find we are talking the dollar down again."[15]

On October 31, after a secret meeting between Baker and Finance Minister Kiichi Miyazawa in San Francisco on September 6, the United States and Japan announced an agreement to coordinate economic policies.[16] The intended message for Germany (and Europe) was clear: if they could not persuade their partners to go along, well then, the United States and Japan, the two biggest economic powers, could make bilateral deals as a G-2. It was a clever ploy, but it collapsed when the Japanese accused Baker of breaking their agreement to keep the dollar-yen rate at 160 to the dollar, the rate prevailing when they had met on September 6.

In early 1987, the dollar was plunging in a true free fall stimulated by Baker's desperate effort to trim the American trade deficit without succumbing to new protectionist trade legislation.

The underlying reality was that the system of international coordination highly touted after the seeming success of the Plaza Accord was fast rupturing. The Germans and Japanese refused to supply the kind of global stimulus Baker demanded, so Baker tried to get the job done by pushing the dollar down. An official at the German embassy in Washington grumbled: "The Americans are trying to solve a political problem—the threat of protectionism—by letting the dollar go."[17]

Volcker, who sublimated his reservations over the Plaza Accord's impact on the dollar, this time didn't try to hide his displeasure. A split between Baker and Volcker was thought by economic guru Henry Kaufman to be "a very serious, disturbing development. We seem to be showing a divided position on economic issues. That doesn't instill global confidence in our management."[18] Kaufman was making a subtle point, clear to the sophisticated financial markets but not so well understood in government: policy disagreements among top officials can quickly generate panic. And market players generally protect themselves by selling stocks and bonds. The pack response can produce sharp declines, even a collapse.

Baker didn't call off his talk-the-dollar-down campaign until he met with five of the other six finance ministers of the G-7 in Paris, February 21 and 22, 1987, in the Louvre Palace, the ornate and gilded main hall of the French Ministry of Finance on the famed rue de

Rivoli, before that ministry was moved across the river to a less handsome home on the left bank.[19]

The Louvre communiqué said that Japan and Germany would make an effort to stimulate their economies in an effort to relieve the huge U.S. trade deficit. In return, Baker pledged, along with the others, to intervene in the markets to stabilize rates "around current levels." Baker told me he was pleased by the headline on my *Washington Post* Monday morning story after the weekend meeting: "Finance Heads Agree to Stop Dollar's Fall—Leading Industrial Nations View Co-operation."[20] He didn't mention or acknowledge that, in less than two years, the major powers had reversed the deal they had struck at the Plaza Hotel: there, they had agreed to drive the dollar down. The trade deficit/surplus problem had not been settled by the sharp decline in the value of the dollar; the American budget deficit was still rising; and German as well as Japanese businessmen were grousing that the higher-valued mark and yen were costing them market shares abroad. So at the Louvre in early 1987 the powers pledged what each of the others wanted to hear in order to assure currency "stability": the United States would curb its budget deficit, Japan and Germany would boost their domestic expansion, and once again the cooperative process might earn respect from financial markets.

The Louvre accord didn't last long. Despite the pledges made in Paris, the dollar began to fall again, and markets were visibly shaken. The canny Akio Morita of Sony Corporation put it to me this way: "You [Americans] should worry about the dollar. It is not a good sign when it goes down so far—it means that everybody's investments in America are worth less than before."[21]

AS HIS EFFORTS TO BRING about international economic cooperation crumbled, Baker began to develop a special hostility toward his opposite number in Bonn, Finance Minister Gerhard Stoltenberg. Baker had been temporarily reassured when German economics minister Martin Bangemann told an OECD meeting in Paris in May 1987 that Germany would act to stimulate its economy if its economic growth rate fell below 2 percent in June.[22]

A palpable tension in global financial markets emerged during the fall of 1987. Despite pressure from Japan and Europe, the American budget deficit remained unchecked, was still out of control, and Baker continued to reject calls to liberalize his stiff-necked "case-by-case" approach to alleviating the debt crisis in the Third World. As the global economy stumbled along, hampered by a weakened American presence, the stock markets, which had been enjoying a huge speculative boom, began to throw off warning signals. Investors had been confused, among other things, by a startling suggestion Baker tossed out on October 1, during the IMF annual meeting—with no prior consultation among his fellow G-7 finance ministers—that gold, after being banned from the monetary system for decades, be brought back in as a vague disciplinary force.[23]

On Wednesday, October 14, the Dow Jones industrial average dropped a record ninety-five points. The next day, the index dropped another 57.61 points, in one of the heaviest trading volume days ever, as New York's Chemical Bank raised its prime lending rate. And about fifty of those fifty-seven points were lost in the final thirty minutes of trading, just two hours after Baker met with reporters at the White House, following a consultation with Reagan, to announce that the economy "looks fundamentally sound."[24]

The ironic parallel between such soothing words and those uttered by John D. Rockefeller as the market crashed in 1929—"My son and I are buying sound common stocks"—seemed lost on Baker. He pointed out that the ninety-five point drop on Wednesday was "only" 3.8 percent in percentage terms, and that the market remained at high levels. Baker conceded that "there are some question marks out there about the economy," but nothing "to warrant 'Apocalypse Now' worries or scenarios."[25] Baker was not alone in trying to sound optimistic: there were reassuring statements as well from Greenspan and Sprinkel. But while Baker was trying to reassure financial markets, he couldn't resist taking another dig at rising interest rates in Germany, which, he complained, did not conform to the spirit of recent international agreements.

In just a few days, Baker would be proved dead wrong, if an apocalypse can be measured by a 508-point crash of the stock market in one day. And although he would bitterly deny it, he was himself partially responsible by so clearly demonstrating that international amity was in a fragile state.

Baker had a right to be concerned by Germany's hard-nosed policy; indeed, Germany's partners in Europe were equally frustrated. But Baker kept up a public barrage, with no apparent result except to convince financial markets that the major powers couldn't handle a developing financial crisis.

On Friday, October 16, Baker leaked word that the United States "will not follow them [the Germans] into deflation" by boosting American interest rates. A high official, while denying that Baker was trying to force the dollar down, said when asked if the United States could tolerate a lower dollar "if the markets took it there," responded: "Yes, if the Germans don't stop squeezing their economic growth."[26] That day, the Dow Jones industrial index closed at 2,246.74, down more than 100 points—a blow so staggering that market expert Henry Kaufman predicted on *Meet the Press* on Sunday, October 18, that the market would recover, or at least, stabilize at the opening on Monday.[27]

But on Sunday, *The New York Times* carried a story quoting "senior Administration officials" as saying that the United States, fed up with German intransigence over the interest rate question, would allow the dollar to fall. The "senior Administration official" was the usual formulation for a Baker quote, supplied on background. On the same *Meet the Press* show on which Kaufman appeared, Baker would not respond directly to questions about the *Times* story. But he answered a question from panelist R. W. (Johnny) Apple of the *Times* this way:

> We have a Louvre agreement that we arrived at in Paris—that we agreed to in Paris—the seven major industrial nations of the world. We have had extraordinary exchange rate stability since then, something that many people didn't think was possible. That Louvre agreement is still operative. We would never change that policy without first making sure at least that we've notified and discussed it with our trading partners. But on the other hand, we will not sit back in this country and watch surplus countries jack up their interest rates and squeeze growth worldwide on the expectation that the United States somehow will follow by raising its interest rates. Now, that is all I have said. That is the totality of what I have said. Notwithstanding, if I may say so, some stories that attribute comments from unidentified senior Administration officials.[28]

Baker's assertion that "we will not sit back" while Germany raised interest rates spelled the death of the Louvre agreement and, with that, effective international cooperation. Most market analysts were convinced that Baker's performance on *Meet the Press* was a contributory factor to the depth of the October 1987 crash.

It was not Jim Baker's finest hour.

To be sure, no single factor can ever explain a break of 508 points on the Dow Jones industrial index. The crash on Black Monday in 1987 also represented investors' reactions to the huge run-up in stock prices to the point where dividend yields on stocks were, on the average, only a fraction of the return on bonds—a sure sign that stocks would turn down. But Baker's words indicated that the major powers, who clearly would have to act together to stem a financial crisis, might be too far apart.

★   ★   ★

MONDAY, OCTOBER 19, 1987, was Black Monday on Wall
Street, with wild gyrations never before recorded. On Friday, the
Dow Jones industrial index had closed at 2,246.74, down more than
100 points. On Monday, the collapse gained speed: the market
opened at 2046.74, down almost precisely 200 points. That afternoon
around two o'clock, with trading in many issues suspended because
the gap between the bid and offering prices was so huge, the Dow
Jones industrial average was off about 275 points from the Friday
close.[29] At the same time, Alan Greenspan boarded a commercial
flight in Washington for Dallas, where he was to address the American Bankers Association the next day. Deplaning in Dallas at five
P.M. East Coast time, Greenspan anxiously asked the Dallas Federal
Reserve officer who met him, "How did the market close?"

"Off five-oh-eight," was the response.

"Okay," Greenspan said, a smile breaking out on his face. Wanting, subconsciously, to hear good news, Greenspan for a moment
translated "five-oh-eight" to a loss of a mere 5.08 points—which
would have represented a spectacular recovery from the decline earlier in the day. Then he grasped the ugly truth: there was no decimal
point in "five-oh-eight."[30]

In the three days ending Monday, the Dow Jones index had plummeted almost 700 points, then rebounded almost 300 points from
the Monday lows on Tuesday and Wednesday, including a single-day
record 102-point gain on Tuesday. The stock exchange management
engaged in half-hearted efforts to limit computerized program trading, and in other ways to stem the ability of a handful of sophisticated investors and speculators to determine the course of stock
prices. As recently as January 8, 1986, a slide of thirty-nine points in
the Dow average had been enough to raise serious questions about
computerized program trading. But no safeguards were put in place:
on Black Monday, the index frequently lost or gained thirty-nine
points in thirty-nine minutes. Prices of some stocks moved twenty
points between successive trades—changes that normally take
weeks or months. "[It's] no longer a marketplace as we knew it. I
don't know what to call it. Is it a casino?" asked Wall Street financier
Felix Rohatyn.[31] After the crash, some controls were instituted by
the exchanges designed to brake precipitate gyrations.

While Greenspan was flying to Dallas on Black Monday, Baker
was en route to Stockholm for a long-planned session with Swedish
finance minister Kjell-Olof Feldt. Instead, as news of the market
plunge reached the Baker plane, Baker canceled the meeting with

Feldt and put into the airport at Frankfurt, Germany, where he met for three hours in a hastily arranged emergency session with Stoltenberg and German Bundesbank president Karl Otto Poehl. In a damage-control effort, the three men issued a joint statement, pledging cooperation to hold currencies stable "around current levels," while the German Bundesbank made a token cut in one interest rate. Then Baker flew back to Washington to try to repair or contain the damage.[32]

It was rather late in the game for Baker to try to rebuild confidence in the global "cooperation" process. In fact, the basic dispute between the United States on the one side, and Germany and Japan on the other, on how to manage the global economy was never to be resolved. Through the four Bush years and the first year of the Clinton administration, through Treasury secretaries Nicholas Brady Jr. and former Texas senator Lloyd Bentsen, American international economic policy would remain much the same: keep the pressure on Japan and Germany to accept more "responsibility" for global economic growth, even as America's influence continued to decline.

15

The Japanese Challenge

I N MY YEARS OF REPORTING on the economic scene in Washington and from foreign capitals, only Japan's enormous success story aroused persistent and intense emotions on the part of government officials and the American public alike. While "Japan-bashing" may have been popular, it was counterproductive; it lulled the American public into thinking that if only the Japanese would behave themselves, our economy would magically revive, and employment would boom once again. As former U.S. trade representative William E. Brock quipped: "My nightmare is that Japan does everything I ask it to do, then I wake up, and our deficit stays the same."[1] But even Representative Richard A. Gephardt (D.-Mo.)—the most strident critic of Japan in Congress—admitted during his fruitless effort to win the 1988 Democratic nomination for president that no more than 20 percent of the trade deficit with Japan could be attributed to their "unfair" trading practices.

I have written many columns and articles making these points, with the added note that Japan—and America—nonetheless must abandon any and all nontariff barriers to trade. One result is that I have been accosted on the streets of Washington by complete strangers who bark something nasty about my "approval of unemployment in America" so long as it benefits "your friends" in Japan. The success of the Japanese in marketing goods here had an odd effect on some Americans: they rushed to buy the Toyotas and Sonys because their performance and quality were high. At the same time, they linked Japanese success with American failure. And the connection they tended to make was not that we might have been doing something wrong—but that the Japanese must be taking unfair advantage. They failed to consider that, in the postwar period, Japan placed its bets on industrial and technological development, while America, especially under Presidents Jimmy Carter and Ronald Reagan, devoted too much of its financial and human resources to military competition with the Soviet Union. Today, it is little solace that we have won the cold war with the Soviet Union only to realize that we are losing on another front, against Japan, in terms of trade and markets.

The seeds for the great trade dispute with Japan that erupted in the 1970s and 1980s were sown in the aftermath of the Second World War, when General Douglas MacArthur established the official exchange rate for Japanese currency at 360 yen to the dollar, a deliberate undervaluation designed to give recovering Japanese exporters a leg up in world markets. In effect, the cheap yen policy was part of America's enlightened postwar generosity toward Japan, parallel to the much more highly publicized Marshall Plan for Europe's reconstruction. The American policy succeeded beyond anyone's imagination in helping to revive Japan and Europe—a credit to America that is much better understood and acknowledged in Europe and Japan than here at home. By the time John F. Kennedy campaigned for office in 1960, fifteen years after the world war, Europe's reconstruction was almost complete, and key nations on the Continent had entered a period of dynamic growth that caused an envious young president to demand that his economists find out for him what Europe's economic "secret" was.[2]

Japan, meanwhile, which had a rocky industrial start in the immediate postwar years selling products widely seen as cheap, shoddy, or unreliable, achieved its "economic miracle" in the 1960s, benefiting from the genius of economist Saburo Okita, director of the Economic Planning Agency. Okita helped create what Japanese politicians called the Income Doubling Plan, a strategy boldly anticipating that the island nation could double its national income or production in short periods of perhaps two to four years. The Japanese economic plan, focusing on a radically new management style, for decades would baffle and frustrate American and European competitors.[3]

For America, as historian Ezra F. Vogel suggested, the reality difficult to accept was that, sometime in the mid-1980s, Japan slipped ahead of the United States in numerous critical economic sectors, especially consumer electronics. And with great advances in applied high technology, Japan at least began to rival the United States as the world's dominant economic power. In his fine 1979 book *Japan as No. 1: Lessons for America*, Vogel suggested that it was in America's interest to acknowledge that the Japanese industrial success story could be attributed to "superior planning, organization, and effort," and to learn from "the Japanese example." When I discussed Vogel's book with Professor Masao Kunihiro, a Japanese scholar who was also a popular TV personality in Japan, he observed: "You [Americans] taught us that if we'd build a better mousetrap, the world would make a path to our door."4

This was a reality with which the American ego found it difficult to cope. "America is just not ready to accept Japan as a power equal to itself," a Japanese ambassador to Washington confided. In the tense atmosphere that dominated U.S.-Japanese relations at the beginning of the Clinton era, a public statement along such lines likely would result in the end of the Japanese diplomat's career. But Americans would do well to look realistically at Japan's growing global influence, and understand better the degree to which the two countries have become interdependent. Justin L. Bloom, whom I met in Tokyo in the early 1980s when he was the science expert at the American embassy, has warned that "the worst mistake" American politicians or business leaders can make "is to underestimate Japan's technical capacity and determination to succeed." The right strategy, Bloom suggested, is to give Japan credit for its achievements, and treat it with the same respect and absence of suspicion we accord our European allies.5

THIRTY YEARS AGO, *Fortune* ran an article entitled "Japan: Help Needed," because Japanese imports were far exceeding exports. But just three years later, in 1957, John C. Davenport wrote in the same magazine that "defeated in war, stripped of colonies, never rich in resources, Japan has emerged as the foremost industrial power in Asia."6 Soon Japanese products came to be regarded as highly reliable and of the best quality. Whereas Japanese manufacturers had earlier attempted to hide the "Made in Japan" label, it was now a mark of distinction. American companies, in fact, began to put their own labels on Japanese brands. When President Ford, matching Japanese custom, gave portable tape-recorders as gifts to Japanese officials on a trip to Tokyo in 1974, the Japanese found "Made in Japan" concealed beneath an American firm's trademark.7

From its slow start at the end of the war, Japanese companies established themselves as major exporters of textiles. They ventured into pearls, bicycles, canned fish, and sewing machines. In mid-1951, Japanese manufacturers held an eighteen-day trade fair in Seattle displaying 8,000 items, including cameras and binoculars that, according to *Business Week*, ranked as equal to American products.[8] Six years later, *Business Week* boosted its evaluation of Nikon and Canon cameras, which it said were just as good as the fabled Leicas or Hasselblads.[9] In the Kennedy-Johnson years, the growing American balance of payments deficit with Japan, still small in absolute numbers, became a divisive political issue. The surge into consumer electronics and automobiles in the 1970s and 1980s would make Japan a leading economic power, able to penetrate markets in North America, Europe, and elsewhere in Asia.

I first visited Japan in 1976 on a reporting assignment for *The Washington Post*, and have returned for one or two such tours almost every year since then, each time learning more of Japanese culture, habits, customs, and ambitions—and each time coming home reinforced in my belief that much of the palpable hostility among Americans toward Japan is rooted in the fact that relatively few Americans have taken the trouble to truly understand the Japanese. To be sure, much of the bitterness toward Japan stems from its deceitful attack on Pearl Harbor on December 7, 1941, and the wartime depiction of the Japanese as beasts or worse—strange little yellow people ready to commit hara-kiri for their emperor. Our image of Japan during the war and even in the postwar years was shaped by Hollywood as much as by any other force. Hollywood portrayed the Germans "as gentlemen with whom it was possible to deal as equals. . . . Japanese soldiers . . . were almost universally cruel and ruthless. Japanese were short, thin, and wore spectacles. They were tough but devoid of scruples. In almost every film showing American-Japanese battles, the enemies broke the rules of civilized warfare."[10]

To what extent Hollywood's concept of the Japanese warrior is based on the real world, and to what degree it represented, in part at least, a rationale for the unexpectedly difficult battle put up by an underrated enemy, is hard to determine. But much of the current bitterness over Japan's economic success surely is rooted in memories of the war.

One of the most important books ever written on Japan is *The Chrysanthemum and the Sword*, by cultural anthropologist Ruth Benedict—who was assigned by the Office of War Information in 1944 "to spell out what the Japanese were like." In the book that resulted from that assignment, Benedict cited the enormous contradictions in the enemy population that provided the basis for the book's title.[11] She noted that Japan lavished attention on art and the "cultivation of chrysanthemums," but also was devoted to the cult of the sword and the top prestige of the warrior." Both, Benedict found, were true sides of the typical Japanese, who was brave but timid; aggressive and unaggressive; militaristic and aesthetic; insolent and polite; rigid and adaptable; disciplined yet insubordinate. But in the postwar period, the harsher images conjured up by the sword are the ones that reappeared with regularity not only in the subsequent literature but in the perceptions of businessmen and officials who were required to deal with the Japanese government and its corporations.

For example, some high officials openly accused the Japanese not merely of dumping their products at below-cost prices but of stealing American patents. A U.S. senator—Republican John C. Danforth of Missouri—was so convinced that it was a waste of time to discuss trade issues with Japan that, beginning in the early 1980s, he refused to see Japanese cabinet officers who sought to pay courtesy calls. Malcolm Baldrige, secretary of commerce under Ronald Reagan, demanded not only that Japan amend its protectionist instincts but actually change its culture in areas where it grated on American sensitivities. And in an incident that stunned his hosts (as well as attending reporters), Donald Regan, Reagan's first secretary of the Treasury, angrily banged the lectern at the Tokyo Press Club, on one of his first official visits to Japan, demanding that the central bank stop propping up the Japanese yen, although he should have known the bank was doing no such thing. There were reasons to be disturbed about the persistent Japanese trade surpluses, but yen manipulation at that point wasn't one of them.

The issues were more complex, and on one of my first visits to Japan I had the good fortune to learn about them from John K. Emmerson, a gifted American foreign service officer whose experience in Japan dated back to the rise of militarism in the 1930s. He returned to Japan immediately after the war, and again during Japan's economic resurgence in the 1960s when he was the deputy chief of mission at the American embassy in Tokyo. After his retirement, Emmerson kept a summer home in Nikko, the mountain site about ninety miles north of Tokyo where shrines to Japan's first shoguns are maintained. I had the great privilege of spending a day with Emmerson at his home in Nikko in 1976. As an old "China hand" and then "Japan hand," Emmerson was an invaluable, balanced source on the history and genesis of the U.S.-Japanese relationship.

He understood that tensions between Japan and the United States were rising, that communication was far from perfect, and that "perception by each of the other's vital interests in a changed world is still not complete."[12] He also understood, as he would later write, that Japan "could not live without resources and markets and that China and Southeast Asia were the logical areas of opportunity. The Japanese discovered that a land war in China was a mistake (we also later found out about land wars in Asia), that colonialism was outmoded, and that sending armies and navies for resources and markets did not work."[13]

Communication and miscommunication play a significant and often ignored role in the troubled U.S.-Japan relationship. Emmerson told me during that conversation in Nikko that the dropping of the atomic bombs by the United States on Hiroshima and Nagasaki in 1945 might have been averted if the Joint Chiefs of Staff had the language capacity properly to understand the Japanese response to the American demand for surrender before the bombs were dropped. The Japanese were trying to surrender, in response to the American ultimatum, Emmerson was convinced, but, in the attempt to save face, had been deliberately vague. Thus the Japanese desire to end the war was misread by American intelligence officers.

The subtle shades of meaning in the Japanese language make it difficult for the *gaijin* (foreigner) to comprehend fully, no matter how extensively he or she has studied. For example, there are dozens of ways of interpreting *hai*—supposedly the word for "yes." But I discovered quickly that *hai* doesn't really mean "yes"—it is more like "I hear you" or "I acknowledge what you say." Herbert Passin, a Columbia University anthropologist and student of the Japanese language, believes that there are even greater differences between the English "no" and the Japanese *iie*, which conveys something much more emphatic than simple disagreement. The Japanese apparently feel that a sharp negative response is rude or hostile—and their hesitancy to offer a simple and direct no can be confusing. Yet, Passin contends, the Japanese can be more direct when they choose to be, despite traditional Japanese concepts of *wa* (harmony) and a decided preference for ambiguity. Western businessmen usually complain that they often don't know exactly where they stand in a negotiation. Passin cites the advice that one well-known consultant gives to his clients when they go to Tokyo: "Never take a smile for yes; never take yes for an answer."[14]

KNOWING A LITTLE JAPANESE can have interesting consequences. Chatting with my friend Tadashi Yamamoto, director of the Japanese Center for Cultural Exchange, I tried out a few words

and phrases I had added to my limited, tourist-oriented Japanese vocabulary. Yamamoto, educated at Marquette University in Milwaukee and a keen student of American government and politics,
responded: "Bart, I think you've gone about as far as you should go in
studying Japanese."

Had my pronunciation been so bad? I wondered.

"No," Yamamoto said, "but we Japanese believe that the more
you know of our language, the greater the searchlight you have into
our minds." This unintentionally revealing remark quite accurately
reflects a strong Japanese national feeling that the outsider, the *gaijin*, is a contaminating intruder. While Japanese officials routinely
complain that one reason for business and trade tensions is that
Americans make too little effort to understand their complicated
language, they are in fact not unhappy with the result. Tadashi
Yamamoto's message to me was that *gaijins* who speak Japanese flu-
ently become a threat to the established system.

Therefore, the Japanese make sure that no *gaijin* is allowed to get
too close.[15] It's only rarely that a *gaijin* is invited to a Japanese home;
nor are invitations to one's home casually extended to other Japanese outside one's immediate family. In fact, when this issue came
up in 1976 during a discussion with Dr. Shinichi Ichimura, then director of the Center for Southeast Asia Studies at Kyoto University,
I was surprised to hear that, while he had had foreign guests in his
home, he had never met the wife of his closest Japanese colleague at
the university over the prior twenty years.

On my visits to Japan, I have only barely begun to explore the
complexities of a culturally, racially, and linguistically unique population whose recorded history covers more than fifteen centuries.[16]
Nonetheless, I have learned enough to know that the average American is badly informed about Japan, and while American businessmen
and many analysts often protest that Japan is somehow "different,"
little effort has been made by Americans to understand the differences.

For one thing, modern-day Japan is still a hierarchical society, a
residue of a caste system that goes back many centuries. Americans
get a glimpse of the system through the custom of exchanging—with
the correct angle of bow—business calling cards, or "name cards,"
when being introduced to a Japanese for the first time. It is only by
this means that a Japanese can learn immediately where a new ac-
quaintance ranks in his own business, profession, or government service—and thus whether he should be deferential to you or you to
him. Sophisticated Western businessmen these days are careful to
carry their own "name cards," translated on one side into Japanese.

The hierarchical system has less attractive elements, including a lower status for women, who are supposed to walk several steps behind their husbands and who—until very recently—have been relegated to educational opportunities far below those available to men.

James C. Abegglen, who in the mid-1960s founded the Tokyo office of the investment advisory firm the Boston Consulting Group, observes that most Western efforts to explain Japan's extraordinary success revolve around either the "benign conspiracy" theory or the "sinister conspiracy" theory. According to the first, Japanese society holds advantages through its racial homogeneity and dedication to a hard work ethic that generates higher productivity than in the West. According to the second, there is collusion among the Japanese government and major companies to achieve global dominance, masterminded by the fabled and wicked Ministry of International Trade and Industry (MITI). In an insightful book, *Kaisha: The Japanese Corporation*, Abegglen and George Stalk Jr. contend that neither theory addresses the simple reality that it is the company, not the government or societies, that competes for markets.[17] Abegglen and Stalk convincingly demonstrate that the successful Japanese companies make their mark by following certain fundamentals, many of which can be adopted by American or European companies determined to do so.

This matches the conclusion of an impressive, lifetime body of work by the American management genius W. Edwards Deming Jr., whose advice was scorned by American companies in the 1950s. But Deming sold Japan on the concept that quality is not produced by an American-style inspection system that rejects faulty products but by a control system that gets it right the first time. Deming, a statistician on General MacArthur's staff in postwar Japan, first took his message to Japanese business leaders in July 1950. Deming was invited to lecture on the basics of quality control at an eight-day seminar for Japanese engineers, and in that series of lectures he convinced the Japanese that an emphasis on quality could make them a force in world markets. In recent years, some American companies were reeducated by Deming, who earned belated respect here. But what until recently was a novelty here is almost a religion there.

Another important milestone was a series of lectures by another American, Joseph M. Juran, in July 1954. In a recent article, Juran says that Japan would have achieved world quality leadership without his and Deming's lectures. But "we did provide them a jump start, without which the Japanese would have been put to more work, and the job might have taken longer, but they would still be ahead of the United States in the quality revolution."[18]

In Japan, Deming and Juran are national heroes, and only belatedly, in the 1980s, did they receive proper recognition in America.
Less than a year after Deming's first lectures in Japan, in June 1951,
the Deming Prize for outstanding achievement was instituted.[19]
More than thirty years later, an equivalent American prize, named
for the late Malcolm Baldrige, was begun to encourage higher American quality.

As Abegglen and Stalk see it, the successful Japanese company
has a bias for growth; a preoccupation with the action of its competitors; and a willingness to exploit in a ruthless way any competitive
advantage that will increase its market share. And the Japanese company chooses corporate, financial, and personnel policies consistent
with achieving those goals. A Japanese company often is willing to
export even if there is no profit, simply to establish itself in the market. The Japanese preoccupation with growth is pursued ruthlessly
in an effort to grind competitors down and out. For example, in the
late 1950s, seeking domestic supremacy, Honda boosted its production of motorcycles 50 percent higher than demand in order to force
Tohatsu, then the leading motorcycle manufacturer, out of business.
Eventually, not only Tohatsu but forty-five other Japanese motor-
bike manufacturers bit the dust.

Abegglen, one of the keenest foreign observers of Japan resident
in Tokyo, notes that the Japanese manufacturer doesn't sit on his
hands waiting for demand to develop, spurring output. The attitude
of the typical Japanese company is that the possibility of falling behind a competitor is a bigger danger than depressed profits: "They
say, 'Be better, not behind. And if not better, be different.' "[20] Akio
Morita, chairman of the highly successful Sony Corporation, told me
a story, perhaps apocryphal, that underscores Abegglen's point that
the Japanese don't wait for demand to generate. There was a European book publisher, Morita smiled, who acquired a valuable manu-
script and, after concluding he could sell 100 copies, produced only
ninety-nine. Wrong approach, said Morita: "We would keep printing
those books and sell as many as we could. The more we printed, the
cheaper the price would be, and with promotion and education, we
could create more demand, and put more books into the hands of
more and more people.[21]

The growth bias of the typical Japanese company is vividly illustrated in the field of consumer products, large and small. When the
domestic Japanese auto market appeared to reach a point of satura-
tion in 1979, Toyota's and Nissan's response was to double the rate
of new product introduction, boost distribution outlets by 15 percent, and add to advertising budgets. Rather than cut production

when demand falls off, Japanese companies cut prices, expand the variety of choices—and increase production, while keeping payrolls intact.

What should be troubling all of us is that, in our reaction to Japan's economic success, some of us betray a racial bias—perhaps a hangover from the war. Especially galling to those who perceive Japan as a threat is that quality has not always been a hallmark of Japanese production. Japan, the way America viewed that far-away nation in the mid-1960s, made cheap toys and cars that didn't run very well. America scoffed at the notion that it had anything to fear from the Japanese. Were they not a nation of copycats, dependent on America's genius for inventions and ideas? Skeptics smirked that if the Japanese dropped an American prototype on their way back to Tokyo, the resultant dent would show up in the Japanese copies.

Overconfident American businessmen and their opposite numbers in Europe didn't give credit to the Japanese genius for taking the best wherever they find it and improving on the idea or design— especially devising commercially profitable consumer applications. The classic case was the willingness of American firms (Ampex and RCA) and the Phillips company in Europe in the early 1960s to license their videocassette recorder (VCR) patents to Japan. The Western companies had only business or industrial uses in mind, but Akio Morita had the vision of making the bulky Western VCRs into a unit small enough for the home TV viewer, a goal that American companies had never imagined.[22] Later, in 1990, Morita and the Sony team would see the logic in buying Columbia Pictures to provide the inventory of movies for Sony's standard VCRs and a smaller 8-mm. version. The failure of American producers to understand the potential of the VCR stands not only as one of the monumental business/ industrial goofs of all time but also as a symbol of how American management relied on comforting stereotypes of Japan to convince themselves they had nothing to fear from competition from Japan.

Another example of Japanese managerial skills that earned them an advantage in the 1960s and 1970s is the development of ceramic engines and engine parts. In the mid-1960s, a British scientific journal published one of the first detailed articles on the exciting prospect that automotive engines could be made of lightweight, thermal-efficient ceramic material instead of metal, with about a 30 percent saving in fuel consumption. What's more, such an engine would almost never wear out.

No one in Britain or elsewhere in the West paid attention to this seemingly Buck Rogers notion. But the article came to the attention of Japanese companies and the Japanese government.[23] The potential for the industrial use of ceramics was one element leading to their commitment of $460 million to R&D on all "new function elements" over a ten-year period. Lionel H. Olmer, an undersecretary of commerce, brought the ceramic example to my attention in 1983 when he drove the world's first car with a ceramic engine on the grounds of the Kyocera Corporation. "It's an experimental model—but it works, that's the main point," Olmer said. Kyocera was already producing ceramic components for diesel engines. In a report to the Commerce Department, Olmer noted: "It is anticipated that ceramic parts—including turbine blades—will be usable in ships and aircraft, eventually." Any company in any country could have pursued the idea of a ceramic engine. But it was a Japanese company that pressed ahead, its emphasis on innovation and new ideas importantly backed by government encouragement and money.

At the beginning of the 1980s, it was only the rare American company, such as Apple Computer, that dared follow the Japanese example. When recession hit America in 1975–76, the semiconductor industry cut back its investment in new products, while the Japanese plunged relentlessly ahead. That enabled them to take the lead in new microchips, at least temporarily swamping the American and European markets—only to be accused of "dumping" below cost by Clyde V. Prestowitz Jr., who was counselor on Japanese affairs to Secretary of Commerce Malcolm Baldrige.

A DECADE AFTER trade problems with the Japanese had begun to surface in the Kennedy-Johnson years, Richard Nixon—against the advice of free-traders within his administration—decided it was politically expedient to protect the American textile industry from Japanese competition, touching off the first of a series of bitter and unproductive economic shootouts with Japan.[24]

To fight off what then began to be perceived as a dangerously undervalued yen, Nixon forced the Japanese currency to rise by devaluing the dollar, and for a time imposed a 10 percent import surcharge aimed primarily at Japan. As part of the wholesale realignment of currencies following the Smithsonian Agreement, the yen was revalued in 1971 to 308 to the dollar. Theoretically, an increase in the value of a nation's currency is supposed to make that nation's exports more costly in world markets, hence less competitive. At the same time, a revaluation—making a currency worth more in terms of some other nation's paper money—ought to make imports cheaper. For example, at 300 yen to the dollar, a 90,000-yen Japanese color TV set would cost an American wholesaler $300. But if the yen increased in value so that 225 were worth a dollar, then the same 90,000-yen TV would cost the American buyer $400. Presumably, since the Japanese TV would carry a higher price tag (in dollars), American distributors would look for cheaper alternatives and Japanese sales would fall off.

The reverse, it was expected, should work to make imports of American goods into Japan more attractive. At 300 yen to the dollar, a Japanese importer would need 90,000 yen to buy $300 worth of Johnnie Walker scotch. But at 225 yen to the dollar, the Japanese buyer would need only 67,500 yen to buy $300 worth of scotch. Or 90,000 of the higher-valued yen would buy $400 worth of scotch.

Thus the theory holds that the costlier yen would discourage sale of Japanese goods and encourage imports of American products. But there is a gap between theory and the real world: exchange rate changes don't affect trade patterns so precisely because there are other forces at work. Japanese exporters faced with an appreciating yen countered by boosting efficiency or accepting a lower profit margin—or both—in order to maintain market share—one of their basic goals, as detailed by analyst Abegglen.

A reduction of 25 percent in the yen price of a Japanese TV set to 67,500 would keep the cost to the American buyer stable, at $300, if the yen traded at 225 to the dollar. Having established a reputation for quality, the Japanese manufacturer might maintain most of his market share without such a drastic cut. A 20 percent cut, to 76,500 yen, for example, would equal a dollar price (at 225 to the dollar) of $340, or close to the original price.

Meanwhile, exporters who might benefit from a depreciating currency often raise their prices in an effort to boost profits instead of using the leverage provided by the cheaper exchange rate to boost their market shares.

Thus the lesson of the 1970s—and it was never learned well—was that there is no straight-line relationship between exchange rates and trade balances. What happened, in fact, after the Nixon-induced revaluation of the yen in 1971 was that the industrious Japanese companies, and also European ones, tightened their belts, cut their costs where possible—and continued to build up surpluses.

"I'm not concerned about the appreciation of the yen," Systems International, Inc., president T. Yoshitami Arai shrewdly observed in 1977. "Most Japanese companies doing export business can always increase their productivity. We don't have the problem that you do, and Europe does, where your labor unions are concerned with ideology. Here, their sole concern is to make the company successful."[25] He estimated in 1977 that it would take American exporters two to three years to break into the Japanese market, "sending their best, high-caliber executives, building inventories and service and distribution organizations. I don't think your firms are willing to make that kind of commitment."[26]

Examples of Japanese attention to quality, and a longtime American failure to understand either quality or the need to conform to the demands of the Japanese consumer, abound. Sony boss Morita noted that his company designed and packaged its products "to suit the tastes of the people of each [importing] country." But he told me of an American company selling kitchen appliances in Japan through the Sony Trading Company that for five years had refused to adapt its standard 110-volt motor to Japan's 100-volt system. Sony was compelled to attach its own transformers to the American appliances to make them salable.[27]

On a larger scale, the abysmal failure of the Big Three automobile companies to sell cars in Japan in the postwar era can be attributed as much to Detroit's failure to supply right-hand drive cars for Japan's British-style road system as to Japanese import barriers. The few cars sold in Japan were gas-guzzling monsters, unsuited for Japan's narrow roads, generally unsupported by an adequate dealer-servicing system. Thus, when a team of Buick engineers and managers visited a dealership in Tokyo in the late 1970s—one of the very few such outlets for American cars in Japan—they were astonished to find a huge repair facility. Asked how he had managed to build up such an apparently successful service business, the Japanese dealer explained to the embarrassed Buick team that they were looking not at a repair facility but at a reassembly plant, where poorly designed Buicks were torn down, then reassembled to Japanese standards.[28]

While Japanese consumers turned up their noses at Detroit's offerings, Americans stood in line for Japanese cars—even when the price advantage was with Detroit. At the start of the Reagan years, the American auto industry, strongly supported by the United Auto Workers, persuaded Japan to place "voluntary" quotas on car exports to give Detroit time to "catch up" with Japanese technological advances in the art of auto manufacturing. But the "voluntary" quotas on Japanese cars simply allowed the big Japanese companies such as Toyota and Nissan to raise their prices—which eager American consumers willingly paid, having determined by the trial-and-error method that Japanese cars were of superior quality and supported by more agreeable service departments than their American competitors were willing to provide.

In terms of efficiency, Japanese auto factories left Detroit behind in a cloud of dust. By skillful use of robots, along with the *kanbei* (just-in-time) coordination of parts delivery, they have achieved impressive results. Despite the traffic congestion on the fifty-mile corridor between Tokyo and Yokohama, for instance, suppliers in the capital magically delivered parts to Nissan's highly automated Zama assembly plant in Yokohama (closed in 1993 because of global overcapacity) on schedule literally minutes before they moved onto the lines.

In a classic case of failed strategy and judgment, most American auto companies, instead of taking advantage of the price disparity to recapture a lost share of market, used higher Japanese prices as an umbrella to raise their own prices. It was a lost opportunity, never regained during the 1980s.

American unions began to argue that, if the Japanese were going to sell so many cars in the American market, they should be required to build them here, thereby providing jobs for American workers. Fearing restrictive legislation if they failed to take the hint, the major Japanese companies invested huge sums in from-the-ground-up auto facilities—and soon were producing cars in America of quality equal to or better than those produced in Japan.

If there is a certain arrogance to Arai's comments implying a superior Japanese work ethic, there also is an underlying truth. The complexities of the Japanese system became clear when I visited a foreman who worked at the Zama plant in the course of my research for a series on Japanese unions, which are mostly company unions. I had managed to get Nissan's permission to interview the foreman at his home, a tidy residence (small by American standards), but packed with modern electronic appliances of all kinds. We talked, through an interpreter, about the role of his union in negotiating wages and working conditions. I had many questions dealing with his own role as foreman in representing his fellow employees. He answered them patiently, and then, smiling, offered a comment that I've never forgotten: "Mr. Rowen, I'm a member of the union, but I think you forget, I am also a member of the company."

That concept, according to which the Japanese worker identifies himself with the company, is one of the reasons for Japan's extraordinary success. Contrast it with the often-heard, frustrated refrain common among white- and blue-collar workers in America: "It's their company!" Although things are changing in today's Japanese culture, especially among younger men and women seeking greater creature comforts, there remains a strong commitment among Japanese workers to the success of the company, especially among male employees who have lifetime job security. Equally, there is a strong paternalistic feeling among top managers and owners, who equate the company with family.

Tasuku Asana, an economics professor who doubles as a Japanese network television commentator, suggests that the Japanese public "thinks it is being blamed for working very hard and doing very right." Many Japanese, sensitive to the wisecrack by former European trade negotiator Sir Roy Denman to the effect that they are a nation of "workaholics who live in rabbit hutches," snap back at the lazy European ethic that tolerates a virtual close-down of business around the three-hour, three-glass-of-wine lunch hour. "What's wrong with working harder and taking a shorter lunch?" asks Tadashi Yamamoto.

BY THE TIME JIMMY CARTER had taken office in 1977, trade tensions with Japan had broken out in full fury and Ambassador Mike Mansfield's frequently voiced admonition that the "United States-Japan relationship is the most important bilateral relationship in the world" was falling on deaf ears. The Japanese "economic miracle" was in full bloom: its exporting companies successfully marketed huge quantities of television sets, cars, and other manufactured goods here, while its importers bought mostly food and raw materials. Angrily, U.S. trade representative Robert Strauss's deputy, Alan W. Wolff, echoed a complaint that became familiar: "With respect to Japan, we're a developing country." The Japanese surplus in 1977 was about $8 billion, and would rise to $15 billion in 1978. Wolff went on to argue a theme that would be taken up by the American labor movement, and subsequently over the following decade and a half by Democratic politicians frustrated by Japan's success: "As Japan increases its market share in the United States . . . it is difficult to explain to unemployed workers in industries why it is that U.S. manufactured goods cannot be sold in substantial quantities in Japan."[29]

There is little doubt that part of the answer lies in a special Japanese brand of protectionism that blends an almost total defensive shield for Japanese farmers, especially for rice, beef, and citrus crops, with an internal old-boy network known as *keiretsu*, under which banks, manufacturers, and distributors either deal exclusively with or heavily favor suppliers and subcontractors within their own particular "family" of businesses. Total loyalty is expected: a teller working for a bank whose *keiretsu* includes the Asahi beer company is expected to drink Asahi beer, not the competitive Kirin beer. But at a more significant level, the *keiretsu*—a linear descendant of the prewar cartels known as *zaibatsu*,[30] theoretically dissolved during the MacArthur occupation—keep out newcomers, Japanese or foreign.

The *keiretsu* operates as effectively against an upstart Japanese company as it does against an American entrepreneur. According to legend, when Morita couldn't crack the Matsushita *keiretsu* that had a hammerlock on domestic sales of TVs and appliances, he had to seek help for Sony from the emperor himself, who cleared the way for Sony's and Morita's huge success. Morita merely smiled when asked whether this story was a convenient fiction or true. What is highly probable is that Morita brought pressure through one of the powerful Japanese political factions that controlled the ruling Liberal Democratic Party in Japan.

Morita, the first Japanese industrialist to open a major production facility in America—for consumer TV products, in San Diego—was convinced that a basic reason why more American manufacturers hadn't duplicated the success of Texas Instruments and IBM in Japan is that they hadn't been willing to put the same kind of money and sweat into it that he put into researching consumer preferences and setting up his own distribution system. The typical American company, Morita said, is too concerned with short-term profits, not the long-term success of the company. "In your country," Morita told me, "management always has to worry about profitability, and at the top—even at the very top—executives can be dismissed."[31]

In an earlier time, Japanese politicians were sensitive to the probability that their economic success abroad would bring them into conflict with the rest of the world, and especially with their patron, the United States. In the fall of 1976, Japanese government officials began to report as "good news" any hint that their growing surplus in exports of cars, color TVs, and other electronic equipment was beginning to slow down.

Michiya Matsukawa, a Japanese vice minister for finance, argued during that period that a "turning point" had been reached, meaning that Japan would have a trade surplus of only $6 billion to $7 billion for 1976, compared to $8 billion in 1975. Matsukawa fretted that Japanese color TV makers were making "unrealistic" inroads in the American market, and warned that it would be unhealthy if the American color TV market were wiped out in the same way that the American black-and-white TV market had been decimated by Asian competitors. "I tell [Japanese exporters] that trade must be balanced, and they must keep the larger relationship in mind."[32] Matsukawa proved to be wrong: the Japanese trade surplus continued to rise. Moreover, the penetration of the American color TV market increased to the point where American producers were all but wiped out, a result that had a dramatic effect in concentrating American hostility to Japan.

Former Treasury secretary John Connally, in his brief and unsuccessful bid for the Republican presidential nomination in 1980, developed a classic form of the Japan-bashing theme. "If the Japanese don't want our $5-a-pound beef, and if they don't want our [Rio Grande] Valley citrus," Connally said in one rabble-rousing speech, "then let 'em eat their mandarin oranges and keep their cars parked in their streets—because they're not going to send them here."[33]

This simplistic argument had a wide appeal: after all, Japan has made many promises to open markets and abandon its protectionist practices that it failed to keep, or kept only after persistent *gaiatsu*, or external pressure. The reality that it was not primarily unfair Japanese trade practices that created the huge American trade deficits did not counter the truth that all unfair trade practices are indefensible and a threat to global well-being. Moreover, as many Japanese critics complained—a notable example was the Maekawa Commission report in the mid-1980s—their country's huge trade surpluses, generating enormous national wealth, were built up at the expense of creature comforts and amenities by a government concentrating instead on benefits to and favors for industry. If the American bias was toward the consumer, the Japanese bias was toward business and industry.

Even as it rose toward the peaks of its economic might, Japan in the late 1970s and early 1980s was driven by a sense of global insecurity, rooted in its island nation status and a commitment that it needed to "export or die." Its leaders protested that, on a global scale, Japan was still weak. In 1979, at a breakfast hosted by Katharine Graham at her Georgetown residence, Japanese prime minister Masayoshi Ohira complained that Americans thought of Japan as a major power. "There are some differences in perception," he said, "and we don't necessarily feel we are a very strong economy." He conceded that Japan has a large gross national product, but said "the strength of a country should be measured not only in terms of flow, but in terms of stock." That was a backdoor admission that in terms of housing, parks, and other consumer amenities available in Europe and America, Japan was far behind.[34] In truth, of course, Ohira represented a rich country pleading poverty.

Ohira argued that Japan needed more time to adapt to pressures from the West to provide greater access to the Japanese market. Yet Japan pressed ahead into high-technology areas, offering generous subsidies to its companies that successfully penetrated the more open American market. As trade and defense expert Ellen L. Frost observed, "It is time for Japan to abandon a small-nation mentality, declare victory, and begin to enjoy some of the fruits of its success."[35]

In his book *Trading Places: How We Allowed Japan to Take the Lead*, which won a wide following, Clyde Prestowitz argued that "of all the Japanese advances into the U.S. market . . . none was so significant or had such later consequences as their conquest of the television industry."[36] Prestowitz contended that American TV manufacturers such as RCA, General Electric, and Zenith, which had a huge technological lead over the Japanese, made a tremendous blunder in licensing their patents to Japan. They were impelled to do this, he says, because the Japanese had blocked their access to the Japanese market, and licensing was the only way to get financial benefits. Moreover, Prestowitz charged, the U.S. government encouraged such licensing to keep "Japan in the Western camp, even if that meant making economic concessions."[37] The argument is frequently made, by Prestowitz and other critics of American policy toward Japan since the mid-1970s, that that policy has been driven by the State Department's determination to keep Japan within the American geopolitical orbit, even at the expense of American companies that suffered from unfair competition.

Prestowitz and Selig S. Harrison of the Carnegie Endowment suggested in a 1990 *Foreign Policy* article that inasmuch as the Soviet empire no longer exists as a threat to American security, the United States can respond to any worrisome Japanese trade actions on a case-by-case basis, not worrying about upsetting critical U.S.-Japanese security relationships in the Pacific. Harrison later added: "I think that the line we take [in the article] is the best way to sort things out so that the destructive type of Japan-bashing is redirected."[38]

Ultimately, according to the Prestowitz view, Japanese collusion, dumping, and outright fraud, combined with American government reluctance to protect its own companies and the marketing mistakes of those companies, resulted in total foreign dominance of the TV market here. This led to a flight of American producers to more favorable manufacturing environments in Taiwan and Mexico, and an unwillingness to take on the marketing of new electronic products, such as the VCR.

There is little doubt that the Japanese economy has relied on technology imported from America and Europe. But Prestowitz skips over a key element in a one-sided account of how the Japanese bested us in color TVs, VCRs, and other consumer products: Americans and Europeans were happy to license technology to Japan because, in their arrogant way, they considered Japan a nation of copiers, not innovators. The evidence is that Western producers missed the boat: the Japanese once again proved that, while Americans may be unsurpassed in technological innovation, they—the Japanese—have no superior in adapting that technology for its ultimate marketability.

In the period from 1951 to 1984, Jim Abegglen and George Stalk calculated in their book on the Japanese corporation, Japanese companies entered into 42,000 contracts for the importation of foreign technology, "representing the best of the technology available in the world, identified after thorough and painstaking study by teams of Japanese of the relative merits of competing technologies."[39] This was a brilliant move, at a very low cost—no more than $17 billion. It backfired on the foreign companies that sold these rights and licenses, content to rack up what they regarded as extra profits, and dubious that the Japanese could turn the knowledge into competitive—to say nothing of better—products. Increasingly, Abegglen told me, the Japanese companies—highly competitive among themselves—began to boost their own expenditures for research and development, again catching competitors in the West by surprise with what they could achieve.[40]

There are two general competitive approaches among the major Japanese companies. The huge Matsushita combine, for example, tends to allow its competitors to experiment with new products and new concepts. Once a competitor has put a successful new product on the market, Matsushita sweeps in with a state-of-the-art model backed by huge investment, designed to make itself the volume leader in two to three years.

In the other pattern, exemplified by Sony, a Japanese company tries to develop new products or variations of old ones. Thus once Matsushita's VHS recording system became preferred to Sony's technically superior Betamax, Sony gave up the Betamax VCRs, produced its own VHS machine, and moved on to high-quality components in audiovisual electronics and into niche markets like the Walkman and Watchman.

All Japanese companies fall into or somewhere between the two competitive philosophies—but they all respond in some way to a new initiative by a competitor. By way of contrast, managements in America and Europe move more carefully to meet the competition of other companies. Inaction is often rationalized on the excuse that the expenditures are too steep or prospects too chancy. The Japanese go all out, and the results are painfully apparent.

There can be little doubt that Japan protected its infant industries by throwing up barriers to competitors from abroad—and unfairly kept those barriers in place long after they should have been removed. But Americans who complained about "unfair trading practices" were wrong to assume that Japanese protection was the only source of its great economic success in the postwar era. Average real economic growth rates of 10.2 percent in the 1960s, 5.6 percent in the 1970s, and 4.0 percent in the 1980s[41] must be credited as well to a national work ethic to get it done right the first time. As W. Edwards Deming explained tirelessly over the years, Japanese work habits coupled with brilliant Japanese managerial systems gave Japanese manufactured products, from cars to computer chips, a qualitative edge over American and European products, helping to push Japan's per capita income in 1987 to $19,553—above America's $18,570 and West Germany's $18,373.[42]

Still vigorous, articulate, and lecturing almost to the moment of his death at age ninety-three in December 1993, Deming sadly noted the decline in the American economy since 1920, when through mass production it made fully half the manufactured products of the world. "Anything made in America was top quality. Anywhere in the world, if you knew the shopkeeper, he might reach under the counter and get an American product for you," he said.[43]

Deming's lesson, and how it was applied, was graphically explained to me in the 1980s by Kesike Yawata, general manager of the Nippon Electric Company, one of the giants in Japanese electronics: "The quality-control question is probably answered this way: the American quality-control philosophy is one of detection, and the Japanese philosophy is one of prevention. It's not a question of which system is right or wrong. Probably the American way fits the American tradition and culture better, and the Japanese way fits the Japanese environment better." Yawata was being polite: the Japanese quality control system was clearly better than America's—because its goal was to get it right the first time, a goal that forward-looking American firms began to set for themselves. The Ford Motor Company adopted the slogan "Quality Is Job One," and the competition grew intense for the Baldrige Prize.

Japanese companies and unions, in interviews I conducted in 1981, cited statistics indicating that the average Japanese worker had produced thirty-three cars in 1977 against twenty-six for the American autoworker in the same year. A productivity study in 1983 reported that by 1980 the Japanese output per worker had soared to fifty a year, while the American average had dropped to twenty-four.[44] Pushed by competition from Japanese quality products over the past ten to twenty years, American industry has improved considerably—but not enough. There is still a willingness among politicians, especially protectionist Democrats, to chalk up Japanese success to "unfair trade practices" rather than to new methods of production and management. Deming had little patience for such protectionist dogma. "Who do you think will be ahead five years from now?" Deming asked. "Knowledge crosses borders without visas," he said, "and there is no substitute for knowledge. What does [an American] school of business teach? They teach the present system, how to get jobs in it, how to perpetuate what we have. That's exactly what we don't want. The school of business ought to educate people for the future, the transformation—but how could they? That would require knowledge. And who has that knowledge?"[45]

Deming was not an optimist: he believed that American managers, who must take the basic responsibility for control of quality and boosting productivity, were too stubborn to make the necessary changes, a view parallel to one expressed by Richard Darman in 1986, when he was deputy secretary of the Treasury. Corporate executives, Darman said, had become "bloated, risk-averse, inefficient, and unimaginative," adding that their failures are largely responsible for the nation's inability to compete with Japan and other foreign producers. In two widely quoted speeches, roundly criticized by business executives, Darman charged that American business leaders had become part of a "corpocracy," unwilling to plan for America's future with the intensity evidenced by some of their competitors. "They showed . . . a general slowness of foot that left them, like Sonny Liston, sitting in a corner on a stool when the bell rang for the crucial rounds."[46]

16

The Threat of
Isolationism

IN AN EFFORT TO LOOK at longer-range solutions—patchwork efforts such as "voluntary quotas" on Japanese cars had done little to reduce the hefty Japanese trade surplus—the United States persuaded Japan in 1989 to undertake talks on the underlying patterns of behavior in each country that help generate Japanese surpluses and American deficits. These were awkwardly labeled the Structural Impediments Initiative (SII), and drifted along, with little success, for the balance of the Bush administration.

On the Japanese side, by way of example, structural impediments included the *keiretsu*, or "old boy" networks that kept business relationships within a tight inner circle; an old-fashioned distribution system that preserved "mom and pop" stores at the expense of supermarkets where Americans could better compete; and a deliberately slowed-down system of patent authorization that kept new ideas from abroad at a competitive arm's length.

American impediments to freer trade were officially defined to include an abysmally low savings rate; an extraordinarily high budget deficit that helped feed imports; and a weak educational system at grade and high school levels that was one factor in putting American companies at a competitive disadvantage with better-trained foreign workers.

Removing these impediments would require basic changes in both countries—changes that would be difficult to achieve even if both sides really wanted to. Breaking down the cultural *keiretsu* ties that had lasted for generations would be no easy task—for Japanese companies as well as American companies that happened to be outside the circle. And one doesn't have to live "inside the Beltway" to know that talking a budget deficit reduction game is easier than actually achieving it. Nonetheless, because negotiators for the Bush administration and the government of Prime Minister Toshiki Kaifu understood that much was at stake, some progress was made in 1991 when President Bush lifted the "unfair trading nation" status pinned on Japan the year before.

Yet unreconstructed American trade hawks such as Missouri's Senator John Danforth and Representative Richard Gephardt—Republican and Democrat, respectively—could not accept the slow-motion gains of the SII talks as a solution to the trade deficit problem. Both hammered President Bush and his trade representative, Carla A. Hills, for not hitting Japan harder. Gephardt, with newly won status as House majority leader, howled that the president was gutless: "At every juncture we have to drag the administration to its feet and prop it up." That was a shopworn line out of Gephardt's failed campaign for the Democratic presidential nomination in 1988. It shouldn't have fooled the 3,700 autoworkers in St. Louis whom Gephardt said faced layoffs because the administration "doesn't fight for them." Danforth made it a bipartisan pitch (at least in Missouri), saying he found the decision to lift the "unfair" label from Japan to be "deeply disappointing and a serious tactical mistake."[1]

Politicians such as Danforth and Gephardt don't really give a hoot about building a sensible national trade policy, but continue to bash Japan so as to pander to narrow constituencies at home. They pursue what some American trade negotiators dub the "black ship" approach, which holds that the right way to deal with Japan is to go in and bust open their markets at whatever the cost. If the Japanese don't knuckle under, then you retaliate—and hard. The Bush team took a more sophisticated, middle-of-the-road approach, not only rejecting the "black ship" philosophy but abandoning the softer tone of the "Chrysanthemum Club," which called for a hands-off policy in the hope that—given time—Japan would act less mercantilistic and more like America. Bush and Ambassador Hills used the tough bargaining weapons created by Danforth, Gephardt, and others in the Omnibus Trade and Competitiveness Act of 1988 to prod new agreements out of Japan, while establishing as their top priority the progress of negotiations to expand global trade rules under the General Agreement on Tariffs and Trade (GATT) that had begun in Uruguay in 1986 and were finally completed in 1993.

But skepticism over the SII approach was justified. It was always misleading to suggest that the way to cure the U.S. bilateral deficit with Japan was to force it to give up unfair trading practices. Even Gephardt had conceded during his failed presidential campaign that not more than 20 percent of the U.S. trade deficit with Japan was traceable to obstacles to free trade maintained by Japan; the much larger balance was caused by weaknesses in the American political and economic structure at home. The big trade deficit was made in America, not made in Japan. Yet Gephardt was unable to let go of his fixation with Japan. In 1989, he had proposed an amendment to the Omnibus Trade Act that would have required the president to undertake automatic retaliation against any major nation that racked up persistent trade surpluses with the United States.[2] Although Gephardt failed to put this overly restrictive amendment through, he did succeed in getting a lesser but still strong negotiating tool into the law that became known as Section "Super 301." This section, operative for a period of two years, gave the president the authority—to be used flexibly—to take retaliatory action against trading practices that he concluded were unfair.

Sanctions were ultimately taken against Japan and a few other nations, although Super 301 was condemned in Europe and Asia as an arrogant, unilateral approach designed to impose American economic values on the rest of the world. And although denounced, as well, as incompatible with the multilateral rules of GATT, Super 301 did in fact appear to open some markets that had been closed to American manufacturers. Super 301 helped American companies penetrate the Japanese market for cellular telephones, supercomputers, and semiconductors.[3]

Super 301 was also useful in generating access to the South Korean market, and those of a few other Third World nations, which, under pressure from Super 301, took "voluntary" steps to simplify their import restrictions rather than risk being stigmatized as "unfair" under Super 301. But rightful access to others' markets, and Japan's continued success in America—especially in the profitable auto market—were two different things. The continuing popularity of Japanese cars among American consumers frustrated Gephardt. In his home state, the declining American auto industry closed some plants, and unemployment among autoworkers was high. Gephardt decided that it was time to emulate Europe's effort to put a cap on Japanese penetration of its car market by trying to limit imports to a flat 1 million a year for an eight-year period.

To accomplish a similar "results oriented" target, Gephardt in the fall of 1991 proposed a new and tougher version of his failed 1989 amendment. "Gephardt II" would "put teeth in Super 301," he said, by insisting on precise reciprocity of treatment, and severely limiting the president's discretion on retaliation issues. If the president refused to act against Japan or any other country that enjoyed persistent, large trade surpluses in major industries such as autos, the president would be ordered to give Congress "a game plan, for action that includes clear, measurable milestones for success," Gephardt told a group of trade experts.[4] Such a "milestone" could be a specific number of foreign cars (American and others) that Japan would be required to buy. If the "quota" were not met, then under Gephardt's new proposal retaliation in the form of shutting off or penalizing Japanese sales here would be the result.

Gephardt's tough proposal triggered a spirited debate, mostly critical. Paula Stern, former chair of the International Trade Commission who had formed her own trade advisory company, the Stern Group, said: "When you get to retaliation, that means that negotiations have failed, and everybody loses."[5] The most telling criticism of the Gephardt approach came from Gary C. Hufbauer, an expert on international trade and a professor at Georgetown University. If the United States could establish its own rules to force access to Japan's market by retaliation, "is it right for Australia and New Zealand and others to retaliate against the United States to get access to our markets? We have a lot of closed markets, too." Gephardt had no direct response for Hufbauer, acknowledging only that the United States had some trade practices "that can be complained about." But our record was much better than others, he insisted.[6]

CONGRESS'S INSTINCTS TO "get tough" on trade were frustrated by the broad support given in the Reagan and Bush years to a laissez-faire approach, with occasional departures triggered by political realities. Thus, in 1985, as protectionist sentiment swelled in Congress—mostly against Japan—James Baker, chief of staff, traded jobs with Secretary of the Treasury Donald Regan and began a desperate search for a way to protect free trade. Baker was persuaded by his deputy secretary, Richard Darman, that since the lion's share of the trade deficit could be attributed to the overvalued dollar, a new policy should be formulated, dumping the do-nothing Reagan-Regan policy. With Darman at his elbow, and profiting from a tutorial on global economics from C. Fred Bergsten, former assistant secretary of the Treasury under Carter, Baker grasped the vital fact that an overvalued dollar—which Reagan and Regan mistakenly took as a sign of American vitality—was in fact strangling American exports and boosting the trade deficit. They would seek a pact with other major nations to push exchange rates closer to where they really belonged.

Baker and Darman understood in the spring of 1985 not only that some way had to be found to devalue the dollar, but also that America had to share global leadership with Japan and Europe.[7] Aided by the fact that the dollar had begun to edge downward from the peaks reached in January 1985, Baker secretly set in process the strategy that resulted in the Plaza Accord of September 22, 1985, when he and Federal Reserve Board chairman Paul A. Volcker met with the finance ministers and central bankers of West Germany, Japan, England, and France—the Group of Five—to depress the dollar and drive up the value of the other currencies.

The Japanese yen, which had been floating at a cheap rate, around 240 to the dollar, would rise in a spectacular way, so that as few as 200 would be worth a dollar within a few months. And for the first time, the European nations, in a coordinated way, agreed that their currencies had to be valued upward.

Less than a month after the announcement of the Accord, Baker testified that the dollar had dropped 7 percent against European currencies and 10 percent against the yen.[8] By Thanksgiving, the yen had broken below 200 to the dollar, and Mulford was saying that the "U.S. would welcome further orderly appreciation of nondollar currencies over time. . . . But we do not want to see any precipitate changes. That's important."[9] But by mid-December, the dollar was down 13 percent against the German mark and 16 percent against the yen.

As the other partners resisted further appreciation of their currencies—because it made their exports more expensive in global markets—Baker relentlessly pushed for more. There was more to do in coordinating policy among trading partners, Baker said in February 1986. "We must never again permit wild currency swings to cripple our farmers and other exporters."[10] Finally, on March 4, Baker reported that the dollar had come down 30 percent against the yen and deutsche mark since the meeting at the Plaza Hotel, and for the first time signaled that was enough: he didn't say that a further decline in the dollar was necessary.[11]

The next several months witnessed a continued fall of the dollar, and increasing worries expressed by Fed chairman Volcker that the dollar might slip into a "free fall" that would stir, among investors, a loss of confidence in the United States. Volcker acknowledged in remarks released April 2 that this fear had contributed to his objections, on February 24, to a cut in the discount rate, which he calculated would accelerate the rate of the dollar's decline in the exchange markets.¹² The next day, aware that Volcker's now-public worries would make markets nervous, Baker gave an interview to Reuters saying that his effort to talk the dollar down was coming to an end. But the intricate game of chess wasn't over.

On April 4, Baker called me to his office to announce: "We have no target for the dollar. The decline since the Plaza has been very orderly. It's been accomplished in a moderate and orderly way, and we're very pleased with it." The same day he told NBC that "There might well be a point beyond which we would not want to see the dollar go [down] further. But it serves no purpose for me to speculate about that or hypothesize about it. All that does is tip off the speculators. . . ." Baker, in these rare on-the-record remarks on the dollar, was trying to respond to Volcker's fears by suggesting that he was no longer trying to push the dollar down further; on the other hand, he didn't want to say "positively"—he wanted to keep the market guessing.

Jim Baker manipulated the press successfully in his and his administration's own interests by rarely talking to a reporter on the record. He didn't mind the use of a tape recorder, but the understanding was that only "a high official" or a "senior administration official" would be quoted. On his travels Baker adopted the Kissinger device of allowing quotes from a "senior official" aboard his plane. The thin disguise didn't fool many readers, but Baker, like Kissinger, could always deny he was accurately quoted if a question came up.

By the time of the May Tokyo economic summit, the dollar was at a low of 165 against the yen. Japanese officials, who had pledged to their business leaders that the slide would be halted at various post-Plaza stages—at 220 yen, then 200, then 180—were distraught. But Baker rejected all Japanese pleas to "stabilize" the yen until the end of May. Finally, on June 3, Baker abandoned further talk of a declining dollar, and said in a formal speech that stability of exchange relationships was now desirable.¹³

Subsequent meetings after the Plaza—broadened to the Group of Seven, which included Italy and Canada—attempted to manage currency relationships for the next several years, requiring a blending of fiscal and monetary policies and an unstated, but perceptible, yielding of national sovereignty. Yet Baker and Darman were realists: although the Group of Five's 1985 Plaza Accord, followed by a decision in 1986 at the Tokyo summit to move away from freely floating rates to a partially managed currency system, represented a basic rejection of the laissez-faire posture that American presidents had followed since 1973, they knew that no major nation would yield too much of its sovereignty on these matters. The progress, they would say repeatedly, could come only in limited, incremental steps.[14]

Baker's immediate goal for the Plaza Accord was to deflate the power of congressional protectionists. And in that he succeeded: as the dollar slid, as Baker stonily demanded "more," as protectionist legislation was shelved, Baker won worldwide plaudits as a masterful politician.

It wasn't unanimous. Martin Feldstein, a brilliant Republican economist who had been one of Reagan's Economic Council chairmen in the first term, got under Baker's skin by pointing out that the process of dollar devaluation had started through normal market activity in January 1985. Thus the Plaza Accord accelerated a trend already under way but was not responsible, alone, for any beneficial effects. Feldstein was right, but a bit harsh: without the Plaza Accord, the decline in the dollar would not have been dramatic enough to short-circuit protectionist legislation in 1985 and 1986.

Yet the Plaza Accord fell well short of Baker's other expectations. Indeed, although the Accord is cited by Republican historians as one of Baker's major achievements during his stewardship of the Treasury, it represented, in the long run, an enormous failure. By giving Japan an incentive to become more productive, the high yen actually made Japanese companies more efficient, and enabled the country to pile up huge cash reserves that allowed it to embark on an investment and acquisition policy that raised hackles in the United States. In the end, the appreciated yen did not serve its main purpose, which was to reduce the huge Japanese trade surplus with the United States, although defenders of exchange rate management such as Bergsten argued that the American balance of payments account, which had shown a surplus of $6.9 billion in 1982 and then had turned into a spectacular deficit of $122.3 billion in 1985, could have touched $300 billion without the Plaza Accord. Instead, after peaking at $160.2 billion in 1987, the deficit fell as low as $92.1 billion in 1990 before turning up again. Nonetheless, the global balance of payments deficit remained huge, albeit a smaller percentage of gross domestic product than it had been—and the deficit with Japan was a bigger part than ever of the total U.S. deficit. Despite the disappointments that later ensued, the Plaza Accord, and the subsequent agreements to establish target zones for exchange rates at the Tokyo summit and at the Louvre in the spring of 1987, represented a reversal of Reagan's "benign neglect" of the dollar in his first term and was welcomed by America's partners in Europe. Beyond that, as Yoichi Funabashi pointed out in his study of the Baker strategy, the other participants at the Plaza Hotel meeting joined in also "out of fear of the destructive efforts of protectionism and of recession caused by unsustainable imbalances."[15]

Baker is a fierce defender of the wisdom of the Plaza Accord, and the agreements that followed in the next few years. He said in an interview as he prepared to leave the Treasury to take over the Bush campaign in 1988: "Suppose we hadn't held the Plaza meeting. Can you imagine where we'd be today on the trade deficit?" Bergsten, an important influence in shaping Baker's and Darman's views in 1985, remains committed to the belief that exchange rate differentials are an important element in stabilizing trade accounts between nations. But he now admits that exchange rate manipulation is only one part of the equation. To the surprise of many of his colleagues, Bergsten came around to the need to accept the inevitability of a certain amount of managed trade regulations to force Japanese to cut its trade surplus.[16]

FROM THE PLAZA ACCORD through September 1990—a full five years—the dollar's foreign exchange value fell by 42.2 percent. MIT economist Paul R. Krugman concluded that by depressing the dollar by that amount, the Plaza Accord had worked effectively "to achieve substantial corrections" in the trade imbalances among the three powerhouse industrial nations.

Yet questions remain: If America's trade deficit had been trimmed back, how much credit should go to a cheaper dollar? And what about the disadvantages of a cheaper dollar?

At the time of the Plaza Accord, the U.S. merchandise trade deficit had crossed the $100 billion mark for the first time in 1984, at $112 billion, and was rising.[17] Most of the bulge in the deficit was attributed to a 44.7 percent rise in the dollar since 1980 that Ronald Reagan and Treasury Secretary Donald Regan applauded as good for America. Yet a clearly overvalued dollar was discouraging exports (it cost foreigners more dollars to buy American goods) and was sucking in imports like a huge vacuum cleaner.

Today, despite Krugman's accolade, the Plaza Accord looks less brilliant to many scholars. Even though the dollar weakened and the yen and German mark strengthened, the U.S. trade deficit, at $122.1 billion in 1985, rose for two years, hitting a peak of $159.5 billion in 1987, and only then started to decline. There was a similar pattern in the less-publicized but marginally more important current account deficit, which includes trade in services as well as merchandise.

High-profile events such as Sony's purchase of Columbia Pictures and the Mitsubishi investment in Rockefeller Center as well as major investments in American companies led to the well-publicized fear that Japan was buying up America. The case was made in a best-selling 1988 book by Susan and Martin Tolchin, which attempted to be even-handed, pointing out the positive job-creating side of Japanese investment in many states. But the theme was essentially negative. In an epilogue to the paperback edition of their book, the Tolchins summed up the anti-foreign-investment case this way: "The nation was selling off its assets faster than it was selling its products."[18]

The Tolchins' book captured the uneasy feelings among Americans about Japan's new ability, as a result of its new wealth, to acquire some of America's "crown jewels." But it has never been clear to me why the average American should feel more comfortable with the wealthy Rockefeller family drawing dividends from its ownership of the famed New York office complex than it would be with wealthy Japanese as the principal owners and the Rockefellers reduced to a minority share. But with widespread publicity given to each new Japanese acquisition in the 1980s, it was plain that while Americans could tolerate—indeed, not even notice—British, Dutch, Canadian, or French ownership of huge assets here, they drew the color line at the Japanese.

Until 1992, Britain owned more American investments than any other country, and the Netherlands ran a close second. In 1990, Britain held about 27 percent of foreign direct investment, against Japan's 21 percent.[19] But Japan caught up and passed Britain in 1992, according to a study by the Arthur Andersen accounting company, released December 15, 1993.[20] Japan's total direct investment in 1992 reached $96.7 billion of a $419.5 billion total, or a 23 percent share, against Britain's 22.6 percent share. But Andrew Kane of the Arthur Andersen company said that Britain may have yielded the lead only "temporarily," because Britain in 1993 was recovering from a recession while the Japanese economy was still in a decline.

Michael H. Armacost suggested that the Japanese contributed to American intolerance of their investments in the United States by inattention to local customs, failure to phase in American managers at top levels, and an obvious prejudice against American blacks as candidates for jobs in their factories here.

Yet the Tolchins' book, rated by *Business Week* as one of the ten best business books of 1988, played an important role in forming American public opinion on the "Japan problem." The Tolchins viewed the cumulative total of all foreign investment as a threat not only to the American economy but to American security. Their essential argument was that a growing dependence on foreign investment—with Japan fast gaining ground on the British, Canadians, and Dutch—would lead "to a loss of freedom as foreigners gain economic and political leverage over the lives of Americans." Just how that loss of freedom would take place was never documented. In the 1993 Arthur Andersen report, Kane minimized the influence of Japanese investments on the American economy, which he labeled deceptively small: "As of 1990, Japanese investors owned only about 2 percent of the net worth of U.S. companies (excluding financial institutions), and 2 percent of manufacturing assets, accounting for less than 0.4 percent of the U.S. [GDP]."[21]

Nonetheless, to the extent that anyone worried that foreigners would somehow gain leverage over the lives of Americans through their investments here, it became a concern that it would be the Japanese who exercised that power.

Much of the newly gained wealth of individual Japanese businessmen was poured into American real estate—in Hawaii and on the mainland. The story of one Genshiro Kawamoto, who in 1987 made headlines by cruising the streets of Honolulu in a custom-built white Rolls-Royce, spotting homes that he would later buy, illustrated the concern. By 1988, Kawamoto owned 160 properties, including the late industrialist Henry Kaiser's posh establishment, for which Kawamoto paid more than $40 million.[22] But by 1992 and 1993, as real estate values in America plunged, these excesses showed only that in many cases, it turned out that the American sellers, rather than the Japanese buyers, had made the better deals.

The problem does not reside in Japanese investment here. It lies, rather, in the barriers Japan puts up to American investment there. Cynthia Day Wallace of CSIS makes clear that there is something wrong in a relationship when Japanese investment in the United States in 1989, according to Commerce Data, hit $12.7 billion, against U.S. direct investment in Japan of only $170 million. That's a ratio of 71–1. The cumulative Japanese investment position— $66.1 billion—was about four times the American investment of $17 billion in Japan.[23]

Japan has "simply hung on too long to postwar protectionist practices that were expedient at the time but that have since been outgrown," Wallace says. Even if, as Japanese economists argue, Japanese investment has sharpened America's competitive edge, the time has come for Japan to drop all barriers to foreign investment.

By 1988, with the U.S. deficit stil higher than it was in 1985, the Plaza Accord's political magic had worn off. Baker could water down, but couldn't head off, an aggressive trade bill that year, the Omnibus Trade Act of 1988. In fact, Baker began to brag publicly that the Reagan administration was being tough on its trading partners.

Spurred by the higher yen, Japan became more efficient at home, and accumulated huge cash resources that led to what some called the big "fire sale"—high-profile physical acquisitions in the United States. Japan's global surplus in 1992 and 1993 moved well past $100 billion, of which half was with the United States. As a percentage of GDP, that was less than at the time of the Plaza Accord, but big enough to strengthen the "managed trade efforts" of a new Democratic administration intent on gaining "market access" to Japan.

As for Germany's shift from a surplus peaking at $58 billion in 1989 into deficits of $19.57 billion in 1991 and $25.56 billion in 1992,[24] this was due more to unification with East Germany than to a stronger deutsche mark, as Paul Krugman agrees.

Krugman's strongest argument is that, with a weaker dollar, the U.S. trade deficit declined from a peak of $160 billion in 1987 (3.5 percent of gross domestic product) to an annual rate of $42 billion (0.8 percent of GDP) in the first half of 1991. Since Krugman's study in 1990, the trade deficit has turned up again, to $96.14 billion in 1992, but at a comfortably low level of just 1 percent of GDP.[25] In terms of American policy goals, that, by any accounting, *is* an achievement for lower exchange rates. But that is just part of the story. William Cline of the Institute for International Economics has done studies that show that the Bush recession of 1990 also played a major role: as the economy weakened, consumers cut their spending on imported as well as domestically produced goods.

THE PERSISTENCE OF JAPAN'S trade surplus throughout the late 1980s, despite all efforts by the Reagan and Bush administrations to persuade Japan to change its ways—while holding back the sterner measures that Democratic politicians advocated—touched off bitter resentment in Japan. The Japanese instinct to defer to the United States was increasingly attacked by a new generation of Japanese politicians who yearned for greater independence from "Big Brother" America.

Japan's new aggressive noises reached a crescendo when a popular Japanese nationalist, Shintaro Ishihara, suggested in a taunting book written with Sony's Akio Morita, *The Japan That Can Say No: Why Japan Will Be First Among Equals,* that Japan could exert power by withholding its modern technology, especially sophisticated computer chips, from America—and, if necessary, blackmail America by offering its secrets to the Soviets. The book was first published in

Japan in 1989 but didn't attract attention here until a bootleg edition in English made the rounds in Washington.²⁶ It appeared as *The Japan That Can Say No: The New U.S.-Japan Relations Card,* mimeographed and distributed by the office of Representative Mel Levine (D.-Cal.), a vigorous critic of Japan. Morita's part of the book was largely a repetition of earlier speeches in which he said that America's trade and economic problems were its own fault, not Japan's. Embarrassed by the storm kicked up in this country by Ishihara's more trenchant language, Morita labeled Ishihara an extremist and refused to be part of the authorized English version published by Ishihara in 1991.

Ishihara's basic message was that Japan had become strong enough, through its superior technology, to drop its dependency on the United States. "We need Asia more than we need the United States," he wrote. He assailed Japanese prime minister Yasuhiro Nakasone for giving away Japanese technology: "All he got in return was Reagan's friendship. Nakasone bragged about being on a first-name basis with President Reagan, and the media played up the 'Ron-Yasu' connection. In fact, it was a one-way relationship. Nakasone was a yes-man to Reagan and betrayed our vital national interests."

Although Japanese officials and businessmen were quick to say privately that Ishihara was out of the mainstream of Japanese political thinking, none of them thought it wise to take him on publicly. Ishihara had touched a responsive chord among Japanese fed up with what they viewed as American arrogance. In the first national election after his book appeared, Ishihara was easily reelected to parliament.

The lesson to be learned from Ishihara is that America desperately needs to pay more attention to Japan—and to Asia. A narrow-minded focus on trade and commercial issues only strengthens a nascent militarist-nationalist instinct among the Japanese. Richard Halloran, a long-time on-the-scene observer, argues that, short of an American withdrawal from Asia coupled with aggressive moves by Japan's neighbors, "Japan will remain an economic giant and a military pygmy. . . ."²⁷ It's not likely that either an American withdrawal or an attack will take place. But short of such dire events, a continual drumbeat of denigration or bashing can only help embolden those Japanese who prefer the sword to the chrysanthemum.

In 1992, Morita further distanced himself from the crude arguments made by Ishihara with a dramatic proposal that took Japan by storm.²⁸ In an article in a Japanese monthly magazine, he said that Japanese companies should abandon "their single-minded pursuit of economic efficiency and success in the market." The production genius who made Sony a global household word contended in this article that Japanese companies must quit "invading" Europe and America, and instead give thought to the negative impact they were having in foreign markets. "Japanese companies should be aware that European and American tolerance of Japanese business practices is reaching its limit at the moment," Morita said. Morita's go-slow counsel—in effect, he would junk the aggressive, price-cutting, low-profit-margin strategy that had brought huge success to Japanese manufacturers—was not well received in a Japan that was facing an economic slowdown.

But Morita, sensing the rising anti-Japanese sentiment not only in America but in Europe and in the fast-developing nations in Southeast Asia, concluded that Japan must play more by the rules set in Europe and America. "By 'rules,' I mean an approach which gives greater priority to the freedom of each individual member of a company than to victory in the marketplace," he wrote. And Japan had to begin to attend to the needs of workers for more vacation time, and to the quality of life for consumers. There is little doubt that Japanese consumers, who feel that their living standards have been kept too low, were a key factor in the defeat of the Liberal Democratic Party in July 1993.

Morita had issued a warning that unless Japan's success was checked, even at the cost of giving up proven competitive techniques—in effect, letting competitors back in the game—America and Europe would take unilateral steps that would be even more oppressive.[29]

THROUGHOUT THE BUSH ADMINISTRATION, presidential free-trade rhetoric was adjusted to political circumstances. Despite a laissez-faire bloc dominated by Bush's first chief of staff, John Sununu, and Economic Council chairman Michael J. Boskin, Bush bent to business pressures for intervention on autos when he took his ill-fated trip to Tokyo early in 1992, and earlier when he agreed to set up Sematech, a tax-aided consortium of private American companies intended to generate technological gains in semiconductors as a way of fending off Japanese competition.

Where to draw the line in such ventures into industrial policy— the picking of "winners" and "losers"—is a perplexing issue. The effort to solve the problems of domestic companies involves risks. When Gephardt made his pitch for a beefed-up Super 301, a European Community official, Corrado Pirzio-Biroli, made the subtle point

that the United States could not retaliate against a foreign trade partner "without helping some domestic firms and hurting others." A
dramatic illustration of what Pirzio-Biroli had in mind came in 1991
when the U.S. International Trade Commission (ITC), responding to
pressure from American producers of the flat-panel displays used in
computer laptops, imposed duties on imported panels, agreeing with
the contention of the domestic makers that the imported panels
were being dumped below Japanese producer costs.

But an American industry of flat-panel producers was only a fan-
tasy industry: no American company had ever been able to churn out
defect-proof panels to match those produced by Sony and other foreign makers. The result was that laptop computer makers such as
Apple and IBM, instead of paying the newly imposed duties for imported panels, moved some of their assembly operations overseas.[30]
In time, the idiotic display-panel strategy was abandoned.

THE BOTTOM LINE IS that America is suffering from a bad case of
injured ego. It was a blow to the national psyche to learn that the
best-selling car in American in 1989 was the Honda Accord. Even
though the Honda Accord, made in Ohio, has more American material content and labor input than Japanese, it is a telling symbol of
Japan's success, a far cry from the days when General Motors' famous TV commercial could tout "baseball, hot dogs, apple pie, and
Chevrolet" as the quintessence of the American dream.

"Americans are shocked to learn that Japan, the good little ally
for which they felt condescending affection, is marching toward
worldwide hegemony regardless of American interests. Japanese are
equally shocked to learn that the United States, the big bumbling
ally they both admire and disdain, will no longer act invariably as
they wish," writes Robert Elegant.[31]

Critics such as James Fallows, a prominent American journalist,
in a widely-quoted series for *The Atlantic* said that Japan, (even for
its own good) ought to be "contained."[32]

The danger of such "loose talk," Bush's ambassador to Japan, Michael Armacost, said in a 1990 interview in the *Japan Times*, "is that
containment language evokes metaphors of resisting a geopolitical
adversary. It's the language of the cold war. It does not define the
problem. Japan is a challenge to the U.S. in the sense that you remind
us that the economic fundamentals count—that savings, investment, productivity, attentiveness to commercial application of technology count in the marketplace."[33]

By 1990, the balance began to change, and Japan—next to Canada, the United States' second-largest trading partner—bought more American manufactures than England, France, and Germany combined as Japan began to drop some of the trade barriers it had put in place to protect growing industries from American and European competition.

During the late 1980s and early 1990s, frustrations among American industrialists whose products still did not measure up to the Japanese led to a rising crescendo of America-firstism, culminating in what may have been the most disastrous foreign mission ever undertaken by an American president. In January 1992, George Bush led a delegation of American businessmen to pressure Japanese prime minister Kiichi Miyazawa and leading Japanese manufacturers to increase their purchases of American computers and auto parts.[34] Prominent on the presidential plane were the chairmen of General Motors and the Ford Motor Company. They were met in Tokyo by Chrysler's Lee Iacocca, one of America's leading Japan-bashers, who added the arrogant touch of flying over in his Chrysler jet. The ironic spectacle of America's Big Three auto executives—whose salaries and stock option privileges ran into the millions of dollars annually while their companies had to declare the biggest losses in history in 1991—trying to unload in Japan cars they had been unable to sell in America was not lost on perceptive citizens in the United States as well as in Japan. The Bush mission escalated bad feelings that threatened to explode beyond trade issues.[35]

The only plausible rationale for the ill-advised trip was the hope of White House political advisers that it might help Bush recover a few lost points in popularity polls. Had Bush really wanted to showcase America's productive skills, he could have surrounded himself with CEOs from America's resurgent high-technology industries, much admired in Japan. But he chose autos, because that's where the political pressure originated. His "trade mission," as the Japanese press derisively referred to it, was an utter disaster: here was an American president, until then professing a belief in free markets, who had become desperate enough about his reelection prospects to beg for a bailout from a major trading partner. He talked of achieving "jobs, jobs, jobs" by somehow getting Japan to buy more of America's products.[36] But the only logical outcome of his trade mission could be Japanese voluntary restraints on exports, which would result in higher prices for consumers. Despite his pitiful reach into the protectionist bag of tricks, the Japanese still preferred Bush to the potential devil they didn't know among the Democratic candidates, all of whom sounded—to one degree or another—like advocates of some form of managed trade.

In a fitting symbol of America's weakening position, televised around the world, Bush suddenly became ill at a state dinner held for him by Prime Minister Miyazawa and vomited into the lap of the diminutive Japanese leader, seated next to him. Yet, when he got back home, Bush made a joke of throwing up on the prime minister of Japan. Incredibly, there was even an allusion to it in Bush's State of the Union message a few weeks later.

The Bush visit was an equally embarrassing event for Miyazawa, under pressure at home because of the early signs of a receding domestic economy and a newly exploding financial scandal. Exasperated by what he considered the ultimate insult of converting a high-level diplomatic meeting into a trade mission with domestic American political overtones ahead of the 1992 presidential campaign, Miyazawa lashed back with bitter comments on the lack of a proper work ethic in the U.S. labor force. Miyazawa, a former finance minister with a good understanding of the American economy, told a budget committee in the Japanese Diet that Americans were losing their drive "to live by the sweat of their brow." Miyazawa had long felt, he said, that America was suffering because so many of its college graduates chose Wall Street over manufacturing careers. Yoshio Sakurauchi, speaker of the House, added fuel to the fire when he said that America had become "Japan's subcontractor," and that 30 percent of U.S. workers were illiterate.[37] These harsh words brought to mind Prime Minister Yasuhiro Nakasone's 1986 comment to members of his party in 1986 that America was being held back by the low educational level and limited intellectual achievements of blacks and other minorities in the American labor force. "Japan is now a highly educated and a fairly intelligent society, much more so than America, on the average. In America, there are quite a few black people, Puerto Ricans, and Mexicans. On the average it [the intelligence level] is still very low. . . . In America, even now, there are many black people who do not know their letters," he said. Michigan Democratic senator Donald Riegle retorted that Sakurauchi's attitude was much like the "view the Japanese held the day its warplanes struck Pearl Harbor. Their arrogance was gone by 1945."[38]

Miyazawa, whose political career in Japan suffered at times because he was considered by the average Japanese politician to be too friendly to America, hit a raw nerve because he was partially right. If he exaggerated the loss of the work ethic in America, he was correct that the quality of the American labor force had slipped: many American workers were now inadequately trained, and as W. Edwards Deming had said earlier, American product quality had gone downhill. The financial lures offered to bright college graduates by the better-paying financial institutions in a go-go decade had crimped the efficiency of the American manufacturing sector. The normally gracious Miyazawa would later apologize for his undiplomatic words.

The immediate result of Miyazawa's needling was a barrage of "Buy American" and other neoisolationist activities. Ultraconservative columnist Pat Buchanan, capitalizing on the opportunity presented by a declining economy and George Bush's failure to respond with some kind of recovery program, threw his hat into the ring for the Republican presidential nomination, demanding that the GOP "put America first." He called Bush a "globalist" who would place a vague concept of a new world order above the need to secure America's "wealth and power."[39] (Similar, if not so extreme, protectionist views were offered by hopefuls for the 1992 Democratic nomination.)

The hysteria generated by the America-firsters spilled over into the business world. Gephardt proposed a plan to cut Japanese car sales by 250,000 a year unless Japan slashed its overall trade surplus with the United States by 20 percent a year for the next five years. Such a draconian approach, of course, could cripple the $9 billion Japanese-owned car industry in the United States, responsible not only for creating upward of 100,000 American jobs but for forcing Detroit into the twentieth century of quality carmaking.[40]

In a burst of anti-Japanese sentiment, the town board of Greece, New York, a Rochester suburb, attracted nationwide attention by canceling a plan to buy a $40,000 hydraulic excavating machine with a Japanese nameplate, Komatsu. Instead, the town voted to spend an extra $15,000 for a similar machine from John Deere, an old-line American company.[41] Then the town elders learned to their embarrassment that the Komatsu machine was made in Illinois by Dresser Industries of Dallas, mostly of American parts, in a joint venture with Komatsu of Japan. But the John Deere machine—although it had an engine made in Ohio—was actually manufactured in Japan! The town wound up renting the Komatsu.[42]

The Monsanto Chemical Company of St. Louis, Missouri, took a different approach as the isolationist fervor burned. It offered each of its 12,000 workers up to $1,000 cash to buy, within six months, a new 1992 model car produced in America. The Monsanto "Buy American" initiative, known as the "Project Get Rolling" campaign, seemed a particularly insidious and coercive pressure: The worker who snubbed the company offer, and bought a foreign car, risked the displeasure of the people who paid his or her salary. At Monsanto, 3,167 workers, or 28 percent of the workforce, accepted the offer, buying $53 million worth of American cars.⁴³

It wasn't hard for the American public to figure out that no one would have to offer a bonus to buy an American car if it were just as good as a competing foreign product. Monsanto, if its goal was to pump up the American economy, would have done better to give each worker a $1,000 bonus and let him or her spend the money as he or she chose. The worst part of the "Buy American" delusion that spread over the country in the early part of 1992 was that if companies making subpar products were bailed out either by the "Buy American" route or artificial trade barriers to better products, they would have no incentive to become competitive.

There is little doubt that, under the pressure of Japanese competition, the Big Three have made spectacular improvements in the quality of their automobiles. Ford, in particular, is judged by independent experts to have made extraordinary strides. Still, in the early 1990s there was some catching up to do: after nine years of protection through the imposition of "voluntary" quotas on Japanese cars, Detroit had about matched European quality but not equaled the Japanese. Yet both American car producers and the unions have learned a good deal from the Japanese. The experiment at the NUMMI auto plant in Fremont, California—a former General Motors plant that had racked up the worst absenteeism record and produced cars of the worst-known quality—was judged by all a success.⁴⁴ Operated jointly by GM and Toyota, the plant opened after being shut down for two years, rehired the former UAW employees who had worked for GM, and, using the Japanese team concept, produced a successful car with two different nameplates—one for Toyota and one for GM. Some NUMMI employees told Donald Ephlin of the National Planning Association: "I am working harder than I used to, but I enjoy it more."⁴⁵ The General Motors separate experiment with its Saturn division, in Tennessee, also emphasized greater worker participation, relying on the team rather than the individual worker. It too was another groundbreaking experiment that seemed to be successful.⁴⁶

AMERICA CAN REGAIN its competitive edge only by reversing its field—by spending more money on investment than on consumption, as recommended by Bill Clinton during the 1992 election campaign.⁴⁷ Economists generally agree that it has been America's inability to save as much as do the Japanese and Germans that is dulling our competitive edge. For twenty years or more, the main problem with the U.S. economy has been that we underspent on investment—especially on human resources—and overspent on consumption.[48]

America's consumption binge over the last decade is detailed in a brilliant book by Juliet B. Schor, *The Overworked American*. She argues that Americans have been trapped in an "insidious cycle of work-and-spend," in order to generate the income they need for lavish consumption. "When the South Street Seaport Museum in New York City opened in the early 1980s as a combination museum-shopping center, its director explained the commercialization as a bow to reality: 'The fact is that shopping is the chief cultural activity in the United States.'"[49] Think about that and you get embarrassed—the highest form of cultural activity is at the shopping mall, not at schools, museums, the library, or the concert hall. Further, however impolitic Prime Minister Miyazawa may have been, the truth is that American labor has been losing out in the competition with workers in Europe and Japan not because of a poor work ethic but because it is not as well educated as it should be—and the situation threatens to get worse as more and more sophisticated technologies are introduced on the factory floor. The most dramatic increases in skills are required of the nation's nonsupervisory workers who actually make the products and deliver the services.

Anthony Carnevale, chief economist of the American Society for Training and Development, points out that 70 percent of the workforce that will be in American plants, offices, and showrooms in the year 2000 are already on the job, and will need retraining to work in an environment of high-performance systems utilizing high technologies.[50] Carnevale estimates that American industry spends $30 billion a year on training, which sounds like a lot but doesn't go all that far. Only one in thirteen American employees have ever benefitted from retraining by their employers. American autoworkers receive about one-third the training given to Japanese autoworkers. In the past, according to Carnevale, American companies competed for business on the basis of their productivity—the ability to mass produce goods or services at low prices. But in today's global economy, which takes advantage of new technologies, the test for success depends not only on price advantage but on the ability of companies and their workers to meet new standards of quality, customization, convenience, and timeliness.[51]

*   *   *

THERE IS A VIEW AMONG some industrial policy advocates, such
as Pat Choate, a writer who once worked for TRW, that bilateral-
ism—he calls it "tailored trade"—is the way and wave of the future.
Choate and others believe "free trade" on a multilateral basis to be
an anachronism, with the United States the last believer or practi-
tioner. "Free trade is a useful economic abstraction for teaching the
principles of economics, but it is destructive as national policy because it does not exist," he claims.[52] The tailored-trade advocates—
the newer buzzword is now "managed trade"—would apply
sanctions to those countries, notably Japan, not conforming to
American priorities, and accept regional trading blocs as the wave of
the future. Often, these views are referred to as part of "revisionist"
theory, popularized by Dutch journalist Karel van Wolferen, who
contends that Japan is not a responsible partner—indeed, that Japan
does not pursue a capitalist, free-market economy in the American
and European tradition.[53] Van Wolferen, Choate, Fallows, and their
revisionist followers, including numerous politicians, would set up
import targets that Japan would have to achieve—or else. The matter
for negotiation, according to Choate, "is the terms of reciprocal market access—the global tit-for-tat."

"Managed trade," "results-oriented trade," "reciprocal market
access"—all are euphemisms for protectionism, distinctions without a difference. "The Japan-bashing reflex of the revisionist school
of thought comes precariously close to the ostrich's way of coping
with danger, write Henrik and Michele Schmiegelow.[54]

The advent of the Clinton administration heralded the arrival to
positions of power of many committed managed trade advocates, including Clinton's Council of Economic Advisers chair, Laura D'Andrea Tyson. An expert on trade in high technology from the
University of California at Berkeley, Tyson is a symbol of those who
see the need for a more direct role for government to intervene on
behalf of American business—at least in some strategic areas. Her
appointment to head the CEA broke a long string of successive chairmen, Democrats as well as Republican, who were more committed
to free and open trade. Clinton's surprise appointment of Tyson
alarmed many who feared she would be in the vanguard of a new
protectionist wave.

But Tyson's arguments clearly appealed to Clinton, who met her
for the first time in September 1992 at a Little Rock meeting where,
it is agreed by other and better known participants, including Robert
R. Reich, a professor at the John F. Kennedy School of Government at
Harvard and original "friend of Bill" going back to days at Oxford,
that she delivered an outstanding and convincing briefing. Tyson

had written that between 1970 and 1989 Japan's share of global exports of science-based industries more than doubled, from 7 percent to 16 percent of the world total, while the U.S. share fell from 30 percent to 21 percent, and the European community's share fell from 47 percent to 38 percent.[55]

This erosion of America's high-technology base worried Tyson, who called for a "defensive" response, which would embody a "cautious activist" agenda for maintaining American competitiveness in a world where others do not hesitate to manipulate trade and "target" foreign markets.[56] Tyson's views were strongly supported within the Clinton administration by Secretary of Commerce Ron Brown, and Trade Representative Mickey Kantor.

Reich, now Clinton's secretary of labor, has a different perspective on the future of American industry. In a provocative book, *The Work of Nations,*[57] Reich pointed out that major manufacturers have begun to lose a distinctive national identity, a theme articulated earlier, in a slightly different way, by a Japanese expert, Kenichi Ohmae, a McKinsey & Company analyst.

"Who is us?"—that's the rhetorical question Reich propounds. His answer is that "us" is "the American workforce, the American people, but not particularly the American corporation. The implications of this new answer are clear: if we hope to revitalize the competitive performance of the United States economy, we must invest in people, not in nationally defined corporations."[58]

Ohmae is on the same track. He argued that "by being a global player, [today's international] corporations can make money in Japan, Europe, or the United States. . . . Corporations must serve their customers, not governments."[59] Reich and Ohmae have thus altered the terms of the debate on competitiveness. Much of the emotional concern about America's large global trade deficit and the foreign investment "invasion" is based on the assumption that trade red ink and foreign takeovers represent the loss of American jobs.

But the "Who Is Us?" concept suggests that is a flawed view: American jobs are wiped out not by competition from foreign producers but by American companies moving their facilities abroad in the search for cheap and nonunionized labor, while American jobs are created by foreign companies. To be sure, to benefit American competitiveness, the jobs created by foreign money must not be mere assembly jobs but jobs that add value to products made by American workers who gain new skills and training.

Indeed, the huge investments made in America in the decade of the 1980s by Japan—and by Canada, Germany, England, and others—have been of enormous benefit to the American economy, gen-

erating jobs and forcing domestic industry—such as the backward
auto companies—to upgrade their skills. Reich's thesis is that, in
seeking to build a more competitive America, ownership of corporations (to generate earnings for the nation's citizens) and financial
control of corporations (to assure that they will act in the best interests of the United States) are less important than assuring steady
gains in the competitiveness of American workers.

As to putting national interests ahead of shareholder interests,
Reich reminds us that, except in wartime, "American-owned companies are under no special obligation to serve national goals." To be
sure, Reich won't satisfy skeptics who believe that foreigners, especially Japan, keep their best and newest technology at home. And
indeed, as Todd Hixon and Ranch Kimball of the Boston Consulting
Group wrote in the *Harvard Business Review* in a companion piece
to the Reich article "Who Is Us?" that preceded his *The Work of
Nations*, if foreign investors come here only to win market share in
America and leave the best technology back home, they don't
sharpen our competitive edge.[60] Nor does America gain by opening
its doors to foreign corporations, such as Airbus Industries, which is
heavily subsidized by a number of European governments. Reich's
highly pragmatic point is that since American firms, like most mul-
tinationals, are set up for profit maximization and not for the development of the American workforce, our policy should be to
encourage any company, foreign or domestic, interested in building
capital in the United States. Instead, our distorted trade policy, channeled by the narrow-mindedness of the 1988 Omnibus Trade Act, is
focused on opening up foreign markets to American companies,
many of which are already well entrenched abroad.

The Clinton administration, putting aside Bush's laissez-faire
policies, initially floundered in establishing a new trade policy, then
accelerated the effort to open the Japanese market, establishing numerical quotas if necessary—an aggressive ploy that risked a break in
U.S.-Japanese relations.

This was an ill-advised strategy, an open invitation to a collison
with Japan at a strange time, and hardly in the United States' broader
and long-term interest: the U.S. economy was in recovery from the
Bush 1990–92 recession. Although the business upturn lagged below
the pace of other postwar recoveries—by some measures, by as much
as half—it was, nonetheless, an improvement evidenced by new efficiency among American companies, compared with their rivals in
Europe and Japan. In early 1994 both Europe and Japan were still
suffering from painful recessions, and it seemed inappropriate for the
Clinton administration to be arguing that selected American indus-

tries needed Washington's help to push their way into the Japanese market. It was a case that perhaps had more merit, say, for the automobile industry in its down years of the 1980s when it suffered, mostly because of its own mistakes, from competition with Toyota and Nissan. Nonetheless, the Clinton administration vigorously pursued a narrow, mercantilist objective to the point where Japanese prime minister Morihiro Hosokawa was forced to say "No," in an unprecedented, open break with the United States. That Clinton would have unyieldingly insisted on the "results oriented" approach risked a weakening of the overall bilateral relationship with Japan, crucial to peace in the Pacific. It ignored the possibility that the forty-five-year-old Japanese leader, who has already taken Japan part of the way along a path of major political and social change, would lose his hold on a fragile coalition government. But prodded by Democratic hardliners on Capitol Hill, whose support he needed for his domestic legislative program, Clinton passed up the window of opportunity presented by the favorable economic climate vis-à-vis Japan, and restored Super 301 by administrative order. He could have looked past sector-by-sector arguments with Japan to a better strategy: first, continuation of pressure on Hosokawa to stimulate the domestic economy in Japan, which would boost the standard of living for its citizens and—incidentally—generate demand for imported goods; and second, dilution of the obsession with Japan by attention to the challenges presented by the emerging markets elsewhere in Asia. This, in fact, was the strategy that had been recommended by Clinton's Secretary of Treasury Lloyd Bentsen. In the tense diplomatic situation as it existed early in 1994, the best hope was that cooler heads would prevail in both Tokyo and Washington.

Even if some truce emerges between the Clinton administration and Hosokawa (or any successor), the issue is symptomatic of an ugliness in some sectors of American society. Indeed, the bitterness of more than a few Americans toward Japan is reminiscent of McCarthyism—an effort by some, including well-known authors, to depict Japan as an implacable enemy of the United States with the collateral labeling of any who challenge them as unpatriotic.

The America-first theme, in any of its permutations, is self-defeating and counterproductive: if politicians hammer away at it persistently, they may convince the public that there is an easy fix to America's economic malaise. People will believe that all of our economic problems can be blamed on our trading partners, especially Japan, not us—that all we have to do is face down our partners, get a "level playing field," and not do the hard job of fixing what's wrong here at home.

Aftermath

THE REAGAN COUNTERREVOLUTION widened the gap in America between the rich and poor, a consequence understood at the time by just a handful of Democrats. Henry Reuss, a liberal from Wisconsin, was one of them, a lonely voice in the House of Representatives who pointed out that the combination of huge tax cuts at the top of the income scale and new, generous depreciation allowances for business, coupled with higher Social Security taxes and reductions in social programs, would further skew income distribution from the bottom 60 percent of taxpayers to the top 10 percent. In addition, the major increase in military budgets would attract investment in the booming, capital-intensive arms industries in the Sun Belt, while hard-hit blue-collar areas in the Midwest likely would suffer further.

Reaganomics put the New Deal and the Great Society in reverse gear. With George Bush's help, it stayed that way for twelve years, until Bill Clinton's budget and tax package forced a mild redistribution, with higher taxes on upper-income families and a larger "earned income credit" for wage earners under $27,000 a year.

Yet, on balance, the Clinton package was not, as *Time* magazine argued, a total reversal of Reaganomics: upper-bracket earners had enjoyed huge accumulations of wealth over the twelve-year reigns of Reagan and Bush. The Clinton budget of 1993, with a modestly more progressive tax system, was only a small step in redressing the balance.[1]

At the end of his two terms, Reagan left a weakened America to George Bush, who, choosing to ignore a deteriorating economy at home, had to pass the tin cup to America's allies to support the military operation in the Persian Gulf in 1991 against Saddam Hussein.

His own failed presidency having done little to resolve America's multiple problems, Bush bequeathed to Clinton the complex assignment of restoring some sense of fiscal balance by reducing the federal budget deficit, which required Clinton to opt for substantial increases in taxes across the board while reforming the health insurance system.

In the late 1980s, the international cooperation system as carefully crafted by Baker and Darman fell on hard times, and failed most of its key challenges. Until settled late in 1993, Europe and the United States for eight years indulged their special interests by allowing a trade war over agricultural products to frustrate creation of broader new rules and coverage under the General Agreement on Tariffs and Trade. The United States and Japan continued to scrap over trade imbalances that persisted despite the Plaza, Tokyo, and Louvre agreements to manage currency fluctuations; and Third World nations continued to be crushed by the burden of their international debt until the deflation during the Bush regime forced interest rates sharply lower.

The sheer magnitude of the deficit/debt problem that confronted Clinton as he took office far exceeded those that Carter bequeathed to Reagan. Moreover, businesses and consumers had also piled up huge debts in the 1980s that they, like the federal government, are now trying to work off.

In "the good old days," the Federal Reserve Board—which typically helped to bring on recessions by keeping interest rates too high (as it did once again in the latter days of the Bush administration until mid-1989)—could turn on the low-interest-rate switch and jumpstart the economy again. Now, it's not so simple: Not only are consumers and businessmen not anxious to take on new debt, they are worried by the country's and their own long-term future. Thus, from June 1989 through October 1993, the Federal Reserve Board took twenty-four easing steps that helped corporations and individuals reduce the interest rate burden.[2] But in terms of stimulating the economy, the old magic seemed to have lost some of its potency. Perversely, low interest rates caused a crimp in the living standards of the elderly and others who had invested their savings conservatively in Treasury bills and certificates of deposit, the interest yield on which in some cases dropped in 1993 to zero or less after taking account of inflation.

As 1994 got under way, a modest business recovery was taking place, sufficient to trigger a reversal of the Fed's easy-money policy. Clearly, the economy was creating more jobs—notably in the services sector—more quickly than the most optimistic Clinton aides had hoped, with a minimum impact on consumer price inflation. Responding to a higher yen that raised Japanese car prices—and to the improved quality of American cars—American buyers turned increasingly to Detroit's offerings. Thus, for at least a short horizon, the American economy under Bill Clinton was enjoying a comfort level that politicians in Europe and Japan could only envy.

Yet, the harsh reality is—and no one knows it better than Clinton—that the United States faces severe, longer-term problems. The president and Congress, even though committed to a steady reduction of the fiscal deficit, must improve the skills of the labor force. That will require greater expenditures by business as well as government.

Will the economy, despite improvement in 1994, be able to generate the kind of high-quality jobs needed in the new technological age? That remains an unanswered question.

A notable phenomenon of the late 1980s and early 1990s was the "downsizing" of the large corporation. Day by day, in monotonous and ominous echoes, companies such as International Business Machine, General Motors, Phillips, Sears, and others announced they would close plants, eliminate thousands of jobs—and more or less carry on production at the same pace.

From the business standpoint, it made sense; from the worker standpoint, it represented a sea change from the good old days, when even a high-school graduate could expect employment of sufficient duration to help him or her fulfill the American dream of raising a family, owning a car, and, over the years of a long-term mortgage, owning a home.

Restoration of such an American dream is extremely unlikely in the short run, and perhaps impossible for many years to come. The deficit remains a constant. Of all the self-inflicted wounds of the past three decades, none has been more harmful than the public debt saddled on the American people by the eight years of Reaganomics, accompanied by an actual decline in real wages.

There had been an actual decline in real weekly U.S. earnings from $315 in 1972 (in 1992 dollars) to a mere $255 in October 1992—a drop of almost 20 percent. As a result, many American families had to turn to more than one breadwinner. Yet, as Clinton Economic Council chair Laura Tyson pointed out, from 1978 through 1991 real median family income showed no change, despite the boost in hours worked.[3]

The right policy prescription is to focus on investment—not just on controlling the federal budget deficit, as important as that is. We need a fiscal thrust—the expenditure of more money in the public sector. That would include rehabilitation of the urban educational system, and a revision of teachers' pay commensurate with the responsibilities they have; revival of revenue sharing to take some of the burdens off state and local governments; and the transfer of large amounts of budget money now committed to defense programs to civilian programs, notably for "infrastructure"—roads, bridges, highways, and the like.

FOR THE NEXT DECADE OR TWO, the American people will be forced to live through a regimen of constrained national budgets. But the next decade or two is not forever. America remains the strongest economic power, but is more dependent on global well-being than it ever was before. America cannot operate, as Reagan in his first term supposed it could, with "benign neglect" of the impact of American policies on the prosperity of other nations. The growing interdependence of nations requires not only the development of a more cohesive, cooperative process than now exists through the combined management of the United Nations and the Group of Seven industrial powers, but in many cases coordinated action. A good example is the need to safeguard the environment as economic power becomes shared around the globe by Third World nations as well as the rich.[4]

One false notion which we must abandon is that America spends too much on foreign aid. We actually spend very little—$16 billion in 1991 for military and civilian aid combined, or 1-plus percent of the budget. The only other developed nation that spends less than we do on foreign aid is Austria. Some of this money, true enough, has accomplished little or fallen into corrupt hands. But in addition to financing the global umbrella that held off the Soviet Union until it collapsed of its own weight, American aid money has helped to wipe out smallpox, reduce infant mortality, advance the cause of women—especially in the distribution of birth control devices and information—and start the green revolution. In all of these areas, the only valid criticism is that we haven't been generous enough.

About half of what we call foreign aid goes to security-related needs in the Middle East and to several NATO countries. Sometimes, critics wrongly consider American shares in the IMF and World Bank as foreign aid, which it is not. It's one of our greatest bargains, as a matter of fact. U.S. investments in the IMF aren't even a budget drain, because we get an equivalent credit on the IMF books for every dollar of our deposits, or "quotas"; and as for the World Bank, for every dollar we've paid in over the last forty-five years, ten dollars have come back here in purchases and contracts for American companies.

THE "GOLDEN AGE" OF America's influence from the end of the Second World War to the beginning of the Vietnam War came about because America had the vision at the end of 1945 to see the need for reconstruction of free societies in Europe and Asia through the Marshall Plan and a special helping hand for Japan. Economic growth soared as we pursued free trade, stable prices, and limited government interference with markets.

Yale professor Paul Kennedy has set the tone for debate on America's future with his now-famous warning that America is falling victim to the same kind of "imperial overstretch" that, in other eras, reduced Spain and England to second-class powers.[5] In the last couple of years, Kennedy's thesis has gained support from those who see not only an American economic decline but an almost mirror-image rise of Japan. Some feel that Japan in many ways is already number one, that Pax Nipponica has been replacing Pax Americana, and that the only question is how much worse for the United States the situation is going to become.

This view is mistaken. American leadership has not been replaced by Japanese leadership, but by a wholly new global regime displacing the cold war in which leadership can be shared.[6] What Kennedy and the "declinist school" he symbolizes forget is that America's real strength is based on its political leadership. Even if America's share of world trade or global production is less than it used to be, the rest of the world still looks to the American president, not to the prime minister of Japan or the chancellor of Germany, to supply that ineffable quality of personal leadership it has come to expect only of the United States. The world wants America to take charge. In the Persian Gulf War, it got such leadership from George Bush when he unified the world's effort to foil Saddam Hussein's grab for oil in the Persian Gulf. But Bush failed miserably when, in effect, he boycotted the Rio summit on the environment, and sent lesser officials to represent the United States. We don't yet know how Bill Clinton will measure up to global demand for him to seize the global reins. But hopeful signs began to emerge at the Tokyo summit in the summer of 1993, and again in the positive role he played in bringing both NAFTA and the GATT trade treaties to successful conclusions, that Clinton understands the global economic issues better than did Bush, despite Bush's exaggerated reputation for skill in the management of foreign affairs.

The United States has repaired some of the weaknesses built up over the last twenty years. Corporate downsizing, however onerous to individuals seeking jobs, has made the American business machine lean and mean in the last decade of the twentieth century. But as a nation, we must spend less on gadgetry and invest more of our public and private resources in people, their health, and their education. American corporate leaders need to take the long-term view that in the '80s made their Japanese counterparts more successful, and concentrate less on short-term profits; in doing so, they will have to cut back on an obscene pattern of self-rewards—huge executive salaries, stock options, and other perks.

None of these reforms will alter the fact that America has suffered a relative decline in its share of global markets, as Japan and Germany, with enormous postwar help from the United States and a genius of their own in producing and marketing quality products, closed the gap. But Germany and Japan will also, inevitably, experience their own problems as others, aided by enormous technological advances that jump borders, catch up. Germany has already felt the unexpected costs of unification with the former East Germany; in 1992–93 Japan experienced its worst recession since the end of the Second World War.

Europe's dream of transforming itself into a single market with a single currency and central bank was shattered by the end of the cold war, which forced the Germans to concentrate instead on their domestic agenda. The Persian Gulf War then exposed Europe's disunity on military/foreign policy. The struggling economies of Cyprus, Malta, Turkey, Poland, and Hungary were not accepted into the twelve-member European Union (successor to the European Community), but Austria, Finland, Sweden, and Norway will join this year, subject to national referenda, reinforcing the divide between Europe's rich and poor.

It becomes increasingly clear that if the nineteenth century, by and large, belonged to the British Empire, and most of the twentieth was dominated by the United States, the twenty-first will be the century for Asia, with perhaps China in the ascendancy. Over the past twenty-five years, according to a recent study by the World Bank, Asia has led the world with spectacular growth. Eight nations— Japan, South Korea, Taiwan, Singapore, Hong Kong, Indonesia, Malaysia, and Thailand—all poor before 1965, have since averaged per capita economic growth just a shade under 6 percent.⁷ The export performance of the eight has been spectacular: their share of the global manufactures' market zoomed from only 9 percent in 1965 to 21 percent in 1990.

Asia presents a challenge to the rest of the world. Its people's talent for analyzing Western consumer markets, and then penetrating them with quality goods, was by and large ignored during the Reagan and Bush years. In a speech at Waseda University in conjunction with the July 1993 economic summit in Tokyo, President Clinton became the first American president to recognize the economic challenge from Asia, and to pledge that he would take it on. Throughout the Reagan and Bush years, America remained wedded to the idea that Europe was "our first overseas interest, with a revitalization of the Americas a close second."⁸ Clinton's Waseda University speech went part of the way to reverse that idée fixe.

Many Americans have had great difficulty accepting the rising economic and military power of other nations, some of which now have nuclear capability, including—in Asia—China and Russia. The ability of Third World nations to produce goods of all kinds at a labor cost a fraction of that in the richer nations has weakened American and European dominance in major manufactured goods, especially in heavy industries such as steel and autos. It will be painful to adjust, but adjust we must: the United States ultimately must abandon labor-intensive industries such as textiles. Europe cannot keep all of its outmoded steel industries. Gracefully, the richer nations must pass on these industries to the less-developed countries, and concentrate on the high-tech industries where they maintain a lead. But in wiping out the jobs of textile workers in America and steelworkers in Europe and others in similar situations, a caring society must preserve the well-being and dignity of those workers. The price may be high, but it's cheaper than the larger costs of preserving such jobs by protectionist tactics.

AN AMERICAN SOCIETY brought up, over the last two decades, to cultivate greed has consumed more than it produced, and borrowed the savings of the rest of the world to pay for its profligate tastes. We have allowed our business and corporate leaders to shuffle paper in the junk bond market instead of grinding away at the dull job of producing goods that other businesses and consumers want to buy. These are serious weaknesses in the American economy and in the American ethos. But if we acknowledge and deal with them, this country will remain the world's leading power because of its unique military, political, and economic potential. American productivity, per capita consumption, and overall wealth still lead the world.

The biggest test for America, as we look back at the long history of self-inflicted wounds and mistakes, is to make sure that they are not repeated. The history of these thirty years is that the same blunders have been made over and over again, from LBJ's refusal to finance war costs with higher taxes, to Nixon's attempts to shift blame for trade deficits onto our trading partners, to Reagan's pursuit of that special combination of voodoo economics positing that lower taxes would increase federal revenues.

As the twentieth century winds down, and we move hesitantly into the twenty-first, our goal should be to share global power with a stronger Japan and Germany, instead of concluding that our interests are so fundamentally opposed that we must collide. With the cold war over, the trend during the 1980s toward the physical integration of the major Western economies is bound to continue, and ultimately that will have to include the former Soviet and Warsaw bloc states as well. Lifting the standard of living the world over would not be a bad outcome: communications, technology, nuclear power, and—more recently—the punctured ozone layer, have combined to make "one world" not a dreamer's slogan but a pragmatic necessity.

Notes

BLUNDER

CHAPTER 1: *Guns and Butter*

1. Therein lies a useful rule for journalists: almost no government official, even while labeling a conversation "off-the-record," expects to see absolutely nothing in print: if he or she did, nothing would be said. The expectation, indeed the plan, is that something will show up in the newspapers, with varying degrees of attribution to "sources" or to otherwise unidentified "officials." But their message gets across. And if reactions turn out to be unfavorable, deniability is readily at hand.

2. Moynihan speech to the Securities Industry Association, The Homestead, Hot Springs, Virginia, May 3, 1982.

3. Kennedy quote, relayed to me by a personal friend of the president.

4. Hobart Rowen, "McNamara Emerges as Economic Czar," *Washington Post*, Nov. 21, 1965.

5. From pages 188–89 of the 1962 Economic Report: "The general guide for noninflationary wage behavior is that the rate of increase in wage rates (including fringe benefits) in each industry be equal to the trend rate of over-all productivity increase. General acceptance of this guide would maintain stability of labor cost per unit of output for the economy as a whole—though not of course for individual industries.

"The general guide for noninflationary price behavior calls for price reduction if the industry's rate of productivity increase exceeds the over-all rate—for this would mean declining unit labor costs; it calls for an appropriate increase in price if the opposite relationship prevails; and it calls for stable prices if the two rates of productivity increase are equal."

6. Rowen, "McNamara Emerges as Economic Czar."

7. Hobart Rowen, "Cost of Vietnam a McNamara Secret," *Washington Post*, June 19, 1966. I attributed this quote then only to a "top" LBJ economist.

8. Hobart Rowen, "LBJ's Economic Aides Were Misled," *Washington Post*, June 23, 1971.

9. Lloyd Norman was diligent, but not flashy; authoritative, but never given to hype, and unappreciated by *Newsweek*. They don't make dedicated reporters like him anymore.

10. Hobart Rowen, "Consider the Cost of Vietnam," *Washington Post*, Nov. 28, 1965.

11. Tom Wicker, "Hey, Hey, LBJ. . . ." *Esquire*, December 1983. Wicker, then covering LBJ for *The New York Times*, heard this chant for the first time late in 1965 or early 1966 on a Johnson trip to New York.

12. Johnson's commitment to the poor and to combating poverty is heatedly debated among his biographers. His later pro-civil rights and antipoverty legislation are an undisputed testament to his real accomplishment. His aide Joseph Califano said: "He thought of the War on Poverty as an extension of the New Deal as helping people get in positions where they could be on their own and where they could pull off their own share of the economic pie" (Merle Miller, *Lyndon: An Oral Biography* [New York: Ballantine Books, 1980], p. 467). On the other hand, writer James Reston Jr. says that as Johnson began as a freshman congressman in 1939, he "was a kid on the make. . . . At this stage of Johnson's career, he possessed no passion toward the poor, the weak, or the colored" (James Reston Jr., *The Lone Star: The Life of John Connally* [New York: Harper & Row, 1989], p. 38).

13. Weidenbaum's doctoral thesis had explained how federal outlays for the Korean War had triggered inflation. As huge government procurement orders pour into the manufacturing system, the first economic impact occurs before the government actually writes a check: in response to orders, production of parts and subassemblies accelerates. That taps the available supplies of raw materials, and labor, as well as financial resources. All such activity shows up first in business inventories, not as actual government spending until the work is completed, before the Treasury actually writes checks to pay for the goods, as delivered. In short, the inflationary effects of the Vietnam buildup had already taken place, even if they were not fully evident in government spending figures. Weidenbaum summarized his theses in *The Wall Street Journal*, Feb. 21, 1966, p. 1.

14. Hobart Rowen, "No Tax Rise—Yet, Administration Says," *Washington Post*, May 6, 1966. Schweitzer was to speak his mind again, even more vigorously, when he called on the Nixon administration to devalue the dollar, earning him the enmity of Treasury Secretary John B. Connally and Undersecretary for Monetary Affairs Paul A. Volcker. See chapters 4 and 5.

15. Neil Sheehan, *A Bright Shining Lie* (New York: Random House, 1988), pp. 536, 579–580.

16. Hobart Rowen, "Vietnam War Supplemental to Force Major Decisions," *Washington Post*, July 24, 1966, and "Vietnam and Tight Money Are Bogeys in Persistent Stock Market Decline," *Washington Post*, July 31, 1966.

17. Hobart Rowen, "High Rates Fail to Dampen Boom," *Washington Post*, Aug. 28, 1966.

18. Schultze defended the budget as showing that the administration was prepared to shift away from economic stimulus toward restraint if conditions in the economy so dictated. But he didn't pretend that the fiscal 1967 budget as it stood was anything but expansionary. See Rowen, "Debate Rages on Inflation Threat," *Washington Post*, Feb. 13, 1966.

19. Former secretary of labor Goldberg, the unions' great bridge to Kennedy, had been yanked off the Supreme Court by Johnson, and dispatched to the United Nations to make room on the bench for Johnson's pal, Abe Fortas. Johnson soft-soaped Goldberg into believing that he could be instrumental in bringing peace to Vietnam. It was a decision Goldberg regretted to the end of his life.

20. Annual meeting of the American Society of Business Editors and Writers, May 9, 1966.

21. James Tobin, "Check the Boom?" *New Republic,* Sept. 3, 1966, pp. 9–14.

22. Hobart Rowen, "Economic Impact . . . ," *Washington Post,* Oct. 9, 1966.

23. Hobart Rowen, "LBJ Gives Up on Steel Hike," *Washington Post,* Aug. 5, 1966. Later, just before the 1968 election, Okun was to write Califano: "We leave behind . . . the unsolved riddle of coupling prosperity with price stability. This will be the biggest overall challenge facing the next administration."

24. Rowen, "LBJ Gives Up on Steel Hike."

25. Okun interview, 1966.

26. He made no public announcement, but Ross, a complex man who later took his own life, made that clear to me in personal conversations.

27. The Economic Report of the President, 1972, p. 195. These are figures for nominal (not price-adjusted) GNP. There was a rapid further increase in GNP (real and nominal, except the real GNP in 1970) each year as the war drained more resources, with the $1 trillion nominal mark passed for the first time in 1971.

28. Weinberg interview, Nov. 23, 1966.

29. Hobart Rowen, "Mills' Message to LBJ: Less Butter Without Guns," *Washington Post,* Sept. 17, 1967.

30. Clark Clifford with Richard Holbrooke, "Serving the President: The Vietnam Years—II," *New Yorker,* May 13, 1991.

31. *Ibid.,* p. 68.

CHAPTER 2 : *The Retreat from Gold*

1. The origins of the Bretton Woods conference have been detailed best by one of its surviving participants, economist Edward M. Bernstein, a former Treasury and IMF official who has written and lectured extensively on the history of the period. It began with German wartime propaganda on the new economic order that Hitler would oversee. John Maynard Keynes, the famous British economist, had been asked by the British Ministry of Information late in 1940 to prepare a plan for a postwar monetary system to counter the Germans' propaganda. Keynes went to work, and by August 1942 completed what came to be known as the Keynes Proposals for an International Clearing Union. Concurrently, under the direction of Treasury official Harry Dexter White, the U.S. Treasury worked out a plan for an International Stabilization Fund and an International Bank for Reconstruction and Development. The British and American initiatives were blended together at the Bretton Woods conference, called by President Roosevelt. See Bernstein's paper, "Keynes and U.S. Foreign Economic Policy," American Economic Association annual meetings, New Orleans, Dec. 28, 1986. Bernstein had been part of the Treasury team at Bretton Woods in 1944, and for almost 50 years down to the present has continued to be "the" authority on such affairs for succeeding generations of Americans. After his Treasury service he was chief economist for the International Monetary Fund; the author of an authoritative newsletter that was must reading for central banks and other experts; and a fellow at the Brookings Institution.

2. See a lucid account of the origins of the Bretton Woods system as well as an account through the 1970s in Robert Solomon, *The International Monetary System, 1945–1981* (New York: Harper & Row, 1982).

3. *Ibid.*, p. 168.

4. Edward M. Bernstein, *The Balance of Payments: Problems and Policies* (Washington, D.C.: EMB, Ltd., Nov. 25, 1966).

5. See Hobart Rowen, "Gold at the Crossroads," *Washington Post*, Mar. 10–14, 1968. Available as a reprint.

6. The Group of Ten at that time consisted of the eight gold pool members—but not including Switzerland—plus Sweden, Japan, and Canada. Switzerland did not formally join the G-10 until 1983, making it, in fact, a G-11.

7. Hobart Rowen, "IMF Achievement at Rio was Great," *Washington Post*, Oct. 7, 1967.

8. *Business in Brief* (Chase Manhattan Bank newsletter, New York), Apr. 4, 1967.

9. Chase Manhattan Bank press release, New York, Apr. 10, 1967, cited in "Chase Manhattan Amends Its Gold Policy Statement," *Washington Post*, Apr. 11, 1968.

10. Larre's designation of the fictional moneylender as Samuel, rather than Pierre, Jean, or André, was probably not accidental.

11. Hobart Rowen, "Estimate of Gold Crisis Loss Set at $1.5 Billion," *Washington Post*, Feb. 16, 1968.

12. Robert D. Hormats, *Reforming the International Monetary System: From Roosevelt to Reagan* (New York: Foreign Policy Association, 1987).

13. Economist James Tobin, back at Yale after his brief stint on the Kennedy CEA, put it this way: "A price increase would merely encourage the further use of resources for extracting a bad substitute for paper money out of the ground."

14. See Rowen, "Gold at the Crossroads."

15. Hobart Rowen, "Memo Triggers Foreign Spending Restrictions," *Washington Post*, Jan. 10, 1968.

16. Hobart Rowen, "Republicans Challenge Gold 'Cover' Proposal," *Washington Post*, Jan. 24, 1968.

17. By the time the gold pool was closed in mid-March 1968, the bite on U.S. gold stocks alone was measured at $2.5 billion, and on the gold pool nations all together at about $3.5 billion. Thus, in the four-month period since devaluation of the British pound, the gold pool had shoveled out about twice the amount of gold dug out of the ground annually.

18. Hobart Rowen, "Pool Formed in 1960 to Help Gold Is Unexpected 'Villain' of Crisis," *Washington Post*, Mar. 11, 1968.

19. In addition to Fowler, Martin, and Schweitzer, the participants at this historic session were: Hubert Ansiaux, governor of the Banque National de Belgique; Dr. Karl Blessing, president of the Deutsche Bundesbank; Guido Carli, governor of the Banca d'Italia; Prof. J. Zijlstra, president of de Nederlansche Bank; Dr. E. Stopper, president of Banque National Suisse; Sir Leslie O'Brien, governor of the Bank of England; and Gabriel Ferras, Bank for International Settlements.

20. Hobart Rowen, "De Gaulle's Gold Plea Stirs Little Concern," *Washington Post*, Mar. 21, 1968.

21. A *London Times* cartoon showed De Gaulle saying, as he steps up to the IMF window with his hand out for cash, next in line after British prime minister Wilson:

"The really humiliating thing about the whole situation . . . is not the complete break-down of my plans . . . and the continuing lack of confidence in the franc, but that we get more like the British every day!"

22. The first allocation of SDRs to member countries was made on Jan. 1, 1970, but "paper gold" has never lived up to its promise or potential; bowing to subsequent hesitancy by succeeding American administrations, which was supported by other conservative governments (especially West Germany), not enough SDRs were issued to cut into the role of the dollar. Third World countries eagerly sought their share of SDRs, which they could exchange for hard currencies. But the United States and Germany, over the years, continued to resist SDR creation as an inflation trigger. All told, less than $30 billion worth of SDRs have been issued, and despite entreaties from poor nations, none has been created since January 1981. According to the IMF, 21.4 billion SDRs were in existence as of Aug. 15, 1990, equal to $29.5 billion, with each SDR worth $1.38 on that date.

23. Giscard d'Estaing interview, *Washington Post*, Sept. 19, 1969. When I first met Giscard d'Estaing in 1962 in his elegant French Treasury office on the rue de Rivoli, we had been discussing economic growth, which at that time was advancing at a faster rate in Europe than in the United States. Economic growth in France had been stimulated by "le Plan," a complex management system that targeted economic results with the cooperation of government, business, and labor. I was on a reporting trip for *Newsweek* to study European techniques for stimulating economic growth, thanks to President Kennedy's interest.

MISMANAGEMENT

CHAPTER 3: *Gradualism and the Final Break with Gold*

1. *Statistical Abstract of the United States 1992* (Washington, D. C.: U. S. Department of Commerce, 1992), p. 456.

2. See Sar A. Levitan and Robert Taggart, *The Promise of Greatness* (Cambridge: Harvard University Press, 1976) for a critique of the Phillips curve and a cogent defense of minimum wage laws.

3. Walker's mother, for her own good reasons, named her son "Charls," without an *e*.

4. The CEA's troubles, it should be noted, were not entirely of Keyserling's making, but that is another long story.

5. Economic Report of the President, 1961, pp. 87–88.

6. The average rate on short-term bank loans to business rose to 8.21 percent in 1969 from 6.68 percent in 1968. For the first half of the decade, this key rate had been 5 percent or less. See Economic Report of the President, 1972, p. 262.

7. Hobart Rowen, "Nixon Surtax Support Decided Budget Plan," *Washington Post*, Jan. 17, 1969.

8. Hobart Rowen, "Hard Line Set Up for Inflation Fight," *Washington Post*, Nov. 20, 1969.

9. Okun interview, November 1969.

10. Hobart Rowen, "More Talk Being Heard About Price-Wage Controls," *Washington Post*, Oct. 10, 1969.

11. Nixon's budget and economic reports were delayed a day, following a cabinet meeting in which Nixon instructed Budget Director Mayo to redo the numbers to show a larger surplus in fiscal 1971.

12. Economic Report of the President, 1972, p. 60.

13. Paul W. McCracken, *Reflections on Economic Advising*, Original Paper 1 (Los Angeles: International Institute for Economic Research, 1976).

14. Hobart Rowen, "Recession Not Likely, Burns Says," *Washington Post*, Feb. 19, 1970.

15. Hobart Rowen, "Political Squabbling Starts Over Nixon Economic Plans," *Washington Post*, Mar. 15, 1970.

16. Hobart Rowen, "Inflation Policy Hit by Burns," *Washington Post*, May 19, 1970.

17. About the only bad publicity Shultz had attracted in a year as secretary of labor resulted from an uncharacteristically harsh attack at a National Bureau of Economic Research dinner on Okun, a committed guidepost advocate.

18. Hobart Rowen, "Incomes Policies Gather Backers," *Washington Post*, May 31, 1970. Among various proposals right on the heels of the Burns initiative were those by Donald S. MacNaughton of the Prudential Insurance Company of America; *Fortune* magazine; the Committee for Economic Development; Wilfred Lewis Jr. of the National Planning Association; the Lionel D. Edie Company; Gaylord A. Freeman Jr., chairman of the board of the First National Bank of Chicago; and many senators and congressmen, including Jacob Javits (R.–N.Y.), Jack Miller (R.–Iowa), and Len Jordan (R.–Idaho), who introduced a bill that would direct the CEA to issue biweekly reports on the implications of important wage and price decisions; and Henry S. Reuss (D.–Wis.) who proposed a bill that would require the CEA to promulgate a set of guideposts. Many others came along later.

19. Hobart Rowen, "Too Much Big Talk About the Economy," *Washington Post*, June 2, 1970.

20. Hobart Rowen, "Nixon Embraces 'Jawboning' in Sharp Policy Turnaround," *Washington Post*, June 18, 1970.

21. Brookings emeritus scholar Walter S. Salant, who had been a fellow OPA employee, also recalled in a letter to the *Washington Post* that Nixon had left the OPA months before nationwide gas rationing was established in 1942.

22. Hobart Rowen, "Nixon Economists Come Under Fire," *Washington Post*, July 1, 1970.

23. Hobart Rowen, "U.S. Economic Picture: Dismal or Optimistic?" *Washington Post*, Sept. 20, 1970.

24. Hobart Rowen, "Schweitzer Stings U.S.," *Washington Post*, Sept. 23, 1970.

25. I met Schweitzer at the Banque de France in 1962. On that occasion, the French police had seen me wander through the bank after my appointment with Schweitzer, taking pictures—without permission. At a time when "plastique" bombs were common and tempers were on edge during student uprisings, the cops took no chances. It took a call to Schweitzer to get me out—without the roll of film.

26. Hobart Rowen, "Kennedy Remarks Result in 'Fuss'," *Washington Post*, Sept. 25, 1970.

27. Hobart Rowen, "Exchange Rate Plans Studied," *Washington Post*, Sept. 14, 1970.

28. The bigger news related to demonstrations by young European radicals who broke windows at the D'Angleterre Hotel, which housed some of the delegates: it was part of the bitterness (fairly or unfairly) being shown to World Bank president Robert S. McNamara, accused of being too little, too late, with aid to poor countries. See "U.S. Economic Picture: Dismal or Optimistic?" *Washington Post*, Sept. 20, 1970.

29. Sherman J. Maisel, *Managing the Dollar* (New York: W. W. Norton, 1973), p. 280.

30. Private conversations in Burns's office at the Fed, December 1970.

31. Hobart Rowen, "Nixon Sets a New Economic Course," *Washington Post*, Jan. 22, 1971. Burn's relationship with Nixon over this period served to increase tensions between him and White House staffers such as Charles W. Colson, who was special counsel to the president and a self described "hatchet man," and Haldeman, who regarded the Fed chairman as too independent, and therefore a danger to Nixon (and to themselves). Just before the Pepperdine speech, one of Nixon's political aides asked me. "Do you know what the Grand Mahatma plans to say?" (Hobart Rowen, "Burns Wields Heavy 'Clout' as Incomes Policy Exponent," *Washington Post*, Dec. 13, 1970.

32. *Wall Street Journal*, July 29, 1971.

33. *International Financial Statistics*, International Monetary Fund, August 1992, p. 538.

34. Instead, he survived a bribery trial—accused of taking $10,000 from the milk industry for a crucial decision when he was secretary of the Treasury—then gave up politics to make a fortune in Texas, only to lose it all in the savings and loan debacle in the late 1980s. In January 1988, declaring bankruptcy, Connally sold his personal possessions at auction and—stripped of his good name and all else except a gutsy spirit—he started over as an economic consultant and adviser. The Texas bravado never disappeared. When I phoned Connally's office in Houston in December 1989 to arrange an interview for this book, I said to his secretary (to make sure I had the right John Connally), "Have I reached the office of the John Connally who was secretary of the Treasury during the Nixon administration?" There was a brief pause, and then, in a dignified voice that indicated my faux pas: "You have reached the office of the John Connally who is the former governor of Texas!" When we met in Houston, he was eager to talk about the old days in Washington, and the backwards projection into the days of his power seemed to restore his spirits.

Connally arranged to pick me up for lunch. It was a bit startling to see him driving his own car—the days of a chauffeured limousine were over. He greeted me like a long-lost friend. He was a bit thinner, and noticeably less ebullient. Walking into an upscale restaurant in Houston, he was visibly buoyed as numerous old acquaintances jumped up to greet him, most addressing him as "Governor." Connally was bitter over James Reston Jr.'s recent and not exactly complimentary biography, *The Lone Star: The Life of John Connally* (New York: Harper & Row, 1989). He said he had refused to talk to Reston, and challenged quotes dealing with conversations Connally was supposed to have had with LBJ. "There were only the two of us in a room. He didn't talk to Johnson, so far as I know, and he sure as hell didn't talk to me. So how the hell can he use a quote?" He would tell all in his own book, he assured me. It was published in 1993, after his death, with Mickey Herskowitz, *In History's Shadow: An American Odyssey* (New York: Hyperion, 1993).

35. Quoted by former assistant secretary of the Treasury (Carter administration) C. Fred Bergsten in interview December 1989. He was one of a group Connally called together after the sweeping decisions at Camp David on August 15, 1971, to freeze wages and prices. At the end of a six-hour brainstorming session. Connally explained his philosophy about foreigners. When I talked to him in Houston at the end of 1989, Connally said he couldn't remember his exact words, but that the Bergsten quote was substantially accurate. "Yeah, that's right," Connally said.

36. Weidenbaum interview, Feb. 27, 1990.

37. Volcker interview, 1989.

38. Hobart Rowen, "Officials Exaggerate GNP In Order to Sell 'Confidence'," *Washington Post*, May 2, 1971.

39. Hobart Rowen, "Klein Lists Stocks to Back Nixon Forecast," *Washington Post*, Apr. 29, 1971.

40. See Hobart Rowen, *Free Enterprisers: Kennedy, Johnson and the Business Establishment* (New York: G.P. Putnam's Sons, 1964); and Hobart Rowen, "America's Most Powerful Club," *Harper's*, July 1960. The exclusive Business Council met behind closed doors with government officials twice a year. The *Harper's* piece was the first to raise the question of the too-cozy relationship of the Council with government officials, and forced some procedural changes during the Kennedy years. Originally called the Business Advisory Council of the Department of Commerce, the Business Council in the 1970s remained a highly influential organization.

41. Weber interview, 1992. Also see Hobart Rowen, "George P. Shultz: Second Wage-Price Freeze Prompted His Resignation," *Washington Post*, Apr. 14, 1974. In the end, Shultz did not actively oppose the August 1971 imposition of a wage-price freeze, but he remained an opponent of controls, and it was Nixon's attempt to reimpose controls, in a later phase in 1973, that led to Shultz's decision to leave the government. Shultz, later to be Ronald Reagan's secretary of state, was a man of great personal integrity and professional detachment; he never offered more than lukewarm support for price-wage controls because he didn't believe in them. With Shultz, convictions counted for something: there came a time in 1972 when Press Secretary Ron Ziegler asked Shultz to pose with a chart on unemployment, so devised that a tiny dip in the monthly jobless rate (from 5.9 to 5.7 percent) looked like a spectacular decline. "It's a dishonest chart, and I won't do it," Shultz quietly told Ziegler. But Ziegler, who had different standards, didn't mind posing with the chart for White House press photographers (Hobart Rowen, "Shultz Carries On," *Washington Post*, May 18, 1972).

42. Paul W. McCracken, *Reflections on Economic Advising*, Original Paper 1 (Los Angeles: International Institute for Economic Research, 1976), p. 3.

43. Connally interview, Houston, Texas, 1989.

44. Robert Solomon, in his *International Monetary System, 1945–81* (New York: Harper & Row, 1982), pp. 184–186, citing journalistic sources, says the key day was August 2, when Connally and George Shultz met with Nixon and decided to abandon "the game of gradualism" in the wake of a steel agreement providing for an 8 percent price increase and a 30 percent, three-year wage hike. Reston, in his biography of Connally, says that Connally shipped a detailed plan to Nixon—the one agreed to later at Camp David—on August 6.

45. Ineptly, Nixon's publicists chose the same name that Lenin had used back in the 1920s.

46. Connally interview, 1989. A similar account, but with different words attributed to Connally, is contained in Reston's *The Lone Star: The Life of John Connally.*

47. Connally interview, 1989. The Dow Jones industrial index recorded the biggest single day's jump in history (to that time) on Monday, August 16, rising almost thirty-three points to 888.95. The low during the year was 797.97 on November 13, as the debate with the Allies continued on a reasonable level of exchange rates.

48. Herbert Stein, *Presidential Economics* (New York: Simon & Schuster, 1984), pp. 156–57.

49. Hobart Rowen, "Nixon Muted Economy Issues," *Washington Post*, Nov. 5, 1972.

50. Those who did attend the Camp David meetings and press conferences were Treasury Secretary John Connelly; Undersecretary for Monetary Affairs Paul A. Volcker; Office of Management and Budget director George P. Shultz; Federal Reserve

Board chairman Arthur F. Burns; Economic Council chairman Paul McCracken; Secretary of Commerce Peter Peterson; White House aide Bob Haldeman; CEA member Herbert Stein; and White House speechwriter William Safire, who kept notes of who said what, and later drafted the official announcement.

51. Hormats interview, Nov. 28, 1989. See also Paul Volcker and Toyoo Gyohten, *Changing Fortunes: The World's Money and the Threat to American Leadership* (New York: Times Books, 1992). Volcker, commenting on the absence of State Department officials at Camp David, says that Nat Samuels, undersecretary of state for economic affairs, was on vacation, and that Kissinger, he later learned, "was on secret negotiations on Vietnam."

CHAPTER 4: *A Question of Control*

1. Bergsten interview, 1991.

2. Connally interview, 1989.

3. Volcker interview, 1989.

4. Hormats interview, December 1989. In 1971, Hormats was a Kissinger aide at the NSC.

5. Weidenbaum interview, Feb. 27, 1990. Weidenbaum recalls that on at least one occasion, Connally let Haldeman cool his heels in his outer office before having him ushered in.

6. Howard Wachtel, *The Money Mandarins* (New York: Pantheon Books, 1986), p. 85.

7. Hobart Rowen, "Rep. Reuss Suggests Devaluation of Dollar," *Washington Post,* Sept. 22, 1971.

8. Reuss interview, Sept. 21, 1971.

9. Connally interview, 1989.

10. *Ibid.*

11. I accompanied Connally to Munich to cover his debut before a European audience at the American Bankers Association's International Monetary Conference. Amazingly, this was Connally's first trip to Europe. Conscious of the need to nurse the American supply of gold, which was being tapped by dollar holders such as France, Connally wished he could strike back. While the two of us were walking alone through a beautiful cathedral outside Munich on a tour arranged by the ABA, Connally called my attention to the gilded, illuminated frescoes on the ceiling, and said: "Goddamn, see that gold up there? I just wish I could grab a chunk of that and bring it back home."

12. Hobart Rowen, "Considering the Price of Gold," *Washington Post,* Sept. 23, 1971.

13. Hobart Rowen, "Devaluation: Presidential Midas Touch," *Washington Post,* Dec. 20, 1971.

14. Connally interview, 1989. Essentially the same account is given by James Reston Jr. in *The Lone Star.* Reston attributes it to a Connally interview with author Martin Mayer. See pp. 430–431.

15. Paul Volcker and Toyoo Gyohten, *Changing Fortunes: The World's Money and the Threat to American Leadership* (New York: Times Books, 1992). In Gyohten's version, the Japanese finance minister told Connally that his predecessor who had agreed to a 17 percent revaluation had been assassinated.

16. *Ibid.,* p. 89.

17. Martin E. Weinstein, *The Human Face of Japan's Leadership: Twelve Portraits* (New York: Praeger, 1989).

18. The Group of Seven includes the United States, West Germany, Japan, England, France, Italy, and Canada. The Group of Ten—now actually eleven with the inclusion of Switzerland—include the Big Seven plus the Netherlands, Belgium, and Sweden.

19. Note this extract of the June 23, 1972, tape of conversations between Nixon and Haldeman, the one that revealed that Nixon personally had ordered a cover-up of the illegal entry into the Watergate headquarters of the Democratic Party six days after it happened on June 17, 1972:

Haldeman: Did you get the report that the British floated the pound?

Nixon: I don't think so.

Haldeman: They did.

Nixon: That's devaluation?

Haldeman: Yeah. [White House assistant Peter] Flanigan's got a report on it here.

Nixon: I don't care about it. Nothing we can do about it.

Haldeman: You want a run-down?

Nixon: No, I don't.

Haldeman: He argues it shows the wisdom of our refusal to consider convertibility until we get a new monetary system.

Nixon: Good. I think he's right. It's too complicated for me to get into. (unintelligible) I understand.

Haldeman: [Fed chairman Arthur] Burns is concerned about speculation about the lira.

Nixon: Well, I don't give a fuck about the lira.

20. Kim McQuaid, *Big Business and Presidential Power* (New York: William Morrow, 1982), pp. 269–70.

21. Burns interview, 1972.

22. Hobart Rowen, "Phase II Success Depends on Discipline of 2–3% Goal," *Washington Post*, Oct. 17, 1971.

23. Hobart Rowen, "Nixon-Connally Economic Goals Miss Target Here and Abroad," *Washington Post*, Nov. 21, 1971.

24. *Ibid.*

25. Hobart Rowen, "Departing McCracken Sees Controls Lingering," *Washington Post*, Dec. 31, 1971.

26. "The Playboy Interview," *Playboy*, February 1973, p. 51.

27. Hobart Rowen, "The Politics of Controls," *Washington Post*, Jan. 13, 1972.

28. Walter W. Heller, in National City Bank of Minneapolis newsletter.

29. Testimony before the Joint Economic Committee, Feb. 18, 1972.

30. Hobart Rowen, "Okun Hits Cut in Employment Goal," *Washington Post*, Feb. 19, 1972.

31. Hobart Rowen, "Meany Failed to Work for Pay Board Goals," *Washington Post*, Mar. 26, 1972.

32. Connally had this explanation of his exit from the Treasury job: He had told Nixon that he would keep the existing staff at Treasury, and that he would be completely loyal to him and to his policies—on one condition, that he had absolute control of the Treasury. The bargain was kept until one day in 1972, when he picked up the newspapers and found that Romana Acosta Banuelos, an Hispanic woman, had been named Treasurer of the United States, a post within his department. Connally called Haldeman, reminded him of Nixon's commitment, and warned that, if it ever happened again, "I'm out of here."

Haldeman apologized, and offered to withdraw the appointment. But Connally said the Banuelos appointment would go through because if word were to leak out, as it inevitably would, that Connally didn't want Banuelos, he would be accused of being prejudiced against Hispanics and women. He warned Haldeman that it better not happen again. When later in 1972, he discovered that Assistant Treasury Secretary Edwin Cohen was at the White House working out tax legislation with Haldeman, Connally said, "I quit."

33. Margaret Garritsen de Vries, *The International Monetary Fund, 1972–78: Cooperation on Trial,* 3 vols. (Washington, D.C.: International Monetary Fund, 1985).

34. Hobart Rowen, "Phase II's Glow Dims," *Washington Post,* Mar. 2, 1972.

35. Hobart Rowen, "Can Mr. Nixon Stand Economic Success?" *Washington Post,* July 30, 1972.

36. Documents dated July 24, 25, 26, 1972, obtained through the Freedom of Information Act, in possession of the author. The Stein memo to Butterfield and Clawson was triggered, he said, by an offensive column of mine dated July 23 that said the "the federal budget is out of control," with the prospect that it could be well in excess of $30 billion, compared to the last revised official estimate of a deficit of $27 billion. I had cited a Goldman, Sachs analysis that showed receipts going down, expenditures up, and a possible deficit range of $35–$38 billion. In the end, the deficit turned out to be well below either the Goldman, Sachs or Nixon estimates, at $14 billion, mainly because revenues turned out to be higher.

But what really sent Stein up the wall was my comment to Clawson, which he included in the memo to Butterfield, that Stein in testimony to the Joint Economic Committee the day after my column was published said he couldn't argue "with the thrust of it."

That triggered the "implacable and unscrupulous" line in Stein's July 26 memo. He cited from the transcript, in which he said he didn't accept "the Goldman, Sacks [sic]–Rowen revenue estimates." He went on to quote his own words, in which he objected to a single figure in the long Goldman, Sachs tally. Then he told Henry Reuss, chairman of the Joint Economic Committee: "Otherwise, the figures that are presented in that column are a good statement of the problem. We don't disagree with the problem. We don't disagree that there is a danger that if we don't control some of these things, stop some of these things, there can be a larger deficit." That was Herb Stein quoting Herb Stein, essentially confirming what I had told Clawson.

On July 24, 1972, I received a friendly, half-embarrassed call from Clawson, a former *Washington Post* colleague with whom I had occasionally shared bylines (if not always the same political instincts). I could tell that Clawson was acting under orders. He had been instructed to relay a complaint from Stein about a column that appeared the day before in which I suggested that a Stein National Press Club speech attacking George McGovern, who then was aspiring to the Democratic presidential nomination, went beyond "the traditional nonpartisan, nonpolitical role" of the CEA chairman. Clawson also said on the phone that another White House official (he didn't identify him, but it was Ehrlichman) had observed that I could not be expected to be objective because my son Jim five years earlier had married McGovern's daughter Susan. Clawson also incorporated a reference to that in his memo to Butterfield.

I told Clawson that I was remaining objective, despite my son's connection to the McGovern family; that my columns of comment on McGovern's economic program—some of them critical—were spread on the record for anyone to see.

37. Bruce Oudes, *"From: The President": Richard Nixon's Secret Files* (New York: Harper & Row, 1989).

38. Hobart Rowen, "The Future of Controls, *Washington Post,* Nov. 2, 1972.

39. Hobart Rowen and James L. Rowe Jr., "Progress Seen on Economy," *Washington Post*, Aug. 13, 1972.

40. For the Walker proposal, see "Controls After Phase II." For McGovern's plan, and a discussion of the Ackley proposal, see Hobart Rowen, "McGovern's Plan For Pay, Prices: Too Weak for '73," *Washington Post*, Sept. 17, 1972. Essentially, McGovern proposed jawboning, buttressed by a White House Review Board with legal enforcement by the president for "flagrant violations" only. Ackley, with some support from Heller and Okun, had come to believe that the Nixon program was too comprehensive.

41. Hobart Rowen, "Controls Given Priority," *Washington Post*, Nov. 11, 1972.

42. Hobart Rowen, "Nixon Vows a 'Big Stick' on Phase III," *Washington Post*, Feb. 8, 1973.

43. Hobart Rowen, "Investors Spurn Stocks; Savers Jilt S&Ls," *Washington Post*, Mar. 23, 1973.

44. Hobart Rowen, "World Money Crisis Advancing to Climax," *Washington Post*, Feb. 9, 1973; "U.S. Devalues Dollar 10 Per Cent," Feb. 13, 1973; "Devaluation Eases Monetary Tension," Feb. 14, 1973.

45. Hobart Rowen, "The Danger of Perpetuating Past Mistakes," *Washington Post*, Apr. 26, 1973.

46. Hobart Rowen, "George Shultz: Looking Back on 5 Years in Government," *Washington Post*, Apr. 14, 1974.

47. Hobart Rowen, "Playing with Economics," *Washington Post*, Jan. 21, 1982. The Stein quote comes from his article in *The Conference Board*, the thrust of which was that presidents tend to become their own chief economists.

48. Sherman J. Maisel, *Managing the Dollar* (New York: W.W. Norton, 1973).

CHAPTER 5 : *OPEC Shocks the World*

1. Benjamin Shwadran, *Middle East Oil Crises Since 1973* (Boulder, Colo.: Westview Press, 1986), p. 49.

2. Colin Legum, ed., *Middle East Contemporary Survey*, vol. 4, 1979–90 (New York and London: Holmes & Meier Publishers, 1982), p. 295.

3. *The Persian Gulf—1974: Money, Politics, Arms and Power*, Hearings, House Committee on Foreign Affairs, Subcommittee on the Near East and South Asia, July 30, August 5, 7 and 12, 1974 (Washington D.C.: U.S. Government Printing Office, 1975), p. 65.

4. Singer, then at the University of Virginia, made this and other points challenging the view that oil would always move up in price in his *Free Market Energy* (New York: Universe Books, 1984).

5. James E. Akins, "Oil Crisis: This Time the Wolf Is Here," *Foreign Affairs*, April 1973, p. 462.

6. J. B. Kelly, *Arabia, the Gulf, & the West* (New York: Basic Books, 1980). Kelly's book, subtitled "A Critical View of the Arabs and Their Oil Policy," is the best history of postwar events in the Gulf and the development of OPEC policy.

7. Shwadran, *Middle East Oil Crises*, p. 49.

8. *Ibid.*, p. 44.

9. Robin Wright, *In The Name of God: The Khomeini Decade* (New York: Simon & Schuster, 1989), pp. 51–52.

10. Sheik Rustum Ali, a Bangladeshi diplomat stationed in Washington, in a Ph.D. dissertation for American University suggested a dual price system for the "Fourth World"—the poor countries without oil resources.

11. Hobart Rowen, "Pushing the Cartel to Bolster Its Aid," *Washington Post*, Aug. 17, 1975, and " 'Fourth World' Held Victim of OPEC's 400% Price Hike," *Washington Post*, Aug. 18, 1975.

12. Testimony before the Senate Appropriations Committee, Mar. 20, 1974.

13. American Economic Association meeting, 1973.

14. Eliyahu Kanovsky, *Saudi Arabia's Dismal Economic Future: Regional and Global Implications* (Tel Aviv: The Dayan Center for Middle Eastern and African Studies, The Shiloah Institute, Tel Aviv University, 1986).

15. Hobart Rowen, "Soaring Oil Costs Threaten to Swamp World Economy," *Washington Post*, Dec. 30, 1973.

16. *Ibid.*

17. *Ibid.*

18. Data compiled by Stuart Tucker for the Overseas Development Council. As originally published by ODC, the figure was $53 billion—a bit misleading, as Tucker agreed in a conversation with me, because it included nearly $14 billion for our imports of oil.

19. Hobart Rowen, "The Energy Crisis: Who's in Charge:" *Washington Post*, June 28, 1973.

20. Hobart Rowen, "The Future of the Energy Czar," *Washington Post*, Feb. 14, 1974. Simon's calculation, later endorsed by such worthies as Kissinger and German finance minister (later chancellor) Helmut Schmidt, was based on an interest rate of 8 percent, meaning that the price of oil would have to rise to $21.59 over the decade to equal the investment return from a $10 per barrel price in 1974. As it turned out, oil rose well over $21.59, then plunged below $10, and in late 1989 was under $18 a barrel, or below 1974 prices adjusting for inflation. In 1993, crude oil prices ranged between $14 and $16 a barrel.

21. An account of this and other elements in the Simon vs. Ash and Stein debate is given in a story by Carroll Kilpatrick and Hobart Rowen in "Energy Chief Is Disputed by Stein and Ash," *Washington Post*, Feb. 14, 1974. Simon's "cotton-pickin' " phrase was an adaptation of a comment made by Simon's boss, Treasury Secretary George Shultz, in September 1973 after presidential counselor Melvin Laird hinted that there might be a tax increase. Shultz, in Japan, when told of Laird's comment, snapped that "Laird should keep his cotton-pickin' hands off economic policy."

22. Hobart Rowen, "Energy Parley Responds to Economic Facts," *Washington Post*, Feb. 17, 1974.

23. Hobart Rowen, "The Oil Crisis Will Continue," *Washington Post*, Mar. 21, 1974. With great foresight, Peter G. Peterson, Nixon's former secretary of commerce, who had left—untainted by Watergate—to head Lehman Brothers, noted that the pressure Europe and Japan were feeling to boost exports to help pay their oil bills "may wipe out the advantage the United States increasingly enjoyed during 1973 from an undervalued dollar, and restore roughly the same conditions that existed prior to August 15, 1971, when American goods encountered serious problems of price competition in world markets."

24. Hobart Rowen, "Study Accepts OPEC Prices," *Washington Post*, July 22, 1975.

25. *Ibid.*

26. Shwadran, *Middle East Oil Crises*, p. 81.

27. McNamara complained to Kay Graham that I had accused him of anti-Semitism—which I had not—and that my reporting at the bank amounted to "a waste of $50,000 worth" of eleven of his senior vice presidents' time. I'm not certain whether McNamara's complaints came after or during the publication of the series. I

suspect that they began after the first few had appeared, because the later articles (for no apparent reason I could divine at the time) disappeared from page one.

Post editors were caught in a bind between their approval for and praise of my reporting and a natural desire not to buck Kay's well-known sense of loyalty, based on old family friendships, to McNamara.

I supplied Kay with a memo on the origins of the reporting assignment, and a meticulously detailed account of the McNamara interview that I assembled from my handwritten notes. I had delivered copies to all top editors of the *Post*, and to Ombudsman Charles Seib. After reading my account of what had happened, Geyelin urged Kay to drop the matter "and consider the case closed." Bradlee, Simons, and Seib gave her the same advice.

But as I sat across from Kay in her eighth floor office, it was clear that she was disturbed by the whole episode. She wondered whether I had been fair to McNamara—indeed, whether the entire investigation was necessary. I assured her I had been fair, and that the investigation was necessary. I remember saying: "I was over there working for you."

Bank PR man Robert Merriam kept the complaint alive in a meeting with Seib, who told me afterward that the Bank was concerned about future "institutional relationships" between the Bank and *The Washington Post*. That, Seib took as a not-so-subtle hint it would be a good idea if the *Post* turned over my ongoing assignment to cover the Bank to another reporter. Seib told Merriam that as far as he knew, I would continue to cover the Bank, and that he was sure I could be counted on to be fair.

Seib wrote a report clearing me of any suggestion that I had made professional missteps. Seib didn't challenge my integrity, or the overall thrust of the series I had written, but thought the pieces, while raising valid questions about the bank, were "flawed" because "the other side" of the story should have been higher up in the first article. That, of course, is a subjective assessment. I didn't agree, nor did Harry Rosenfeld, as the hands-on editor, nor did other senior editors.

I felt I had unfairly been placed on trial, and my future at the *Post* jeopardized by McNamara. I wrote a memo to Rosenfeld (and the files) on Aug. 19, 1975: "There should be kudos, instead of a kick in the ass and a feeling of insecurity—and the time wasted in writing letters like these."

28. William Safire, *Before the Fall* (New York: DaCapo Press, 1975), p. 192.

29. Hobart Rowen, "McNamara's Role in Meeting Is Questioned," *Washington Post*, July 24, 1975.

30. I kept detailed notes of the conversation with McNamara. In fact, my notetaking was one of the elements that infuriated him. At one point, he said to me: "Do you know what, I think you're insane—go ahead, write it down, I see you writing it down, insane." I responded: "Well Mr. McNamara, that's what you said, you said I was insane, and I'm taking notes, so I wrote it down." He responded: "Well, it's just an expression."

31. Report No. 802. See also Rowen, "Study Accepts OPEC Prices."

32. Kay initiated a discussion of the 1975 contretemps as one case history for a discussion in her book of the relationships of a publisher to the "city room" of a newspaper. She acknowledged she had been unhappy with me because of the McNamara affair, and had withdrawn from the debate with Bradlee and others over my future still unhappy, with the feeling that for the first time, she had "lost one." After that, she said, she never intervened in such an episode—it was unique in her highly successful career at the *Post*.

Kay Graham was distressed to discover that I had been bitter all these years, worried that my advancement at *The Washington Post* might be affected by awareness among her editors that I was in her doghouse. She was genuinely stunned. "I don't mind the tape being on. . . ." she said. "It took me a very long time to realize that in my job, when I say something or looked at something, or even made a joke that misfired, it's taken very seriously. With some degree of justice. But . . . if you haven't worked your way up in management, and you don't know how things work, how somebody at the top impacts somebody, you know . . . And so I didn't understand . . . that if I'm pissed with somebody, and there's a hangover there, that it carries a message beyond what it should, if you see what I mean."

In the intervening years, Kay had forgotten about the McNamara affair. She had been continuously and publicly complimentary about my reporting and writing. But until our conversation in 1991, I had not been able to let go of my resentment.

33. Hobart Rowen, "Raising the Oil Blackmail," *Washington Post*, May 25, 1975.

34. "Die Situation ist sehr angespannt," *Der Spiegel*, Jan. 20, 1975.

35. King Faisal's views were communicated in exclusive interviews with *The Washington Post*'s Jim Hoagland.

36. Akins, "Oil Crisis: This Time the Wolf Is Here."

37. *The Wall Street Journal* put the issue well: "The idea that to crush Israel, they [the Arab nations] would ignore their economic interests, or would turn charitable if Israel were sacrificed, strikes us as a view tinged with romanticism which has so often fogged the Western view of the Middle East" (Editorial, Aug. 21, 1973).

38. Hobart Rowen, "The Oil Cartel and Development Aid," *Washington Post*, May 23, 1974.

39. *Ibid.*

40. Hobart Rowen, "Ford, Oil, and OPEC," *Washington Post*, Oct. 13, 1974.

41. Hobart Rowen, "Driving Toward a Crisis," *Washington Post*, Dec. 24, 1974.

42. Speech to National Economists' Club, reported in the *Washington Post*, Dec. 3, 1974.

43. Greenspan interview during his CEA chairmanship, 1974.

44. "Kissinger on Oil, Food, and Trade," *Business Week*, Jan. 13, 1975, p. 66.

45. Hobart Rowen, "Countering the Cartel," *Washington Post*, Jan. 5, 1975.

46. Hobart Rowen, "Car Trouble," *Washington Post*, May 29, 1975.

47. Hobart Rowen, "Imports' Success Has Detroit Rattled," *Washington Post*, May 25, 1975,

48. Hobart Rowen, "Bigger Cars: The Desire Lingers On," *Washington Post*, Feb. 26, 1976.

49. Testimony by Treasury Secretary Lloyd Bentsen before the Senate Finance Committee, Apr. 20, 1993.

CHAPTER 6 : *Gerald Ford's Recession*

1. Hobart Rowen, "Bidding Farewell to Nixonomics," *Washington Post*, Aug. 11, 1974.

2. Greenspan interview, 1974.

3. *Ibid.*; see also Hobart Rowen, "Ford Speeds Pace of Fight on Inflation," *Washington Post*, Aug. 30, 1974.

4. Connally interview, 1989.

5. Hobart Rowen, ". . . But Mr. Ford Is on the Right Track," *Washington Post*, Aug. 15, 1974.

6. Hobart Rowen, "Needed: 'New Ideas' on the Economy," *Washington Post*, Aug. 22, 1974.

7. Hobart Rowen, "Simon Sees Wage-Price Guidelines," *Washington Post*, Aug. 28, 1974.

8. Hobart Rowen, "Controls Flatly Ruled Out, No Wage-Price Limits, Ford Vows," *Washington Post*, Aug. 29, 1974.

9. In recent years, to conform to international practice, the concept of gross domestic product (GDP) has been substituted for GNP. GDP measures all output within U.S. geographical boundaries. GNP measures output by U.S. residents no matter where they live or own capital. For the United States, the statistical differences between GNP and GDP are trivial enough to be ignored for most purposes.

10. Sprinkel prefers to refer to himself as "Beryl the Pearl"—which makes the point that he pronounces his first name "Burl," not "Ber-al." One of the best profiles of the monetarist ideologue Sprinkel was written by journalist Art Pine, then on *The Wall Street Journal* staff, published July 13, 1982.

11. Hobart Rowen, "Fighting Inflation," *Washington Post*, Sept. 22, 1974.

12. Hobart Rowen, "Ford Pledges Action Plan on Economy," *Washington Post*, Sept. 6, 1974.

13. Milton Friedman, "A Dissenting View," *Newsweek*, Aug. 25, 1975, p. 62.

14. Friedman could get under the skin of his fellow economists, but he was hard to ignore. In 1976, when accepting a special Nobel Prize for economics, Friedman offended the profession once more by saying the award did not represent "the pinnacle of my career." He said when informed of the award that he was of course "delighted," but would not have chosen "the particular seven people who make these awards as the jury to which I would want to submit by scientific work." That was pure Milton Friedman, arrogant to the last syllable, perhaps his way of suggesting that he thought the recognition was long overdue. (*Washington Post*, Oct. 15, 1976.)

15. See Rowen, "Fighting Inflation."

16. Greenspan interview, *Washington Post*, Sept. 12, 1974. See also Hobart Rowen, "Economy: More 'Old Time Religion'?" *Washington Post*, Sept. 12, 1974.

17. Hobart Rowen, "Economic Summit Marked by Discord," *Washington Post*, Sept. 28, 1974.

18. Burns interview, 1974.

19. Testimony to the Joint Economic Committee of Congress, Oct. 10, 1974, reported in Hobart Rowen, "Fed Franklin Aid Was $1.75 Billion," *Washington Post*, Oct. 11, 1974.

20. Hobart Rowen, "Ford's Economic Blinders," *Washington Post*, Nov. 17, 1974.

21. Ford's tax proposals created an unusual split between Brookings director of research Joseph Pechman and Arthur Okun, then Pechman's colleague at the think tank. In testimony before the Joint Economic Committee, Pechman opposed the surcharge, saying it would exacerbate the recession and further distort the tax code. Okun supported the proposals.

22. Hobart Rowen, "Gas Tax, Pay-Price Curb Sidestepped," *Washington Post*, Oct. 9, 1974.

23. Hobart Rowen, "The Economy and George Meany," *Washington Post*, Nov. 14, 1974.

24. Hobart Rowen, "An Economy Too Long Neglected," *Washington Post*, Nov. 7, 1974.

25. Hobart Rowen, "The Economy: 'Time is growing Short,'" *Washington Post*, Dec. 19, 1974.

26. William Watts and Lloyd A. Free, *State of the Nation 1973* (New York: Universe Books, 1973), and *State of the Nation 1974* (New York: Universe Books, 1974).

27. Rowen, "Ford's Economic Blinders."

28. Hobart Rowen, "A Grim '76 Pictured by Ford," *Washington Post*, Feb. 4, 1975.

29. Hobart Rowen, "Ford's Economics: Honest, Misguided," *Washington Post*, Feb. 6, 1975.

30. Hobart Rowen, "Growth In Jobs and GNP," *Washington Post*, June 29, 1975.

31. Saul Klaman, research director of the Mutual Savings Banks Association, had the courage to say: "The taxpayers are making rebates for the home builders, and I don't know whether it's worth it" (Hobart Rowen, "The Tax Bill: It Could Have Been Worse," *Washington Post*, Apr. 3, 1975).

32. Hobart Rowen, "Burns' Policies at Center of Economic Storm," *Washington Post*, Apr. 20, 1975.

33. There are various other definitions of the money supply, known as M-3, M-4, and so on, depending on what is included—savings accounts, certificates of deposit, mutual funds, and other forms of money and near money.

34. Hobart Rowen, "Fed Is Trying to Spur Money Growth," *Washington Post*, May 2, 1975.

35. Hobart Rowen, "Recovery Forecasts Imprecise," *Washington Post*, Apr. 6, 1975.

36. Brimmer interview, quoted in Hobart Rowen, "Arthur Burns Goes Public," *Washington Post*, May 22, 1975.

37. See June 16, 1975, congressional testimony by C. Fred Bergsten, who had been on the National Security Council staff in the Nixon administration, and later would become assistant secretary of the Treasury for international affairs in the Carter administration.

38. Speech to the Society of American Business Writers, May 1975, Washington, D.C.

39. Hobart Rowen, "Simon Seems to Say: Turn the Clock Back," *Washington Post*, Nov. 2, 1975.

40. Arthur M. Okun, *Equality and Efficiency: The Big Tradeoff* (Washington, D.C.: Brookings Institution, 1975). This was an expanded version of Okun's Godkin series of lectures at Harvard in 1974.

41. Friedman, "A Dissenting View."

42. Clausen interview, San Francisco, 1975.

43. Hobart Rowen and Don Oberdorfer, "Financiers Deeply Divided on Effects of N.Y. Default," *Washington Post*, Nov. 9, 1975, p. 1.

44. Hobart Rowen, "U.S. Hints Shift on N.Y. Aid," *Washington Post*, Oct. 3, 1975.

45. Hobart Rowen, "Mr. Ford and New York's Free Tuition," *Washington Post*, Oct. 10, 1975.

46. To be sure, when it comes to City College of New York, I am not a disinterested person: I am a 1938 graduate of CCNY, a unit of what is now known as the City University of New York. But I thought, as Ford bellyached to Abe Beame about free tuition, of the list of City College graduates who had repaid the city and nation many times over for the opportunities that CCNY gave them: Jonas Salk, Felix Frankfurter, Morris Raphael Cohen, Sydney Hook, Ernest Nagel, and George Washington Goethals, to name a few. And here was Ford shamelessly nagging Beame about the costs for CCNY, less than $100 million out of the city's accumulated deficit of $3.2 billion.

47. Hobart Rowen, "Rocky Fears 'Catastrophe,' Asks Congress to Aid N.Y.," *Washington Post*, Oct. 18, 1975.

48. Rohatyn interview, *Newsday*, June 28, 1989.

49. Hobart Rowen, "Ford Tax Cut: Strong Stimulus," *Washington Post*, Oct. 19, 1975.

50. Minneapolis National City Bank newsletter, October 1975.

51. Hobart Rowen, "Group of 12 Economists Backs Tax Cut Extension," *Washington Post*, Nov. 1, 1975. Included in the survey—all but one being former chairmen or members of the Council of Economic Advisers—were Republicans Whitman, McCracken, Stein, William J. Fellner, and Hendrik Houthakker; and Democrats Gardner Ackley, Walter Heller, Arthur Okun, James Duesenberry, James Tobin, Otto Eckstein, and Charles Schultze.

CHAPTER 7 : *The Birth of Economic Summitry*

1. The French version of "stable but adjustable" translated as "fixed but adjustable."

2. Hobart Rowen, "Inflation Curb Said Unlikely," *Washington Post*, Sept. 10, 1973.

3. Robert Solomon, *The International Monetary System, 1945–81* (New York: Harper & Row, 1982).

4. *Ibid.*

5. One smaller issue was settled at Nairobi. J. Dewey Daane, the gregarious governor of the Fed, was nearing the end of his term, but knew that Chairman Burns might not recommend his reappointment to Nixon because he was known to enjoy a night out on the town. Although Daane was working overtime at Nairobi to establish goodwill with Burns, he had the bad luck to escort a beautiful young lady to dinner at the Nairobi Intercontinental Hotel within view of Burns, at dinner in the same restaurant with his wife, Helen, my wife, and me. Daane blanched as he saw Burns, nodded greetings, and moved along. But in a few minutes, he returned alone and, approaching Burns, said: "Arthur, believe it or not, she works for Wells Fargo [the banking company]." Daane didn't wait for a reaction. Had he done so, he would have seen Burns shake his head and laugh. Nixon, on Burns's recommendation, soon appointed Yale professor Henry C. Wallich to replace Daane. Later, discussing this incident, Daane laughed at the recollection and added: "She really did work for Wells Fargo!"

6. Robert Hormats remembers a four-hour meeting among Secretary of Treasury George Shultz, Undersecretary Paul Volcker, and himself (representing Henry Kissinger), facing French finance minister Valery Giscard d'Estaing and Giscard's deputy, Claude-Pierre Brossollet. See Robert D. Hormats, *Reforming the International Monetary System: From Roosevelt to Reagan* (New York: Foreign Policy Association, 1987).

7. Hobart Rowen, "Pact Seen As Aiding Gold Plan," *Washington Post*, Dec. 18, 1974.

8. Henry Kissinger, "Kissinger on Oil, Food and Trade," *Business Week*, July 18, 1973, pp. 59–62.

9. Paul Volcker and Toyoo Gyohten, *Changing Fortunes* (New York: Times Books, 1992), pp. 125, 347–348. See also W. R. Smyser, "Goodbye, G-7," *Washington Quarterly*, Winter 1993, p. 15.

10. The offended, excluded nations, were Italy, Canada, Belgium, the Netherlands, and Sweden. Later, Italy and Canada were added, to form a Group of Seven that parallels the membership of the economic summit nations. But suspicion of the G-5 remains among those excluded; even within the G-5, British and French ministers sometimes feel their place in the high council is an anachronistic hangover from an earlier era of colonial strength. The fact is that for the past decade the international

monetary system has been controlled by a G-3 consisting of the United States, Germany, and Japan.

11. Solomon, *International Monetary System*, p. 269.

12. Yeo recalls that it was his habit to puff away at his cigars in Larosière's handsome office because Larosière, although he didn't smoke, had no objection. He learned only later that Larosière always had the place fumigated after his visits. No. 93 rue de Rivoli was the old site of the French Ministry of Finance, one of the original buildings of the Louvre Museum, in 1988 reclaimed by the Louvre. The Ministry of Finance has now been banished to a monstrous site on the Rive Gauche.

13. Solomon, *International Monetary System*, p. 271.

14. Yeo interview, November 1990.

15. *Ibid.* Yeo had been present on the *Sequoia.*

16. Margaret Garritsen de Vries, *The International Monetary Fund, 1972–1978: Cooperation on Trial,* 3 vols. (Washington, D.C.: International Monetary Fund, 1985), 2: 743.

17. Yeo interview, November 1990.

18. Canada, rejected by Giscard, was included at Ford's insistence in 1976 in Dorado Beach, completing the Group of Seven major nations.

19. Hobart Rowen, "Economic Review By Allies Asked," *Washington Post,* Nov. 12, 1975.

20. Hormats, *Reforming the International Monetary System,* p. 38.

21. *Ibid.,* p. 40.

22. Hobart Rowen, "Summit Ends With Pledge of Recovery," *Washington Post,* Nov. 18, 1975.

23. De Vries, *International Monetary Fund,* 2: 760–762.

24. Hobart Rowen, "Jamaica's Political Turbulence Gets International Audience," *Washington Post,* Jan. 11, 1976.

25. Yeo interview, Kingston, Jan. 9, 1976.

26. The operative section of Article IV—what Yeo called the "drive system" of the agreement—read as follows:

"Recognizing that the essential purpose of the international monetary system is to provide a framework that facilitates the exchange of goods, services, and capital among countries, and that sustains economic growth, and that a principal objective is the continuing development of orderly conditions that are necessary for financial and economic stability, each member undertakes to collaborate with the Fund and other members to assure orderly exchange arrangements and promote a stable system of exchange rates. In particular, each member shall:

"(i) endeavor to direct its economic and financial policies toward the objective of fostering orderly economic growth with reasonable price stability, with due regard to its circumstances;

"(ii) seek to promote stability by fostering orderly underlying economic and financial conditions that do not tend to produce erratic disruption;

"(iii) avoid manipulating exchange rates or the international monetary system in order to prevent effective balance of payments adjustment or to gain an unfair competitive advantage over other members; and

"(iv) follow exchange policies compatible with the undertaking under this section."

27. Tom de Vries, "Jamaica, or the Non-Reform of the International Monetary System," *Foreign Affairs,* Spring 1976.

28. Hobart Rowen, "The Economic Picture: What Effect on Voters?" *Washington Post,* Mar. 25, 1976.

29. Hobart Rowen, "Simon, Stern Foe of Spending, Off on $131,500 Trip," *Washington Post*, Nov. 27; "Simon Says He Got Gifts Abroad, Asks to Buy Them," *Washington Post*, Dec. 11, 1976.

30. Hobart Rowen, "Simon Can't Keep Gifts from Abroad," *Washington Post*, Dec. 18, 1976.

31. Present-day rules are the same, except that if a federal official who receives a gift notes that he would like to buy it, at the time he turns it in within sixty days of receiving it, he will be accorded priority over potential purchases by the states. But government agencies still get first crack at such gifts. Simon's basic problem was that he didn't report the receipt of the gifts in question until someone blew the whistle on him.

32. Simon, I gathered from a mutual friend, was stunned that I had written about his junket to Moscow, and then followed up on the gifts story, inasmuch as he had once invited me to his home for dinner, and to a tennis game with Ford aide Bill Seidman—like Simon, a tennis buff.

33. Conversation with Mrs. Black Oct. 23, 1991, when, as U.S. ambassador to Czechoslovakia, she accompanied President Vaclev Havel on an official trip to Washington.

34. Simon interview, 1975.

35. Hobart Rowen, "Good Times, But Not Yet Boom Times," *Washington Post*, Mar. 14, 1976.

36. Hobart Rowen, "Budget Report Questions Ford Plan, *Washington Post*, Mar. 16, 1976; "Viewing Budget Options," *Washington Post*, Mar. 21, 1976.

37. Hobart Rowen, "Reagan's Economic Ideas," *Washington Post*, Apr. 20, 1976. The Reagan interview, which set out basic tenets of Reaganism that barely changed in later years, was conducted in the VIP lounge of a small airport in Fort Worth, Texas. The April 20 article was one of a series of profiles of all of the candidates for nominations in both parties, based on one-on-one interviews.

38. Hobart Rowen, *The Free Enterprisers: Kennedy, Johnson, and the Business Establishment* (New York: G. P. Putnam's Sons, 1964), p. 285.

39. Private conversation with Okun at the time.

40. Hobart Rowen, "Politics Denied as Motive for Calling Summit," *Washington Post*, Apr. 6, 1976.

41. Lou Cannon, *Reagan* (New York: G. P. Putnam's Sons, 1982), pp. 195–199.

42. Reagan interview.

43. *Ibid.*

44. See testimony by C. Fred Bergsten, then with the Brookings Institution, before the House Banking Committee's international finance subcommittee, June 3, 1976.

45. Hobart Rowen, "Potential Accomplishments of Monetary Summitry Limited," *Washington Post*, June 20, 1976.

46. Hobart Rowen, dispatches from San Juan and Dorado Beach, *Washington Post*, June 26, 27, 28, and 29, 1976.

47. Hobart Rowen, "Seven Nations Unify in Inflation Fight," *Washington Post*, June 30, 1976.

48. Hobart Rowen, "Activist Economic Role is Favored by Brown," *Washington Post*, May 15, 1976.

49. Hobart Rowen, "The Shape of Carter's Economics," *Washington Post*, Apr. 16, 1976.

50. Hobart Rowen, "Democrats Advised to Stress Control of Fiscal Spending," *Washington Post*, Apr. 25, 1976.

51. Hobart Rowen, "Ford's Pragmatic Economics," *Washington Post*, May 2, 1976.

52. Hobart Rowen, "Toward Economic Reform," *Washington Post*, July 15, 1976; "Carter's Team of Economic Advisers," *Washington Post*, July 25, 1976.

53. Jasinowski, joined Carter's staff as staff coordinator on economics after working for the Congressional Joint Economic Committee as a principal drafter of the Humphrey-Hawkins Bill. Other members of the Carter economic "task force" in 1976 included Lawrence Klein and Irving B. Kravis of the University of Pennsylvania; Joseph A. Pechman and Charles Schultze of the Brookings Institution; Stanley Surrey, Michael L. Wachter, Benjamin M. Friedman, and Martin Feldstein of Harvard University; Lester Thurow of MIT; and Richard N. Cooper of Yale University.

54. John Bowles's uncle, Chester A. Bowles, had been a price administrator and ambassador to India in earlier Democratic administrations.

55. *Meet the Press*, July 11, 1976, transcript, p. 24.

56. While all of the Democratic presidential candidates, except Carter, accepted the Humphrey-Hawkins proposals without question, a number of liberal economists, including Carolyn Shaw Bell of Wellesley, Charles C. Holt of the Urban Institute, Charles L. Schultze of the Brookings Institution, manpower expert Sar Levitan of George Washington University, and Melville J. Ulmer of the University of Maryland had the courage to point out that it raised expectations too high. Levitan, for example, demonstrated that the original 3 percent unemployment goal would require an unprecedented 7.5 percent real economic growth rate from 1976 until 1980. Charles Schultze produced a devastating analysis of how "the government of last resort" paying the "prevailing" wage could generate a wild inflation. Yet, in deference to the AFL-CIO, the bill excluded any effort to enforce wage-price guidelines, or in any other ways to encourage wage moderation. Ulmer suggested that a tax increase would be necessary to finance the higher costs of large-scale public employment. See Hobart Rowen, "Re-thinking the Humphrey-Hawkins Bill," *Washington Post*, May 27, 1976, and "Rescue Attempts for the Full Employment Bill," *Washington Post*, June 17, 1976.

57. Republican platform, Kansas City Convention, 1976.

58. Hobart Rowen, "The GOP's 'Steady-as-You-Go' Economy," *Washington Post*, Aug. 19, 1976.

59. George McGovern, "Memo to the White House," *Harper's*, October 1977.

60. Office of Management and Budget director James T. Lynn estimated the cost of new initiatives in the Democratic platform at $100 billion, and Treasury Secretary Simon raised the ante to $200 billion. See Hobart Rowen, "Carter Unit Maps Battle with GOP on the Economy," *Washington Post*, Aug. 22, 1976.

61. The effort to cast Carter in a conservative mold even embraced the first mention of supply-side economics, normally associated with Ronald Reagan. Carter's advisers brought it up that summer of 1976. Five years before Reagan's inaugural, as they began planning how to do battle with Gerald Ford on economic issues, the Carter staff convinced their candidate that Ford had been so preoccupied with managing the demand side of the economy he had ignored "the crucial question of the supply side." That phrase was used by Carter aides, and appeared in a *Washington Post* story Aug. 22, 1976, after conversations I had in Atlanta. Their plan was to stress John Dunlop's argument that one cause of inflation was inattention to the supply side of the economic equation: inflation is accelerated, the argument goes, because of bottlenecks that occur either because of labor or capital shortages, or because of obstacles put in the way of the most efficient operation of the government, business, or unions. An

earlier effort to challenge such "sacred cows" that institutionalize inflation had also been recommended to President Nixon by a member of his Council of Economic Advisers, Hendrik Houthakker.

Mondale warned Carter that he needed to be realistic about pushing such supply-side, anti-inflation remedies on Capitol Hill. But Carter told Mondale that if he got the kind of mandate he was hoping for in November, perhaps some of the things that hadn't seemed feasible or realistic would prove to be realistic. That would turn out to be little more than wishful thinking.

62. Hobart Rowen and James L. Rowe Jr., "Jobless Rate Increases to 7.9 Per Cent," *Washington Post*, Sept. 4, 1976.

63. Hobart Rowen, "Labor Gears Up to Aid Carter," *Washington Post*, Sept. 5, 1976.

64. Hobart Rowen, "Another Oil Price Boost: Complacency and Consequences," *Washington Post*, Oct. 28, 1976.

DRIFT

CHAPTER 8 : *Jimmy Carter's Ineptitude*

1. James Fallows, "The Passionless Presidency," *Atlantic*, May 1979.

2. Mark Siegel, "The Carter Example," *New Democrat*, published by the Democratic Leadership Council, January 1993. Siegel was outlining Carter's decision-making patterns as a model for Bill Clinton to avoid.

3. Speech to National Economists Club, Washington, D. C., May, 1977.

4. For a good academic explanation of this dilemma, see the May 1977 commencement address at the University of North Carolina by economist Edward M. Bernstein.

5. Hobart Rowen, "Carter Backed by Greenspan," *Washington Post*, May 1, 1977.

6. Carter was perceived by conservative supporters as having tilted to the left with a series of liberal appointments to subcabinet jobs. See Richard M. Scammon and Ben J. Wattenberg, "Jimmy Carter's Problem," *Public Opinion*, March/April 1978.

7. Hobart Rowen, "Germany: The Fat Cat in Left-Leaning Europe," *Washington Post*, May 19, 1977.

8. Strauss interview, 1990. He continued: "Helmut has become too critical of everybody. He and former Japanese prime minister Fukuda founded this former heads of government group—former Canadian prime minister Trudeau is on it. I think he couldn't get Ford, and didn't want Carter, so he asked me to sit on it. I finally got out of it—they were just reliving the [old] days, it didn't mean anything."

9. Hobart Rowen, "AFl-CIO Mounts Bitter Attack on Carter's Policies," *Washington Post*, Apr. 6, 1977.

10. Hobart Rowen, "2-Point Inflation Cut is Sought by '80," *Washington Post*, Apr. 16, 1977.

11. It is interesting to note, in retrospect, that Lance's "if it ain't broke, don't fix it" observation dealt initially with proposals to reform the banking and savings and loan industries. Lance resisted proposals to improve the regulatory system because, he said, no depositor had ever lost "a dime" despite then-prevalent bank failures.

12. Hobart Rowen, "Nostalgia in Shanghai—Blumenthal Tours Boyhood Ghetto Home," *Washington Post*, Mar. 4, 1979. There have been few stories in my career that gave me greater professional satisfaction than this one. From a handful of reporters with Blumenthal, he could take only three on a five-hour walking tour—and I pulled the short straw to represent print journalists. After dictating a twenty-minute, full-pool report for my colleagues, I dictated a story, from notes, over then fragile telephone lines, which made page one of the *Post*.

13. Hobart Rowen, "Blumenthal, Appearance and Reality," *Washington Post*, Feb. 25, 1979.

14. Eizenstat interview, Dec. 21, 1991.

15. Bosworth interview, 1993.

16. Hobart Rowen, "Budget-Boss Lance: 'If it Ain't Broke, Don't Fix It'," *Washington Post*, Dec. 23, 1976.

17. Blumenthal interview.

18. Eizenstat interview.

19. Strauss has attained his goal of being at the center of Washington power politics over the last twenty years by maintaining close ties with Republicans without offending the leaders of his own party. It's hard to think of another ex-chairman of the Democratic Party who would have been sent by Republican president Bush as ambassador to the Soviet Union, and then to Russia, in 1991 at the very peak of an international crisis. The day after his nomination, Strauss—accessible as always to a journalist—quipped: "I'm no Russian expert, but I've never had a job yet that I understood when I went into it. I may not be very deep, but I'm a quick study."

20. All Strauss quotes from interview, March 1991. Corroborated in broad outline, if not in exact words, in February 1991 interview with Owen, who initially volunteered the basic outline of how Strauss got to the 1977 London summit.

Later, in the Bush administration, Strauss as a concerned private citizen urged Trade Representative Carla Hills to follow his precedent at the Houston summit in 1990. But while Hills was invited to Houston by Bush, she stayed on the sidelines and helped shape a compromise that loosened up stalled negotiations on the Uruguay Round of trade negotiations. But neither she nor Commerce Secretary Robert A. Mosbacher made it inside the summit hall.

21. Hobart Rowen, "Schmidt Sees Economic Summit as Endorsing W. German Stance," *Washington Post*, May 14, 1977.

22. Carter economic adviser Schultze did not rate an invitation to the 1976 London summit.

23. Rowen, "Schmidt Sees Economic Summit as Endorsing W. German Stance."

24. Hobart Rowen, "Japan Taking Indirect Approach on Trade," *Washington Post*, May 1, 1977.

25. Hobart Rowen, "Mercantilism Feared in the Ascendancy Again," *Washington Post*, May 15, 1977; "Europe Places Economic Self-Interest over Summit Ideals," *Washington Post*, May 22, 1977; "U.S. to Resist Spread of Import Quota Curbs," *Washington Post*, June 3, 1977.

26. Rowen, "Europe Places Economic Self-Interest Over Summit Ideals."

27. Hobart Rowen, "Barre Pressed 'Organized Free Trade' in Talks with Carter," *Washington Post*, Sept. 18, 1977.

28. Addresses to the American Newspaper Publishers Association, Sept. 14, 1977, and to the Detroit Economic Club, Oct. 4, 1977.

29. Martin N. Baily and Arthur M. Okun, eds., *The Battle Against Unemployment and Inflation: Problems of the Modern Economy*, 3d ed. (Washington, D.C.: Brookings Institution, 1982), p. viii.

30. Hobart Rowen, "The Tax-Cut Dilemma," *Washington Post*, May 11, 1978.

31. Hobart Rowen, "No Rave Reviews on Carter's Economic Record," *Washington Post*, Jan. 1, 1978.

CHAPTER 9: *The Failure to Control Inflation*

1. See former Wage Stabilization Board chairman Arnold Weber, in *Exhortations and Controls: The Search for a Wage-Price Policy, 1945–71*, ed. Craufurd D. Goodwin

(Washington, D.C.: Brookings Institution, 1975), pp. 378–80: "Wage-price policy in the United States has now undergone thirty years of trial and error, and it is fair to say that there has been as much of the latter as the former. . . . The organizational arrangements for carrying out wage-price policy have had all the continuity of a pickup volleyball team. . . . The notion that wage-price policy can be global and employed to control the general level of wages and prices effectively should be rejected."

See also John Sheahan, *The Wage-Price Guideposts* (Washington, D.C.: Brookings Institution, 1967), p. 196: "The American economy . . . worked distinctly better than usual in the early 1960s when rising demand was combined with the guideposts. As compared to the 1950s, production increased faster, and the rate of increase in prices slowed down. The restraint on prices and wages achieved by the guideposts was a junior partner in this achievement."

2. Hobart Rowen, "Tough Time Selling Wage Guidelines to Labor," *Washington Post*, Sept. 17, 1978.

3. Hobart Rowen, "Meany Suggests Mandatory, Not Voluntary, Wage-Price Plan," *Washington Post*, Oct. 11, 1978.

4. Hobart Rowen, "Blumenthal Pledges Aid for Dollar," *Washington Post*, Aug. 18, 1978.

5. Hobart Rowen, "Inflation: The Worst Is Yet to Come," *Washington Post*, Mar. 16, 1978.

6. Speech to the Economic Club of Chicago, Oct. 6, 1977.

7. *Ibid.*

8. Eizenstat interview, Dec. 21, 1991.

9. Hobart Rowen, "Arthur F. Burns—Strong, Outspoken, and Out of Favor," *Washington Post*, Dec. 29, 1977.

10. Hobart Rowen, "Farewell from Fed Chairman: Sell Gold to Save the Dollar," *Washington Post*, Apr. 1, 1978.

11. Among the favorite notions of the day were TIP plans—TIP being the acronym for tax-oriented income policies. Two of the best known and most widely debated were offered by Arthur M. Okun and Henry C. Wallich, in conjunction with Sidney Weintraub. Okun would have used the tax system as a "carrot"—tax rebates to induce companies and unions to moderate wage demands. Wallich and Weintraub would have used a "stick" to accomplish the same end. They would have set a numerical wage guidepost, and corporations that offered more generous pay increases would be penalized by higher taxes. See Hobart Rowen, "The TIP Carrot or the TIP Stick," *Washington Post*, Apr. 30, 1978.

12. Hobart Rowen, "Blumenthal: Inflation Top Worry; Japan Current Account Surplus Up," *Washington Post*, Mar. 15, 1978.

13. Hobart Rowen, "Miller Not Ready to Give in on Move to Tighter Money," *Washington Post*, Apr. 15, 1979.

14. Hobart Rowen, "Guidelines That Pinch," *Washington Post*, May 7, 1978.

15. Hobart Rowen, "Uncle Sam's Credibility in the Inflation Fight," *Washington Post*, Mar. 30, 1978.

16. *Meet the Press*, Mar. 5, 1978.

17. Hobart Rowen, "U.S. Gold Will Be Put on Auction Block to Bolster Dollar, Reduce Trade Deficit," *Washington Post*, Apr. 20, 1978.

18. Hobart Rowen, "Blumenthal Pledges Aid for the Dollar," *Washington Post*, Apr. 22, 1978.

19. Hobart Rowen, "Miller and the Turning Point," *Washington Post*, Aug. 6, 1978.

20. Hobart Rowen, "Major U.S. Banks Jump Prime Rate to 11.5 Per Cent," *Washington Post*, Nov. 25, 1978.

21. In typical fashion, Robert Strauss exulted: "This gives him additional muscle across the board. Why, the fallout even can affect the price of beans in Peoria" (Hobart Rowen, "The World Looks Anew at Carter," *Washington Post*, Sept. 21, 1978).

22. When Shultz was secretary of the Treasury, he also was designated as chief economic adviser, and he knew how to use his authority. Once, Nixon's secretary of defense, Melvin Laird, tossed off a few bon mots about the economy on a trip to Tokyo. When the story moved on the wires, Shultz was asked about Laird's comment and snapped: "He better keep his cotton-pickin' hands off!" That was the end of Laird's intervention in economic policy.

23. Hobart Rowen, "If Only Blumenthal Could Join the Team," *Washington Post*, Aug. 8, 1978.

24. *Ibid.*

25. Robert D. Putnam and Nicholas Bayne, *Hanging Together: The Seven-Power Summits*, (Cambridge, Mass.: Harvard University Press, 1984), p. 80.

26. Hobart Rowen, "Toward a Shift in Economic Power," *Washington Post*, July 20, 1978.

27. W. R. Symser, "Goodbye, G-7," *Washington Quarterly*, Winter 1993, p. 18.

28. Owen interview, 1991.

29. Clyde V. Prestowicz Jr., *Trading Places: How We Allowed Japan to Take the Lead* (New York: Basic Books, 1984), pp. 251–252.

30. Strauss interview.

31. Strauss tells me that, before he engaged Giscard, he whispered to Carter, asking whether he should back off. Carter, Strauss said, "told me to use my own judgment."

32. According to both Strauss and Owen, British prime minister James Callaghan turned to Foreign Secretary David Owen and asked: "Do you know who Dizzy Dean is?" Owen confessed he didn't. But Callaghan did. "Dizzy Dean," Callaghan told his minister, "is a pitcher for the St. Louis Cardinals who won the World Series last year against the Detroit Tigers."

33. Hobart Rowen, "Too Many Goodies to the Trade Sharks?" *Washington Post*, June 14, 1979.

34. Hobart Rowen, "Treasury Official Is Optimistic," *Washington Post*, Sept. 21, 1978.

35. American (or other nations') quota deposits for the IMF involve no significant budget outlay, in contrast to shares bought in the World Bank. For each dollar deposited in the IMF, the United States receives an equivalent interest-bearing credit on the IMF's books, based on a basket of other major currencies. The only loss, which would likely be temporary, would come about through fluctuations in exchange rates.

A small share of World Bank commitments, on the other hand, must actually be transferred to the Bank. The much larger share is "on call," against emergencies. A practical point to remember is that World Bank expenditures provide the United States with huge leverage: since the U.S. share is about 20 percent, each dollar of funding for the World Bank provides about $5 in total lending power for the Bank. Moreover, Bank figures indicate that over the years, U.S. expenditures for the Bank are more than matched by spending in the United States for equipment and services by the recipients of Bank loans and grants.

36. Hobart Rowen, "IMF Given U.S. Pledge on the Dollar—Carter Promises Anti-Inflation Plan Will Cut Oil Use," *Washington Post*, Sept. 26, 1978.

37. Larre interview, Oct. 6, 1978.

38. Hobart Rowen, "Inflation and the Conservative Trend," *Washington Post,* Oct. 12, 1978.

39. *Ibid.*

40. Solomon interview, Nov. 19, 1978.

41. Hobart Rowen, "Increasing Confidence in Carter Dollar Plan," *Washington Post,* Nov. 19, 1978.

42. Hobart Rowen, "A Do-Nothing Oil Policy," *Washington Post,* Feb. 22, 1979.

43. Hobart Rowen, "A Made-in-Riyadh U.S. Energy Policy," *Washington Post,* Apr. 1, 1979.

44. Erwin C. Hargrove and Samuel A. Morley, eds., *The President and the Council of Economic Advisers: Interviews with the CEA Chairman* (Boulder, Colo.: Westview Press, 1984), p. 485. Schultze leaked his effort to stir Miller into anti-inflation action to my colleague at the *Washington Post,* John Berry, considered the town's best reporter on Federal Reserve affairs.

45. Miller interview, April 1979.

46. The sponsors were Lloyd Cutler, senior partner of the law firm Cutler and Pickering; former secretary of the Navy Paul Ignatius; and former secretary of the Air Force Eugene Zuckert.

47. *Public Papers of the Presidents of the United States, 1979, Jimmy Carter,* Bk. 2 (Washington, D.C.: U.S. Government Printing Office, 1980), pp. 1235–41.

48. Hobart Rowen, "A Hollow Ring," *Washington Post,* July 19, 1979.

49. Hobart Rowen, "Leadership—on Empty," *Washington Post,* June 21, 1979.

50. Quoted by Martin Schram in "Gas Crisis: Color the White House Bluer," *Washington Post,* July 1, 1979.

51. Hobart Rowen, "Carter Leaves for Tokyo; Energy Is Summit Issue," *Washington Post,* June 24, 1979.

52. Schram, "Gas Crisis."

53. Giscard d'Estaing interview in *Newsweek,* July 2, 1979, published in news reports June 28, 1978.

54. Hobart Rowen and Edward Walsh, "Tokyo Summit Adopts Joint Oil Import Curbs; Tokyo Summit Sets Oil Import Limits," *Washington Post,* June 30, 1979.

55. Hobart Rowen, "Pep Rally," *Washington Post,* July 12, 1979.

56. Eizenstat interview, Jan. 3, 1993.

57. Eizenstat interview, Dec. 21, 1991. My view at the time was in opposition to deregulation; but I nonetheless favored allocation or rationing of supplies.

58. Hobart Rowen, "Tough Talk Needs Follow-Through," *Washington Post,* July 8, 1979.

59. Hobart Rowen, "Blumenthal: 'Schizophrenia' Crippled Economic Policy," *Washington Post,* Oct. 30, 1979.

60. Hobart Rowen, "Kreps: Introspective Farewell," *Washington Post,* Nov. 3, 1979.

61. Hobart Rowen, "Bloopers Abounded as Events Caught up to Carternomics," *Washington Post,* Jan. 18, 1981.

GREED

CHAPTER 10: *Voodoo Economics and the Triumph of Greed*

1. Thomas H. Stanton, *A State of Risk* (New York: HarperCollins, 1991). This by far is the most authoritative account of the problems of government-sponsored enterprises (GSEs).

2. Neither Mundell nor Laffer became part of the Reagan administration.

3. Hobart Rowen, "Stockman's Snake Oil," *Washington Post*, Apr. 17, 1986.

4. David A. Stockman, *The Triumph of Politics: The Inside Story of the Reagan Revolution* (New York: Avon Books, 1987).

5. Speech to the Washington Press Club, Washington, D. C., Jan. 27, 1982, reproduced in Daniel Patrick Moynihan, *Came the Revolution* (New York: Harcourt Brace Jovanovich, 1988).

6. Donald T. Regan, *For the Record: From Wall Street to Washington* (New York: Harcourt Brace Jovanovich, 1988).

7. Leutwiler interview, Zurich, reported in Hobart Rowen, "Keeping Watch on Reaganomics," *Washington Post*, June 4, 1981.

8. Hobart Rowen, "Economic Leaders Abroad View a Flailing and Uncertain U.S.," *Washington Post*, June 7, 1981.

9. Donald R. Sherk, "U.S. Policy Toward the Multilateral Development Banks," *Washington Quarterly*, Summer 1993.

10. Hobart Rowen, "Putting the Heat on Volcker," *Washington Post*, Aug. 13, 1981.

11. Hobart Rowen, "The CEA Gets a Reprieve," *Washington Post*, Mar. 3, 1985.

12. Kathryn M. Dominguez and Jeffrey A. Frankel, *Does Foreign Exchange Intervention Work?* (Washington, D.C.: 1993) Institute for International Economics, p. 9. The authors challenge the still-conventional wisdom that exchange rate intervention is largely ineffective.

13. Hobart Rowen, "Volcker Sees Room for Tax Cut Now—Fed Chairman Says Monetary Policy Won't be Changed," *Washington Post*, June 6, 1981.

14. Hobart Rowen, "Tough to Buck Popular President—Democrats Unhappy with Economic Program, but Toss in the Towel," *Washington Post*, May 3, 1981.

15. Lou Cannon, *Reagan* (New York: G.P. Putnam's Sons, 1982).

16. Hobart Rowen, "Testing Period Starts for Reagan Policies," *Washington Post*, Aug. 2, 1981.

17. *Midyear World Economic Outlook*, International Monetary Fund, July 1981.

18. 1992 Economic Report, Council of Economic Advisers, Washington, D.C., p. 332.

19. Benjamin Friedman, *Day of Reckoning* (New York: Random House, 1988). Friedman's book on explosion of the national debt under Reagan is one of the most lucid accounts of how the supposed supply-side magic went wrong.

20. This quote was attributed to Regan by his friend James Miller, former Budget Bureau chief for Ronald Reagan, in an interview with the author.

21. Miller telephoned me to challenge the accuracy of Seidman's recollection of these events when the substance of his comments was reported in the *Washington Post* in a column of mine, "Seidman's Honesty an Embarrassment to Bush." He denied having written Seidman that he was "a disloyal Reaganite," but couldn't be sure he hadn't said something to that effect in a conversation. When I checked with Seidman after Miller's call, Seidman supplied texts of OMB letters and memos that essentially support the charge that Miller attempted to shrink the FDIC supervisory staff. One of the OMB letters was signed by Miller's chief deputy, not by Miller himself. But as Seidman observed to me, the deputy's letter would not likely have been sent without Miller's approval. A few days after the column appeared, a letter of protest was submitted to the *Post*, signed by Mrs. Miller. It said the column had damaged Miller's reputation. It claimed that I had misquoted Seidman, and that Seidman had confirmed that to the Millers. When I checked again, Seidman told me that was not true, and

supplied additional documents to substantiate the charge of attempted interference. This information was conveyed to Mrs. Miller by the *Post* Letters to the Editor staff. Her letter was not published.

22. Greenspan testimony Joint Economic Committee, January 1981.

23. Hobart Rowen, "Fed Governors Dispel Some Fantasies About 'Real' Interest Rate; Fed Board Has No Illusion About 'Real' Interest Rate," *Washington Post,* June 28, 1981. See also Edward J. Kane, *The S&L Insurance Mess: How Did it Happen?* (Washington, D.C.: Urban Institute, 1989), pp. 75–79.

24. Hobart Rowen, "Conference on Thrifts Warned Against Federal Bail-Outs," *Washington Post,* Oct. 30, 1981.

25. Hobart Rowen, "2 of 3 S&Ls Are Insolvent," *Washington Post,* Oct. 29, 1981.

26. *Ibid.*

27. Kane, *The S&L Insurance Mess,* pp. 6–7.

28. Hobart Rowen, "All-Saver Bill Is Anything But," *Washington Post,* July 5, 1981.

29. *Ibid.*

30. *Meet the Press* transcript, June 28, 1981, p. 8.

31. Hobart Rowen, "No Increase in Passbook Rates Due; Passbook Rate Rise Unlikely; Reagan Cites Drain Out of Accounts Into All-Savers," *Washington Post,* Oct. 17, 1981.

32. Testimony before the House Ways and Means Committee, Feb. 22, 1989.

33. William Greider, *Who Will Tell the People: The Betrayal of American Democracy* (New York: Simon & Schuster, 1992), p. 91.

34. Seidman interview, June 30, 1990.

35. Hobart Rowen, "Institutions Add Services, Boost War for Deposits," *Washington Post,* July 20, 1973.

36. Hobart Rowen, "Could Our Bank System Crumble?—Greed, Speculation and Fads Push It Closer to the Edge," *Washington Post,* Aug. 22, 1982.

37. Seidman interview, 1990.

38. Keating's own view of whether he extracted a service in exchange for his money: "One question is whether my financial support in any way influenced several political figures to take up my cause. I want to say in the most forceful way I can: I certainly hope so."

39. Greenspan, at the time he advised a law firm representing Lincoln, was president of Townsend-Greenspan, an economic consulting company. He gave the opinion that S&Ls should be allowed to make direct investments in real estate—a practice that the FHLBB was questioning at the time the Keating Five took up his cause. In an interview with Jerry Knight of *The Washington Post,* on Nov. 3, 1989, Greenspan said he was "surprised and distressed" by what had happened to Lincoln since 1985.

40. Glenn separately asked for a meeting at the *Post* with Katharine Graham and senior editors, during which he made the same arguments and registered the same complaint about my column with Mrs. Graham.

41. All three senators insist they did nothing wrong, merely performed their senatorial duties for a constituent who claimed he was being railroaded by the government. After a Senate Ethics Committee hearing, Cranston, Riegle, and DeConcini were only mildly chastised, and Glenn and McCain got off even more lightly. Cranston blamed his retirement on his illness with prostate cancer.

42. Economist Andrew F. Brimmer, a former governor of the Federal Reserve, estimated in January 1994 that the collapse of the S&L industry in the late 1980s "may ultimately cost American taxpayers between $150 billion and $175 billion on a pre-

sent value basis." See "Raiders and Regulators—Enterprise Subversion and Specula-
tion in the Savings and Loan Crisis," a paper presented to the Society of Government
Economists and the North American Economics and Finance Association, Boston,
Mass., January 5, 1994.

43. Testimony before the House Ways and Means Committee, Feb. 22, 1989.

44. Report by Jeff Gerth in *The New York Times*, Jan. 1, 1990.

45. Ronnie Dugger, "Blitzing the American Dream," *Texas Observer*, Dec. 15,
1989.

46. *Ibid.*

47. See *New York Times, Washington Post,* and *Wall Street Journal* accounts July
8, 1982; also Hobart Rowen, "After the Penn Square Fiasco," *Washington Post*, July
15, 1982.

48. Rowen, "After the Penn Square Fiasco."

49. Heimann interview, 1989.

50. Rowen, "Could Our Banking System Crumble?

51. Hobart Rowen, "Where Were the Bank Regulators?" *Washington Post*, May
27, 1984.

52. Press release, Department of the Treasury, Washington, D.C.

53. Hobart Rowen, "The 'Too Big to Fail' Trap—How the Federal Deposit Insurance System Has Been Abused Since 1945," *Washington Post*, Aug. 1, 1991.

54. Golembe interview, July 1991.

55. *Ibid.*

56. Edward J. Kane, "The Dangers of Capital Forbearance: The Case of FSLIC and
the Zombie S&Ls," paper prepared for conference on Contemporary Policy Issues,
Aug. 5, 1986.

57. Kane paper written for the National Center on Financial Services, University
of California, June 23, 1986.

58. William Niskanen, *Reagonomics: An Insider's Account of the Politics of the
People* (New York: Oxford University Press, 1988), p. 206.

59. Kane, *The S&L Insurance Mess.*

60. This policy had been adopted in an emergency as President Carter's control of
the economy faltered, and Volcker, called back from an IMF/World Bank meeting in
Belgrade, took charge. See accounts Oct. 9, 10, 11, 1979, *Washington Post;* also Hobart
Rowen, "Volcker's Revolution," *Washington Post*, Oct. 11, 1979. For relationship
of the "new operating procedure" to the S&L crisis, see *Washington Post*, June 28,
1981.

61. Gramley interview, June 27, 1981.

62. Michael Binstein in an article from *Regardie's*, reprinted in the *Business Journalist*, published by the Society of American Business Editors and Writers, August
1989. Binstein wrote extensively on the S&L issue, including a special report on Lincoln Savings and Loan and its relationships to the Keating Five for *The Washington
Post*, May 15, 1988, "A Study in Power; How S&L War Led Senators to Pressure
Regulators."

63. Binstein, "A Study in Power."

64. *Ibid.*

65. "America's Insurers—No Thrifts Crisis, This," *The Economist*, Apr. 20, 1991,
pp. 78–80.

66. *Controlling the Risks of Government-Sponsored Enterprises* (Washington,
D.C.: Congressional Budget Office, April 1991).

67. Thomas H. Stanton, *A State of Risk* (New York: HarperCollins, 1991).

68. Hobart Rowen, "Private Profits, Public Risks," *Washington Post*, Nov. 21, 1991.

69. Stanton interview, 1991.

70. See *Controlling the Risks*.

71. Hobart Rowen, "It's Time to Curb Federally Backed Enterprises," *Washington Post*, May 20, 1990. Darman later incorporated these estimates in the budget document for fiscal 1992 sent to Congress in January 1991.

72. "Market Sees That Junk Bonds Are, Well, Junk," letter to the *New York Times*, May 13, 1990, by Louis Lowenstein, Simon H. Rifkind Professor of Law, Columbia University, New York.

73. Giuliani interview in *Barron's*, Nov. 26, 1990.

74. Kaufman interview, 1991.

75. Michael Quint, "Regulatory Shift Allows U.S. Banks to Trade Stocks," *New York Times*, Sept. 21, 1990.

76. Hobart Rowen, "Bankers' Nightmare: A Plague of Mexicos," *Washington Post*, Sept. 23, 1982. Although *The Wall Street Journal* was enterprising in developing the GRH story, it was unaccountably buried on p. 16 of its Sept. 17, 1982 edition.

77. Hobart Rowen, "Salomon Scheme Provides Lesson on Regulation," *Washington Post*, Aug. 25, 1991, and "Salomon Saga," *Washington Post*, Sept. 12, 1991.

78. Interview with Wall Street trader who preferred to stay anonymous.

79. Tom Wolfe, *Bonfire of the Vanities* (New York: Farrar Straus Giroux, 1987).

80. Buffett testimony before the House Subcommittee on Telecommunications and Finance, Sept. 4, 1991.

81. Hobart Rowen, "Things Will Never Be the Same for Salomon Brothers," *Washington Post*, Sept. 12, 1991.

82. Hobart Rowen, "Salomon Scheme Provides Lesson on Regulation," *Washington Post*, Aug. 25, 1991.

83. For example, Robert A. Altman, president of BCCI, and Clark Clifford, chairman of BCCI, were not found guilty of complicity in the scandal surrounding their bank. But the BCCI case remains a mystery.

CHAPTER 11: *Oil and Its Discontents*

1. At its peak in 1977, OPEC production was 31 million barrels a day.

2. Hobart Rowen, "Pressure Behind AWACS Was Crass Business Greed," *Washington Post*, Nov. 8, 1981.

3. These synthetic "editorials" are among the most subtle pieces of business propaganda, and I question whether it is good journalistic practice to allow companies, labor unions, or other special interests to buy space on op-ed pages or in other opinion/analytical parts of news journals.

4. Benjamin Shwadran, *Middle East Oil Crises Since 1973* (Boulder, Colo.: Westview Press, 1986), p. 172.

5. *Facts and Figures of Japan* (Brooklyn, N.Y.: Revisionist Press, 1989), p. 29.

6. Ostry and Oppenheimer interviews.

7. Hobart Rowen, "OPEC's Out of the Driver's Seat," *Washington Post*, Feb. 11, 1982.

8. Hobart Rowen, "Oil, Oil Everywhere . . . ," *Washington Post*, Mar. 4, 1982. Other analysts were less bearish than Neustein, but all agreed that whatever the bargain Du Pont and Big Steel thought they were getting, it had been limited by declining oil prices. Du Pont stood to be especially hard hit by the lower value of the coal proper-

ties it had picked up in the Conoco deal. At $25 oil, said a Paine Webber analyst, "you can shut down most of Appalachia. At $20, it's finished."

9. Hobart Rowen, "OPEC's Arrogant Blackmail Changed Disaster Into Glut," *Washington Post,* Apr. 4, 1982.

10. Eliyahu Kanovsky, "Middle East Oil Power: Mirage or Reality?" in Haleh Esfandiari and A. L. Udovitch, eds., *Economic Dimensions of Middle Eastern History* (Princeton, N.J.: Darwin Press, 1990).

11. See U.S. Department of Energy, *Monthly Energy Review,* various issues, cited in Kanovsky, "Middle East Oil Power."

12. Geologists have badly and consistently underestimated future global oil supplies. For example, Kanovsky notes that substantial oil discoveries were still being made in the North Sea in 1988 despite repeated predictions that North Sea oil supplies would soon level off. According to *The Economist,* Nov. 21, 1987, more North Sea oil was discovered in 1987 than in any year since 1975.

13. Kanovsky, "Middle East Oil Power," p. 38.

14. Robert Stobaugh and Daniel Yergin, "After the Second Oil Shock: Pragmatic Energy Strategies," *Foreign Affairs,* Spring 1989.

15. Senate Committee on Energy and Natural Resources, *The Geopolitics of Oil,* December 1980.

16. Eliyahu Kanovsky, *Saudi Arabia's Dismal Economic Future: Regional and Global Implications* (Tel Aviv: Dayan Center for Middle Eastern and African Studies, Tel Aviv University, 1986).

17. International Monetary Fund Annual Report, September 1982.

18. Kanovsky's view: "The Saudis are on a collision course between rising expenditures and falling revenue, and their ability to control these trends is very limited."

19. For example, see testimony by former secretary of defense James Schlesinger, Senate Committee on Energy and Natural Resources, "The Geopolitics of Oil," December 1980.

20. Hobart Rowen, "Singing OPEC's Tune," *Washington Post,* Aug. 2, 1990.

21. Transcript of *MacNeil/Lehrer Newshour,* July 25, 1990.

22. Address to the annual Henry Jackson Award dinner of the Jewish Institute for National Security Affairs, Oct. 29, 1991. According to a JINSA news release, Cheney "offered a public 'thank you' to fellow dinner guest General David Ivry, now the Director General of the Israeli Ministry of Defense, [who had led the 1981 raid] for 'the action Israel took in 1981 with respect to the Baghdad reactor.'" Cheney was too diplomatic to note that his predecessor at the Pentagon, Caspar Weinberger, was so infuriated at the Israelis at the time of the raid that he urged Reagan to apply sanctions against Israel.

23. Hobart Rowen, "More than Oil Is at Stake," *Washington Post,* Sept. 16, 1990.

24. *Ibid.*

25. Hobart Rowen, "Invasion Pushing Bush Toward His Biggest Test," *Washington Post,* Aug. 5, 1990.

26. *International Financial Statistics Yearbook* (Washington, D.C.: International Monetary Fund, 1992).

27. Eliyahu Kanovsky, "Make Haste Slowly in Peace Talks," *Jerusalem Post,* Sept. 24, 1992.

CHAPTER 12: *The Folly of Deregulation*

1. Susan J. Tolchin and Martin Tolchin, *Dismantling America: The Rush to Deregulate* (Boston: Houghton Mifflin Company, 1983), p. 248.

2. Testimony before the House Committee on Public Works and Transportation's Subcommittee on Aviation Regulatory Reform, 95th Congress, 1st session, Oct. 5–19, 1977.

3. *Ibid.*

4. Alfred E. Kahn, testimony before the Senate Committee on Commerce, Science and Transportation, oversight hearing on Airline Concentration at Hub Airports, Sept. 22, 1988.

5. *Ibid.*

6. *Ibid.*

7. Hobart Rowen, "Air Fares: Higher and Higher," *Washington Post*, Nov. 17, 1988.

8. *Ibid.*

9. Speech to the British-American Chamber of Commerce, New York, Mar. 24, 1993.

10. Paul S. Dempsey, *The Social and Economic Consequences of Deregulation* (Westport, Conn.: Greenwood Press, 1989). For historical references in this chapter, I have relied on Professor Dempsey's extensive studies, notably his "Rise and Fall of the Civil Aeronautics Board: Opening Wide the Floodgates of Entry," *Transportation Law Journal* (University of Denver College of Law), 11:1 (1979).

11. Dempsey, "Rise and Fall of the Civil Aeronautics Board."

12. Steven A. Morrison and Clifford Winston, "Airline Deregulation and Public Policy," *Science*, Aug. 18, 1989.

13. *The HarperCollins Dictionary of Economics* (New York: HarperPerennial, 1991).

14. Dempsey testimony, National Commission to Ensure a Strong Competitive Airline Industry, Washington, D.C., June 1, 1993, p. 97.

15. Dempsey, *Social and Economic Consequences*, p. 119.

16. Kahn interview, 1983. Similar statements appear in Kahn's writing, and in correspondence in which Kahn critiqued my writings opposing deregulation.

17. Unpublished letter from Donald I. Baker, former assistant attorney general for antitrust, to *The Washington Post*, dated Sept. 16, 1986. Copy sent to author.

18. Alfred E. Kahn, "The Flying Monopoly Game," *Washington Post*, Aug. 26, 1986.

19. Hobart Rowen, "American's Solo Flight," *Washington Post*, Mar. 14, 1983.

20. Paul Stephen Dempsey, "Fear of Flying Frequently," *Newsweek*, Oct. 5, 1987.

21. "Airlines' Passengers Waging Guerrilla War on High Fares," *New York Times*, June 19, 1993, p. 1.

22. James Popkin, "Two Is Cheaper than One," *U.S. News & World Report*, Nov. 16, 1992, p. 102. The article explains how travelers who fly frequently between the cities could manipulate their travel dates and theoretically use all four portions of the two excursion tickets, saving $1,012 from the cost of two unrestricted round-trip tickets. The airlines, naturally, are seeking ways of foiling such ploys, primarily by tracking the tickets purchased through computers, and trying to bill travel agents for the difference. But according to Popkin, "back to back" ticketing appears to break no laws.

23. Conversation with Heller, who used this story frequently in speeches to debunk excessive reliance on statistical averages.

24. Donald R. Bartlett and James B. Steele, *America: What Went Wrong?* (Kansas City: Andrews and McMeel, 1992), chart, p. 110.

25. *Runxheimer Reports on Travel Management* (Northport, Ill., 1989).

26. Rowen, "American's Solo Flight."

27. Hobart Rowen, "Airline Oversight in Hindsight," *Washington Post,* July 23, 1993.

28. Paul Stephen Dempsey, "Airlines, Aviation and Public Policy: The Need for Regulatory Reform," address to the National Commission to Ensure a Strong Competitive Airline Industry, Commerce Department auditorium, June 1, 1993.

29. Morrison and Winston have written extensively in defense of deregulation, including *The Economics of Deregulation* (Washington, D.C.: Brookings Institution, 1986), and "Airline Deregulation and Public Policy," *Science,* Aug. 18, 1989.

30. "Deregulation Is Ruining Airlines, Swelling Fares, Study Says," *Aviation Daily,* Apr. 6, 1993.

31. Dempsey testimony, National Commission to Ensure a Strong Competitive Airline Industry.

32. Hobart Rowen, "The Eastern Episode's Big Lesson," *Washington Post,* Mar. 19, 1989.

33. Sasser interview, 1986.

34. Paul Stephen Dempsey, "With Deregulation, Big Get Bigger," *Philadelphia Inquirer,* Dec. 19, 1987, p. A9.

35. Statement for *Common Cause* magazine, January/February 1987. See also Dempsey, "The Social and Economic Consequences of Deregulation."

36. "Deregulation Gone Haywire," *Atlanta Journal and Constitution,* Nov. 27, 1983.

37. James E. Rowen is my son. His writings on airline deregulation have been totally independent of my own work, and much more exhaustive on air safety. His investigative series on air safety, "The Fatal Flaws in Flying," ran in the *Milwaukee Journal* from Dec. 15 through Dec. 22, 1985; Eichel's "How Deregulation Increased the Strain on Air Safety," appeared in *The Philadelphia Inquirer,* Dec. 6, 1989.

38. Richard B. McKenzie, "Airline Deregulation and Air Travel Safety" (St. Louis: Center for the Study of American Business, Washington University, 1991), p. 5.

39. James Rowen, "Air Florida: Too Big Too Fast," *Milwaukee Journal,* Dec. 15, 1985.

40. McKenzie, "Airline Deregulation and Air Travel Safety," p. 5.

41. Hobart Rowen, "Re-regulate the Airlines," *Washington Post,* Sept. 19, 1987.

42. Alfred E. Kahn and Daniel M. Kasper, "Airline Safety Without Reregulation," *New York Times,* Apr. 14, 1986.

43. Hobart Rowen, "The Extra Maintenance Dollar," *Washington Post,* May 5, 1988.

44. Comment made on the *Diane Rehm Show,* WAMU-FM radio, American University, June 1988.

45. Quoted in Eichel, "How Deregulation Increased the Strain on Air Safety."

46. Morrison and Winston, "Airline Deregulation and Public Policy."

47. Donald I. Baker unpublished letter, Sept. 16, 1986.

48. Report by National Transportation Safety Board, Jan. 15, 1993.

49. Kahn letter to *The New York Times,* 1986.

50. James Rowen, "Deregulation Fears Now Seem Justified," *Milwaukee Journal,* Dec. 22, 1985. Clark's memo went on to say that maintenance of aircraft, and training of workers for maintenance duties, were areas that could suffer after deregulation "in any economic pinch."

51. Statement by Thayer for *Common Cause* magazine, January/February 1987.

52. Tolchin and Tolchin, *Dismantling America: The Rush to Deregulate.*

53. Alfred E. Kahn, "I Would Do It Again," *Regulation,* an American Enterprise Institute Journal on Government and Society, 1988, no. 2, p. 26.

54. Frederick C. Thayer, "Let's Reregulate the Deregulated Airlines," *Los Angeles Times,* Sept. 11, 1986. Thayer is the author of *Rebuilding America: The Case for Economic Regulation* (New York: Praeger, 1984).

55. National Transportation Safety Board tables published Jan. 15, 1993, and revised May 25, 1993, press release SB 93-02A.

56. The Clinton administration doesn't appear to have any ideological hang-ups that would force it to stick to deregulation in some sanctimonious bow to the mythology of free and untrammeled markets. Moreover, reflecting his dedication to the view that government must play a more active role in supporting American industry—especially high-tech industries that help build American export strength—Clinton has pointedly singled out aerospace for special attention. His secretary of transportation, Federico Peña, is a realist, who came down hard on Northwest Airlines when it attempted to run Reno Air, a brash small newcomer, out of one of its markets.

The Baliles Commission, after a series of public hearings, issued a draft report in July 1993, concluding that U.S. civil aviation was "in abysmal financial condition" and that the aerospace industry "was reeling financially and structurally" from the combined impact of the airlines' troubles and cuts in the defense budget. The commission recommended tax relief, liberalization of rules governing foreign ownership, and other steps that might help the industry. And while rejecting a return to the old CAB system of complete regulation of fares and routes, it adopted, by a 14-1 vote—only commission member and former CAB chairman Robson voted against it—a proposal to establish an advisory committee to the secretary of transportation to determine whether an airline's financial condition "poses risks to the public or the industry." It could be created without resort to new legislation. By posing this innovative idea, the commission became the first government body since 1978 to question the wisdom of airline deregulation. Oversight of an airline's financial condition would establish enough of a government presence to trouble conservative deregulators such as Robson.

Robson who had been deputy Treasury secretary in the Bush administration after heading the CAB under Ford, and is now a fellow at the Heritage Foundation, a conservative think tank in Washington, told me that not only would a new advisory committee be one more unnecessary agency in an overgrown Washington bureaucracy, but it would be "a step in the wrong direction, back to a form of regulation. It's a crack in the door, although a small one, in the direction of a regulated environment."

The commission, for all of its good intentions, quietly went out of being in 1993 without having accomplished a great deal. The airline industry remains seriously troubled, and has begun to look for an infusion of new capital, not only from abroad but from its own employees. Discussions were under way at the end of the year between United Airlines and its employees on the possibility that employees would become the majority owners of the airline, in exchange for making $5 billion worth of concessions on pay and work rules that would enable United to compete with the bargain rates offered by smaller, no-frills carriers such as Southwest Airlines.

A friendlier relationship between airline managements and their workers would certainly help. But the enormous problems generated or surfaced by deregulation, including congestion at airports and declining quality of service, remain. The airline industry, having been deregulated, is not likely to ever go back to a fully regulated system. But clearly, there is need for greater government oversight, if for no other reason than to prevent the airlines' suicidal propensity to indulge in fare wars.

CHAPTER 13: *Third World Agonistes*

1. I later learned that Baker's message was delivered by his long-time confidante and public relations aide, Margaret Tutwiler.

2. Edward R. Fried and Philip H. Trezise, "Third World Debt: Phase Three Begins," *Brookings Review*, Fall 1989. The "Baker 17" countries include: Argentina, Bolivia, Brazil, Chile, Colombia, Costa Rica, Ecuador, Ivory Coast, Jamaica, Mexico, Morocco, Nigeria, Peru, Philippines, Uruguay, Venezuela, and Yugoslavia.

3. Hobart Rowen, "Forgive the Debts," *Washington Post*, Feb. 26, 1987.

4. Quoted from Oct. 16, 1984, *Wall Street Journal* by Christine Bindert of Shearson-Lehman Brothers at a joint conference sponsored by the Subcommittee on Economic Goals and Intergovernmental Policy of the Joint Economic Committee and the Congressional Research Service, Nov. 13, 1984; Joint Committee print 98-284, 98th Congress, 2d session, p. 35.

5. Hobart Rowen, "Loose Lending and the World Debt Crisis," *Washington Post*, Sept. 19, 1982. Kaufman is often linked with his Wall Street friend Albert Wojnilower of the First Boston Corporation as "Dr. Doom and Dr. Death." When asked which of the pessimistic pair he is, Kaufman usually responds, cheerfully: "I'm Doom."

6. William R. Cline, "The International Debt Problem," unpublished paper, 1992.

7. Rowen, "Loose Lending and the World Debt Crisis."

8. Paul Volcker and Toyoo Gyohten, *Changing Fortunes: The World's Money and the Threat to American Leadership* (New York: Times Books, 1992).

9. Hobart Rowen, "Emminger Asks Curbing Third World Spending," *Washington Post*, Sept. 23, 1982.

10. Hobart Rowen, "Bank Ministers Meeting Amid World Trauma," *Washington Post*, Aug. 29, 1982.

11. Leutwiler interviews, Dec. 21, 1992, and Mar. 6, 1993.

12. Sir Harold Lever, longtime private counselor to a series of British governments, had confided to me on a visit to his glamorous London apartment in May 1981 that Poland was defaulting on about $20 billion in loans from Western banks. "We have to paper this over, or it would ruin the banks—and have little effect on Poland," Sir Harold said. I reported his concern in a *Washington Post* column June 4, 1981.

13. Leutwiler interviews.

14. *Ibid.*

15. Nora Lustig, *The Mexican Economy in the Eighties: An Overview* (Washington, D.C.: Brookings Institution, 1989).

16. Hobart Rowen, "Interest Break Halts Dollar's Rise," *Washington Post*, Oct. 8, 1982, and "Changing Course," Oct. 14, 1982.

17. Volcker and Gyohten, *Changing Fortunes.*

18. Rowen, "Loose Lending and the World Debt Crisis."

19. *Ibid.*

20. Karin Lissakers, *Banks, Borrowers, and the Establishment: A Revisionist Account of the International Debt Crisis* (New York: Basic Books, 1991), p. 83; postscript, 1993 edition.

21. *Ibid.*

22. Rowen, "Loose Lending and the World Debt Crisis."

23. Pedro-Pablo Kuczynski, *Latin American Debt* (Baltimore: Twentieth Century Fund and Johns Hopkins University Press, 1988).

24. Hobart Rowen, "Banks Reduce Third World Lending," *Washington Post*, Nov. 9, 1982.

25. Edward M. Bernstein, "The Latin American Debt Problem and the United States," paper presented at the University of North Carolina, Feb. 21, 1989.

26. Hobart Rowen, "Kissinger Asks Fast Financial Action," *Washington Post*, Sept. 21, 1982.

27. Hobart Rowen, "Nine Major Banks Highly Exposed on Third World Loans," *Washington Post*, Oct. 24, 1982.

28. Hobart Rowen, "Protectionism, World Debt Crisis Intertwined," *Washington Post*, Nov. 14, 1982.

29. Schulmann, later managing director of the Institute for International Finance—a banker's lobby in Washington—became a member of the governing council of the German Bundesbank in 1992. The remarks quoted here were made during an economic conference jointly sponsored by the Global Independence Center of Philadelphia and the Group of Thirty, Philadelphia, Nov. 8, 1982.

30. Keynote address to economic conference jointly sponsored by the Global Independence Center of Philadelphia and the Group of Thirty, Philadelphia, Nov. 8, 1982.

31. Cline prepared these figures for *The Washington Post* from Federal Reserve Board data; published by the *Post* Oct. 24, 1982. The "Big Nine" at that time were: Bank of America, Chase Manhattan, Citicorp, Manufacturers Hanover Trust, Bankers Trust, Chemical Bank, First Chicago, Continental Illinois, and Morgan Guaranty.

32. James L. Rowe Jr., "Interest-Rate Spread Seen Giving Big Banks Healthy Earnings," *Washington Post*, Sept. 19, 1982.

33. Ishrat Husain and Ishac Diwan, eds., *Dealing with the Debt Crisis* (Washington, D.C.: World Bank, 1989). This report on a January 1989 symposium on the debt crisis is an invaluable compendium of expert views on the origins and potential solutions of the problem.

34. Even in 1986, Wriston stuck with the belief that bankers had done well in judging risk. See Walter B. Wriston, *Risk and Other Four-Letter Words* (New York: Harper & Row, 1986).

35. Kaufman and Rohatyn quotes from interviews in 1982. See also Hobart Rowen, "Could Our Bank System Crumble?" *Washington Post*, Aug. 22, 1982.

36. Rowen, "Could Our Bank System Crumble?"

37. *Financial Times*, July 30, 1992.

38. Henry C. Wallich, "Perspective on the External Debt Situation," address to the annual meeting of the American Economic Association, Dallas, Texas, Dec. 28, 1984.

39. John T. Cuddington, "The Extent and Causes of the Debt Crisis of the 1980s," in Husain and Diwan, eds., *Dealing with the Debt Crisis*.

40. Kucyznski, *Latin American Debt*.

41. Testimony by William R. Cline of the Institute for International Economics at joint conference sponsored by Subcommittee on Economic Goals and Intergovernmental Policy of the Joint Economic Committee and the Congressional Research Service, Nov. 13, 1984; Joint Committee print 98–284, 98th Congress, 2d session, p. 2.

42. Roy Culpeper, "Beyond Baker: The Maturing Debt Crisis," The North-South Institute, Ottawa, Canada, May 1987.

43. William R. Cline, "The Baker Plan and Brady Reformulation: An Evaluation," in Husain and Diwan, eds., *Dealing with the Debt Crisis*.

44. Hobart Rowen, "Aid Plan for Africa Withdrawn," *Washington Post*, Oct. 7, 1985.

45. Hobart Rowen, "The Second Most Powerful Person in the Country," *Washington Post*, Oct. 24, 1985.

46. *Meet the Press*, Oct. 13, 1985.

47. Percy S. Mistry, "Third World Debt—Beyond the Baker Plan," unpublished paper, April 1987.

48. John Burgess and Hobart Rowen, "U.S. Unveils Plan to Ease Crisis of Debtor Nations," *Washington Post*, Oct. 8, 1985; Hobart Rowen, "Reaction Mixed to Debt Plan," *Washington Post*, Oct. 9, 1985.

49. Testimony to the Senate Banking Committee, May 14, 1986.

50. Bill Bradley, "A Proposal for Third World Debt Management," speech at conference sponsored by Smick Medley & Associates, Zurich, Switzerland, June 29, 1986. See also Hobart Rowen, "Senator Outlines Third World Debt Proposal," *Washington Post*, June 30, 1986, and "Write Off Some Third World Debt," *Washington Post*, July 10, 1986.

51. Jeane Kirkpatrick, "Consider the Bradley Plan," *Washington Post*, July 21, 1986.

52. Speech to the National Press Club, Washington, D.C., July 24, 1986.

53. For details, see table published by the *National Journal*, Aug. 9, 1986, p. 1934.

54. Hobart Rowen, "Clausen Saga Comes to End," *Washington Post*, Oct. 13, 1985.

55. *Ibid.*

56. Annual address to the IMF/World Bank meeting, Seoul, Oct. 8, 1985.

57. Hobart Rowen, "Debt Plan Seen Prodding World Bank on Loans," *Washington Post*, Oct. 10, 1985.

58. Clausen interview with Hobart Rowen, in *Institutional Investor*, June 1985.

59. Clausen—who had never been to Africa while he was in the private banking business—became passionate after a few trips as president of the World Bank on the need to alleviate poverty—especially for the "poorest of the poor" nations served by the Bank's concessional-aid arm, the International Development Association (IDA). That triggered a battle royal with the Treasury over funds for IDA, which the Reagan administration had been cutting back from levels established under Carter. Clausen wanted $12 billion for IDA, of which the U.S. contribution, 25 percent, would be $3 billion. Don Regan argued that $9 billion was enough, cutting the U.S. contribution to $2.25 billion, or $750 million a year, a budget saving of $250 million annually. Clausen then undertook to pressure Reagan in a way that assured his demise. Troubled by what he considered Don Regan's penny-pinching, Clausen arranged to have British prime minister Margaret Thatcher and other European heads of government to write directly to President Reagan to ask for a full $3 billion contribution from the United States. The ploy didn't work, but Regan never forgave Clausen. Moeen Qureshi, a Bank vice president who over the years was one of the Bank's best and most devoted officials and after his retirement from the bank was the interim prime minister of Pakistan for ninety days in 1993, also paid a price. Qureshi, publicly critical of the U.S. downhold on IDA, had acted as Clausen's emissary to Thatcher. Thus, when Clausen named Qureshi as executive head of the Bank's International Finance Corp. (the private-lending arm), Regan vetoed Qureshi. Not to be outdone, when Regan proposed a Latin American, Clausen refused Regan's pick, and both Clausen and Regan then agreed on Sir William Ryrie, a former British Treasury official, to run the IFC.

60. Timothy B. Clark, "Tackling the Debt Crisis," *National Journal*, Aug. 9, 1986, p. 1934.

61. Hobart Rowen, " 'Debt Relief' Gets a Cautious Nod," *Washington Post,* Oct. 8, 1987.

62. United Nations Association of the United States of America press release, August 29, 1988, embargoed until September 7, 1988; and "Third World Debt: A Reexamination of Long-Term Management," report of the Third World Debt Panel of the Economic Policy Council of UNA-USA, September 7, 1988.

63. Richard E. Feinberg, "How to Reverse the Defunding of Latin America by the Multilateral Lending Agencies," Overseas Development Council internal paper, Sept. 15, 1988 draft. Feinberg noted that the Reagan administration had conducted a long and debilitating battle with the Inter-American Development Bank, which Baker considered to be incompetent, and thereby blocked efforts of Canada and European nations to expand the IDB's lending potential. Baker stalled the IDB's search for new capital, even though, according to Feinberg, the IDB management acceded to American demands that handpicked personnel from Treasury be placed in key policy positions. The Latin American member nations of IDB refused Baker's demands that the United States be given virtual veto power over individual loans.

64. Hobart Rowen, "Debt Relief That Adds Up," *Washington Post,* Mar. 9, 1989.

65. James L. Rowe Jr., "Financial Firemen Face Another Frantic Year," *Washington Post,* Jan. 15, 1984.

66. Testimony to the House Banking Subcommittee on International Development, Finance, Trade and Monetary Policy, September 1989. Also see Eugene Rotberg, "The State of Play," *Annual Meeting News,* International Media Partners, Washington, D.C., Sept. 28, 1989.

67. Shafiqul Islam, "Beyond Brady: Toward a Strategy for Debt Reduction," a paper presented at the Third World Scientific Banking meeting, Dubrovnik, Yugoslavia, June 1989.

68. Husain and Diwan, eds., *Dealing with the Debt Crisis.*

69. John Cavanagh and Robin Broad, who were visiting research associates at the University of the Philippines in 1989, have documented the environmental degradation and the crushing debt burden—with virtually no relief—of that poor country. Some 12 million people throw their domestic waste into Manila Bay. Neither the World Bank nor the IMF, as they exploited the natural resources of the Philippines for the benefit of foreign investors, paid attention to what they were doing to the environment and to the condition of the people who live there. In a letter to me dated Feb. 11, 1989, Cavanagh and Broad wrote: "In Philippine tourist spots, one cannot sit idly for more than brief spells before a Filipino—usually a child—approaches to sell anything from shells to food to clothing to themselves."

70. Morse interview, 1989.

71. Communiqué, 1988 Toronto Economic Summit.

72. Jeffrey D. Sachs, "Making the Brady Plan Work," *Foreign Affairs,* Summer 1989.

73. Nathaniel C. Nash, "Latin Debt Load Keeps Climbing Despite Accords," *New York Times,* Aug. 1, 1992.

74. Lissakers, *Banks, Borrowers, and the Establishment,* pp. 266–267 of the 1993 edition.

CHAPTER 14: *End of an Era*

1. Yoichi Funabashi, *Managing the Dollar: From the Plaza to the Louvre* (Washington, D.C.: Institute of International Economics, 1988), p. 10.

2. I did a bit to redress that imbalance by asking Baker to see German reporter Klaus Engelen, which Baker did, and Engelen got an interview featured by his paper.

3. Testimony before the Senate Banking Committee, February 1986.

4. A leading theorist on the possibility that a sharp drop in the dollar would lead to a recession was Stephen Marris, then with the Institute for International Economics.

5. Interview, 1986.

6. Bergsten interview, 1990.

7. Hobart Rowen, "Ministers Downplay Dispute," *Washington Post*, Oct. 27, 1986.

8. Hobart Rowen, "2d Global Rate Fix Unlikely," *Washington Post*, Mar. 23, 1986, and "Volcker's Dilemma," *Washington Post*, Mar. 23, 1986.

9. Rowen, "2d Global Rate Fix Unlikely."

10. Interview, 1986.

11. Angell interview. See also Hobart Rowen, "Problems Remain at the Fed," *Washington Post*, Apr. 6, 1986.

12. Hobart Rowen, "Forcing the Issue at the Fed," *Washington Post*, June 19, 1986.

13. Hobart Rowen, "Volcker Hints Germans Should Lead Rate Cuts," *Washington Post*, June 5, 1986.

14. Data provided by the Institute for International Economics, Washington, D.C., and cited in Hobart Rowen, "How Baker Talked the Dollar Down," *Washington Post*, June 8, 1986.

15. *Ibid.*

16. Funabashi, *Managing the Dollar*, p. 53.

17. Hobart Rowen, "Beyond the Currency Controversy," *Washington Post*, Jan. 18, 1987.

18. *Ibid.*

19. Italy didn't attend, its ego having been ruffled by exclusion, as usual, from the G-5 dinner among the United States, France, Japan, Germany, and England on Feb. 21. Canada, the other "junior" member, also did not go to the dinner, but took its place at the sessions each day. Thus the Louvre G-7 meeting turned into a G-6.

20. Conversation with Baker.

21. Morita interview, April 1987.

22. Hobart Rowen, "Germany Agrees to Expand Economy," *Washington Post*, May 14, 1987.

23. Hobart Rowen, "For Baker Gold Would Add 'Discipline,'" *Washington Post*, Oct. 2, 1987.

24. Hobart Rowen "Stocks Plunge After Bank Raises Prime Lending Rate," *Washington Post*, Oct. 16, 1987.

25. *Ibid.*

26. Hobart Rowen, "Bonn Gets Warning About High Rates," *Washington Post*, Oct. 17, 1987.

27. *Meet the Press*, transcript, Oct. 18, 1987.

28. *Ibid.*

29. Chart, *Wall Street Journal*, Oct. 20, 1987.

30. Interview with long-time Fed public relations chief Joseph R. Coyne, who accompanied Greenspan on the Black Monday flight to Dallas.

31. Hobart Rowen, "The Stock Market Will Never Be the Same." *Washington Post*, Oct. 25, 1987.

32. Hobart Rowen, "Reagan, in Bid to Restore Confidence, Cites Global Co-operation," *Washington Post*, Oct. 21, 1987.

CHAPTER 15 : *The Japanese Challenge*

1. Interview with author, 1982.

2. See Hobart Rowen, *The Free Enterprisers: Kennedy, Johnson and the Business Establishment* (New York: G. P. Putnam's Sons, 1964).

3. Okita died on Feb. 9, 1993. A basic reference on the workings of the Japanese economy is the Brookings Institution's *Asia's New Giant: How the Japanese Economy Works*, edited by Hugh Patrick and Henry Rosovsky, February 1976. Also see Saburo Okita's *Japan's Challenging Years: Reflections on My Lifetime* (Canberra: Australia-Japan Research Centre, 1983).

4. Hobart Rowen, "Lessons, Made in Japan," *Washington Post*, June 28, 1979.

5. Justin L. Bloom, "Japan as a Scientific and Technological Superpower," the U.S. Department of Commerce National Technical Information Service, Copyright 1990 by Justin L. Bloom.

6. John C. Davenport, "In Japan, It's 'Jimmu Keiki,' " *Fortune*, July 1957, p. 107.

7. *Newsweek*, Dec. 2, 1974, p. 26.

8. *Business Week*, July 7, 1951, p. 148.

9. *Business Week*, Sept. 7, 1957, p. 158.

10. Gregory D. Black and Claton R. Koppes, "OWI Goes to the Movies," *Foreign Service Journal*, August 1974."

11. The fruits of Ruth Benedict's wartime assignment were published in 1946 by the Riverside Press, Cambridge, Mass. *The Chrysanthemum and the Sword* has provided a basis for understanding Japan for several generations of writers and scholars. Although its original rationale was to answer questions about a little-known and little-understood enemy power, it remains must reading for anyone interested in present-day Japan. Any businessman or tourist who visits Japan without first reading *The Chrysanthemum and the Sword* does not have adequate preparation for his or her encounter with Japan and the Japanese.

12. John K. Emmerson, *The Japanese Thread: A Life in the U.S. Foreign Service* (New York: Holt, Rinehart and Winston, 1978), p. 398.

13. *Ibid.*, pp. 393–394.

14. Herbert Passin, *Japanese and the Japanese: Language and Culture Change* (Tokyo: Kinseido, 1980), p. 136.

15. The private nature of the Japanese persona was brilliantly described by my former colleague Richard Halloran in his *Japan: Images and Realities* (New York: Alfred A. Knopf, 1969). Halloran, who covered Japan for *The Washington Post* and *Business Week*, was one of the first to understand that the early days of Japan's role as a subservient client state of the United States were numbered. Read fresh today, his book retains all of its initial impact.

16. Frank Joseph Shulman, *Japan*, World Bibliographical Series, vol. 103. (Oxford, England: Clio Press, 1990).

17. James C. Abegglen and George Stalk Jr., *Kaisha: The Japanese Corporation* (New York: Basic Books, 1985), should be required reading for all American corporate and government officials who deal with Japan.

18. Joseph M. Juran, "Made in U.S.A.: A Renaissance in Quality," *Harvard Business Review*, July-August 1993, p. 42.

19. *Ibid.*, p. 43.

20. Abegglen interview, 1980.

21. Morita interview, 1985. Morita also used this or a variation of the story in speeches to international business groups.

22. Abegglen and Stalk, *Kaisha*, p. 7.

23. Hobart Rowen, "The Ceramic Example," *Washington Post*, Feb. 17, 1983.

24. Hobart Rowen, "The Secret Ways of Protectionism," *Washington Post*, July 8, 1970.

25. Arai interview, Tokyo, November 1977.

26. Hobart Rowen, "Japan Tries Harder, But Who Appreciates the Yen?" *Washington Post*, Nov. 13, 1977.

27. Morita interview, Tokyo, October 1977.

28. William G. Ouchi, *Theory Z: How American Business Can Meet the Japanese Challenge* (Reading, Mass.: Addison-Wesley, 1981).

29. Speech in New York, quoted in *The Washington Post*, Dec. 11, 1977.

30. *Zaibatsu* is translated as "Financial cliques," according to author Richard Halloran. See his *Japan: Images and Realities*, p. 49.

31. Morita interview, November 1977.

32. Matsukawa interview, Tokyo, September 1976.

33. Hobart Rowen, "Protectionist Poison," *Washington Post*, May 24, 1979.

34. Transcript, Ohira breakfast, May 20, 1979. See also Hobart Rowen, "Ohira Optimistic on Eve of Talks at White House," *Washington Post*, May 21, 1979.

35. Frost interview, Osio, Japan, 1986. Ellen Frost is currently counselor to Mickey Kantor, U.S. trade representative in the Clinton administration.

36. Clyde V. Prestowitz Jr., *Trading Places: How We Allowed Japan to Take the Lead* (New York: Basic Books, 1988), p. 200.

37. *Ibid.*

38. Selig S. Harrison and Clyde Prestowitz, "Pacific Agenda: Defense or Economics," *Foreign Policy*, Summer 1990. Harrison's later comment was in a personal letter to me, cited in my *Washington Post* column, "Reforging U.S. Ties With Japan," Nov. 10, 1991.

39. Abegglen and Stalk, *Kaisha*.

40. Abegglen interview, Tokyo, 1984

41. Statistics supplied by the Japanese embassy in Washington.

42. *Japan 1990: An International Comparison* (Tokyo: Keizai Koho Center, 1990), p. 12.

43. Interview with Deming, May 1991. Deming also made remarks on the decline in American power since the 1920s on July 22, 1991, in a special appearance at a bipartisan audience of Congress members and staffers, assembled by Representative Newt Gingrich (R.–Ga.). An account is contained in my *Post* column for July 25, 1991.

44. Harbour Associates, Berkley, Michigan.

45. Address to congressional seminar chaired by Representative Newt Gingrich, July 22, 1991.

46. Speeches to the Japan Society, New York, Nov. 7, 1986 and to the Harvard Business School, Nov. 24, 1986.

CHAPTER 16: *The Threat of Isolationism*

1. Hobart Rowen, "The Wrong Way to Deal With Japan," *Washington Post*, May 3, 1990.

2. Hobart Rowen, "Gephardt II's Meat-Ax Approach to Trade," *Washington Post*, Sept. 15, 1991.

3. Laura D'Andrea Tyson, *Who's Bashing Whom? Trade Conflict in High-Technology Industries* (Washington, D.C.: Institute for International Economics, 1992).

4. Speech to Institute for International Economics, Washington, D.C., September 1991.

5. Rowen, "Gephardt II."

6. Ibid.

7. Hobart Rowen, "Baker's Legacy at Treasury," Washington Post, Aug. 11, 1988.

8. Baker testimony to the Senate Foreign Relations Committee, Oct. 13, 1985.

9. Washington Post interview with Mulford, Nov. 26, 1985.

10. Briefing on the budget, Feb. 5, 1986.

11. Baker speech at Civic Center, Peoria, Illinois.

12. In a report to the Senate Finance Committee released Apr. 2, 1986, Volcker said the dollar had been dropping "fairly rapidly, and it was likely, in the circumstances, that a significant easing [of interest rates] . . . would risk a cumulative decline."

13. American Bankers Association meeting in Boston, June 3, 1986.

14. Baker and Darman interviews, 1986.

15. Yoichi Funabashi, Managing the Dollar: From the Plaza to the Louvre (Washington, D.C.: Institute for International Economics, 1988).

16. Bergsten interviews, 1986.

17. Economic Report of the President, 1992, p. 412.

18. Martin and Susan Tolchin, Buying Into America: How Foreign Money is Changing the Face of Our Nation (New York: Times Books, 1988).

19. Mack Ott, "Foreign Investment in the United States," in David R. Henderson, ed., The Fortune Encyclopedia of Economics (New York: Warner Books, 1993).

20. Karl Schoenberger, "Japan Tops Britain in U.S. Investment," Los Angeles Times, Dec. 16, 1993.

21. Ibid.

22. Kevin Phillips, The Politics of Rich and Poor (New York: Random House, 1990).

23. Cynthia Day Wallace et al., Foreign Direct Investment in the 1990s (Netherlands: Dordrecht-Nijhoff, 1990).

24. International Financial Statistics (Washington, D.C.: International Monetary Fund, 1993), p. 244.

25. Ibid., pp. 554, 556.

26. Shintaro Ishihara, The Japan That Can Say No: Why Japan Will Be First Among Equals (New York: Simon & Schuster, 1991).

27. Richard Halloran, Chrysanthemum and Sword Revisited: Is Japanese Militarism Resurgent? (Honolulu, Hawaii: East-West Center, 1991).

28. Akio Morita, "A New Management Philosophy," Bungie Shunju, January 1992.

29. Morita interview, 1992.

30. Kenneth T. Walsh, Gloria Borger, Susan Dentzer, and Carla Anne Robbins, "The 'America First' Fallacies," U.S. News & World Report, Feb. 3, 1992.

31. Robert Elegant, Pacific Century: Inside Asia Today (New York: Crown Publishers, 1988).

32. James Fallows, "Containing Japan: Japan's One-Sided Trading Will Make the U.S.-Japanese Partnership Impossible to Sustain—Unless We Impose Limits on Its Economy," Atlantic, May 1989.

33. Hobart Rowen, "Why Friendship Between Japan, U.S. Is Cooling," Washington Post, Feb. 2, 1990.

34. "The 'America First' Fallacies," U.S. News & World Report, Feb. 3, 1992. This

was an outstanding piece of in-depth journalism by Kenneth T. Walsh, Gloria Borger, Susan Dentzer, and Carla Anne Robbins, supplemented by an editorial, "The American Isolationist Mirage," by Michael Barone.

35. Hobart Rowen, "Buying American," *Washington Post,* Feb. 5, 1992; Don Oberdorfer, "U.S.-Japan Relations Seen Suffering Worst Downturn in Decades," *Washington Post,* Mar. 1, 1992.

36. Hobart Rowen, "Bush's Trip Will be Costly for Consumers," *Washington Post,* Jan. 12, 1992.

37. These harsh words brought to mind Prime Minister Yasuhiro Nakasone's 1986 comment to members of his party in 1986 that America was being held back by the low educational level and limited intellectual achievements of blacks and other minorities in the Ameican labor force. "Japan is now a highly educated and a fairly intelligent society, much more so than America, on the average. In America, there are quite a few black people, Puerto Ricans, and Mexicans. On the average it [the intelligence level] is still very low. . . . In America, even now, there are many black people who do not know their letters," he said. Hobart Rowen, "Nakasone Shot Himself in the Foot," *Washington Post,* Sept. 25, 1986, and "Thanks (?), Mr. Nakasone," *Washington Post,* Oct. 5, 1986.

38. John Schwartz, "The Push to 'Buy American'," *Newsweek,* Feb. 3, 1992.

39. *Ibid.*

40. "The 'America First' Fallacies."

41. Schwartz, "The Push to 'Buy American.' "

42. *Rochester Democrat and Chronicle,* Jan. 25, 1992; *Rochester Times-Union,* July 10, 1992.

43. Data supplied by Monsanto press affairs office, which reported acceptances exceeded management's expectation that about 1,200 workers would participate, buying $20 million worth of American cars.

44. James A. Auerbach and Jerome T. Barrett, eds., *The Future of Labor-Management Innovation in the United States* (Washington, D.C.: National Planning Association, 1993).

45. *Ibid.*

46. *Ibid.*

47. Bill Clinton and Al Gore, *Putting People First* (New York: Times Books, 1992).

48. A congressional panel headed by senators Sam Nunn (D.-Ga.) and Pete Domenici (R.-N.Mex.), and working with the Center for Strategic and International Studies (CSIS), a Washington think tank, published a detailed study in 1992 on how the tax system might be changed to concentrate on consumption. See Eric Pianin, "Bipartisan Panel Unveils Radical Plan for Deficit: System Would Tax Consumption, Aid Investors," *Washington Post,* Oct. 1, 1992.

49. Juliet B. Schor, *The Overworked American: The Unexpected Decline of Leisure* (New York: Basic Books, 1993).

50. Carnevale testimony, Senate Committee on Labor and Human Resources, Jan. 16, 1992.

51. *Ibid.*

52. Pat Choate and J. K. Linger, *The High-Flex Society: Shaping America's Economic Future* (New York: Alfred A. Knopf, 1986), p. 63.

53. Karel van Wolferen, *The Enigma of Japanese Power: The First Full-Scale Examination of the Inner Workers of Japan's Political/Industrial System* (New York: Alfred A. Knopf, 1989).

54. Michele and Henrik Schmiegelow, *Strategic Pragmatism: Japanese Lessons in*

the Use of Economic Theory (New York: Praeger, 1991). Henrik is a German foreign service officer, Michele is an economics professor.

55. Paulo Guerrieri and Carlo Milana, "Technology and Trade Competition in High-Tech Products," BRIE Working Papers 54, University of California, Berkeley, October 1991—cited in Tyson, *Who's Bashing Whom?*, p. 19.

56. Tyson, *Who's Bashing Whom?*

57. Robert R. Reich, *Work of Nations* (New York: Knopf, 1991).

58. *Ibid.*

59. Kenichi Ohmae, *The Borderless World: Power and Strategy in the Interlinked Economy* (New York: HarperCollins, 1990).

60. *Harvard Business Review*, January/February 1990.

AFTERMATH

1. The *Time* magazine cover for Aug. 16, 1993, after passage of the Clinton budget, showed Reagan upside down, with the cover story line reading: "Overturning the Reagan Era—It's painful, messy and modest, but Clinton's budget signals a new course for America."

2. *Economic Perspective: Week of October 4* (New York: Aubrey G. Lanston & Co., Inc., 1993).

3. Tyson interview.

4. Alfred Reifman, *America in Economic Decline?* (Washington, D.C.: Congressional Research Service, Library of Congress, 1989).

5. Paul Kennedy, *The Rise and Fall of the Great Powers* (New York: Random House, 1987).

6. For a full explication of this view, see Henry R. Nau, *The Myth of America's Decline* (New York: Oxford University Press, 1990).

7. *The East Asian Miracle* (Washington, D.C.: World Bank, 1993).

8. Paula Stern, "U.S. Economic Policy in Asia at a Crossroads," a paper prepared for the U.S.-Thai Leadership Council, Bangkok, Mar. 7, 1993.

Bibliography

BOOKS

Aaron, Henry J., ed. *Setting National Priorities: Policy for the Nineties.* Washington, D.C.: The Brookings Institution, 1990.

Aaron, Henry J., and Charles L. Schultze, eds., *Setting Domestic Priorities: What Can Government Do?* Washington, D.C.: The Brookings Institution, 1992.

Abegglen, James C., and George Stalk Jr. *Kaishi: The Japanese Corporation.* New York: Basic Books, 1985.

Adams, Walter E., and James W. Brock. *Dangerous Pursuits: Mergers and Acquisitions in the Age of Wall Street.* New York: Pantheon Books, 1989.

Aliber, Robert Z. *The Multinational Paradigm.* Cambridge, Mass.: MIT Press, 1993.

Baumol, William J., Sue Anne Batey Blackman, Edward N. Wolff, et al. *Productivity and American Leadership: The Long View.* Cambridge, Mass.: MIT Press, 1989.

Ben-Dasan, Isaiah. *The Japanese and the Jews.* Translated from the Japanese by Richard L. Gage. New York and Tokyo: John Weatherhill, 1972.

Bergsten, C. Fred. *America in the World Economy: A Strategy for the 1990s.* Washington, D.C.: Institute for International Economics, 1988.

Bergsten, C. Fred. *The Dilemmas of the Dollar: The Economics and the Politics of United States International Monetary Policy.* New York: New York University Press, 1975.

Bhagwati, Jagdish. *Protectionism.* Cambridge, Mass.: MIT Press, 1988.

Bloom, Justin L. *Japan as a Scientific and Technological Superpower.* Washington D.C.: The Department of Commerce National Technical Information Service, 1990.

Bosworth, Barry P. *Saving and Investment in a Global Economy.* Washington, D.C.: The Brookings Institution, 1993.

Brock, William, and Robert Hormats, eds. *The Global Economy: America's Role in the Decade Ahead.* New York: W. W. Norton, 1990.

Brown, Lester R. *State of the World, 1992.* New York: W. W. Norton, 1992.

Brzezinski, Zbigniew. *The Fragile Blossom: Crisis and Change in Japan.* New York: Harper & Row, 1972.

Burns, Arthur F. *Reflections of an Economic Policy Maker.* Washington, D.C.: The American Enterprise Institute for Public Policy Research, 1978.

Burstein, Daniel. *Yen: Japan's New Financial Empire and Its Threat to America.* New York: Simon & Schuster, 1988.

Cannon, Lou. *President Reagan: The Role of a Lifetime.* New York: Simon & Schuster, 1991.

Cannon, Lou. *Reagan.* New York: G. P. Putnam's Sons, 1982.

Caro, Robert A. *The Years of Lyndon Johnson: Means of Ascent.* New York: Alfred A. Knopf, 1990.

Carter, Jimmy. *Keeping Faith: Memoirs of a President.* New York: Bantam Books, 1982.

Caves, Richard E., and Masu Uekusa. *Industrial Organization in Japan.* Washington, D.C.: The Brookings Institution, 1976.

Choate, Pat. *Agents of Influence.* New York: Alfred A. Knopf, 1990.

Choate, Pat, and J. K. Linger. *The High-Flex Society.* New York: Alfred A. Knopf, 1986.

Christopher, Robert C. *The Japanese Mind: The Goliath Explained.* New York: Linden Press/Simon & Schuster, 1983.

Cline, William R. *American Trade Adjustment: The Global Impact.* Washington, D.C.: Institute for International Economics, 1989.

Cline, William R. *International Debt: Systemic Risk and Policy Response.* Washington, D.C.: Institute for International Economics, 1984.

Clinton, Gov. Bill, and Sen. Al Gore. *Putting People First: How We Can All Change America.* New York: Times Books, 1992.

Dertouzos, Michael L., Richard K. Lester, and Robert M. Solow. *Made in America: Regaining the Productive Edge.* Cambridge, Mass.: MIT Press, 1989.

Dempsey, Paul Stephen, and Andrew R. Goetz. *Airline Deregulation and Laissez-Faire Mythology.* Westport, Conn.: Quorum Books, 1992.

Denison, Edward F. *Accounting for Slower Economic Growth.* Washington, D.C.: The Brookings Institution, 1979.

Denison, Edward F. *Why Growth Rates Differ.* Washington, D.C.: The Brookings Institution, 1967.

Derian, Jean-Claude. *America's Struggle for Leadership in Technology.* Translated by Severen Schaeffer. Cambridge, Mass.: MIT Press, 1990.

Destler, I. M., and C. Randall Henning. *Dollar Politics: Exchange Rate Policymaking in the United States.* Washington, D.C.: Institute for International Economics, 1989.

De Vries, Margaret Garritsen. *Balance of Payments Adjustment, 1945 to 1986: The IMF Experience.* Washington, D.C.: The International Monetary Fund, 1987.

Dobson, Wendy. *Economic Policy Coordination: Requiem or Prologue?* Washington, D.C.: Institute for International Economics, 1991.

Dornbusch, Rudiger, Anne O. Krueger, Laura D'Andrea Tyson, Robert Z. Lawrence, and Charles L. Schultze, eds. *An American Trade Strategy: Options for the 1990s.* Washington, D.C.: The Brookings Institution, 1990.

Dugger, Ronnie. *On Reagan: The Man & His Presidency.* New York: McGraw-Hill, 1983.

Edsall, Thomas Byrne, with Mary D. Edsall. *Chain Reaction: The Impact of Race, Rights, and Taxes on American Politics.* New York: W. W. Norton, 1991.

Elegant, Robert. *Pacific Destiny: Inside Asia Today.* New York: Crown Publishers, 1990.

Emmerson, John K. *The Japanese Thread: A Life in the U.S. Foreign Service.* New York: Holt, Rinehart & Winston, 1978.

Friedman, Benjamin M. *Day of Reckoning: The Consequences of American Economic Policy Under Reagan and After.* New York: Random House, 1988.

Funabashi, Yoichi. *Managing the Dollar: From the Plaza to the Louvre.* Washington, D.C.: Institute for International Economics, 1988.

Gabor, Andrea. *The Man Who Discovered Quality.* New York: Times Books, 1990.

Galbraith, James K. *Balancing Acts: Technology, Finance and the American Future.* New York: Basic Books, 1989.

Galbraith, John Kenneth. *The Anatomy of Power.* Boston: Houghton Mifflin, 1983.

Galbraith, John Kenneth. *The Great Crash of 1929.* 3d ed. Boston: Houghton Mifflin, 1972.

Galbraith, John Kenneth. *Money: Whence It Came, Where It Went.* Boston: Houghton Mifflin, 1975.

Galbraith, John Kenneth. *A Short History of Financial Euphoria.* Nashville: Whittle, 1990.

Garten, Jeffrey E. *A Cold Peace: America, Japan, Germany, and the Struggle for Supremacy.* New York: Times Books, 1992.

Goodwin, Craufurd D., ed. *Exhortation & Controls: The Search for a Wage-Price Policy, 1945–1971.* Washington, D.C.: The Brookings Institution, 1975.

Graham, Edward M, and Paul R. Krugman. *Foreign Direct Investment in the United States.* Washington, D.C.: Institute for International Investment, 1989.

Greider, William. *The Trouble with Money.* Nashville: Whittle, 1989.

Greider, William. *Who Will Tell the People? The Betrayal of American Democracy.* New York: Simon & Schuster, 1992.

Halberstam, David. *The Reckoning.* New York: William Morrow, 1986.

Hall, Edward T., and Mildred Reed Hall. *Hidden Differences: Doing Business with the Japanese.* Garden City, N.Y.: Anchor Press/Doubleday, 1987.

Halloran, Richard. *Japan: Images and Realities.* New York: Alfred A. Knopf, 1969.

Hargrove, Erwin C., and Samuel A. Morley, eds. *The President and the Council of Economic Advisors: Interviews with CEA Chairmen.* Boulder and London: Westview Press, 1984.

Harris, Seymour E., ed. *The New Economics: Keynes' Influence on Theory and Public Policy.* New York: Alfred A. Knopf, 1952.

Heginbotham, Erland. *Asia's Rising Economic Tide: Unique Opportunities for the United States.* Washington, D.C.: National Planning Association, 1993.

Heller, Walter W. *The Economy: Old Myths and New Realities.* New York: W. W. Norton, 1976.

Hinshaw, Randall. *the Unstable Dollar.* New Brunswick, N.J.: Transaction Books, 1988.

Hinshaw, Randall, ed. *International Monetary Issues After the Cold War: A Conversation among Leading Economists.* Baltimore and London: The Johns Hopkins University Press, 1993.

Hofheinz, Roy Jr., and Kent E. Calder. *The Eastasia Edge.* New York: Basic Books, 1982.

Homer, Sidney, and Richard Sylla. *A History of Interest Rates.* 3d ed., with a foreword by Henry Kaufman. New Brunswick and London: Rutgers University Press, 1991.

Hormats, Robert D. *American Albatross: The Foreign Debt Dilemma.* New York: Priority Press, 1988.

Hormats, Robert D. *Reforming the International Monetary System, from Roosevelt to Reagan.* New York: Foreign Policy Association, 1987.

Hufbauer, Gary C., and Jeffrey J. Schott. *NAFTA: An Assessment.* Washington, D.C.: Institute for International Economics, 1993.

Husain, Ishrat, and Diwan Ishac, eds. *Dealing with the Debt Crisis.* Washington, D.C.: The World Bank, 1989.

Ishihara, Shintaro. *The Japan That Can Say No.* New York: Simon & Schuster, 1989.

Ishikawa, Kaoru, ed. *QC Circle Koryo: General Principles of the QC Circle.* Tokyo: Union of Japanese Scientists and Engineers (JUSE), 1970.

Johnson, Chalmers. *Comparative Capitalism: The Japanese Difference.* Berkeley: Haas School of Business, University of California, 1993.

Kahn, Herman, and Thomas Pepper. *The Japanese Challenge.* New York: Thomas Y. Crowell, 1979.

Kane, Edward J. *The S&L Insurance Mess: How Did It Happen?* Washington, D.C.: The Urban Institute Press, 1989.

Kaufman, Henry. *Interest Rates, the Markets, and the New Financial World,* New York: Times Books, 1986.

Kelly, J. B. *Arabia, the Gulf & the West: A Critical View of the Arabs and Their Oil Policy.* New York: Basic Books, 1980.

Kemmerer, Edwin Walter. *The ABC of the Federal Reserve System.* Princeton: Princeton University Press, 1926.

Kotkin, Joel, and Yoriko Kishimoto. *The Third Century: America's Resurgence in the Asian Era.* New York: Crown Publishers, 1988.

Kotz, Nick. *Wild Blue Yonder: Money, Politics and the B-1 Bomber.* New York: Pantheon Books, 1988.

Krugman, Paul. *The Age of Diminished Expectations: U.S. Economic Policy in the 1990s.* Washington, D.C.: Washington Post Co., 1990.

Kuczynski, Pedro-Pablo. *Latin American Debt.* Baltimore, Md.: The Johns Hopkins University Press, 1988.

Kuttner, Robert. *The End of Laissez-Faire.* New York: Alfred A. Knopf, 1991.

Lekachman, Robert. *The Age of Keynes.* New York: Random House, 1966.

Lissakers, Karin. *Banks, Borrowers, and the Establishment.* New York: Basic Books, 1991.

Maisel, Sherman J. *Managing the Dollar.* New York: W. W. Norton, 1973.

Malabre, Alfred L., Jr. *Lost Prophets: An Insider's History of the Modern Economists.* Boston, Mass.: Harvard Business School Press, 1994.

Marris, Stephen. *Deficits and the Dollar: The World Economy at Risk.* Washington, D.C.: Institute for International Economics, 1985.

Mason, Edward S., and Robert E. Asher. *The World Bank Since Bretton Woods.* Washington, D.C.: The Brookings Institution, 1973.

McQuaid, Kim. *The Anxious Years: America in the Vietnam-Watergate Era.* New York: Basic Books, 1989.

McQuaid, Kim. *Big Business and Presidential Power from FDR to Reagan.* New York: William Morrow, 1982.

Miller, Merle. *Lyndon: An Oral Autobiography.* New York: Ballantine Books, 1980.

Moynihan, Daniel Patrick. *Came the Revolution: Argument in the Reagan Era.* San Diego and New York: Harcourt Brace Jovanovich, 1988.

Nau, Henry R. *The Myth of America's Decline.* New York: Oxford University Press, 1990.

Nau, Henry R., ed. *Domestic Trade Politics and the Uruguay Round.* New York: Columbia University Press, 1989.

Neikirk, William R. *Volcker: Portrait of the Money Man.* New York: Congdon & Weed, 1987.

Nivola, Pietro S. *Regulating Unfair Trade.* Washington, D.C.: The Brookings Institution, 1993.

Ohmae, Kenichi. *The Borderless World: Power and Strategy in the Interlinked Economy.* New York: HarperCollins, 1990.

Okita, Saburo. *Japan's Challenging Years*. Adapted from the Japanese by Graeme Bruch with assistance of Ann Nevile. Canberra: Australia-Japan Research Centre, 1983.

Okita, Saburo. *A Life in Economic Diplomacy*. Abridged from the Japanese by Dani Botsman. Canberra: Australia-Japan Research Centre, 1993.

Okita, Saburo. *Steps to the 21st Century*. Tokyo: The Japan Times, 1993.

Okun, Arthur M. *Economics for Policymaking: Selected Essays of Arthur M. Okun*. Edited by Joseph A. Pechman. Cambridge, Mass.: MIT Press, 1983.

Ouchi, William G. *Theory Z: How Americans Can Meet the Japanese Challenge*. Reading, Mass.: Addison-Wesley, 1981.

Palmer, John L., and Isabel V. Sawhill. *The Reagan Experiment*. Washington, D.C.: The Urban Institute Press, 1982.

Palmer, John L., and Isabel V. Sawhill. *The Reagan Record*. Cambridge, Mass.: Ballinger, 1984.

Passin, Herbert. *Japanese and the Japanese Change: Language and Culture Change*. Tokyo: Kinseido, 1980.

Phillips, Kevin P. *The Politics of Rich and Poor*. New York: Random House, 1990.

Phillips, Kevin P. *Staying on Top: The Business Case for a National Industrial Policy*. New York: Random House, 1984.

Porter, Michael E. *The Competitive Advantage of Nations*. New York: Free Press, 1990.

Prestowitz, Clyde V., Jr. *Trading Places: How We Allowed Japan to Take the Lead*. New York: Basic Books, 1988.

Putnam, Robert D., and Nicholas Bayne. *Hanging Together: The Seven-Power Summits*. Cambridge, Mass.: Harvard University Press, 1984.

Regan, Donald T. *For the Record: From Wall Street to Washington*. New York: Harcourt Brace Jovanovich, 1988.

Reich, Robert B. *The Work of Nations*. New York: Alfred A. Knopf, 1991.

Reischauer, Edwin O. *The Japanese*. Cambridge Mass.: Harvard University Press, 1977.

Reston, James, Jr. *The Lone Star: The Life of John Connally*. New York: Harper & Row, 1989.

Roosa, Robert V. *The Dollar and World Liquidity*. New York: Random House, 1967.

Rose, Richard. *The Postmodern President*. Chatham, N.J.: Chatham House, 1988.

Rosecrance, Richard. *America's Economic Resurgence: A Bold New Strategy*. New York: Harper & Row, 1990.

Rowen, Hobart. *The Free Enterprisers: Kennedy, Johnson and the Business Establishment*. New York: G. P. Putnam's Sons, 1964.

Schlossstein, Steven. *The End of the American Century*. New York: Congdon & Weed, 1989.

Schmiegelow, Michele, and Henrik Schmiegelow. *Strategic Pragmatism:*

Japanese Lessons in the Use of Economic Theory. New York: Praeger, 1989.

Schultze, Charles L. *Memos to the President: A Guide Through Macroeconomics for the Busy Policymaker.* Washington, D.C.: The Brookings Institution, 1992.

Sewell, John W., Stuart K. Tucker, et al. *Growth, Exports, & Jobs in a Changing World Economy: Agenda, 1988.* New Brunswick, N.J.: Transaction Books, 1988.

Sheahan, John. *The Wage-Price Guideposts.* Washington, D.C.: The Brookings Institution, 1967.

Sheehan, Neil. *A Bright Shining Lie.* New York: Random House, 1988.

Shultz, George P. *Turmoil and Triumph: My Years as Secretary of State.* New York: Charles Scribner's Sons, 1993.

Shwadran, Benjamin. *Middle East Oil Crises Since 1973.* Boulder, Colo.: Westview Press, 1986.

Singer, S. Fred, ed. *Free Market Energy.* New York: Universe Books, 1984.

Solomon, Robert. *The International Monetary System, 1945–1981.* New York: Harper & Row, 1982.

Stanton, Thomas H. *A State of Risk: Will Government-Sponsored Enterprises Be the Next Financial Crisis?* New York: HarperCollins, 1991.

Stein, Herbert. *Presidential Economics: The Making of Economic Policy from Roosevelt to Reagan and Beyond.* New York: Simon & Schuster, 1984.

Tolchin, Martin, and Susan J. Tolchin. *Buying into America.* New York: Times Books, 1988.

Tolchin, Martin, and Susan J. Tolchin. *Selling Our Security: The Erosion of America's Assets.* New York: Alfred A. Knopf, 1992.

Tolchin, Susan J., and Martin Tolchin. *Dismantling America: The Rush to Deregulate.* Boston: Houghton Mifflin, 1983.

Van Wolferen, Karel. *The Enigma of Japanese Power.* New York: Alfred A. Knopf, 1989.

Tyson, Laura D'Andrea. *Who's Bashing Whom? Trade Conflict in High-Technology Industries.* Washington, D.C.: Institute for International Economics, 1992.

Vogel, Ezra F. *Comeback, Case by Case: Building the Resurgence of American Business.* New York: Simon & Schuster, 1985.

Vogel, Ezra F. *Japan as Number One: Lessons for America.* New York: Simon & Schuster, 1979.

Volcker, Paul, and Toyoo Gyohten. *Changing Fortunes: The World's Money and the Threat to American Leadership.* New York: Times Books, 1992.

Yergin, Daniel. *The Prize: The Epic Quest for Oil, Money, and Power.* New York: Simon & Schuster, 1991.

Wachtel, Howard M. *The Money Mandarins: The Making of a Supranational Economic Order.* New York: Pantheon Books, 1986.

Williamson, John, ed. *The Political Economy of Policy Reform.* Washington, D.C.: Institute for International Economics, 1994.

Wright, Robin. *In the Name of God: The Khomeini Decade.* New York: Simon & Schuster, 1989.

ARTICLES, PAMPHLETS, SPEECHES

Angell, Wayne D. *Reflections on Monetary Policy.* Remarks at the Downtown Economists Club, New York, Oct. 5, 1993.

Arndt, Sven W., and Robert W. Dunn Jr. *NAFTA Faces the Congress—Issues and Prospects.* A Lowe Institute Policy Study, Claremont McKenna College, Claremont, Calif., September, 1993.

Bernstein, Edward M. *Structural Problems and Economic Policy.* Washington, D.C.: EMB Ltd., Jan. 16, 1979.

Bhagwati, Jagdish. "Beyond NAFTA: Clinton's Trading Choices." *Foreign Policy,* Summer 1993.

Cole, Robert E. "U.S. Quality Improvement in the Auto Industry: Close but No Cigar," *California Management Review* 32 (Summer 1990).

Courtis, Kenneth S. "Challenges Across the Pacific: Asia's New Agenda and Issues for the United States." Testimony before the House Committee on Foreign Affairs, Washington, D.C., Feb. 17, 1993.

Courtis, Kenneth S. "Japan's Next Leap Forward." *Asia, Inc.* December 1992.

Fallows, James. "The Passionless Presidency—The Trouble with Jimmy Carter's Administration." *Atlantic,* May 1979.

Feigenbaum, Armand V. "Quality: The Strategic Business Imperative," *Quality Progress,* February 1986.

Fosler, Gail D. *North American Outlook, 1993–94.* Ottawa and New York: The Conference Board of Canada, 1993.

Funabashi, Yoichi. "The Asianization of Asia." *Foreign Affairs,* November/December 1993.

Garten, Jeffrey E. *Japan, Germany and the American Election.* Remarks at the University of California, Berkeley, Sept. 14, 1992.

Goetz, Andrew R., and Paul Stephen Dempsey. "Airline Deregulation Ten Years After: Something Foul in the Air." *Journal of Air Law and Commerce* 54:4 (1989).

Healey, Denis. "The World Economy in the 1980s." *McKinsey Quarterly,* Winter 1981.

Ipsen, Erik. "The Brady Plan's Enforcer." *Institutional Investor,* July 1989.

Islam, Shafiqul. *Political Cold War in Russia and the American Response.* New York: Council on Foreign Relations, Mar. 19, 1993.

Islam, Shafiqul. *Western Assistance to Russia.* New York: Council on Foreign Relations, Apr. 14, 1993.

Ito, Kan. "Trans-Pacific Anger." *Foreign Policy,* Spring 1990.

Johnson, Sheila K. *American Attitudes Toward Japan, 1941–1975.* Policy

Study 15. Washington, D.C., and Stanford: American Enterprise Institute for Public Policy Research and the Hoover Institution, 1975.

Juran, Joseph M. "Made in the U.S.A.: A Renaissance in Quality," *Harvard Business Review*, July/August 1993.

Kanovsky, Eliyahu. "Middle East Oil: An Economic Analysis." In *Middle East Contemporary Survey*, vol. 4: *1979–80* New York: Holmes & Maier, 1982.

Kanovsky, Eliyahu. "The Diminishing Importance of Middle East Oil." In *Middle East Contemporary Survey*, vol. 5: *1980–81* New York: Holmes & Maier, 1983.

Kanovsky, Eliyahu. *The Economic Consequences of the Persian Gulf War: Accelerating OPEC's Demise.* Washington, D.C.: Washington Institute for Near East Policy, 1992.

Kanovsky, Eliyahu. *The Forgotten Dimension: Economic Developments in the Arab Countries and Their Possible Impact on Peace Agreements.* Ramat Gan, Israel: Bar-Ilan Center for Strategic Studies, December 1992.

Kanovsky, Eliyahu. "A Long Look at Long-Term Security." *Jerusalem Post*, Jan. 15, 1993.

Kaufman, Henry. *Beyond the Business Cycle: New Developments in Business and Finance.* Remarks delivered to the Chapman University Economic Forum, Irvine, Calif., Apr. 29, 1993.

Knowles, James W., and Charles B. Warden Jr. *The Potential Economic Growth in the United States.* Study Paper No. 20, Joint Economic Committee, 86th Congress, 2d Session. Washington, D.C.: U.S. Government Printing Office, Jan. 30, 1960.

Kramer, Michael. "The Velvet Hammer—Secretary of State James Baker Is a Gentleman Who Hates to Lose." *Time*, Feb. 13, 1989.

McCracken, Paul W. *Reflections on Economic Advising.* International Institute for Economic Research. Ottawa, Ill.. Green Hill Publishers, n.d.

McNamee, Mike. "Greenspan's Moment of Truth." *Business Week*, July 31, 1989.

Mead, Walter Russell. "The United States and the World Economy." *World Policy Journal*, Summer 1989.

Menil, George de, and Anthony N. Solomon. *Economic Summitry.* New York: Council on Foreign Relations, 1983.

Murray, Alan. "Once-Cozy White House and Fed Are at Odds, and Slowing Economy Portends Worse to Come." *Wall Street Journal*, Dec. 28, 1989.

Nye, Joseph D., Jr. "Coping with Japan." *Foreign Policy*, no. 89, Winter 1992–93.

Ohashi, Ryosuke. "Philosophical Reflections on Japan's Cultural Context." *Japan Echo* (Tokyo) 16 (Spring 1989).

Olson, James E. "The Quality Challenge." *Quality Progress*, February 1986.

Packard, George R., and William Watts. *The United States and Japan: American Perspectives and Policies.* Washington, D.C.: Potomac Associates, The School of Advanced International Studies, 1978.

Porter, Michael E. "Japan Isn't Playing by Different Rules." *New York Times*, July 22, 1990, p. F13.

Reich, Robert B. "The Economic of Illusion and the Illusion of Economics." *Foreign Affairs* 6:3 (1988).

Rowen, Hobart. "Gold at the Crossroads." *Washington Post*, Mar. 10–14, 1968.

Rowen, Hobart. "Prosperity, Growth, and Quality: The Threat from Protectionist Policies." *Quality Progress*, February 1986.

Safire, William. "Bush's Gamble." *New York Times Magazine*, Oct. 18, 1992.

Sherk, Donald R. "U.S. Policy Toward the Multilateral Development Banks." *Washington Quarterly* 16 (Summer 1993).

Spencer, Edson W. "Japan as Competitor." *Foreign Policy*, Spring, 1990.

Stern, Paula. *U.S. Economic Policy in Asia at a Crossroads*. Address to U.S. Thai Leadership Council, Bangkok, Mar. 7, 1993.

Stern, Paula. *A U.S. Trade Policy for the Pacific Century*. Washington, D.C.: Progressive Policy Institute, Nov. 11, 1993.

Stokes, Bruce. *Japanese Investment in the United States: Its Causes and Consequences*. New York: Japan Society, 1988.

Stokes, Bruce. "Tilting Toward Asia." *National Journal*, July 11, 1992.

Tasker, Peter. "The End of Japan, Inc." *Wall Street Journal*, June 30, 1993.

Tucker, Robert W. "Oil & American Power—Three Years Later." *Commentary*, January 1977.

Tucker, Robert W. "Oil and American Power—Six Years Later." *Commentary*, September 1979.

Tucker, Stuart K. "U.S. Exports to Developing Countries: Analysis and Projections." Prepared for the Overseas Development Council, Washington, D.C., February 1992.

Von Furstenberg, George M., and Joseph P. Daniels. "Can You Trust G-7 Promises?" *International Economic Insights*, September/October, 1991.

Wilson, Vincent, Jr. "The Best Response to OPEC is to Fight Fire with Fire." *Washington Star*, Aug. 17, 1975.

Wilson, Vincent, Jr. "The Unforced Errors of Nicholas Brady." *The Economist*, June 24, 1989.

REPORTS

Auto Situation: 1980. Report by the Subcommittee on Trade, House Ways and Means Committee, Committee Print, 96th Congress, 2d Session. Washington, D.C.: U.S. Government Printing Office, June 6, 1980.

United States-Japan Trade Report. Subcommittee on Trade, House Ways and Means Committee, Committee Print, 96th Congress, 2d Session. Washington, D.C.: U.S. Government Printing Office, Sept. 5, 1980.

Rethinking Japan Policy. U.S.-Japan Study Group, Carnegie Endowment for International Peace. Washington, D.C., 1993.

The Developing World: Danger Point for U.S. Security. A report to the Arms

Control and Foreign Policy Caucus, U.S. Congress, Washington, D.C., Aug. 1, 1989.

The Maastricht Agreement on Economic and Monetary Union in the European Community. Annual Report, The International Monetary Fund, Washington, D.C., pp. 47–48.

The Economic and Budget Outlook: An Update. Washington, D.C.: Congressional Budget Office, August 1989.

Report of the Presidential Task Force on Market Mechanisms. Nicholas F. Brady, chairman. Washington, D.C.: U.S. Government Printing Office, Jan. 8, 1988.

America's Agenda—Rebuilding Economic Strength. A report by the Cuomo Commission on Competitiveness, Lewis B. Kaden, chairman; Lee Smith, director and editor, Armonk, N.Y.: M. E. Sharpe, Inc., 1992.

Index

HOBART ROWEN has reported for *The Washington Post* on economics for nearly thirty years. He has been on the scene in Washington, D.C., since the Second World War, and has achieved national recognition for his reporting and commentary on business news in the nation's capital. In 1961, Hobart Rowen won the Sigma Delta Chi Distinguished Service Award for Magazine Reporting—the top honor in the field. In 1985, he was cited as the best newspaper business reporter in the nation in the *Washington Journalism Review*'s Best in the Business competition. He is the author of *The Free Enterprisers: Kennedy; Johnson, and the Business Establishment.* He lives in Chevy Chase, Maryland.

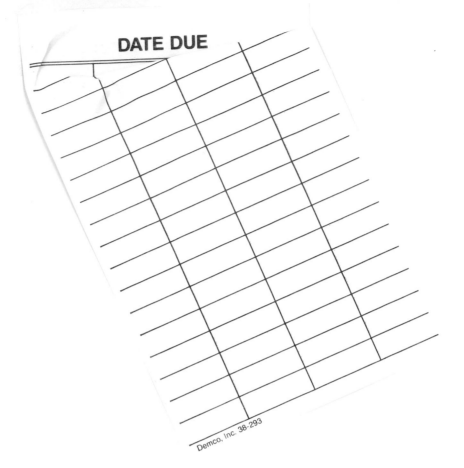

DATE DUE

Demco, Inc. 38-293